THE BARBOUR COLLECTION OF CONNECTICUT TOWN VITAL RECORDS

THE BARBOUR COLLECTION OF CONNECTICUT TOWN VITAL RECORDS

MILFORD 1640–1850

NEW CANAAN 1801–1854

NEW HARTFORD 1740–1854

Compiled by
Jan Tilton

General Editor
Lorraine Cook White

Copyright © 2000
Genealogical Publishing Co., Inc.
Baltimore, Maryland
All Rights Reserved
Library of Congress Catalogue Card Number 94-76197
International Standard Book Number 0-8063-1641-1
Made in the United States of America

INTRODUCTION

As early as 1640 the Connecticut Court of Election ordered all magistrates to keep a record of the marriages they performed. In 1644 the registration of births and marriages became the official responsibility of town clerks and registrars, with deaths added to their duties in 1650. From 1660 until the close of the Revolutionary War these vital records of birth, marriage, and death were generally well kept, but then for a period of about two generations until the mid-nineteenth century, the faithful recording of vital records declined in some towns.

General Lucius Barnes Barbour was the Connecticut Examiner of Public Records from 1911 to 1934 and in that capacity directed a project in which the vital records kept by the towns up to about 1850 were copied and abstracted. Barbour previously had directed the publication of the Bolton and Vernon vital records for the Connecticut Historical Society. For this new project he hired several individuals who were experienced in copying old records and familiar with the old script.

Barbour presented the completed transcriptions of town vital records to the Connecticut State Library where the information was typed onto printed forms. The form sheets were then cut, producing twelve small slips from each sheet. The slips for most towns were then alphabetized and the information was then typed a second time on large sheets of rag paper, which were subsequently bound into separate volumes for each town. The slips for all towns were then interfiled, forming a statewide alphabetized slip index for most surviving town vital records.

The dates of coverage vary from town to town, and of course the records of some towns are more complete than others. There are many cases in which an entry may appear two or three times, apparently because that entry was entered by one or more persons. Altogether the entire Barbour Collection--one of the great genealogical manuscript collections and one of the last to be published--covers 137 towns and comprises 14,333 typed pages.

TABLE OF CONTENTS

MILFORD 1

NEW CANAAN 207

NEW HARTFORD 243

ABBREVIATIONS

adm. fr..............admitted as a freeman
ae......................age
b........................born, both
bd......................buried
B. G..................Burying Ground
d........................died, day, or daughter
decd..................deceased
f.........................father
h........................hour
int. pub.............intention published
J.P.....................Justice of Peace
m......................married or month
res.....................resident
s........................son
s.b.....................stillborn
w......................wife
wid....................widow
wk.....................week
y........................year

THE BARBOUR COLLECTION
OF CONNECTICUT TOWN
VITAL RECORDS

MILFORD VITAL RECORDS
1640 - 1850

	Vol.	Page

ADAMS, Edward, tanner, came to Milford, 1646 — ES 176
    Elizabeth, m. James **BRISCOE**, June 1, 1699, by Hon. Robert
        Treat, Dept. Gov. — 1 80
    Elizabeth, d. William, b. Mar. 3, 1704/5 — 1 29
    Elizabeth, d. William, b. Mar. 3, 1704/5 — OL 62
    Nathaniel, lawyer, of Green Farms, Fairfield, Co., Conn., m.
        Jerusha **BULL**, d. Henry & Harriet, [   ] — 1 174
    Samuel, s. William, b. May 3, 1706 — 1 29
    Samuel, s. William [& Elizabeth], b. May 3, 1706 — OL 62
    William, s. William, b. June 3, 1708 — 1 29
    William, s. William, b. June 3, 1708 — OL 63
    William, d. [   ], 1787 (non resident) — SM 35
    William, d. July [   ], 1795, at Hartford (non resident) — SM 57
ADKINS, -----, m. William **GOLD**, Apr. 12, 1716, by Jon[a]th[an]
    Law, J.P. — OL 80
ADKINSON, Rebecca, m. Thomas **CAMFIELD**, Feb. 26, 1679, by
    Major Treat, Dept. Gov. — OL 36
ALBERS, Hantz, came to Milford, [   ] — ES 176
ALLEN, ALEN, [see also **ALLIN** & **ALLYN**], Abigail, d. Gideon,
    b. [   ] — OL 37
    Abigail, d. Sarah, bp. 1688* *(Sept. 9, 1688 hand printed in
        original manuscript) — ES 238
    Abigail, Mrs., m. John **SHEPARD**, Oct. 8, 1707, by Capt.
        Sam[ue]ll Eells, J.P. — OL 61
    Abigail, Mrs., m. John **SHEPARD**, Oct. 9, 1707, by Samuel
        Eells, J.P. — 1 28
         — 1 65
    Edward, s. Lieut. George, b. Mar. 1, 1713/14 — ES 238
    Edward, s. Geo[rge], b. Mar. 1, 1714 — ES 180
    Edward, Col., d. [   ], 1778, at Woodbury — BP 83
    Edward, d. [   ], 1840, ae. 12 — SM 12
    Elijah, formerly of Milford, d. Mar. [   ], 1777 — ES 238
    Frances, d. Mrs. [   ], bp. 1676 — ES 238
    Frances, w. Capt. George A., bp. 1728 — BP 80
    Gabriel, Capt., d. [   ], 1838, ae. 85
    George, m. Frances **ARNOLD**, Nov. 20, 1707, by Capt. Samuel
        Eells, J.P. — 1 28
    George, m. Frances **ARNOLD**, Nov. 20, 1707, by Sam[ue]ll
        Eells, J.P. — OL 61
         — ES 238
    George, s. [Geo[rge], b. May 5, 1715 — 1 65
    George, s. Lieut. George, d. May 5, 1719 — 1 17
    George, s. Gideon, b. [   ] — OL 34
    Georg[e], s. Gideon, b. [   ] — ES 104
    George, [s. Gideon & Sarah], b. [   ] — ES 238
    Gideon, s. Sarah, bp. 1678
    Gideon, m. Sarah **PRUDDEN**, d. Rev. Peter & Johannah,

BARBOUR COLLECTION

	Vol.	Page
ALLEN, ALEN, [see also ALLIN & ALLYN], (cont.)		
[ ], d. [ ], 1690	ES	104
G----*, m. Sarah PRUDDEN, d. Peter, [ ]		
*(Gideon)	ES	182
Gideon, [s. Gideon & Sarah], b. [ ]	ES	104
Hannah, d. Gideon, b. Oct. 6, 1685	1	21
Hannah, d. Gideon, b. Oct. 6, 1685	OL	42
Hannah, d. Sarah, bp. 1685	ES	238
Hannah*, Mrs., d. Nov. 14, 1798 *Note by N. G. Pond says probably "Hannah ALLING"	SM	65
Hawks, came to Milford, 1645	ES	176
Henry, s. George, of Weymouth, in Boston, 1635, Sandwich, Mass., 1637, Plymouth; d. 1648; Will at Plymouth	1	6
Henry, came to Milford, 1645	ES	176
Henry, s. Henry, b. May 2, 1674	OL	27
Henry, s. Mrs. [bp.], 1674	ES	238
John, s. Sarah, bp. 1680	ES	238
John, s. Gideon, b. Feb. 19, 1682	1	19
John, s. Gideon, b. Feb. 19, 1682	OL	40
Josiah, s. George, b. Jan. 10, 1708	1	29
Josiah, s. George, b. Jan. 10, 1708/9	OL	64
Keziah, m. John PLUMB, Mar. 27, 1723, by Sam[ue]l Andrews, Rev.	1	73
Mary, d. Benony, b. Oct. 21, 1663	OL	16
Mary, d. Henry, b. Aug. 2, 1700	1	23
Mary, d. Henry, b. Aug. 2, 1700	OL	48
Mary, Mrs. of New Haven, m. Miles MERWIN, of Milford, Nov. 11, 1730, by Sam[ue]ll Bishop, J.P. Witnesses Stephen Trowbridge, Joseph Miles	1	88
Mehetabel, Mrs., d. [ ], 1805	BP	11
Mercy, d. Henry, b. July 4, 1703	1	23
Mercy, d. Henry, b. July 4, 1703	OL	48
Mercy, m. Sam[ue]ll BALDWIN, s. Sam[ue]ll, 3rd, Dec. 25, 1723, by Sam[ue]ll Eells, Asst.	1	90
Noble, m. Sarah [LAMBERT, d. Frederic & Sally], [ ]	1	50
Ruth, m. Joseph NORTHROP, shoemaker, June 10, 1725	1	46
Ruth, m. Joseph NORTHROP, June 10, 1725, by Sam[ue]ll Eells, Asst.	1	103
Ruth, d. Sam[ue]ll, of New Haven, m. Dan HINE, of Milford, Feb. 18, 1756, by Rev. Benjamin Woodbridge, of Amity	1	135
Sarah, d. Benony, b. Oct. 5, 1660	OL	18
Sarah, had s. Gideon, bp. 1678 & s. John, bp. 1680	ES	238
Sarah, had d. Hannah, bp. 1685; had d. Abigail bp. 1688	ES	238
Sarah, dismissed from 3rd Ch. in Boston, 1696 & received here	ES	238
Sarah, of Fairfield, m. Gov. Jonathan LAW, [ ], 1725; d. Jan. 17, 1727	ES	130
-----, [his] ch. in North Milford, d. [ ], 1806	BP	14
ALLING, see also ALLEN & ALLYN], Anna, of East Haven, m. Nathan PLATT, of Milford, Sept. 21, 1771, by Noah Willeston	1	160
Edward, s. Lieut. Geo[rge], b. [ ], 1719	ES	238

	Vol.	Page
ALLING, [see also **ALLEN** & **ALLING**], (cont.)		
Hannah, see Hannah **ALLEN**	SM	65
ALLYN, ALLEYNE, ALLYNE, ALYNE, [see also **ALLEN** & **ALLING**], Henry, s. George & Catharine, of Sandwich, Mass. In 1637 was in Sandwich, Mass. his brothers were Ralph, George, Samuel, William, Matthew & five others; d. 1648	1	11
Henry, s. Henry, b. May 2, 1674	1	13
Josiah, s. George, d. Apr. 5, 1709	1	43
Josiah, d. Apr. [ ], 1709 (s. George)	OL	89
Mary, d. Henry*, b. Oct. 21, 1663 *(This Henry **ALLEN** was son of George of Weymouth, in Boston, 1635, Sandwich Mass., 1637, Plymouth 1641; d. 1648, Will at Plymouth)	1	6
Mercy, d. Henry, b. Oct. 8, 1671	1	11
Mercy, d. Henary, b. Oct. 8, 1671	OL	24
Merian, d. Benony, b. Apr. 20, 1669	OL	21
Merriam, d. Henry, b. Apr. 20, 1669	1	9
Obadiah, of Mattabeseak, m. Elizabeth **SAMFORD**, d. Thomas, of Milford, Oct. 21, 1669, by John Clarke, Commissioner	1	10
Obadiah, of Mettabeseck, m. Elizabeth **SAMFORD**, d. Thomas, of Milford, [ ], 1669, by John Clark, Com.	OL	22
Sarah, d. Henry, b. Oct. 5, 1660	1	8
ALSOP, ALSOPP, Elizabeth, m. Richard **BALDWIN**, a first settler, [ ] See 1st Church Records	1	111
Elizabeth, adm. Church Feb. 5, [1643]; Since m. Richard **BALDWIN** [ ]	OL	98
Eliza[beth], m. Richard **BALDWIN**, [ ]; d. Mar. [ ], 1664	ES	238
AMES, Elias, s. Joseph & Margaret, b. May 8, 1756	1	138
Joseph, m. Marg[a]ret **SMITH**, May 30, 1754, Witnesses: John Fowler, David Baldwin	1	138
ANDERSON, William, d. [ ], 1829, ae. 25	BP	59
-----, his s. [ ], d. Aug. 17, 1790, ae. 10 days	SM	42
ANDREWS, ANDREW, Abigail, oldest ch. of Samuel, m. Gov. [ ] **LAW**, [ ]; d. same year, ae. 20	ES	118
Abigail, [d. Rev. -----], b. June [ ], 1686	ES	238
Abigail, d. Rev. S. A., bp. June 23, 1686	ES	238
Abigail, d. Rev. S[amuel], bp, 1687; d. Sept. 25, 1724	ES	238
Abigail, [w. Rev. Samuel], adm. to Ch. 1691; d. Dec. 5, 1727	ES	238
Abigail, [d. Thomas A.], b. [ ], 1695	1	27
Abigail, m. Jonathan **LAW**, Aug. 1, 1706, by Lieut. Gov. Treat	OL	56
Abigail, m. Jonathan **LAW**, Aug. 1, 1706, by Lieut. Gov. Treat	ES	130
Abigail, m. Gov. Jonathan **LAW**, Aug. 2, 1706; d. Sept. 25, 1724	ES	238
Abigail, [d. Samuel, Jr.], [ ], 1723	1	78
Abigail, d. Sam[ue]ll, Jr., b. Feb. 6, 1723/4	SM	62
Elias, his d. [ ], d. Oct. 25, 1797	ES	238
Eliza, [d. Rev. Samuel], 1690	BP	47
Eliza, d. [ ], 1822, North Milford	OL	37
Elizabeth, d. Thomas, b. Nov. 4, 1679	ES	238
Elizabeth, [d. Rev. -----], b. June [ ], 1690	ES	238
Elizabeth, d. [Samuel], bp. 1728	ES	238
Elizabeth Ann, d. Samu[e]ll & Elizabeth, b. Sept. 26, 1749	1	127

BARBOUR COLLECTION

	Vol.	Page
ANDREWS, ANDREW, (cont.)		
Eunice, d. Sam[ue]l, Jr., b. Aug. 16, 1720	1	69
Eunice, d. Sam[ue]l, Jr., [ ], 1720	ES	238
Eunice, w. S[amuel], Jr., adm. to Ch. 1727	ES	238
Eunice, wid. Sam[ue]l, Jr., m. Gov. Jonathan **LAW**, 1730	ES	130
Eunice, Mrs. m. Jonathan **LAW**, Jr., b. of Milford, Jan. 11, 1736/7, by Jon[a]th[an] Law, Dept. Gov.	1	104
Eunice, wid. Samuel, m. Gov. ----- LAW, [ ]	ES	118
Eunice Hall, d. Sam[ue]ll, b. Feb. 17, 1751/2 O.S.	1	131
Hannah, twin with Mary, d. Thomas, b. Jan. 13, 1683	1	18
Hannah, twin with Mary, d. Thomas, b. Jan. [ ], 1683	OL	38
Hannah, [d. Rev. -----], b. Nov. [ ], 1704	ES	238
Hannah, d. Sam[uel] A., b. N[ ], 1704	ES	238
Jane, twin with Mary, d. Sam[ue]l, b. [ ], 1696; d. Feb. 1, 1696	ES	238
Jane, d. Sam[ue]l, bp. 1697	ES	238
Jane, d. Sam[ue]l, b. [ ], 1699	ES	238
Jane, [d. Rev. -----], b. Apr. [*], 1699 *(16 hand printed in original manuscript)	ES	238
John, s. Tho[ma]s A., b. F[eb] [ ], 1685	ES	238
John, [s. Rev. -----], b. [ ], 1694, d. [ ], 1714	ES	238
John, [s. Samuel & Eunice], b. [ ], d. [ ], 1714, ae. 20	ES	118
John, s. Rev. S[amuel], [ ], 1714; d. young	ES	238
Jonathan, s. Sam[ue]l A., b. [ ], 1701	ES	238
Jonathan, s. Sam[ue]l, bp. 1701	ES	238
Jonathan, [s. Rev. -----], b. Aug. [ ], 1701	ES	238
Jonathan, m. Elizabeth **SMITH**, Jan. 5, 1726/7, by Rev. Sam[ue]ll Andrews	1	82
Jonathan, m. Eunice **BALDWIN**, Apr. 20, 1758, by Rev. Benjamin Woodbridge, of Amity	1	163
Mary, twin with Hannah, d. Thomas, b. Jan. 13, 1683	1	18
Mary, twin with Hannah, d. Thomas, b. Jan. [ ], 1683	OL	38
Mary, [d. Rev. -----], b. July 24, 1696	ES	238
Mary, twin with Jane, d. Sam[ue]l, b. [ ], 1696	ES	238
Mary, d. Sam[ue]l, bp. 1699	ES	238
Mary, m. Benjamin **PRITCHARD**, Jr., Jan. 20, 1712/13, by Samuel Eells, Asst.	1	91
Mary, d. June 15, 1785, ae. 7	SM	29
Rebecca, d. Thomas A., b. May [ ], 1693	ES	238
Ruth, d. Tho[mas] A., b. [ ], 1690	ES	238
Samuel, son-in-law of [Gov. Robert], [ ]	ES	238
Samuel, from Cambridge; ordained Nov. 18, 1685; d. July 24, 1738	ES	57
Sam[ue]l, s. Rev. S[amuel], bp. 1688; adm. to Ch. 1713; d. Apr. 26, 1728	ES	238
Samuel, [s. Rev. -----], b. Sept. [ ], 1688; d. Sept. 25, 1724	ES	238
Samuel, Jr., [s. Rev. Samuel], b. Sept. [ ], 1688; m. Eunice **HALL**, of Wallingford, Dec. 9, 1719; d. Aug. 26, 1728	ES	238
Samuel, Jr., of Milford, m. Eunice **HALL**, of Wallingford, Dec. 9, 1719, by Capt. John Hall, of Wallingford, J.P.	1	69
Sam[ue]l, Jr., m. Eunice **HALL**, [ ], 1719	ES	238
Sam[uel], 3rd, [s. Sam[ue]l, Jr. & Eunice], b. Aug. [ ], 1720	ES	238

MILFORD VITAL RECORDS

	Vol.	Page
ANDREWS, ANDREW, (cont.)		
Sam[uel], s. S[a]m[ue]l, Jr., b. [ ], 1720	ES	238
Samuel, s. Samuel, Jr., b. Feb. 25, 1721/2	1	68
Samuell, s. Sam[ue]ll, Jr., b. Feb. 25, 1722	1	78
Samuel, oldest s. of Rev. Samuel, m. Eunice -----, [ ]; d. Sept. 25, 1724	ES	118
Samuel, m. Mrs. Elizabeth **HARPIN**, Nov. 3, 1748, by Jonathan Law, Gov.	1	127
Sam[ue]ll & w. Elizabeth, adm. to Ch. 1754	ES	238
Samuel, Rev. supposed to have been near Boston, 1756(?), d. Jan. 24, 1738, ae. 82; had been 52 years pastor of the Church; was 2nd Pres. Of Yale College. His w. [ ] d. Dec. 5, 1727, by who he had 4 sons, 5 daughters, only one son Jonathan survived him	ES	118
Samuel, his s. [ ], d. Jan. 10, 1776	SM	5
Samuel, his s. [ ], d. Dec. [ ], 1781	SM	22
Samuel, his infant s. [ ], d. Apr. 25, 1786	SM	31
Samuel, his w. [ ], d. May 11, 1786, ae. 36	SM	31
Samuel, d. Feb. 13, 1787	SM	33
Samuel, his d. [ ], d. Oct. 7, 1787, ae. 7	SM	34
Sarah, m. Samuel **NORTHROP**, Feb. 25, 1713/14, by Jonathan Law, J.P.	1	35
Sarah, m. Sam[ue]ll **NORTHROP**, Feb. 25, 1713/14, by Jon[a]th[an] Law, J.P.	OL	75
Sarah, [d. Samuel, Jr.], [ ], 1725	ES	238
Sarah, d. Sam[ue]ll, Jr., b. Mar. 27, 1726	1	78
Thomas, s. Thomas, b. Sept. 10, 1681	OL	37
William, [s. Rev. -----], b. May [ ], 1692; d. May 2, 1712	ES	238
William, s. Samuel, d. May 2, 1712	1	44
William, s. Samuel, d. May 2, 1712	OL	90
William, [s. Samuel & Eunice], b. [ ]; d. May 2, 1712, ae. 20	ES	118
W[illia]m, s. Rev. Sam[ue]l, d. May 2, 1712	ES	238
W[illia]m, s. Rev. S[amuel], [ ], 1712; d. young	ES	238
William, had negro girl d. Feb. 1, 1776	SM	5
William, his 1st w. [ ], d. Feb. 18, 1787	SM	33
William, d. July 30, 1796	SM	59
-----, wid., d. [ ], 1815, at N. Milford	BP	30
ARNOLD, Abigail, m. Jonathan **LAW**, Feb. 14, 1704/5; d. Dec. 14, 1705	OL	56
Abigail, m. Gov. Jonathan **LAW**, Feb. 14, 1705; d. Dec. 14, 1705	ES	130
Frances, m. George **ALLEN**, Nov. 20, 1707, by Capt. Samuel Eells, J.P.	1	28
Frances, m. George **ALLEN**, Nov. 20, 1707, by Sam[ue]ll Eells, J.P.	OL	61
John, d. Aug. 15, 1783, ae. 50	SM	26
John, pd. £5 for not procuring men for Continental Army	1	55
Jonathan, Rev. of West Haven, m. Abigail **BEARD**, of Milford, d. John & Abigail, Apr. 4, 1728, by Sam[ue]ll Eells, Asst.	1	82
Jonathan, Rev. of West Haven, m. Mrs. Sarah **MILES**, July 29, 1728, by Sam[ue]ll Eells, Asst.	1	82
Joseph, d. Jan. [ ], 1777, taken dead from a British Ship	SM	9
-----, wid., d. [ ], 1813	BP	26

	Vol.	Page
ASHBAND, [see under **ASHBORN**]		
ASHBORN, ASHBAND, ASHBUN, Abigail, d. John & Hannah, b. July 29, 1764	1	149
Abigail, Miss d. [ ], 1807	BP	15
Joseph, came to Milford, [ ]	ES	176
Mary, d. John & Hanna, b. May 21, 1766	1	155
Mary (Holt), wid. of Joseph, d. Aug. 26, 1750	1	127
Thankfull, d. Joseph, m. William **CHARLES**, Apr. 18, 1739, by Roger Newton, Asst.	1	119
ASTWOOD, Hannah, see Hannah **FREEMAN**	OL	99
Hannah, see Hannah **FAIRMAN** or **FREEMAN**	ES	238
John, original member of First Church gathered at New Haven Aug. 22, 1739	ES	57
John, Capt., 1644	ES	40
John, Capt. Agent to England, 1653, d. July [ ], 1654, in England (one of the first planters)	ES	16
John, d. [ ], 1654, in England	OL	97
Sarah, w. John, adm. Church Aug. 2, [1640]; bd. Nov. 13, 1669	OL	97
Sarah, w. John, d. Nov. 13, 1669	ES	238
-----, Capt. d. [ ], in London	ES	17
ATKINS, Mary, m. William **GOLD**, Apr. 12, 1716, by Jonathan Law, J.P.	1	37
ATWATER, Allan, d. [ ], 1803, ae. 19 (No. 21)	BP	7
Allen, d. Aug. 23, 1803, ae. 19	SM	78
Amos, Priv., member of Capt. Samuel Peck's Co., Milford 1776	1	54
David, his w. [ ], d. [ ], 1816; his child d. [ ], 1816	BP	34
David, d. [ ], 1823	BP	49
David, d. [ ], 1839, ae. 32, at Petersburg, Va.	BP	81
Elnathan, d. [ ], 1817, ae. 24, Canton	BP	36
Elnathan, d. [ ], 1840, ae. 25	BP	83
Esther, Mrs., d. [ ], 1817	BP	36
John, Priv., member of Capt. Samuel Peck's Co., Milford, 1776	1	54
Joshua, s. Joshua, b. Apr. 10, 1658	1	3
Joshua, s. Joshua, b. Apr. 10, 1658	OL	11
Jotham*, Priv., member of Capt. Samuel Peck's Co., Milford 1776 *(Killed or taken)	1	54
Polly, d. Dea. W[illia]m, d. [ ], 1805, ae. 16 y.	BP	10
Susan, d. [ ], 1840, ae. 20	BP	83
William, his 1st w. [ ], d. Nov. 30, 1784, ae. 30	SM	28
William, his s. [ ], d. Nov. 25, 1790	SM	44
W[illia]m, his infant d. [ ], d. Feb. 27, 1796	SM	58
William, Dea., his 2nd w. [ ], d. Sept. 6, 1800, ae. 47	SM	70
William, his d. [ ], d. Feb. 4, 1805, ae. 7	SM	82
William, his infant ch. d. [ ], 1815	BP	28
W[illia]m, Dea., d. [ ], 1816, ae. 70	BP	34
W[illia]m, d. [ ], 1816	ES	94
W[illia]m, his ch. d. [ ], 1822	BP	47
William, d. [ ], 1839, ae. 64	BP	81
-----, came to Milford, 1655	ES	176
ATWOOD(?), -----, wid., d. [ ], 1836, d. at Bridge[port]	BP	75
AUSTIN, Caleb, Dr., d. [ ], 1822	BP	47
-----, Dr. his wid. [ ], d. [ ], 1839, ae. 86	BP	81

	Vol.	Page
BAILEY, BAYLEY, Charity, m. Moses STILSON, Mar. 17, 1704/5, by Sam[ue]ll Eells, J.P.	OL	53
Elizabeth, m. Joseph PLUM, Dec. 5, 1709, by Jonathan Law, J.P.	1	31
Elizabeth, m. Joseph PLUM, Dec. 5, 1709, by Jon[a]th[an] Law, J.P.	OL	67
Tho[ma]s, came to Milford, 1646	ES	177
BAKER, Hannah, d. Thomas, bp. [1650, by Rev. Peter Prudden]	OL	103
John, s. Tho[mas], d. [ ], 1684	ES	238
T., removed to East Hampton, 1650	ES	17
Thomas, d. [ ], (One of the first planters)	ES	16
Thomas, adm. Church Dec. 12, [1643]; dismissed to East Hampton, L.I.	OL	98
BALDWIN, Aaron, twin with Moses, s. James, b. Apr. 15, 1705	1	25
Aaron, twin with Moses, s. James, b. Apr. 15, 1705	OL	53
Abel, s. Amos, b. Sept. 8, 1771	1	160
Abel, m. [ ], 1802 (No. 22)	BP	6
Abel, s. Nathan, d. Sept. 9, 1802	SM	75
Abiel, s. Sam[ue]ll, b. Nov. 26, 1724	1	79
Abigail, w. Nathaniel, adm. Church June 9, [1644]; d. Mar. 22, 1648	OL	98
Abigail, d. Nathaniel, bp. [1648, by Rev. Peter Prudden]	OL	103
Abigail, w. Nath[anie]l, d. [ ], 1648	ES	238
Abigail, d. Timothy, bp. [1650, by Rev. Peter Prudden]	OL	104
Abigail, d. John, b. Nov. 15, 1658	1	3
Abigaile, d. John, b. Nov. 15, 1658	OL	11
Abigail, m. Joseph PECK, Jr., Jan. 14, 1706/7	1	27
Abigail, m. Joseph PECK, Jr., Jan. 14, 1706/7	OL	59
Abigail, d. David, b. Nov. 20, 1709	1	31
Abigail, d. David, b. Nov. 20, 1709	OL	68
Abigail, m. Samuel TERRELL, Jr., Aug. 17, 1710, by Jonathan Law, J.P.	1	33
Abigail, m. Samuel TERRELL, Jr., Aug. 17, 1710, by Jon[a]th[a]n Law, J.P.	OL	70
Abigail, d. Jon[a]th[an], Jr. & Mary, b. Feb. 17, 1716	1	71
Abigail, m. Thomas BADLWIN, Jan. 7, 1724/5, by Sam[ue]ll Eells, Asst.	1	82
Abigail, d. Thomas [& Abigail], b. Feb. 1, 1727/8	1	82
Abigail, d. Andrew, b. Aug. 20, 1760	1	163
Abigail Ann, [d. Beard & Sybel], b. Feb. 3, 1812	1	177
Abner, s. David, b. Sept. 8, 1720	1	69
Abraham, s. Charles, b. Feb. 28, 1733	1	119
Abraham, s. Charles, b. Feb. 18, 1733/4	1	100
Abraham, his w. [ ], d. Nov. 27, 1780	SM	20
Abraham, [s. Beard & Sybel], b. June 8, 1815	1	177
Adolphus, his child d. [ ], 1831	BP	64
Allexander, s. Richard & Hannah, b. Aug. 5, 1732	1	111
Alsop, s. Theophilus, b. Feb. 1, 1741/2	1	111
Amos, m. Mary Emeline (LAMBERT) WILCOX, [ ]; her 2nd husband	1	52
Amos, pd. £5 for not procuring men for Continental Army	1	55
Amos, m. Sybyl BALDWIN, Sept. 30, 1756, by Rev. Sam[ue]ll Whittlesey	1	136

BALDWIN, (cont.)

	Vol.	Page
Amos, s. Amos, b. Aug. 27, 1763	1	148
Amos, d. June 24, 1785, ae. 51	SM	29
Amos, his child d. [ ], 1828	BP	57
Amos, his child d. [ ], 1831	BP	64
Amy, d. Charles, b. Sept. 7, 1736	1	119
Amy, [d. Beard & Sybel], b. Feb. 14, 1801	1	177
Andrew, s. Timothy, b. Mar. 1, 1724	1	80
Andrew, m. Ann **MERWIN**, May 23, 1753, by Nathan Baldwin, J.P.	1	133
Ann, d. Caleb & Ann, b. Nov. 15, 1733	1	96
Ann, m. Amos **NORTHROP**, Dec. 16, 1741, by Sam[ue]ll Gunn, J.P.	1	112
Ann, m. Richard **HOLLINGWORTH**, b. of Milford, June 16, 1755, by Sam[ue]ll Eells, Asst.	1	117
Ann, d. Andrew, b. Sept. 3, 1758	1	163
Annah, d. David, b. Apr. 13, 1718	1	63
Anne, d. Timothy, bp. [1655, by Rev. Peter Prudden]	OL	105
Anne, d. Tim[othy], d. July 21, 1655, ae. 3 wks.	ES	238
Asahel, pd. £5 for not procuring men for Continental Army	1	55
Ashbel, his mark for cattle recorded Feb. 12, 1794	1	172
Avis, wid., d. Jan. 26, 1813, ae. 75	BP	25
Avis, d. [ ], 1836, ae. 76	BP	74
Beard, b. June 9, 1774	1	177
Benjamin, s. Joseph, bp. [1644, by Rev. Peter Prudden]	OL	101
Caleb, s. Samuel, b. July 26, 1704	1	26
Caleb, s. Samuel, b. July 26, 1704	OL	53
Caleb, Jr., m. Ann **TIBBALLS**, Jan. 29, 1729, by Sam[ue]ll Eells, Asst.	1	86
Caleb, s. Caleb & Ann, b. Mar. 30, 1740	1	110
Catharine, d. Thad[deus], d. [ ], 1802 (No. 27)	BP	6
Caty, d. Andrew, b. Sept. 2, 1764	1	163
Charles, s. Richard, b. Jan. 24, 1704/5	1	25
Charles, s. Richard, b. Jan. 24, 1704/5	OL	52
Charles, m. Sarah **BALDWIN**, Aug. 6, 1730, by Sam[ue]ll Eells, Asst.	1	93
Charles, d. Jan. 31, 1783	SM	25
Charles, [s. Beard & Sybel], b. Mar. 10, 1799	1	177
Cloe, d. Henry & Lydiah, b. Jan. 17, 1761	1	144
Comfort, d. Ens. Nathan, b. Dec. 26, 1729	1	84
Comfort, d. Henry & Lydia, b. Dec. 19, 1757	1	138
Comfort, d. Dec. 29, 1784, ae. 6 y.	SM	28
Comfort, d. Thaddeus, d. Sept. 30, 1802, ae. 12	SM	75
Comfort, Miss, d. [ ], 1807	BP	16
Comfort, [ch. of Beard & Sybel], b. July 14, 1807	1	177
D. L., his child d. [ ], 1824, ae. 4 m.	BP	50
Daniel, s. [Nathaniel], bp. [1644, by Rev. Peter Prudden]	OL	101
Daniel, m. Elizabeth **BOTCHFORD**, d. Henry, b. of Milford, June 25, 1665, by Benjamin Ffenn, Magestrate	OL	17
Daniel*, m. Elizabeth **BOCHFORD**, d. Henry, June 27, 1665, by Benj[amin] Ffenn, Magistrate *(First written "Samuel")	1	6
Daniel, s. Daniel, b. July 2, 1666; d. same month 23, [1666]	1	17
Daniel, s. Daniel, b. July 2, 1666; d. 23rd day of same month	OL	34

MILFORD VITAL RECORDS

	Vol.	Page
BALDWIN, (cont.)		
Daniel, s. Daniel, b. Mar. 3, 1667/8	OL	20
Daniel, s. Daniel, b. Mar. 3, 1668	1	17
Daniel, s. Daniel, b. Mar. 3, 1668	OL	34
Daniel, s. Daniel, b. Mar. 3, 1668/9	1	8
Daniel, had d. [ ], b. Aug. 3, 1672 (is now decd.)	1	12
Daniell, his d. [ ], b. Aug. 3, 1672; is now decd.	OL	25
Daniel, s. Nathaniel, Sr., d. Feb. 5, 1711/12	OL	90
Dan[ie]ll, his w. [ ], d. [ ], 1813	BP	25
Daniel, d. [ ], 1821, ae. 30	BP	44
Daniel, d. [ ], 1823	BP	49
David, Maj. pd. £5 for not procuring men for Continental Army	1	55
David, pd. £5 for not procuring men for Continental Army	1	55
David, s. Joseph, bp. [1651, by Rev. Peter Prudden]	OL	104
David, m. Mary **STREAME**, d. Ens. John, Nov. 11, 1674, by Capt. Thomas Topping	1	14
David, m. Mary **STREAME**, d. Ens. John, Nov. 11, 1674, by Thomas Tapping	OL	28
David, m. Abigail **WILKINSON**, Feb. 12, 1707/8, by Capt. Eells, J.P.	OL	63
David, m. Abigail **WILKINSON**, Feb. 20, 1707/8, by Capt. Samuel Eells, J.P.	1	29
David, s. David, b. Nov. 3, 1708	1	31
David, s. David, b. Nov. 3, 1708	OL	67
David, s. David, d. Dec. 24, 1708	1	43
David, s. David, d. Dec. 24, 1708	OL	89
David, s. Nathaniel, Sr., d. Feb. 5, 1711/12	1	43
David, s. David, b. Oct. 23, 1712	1	34
David, s. David, b. Oct. 23, 1712	OL	74
David, s. Daniel, b. Sept. 28, 1713	1	79
David, s. Nathan, [ ], 1724	ES	238
David, s. Thomas [& Abigail], b. Mar. 10, 1725/6	1	82
David, s. Andrew, b. Nov. 10, 1755	1	163
David, Maj. m. Elioce **MULET**, Feb. 2, 1764. Witnesses; Lewes Mulet, Jr., Mary Mulet	1	156
David, Maj., m. Alice **MALLETT**, [ ], 1764	ES	238
David, heard of death Feb. 5, 1780	SM	19
David, Major, d. May 4, 1784, ae. 60	SM	27
David, Major, d. 1784	ES	41
David, d. June 21, 1789, ae. 63	SM	40
Deborah, d. Thomas, b. Jan. 25, 1716/17	1	63
Ebenezer, s. Ebenezer, b. Dec. 2, 1716	1	38
Ebenezer, s. Ebenezer, b. Dec. 2, 1716	OL	83
Edward, s. Richard, b. Oct. 1, 1707	1	28
Edward, s. Richard, b. Oct. 1, 1707	OL	62
Edward, m. Elizabeth **HINE**, Dec. 6, 1733, by Sam[ue]ll Eells, Asst.	1	119
Edward, s. Amos & Sybyl, b. Apr. 19, 1758	1	129
Edward, d. Apr. 4, 1778, ae. 70	SM	15
Edward, his d. [ ], d. July 10, 1801, ae. 13	SM	72
Edward, d. [ ], 1838, ae. 80	BP	80
Elias, s. Isaac [& Philene], b. Jan. 16, 1773	1	163
Elihu, s. Maj. David [& Elioce], b. Nov. 28, 1767	1	156

	Vol.	Page
BALDWIN, (cont.)		
Elihu, his 1st w. [ ], d. Oct. 9, 1784	SM	28
Elihu, d. Sept. 13, 1795, at Baltimore (Heard of death)	SM	55
Elihu, d. [ ], 1817, ae. 87	BP	36
Elijah, s. Timothy, b. Sept. 11, 1740	1	118
Elijah, [s. Beard & Sybel], b. Mar. 2, 1797	1	177
Elijah, d. [ ], 1819, ae. 30	BP	39
Elizabeth, d. Richard, bp. [1644, by Rev. Peter Prudden]	OL	101
Elizabeth, d. Joseph, bp. [1645, by Rev. Peter Prudden]	OL	101
Elizabeth, d. John, bp. [1649, by Rev. Peter Prudden]	OL	103
Elizabeth, m. Zachariah **BURWELL**, Nov. 18, 1663 "They removed to Newark, N.J., as appears by records of deed Leb. 4, P. 258"	1	5
Elizabeth, m. Zachariah **BURWELL**, Nov. 18, 1663; settled in Newark, N.J.	OL	15
Elizabeth, d. Richard, b. Oct. 22, 1666	OL	18
Elizabeth, d. Daniel, b. Apr. 18, 1670	1	17
Elizabeth, d. Daniel, b. Apr. 18, 1670	OL	34
Elizabeth, d. Daniel, b. Apr. 24, 1670	1	10
Elizabeth, d. Daniel, b. Apr. 24, 1670	OL	22
Elizabeth, wid., m. Lieut. William **FFOWLER**, widower, Nov. 1, 1670, by John Clarke, Commissioner	1	10
Elizabeth, wid., m. Lieut. William **FOWLER**, widower, Nov. 15, 1670, by John Clark, Com.	OL	23
Elizabeth, d. Nathaniel, b. June 9, 1672	1	12
Elizabeth, d. Nathaniel, b. June 9, 1672	OL	25
Elizabeth, d. Josiah, b. Dec. 19, 1672	1	12
Elizabeth, d. Josiah, b. Dec. 19, 1672	OL	25
Elizabeth, d. Silvanus, b. Mar. 29, 1673	1	12
Elizabeth, d. Silvanus, b. Mar. 29, 1673	OL	25
Elizabeth, d. James, b. Mar. 21, 1697	1	20
Elizabeth, d. James, b. Mar. 21, 1699	OL	43
Elizabeth, m. John **MARVIN**, Jan. 6, 1704/5, by Capt. Samuel Eells, J.P.	1	26
Elizabeth, m. John **MARWIN**, Jan. 6, 1704/5, by Capt. Sam[ue]ll Eells, J.P.	OL	53
Elizabeth, m. Enos **CAMP**, Sept. 28, 1710, by Joseph Treat, J.P.	OL	69
Elizabeth, m. John **HINE**, May 3, 1716	1	39
Elizabeth, m. John **HINE**, May 3, 1716	OL	84
Elizabeth, d. Joshua, b. [ ], 1728	ES	238
Elizabeth, d. Stephen & Eunice, b. Sept. 29, 1731	1	90
Elizabeth, d. Stephen & Eunice, b. Sept. 29, 1731	1	91
Elizabeth, d. Edward, b. July 2, 1750	1	128
Elizabeth, d. Amos, b. Aug. 30, 1767	1	155
Elizabeth, d. Maj. David [& Elioce], b. Oct. 20, 1768	1	156
Elnathan, his s. & d. [twins], b. & d. Nov. 11, 1784	SM	28
Elnathan, his twin d. [ ], d. June 19, 1788	SM	36
Elnathan, his twin d. [ ], d. June 20, 1788	SM	36
Elnathan, his w. [ ], d. [ ], 1808	BP	18
Elnathan, his ch., d. [ ], 1831	BP	64
Elnathan, d. [ ], 1832, ae. 87	BP	68
Enoch, s. Thomas, b. Nov. 29, 1712	1	63
Enoch, s. Timothy, b. Oct. 6, 1736	1	118

	Vol.	Page

BALDWIN, (cont.)

Esther, d. Nathaniel, Sr., b. Nov. 14, 1676	1	15
Esther, d. Nathaniell, Sr., b. Nov. 14, 1676	OL	30
Esther, d. Nathaniel, Sr., b. May 21, 1683	1	19
Esther, d. Nathaniel, b. May 25, 1683	OL	42
* *(Elizabeth, w. Richard, d. Mar. [ ], 1664 hand printed in original manuscript)	ES	238
Esther, [twin with Rachel], d. Jon[a]th[an], Jr. & Mary, b. Mar. 17, 1720; d. May 9, 1720	1	71
Easther, m. Benjamin **BULL**, Dec. 22, 1748, by Rev. Sam[ue]ll Whittlesey	1	152
Esther, d. [ ], 1801 (No. 21)	BP	3
Ethel, her child d. [ ], 1830, ae. 12	BP	61
Eunice, d. Noah [& Thankfull], b. Jan. 12, 1733/4	1	98
Eunice, d. Theophilus, b. Apr. 20, 1738	1	107
Eunice, m. Jonathan **ANDREWS**, Apr. 20, 1758, by Rev. Benjamin Woodbridge, of Amity	1	163
Eunice, d. Andrew, b. June 25, 1767	1	163
Eunice, Miss d. [ ], 1813, ae. 31	BP	31
Eunice, wid., d. [ ], 1824, ae. 95	BP	50
Ezra, s. Jonathan, b. Dec. 1, 1706	1	27
Ezra, s. Jon[a]th[an]n, b. Dec. 1, 1706	OL	58
Frederick, his ch. d. [ ], 1832	BP	67
Freelove, d. Phinehas & Rebeckah, b. Dec. 5, 1728	1	87
Gamaleel, s. Sam[ue]ll, Jr. & Sarah, b. Sept. 11, 1716	1	79
Hannah, d. Joseph, bp. [1644, by Rev. Peter Prudden	OL	101
Hannah, d. Timothy, bp. [1644, by Rev. Peter Prudden]	OL	101
Hannah, d. Timothy, decd., m. Elnathan **BOCHFORD**, widower, Dec. 12, 1667, by Mr. Ffenn, Magistrate	1	8
Han[n]ah, d. Timothy, decd., m. Elnathan **BOXFORD**, widower, b. of Milford, Dec. 12, 1667, by Mr. Ffenn, Magestrate	OL	20
Hannah, d. Nathaniel, b. July 11, 1674	1	13
Hannah, d. Nathaniel, b. July 11, 1674	OL	27
Hannah, m. John **FFISKE**, Jan. 17, 1681, by Major Treat	OL	37
Hannah, w. Jonathan, [ ], 1681	ES	238
Hannah, w. Jonathan, d. June 9, 1693	1	40
Hannah, w. Jonathan, d. June 9, 1693	OL	86
Han[n]ah, d. Joseph, cooper, b. Apr. 10, 1716/17	1	63
Hannah, d. Richard, Jr. & Hannah, b. Mar. 3, 1734/5	1	111
Henry, s. Barnabus, b. Oct. 5, 1702	1	33
Henry, s. Barnabus, b. Oct. [ ], 1702	OL	72
Henry, of Amity, m. Lydia **BOTCHFORD**, of Milford, Feb. 23, 1757 by Sam[ue]ll Whittlesey	1	138
Henry, s. Henry & Lydia, b. Aug. 7, 1759	1	141
Hesekiah, his infant ch., d. [ ], 1815	BP	29
Huldy Allen, d. Enoch & Mary, b. Feb. 17, 1764	1	154
Isaac, pd. £5 for not procuring men for Continental Army	1	55
Isaac, s. David, b. Feb. 22, 1715/16	1	37
Isaac, s. David, b. Feb. 22, 1715/16	OL	80
Isaac, s. Theophilus, b. Apr. 18, 1740	1	111
Isaac, m. Philene **PURDIE**, Dec. 24, 1766, by Benjamin Woodbridge	1	163
Isaac, s. Isaac [& Philene], b. Nov. 24, 1770	1	163

BARBOUR COLLECTION

	Vol.	Page
BALDWIN, (cont.)		
Isaac, his infant s. [ ], d. May 6, 1790	SM	41
Isaac, d. Apr. 17, 1791, ae. 53	SM	45
Isaac, his w. [ ], d. [ ], 1817	BP	37
Isaac, his w. [ ], d. [ ], 1822	BP	47
Isaac, d. [ ], 1823, ae. 60	BP	49
Isaac, his w. [ ], d. [ ], 1828, ae. 24	BP	57
Israel, s. Sam[ue]ll, Jr., b. Oct. 31, 1718	1	79
Jacob, s. Joseph, b. Jan. 20, 1717/18	1	63
Jacob, m. Rebeckah **TERRELL**, Apr. 11, 1744, by Roger Newton, Asst.	1	122
Jared, s. Caleb & Ann, b. Jan. 30, 1731/2	1	94
Jared, his youngest, d. [ ], d. Mar. 11, 1776	SM	5
Jared, his w. [ ], d. [ ], 1823	BP	48
Jared, d. [ ], 1830	BP	61
Jehial, s. Daniel, b. June 21, 1716	1	79
Jeremiah, pd. £5 for not procuring men for Continental Army	1	55
Jeremiah, s. Sergt. Richard, b. Sept. 22, 1660	OL	13
Jeremiah, s. Sergt. Daniel, b. Sept. 10, 1706	1	27
Jeremiah, s. Sergt. Dan[ie]ll, b. Sept. 10, 1706	OL	56
Jerijah, s. Richard, Sr., b. Jan. 19, 1701/2	1	25
Jerijah, s. Richard, Sr., b. Jan. 19, 1701/2	OL	52
Jrejah, member of 2nd Church formed in 1742	ES	87
Joanna, [d. Samuel, s. of Peter], b. Ma[y] 1, 1676	ES	184
Joel, s. Samuel, Sr., b. July 11, 1711	1	33
Joel, s. Samuel, Sr. (wheelwright), b. July 11, 1711	OL	70
Joel, m. Abigail **FENN**, Dec. 26, 1734, by Sam[ue]ll Eells, Asst.	1	106
Joel, s. Joel & Abigail, b. May 21, 1739	1	109
Joel, original member of 2nd Church formed in 1742	ES	87
Joel, d. [ ], 1807, at Charleston, South Carolina	BP	16
Joel, his w. [ ], d. [ ], 1826	BP	54
Joel, d. [ ], 1833	BP	68
Joel, his w. [ ], d. [ ], 1838	BP	79
John, s. Nathaniel, bp. [1644, by Rev. Peter Prudden]	OL	101
John, s. John, bp. [1648, by Rev. Peter Prudden]; adm. Church Mar. 19, 1648	OL	103
John, adm. Church Mar. 19, [1648], bd. June 21, 1681	OL	99
John, s. John, b. Apr. 13, 1657	1	3
John, s. John, Jr., b. Apr. 13, 1657	OL	10
John, s. John, Sr., m. Hannah **BREWER**, d. of Obadiah, of New London, Oct. 30, 1663, by Robert Treat	1	5
John, s. Nathaniel, m. Hannah **OSBORNE**, d. Richard, Nov. 19, 1663, by Robert Treat	1	5
John, s. Nathaniell, m. Han[n]ah **OSBORNE**, d. Richard, Nov. 19, 1663, by Rob[ert] Treat	OL	15
John, s. John, Sr., m. Han[n]ah **BROWEN**, d. Obadiah, of New London, Nov. 30, 1663, by Rob[ert] Treat	OL	15
John, his s. [ ], b. June 2nd week, 1665	1	6
John, Sr., had s. [ ], b. June 2nd week, 1665	OL	16
John, s. Daniel, b. Mar. 26, 1679	1	17
John, s. Daniel, b. Mar. 26, 1679	OL	34
John, [s. Samuel, s. of Peter], b. Ma[y] 20, 1680	ES	184
John, [d.], 1681	ES	18

	Vol.	Page
BALDWIN, (cont.)		
John, d. [ ], 1681	ES	238
John, s. Jonathan, b. May 22, 1683	1	19
John, s. Jonathan, b. May 22, 1683	OL	40
John, d. Mar. 19, 1694, ae. 5 y.	ES	238
John, his child d. [ ], 1837, ae. 14 m.	BP	77
John, Sr., m. Mary **BREWEN**, d. John, Aug. 15, [ ]	OL	7
John, Sr., of Milford, m. Marie **BREWER**, d. of John, [ ]	1	1
Jonathan, s. Joseph, b. Feb. 15, 1649	LL	2
Jonathan, s. Joseph, bp. [1649, by Rev. Peter Prudden]	OL	103
Jonathan, adm. to 1st Ch. 1675	ES	238
Jonathan, m. Hannah **WARD**, Nov. 2, 1677, by John Ward	1	17
Jonathan, m. Hannah **WARD**, Nov. 2, 1677, by Jno Ward	OL	34
Jonathan, s. Jonathan, b. Jan. 31, 1679	1	17
Jonathan, s. Jonathan, b. Jan. 31, 1679	OL	35
Jonathan, s. Jonathan, bp. 1680	ES	238
Jonathan, m. Mary **TIBBALLS**, Sept. 28, 1710, by Samuel Eells, J.P.	1	32
Jon[a]th[an], Jr., m. Mary **TIBBALLS**, Sept. 28, 1710, by Major Sam[ue]ll, Eells, Asst. Witnesses, Sam[ue]ll Tibballs, Anna Smith, Allis Fowler	1	71
Jon[a]th[an], m. Mary **TIBBALLS**, Sept. 28, 1710, by Sam[ue]ll Eells, Asst.	OL	68
Jon[a]th[an], Jr., m. Mary **TIBBALL**, [ ], 1710	ES	238
Jon[a]th[an], s. Jon[a]th[an], Jr. & Mary, b. Sept. 17, 1722	1	71
Joseph, [d.]	ES	16
Joseph, adm. [June] 23, [1644]	OL	98
Joseph, s. Joseph, bp. [1644, by Rev. Peter Prudden]	OL	101
Joseph, s. John, bp. [1651, by Rev. Peter Prudden]	OL	104
Joseph, s. Joseph, b. Oct. 1, 1663	1	6
Joseph, s. Joseph, b. Oct. 6, 1663	OL	15
Joseph, Jr., m. Hannah **BRISCOE**, Mar. 26, 1714, by Joseph Treat, J.P.	1	35
Joseph, Jr., m. Han[n]ah **BRISCO**, Mar. 26, 1714, by Jos[eph] Treat, J.P.	OL	76
Joseph Beard, [s. Beard & Sybel], b. Nov. 29, 1802	1	177
Joshua, s. Sergt. Jonathan, bp. 1691	ES	238
Joshua & his w. [ ], adm. to Ch. 1727	ES	238
Joshua, m. Abigail **BEARD**, Aug. 10, 1773	ES	238
Joshua, d. [ ], 1821, ae. 95	BP	45
Joshua, his wid. [ ], d. [ ], 1832, ae. 82	BP	67
Josiah, s. John, bp. [1648, by Rev. Peter Prudden]; adm. Church Mar. 19, 1648	OL	103
Josiah, s. John, m. Mary **CAMP**, d. Samuel, "sometime, now Mary Law", b. of Milford, June 25, 1666, by Mr. Fenn, Magestrate	OL	19
Josiah, s. John, m. Mary* **CAMP**, d. Edward, of New Haven, now Marcy Ewine (should be Law), June 25, 1667, by Mr. FFenn *(Marcy?)	1	8
Josiah, s. Josiah, b. Mar. 21, 1677	1	16
Josiah, s. Josiah, b. Mar. 21, 1677/8	OL	32
Josiah, d. [ ], 1683	ES	238

	Vol.	Page
BALDWIN, (cont.)		
Justice, m. Ma[r]tha NETTLETON, Nov. 26, 1771, by Rev. Sam[ue]ll Whittlesey	1	160
Justus, d. June 13, 1793, ae. 66	SM	49
Katharine, d. Phinehas, b. Nov. 1, 1731	1	92
Lois, d. Daniel & Patience, b. May 19, 1727	1	82
Louis, d. Jacob, b. Sept. 14, 1747	1	127
Martha, d. Joseph, bp. [1646, by Rev. Peter Prudden]	OL	102
Martha, d. Richard, b. Apr. 1, 1663	1	5
Martha, d. Richard, b. Apr. 1, 1663	OL	15
Martha, m. Samuel NETTLETON, Feb. 8, 1681, by Maj. Treat	1	18
Martha, m. Nath[anie]l NETTESON, Feb. 8, 1681, by Major Treat	OL	38
Martha, m. Enos CAMP, Sept. 28, 1710, by Joseph Treat, J.P.	1	32
Martha, d. Jon[a]th[an], Jr. [& Mary], b. Mar. 23, 1713	1	71
Martha, d. Edward & Elizabeth, b. Feb. 2, 1744/5	1	119
Martha, wid. d. [ ], 1810, ae. 88 y.	BP	20
Mary, d. Samuel, b. Nov. [ ]	OL	7
Mary, m. John BULL, s. Henry & Harriet, [ ]	1	174
Mary, adm. Church, Jan. 9, [1642]. Since m. Robert PLUM, [ ]	OL	98
Mary, w. Timothy, adm. Church Mar. 5, [1643]	OL	98
Mary, d. Timothy, bp. [1643, by Rev. Peter Prudden]	OL	100
Mary, w. [Joseph], adm. Church July 25, [1644]	OL	98
Mary, d. Joseph, bp. [1644, by Rev. Peter Prudden]	OL	101
Mary, w. Tim[othy], d. July 21, 1647	ES	238
Mary, w. Timothy, adm. Church Dec. [ ], 1652	OL	99
Mary, d. Sergt. Richard, b. Nov. 10, 1653	1	1
Mary, d. Richard, bp. [1653, by Rev. Peter Prudden]	OL	104
Mary, w. John, adm. Church Apr. 30, [1653]; d. Sept. 2, 1670	OL	99
Mary, d. John, b. Sept. 7, 1654	1	2
Mary, d. John, b. Sept. 7, 1654	OL	8
Mary, d. John, bp. [1654, by Rev. Peter Prudden]	OL	105
Mary, d. of Timothy, of Milford, m. Benjamin SMITH, s. William, of Huntington, Oct. 21, 1660, by Robert Treat, Magistrate	1	4
Mary, d. Timothy, of Milford, m. Benjamin SMITH, s. William, of Huntington, Oct. 24, 1660, by Robert Treat, Magestrate	OL	13
Mary, d. Josiah, b. Sept. 14, 1670	1	10
Mary, d. Josiah, b. Sept. 14, 1670	OL	23
Mary, d. Daniel, b. Aug. 5, 1672, d. Jan. 1, 1672 [1673?]	1	17
Mary, d. Daniel, b. Aug. 1, 1672, d. Jan. 1, following	OL	34
Mary, [d. Samuel, s. of Peter], b. Aug. 17, 1681	ES	184
Mary, w. Sergt. Timothy, d. Sept. 29, 1703	1	41
Mary, w. Sergt. Timothy, d. Nov. 29, 1703	OL	87
Mary, m. Thomas NEWTON, June 20, 1704, by Thomas Clark, J.P.	1	79
Mary, m. Thomas NEWTON, s. Rev. [ ], June 20, 1704; d. May 29, 1744	ES	238
Mary, d. Jon[a]th[an], Jr. & Mary, b. Sept. 8, 1711	1	71
Mary, wid., d. May 28, 1712	1	44
Mary, wid., d. May 28, 1712	OL	91
Mary, d. Nathan, b. July 12, 1714	1	39

	Vol.	Page
BALDWIN, (cont.)		
Mary, d. Nathan, b. July 12, 1714	OL	91
Mary, d. Ebenezer, b. Feb. 11, 1714/15	1	38
Mary, d. Ebenezer, b. Feb. 11, 1714/15	OL	83
Mary, d. Timothy, b. Feb. 10, 1722	1	80
Mary, d. Theophilus & Dorothy, b. Dec. 28, 1743	1	118
Mary, [d. Beard & Sybel], b. Jan. 2, 1805	1	177
Mehetable, d. Obadiah, b. Feb. 21, 1702/3	1	23
Mehittabel, d. Obadiah, b. Feb. 21, 1702/3	OL	48
Mehetabeel, m. Benj[ami]n **BUNNELL**, Apr. 13, 1726, by Jon[a]th[an] Law, Dept. Gov.	1	81
Mercy, m. Azariah **CANFIELD**, Feb. 26, 1719/20, by Major Sam[ue]ll Eells, Asst.	1	75
Mercy, d. Sam[ue]ll [& Mercy], b. Nov. 1, 1724	1	90
Merrett, d. [ ], 1815	BP	28
Mildred, w. Lieut. Silvanus, d. Jan. 6, 1711/12	1	43
Mildred, w. Lieut. Silvanus, d. Jan. 6, 1711/12	OL	90
Miles, s. Andrew & Ann, b. Apr. 22, 1754	1	133
Moses, twin with Aaron, s. James, b. Apr. 15, 1705	1	25
Moses, twin with Aaron, s. James, b. Apr. 15, 1705	OL	53
Naoma, d. Jacob [& Rebeckah], b. Nov. 6, 1747	1	122
Naomi, d. Jacob, d. Nov. 4, 1750	1	127
Nathan, m. Elizabeth **ROGERS**, July 31, 1712, by Samuel Eells, J.P.	1	34
Nathan, m. Elizabeth **ROGERS**, July 31, 1712, by Sam[ue]ll Eells, Asst.	OL	74
Nathan, s. Nathan, Jr., b. June 13, 1715	1	36
Nathan, s. Nathan, Jr., b. June 13, 1715	OL	78
Nathan, m. Elizabeth **FORD**, June 24, 1715, by Major Eells, Asst.	1	36
Nathan, m. Elizabeth **FFORD**, June 24, 1715, by Major Eells, Asst.	OL	77
Nathan, s. Nathan, b. Dec. 12, 1716	1	39
Nathan, s. Nathan, b. Dec. 12, 1716/17	OL	84
Nathan, 1st J.P., b. Dec. 13, 1717	ES	185
Nathan, Capt., 1737	ES	41
Nathan, Jr., d. [ ], 1803 (1808? See Probate Files)	BP	7
Nathan, Jr., d. Mar. 30, 1803 (1808? See Probate Files)	SM	77
Nathan, d. [ ], 1804, ae. 83 (No. 14)	BP	9
Nathan, d. May 9, 1804	SM	80
Nathan, his ch. d. [ ], 1825	BP	52
Nathan, his infant d. [ ], 1837	BP	77
Nathan Andrew, [s. Beard & Sybel], b. Aug. 17, 1821	1	177
Nathaniel, cooper, b. of Timothy, d. [ ], (One of the first planters)	ES	16
Nathaniel, s. Nathaniel, bp. [1645, by Rev. Peter Prudden]	OL	102
Nathaniel, s. John, bp. [1648, by Rev. Peter Prudden]; adm. Church Mar. 19, 1648; d. Jan. 16, 1671	OL	103
Nathaniel, weaver, m. Hannah **BOTCHFORD**, d. Henry, Mar. 12, 1670/1	1	11
Nathaniel, weaver, m. Hannah **BOTSFORD**, d. Hennary, Mar. 12, 1670/1, by John Clark, Com.	OL	24
Nathaniel, s. Daniel, b. May 14, 1676; d. July 14, 1676	1	17

BALDWIN, (cont.)

	Vol.	Page
Nathaniell, s. Daniel, b. May 14, 1676; d. July 14, 1676	OL	34
Nathaniel, s. Nathaniel, b. Sept. 6, 1676	1	15
Nathaniell, s. Nathaniell, b. Sept. 6, 1676	OL	30
Nathaniell, d. July 5, 1748	1	123
Nathaniel, d. [ ], 1748	ES	238
Noah, [s. Sergt. Jonathan], bp. 1701	ES	238
Noah, of Milford, m. Thankfull **JOHNSON**, of Stratford, Mar. 27, 1733, by Rev. Hez[ekiah] Gold, of Stratford	1	98
Noah, Elder, original member of 2nd Church formed in 1742	ES	87
Noah, Elder, d. Mar. 6, 1784	SM	27
Noah, d. [ ], 1784	ES	94
Obadiah, s. John, b. Oct. 29, 1660	1	4
Obadiah, s. John, Sr., b. Oct. 29, 1660	OL	13
Patience, d. Daniel, b. Oct. 11, 1724	1	79
Peleg, s. Samuel, b. Feb. 11, 1708/9	1	31
Peleg, s. Samuel, b. Feb. 11, 1708/9	OL	66
Peleg, original member of 2nd Church formed in 1742	ES	87
Peleg, his w. [ ], d. July 27, 1776, ae. 62	SM	6
Peleg, Priv., member of Capt. Samuel Peck's Co., Milford 1776	1	54
Peleg, d. Mar. 11, 1797, ae. 88	SM	61
Peleg, his ch., d. [July], 1799	BP	2
Peleg, his d. [ ], d. Aug. 15, 1799, ae. 2 y.	SM	67
Peleg, his d. [ ], d. Feb. 27, 1800	SM	69
Peleg, see Peleg **BENJAMIN**	1	179
Peter, [s. Samuel, s. of Peter], b. F[eb.] [ ], 1672	ES	184
Phebe, d. Sergt. Jonathan, b. Nov. 6, 1704	1	25
Phebe, d. Sergt. Jonathan, b. Nov. 6, 1704	OL	51
Phebe, bapt. 1704	ES	238
Phebe, wid., d. [ ], 1821	BP	44
Phinehas, s. Richard, b. Mar. 1, 1700	1	25
Phinehas, s. Richard, b. Mar. 1, 1700	OL	52
Phinehas, m. Rebeckah **BALDWIN**, Aug. 25, 1727, by Sam[ue]ll Eells, Asst.	1	87
Phinehas, m. Rebecca **BALDWIN**, Aug. 25, 1727	ES	238
Phinehas, m. Rebeccah **BALDWIN**, [ ], 1727	ES	238
Phinehas, his ch., d. [ ], 1805	BP	11
Phinehas, d. [ ], 1808	BP	17
Polly Esther, d. [ ], 1827, ae. 23	BP	56
Rachel, [twin with Esther], d. Jon[a]th[an], Jr. & Mary, b. Mar. 17, 1720	1	71
Rebecca, d. Samuel, b. Nov. 10, 1702	1	26
Rebecah, d. Samuel, b. Nov. 10, 1702	OL	53
Rebeckah, m. Phinehas **BALDWIN**, Aug. 25, 1727, by Sam[ue]ll Eells, Asst.	1	87
Rebecca, m. Phinehas **BALDWIN**, Aug. 25, 1727	ES	238
Rebeccah, m. Phinehas **BALDWIN**, [ ], 1727	ES	238
Rebeckah, m. Richard **SPERRY**, Dec. 6, 1764, by Benjamin Woodbridge	1	153
Rebeckah, d. Isaac [& Philene], b. Sept. 30, 1767	1	163
Rebecca, wid., d. May 5, 1790, ae. 89	SM	41
Remember, d. Josiah, b. Feb. 29, 1679/80	1	17
Remember, d. Josiah, b. Feb. 29, 1679/80	OL	35

MILFORD VITAL RECORDS 17

	Vol.	Page
BALDWIN, (cont.)		
Reuben, s. Jacob [& Rebeckah], b. Sept. 28, 1746	1	122
Richard, a first settler, m. Elizabeth ALSOPP, [ ] see 1st Church Records	1	111
Richard, m. Eliza[beth], ALSOP, [ ]	ES	238
Richard, m. Elizabeth ALSOP, [ ]	OL	98
Richard, adm. Church May 9, [1641]; d. July 23, 1665	OL	98
Richard, d. July 23, 1665 (One of the first planters)	ES	16
Richard, s. John, b. Sept. 27, 1666	1	7
Richard, s. John, Sr., b. Dec. 27, [16]66	OL	18
Richard, s. Silvanus, b. Dec. 14, 1674	1	14
Richard, s. Silvanus, b. Dec. 14, 1674	OL	28
Richard, s. Silvanus, [ ], 1674; Silvanus was son of Richard, 1st	ES	238
Richard, s. Lieut. Silvanus, d. Oct. 11, 1703	1	41
Richard, s. Lieut. Silvanus, d. Oct. 11, 1703	OL	87
Richard, s. Sergt. Zachariah, b. Sept. 10, 1709	1	31
Richard, s. Sergt. Zachariah, b. Sept. 10, 1709	OL	67
Richard, m. Alice BOTSFORD, Oct. 31, 1771, by Rev. Sam[ue]ll Wales	1	161
Richard, his w. [ ], d. [ ], 1822	BP	47
Richard, d. [ ], 1834, ae. 68	BP	71
Samuel, s. John, bp. [1648, by Rev. Peter Prudden]; adm. Church Mar. 19, 1648	OL	103
Samuell, s. Miles, b. June 28, 1661	OL	14
Samuel*, m. Elizabeth BOCHFORD, d. Henry, June 27, 1665, by Benj[amin] Ffenn, Magistrate *(Overwritten to read "Daniel")	1	6
S[a]m[uel], [s. Samuel, s. of Peter], b. Aug. 10, 1673	ES	184
Samuel, s. Daniel, b. Dec. 26, 1673	1	13
Samuel, s. Daniel, b. Dec. 26, 1673	OL	26
Samuel, s. Daniel, b. Dec. 26, 1673; d. Mar. 26, 1674	1	17
Sam[ue]ll, s. Daniel, b. Dec. 26, 1673; d. Mar. 26, 1674	OL	34
Samuel, s. Josiah, b. Mar. 14, 1674/5	1	14
Samuel, s. Josiah, b. Mar. 14, 1674/5	OL	29
Samuel, s. David, b. Dec. 25, 1683	1	19
Samuel, s. David, b. Dec. 25, 1683	OL	40
Samuel, s. Nathaniel, b. Jan. 14, 1684	OL	42
Samuel, s. Nathaniel, b. May 14, 1684	1	19
Sam[ue]l, [s. Samuel, s. of Peter], b. Ju[ne] [ ], 1677; m. Hannah CLARK, [ ], 1705	ES	184
Samuel, s. Samuel, b. Feb. 17, 1700/1	1	26
Samuel, s. Samuel, b. Feb. 17, 1700/1	OL	53
Sam[ue]ll, m. Sarah CARBY, Apr. 9, 1712, by Sam[ue]ll Eells, Asst.	OL	74
Samuel, s. Samuel, b. May 10, 1713	1	34
Sam[ue]ll, s. Sam[ue]ll, b. May 10, 1713	OL	74
Sam[ue]ll, s. Sam[ue]ll, 3rd, m. Mercy ALLEN, Dec. 25, 1723, by Sam[ue]ll Eells, Asst.	1	90
Samuel, s. Sam[ue]l [& Mercy], b. Apr. 10, 1731	1	90
Samuel, d. Jan. 8, 1737/8	1	105
Samuel, Jr., s. Samuel, of Milford, m. Abigaill HUMPHREY-VILLE, of New Haven, Jan. 8, 1753, by Rev. Benjamin		

BALDWIN, (cont.)

	Vol.	Page
Woodbridge, of Amity	1	131
Samuel, d. [ ], 1778	SM	16
Samuel, s. Elihu & Phebe, b. June 20, 1792	1	173
Samuel, his infant ch. d. [ ], 1815	BP	30
Sarah, d. Timothy, bp. [1645, by Rev. Peter Prudden]	OL	101
Sarah, d. Richard, bp. [1649, by Rev. Peter Prudden]	OL	103
Sarah, d. Joseph, b. Nov. 6, 1653	1	1
Sarah, d. Joseph, b. Nov. 6, 1653	OL	7
Sarah, d. Joseph, bp. [1653, by Rev. Peter Prudden]	OL	104
Sarah, d. John, b. Dec. 25, 1655	1	2
Sarah, d. John, b. Dec. 25, 1655	OL	9
Sarah, d. John, bp. [1655, by Rev. Peter Prudden]	OL	105
Sarah, d. John, b. [ ] 20, 1663	1	6
Sarah, m. Samuel **BUCKINGHAM**, Dec. 12, 1663, by Mr. Ffenne, Magistrate	1	6
Sarah, m. Samuell **BURLINGHAM***, b. of Milford, Dec. 12, 1663, by Mr. Fenn, Magestrate *(Probably "BUCKINGHAM")	OL	16
Sarah, d. Timothy, m. Samuel **BUCKINGHAM**, s. Thomas, Dec. 14, 1663, by Mr. Benjamin Ffenne	1	5
Sarah, d. Timothy, m. Daniell **BURLINGHAM***, s. Thomas, decd., Dec. 14, 1663, by Benjamin Ffenn *(Samuel **BUCKINGHAM**)	OL	15
Sarah, d. John, b. [ ] 20, 1663	OL	15
Sarah, d. wid. Elizabeth, m. Samuel **RIGGS**, of Pagussie, June 14, 1667, by Samuell Shearman, Magistrate	1	8
Sarah, d. wid. Elizabeth, of Milford, m. Samuel **RIGGS**, of Pagosis, June 14, 1667, by Samuel Sherman, Magestrate	OL	20
Sarah, s. [sic] Josiah, b. Mar. 29, 1668	1	8
Sarah, d. Josiah, b. Mar. 29, 1668	OL	20
Sarah, d. Silvanus, b. Aug. 15, 1677	1	16
Sarah, d. Silvanus, b. Aug. 15, 1677	OL	32
Sarah, d. Lieut. Silvanus, d. Sept. 24, 1703	1	41
Sarah, d. Lieut. Silvanus, d. Sept. 24, 1703	OL	87
Sarah, d. Sergt. Zachariah, b. June 9, 1706	1	27
Sarah, d. Sergt. Zachariah, b. June 9, 1706	OL	58
Sarah, w. Daniel, d. Dec. 18, 1710	1	43
Sarah, w. Daniel, d. Dec. 18, 1710	OL	89
Sarah, d. Joseph, b. Jan. 10, 1713/14	1	35
Sarah, d. Joseph, Jr. [& Hannah], b. Jan. 10, 1713/14	OL	76
Sarah, d. Thomas, b. Aug. 29, 1715	1	63
Sarah*, had d. Sarah, b. July 30, 1721; d. June 19, 1722 *(Probably "Samuel")	1	79
Sarah, d. Sarah*, b. July 30, 1721; d. June 19, 1722 *(Probably Samuel")	1	79
Sarah, m. Charles **BALDWIN**, Aug. 6, 1730, by Sam[ue]ll Eells, Asst.	1	93
Sarah, d. Charles & Sarah, b. Apr. 2, 1731	1	93
Sarah, d. Charles, b. Sept. 17, 1741	1	119
Sarah, d. Andrew, b. Aug. 4, 1763	1	163
Sarah, d. Isaac [& Philene], b. May 2, 1769	1	163

	Vol.	Page
BALDWIN, (cont.)		
Sarah, wid., d. Sept. 20, 1790, ae. 84	SM	42
Sarah, d. [ ], 1804	BP	10
Sibella, d. Sam[ue]ll [& Mercy], b. Nov. 22, 1728	1	90
Sile, s. Richard, b. [ ], 1646; d. [ ], 1727	ES	238
Silva, m. Mildred **PRUDDEN**, d. Peter, [ ]	ES	182
Silva, s. Richard, bp. [1646, by Rev. Peter Prudden]; d. in the beginning of June, 1727	OL	102
Silva, s. Silva, s. of Richard, bp. [ ], 1679	ES	238
Silva, s. Richard, d. [ ], 1727, ae. 83	ES	176
Silvanus, s. Richard, 1ˢᵗ, [ ]	ES	238
Silvanus, Lieut., m. Mildred **PRUDDEN**, d. Rev. Peter & Johannah, Sept. 19, 1671	ES	104
Silvanus, m. Mildred **PRUDEN**, b. of Milford, Sept. 20, 1671, by Benjamin Ffenn, Asst.	OL	24
Silvanus, m. Mildred **PRUDEN**, Sept. 12, [ ], by Benj[amin] Ffenne, Asst.	1	11
Silvanus, s. Silvanus, b. Nov. 30, 1679	1	17
Silvanus, s. Silvanus, b. Nov. 30, 1679	OL	34
Silvanus, s. Lieut. Silvanus, d. Oct. 20, 1703	1	41
Silvanus, s. Lieut. Silvanus, d. Oct. 20, 1703	OL	87
Silvanus, s. Barnabus, b. Sept. 17, 1706	1	33
Silvanus, s. Barnabus, b. Sept. 17, 1706	OL	72
Silvanus, s. Barnabus, b. Nov. 15, 1706	1	80
Silvanus, m. Mary **FRENCH**, d. of Frances, of Derby, Apr. 18, 1734, by Rev. Daniel Humpheres, of Derby	1	99
Solomon, his w. [ ], d. Apr. 23, 1785, ae. 46	SM	29
Solomon, d. July 4, 1798, ae. 60	SM	64
Stephen, s. Zachariah, b. Oct. 11, 1693	1	20
Stephen, s. Zachariah, b. Oct. 11, 1701	OL	43
Stephen, m. Eunice **FOWLER**, Sept. 15, 1730, by Roger Newton, J.P.	1	87
Stephen, d. Mar. 29, 1788, ae. 89	SM	36
Susannah, m. John **BURWELL**, Jan. 2, 1717/18, by Major Eells, Asst. Witness John Fflower	1	66
Susannah, d. Joel [& Abigail], b. May 18, 1736	1	106
Susannah, m. Peter **HEPBURN**, Dec. 16, 1753, by Nathan Baldwin, J.P.	1	139
Sibbell, d. Edward & Elizabeth, b. July 15, 1740 (Sybil)	1	119
Sybyl, m. Amos **BALDWIN**, Sept. 30, 1756, by Rev. Sam[ue]ll Whittlesey	1	136
Sibball, d. Amos, b. Aug. 25, 1773	1	164
Sybel, b. Aug. 21, 1777	1	177
Sybyl, Mrs., d. [ ], 1802	BP	6
Sibel, wid., d. Dec. 9, 1802	SM	76
Sybel Elizabeth, [d. Beard & Sybel], b. Sept. 29, 1818	1	177
Temperance, d. Richard, bp. [1651, by Rev. Peter Prudden]	OL	104
Temperance, d. Richard, decd., m. Nathan **BURWELL**, s. Samuel, decd., Jan. 14, 1673, by Major Treat	1	13
Temperance, m. Nathan **BURWELL**, s. John, decd., b. of Milford, Jan. 14, 1673, by Major Treat	OL	26
Temperance, d. Zachariah, b. May 11, 1675	1	20

BALDWIN, (cont.)

	Vol.	Page
Temperance, d. Zachariah, b. May 9, 1703	OL	43
Thaddeus, s. Caleb & Ann, b. Feb. 16, 1735/6	1	103
Thaddeus, his ch., d. Oct. 20, 1784	SM	28
Thad[deus], his d. [ ], d. [ ], 1801	BP	4
Thaddeus, his d. [ ], d. Dec. 5, 1801, ae. 15	SM	73
Thaddeus, d. [ ], 1825	BP	52
Thaddeus, his wid. [ ], d. [ ], 1833	BP	69
Thankfull, d. Eben[eze]r, b. Apr. 18, 1719	1	68
Thankfull, wid., d. Feb. 6, 1802	SM	74
Theophilus, s. Richard, b. Apr. 26, 1659	1	3
Theophilus, s. Richard, b. Apr. 26, 1659	OL	11
Theophilus, m. Elizabeth CANFIELD, Feb. 8, 1682, by Major Treat	1	18
Theophilus, m. Elizabeth CANFIELD, Feb. 8, 1682, by Major Treat	OL	38
Theophilus, s. Theophilus, b. Nov. 27, 1735	1	102
Theophilus, s. Theophilus, b. Nov. 27, 1735	1	104
Theophilus, s. Richard & Alice, b. July 21, 1772	1	161
Thomas, m. Jerushah CLARKE, Jan. 17, 1711/12, by Samuel Eells, Asst. Witnesses, John Fowler, Susannah Fowler	1	63
Thomas, m. Abigail BALDWIN, Jan. 7, 1724/5, by Sam[ue]ll Eells, Asst.	1	82
Timothy, adm. Church Mar. 5, [1643]	OL	98
Timothy, s. Timothy, b. June 12, 1658	1	3
Timothy, s. Timothy, b. June 12, 1658	OL	11
Timothy, d. July 18, 1664	ES	16
Timothy, Sergt., d. Dec. 8, 1703	1	41
Timothy, Sergt., d. Dec. 8, 1703	OL	87
Timothy, of Milford, m. Zerviah JOHNSON, of Derby, July 22, 1719, by Sam[ue]ll Bishop, J.P.	1	79
Timothy, s. Timothy, b. Dec. 13, 1722	1	80
William Clarke, [s. Beard & Sybel], b. Apr. 11, 1810	1	177
Zachariah, s. Sergt. Richard, b. Sept. 22, 1660	1	4
Zachariah, m. Sarah MARVIN, Aug. 25, 1708, by Thomas Clarke, J.P.	1	30
Zachariah, m. Sarah MARWIN, Aug. 25, 1708, by Thomas Clark, J.P.	OL	64
Zachariah, s. Zachariah, b. Mar. 27, 1709	1	30
Zachariah, s. Zachariah [& Sarah], b. Mar. 27, 1709	OL	64
Zachariah, d. May 31, 1722	1	83
Zachariah (Dept.), d. M[ ] 31, 1722	ES	238
-----, his infant child d. [ ], 1828	BP	57
-----, d. [ ], 1829	BP	60
-----, d. Stephen, m. [Benjamin BULL], [ ]	1	45
BANFORD, Mary, see under Mary SANFORD	SM	11
BARBER, Charlotte, d. Azariah, b. Nov. 19, 1790; m. Treat LAMBERT, [s. Nehemiah & Sarah], [ ]	1	50
BARD, [see also BEARD], Ebenezer, twin with Jeremiah, s. John, b. Apr. 16, 1672	OL	24
Jeremiah, twin with Ebenezer, s. John, b. Apr. 16, 1672	OL	24
Joseph, s. John, b. July 20, 1666	OL	17

	Vol.	Page
BARD, [see also **BEARD**], (cont.)		
Samuel, s. John, b. Feb. 4, 1669	OL	22
BARKER, James, drafted for Continental Army (but not marched)	1	58
BARLOW, J., his s. [ ], d. May 31, 1795	SM	55
BARNES, BARNS, BARN, [see also **BURN**], Abraham, Priv., member of Capt. Samuel Peck's Co., Milford 1776	1	54
James, his w. [ ], d. [ ], 1833 (Perhaps **BURN**?)	BP	70
Louisa, d. [ ], 1827, ae.]0	BP	56
Mary, d. of Anson B., of N.H., m. Benjamin Lott **LAMBERT**, [s. Benjamin Lott & Eunice], Nov. 4, 184[ ]; d. Aug. 20, 1847	1	53
Rebeccah, of Farmington, m. Thomas **SANFORD**, of Milford, Sept. 29, 1713, by Rev. Sam[ue]ll Whitman, of Farmington	1	73
BASSETT, BASSET, BASSIT, Catharine, her infant s. [ ], d. Jan. 26, 1790	SM	41
Dan, his infant ch., d. [ ], 1818	BP	38
David, d. [ ], 1803, at Sea in Capt. Peck's vessel	BP	7
David, d. Feb. [ ], 1803, at Seaboard Peck	SM	77
David, his ch., d. [ ], 1804	BP	9
David, infant, d. July 28, 1804	SM	80
David, his ch., d. [ ], 1826	BP	55
Edward, s. Edward & Sarah, b. Mar. 13, 1776	1	170
Edward, his s. [ ], d. May 5, 1782	SM	23
Edward, his w. [ ], d. Feb. 17, 1798, ae. 43	SM	63
Elias, s. Edward & Sarah, b. Mar. 17, 1780	1	170
Isaac, his d. [ ], d. Sept. 17, 1793, ae. 27	SM	50
Isaac, his twin d. [ ], d. Mar. 8, 1796	SM	58
Isaac, had twin d. [ ], d. June 23, 1796	SM	59
John, his ch., d. [ ], 1820	BP	42
Jonah, his ch., d. [ ], 1818	BP	38
Jonah, his ch., d. [ ], 1830, ae. 2	BP	62
Josiah, m. Allice **CAMFIELD**, Apr. 25, 1717	1	66
Josiah, s. Josiah, b. Oct. 14, 1719	1	66
Josiah, s. Edward & Sarah, b. Mar. 10, 1783	1	170
Marcus, d. [ ], 1815, ae. 24 y.	BP	29
Mary, d. [ ], 1802, ae. 87	BP	6
Mary, d. Sept. 19, 1802, ae. 87	SM	75
Mahctabeel, d. Edward & Sarah, b. Apr. 24, 1778	1	170
Merrett, his infant d. [ ], 1837	BP	77
Nehemiah, d. [ ], 1830	BP	61
Samuel, Priv., member of Capt. Samuel Peck's Co., Milford 1776	1	54
Samuel, Jr., his s. [ ], d. Dec. 14, 1795	SM	56
Samuel, d. [ ], 1806, ae. 82	BP	14
Sam[ue]ll, his wid., d. [ ], 1815, ae. 86	BP	28
Sarah, m. Walter **LEWIS**, Nov. [ ], 1728, by Sam[ue]ll Eells, Asst.	1	90
Sarah, d. Edward & Sarah, b. Dec. 21, 1774	1	170
-----, wid., her child d. [ ], 1806, [ae.] 6	BP	14
BAYLEY, [see under **BAILEY**]		
BEACH, BEECH, Abigail F., d. [ ], 1838, ae. 15	BP	80
Abraham, of Goshen, d. Jan. [ ], 1777	SM	9
Alexander, drafted for Continental Army as Jonathan Clark's man	1	58

	Vol.	Page

BEACH, BEECH, (cont.)
Amey Wetmore, d. Sam[ue]ll & Mary, b. Mar. 30, 1761	1	161
Benajah, s. Sam[ue]ll & Mary, b. Mar. 24, 1752	1	161
Benjamin, his w. [ ], d. [ ], 1837, ae. 25	BP	78
Dennis, his infant d. [ ], 1837	BP	77
Eleanor, m. Joseph STONE, May 11, 1753, by Rev. Sam[ue]ll Whittlesey	1	139
Elizabeth, d. Sam[ue]ll & Mary, b. Aug. 23, 1758	1	161
Hannah, d. Thomas, b. May 13, 1734	1	102
Hannah, d. Sam[ue]ll & Mary, b. July 27, 1771	1	161
Hezekia[h], s. Thomas, b. May 27, 1662	OL	14
John, s. Thomas, b. Oct. 19, 1655	1	2
Landa, his w. [ ], d. [ ], 1823, ae. 36	BP	49
Landa, d. [ ], 1824, ae. 97	BP	50
Mary, d. Thomas, b. Dec. 27, 1657	1	3
Mary, d. Thomas, b. Dec. 27, 1657	OL	10
Mary, d. Sam[ue]ll & Mary, b. Oct. 18, 1754	1	161
Naomy, d. Sam[ue]ll & Mary, b. Jan. 15, 1769	1	161
Samuel, s. Thomas, b. June 5, 1660	1	4
Samuell, s. Tho[ma]s, b. June 5, 1660	OL	12
Samuel, s. Thomas, b. Aug. 10, 1729	1	90
Samuel, s. Thomas, b. Aug. 10, 1729	1	102
Sarah, d. Sam[ue]ll & Mary, b. Nov. 17, 1765	1	161
Susannah, d. Sam[ue]ll & Mary, b. June 12, 1756	1	161
Thaddeus, his s. [ ], d. Oct. 29, 1784	SM	28
Tho[ma]s, came to Milford, 1658	ES	176
Thomas, d. Sept. 11, 1779	SM	18
Thomas, his w. [ ], d. May 22, 1783, (Heard of death at Long Island)	SM	25
Thomas, his infant, s. [ ], d. May 25, 1788	SM	36
W[illia]m, his infant d. [ ], 1835 (From New York)	BP	72
Zopher, s. Thomas, b. May 27, 1662	1	5

BEARD, [see also BARD], A, Col., d. [   ], 1826 — BP 54
Abigail, d. John, b. Nov. 28, 1706	OL	63
Abigail, d. John, b. Dec. 28, 1706	1	29
Abigail, of Milford, d. John & Abigail, m. Rev. Jonathan ARNOLD, of West Haven, Apr. 4, 1728, by Sam[ue]ll Eells, Asst.	1	82
Abigail, d. Joseph [& Sarah], b. Apr. 21, 1740	1	113
Abigail, m. Joshua BALDWIN, Aug. 10, 1773	ES	238
Abigail, d. Sept. 11, 1787, ae. 26	SM	34
Andrew, pd. £5 for not procuring men for Continental Army	1	55
Andrew, his s. [ ], d. Sept. 7, 1785, ae. 9 m.	SM	29
Andrew, his d. [ ], d. Feb. 27, 1793, ae. 2 m.	SM	49
Andrew, d. [ ], 1838, ae. 86	BP	79
Ann, m. John EELLS, [ ], 1728	ES	238
Anna, d. Jeremiah, b. June 30, 1701	1	20
Anna, d. Jeremiah [& Mary], b. June last day, 1701	OL	43
Anna, m. John EELLS, Jan. 11, 1727/8, by Sam[ue]ll Eells, Asst.	1	86
Anna, m. John EELLS, Jan. 11, 1728	ES	238
Benjamin, s. Joseph, b. Mar. 12, 1713/14	1	39
Benjamin, s. Joseph, b. Mar. 12, 1713/14	OL	91
Deborah, d. Samuel, b. Oct. 14, 1699	1	22

	Vol.	Page

BEARD, [see also **BARD**], (cont.)

	Vol.	Page
Deborah, d. Samuel, b. Oct. 14, 1699	OL	47
Ebenezer, twin with Jeremiah, s. John, b. Apr. 16, 1672	1	11
Ebenezer, s. John, d. Aug. 24, 1624 [1674]	1	14
Ebenezer, s. John, d. Aug. 24, 1674	OL	28
Ebenezer, d. Aug. 24, 1674	ES	238
Elizabeth, d. John, b. Sept. 20, 1656	1	3
Elizabeth, d. John, b. Sept. 20, 1656	OL	9
Ephraim, pd £5 for not procuring men for Continental Army	1	55
James*, s. John, b. Dec. 4, 1661 *(Probably "James")	1	4
James, s. John, b. Dec. 4, 1661	OL	14
James, s. Samuel, b. Feb. 4, 1702/3	1	22
James, s. Samuel, b. Feb. 4, 1702/3	OL	47
James, d. [ ], 1709	ES	238
James, his w. [ ], d. [ ], 1821, ae. 50	BP	44
Jeremiah, twin with Ebenezer, s. John, b. Apr. 16, 1672	1	11
Jeremiah, [ ], 1681	ES	238
Jeremiah, m. Martha **PETTET**, May 26, 1697, by Tho[mas] Clarke, Justice	1	20
Jeremiah, m. Mary **PETTIT**, of Stratford, May 26, 1697, by Thomas Clark, J.P.	OL	43
Jno, adm. to Ch. 1703	ES	238
John, s. John, b. June 27, 1654	1	1
John, s. John, b. June 27, 1654	OL	8
John, Capt., 1670	ES	40
John, Capt., d. Sept. [ ], 1690	ES	238
John, s. Joseph, b. Mar. 28, 1702	1	22
John, s. Joseph, b. Mar. 28, 1702	OL	45
John, m. Abigail **HOLLINGWORTH**, Mar. 15, 1704/5, by Thomas Clark, J.P.	1	25
John, m. Abigail **HOLLINGWORTH**, Mar. 15, 1704/5, by Thomas Clark, J.P.	OL	53
John, d. Aug. 24, 1708	1	43
John, d. Aug. 24, 1708	OL	89
John, m. Martha **BURWELL**, Jan. 30, 1728/9	1	84
John, s. John & Martha, b. Dec. 27, 1729	1	84
John, his s. [ ], d. Sept. 29, 1794	SM	52
John, d. [ ], 1826	BP	54
John, his wid. [ ], d. [ ], 1834	BP	71
Joseph, s. John, b. July 20, 1666	1	7
Joseph, m. Sarah **SAMFORD**, Apr. 10, 1703, by Robert Treat, Dept. Gov.	1	22
Joseph, m. Sarah **SANFORD**, Apr. 10, 1703, by Rob[er]t Treat, Dept. Gov.	OL	45
Joseph, m. Sarah **SMITH**, June 27, 1706, by Capt. Samuel Eells, J.P.	1	29
Joseph, m. Sarah **SMITH**, June 27, 1706, by Sam[ue]ll Eells	OL	62
Joseph, s. Joseph, b. May 28, 1707	1	29
Joseph, s. Joseph [& Sarah], b. May 28, 1707	OL	62
Joseph, his marks for cattle recorded Aug. 27, 1733	1	95
Joseph, m. Sarah **PLATT**, June 22, 1737, by Sam[ue]ll Eells, Asst.	1	113

	Vol.	Page
BEARD, [see also **BARD**], (cont.)		
Joseph, s. Joseph & Sarah, b. July 6, 1751; d. Aug. 30, 1751	1	129
Joseph, d. Feb. 19, 1779	SM	17
Martha, wid. [d.]	ES	16
Martha, wid., adm. Church Nov. 1, [1640]	OL	97
Martha, m. John **STREAME**, Dec. 20, 1649, by Capt. Asa Woods	LL	1
Martha, d. Sept. 2, 1788, ae. 30	SM	37
Mary, d. John, b. Nov. 12, 1658	1	3
Mary, d. John, b. Nov. 12, 1658	OL	11
Mary, d. Jeremiah, b. Apr. 9, 1706	1	27
Mary, d. Jeremiah, b. Apr. 9, 1706	OL	58
Mary, d. Joseph, b. Apr. 7, 1710	1	32
Mary, d. Joseph, b. Apr. 7, 1710	OL	70
Mary, d. Joseph, b. Feb. 26, 1742/3	1	117
Nathan, s. Sergt. Samuel, b. Feb. 14, 1705/6	1	28
Nathan, s. Sergt. Sam[ue]ll, b. Feb. 14, 1705/6	OL	60
Samuel, s. John, b. Feb. 4, 1669/70	1	10
Samuel, m. Sarah **CLARK**, July 8, 1696, by Thomas Clark, J.P.	1	25
Samuel, m. Sarah **CLARK**, July 8, 1696, by Thomas Clark, J.P.	OL	52
Samuel, s. Samuel, b. Apr. 8, 1697	1	22
Samuel, s. Sam[ue]ll, b. Apr. 8, 1697	OL	47
Samuel, his 1ᵗ w. [ ], d. Apr. 21, 1791, ae. 21	SM	45
Sarah, d. John, b. July 22, 1675	1	15
Sarah, d. John, b. July 22, 1675	OL	29
Sarah, d. Jeremiah, b. Apr. 4, 1698	1	20
Sarah, d. Jeremiah [& Mary], b. Apr. 4, 1698	OL	43
Sarah, w. Joseph, d. Mar. 4, 1702/3	1	40
Sarah, w. Joseph, d. Mar. 4, 1702/3	OL	86
Sarah, w. John, d. Sept. 19, 1703	OL	87
Sarah, w. John, d. Sept. 29, 1703	1	41
Sarah, d. John, d. Oct. 21, 1703	1	41
Sarah, d. John, d. Oct. 21, 1703	OL	87
Sarah, d. Joseph, b. Sept. 10, 1708	1	32
Sarah, d. Joseph, b. Sept. 10, 1708	OL	70
Sarah, d. Joseph [& Sarah], b. June 9, 1738	1	113
Sara, m. Sam[ue]ll **PRUDDEN**, Jr., b. of Milford, Feb. 25, 1741/2, by Rev. Sam[ue]ll [ ]	1	112
Sarah, w. Joseph, d. Aug. 30, 1751	1	129
Timothy, drafted for Continental Army	1	58
-----, had negro Tim, d. July 27, 1787	SM	34
-----, wid., d. [ ], 1814, ae. 87	BP	26
BEARDSLEY, BEARDSLEE, BEAZLEY, Charles, Dr., d. [ ], 1822, at Newtown	BP	47
John, d. Feb. 17, 1803	SM	77
Samuel, his child d. [ ], 1828	BP	58
Sam[ue]l, his child d. [ ], 1828, ae. 4 d.	BP	58
Thomas, m. Elizabeth **HERVEY**, May 20, 1649/50, by Capt. Asa Woods	LL	2
-----, Mr., d. [ ], 1803, ae. 79 (No. 5)	BP	7
BEARS, [see under **BEERS**]		
BEERS, BEARS, Anne, d. David & Anne, b. Jan. 6, 1730/1	1	111
Benjamin, s. David & Ann, b. Apr. 23, 1736	1	111
Benjamin, Jr., d. Oct. 23, 1776, ae. 17	SM	8

	Vol.	Page
BEERS, BEARS, (cont.)		
Benjamin, his w. [ ], d. Jan. 18, 1777	SM	10
Benj[amin], d. [ ], 1799, ae. 67	BP	2
Benjamin, d. Oct. 25, 1799	SM	68
Benj[ami]n, his infant ch., d. [ ], 1816	BP	34
David, s. David & Anne, b. July 30, 1728	1	111
James, s. [James & Martha], [ ]	ES	18
James, Came to Milford, 1638	ES	176
Jere, Came to Milford, 1638	ES	176
Jeremiah, [s. James & Martha], [ ]	ES	18
John, Came to Milford, 1638	ES	176
John, s. Samuel, b. Oct. 19, 1655	OL	9
John, his ch., d. [ ], 1813	BP	31
John, d. [ ], 1838	BP	80
John, s. James & Martha, [ ]	ES	18
Martha, wid. James, d. June 1, 1647	ES	18
Martha, wid. of James with her sons John, James, & Jeremiah and three daughters, came with the first fifty families and had equal share with other planters; d. June 1, 1647	ES	18
Mary, d. David & Anne, b. Sept. 10, 1726	1	111
Thomas, d. Apr. [ ], 1782, (Was not in Milford at time of death)	SM	24
BEAZLEY, [see under **BEARDSLEY**]		
BECHFORD, [see under **BOTSFORD**]		
BEEBEE, Joel, drafted for Continental Army	1	57
Joel, Priv., member of Capt. Samuel Peck's Co., Milford 1776	1	54
Nath[anie]l, not drafted for Continental Army	1	57
BEECHER, Eleazer, m. Elizabeth **WELCH**, wid., Nov. 31, 1704, by Robert Treat, Dept. Gov.	1	26
Eleazer, m. wid, Elizabeth **WELCH**, Nov. 30, 1704, by Robert Treat, Dept. Gov.	OL	55
Eleazer, s. Eleazer, b. Nov. 4, 1707	1	28
Eleazer, s. Eleazer, b. Nov. 4, 1707	OL	61
Jerushah, d. Eleazer, b. Sept. 1, 1705	1	27
Perushah*, d. Eleazer, b. Sept. 1, 1705 *(Probably "Jerusha")	OL	58
BELDEN, John, d. [ ], 1783. Drowned at Sea	SM	26
John, drafted for Continental Army	1	58
Martha, of Wethersfield, m. Abraham J. H. **DEWITT**, of Milford, Aug. 22, 1792, by Rev. John Marsh, in Wethersfield	1	175
Nancy, d. [ ], 1808, ae. 24	BP	17
-----, Mr., d. [, 1813]	BP	33
BENEDICT, Daniel, of Harwinton, d. Jan. [ ], 1777	SM	9
-----, Mr., d. [, 1813]	BP	33
BENJAMIN, Anna, wid., d. [ ], 1825	BP	52
Barzillai, d. [ ], 1805	BP	12
Mary, d. June [ ], 1779	SM	17
Nathan, his child d. [ ], 1807, ae. 2 y.	BP	15
Nathan, had a stranger d. at his house [ ], 1810	BP	21
Peleg, instead of **BALDWIN**, is on an old payroll of Capt. Samuel Peck's Co.	1	179
BENNETT, BENETT, Daniel, Dea., d. June 21, 1794	SM	53
Jno, Came to Milford, 1651, or 1652	ES	176
-----, Mrs., d. [ ], 1819, ae. 80	BP	40

	Vol.	Page
BENNING, Elizabeth, adm. Church July 18, [1641]. Since m. Mr. **FORDHAM**.	OL	98
Eliz[abeth], m. Mr. [ ], **FORDHAM**, [ ]	ES	238
BENTON, A., removed to Guilford, 1666	ES	17
Andrew, [d.]	ES	18
Andrew, adm. Church Jan. [ ], 1648; dismissed to Hartford	OL	99
Andrew, s. Andrew, bp. [1653, by Rev. Peter Prudden]	OL	104
Hannah, d. Andrew, bp. [1651, by Rev. Peter Prudden]	OL	104
John, s. Andrew, b. Apr. 9, 1650	LL	2
John, s. Andrew, d. May 24, 1650	LL	1
John, s. Andrew, d. May [ ], 1650, ae. 3 or 4 wks	ES	238
John, s. Andrew, bp. [1650, by Rev. Peter Prudden]	OL	103
John, d. May [ ], 1650	ES	238
John, s. Andrew, b. Oct. 7, 1656	1	3
John, s. Andrew, b. [ ], 1656	OL	9
John, d. [ ], 1659, ae. 3 wks.	ES	35
Mary, d. Andrew, b. Apr. 14, 1655	1	2
Mary, d. Andrew, b. Apr. 14, 1655	OL	8
Mary, d. Andrew, bp. [1655, by Rev. Peter Prudden]	OL	105
Samuel, s. Andrew, b. Aug. 15, 1658	1	3
Samuel, s. Andrew, b. Aug. 15, 1658	OL	11
Sarah, [ ] of Andrew, adm. Church Oct. 13, 1650	OL	99
BETHSFORD, [see under **BOTSFORD**]		
BETTS, [see also **BOTS**], Eliza, of Wilton, m. John James [**LAMBERT**], [s. David & Susannah], [ ]	1	53
Goodman, Came to Milford, 1658	ES	176
Hannah, of Norwalk, d. of Thomas, m. Samuel **CAMP**, of Milford, Nov. 13, 1672, by Mr. Olmsted, Comm., in Norwalk	1	12
Hannah, of Norwalk, d. Thomas, m. Samuel **CAMP**, of Milford, Nov. 13, 1672, by Mr. Omstead, Com.	OL	24
John, of Lebanon, m. Mercy **FOWLER**, d. Lieut. [ ]	OL	22
Samuel, s. Thomas, b. Apr. 4, 1660	1	3
Samuell, s. Tho[ma]s, b. Apr. 4, 1660	OL	12
BIDDLE, John, of Glastonbury, d. Jan. [ ], 1777	SM	11
BILL, BILLS, Lavinia, of Lebanon, d. John, m. David **LAMBERT**, s. Jesse & Deborah, July 1, 1727. Settled in Norwalk	OL	54
Lurania, of Lebanon, Conn., d. John & Mercy (Fowler), m. David **LAMBERT**, s. Jesse, from England in 1680, Feb. 1, 1727; moved to Norwalk	1	53
BINGS, Thomas, drafted for Continental Army	1	57
BIRCHARD, Joseph, m. Elizabeth **LAMBERT**, d. Jesse & Deborah, [ ], settled in Norwalk	1	49
BIRD, -----, Mr., d. [,1813]	BP	33
BIRDSEYE, Hannah, d. John, bp. [1642, by Rev. Peter Prudden]	OL	100
John, s. John, bp. [1641, by Rev. Peter Prudden]	OL	100
John, [ ] A[ ] 4, [ ]41	ES	238
John, adm. Church Aug. 23, [1640]; dismissed to Stratford Church Mar. 19, 1649	OL	97
John, removed to Stratford, Aug. 29, 1649	ES	17
John, [d.]	ES	16
Phillipa, w. John adm. Church Aug. 23, [1640]; dismissed to Stratford Church Mar. 19, 1649	OL	97

	Vol	Page

BISCO, [see under BRISCO]
BISHOP, James, of New Haven, m. Elizabeth TOMPKINS, Dec. 12, 1665, by Benjamin Ffenn, Magistrate — 1, 7
 James, of New Haven, m. Elizabeth TOMKIN, of Milford, Dec. 12, 1665, by Benjamin Ffenn, Magestrate — OL, 17
 James, m. Johannah PRUDDEN, wid. Rev. Peter, in the winter of 1683 — ES, 101
 Joanna, m. Rev. Peter PRUDDEN, [   ]; d. [   ], 1686 — ES, 238
BLACKMAN, -----, his child d. [   ], 1830 — BP, 62
BLAGUE, [see under BLAKE]
BLAKE, BLAGUE, Celia B., d. of Allen B., of Winchester, Conn., m. David D. [LAMBERT], [s. Benjamin Lott & Eunice], Aug. 24, [   ]; d. Sept. 7, 1849 — 1, 53
 Jeremiah, of North Lyme, m. Thankfull ROACH, of Milford, July 31, 1739, by Rev. Sam[ue]ll Whittlesey, Jr. (Written "Jeremiah Blange") — 1, 108
 Jeremiah, his w. [   ], d. Mar. 23, 1784 — SM, 27
 Jeremiah, of East Haddam, d. Apr. 3, 1788, ae. 79 — SM, 36
BLANGE, [see under BLAKE]
BLOOMER, Betsey, d. [   ], 1825 — BP, 53
BLOSS, Charles, m. Anne [LAMBERT], [d. Frederic & Sally], [   ] — 1, 50
BLOTCHFORD, [see under BOTSFORD]
BOARDMAN, Josiah, his child d. [   ], 1805 — BP, 11
 -----, Mr. his child d. [   ], 1809 — BP, 19
 -----, Mr., d. [   ], 1813 — BP, 25
 -----, Mrs. Her child d. [   ], 1815, ae. 9 y. — BP, 28
BOICE, Johannah, m. Rev. Peter PRUDDEN, about 1637; came to America (both) 1637; m. 2nd h. James BISHOP, in the winter of 1683 — ES, 101; OL, 97
BOLT, Frances, adm. Church, Feb. 9, [1639/40], at New Haven — ES, 16
 Francis, [d.] [   ], 1646 — ES, 35
 Philip, d. [   ], 1646
BOOTH, BOOTHE, Eliza, d. John & Dencie, of Wallingford, b. Aug. 16, 1815; m. Edward R. LAMBERT, eldest s. Edward A. & Anne, Jan. 1, 1833, by Dr. Harry Croswell — 1, 47
 Eliza, d. John, of Wallingford, Ct., m. Edward Rodolphus LAMBERT, [s. Edward A. & Anne], Jan. 1, 1833, in Trinity Church, New Haven, by Dr. Crosswell — 1, 52
 Walter, Priv., member of Capt. Samuel Peck's Co., Milford 1776 — 1, 54
BOTS*, [see also BETTS], Pitty, m. Charles DEALE, b. of Milford, July 3, 1672, by John Clark, Com. *(BET[T]S?) — OL, 24
BOTSFORD, BECHFORD, BOCHFORD, BETHSFORD, BLOTCHFORD, BOTCHFORD, BOTSHARD, BOXFORD, [see also BOTS], Abiah, d. Timothy, b. Jan. 24, 1711; d. Aug. 18, following — 1, 36; OL, 79
 Abiah, d. Timothy, b. Jan. 24, 1711; d. Aug. 18, following — 1, 124
 Abia, d. Timothy, Jr., b. May 5, 1748
 Alice, m. Richard BALDWIN, Oct. 31, 1771, by Rev. Sam[ue]ll Wales — 1, 161; 1, 38
 Amos, s. Sergt. John, b. Oct. 25, 1711 — OL, 83
 Amos, s. Sergt. Jno, b. Oct. 25, 1711

BOTSFORD, BECHFORD, BOCHFORD, BETHSFORD, BLOTCHFORD, BOTCHFORD, BOTSHARD, BOXFORD, [see also **BOTS**], (cont.)

	Vol.	Page
Annah, d. Elnathan, b. Apr. the last day, 1674	OL	27
Benjamin, drafted for Continental Army	1	57
Christian, d. Henry, b. Aug. 17, 1701	OL	45
Christiania, d. Henry, b. Aug. 17, 1701	1	21
David, s. Sam[ue]ll, b. Aug. [ ], 1713	1	65
David, d. Jan. 21, 1796, ae. 82	SM	58
David, Jr., pd. £5 for not procuring men for Continental Army	1	55
Ebenezer, s. Sam[ue]ll, b. Apr. 6, 1709	1	65
Eli, Capt., d. [ ], 1819	BP	40
Elizabeth, w. Henry, adm. Church, Oct. 4, [1640]	OL	97
Elizabeth, d. Henry, bp. [1643, by Rev. Peter Prudden]	OL	100
Elizabeth, d. Henry, m. Daniel **BALDWIN**, b. of Milford, June 25, 1665, by Benjamin Ffenn, Magestrate	OL	17
Elizabeth, d. Henry, m. Samuel* **BALDWIN**, June 27, 1665, by Benj[amin] Ffenn, Magistrate *(Overwritten to read "Daniel")	1	6
Elizabeth, d. Elnathan, b. Oct. 22, 1665	1	7
Elnathan, s. Henry, bp. [1641, by Rev. Peter Prudden]	OL	100
Elnathan, m. Elizabeth **FFLETCHER**, Dec. 12, 1664, by Benj[amin] Ffenn	1	6
Elnathan, m. Elizabeth **FFLETCHER**, b. of Milford, Dec. 12, 1666	OL	17
Elnathan, widower, m. Hannah **BALDWIN**, d. Timothy, decd., Dec. 12, 1667, by Mr. Ffenn, Magistrate	1	8
Elnathan, widower, m. Han[n]ah **BALDWIN**, d. Timothy, decd., b. of Milford, Dec. 12, 1667, by Mr. Ffenn, Magestrate	OL	20
Elnathan, s. Samuel, b. Sept. 29, 1704	1	25
Elnathan, s. Samuell, b. Sept. 29, 1704	OL	51
Elnathan, Priv., member of Capt. Samuel Peck's Co., Milford 1776	1	54
Elnathan, his w. [ ], d. [ ], 1818	BP	38
Elnathan, d. [ ], 1830, ae. 61	BP	61
Esther, d. Henry, bp. [1647, by Rev. Peter Prudden]	OL	102
Easther, d. Henry, m. Nathaniell **WHEELER**, b. of Milford, June 27, 1665, by Benjamin Ffenn, Magestrate	OL	17
Hannah, d. Henry, bp. [1645, by Rev. Peter Prudden]	OL	102
Hannah, d. Henry, m. Nathaniel **BALDWIN**, weaver, Mar. 12, 1670/1	1	11
Hannahy, d. Hennary, m. Nathaniel **BALDWIN**, weaver, Mar. 12, 1670/1, by John Clark, Com.	OL	24
Hannah, d. Elnathan, b. Apr. 30, 1674	1	13
Hannah, wid., d. Aug. 7, 1706	1	43
Han[n]ah, wid., d. Aug. 7, 1706	OL	89
Hannah, w. Samuel, d. Oct. 29, 1732	1	98
Hannah, Mrs., d. [ ], 1814	BP	26
Henry, adm. Church July 25, [1644]	OL	98
Henry, s. Elnathan, b. Sept. 12, 1676	1	15
Henry, s. Elnathan, b. Sept. 12, 1676	OL	30
Henry, d. [ ], 1686	ES	16
Henry, m. Christiania **GUNN**, Nov. 12, 1700, by Robert Treat,		

	Vol.	Page

BOTSFORD, BECHFORD, BOCHFORD, BETHSFORD, BLOTCHFORD, BOTCHFORD, BOTSHARD, BOXFORD, [see also **BOTS**], (cont.)

	Vol.	Page
Dept. Gov.	1	21
Henry, m. Christian **GUNN**, Nov. 12, 1700, by Rob[er]t Treat, Dept. Gov.	OL	45
Hestter, d. Henry, m. Nathaniel **WHEELER**, June 27, 1665, by Benjamin Ffenn, Magistrate (Written "Hestter **BETHSFORD**")	1	6
Hester, d. Elnathan, b. Oct. 18, 1668	1	9
Hester, d. Elnathan, b. Oct. 18, 1668	OL	21
Heth, d. Apr. 7, 1782 (Was not in Milford at time of death)	SM	24
Hubbard, his child d. [ ], 1829	BP	60
Isaac, s. Timothy, Jr., b. June 14, 1742	1	112
John, s. Elnathan, b. Jan. 8, 1680	OL	36
John, s. Sergt. John, b. Mar. 28, 1708	1	38
John, s. Sergt. John, b. Mar. 28, 1708	OL	83
Jon[a]th[an], s. Sam[ue]ll, b. Mar. 12, 1710	1	65
Lydia, d. Timothy, Jr., b. Sept. 2, 1735	1	102
Lydia, of Milford, m. Henry **BALDWIN**, of Amity, Feb. 23, 1757, by Sam[ue]ll Whittlesey	1	138
Mary, d. Henry, bp. [1643, by Rev. Peter Prudden]	OL	100
Mary, d. Henry, m. Andrew **SAMFORD***, Jr., Jan. 8, 1667, by Mr. Ffenn, Magistrate *(SANFORD)	1	8
Mary, d. Henry, m. Andrew **SAMFORD***, Jr., b. of Milford, Jan. 8, 1667, by Mr. Ffenn, Magestrate *(SANFORD)	OL	20
Mary, d. Elnathan, b. Feb. 11, 1671	OL	24
Mary, d. Elnathan, b. Feb. 11, 1671/2	1	11
Mary, d. Timothy, b. Dec. 21, 1705; d. Jan. 22, following	1	36
Mary, d. Timothy, b. Dec. 21, 1705; d. Jan. 22, following	OL	79
Mary, d. Timothy, b. Mar. 2, 1706	1	36
Mary, d. Timothy, b. Mar. 9, 1706	OL	79
Mary, m. Eleazer **CAMP**, Feb. 30 [sic], 1728 (Probably May 30)	1	84
Mary, m. Eleazer **CAMP**, May 30, 1728, by Sam[ue]ll Gunn, J.P.	1	97
Mary, d. Timothy, Jr., b. Mar. 8, 1736/7	1	104
Mihitabeel, d. Sam[ue]ll, b. Oct. 16, 1715	1	65
Mehetable, m. Benjamin **SMITH**, Jr., June 16, 1747, by Sam[ue]ll Whittlesey, Jr.	1	123
Nathan, s. Timothy, b. Nov. 18, 1713	1	37
Nathan, s. Timothy, b. Nov. 18, 1713	OL	79
Nathan, m. Sarah **COLLINS**, Oct. 6, 1737, by Roger Newton, Asst.	1	104
Ruth, d. Henry, bp. [1649, by Rev. Peter Prudden]	OL	103
Samuel, s. Elnathan, b. July 30, 1670	1	10
Samuel, s. Elnathan, b. July 30, 1670	OL	23
Sarah, d. Elnathan, b. Aug. 10, 1683	1	19
Sarah, d. Elnathan, b. Apr. 10, 1683	OL	42
Sarah, d. Samuel, b. Feb. 11, 1706/7	1	29
Sarah, d. Samuel, b. Feb. 11, 1706/7	OL	63
Sarah, m. Daniel **MERWIN**, Nov. 30, 1710, by Joseph Treat, J.P.	1	35
Sarah, m. Daniel **MERWIN**, Nov. last day, 1710, by Joseph Treat, J.P.	OL	76

BOTSFORD, BECHFORD, BOCHFORD, BETHSFORD, BLOTCHFORD, BOTCHFORD, BOTSHARD, BOXFORD, [see also **BOTS**], (cont.)

	Vol.	Page
Timothy, s. Elnathan, b. Nov. 10, 1678	OL	36
Timothy, m. Mary **PECK**, Feb. 14, 1704/5, by Samuel Eells, J.P.	1	25
Timothy, m. Mary **PECK**, Feb. 14, 1704/5, by Samuel Eells, J.P.	OL	52
Timothy, s. Timothy, b. Apr. 3, 1708	1	36
Timothy, s. Timothy, b. Apr. 3, 1708	OL	79
Timothy, s. Timothy & Mary, m. Lydia **SMITH**, d. Timothy & Elizabeth, b. of Milford, Nov. 21, 1734, by Sam[ue]ll Gunn, J.P.	1	100
Timothy, s. Timothy, Jr., b. Nov. 2, 1738	1	107
-----, wid., d. [ ], 1787 (non resident)	SM	35
-----, Mr. lived to be "above 90 years"	ES	17
BOW, James, his d. [ ], d. Sept. 9, 1788	SM	37
BOWEN, -----, Mr. his child d. [ ], 1811	BP	21
BOWERS, -----, his w. [ ], d. [ ], 1804, ae. 44	BP	9
-----, Mr. his w. [ ], d. July 16, 1804	SM	80
BOWLEY, John, d. [ ], 1803	BP	7
John, d. May 31, 1803	SM	77
BRACE, Mary, m. John **SMITH**, tailor, June 1, 1699, by Robert Treat, Dept. Gov.	1	21
Mary, m. John **SMITH**, tailor, June 1, 1699, by Robert Treat, Dept. Gov.	OL	45
Phebe, m. John **PLATT**, June 27, 1675, by Robert Treat, Dept. Gov.	1	20
Phebe, m. John **PLATT**, June 27, 1703, by Robert Treat, Dept. Gov.	OL	43
[BRACKETT], [see under **BROCKETT**]		
BRADLEY, Allen, Priv., member of Capt. Samuel Peck's Co., Milford 1776	1	54
Cela, his w. [ ], d. [ ], 1836	BP	75
Dennis, m. Lazarus **CLARK**, Dec. 18, 1771, by Rev. Benj[amin] Woodbridge, of Amity. Witnesses Andrew Bradley, David Clark	1	168
Ezekiel, his s. [ ], d. [ ], 1830, ae. 14	BP	62
George, d. [ ], 1820, at the South	BP	42
Israel, his w. [ ], d. [ ], 1811	BP	22
Israel, d. [ ], 1825, ae. 74	BP	52
Levi, his child d. [ ], 1808	BP	18
Levi, his child d. [ ], 1809	BP	18
Lyman, d. [ ], 1830, ae. 40	BP	61
Mary, wid., d. [ ], 1830	BP	62
Mix, Capt., d. [ ], 1816	BP	35
Rebeckah, d. Stephen, b. Feb. 19, 1747/8 O.S.	1	134
Stephen, s. Stephen, b. May 9, 1745	1	133
-----, his twin d. [ ], d. May 16, 1789	SM	39
-----, Mrs., d. Apr. 10, 1800	SM	69
BREWER, BREWEN, Hannah, d. of Obadiah, of New London, m. John **BALDWIN**, s. of John, Sr., Oct. 30, 1663, by Robert Treat	1	5
Marie, d. of John, m. John **BALDWIN**, Sr., of Milford, [ ]	1	1

	Vol.	Page
BREWER, BREWEN, (cont.)		
Mary, d. John, m. John **BALDWIN**, Sr., Aug. 15, [ ] (Written "Mary **BREWEN**")	OL	7
BRIANT, [see under **BRYAN**]		
BRIATT, [see under **BRYAN**]		
BRIGGS, -----, Lieut., d. [ ], 1814 (A soldier wounded at Sacketts Harbor)	BP	27
BRINCON, BRIMSON*, Hannah, d. Richard, of Farmington, m. Samuel **SAMFORD**, s. Thomas, Aug. 16, 1674, by Major Treat *(**BRUNSON**)	1	13
Hannah, d. Richard, of Farmington, m. Samuell **SANFORD**, s. Thomas, of Milford, Apr. 16, 1674, by Major Treat (Written "Hannah **BRINCON**")	OL	27
BRINSMEAD, BRIMSMEAD, Abigail, d. John, b. Mar. 7, 1706/7	1	35
Abigail, d. John, b. Mar. 7, 1706/7	OL	76
Abigail, m. David **GIBSON**, Aug. [ ], 1724, by Major Sam[ue]ll Eells, Asst.	1	75
Abigail, d. John & Abigail, m. David **GIBSON**, Aug. 20, 1724, by Samuell Eells, Asst.	1	90
Ann, d. John & Abigail, b. Feb. 24, 1722/3	1	72
Elizabeth, d. John, b. Mar. 12, 1709/10	1	35
Elizabeth, d. John, b. Mar. 12, 1709/10	OL	76
Elizabeth, m. Phinehas **NORTHROP**, Dec. 9, 1732, by Sam[ue]ll Gunn, J.P.	1	94
John, s. John, b. Oct. 4, 1705	1	35
John, s. John, b. Oct. 4, 1705	OL	76
Mary, d. John, b. July 26, 1714	1	35
Mary, d. John, b. July 26, 1714	OL	76
BRISCOE, BISCO, BRISCO, Abigail, d. Nathaniel, b. Nov. 1, 1684	1	19
Abigail, d. Nathaniel, b. Nov. 1, 1684	OL	41
Abigail, d. James, b. June 26, 1706	1	80
Abigail, m. Ezekiel **NEWTON**, May 21, 1711, by Rev. Grindal Rawson, of Mendam	1	35
Abigail, m. Ezekiel **NEWTON**, May 21, 1711, by Rev. Grindall Rawson, of Mendam	OL	75
Abigail, d. Sam[ue]ll, b. Mar. 1, 1721	1	68
Abigail, d. Samuel, Jr. & Ruth, b. Nov. 9, 1754	1	134
Elizabeth, d. James, b. July 29, 1704	1	80
Hannah, m. Joseph **BALDWIN**, Jr., Mar. 26, 1714, by Joseph Treat, J.P.	1	35
Han[n]ah, m. Joseph **BALDWIN**, Jr., Mar. 26, 1714, by Jos[eph] Treat, J.P.	OL	76
Isaac, s. Sam[ue]ll, b. Feb. 5, 1729/30	1	84
James, s. Nathaniel, bp. [1649, by Rev. Peter Prudden]	OL	103
James, in 1671, destroyed the Indian Fort	ES	14
James, s. Nathaniel, b. Aug. 14, 1673	1	13
James, s. Nathaniel, Aug. 14, 1673	OL	26
James, m. Sarah **WHEELER**, Nov. 6, 1676, by Capt. Tapping	1	15
James, m. Sarah **WHEELER**, Dec. 6, 1676, by Capt. Tapping	OL	30
James, s. James, b. Aug. 25, 1679	1	17
James, s. James, b. Aug. 25, 1679	OL	33
James, m. Elizabeth **ADAMS**, June 1, 1699, by Hon. Robert Treat,		

	Vol.	Page
BRISCOE, BISCO, BRISCO, (cont.)		
Dept. Gov.	1	80
James, s. James, b. Mar. 5, 1715	1	80
John, s. Nathaniel, bp. [1651, by Rev. Peter Prudden]	OL	104
John, s. Samuel, b. June 8, 1715	1	36
John, s. Samuel, b. June 8, 1715	OL	78
John, s. James, b. Apr. 22, 1721	1	80
Joseph, adm. Church Apr. 19, 1649	OL	99
Mary, d. Nathaniel, b. Nov. 15, 1675	1	15
Mary, d. Nathaniel, b. Nov. 15, 1675	OL	29
Mary, d. James, b. Mar. 8, 1701	1	80
Mary, d. Sam[ue]ll & Ruth, b. Oct. 2, 1764	1	149
Mehitable, d. James, b. Oct. 11, 1712	1	80
Nathan, s. Samuel, b. July 15, 1717	1	39
Nathan, s. Sam[ue]ll, b. July 15, 1717	OL	84
Nathan, s. Sam[ue]ll & Ruth, b. Feb. 26, 1762	1	145
Nathaniel, adm. Church Apr. 20, [1644]	OL	98
Nathaniel, s. Nathaniel, bp. [1646, by Rev. Peter Prudden]	OL	102
Nathaniel, m. Mary **CAMP**, d. of wid. Lane, Nov. 29, 1672, by John Clark, Commissioner	1	12
Nathaniel, of Milford, m. Mary **CAMP**, d. wid. Jane, of Milford, Nov. 29, 1672, by John Clark, Com.	OL	25
Nath[anie]l, d. [ ], 1683	ES	16
Nathaniel, s. James, b. June 16, 1708	1	80
Ruth, d. Samuel, b. Nov. 9, 1709	1	31
Ruth, d. Samuel, b. Nov. 9, 1709	OL	66
Ruth, w. Samuel, d. Nov. 17, 1709	1	43
Ruth, w. Samuel, d. Nov. 17, 1709	OL	89
Ruth, d. Sam[ue]ll, Jr., b. Nov. 22, 1750	1	128
Samuel, s. Nathaniel, b. Apr. 4, 1678	1	16
Samuell, s. Nathaniell, b. Apr. 4, 1678	OL	32
Samuel, m. Ruth **SMITH**, Oct. 23, 1707, by Capt. Eells	1	29
Samuel, m. Ruth **SMITH**, Oct. 23, 1707, by Capt. Eells	OL	62
Samuel, m. Abigail **PLATT**, July 3, 1712, by Samuel Eells, Asst.	1	33
Sam[ue]ll, m. Abigail **PLATT**, July 3, 1712, by Sam[ue]ll Eells Asst.	OL	71
Samuel, s. Samuel, b. Sept. 9, 1713	1	34
Sam[ue]ll, s. Sam[ue]ll, b. Sept. 9, 1713	OL	74
Samuel, m. Ruth **NORTHROP**, Dec. 11, 1746, by Rev. Benjamin Woodbridge, of Amity	1	120
Samuel, s. Sam[ue]ll, Jr., b. Jan. 1, 1748/9	1	126
Sam[ue]ll, s. Sam[ue]ll, Jr., d. Aug. 28, 1751	1	128
Sam[ue]ll, s. Sam[ue]ll & Ruth, b. Oct. 4, 1757	1	137
Sarah, d. James, b. Mar. 25, 1678	1	16
Sarah, d. James, b. Mar. 25, 1678	OL	32
Sarah, d. Nathaniel, b. Jan. 22, 1680	OL	36
Sarah, d. James, b. Feb. 23, 1718/19	1	80
Sarah, d. Sam[ue]l, Jr. & Ruth, b. Oct. 11, 1751	1	131
-----, Mrs., d. [ ], 1806, ae. 85	BP	14
BRISTOL, BRISTOLL, Abigail, m. Daniel **TERRELL**, Nov. 27, 1712, by Samuel Eells, Asst.	1	33
Abigail, m. Dan[ie]l **TERRILL**, Nov. 27, 1712, by Sam[ue]ll Eells, Asst.	OL	72

MILFORD VITAL RECORDS 33

	Vol.	Page
BRISTOL, BRISTOLL, (cont.)		
Ann, m. Isaac **HINE**, Jan. 12, 1757, by Rev. Job. Prudden	1	141
Elizabeth, wid., d. [ ], 1816	BP	34
Esther, d. Sam[ue]ll & Esther, b. Jan. 17, 1728	1	83
Hannah, m. Thomas **HINE**, Nov. 9, 1684, by John Nash, Asst.	1	19
Hannah, m. Thomas **HINE**, Nov. 9, 1684, by Jno Nash, Asst.	OL	41
Hester, Miss d. [ ], 1817, ae. about 90	BP	36
Hiel, his s. [ ], d. Mar. 21, 1781	SM	21
Isaac, his d. [ ], d. [ ], 1812, ae. 8 y.	BP	24
Isaac, his w. [ ], d. [ ], 1834, ae. 59	BP	72
Isaac, d. [ ], 1837, ae. 62	BP	78
Jehiel, his child d. [ ], 1802	BP	5
Jehiel, his d. [ ], d. Apr. 24, 1802, ae. 15 m.	SM	74
Jehiel, his w. [ ], d. [ ], 1814	BP	26
Jehiel, d. [ ], 1815	BP	30
Jehiel, his w. [ ], 1839, ae. 60	BP	81
Johnson, his child d. [ ], 1834	BP	71
Johnson, his child d. [ ], 1836	BP	74
Jonathan, d. Sept. 16, 1794, at Sea	SM	52
Mark, d. Mar. 14, 1794, ae. 37	SM	51
Mercy, d. [ ], 1783, at New Milford	SM	26
Naomi, m. Jabez Benedict **BULL**, s. [Jirah & Sibella, [ ]	1	45
Nathan, pd. £5 for not procuring men for Continental Army	1	55
Nathan, Sergt., drafted for Continental Army	1	58
Nathan, Priv., member of Capt. Samuel Peck's Co., Milford 1776; a drummer	1	54
Nathan, of Milford, m. Anne **LAMBERT**, Feb. 3, 1777	1	50
Nathan, Jr., his child d. [ ], 1805	BP	11
Nathan, d. [ ], 1826, ae. 78	BP	55
Nathan, his wid. [ ], d. [ ], 1833, ae. 85	BP	69
Nehe[mia]h, s. Nehemiah & Larania, b. Dec. 25, 1801	1	172
Nehe[mia]h, his s. [ ], d. [ ], 1815, ae. 16	BP	29
Nehemiah, d. [ ], 1832, ae. 63	BP	67
Nehemiah, Jr., his child d. [ ], 1832, ae. 4 y.	BP	67
Nehemiah, d. [ ], 1838, ae. 56	BP	80
Peter, drafted for Continental Army	1	58
Richard, Capt. His w. [ ], d. Nov. 10, 1781	SM	22
Richard, Capt., d. July 30, 1791, ae. 83	SM	46
Sam[ue]l, member of 2[nd] Church formed in 1742	ES	87
Samuel, d. [ ], 1830	BP	63
Wyllys, his infant child d. [ ], 1832	BP	67
Wyllys, his child d. [ ], 1836	BP	74
-----, wid., d. Aug. 1, 1792	SM	48
-----, Mr. his child d. [ ], 1807	BP	16
-----, Mrs., d. [ ], 1822	BP	47
-----, Mrs., d. [ ], 1825	BP	52
BROCKETT, Hezekiah, drafted for Continental Army	1	58
BRONSON, Elisha, of Litchfield, d. Jan. [ ], 1777	SM	9
BROOKS, Bridget, w. William, adm. Church Sept. 8, [1644]; d. June 23, 1663	OL	98
Sarah, d. June 5, 1703, in the 88th y. of her age	1	43
Sarah, d. June 5, 1709, in the 88th y. of her age	OL	89
William, adm. Church June 11, [1648]; dismissed to Fairfield		

	Vol.	Page
BROOKS, (cont.)		
Church	OL	99
W[illia]m, [d.], 1684	ES	18
BROWEN, [see under **BROWN**]		
BROWN, BROWEN, BROWNE, Edw[ard], his child d. [ ], 1832	BP	66
Esther, d. John, bp. [1649, by Rev. Peter Prudden]	OL	103
Han[n]ah, d. Obadiah, of New London, m. John **BALDWIN**, s. John, Sr., Nov. 30, 1663, by Rob[ert] Treat	OL	15
Jno, Came to Milford, 1648	ES	176
John, adm. Church Dec. 9, [1649]	OL	99
John, s. John, bp. [1649, by Rev. Peter Prudden]	OL	103
John, s. John, b. July 12, 1655	1	2
John, s. John, b. July 12, 1655	OL	8
John, d. [ ], 1837, in New Haven, bd. In Milford	BP	77
Joseph, s. John, bp. [1652, by Rev. Peter Prudden]	OL	104
Mary, w. John, adm. Church, Dec. 23, [1649]	OL	99
Mary, d. John, bp. [1649, by Rev. Peter Prudden]	OL	103
Mary, d. John, bp. [1653, by Rev. Peter Prudden]	OL	104
Phebe, d. John, b. July 5, 1660	1	4
Phebe, d. John, b. July 5, 1660	OL	12
Samuel, d. [Dec.] [ ], 1795, (Heard of death; drowned at Long Island)	SM	56
Sarah, d. Jno, b. Aug. 6, 1650	LL	3
Stephen, of Killingly, d. Jan. [ ], 1777	SM	10
Thomas, s. John, bp. [1655, by Rev. Peter Prudden]	OL	105
-----, Capt., d. [ ], 1826	BP	55
-----, Mrs., d. [ ], 1839	BP	82
BRUNSON, Hannah, see under Hannah **BRINCON**		
BRYAN, BRIANT, BRIATT, BRYANT, Abigail, d. Richard, b. Nov. 22, 1663	1	5
Abiga[i]l, d. Richard, b. Jan. 12, 1671	OL	24
Abigail, d. Richard, b. Jan. 12, 1671/2	1	11
Abigail, d. Joseph, [ ], 1719	ES	238
Alexander, agent of the 1st purchase	ES	1
Alex[ander], brother of Richard	ES	238
Alexander, s. Richard, bp. [1654, by Rev. Peter Prudden]; d. 1700	OL	105
Alexander, Ens., agent of the 2nd purchase Oct. [ ], 1660	ES	1
Alexan[de]r, [d.] [ ], 1670	ES	16
Alexander, s. Alexander, Jr., b. June 15, 1677	1	16
Alexander, s. Alexander, Jr., b. June 15, 1677	OL	31
Alexander, s. Alexander, b. Nov. 24, 1682	1	18
Allexander, s. Allexander, b. Dec. 24, 1682	OL	39
Alexander, d. Aug. 19, 1701	1	42
Alexander, d. Aug. 19, 1704	OL	88
Allexander, s. Richard, b. Oct. 13, 1709	OL	72
Alexander, s. R[ichard], bp. 1709	ES	238
Alexander, s. Richard, b. Oct. 13, 1719	1	33
Ann, d. Alexander, Jr., b. Sept. 8, 1674	1	14
Ann, d. Alexander, Jr., b. Sept. 8, 1674	OL	28
Ann, d. Richard, Jr. & Sarah, b. Feb. 19, 1730/1	1	100
Anne, Adm. Church Sept. 13, [1640]; d. Feb. 20, 1661	OL	97
Augustine, s. Alexander, b. Apr. 25, 1694	1	25

	Vol.	Page
BRYAN, BRIANT, BRIATT, BRYANT, (cont.)		
Augustine, s. Alexander, b. Apr. 25, 1694	OL	53
Augustine, s. Alexander, d. Aug. 8, 1705	1	42
Augustine, s. Allexander, d. Aug. 8, 1705	OL	88
Augustine, s. Richard, b. Jan. 28, 1706/7	1	28
Augustine, s. Richard, b. Jan. 28, 1706/7	OL	61
David, [s. Richard & Sarah], [b.] Jan. 14, 1748	ES	238
David, s. Richard & Sarah, b. Feb. 14, 1748	1	158
Ebenezer, s. Alexander, b. Feb. 17, 1690	1	25
Ebenezer, s. Alexander, b. Feb. 17, 1690	OL	53
Ebenezer, m. Esther GOODYEAR, July 15, 1713, by John Allen, Asst.	1	77
Ebenezer, s. Ebenezer, b. Dec. 27, 1718	1	65
Ebenezer, d. Jan. 27, 1777	SM	11
Elijah, drafted for Continental Army	1	57
Elijah, s. Richard & Sarah, b. Sept. 3, 1759	1	158
Elijah, [s. Richard & Sarah, b.] Sept. 3, 1759	ES	238
Elijah, Priv., member of Capt. Samuel Peck's Co., Milford 1776	1	54
Elizabeth, d. Richard, b. Nov. 22, 1663	OL	15
Elizabeth, d. Richard, b. Apr. 19, 1680	OL	36
Elizabeth, wid., m. Robert TREAT, Gov. of Conn., Oct. 22, 1705; d. Jan. following	ES	105
Elizabeth, m. Robert TREAT, Oct. 22, 1705; d. Jan. [ ]	ES	238
Elizabeth, Mrs., m. Robert TREAT, Sr., Oct. 24, 1705, by Rev. Samuel Andrew	1	26
Elizabeth, Mrs., m. Robert TREAT, Sr., Oct. 24, 1705, by Rev. Samuel Andrews	OL	54
Elizabeth, wid., d. [ ], 1802	BP	6
Elizabeth, wid., d. Oct. 14, 1802, ae. 86	SM	76
Esther, Mrs., m. Thomas GIBB, Aug. 20, 1729, by Sam[ue]ll Eells, Asst.	1	95
Esther, m. Tho[mas] GIBBS, Aug. [ ], 1729	ES	238
Esther, wid., d. [ ], 1837, ae. 80	BP	78
Fowler, s. Richard & Sarah, b. Sept. 26, 1765	1	158
Fowler, [ch. Richard & Sarah, b.] Sept. 26, 1765	ES	238
Francis, s. Richard, b. Feb. 13, 1668	1	9
Pfrances, d. Richard, b. Feb. 13, 1668	OL	21
Frances, d. Richard, b. Sept. 22, 1704	1	24
Frances, d. Richard, b. Sept. 22, 1704	OL	49
Francis, m. Jeremiah GILLIT, July 16, 1725, by Sam[ue]ll Eells, Asst.	1	85
Frances, d. Richard, Jr. & Sarah, b. Aug. 16, 1726	1	100
Frances, d. Richard & Sarah, m. Sam[ue]l TREAT, s. Sam[ue]l, Jan. 27, 1751	ES	238
Frances, d. Richard & Sarah, m. Samuel TREAT, s. Samuel, June 27, 1751, by Rev. Samuel Whittlesey	1	127
Frances, d. Richard & Sarah, m. Samuel TREAT, s. Samuel, June 27, 1751	ES	238
Gideon, d. [ ], 1788 (died absent)	SM	38
Gideon, d. [ ], 1788, at Derby	ES	165
Hannah, d. Richard, b. Aug. The last, 1654	1	1
Hannah, d. Richard, b. Aug. The last, 1654	OL	8

	Vol.	Page
BRYAN, BRIANT, BRIATT, BRYANT, (cont.)		
Hannah, d. Richard, bp. [1654, by Rev. Peter Prudden]	OL	105
Hannah, d. Richard, m. John **HERRIMAN**, of New Haven, Nov. 20, 1672, by John Clarke, Commissioner	1	12
Hannah, d. Richard, of Milford, m. John **HERRIMAN**, of New Haven, Nov. 20, 1672, by John Clark, Com.	OL	25
Hannah, d. Richard, b. Jan. 21, 1711/12	1	34
Hannah, d. Richard, b. Jan. 21, 1711/12	OL	72
Ichabod, d. Jan. 12, 1794, ae. 9	SM	51
Isaac, s. Joseph & Juliana, b. Apr. 27, 1780. (He also settled at Mt. Zion, Hancock Co., Ga.)	1	170
Jehiah, Lieut., member of Capt. Samuel Peck's Co., Milford, 1776	1	54
Jehiel, Capt., d. [ ], 1807, ae. 78	BP	16
Jehiel, d. [ ], 1826	BP	54
Jeheil, Capt., d. Apr. 12, 1837	1	178
Jehiel, Capt., d. [ ], 1837, ae. 31	BP	77
John, s. Alexander, b. July 12, 1680	1	18
John, s. Alex[ander], b. July [ ], 1680	OL	35
John, [s. Richard & Sarah, b.], Feb. 24, 1754	ES	238
John, s. Richard & Sarah, b. Feb. 23, 1757	1	158
Jno, his w. [ ], d. [ ], 1815, ae. 62, North Milford	BP	28
Joseph, s. Richard, b. July 15, 1682	1	18
Joseph, s. Richard, b. July 15, 1682	OL	38
Joseph, bp. [ ], 1682	ES	238
Joseph, s. Joseph & Mary, b. May 8, 1721	1	91
Joseph, [s. Joseph], [ ], 1721	ES	238
Joseph, s. Joseph, b. [ ], 1721	ES	238
Joseph, d. Aug. 1, 1742	1	132
Joseph, d. [ ], 1742	ES	238
Joseph, d. Apr. 3, 1751	1	132
Joseph, d. [ ], 1751	ES	238
Joseph, s. Joseph & Juliana, b. Nov. 28, 1769. (He settled at Mt. Zion, Hancock Co., Ga.)	1	169
Joseph, his twin s. [ ], d. Sept. 13, 1776	SM	7
Joseph, Capt., d. Aug. 11, 1783, ae. 38	SM	26
Juliana, d. Joseph & Juliana, b. Sept. 13, 1776	1	169
Martha, m. Joseph **SMITH**, July 5, 1711, by Samuel Eells, Asst.	1	33
Martha, m. Joseph **SMITH**, July 5, 1711, by Sam[ue]ll Eells, Asst.	OL	71
Mary, d. Richard, b. Feb. 15, 1649	LL	2
Mary, w. Richard, adm. Church May 14, [1653]	OL	99
Mary, d. Richard [& Mary], bp. [1654, by Rev. Peter Prudden]	OL	105
Mary, d. Richard, merchant, m. John **MAULBE***, Feb. 28, 1666, by Thomas Clark, Commissioner *(MALTBY?)	1	8
Mary, d. Richard, merchant, m. John **MAULBEE**, merchant, Feb. 28, 1666, by Mr. Clark, Com.	OL	19
Mary, d. [Joseph], [ ], 1730	ES	238
Mary, d. Richard & Sarah, b. Mar. 7, 1736	1	104
Mehetabeel, [twin with Richard], d. Richard & Mehetabeel, b. Aug. 15, 1721	1	98
Mehitabeel, w. Richard, Jr., d. Sept. 16, 1721	1	99
Mehitabel, d. Richard & Sarah, b. May 19, 1745; d. Sept. 4, 1746	1	158
Mehetabel, [d. Richard & Sarah], [b.] May 19, 1745	ES	238
Mehitabel, d. Richard & Sarah, b. Mar. 31, 1752; d. May 12, 1754	1	158

	Vol.	Page
BRYAN, BRIANT, BRIATT, BRYANT, (cont.)		
Mehitabel, d. Richard & Sarah, b. Apr. 14, 1755; d. June 14, 1756	1	158
Nathan, s. Richard, b. Dec. 11, 1714	1	36
Nathan, s. Richard, b. Dec. 11, 1714	OL	78
Oliver, s. Richard & Sarah, b. June 3, 1756	1	158
Oliver, [s. Richard & Sarah, b.] Ju[ ], 14, 1756	ES	238
Oliver, Sergt., member of Capt. Samuel Peck's Co., Milford, 1776	1	54
Oliver, his s. [ ], d. Feb. 6, 1780	SM	19
Oliver, d. [ ], 1832, ae. 76	BP	68
Richard, s. Richard, b. Oct. 1, 1666	1	7
Richard, s. Richard, b. Oct. 8, 1666	OL	18
Richard, m. Mary **WILMOT**, July 15, 1679	1	18
Rich[ard], m. Mary **WILMOT**, July 15, 1679	OL	35
Richard, m. Mehetable **CLARK**, Oct. 20, 1720, by Sam[ue]ll Eells, Asst.	1	68
Richard, [twin with Mehetabeel], s. Richard & Mehitabeel, b. Aug. 15, 1721	1	98
Richard, m. Mrs. Sarah **TREAT**, Mar. 15, 1721/2, by Rev. Sam[ue]ll Andrews	1	100
Rich[ard], d. Jan. 18, 1734	ES	238
Richard, brother of Alexander, d. J[ ] 28, 1734	ES	238
Richard, d. Jan. 18, 1734/5	1	100
Richard, (Town Clerk), d. July 18, 1734/5	ES	238
Richard, Jr., m. Sarah **FOWLER**, Jan. 13, 1742. Witnesses, John Fowler, Mary Fowler	1	158
Richard, m. Sarah **FOWLER**, July 13, 1742	ES	238
Richard, s. Richard & Sarah, b. Dec. 27, 1746	1	158
Richard, [s. Richard & Sarah], [b.] Dec. 29, 1746	ES	238
Richard, Capt., d. March 19, 1776, ae. 55	SM	5
Richard, Col., d. 1776	ES	41
Richard, his d. [ ], m. Joseph **TREAT**, [ ]	ES	238
Richard Smith, s. Joseph & Juliana, b. June 6, 1778	1	170
Samuel, Marshall, drafted for Continental Army	1	57
Samuel, s. Richard, b. Apr. 2, 1660	1	3
Samuell, s. Richard, b. Apr. 2, 1660	OL	12
Samuel, m. Mrs. Martha **WHITING**, d. John Whiting, of Hartford, Dec. 25, 1683, by Maj. John Talcot, Asst.	1	19
Samuel, of Milford, m. Mrs. Martha **WHITING**, d. John Whiting, of Stratford*, Dec. 25, 1683, by Major John *(Overwritten to read "Hartford")	OL	40
Sam[ue]ll, Capt., 1696	ES	40
Sam[ue]ll, s. Richard & Sarah, b. [ ] 15, 1750	1	158
Sam[ue]ll, [s. Richard & Sarah, b.], Jan. 15, 1759	ES	238
Sarah, d. Richard, b. Apr. 24, 1657	1	3
Sarah, d. Richard, b. Apr. 24, 1657	OL	12
Sarah, Mrs., m. Samuel **FITCH**, Oct. 23, 1678, by Major Robert Treat, D.G.	1	16
Sarah, Mrs., m. Samuell **FFITCH**, Oct. 23, 1678, by Major Robert Treat, D.G.	OL	33
Sarah, d. Richard & Sarah, b. June 4, 1723	1	100
Sarah, d. Richard & Sarah, b. May 26, 1744; d. June 17, 1746	1	158
Sarah, d. Richard & Sarah, b. Apr. 24, 1749	1	158

	Vol.	Page
BRYAN, BRIANT, BRIATT, BRYANT, (cont.)		
Sarah, [d. Richard & Sarah], b. Aug. 24, 1749	ES	238
Sarah, m. Benedict LAW, Jan. 4, 1770. Witnesses David Bryan, Susanna Fowler	1	160
Sarah, wid., d. [　　　　], 1803, ae. 79	BP	7
Sarah, wid., d. Feb. 5, 1803	SM	77
Sibella, d. Richard, m. Benedict BULL, of Newport, R.I., s. of Henry, a descendant of Henry Bull, one of the early governors of the colony, Dec. 11, 1716	1	45
Sibella, m. Benedict BULL, Dec. 11, 1716	1	66
Sibella, Mrs., m. Hugh GRAY, [　　　　], by Robert Treat, Dept. Gov.	OL	43
Susannah, Mrs., m. Capt. Roger NEWTON, Apr. 10, 1712	1	34
Susannah, Mrs., m. Capt. Roger NEWTON, Apr. 10, 1712	OL	73
Susannah, m. Col. George NEWTON, s. of supposed Capt. Samuel & grandson, of Rev. Roger, Apr. 10, 1712. Had children Roger, Susannah, Martha	ES	116
Susanna, d. Richard & Sarah, b. Jan. 3, 1762; d. Nov. 15, 1765	1	158
——, wid. Her negro d. Sept. 7, 1777	SM	13
——, Mrs., d. [　　　　], 1823, ae. 93	BP	48
BRYANT, [see under **BRYAN**]		
BUCKINGHAM, Abell, s. Nathaniell, b. May 22, 1745	1	132
Abigail, d. Sam[ue]ll & Silence, b. Nov. 19, 1720	1	70
Abijah, s. Nath[anie]ll, b. June 22, 1735	1	103
Abijah, m. Hannah BYANTON, Jan. 11, 1759*, by Rev. Job. Prudden; Recorded Sept. [　　] *(Probably wrong; conflicts with date of birth of first child)	1	151
Abijah, s. Abijah [& Hannah], b. Feb. 15, 1760; d. June 19, 1761	1	151
Abijah, s. Abijah [& Hannah], b. June 5, 1762; d. Sept. 9, 1764	1	151
Alice, Mrs., d. Feb. 8, 1741/2	1	111
Ann, wid., [　　　　], 1659 and 1662	ES	238
Ann, d. Sam[ue]ll, b. June 17, 1674	OL	27
Ann, d. Capt. Samuel, b. Mar. 6, 1723	1	301
Ann, d. Capt. Sam[ue]ll, b. Mar. 16, 1723	1	124
Ann, d. John, b. Nov. 19, 1739	1	114
Anne, d. Samuel, b. June 17, 1674	1	14
Benjamin, s. John, b. Mar. 5, 1698	OL	54
Benjamin, s. John, b. Mar. 5, 1698/9	1	26
Clement, m. Joseph TREAT, Feb. 25, 1734	ES	238
Clement, m. Joseph TREAT, Sept. 26, 1734, by Roger Newton, J.P.	1	101
Clement, m. Capt. Joseph TREAT, Sept. 26, 1734	1	130
Clement, m. Joseph TREAT, [　　　　], 1734	ES	238
D., Dea. His w. [　　], d. [　　　　], 1830, ae. 85	BP	61
Daniel, m. Hannah FFOWLER, d. of Sergt. William, Nov. 21, 1661, by Matthew Gilbert, Dept. Gov.	1	4
Daniell, m. Sarah FFOWLER, d. Sergt. William, b. of Milford, Nov. 21, 1661, by Matthew Gilbert, Dept. Gov.	OL	14
Daniell*, s. Thomas, decd., m. Sarah BALDWIN, d. Timothy, Dec. 14, 1663, by Benjamin Ffenn *(Probably "Samuel Buckingham")	OL	15
Daniell, s. Sergt. Daniell, b. Jan. 30, 1665	OL	17

MILFORD VITAL RECORDS 39

	Vol.	Page
BUCKINGHAM, (cont.)		
Daniel, s. Sergt. Daniel, b. Jan. 30, 1665/6	1	7
Daniel, Elder, d. May 2, 1711	1	63
Daniel, Elder, d. May 11, 1711	ES	238
Daniel, d. May 2, 1712. "Was Elder in 1st Ch. almost 39 yrs.	ES	238
Daniel, Rev., s. Rev. Daniel, b. Oct. 27, 1713	ES	126
Dan[ie]l, Elder, d. May 2, 1715	ES	238
Daniel, m. Sibbell BULL, Jan. 10, 1773	1	162
Daniel, his w. [ ], d. Mar. 4, 1784, ae. 34	SM	27
Daniel, chosen Dea. June 9, 1789	ES	238
Dan[ie]l, Jr., his child d. [ ], 1814	BP	27
Daniel, Jr., his w. [ ], d. [ ], 1822, ae. 36	BP	47
Daniel, Dea., d. [ ], 1836, ae. 88	BP	76
Daniel, [s. Daniel & Sibball], b. [ ]	1	162
Deborah, d. Sam[ue]ll, b. Mar. 22, 1718	1	64
Eben[eze]r, s. Capt. Sam[ue]ll, b. Dec. 10, 1727	1	124
Ebenezer, Dea., d. Oct. 6, 1795 (non resident)	SM	57
Elizabeth, d. Capt. Sam[ue]ll, b. Apr. 11, 1738	1	124
Elizabeth, wid., d. [ ], 1838	BP	80
Enoch, s. Capt. Sam[ue]ll, b. Dec. 15, 1740	1	124
Ephraim, s. Nath[anie]ll, b. Dec. 6, 1743	1	118
Eph[rai]m, d. [ ], 1825	BP	52
Esther, d. [Thomas], bp. May 30, 1669; dismissed to Seabrook [ ], 1670	ES	238
Esther, m. Richard PLATT, Nov. 7, 1706, by Capt. Eells	1	27
Esther, m. Richard PLATT, Nov. 7, 1706, by Capt. Eells	OL	58
Esther, d. Tho[ma]s, b. Jan. 29, 1725/6; d. July 16, 1726	1	79
Esther, d. Capt. Sam[ue]ll, b. Apr. 17, 1730	1	124
Esther, see also Hester		
Eunice, d. [ ], 1793	SM	50
Gideon, s. Daniel, b. Oct. 4, 1675	1	15
Gideon, s. Josiah, b. Oct. 4, 1675	OL	29
Gideon, s. Elder [ ], [ ], 1675	ES	238
Gideon, m. Sarah HUNT, Feb. 3, 1703, by Robert Treat, Dept. Gov.	1	22
Gideon, m. Sarah HUNT, Feb. 3, 1703/4, by Rob[er]t Treat, Dept. Gov.	OL	47
Gideon, s. Gideon, b. Dec. 24, 1704	1	23
Gideon, s. Gideon, b. Dec. 24, 1704	OL	47
Gideon, b. June 22, 1744; d. Dec. 8, 1809; was Town Clerk, 35 years	ES	132
Gideon, Town Clerk Apr. [ ], 1776	ES	238
Gideon, d. [ ], 1809, ae. 65	BP	19
Hannah, w. Thomas, adm. Church, Feb. 9, [1639/40], at New Haven	OL	97
Hannah, d. Daniell, b. Oct. 11, 1663	OL	16
Hannah, d. Daniel, b. Oct. 11, 1664	1	6
Hannah, d. Samuel, b. Mar. 1, 1670/1	1	10
Hannah, d. Daniell, b. Mar. 24, 1670/1	OL	23
Hannah, d. John, b. Mar. 12, 1701/2	1	26
Hannah, d. John, b. Mar. 12, 1701/2	OL	54
Hannah, m. Joseph TREAT, June 9, 1720, by Sam[ue]ll Eells, Asst.	1	68

	Vol.	Page
BUCKINGHAM, (cont.)		
Hannah, d. of John, m. Joseph **TREAT**, June 9, 1720	1	130
Hannah, m. Joseph **TREAT**, July 9, 1720; d. May 25, 1739	ES	238
Hannah, d. Abijah [& Hannah], b. Jan. 11, 1759 (Date conflicts with marriage of parents)	1	151
Hester, d. Samuel, b. May 4, 1677	1	16
Hesther, d. Samuell, b. May 4, 1679	OL	33
Hester, see also Esther		
Isaac, Capt. [ ], 1768	ES	238
Isaac, his child d. [ ], 1806	BP	13
Isaac, his w. [ ], d. [ ], 1810	BP	20
Jabez, [s. Daniel & Sibball], b. [ ]	1	162
Jared, s. Capt. Sam[ue]ll, b. Sept. 16, 1732	1	124
Jere, d. [ ], 1822, ae. 8	BP	48
Joanna, d. Samuel, b. Dec. 4, 1667; m. Joseph **WATKINS**, of Stratford; m. 2nd Jesse **LAMBERT**; m. 3rd Samuel **CAMP**, of Newark, Nov. 24, 1726	1	49
John, s. Daniel, b. May 13, 1673	1	12
John, s. Daniel, b. May 13, 1673	OL	25
John, d. Nov. 17, 1703	1	42
John, d. Nov. 17, 1703	OL	88
John, m. Keziah **CLARK**, Mar. 25, 1731, by Roger Newton, J.P.	1	96
John, s. John, b. Sept. 27, 1744	1	114
John, 3rd, d. Dec. 25, 1777	SM	14
John, his youngest child d. July 27, 1783	SM	26
John, d. Mar. 3, 1788, ae. 81	SM	36
John, Jr., his w. [ ], d. [ ], 1807	BP	16
John, d. [ ], 1809	BP	18
John, his s. [ ], d. [ ], 1825, ae. 13	BP	52
John, d. [ ], 1831	BP	65
Joseph, s. Nathaniell, b. July 1, 1730	1	86
Joseph, d. [ ], 1808	BP	18
Josiah, s. Daniel, b. Mar. 13, 1677	1	16
Josiah, s. Daniel, b. Mar. 13, 1677/8	OL	32
Josiah, s. Elder [ ], [ ], 1678	ES	238
Josiah, s. Gideon, [ ], 1718	ES	238
Josiah, Capt., d. Oct. 19, 1784, ae. 66	SM	28
Josiah, Sergt., 1765; d. 1784	ES	41
Keziah, wid., d. [ ], 1809, ae. 97	BP	19
Lucy, d. Oct. 11, 1798, ae. 20	SM	64
Mary, d. Thomas, bp. [1643, by Rev. Peter Prudden]	OL	100
Mary, d. Samuel, b. Oct. 3, 1666	1	7
Mary, d. Samuel, b. Oct. 3, 1666	OL	18
Mary, d. Daniel, b. Aug. 27, 1668; m. Ephraim **STREAM**, the first Settler, [ ]	1	9
Mary, d. Daniell, b. Aug. 27, 1668	OL	21
Mary, d. Samuel, b. Mar. 13, 1676/7	1	15
Mary, d. Sam[ue]ll Burlingame, *b. Mar. 13, 1676/7 *(Probably "Buckingham")	OL	31
Mary, wid., m. Ephraim **STRONG**, May 10, 1712, by Capt. Joseph Treat, J.P.	1	76
Mary, m. Gideon **PLATT**, Feb. 28, 1716, by Sam[ue]ll Eells, Asst.	1	83
Mary, d. Thomas, b. Sept. 16, 1724	1	78

	Vol.	Page
BUCKINGHAM, (cont.)		
Nathan, s. Capt. Sam[ue]ll, b. Aug. 20, 1735	1	124
Nathaniel, m. Sarah **SMITH**, May 30, 1728, by George Newton, J.P.	1	86
Nathaniel, s. Nathaniell, b. Mar. 8, 1729	1	86
Nath[anie]l, original member of 2nd Church formed in 1742	ES	87
Nathaniell, s. Nathaniell, d. Sept. 30, 1753	1	132
Nathaniel, Dea., d. Oct. 27, 1780, ae. 80	SM	20
Oliver, s. Nath[anie]ll, b. May 27, 1739	1	109
Oliver, m. Elizabeth **TERRELL**, May 26, 1772, by Job Prudden	1	160
Peter, d. Apr. 19, 1804, ae. 69 (negro)	SM	79
Samuel, s. Thomas, bp. [1641], [by Rev. Peter Prudden]	OL	100
Samuel, m. Sarah **BALDWIN**, Dec. 12, 1663, by Mr. Ffenne, Magistrate	1	6
Samuell, m. Sarah **BALDWIN**, b. of Milford, Dec. 12, 1663, by Mr. Fenn, Magestrate (Written "Samuell Burlingham")	OL	16
Samuel, s. Thomas, m. Sarah **BALDWIN**, d. Timothy, Dec. 14, 1663, by Mr. Benjamin Ffenne	1	5
Samuel, s. Samuel, b. Oct. 7, 1667	1	8
Samuel, s. Samuel, b. Oct. 7, 1667	OL	19
Samuel, s. Samuel, b. Sept. 1, 1668	1	9
Samuell, s. Samuell, b. Nov. 1, 1668	OL	21
Samuel, Sr., d. Mar. 17, 1699/1700	1	40
Samuell, Sr., d. Mar. 17, 1699/1700	OL	86
Sam[ue]l, m. Silence **CLARKE**, May 20, 1714, by Rev. Sam[ue]l Andrews	1	64
Sam[ue]ll, s. Sam[ue]l, b. Sept. 11, 1725	1	79
Samuel, Capt. 1747	ES	41
Samuel, his infant child d. [ ], 1820	BP	41
Sarah, d. Samuel, b. Jan. 8, 1664	1	6
Sarah, d. Samuell, b. Jan. 8, 1664	OL	17
Sarah, m. George **CLARK**, 2nd, Jan. 3, 1705/6, by Robert Treat, Dept. Gov.	1	37
Sarah, m. George **CLARK**, 2nd, Jan. 3, 1705/6, by Robert Treat, Dept. Gov.	OL	81
Sarah, d. Sam[ue]ll, b. Apr. 21, 1716	1	64
Sarah, d. John & Keziah, b. Sept. 13, 1733	1	96
Sarah, d. Nathaniel, b. Feb. 29, 1733/4	1	103
Sarah, wid., d. [ ], 1828	BP	57
Sibbill, d. Nathaniel, b. Sept. 13, 1737 (Sybil)	1	107
Sybell, m. Nathan **NETTLETON**, Nov. 3, 1757, by Rev. Job Prudden	1	137
Sibball, d. Daniel & Sibball, b. Oct. 21, 1773	1	162
Sibel, Jr., d. Sept. 7, 1783, ae. 10	SM	26
Thomas, d. [ ], in Boston	ES	17
Thomas, original member of First Church gathered at New Haven Aug. 22, 1639	ES	57
Thomas, s. Thomas, bp. [1646, by Rev. Peter Prudden]	OL	102
Tho[mas], s. Tho[mas], b. & bp. Oct. 8, 1646	ES	238
Tho[m]s, d. [ ], 1657, in Boston; one of the first planters	ES	16
Tho[mas], d. [ ], 1657, at Boston	ES	238
Thomas, d. [ ], 1657, at Boston	OL	97
Thomas, adm. To 1st Ch. Sept. 24, 1665; dismissed to 1st Ch. of		

	Vol.	Page
BUCKINGHAM, (cont.)		
Seabrook, Oct. [ ], 1670	ES	238
Thomas, s. Daniel, b. Mar. 1, 1670/1	1	10
Thomas, s. Daniell, b. Mar. 1, 1670/1 (Perhaps Mar. 5)	OL	23
Thom[as], s. Dan[ie]l, B., b. M[ ] 5, 1671	ES	185
Tho[mas], s. Daniel, bp. [ ], 1671/2	ES	238
Tho[mas], s. Sam[uel] B., b. June 5, 1672	ES	185
Thomas, s. Samuel, b. June 25, 1672	1	12
Thomas, s. Sam[ue]ll, b. June 25, 1672	OL	24
Thomas, s. Sam[ue]l, bp. [ ], 1672	ES	238
Thomas, m. Mary B. **WOODRUFFE**, Jan. 9, 1723/4, by Sam[ue]ll Eells, Asst.	1	73
Tho[mas], m. Mary **WOODRUFF**, July 9, 1724	ES	238
Thomas, s. Thomas & Mary, b. May 19, 1727	1	81
Tho[mas] & his w. [ ], adm. To Ch. 1730	ES	238
-----, Dr. had negro Tamar, d. Dec. 22, 1790	SM	44
-----, had negro Peter Prime, d. [ ], 1804	BP	9
-----, Mrs., d. [ ], 1806	BP	13
-----, his w. [ ], d. [ ], 1812	BP	23
BUDDINGTON, BUDINGTON, Sam, Capt. his child d. [ ], 1821	BP	44
Theodore, his child d. [ ], 1838	BP	80
Walter, his w. [ ], d. [ ], 1825	BP	53
-----, Mr., d. [ ], 1826, ae. 80	BP	55
-----, Mrs., d. [ ], 1829	BP	60
BULL, Anna, d. Jer[emiah] & Anne, b. Aug. 20, 1781; m. Edward A. **LAMBERT**, 4th s. David, [ ]	1	152
Anne, d. Benjamin & Anne, b. Jan. 30, 1757	1	152
Anne, only child of Jeremiah & Anne (**GUNN**), b. Aug. 20, 1781	1	52
Anne, [d. Jeremiah & Ann], b. Aug. 20, 1782; m. Edward A. **LAMBERT**, s. David, Jan. 16, 1806	1	45
Anne, only child of Jeremiah & Anne (**GUNN**), m. Edward Allyn **LAMBERT**, 6th s. of David & Martha, Jan. 16, 1806, by Bazaleel Pinnio	1	52
Benedict, of Newport, R.I., s. Henry a descendant of Henry **BULL**, one of the early governors of the colony; had two brothers, Joseph & John, who remained in R.I.; m. Sibella **BRYAN**, d. Richard, Dec. 11, 1716	1	45
Benedict, m. Sibella **BRYAN**, Dec. 11, 1716	1	66
Benedick, [twin with Jirah], s. Benedick, b. Oct. 10, 1721	1	69
Benedict & w. Sibella had twins b. Oct. 12, 1721	1	45
Benedict, his child d. [ ], 1803	BP	7
Benedict, his infant s. [ ], d. May [ ], 1803	SM	77
Benedict, his child d. [ ], 1809	BP	19
Benedict, [s. Jabez Benedict & Naomi], b. [ ]; moved to Plymouth, Conn.	1	45
Benjamin, m. [ ] **BALDWIN**, d. Stephen, [ ]	1	45
Benjamin, m. Easther **BALDWIN**, Dec. 22, 1748, by Rev. Sam[ue]ll Whittlesey	1	152
Benj[ami]n, m. Ann **PLATT**, his 2nd w. Apr. 11, 1754, by Sam[ue]ll Whittlesey	1	152
Benj[ami]n, s. Benj[ami]n & Ann, b. Jan. 24, 1755; d. Dec. 6, 1757	1	152

	Vol.	Page
BULL, (cont.)		
Benjamin, s. [Benjamin], b. June 22, 1761; m. [ ], [ ]; had no children	1	45
Benj[ami]n, s. Benj[ami]n & Anne, b. June 22, 1761	1	152
Benjamin, Capt., d. Oct. 4, 1776, ae. 54	SM	7
Benj[amin], 1st. Capt., 1772; d. 1776	ES	41
Benj[amin], chosen Dea. Nov. 29, 1798	ES	238
Benjamin, Dea. Had negro Cuff, d. Dec. 11, 1800	SM	70
Benj[amin], 2d., [Capt.], 1804	ES	41
Betsey, d. Dan[ie]ll, d. Aug. 1, 1796, ae. 2 y.	SM	59
Bryan, d. May 14, 1804, in New York	SM	80
Cornelius, s. Henry & Harriet, b. June 14, 1806	1	174
Daniel, s. [Benjamin], b. Oct. 23, 1763; moved to Plymouth, Conn.	1	45
Daniel, s. Benj[ami]n, b. Oct. 23, 1763; m. Betsey [ ], [ ]; moved to Plymouth, Conn.	1	152
Daniel, his s. [ ], s. b. July 9, 1793	SM	49
Elizabeth, wid., d. [ ], 1836, ae. 55	BP	75
Easther, d. Benjamin & Easther, b. Mar. 11, 1750; m. Matthew **WOODRUFF**, [ ]	1	152
Fame, [ch. of Jabez Benedict & Naomi], b. [ ]; m. [ ]; had children Fame, Jabez, who m. a **LAMBERT** of Virginia & settled in Florida, and Bryan	1	45
Frederick, s. Henry & Harriet, b. Feb. 9, 1786	1	174
Frederick, s. Henry & Harriet, d. Feb. 9, 1798. He was killed by a kick of a horse. (Note says "Mistake of date")	1	174
Frederick, d. Sept. 12, 1798, ae. 13 y.	SM	64
Godsgift, d. Benedict & Sibella, b. Feb. 4, 1724/5	1	77
Harpin, d. [ ], 1822, at Sea	BP	46
Harriet, d. Henry & Harriet, b. Sept. 5, 1787	1	174
Harvey, d. [ ], 1834	BP	71
Henry, see under Benedict **BULL**		
Henry, [s. Jabez Benedict & Naomi], b. [ ], 1754; m. [ ]; had children Frederic; Henry; John, who married and had William; Philip, William Harpin, Cornelius	1	45
Henry, m. Harriet **MERCHANT**, divorced w. of Sam[ue]l & d. of John **HARPIN**, Apr. 7, 1785, by Rev. David Fuller	1	174
Henry, s. Henry & Harriet, b. Sept. 16, 1791	1	174
Henry, Dea., d. [ ], 1819	BP	39
Henry, d. Apr. [ ], 1819	ES	94
J., had strange person d. at his home, [ ], 1813	BP	31
J. B., Dea., d. [ ], 1814, ae. 67	BP	27
Jabez Benedict, [s. Jirah & Sibella], b. Jan. 19, 1747; m. Naomi **BRISTOL**, [ ]	1	45
Jabez Benedict, s. Jirah, b. Jan. 19, 1747/8	1	124
Jabez Benedict, d. Aug. 8, 1814	ES	94
James, Jr., d. [ ], 1826, ae. 29	BP	54
James, d. [ ], 1831, ae. 60	BP	64
Jeremiah, s. Jirah & Sibella (**PECK**), b. Mar. 10, 1757; d. May 24, 1832	1	152
Jeremiah, [s. Jabez Benedict & Naomi], b. Mar. 10, 1757; m. Ann **GUNN**, d. Stephen, Aug. 30, 1780	1	45
Jeremiah, Corp., member of Capt. Samuel Peck's Co., Milford,		

	Vol.	Page
BULL, (cont.)		
1776	1	54
Jeremiah, m. Anne GUNN, Aug. 30, 1780, by Rev. Samuel Wales	1	152
Jeremiah, d. [ ], 1832, ae. 75	BP	67
Jerusha, d. Henry & Harriet, b. Mar. 27, 1798; m. Nathaniel ADAMS, lawyer, of Green Farms, Fairfield. Co., Conn., [ ]	1	174
Jirah, [s. Benjamin], m. Sibella PECK, d. Jeremiah, s. of John, s. of John, [ ]	1	45
Jirah, [twin with Benedick], s. Benedick, b. Oct. 10, 1721	1	69
Jirah, d. [ ], 1823, ae. 48	BP	49
John, s. Henry & Harriet, b. Sept. 5, 1793; m. Mary BALDWIN, [ ]	1	174
John, m. Elizabeth DICKINSON, d. Sylvanus & Mary, [ ]	1	178
Mary, d. Benj[ami]n & Anne, b. July 11, 1758	1	152
Mary Ann, d. Henry & Harriet, b. June 3, 1800; m. Sam[ue]ll WOODHULL, tailor, of Bridgeport, [ ]; settled in Utica, N.Y.	1	174
Mary N., d. [ ], 1812, ae. 12	BP	24
Philip, s. Henry & Harriet, b. Dec. 25, 1795	1	174
Philip, d. [ ], 1822, at Sea	BP	47
Richard Bryan, d. [ ], 1804, in New York	BP	9
S-----, wid., d. Sept. 24, 1776, ae. 83	SM	7
Sarah, [d. Jabez Benedict & Naomi], b. [ ]; m. [ ]. Had ch. Frederika, W[illia]m Atwater, Allen C., Tirah (?), Marcus, Henry	1	45
Sibbell, m. Daniel BUCKINGHAM, Jan. 10, 1773	1	162
Sibel, wid., d. May 21, 1787, ae. 71	SM	33
Sibel, d. Henry & Harriet, b. July 15, 1789	1	174
Sibel, d. Henry & Harriet, d. Sept. 30, 1790	1	174
Sibyl, d. Oct. 1, 1790, ae. 1 y.	SM	43
Sibella, d. Benedict, b. Feb. 24, 1719/20	1	66
William, s. John, see under Henry BULL	1	45
William Harpin, s. Henry & Harriet, b. Dec. 26, 1802	1	174
-----, Col, b. June 21, 1761	ES	238
-----, Col, d. [ ], 1826, ae. 64	BP	55
-----, his child d. [ ], 1833	BP	69
BUNNELL, BUNNLE, Abigail, d. Benj[amin] [& Mehetabeel], b. Dec. 3, 1726	1	81
Abigail, d. Benja[mi]n, d. May 14, 1728	1	93
Abigaill, [twin with Isaac], d. Benjamin & Mehitabeel, b. June 12, 1734	1	100
Benj[ami]n, m. Mehetabeel BALDWIN, Apr. 13, 1726, by Jon[a]th[an] Law, Dept. Gov.	1	81
Benjamin, s. Benjamin, b. Mar. 7, 1731/2	1	93
Charles, s. Benj[ami]n, b. Sept. 15, 1738	1	111
Hannah, [twin with Margat], d. Gershom, b. June 15, 1729	1	83
Isaac, [twin with Abigaill], s. Benjamin & Mehetabeel, b. June 12, 1734	1	100
Louis, d. Benj[ami]n, b. Sept. 18, 1740	1	111
Luke, s. Benjamin, b. Sept. 20, 1736	1	104
Lydia, of Milford, m. Ffrancis FFRENCH, of Pagasset, (Derby)		

	Vol.	Page
BUNNELL, BUNNLE, (cont.)		
Apr. 10, 1661	1	4
Lydia, of Milford, m. Frances **FRENCH**, of Paganick, Apr. 10, 1661	OL	14
Margat, [twin with Hannah], d. Gershom, b. June 15, 1729; d. July 2, 1729	1	83
Mary, d. Samuel, b. Apr. 6, 1663	OL	20
Mary, d. Samuel, b. Oct. 20, 1667	OL	20
Mehetabeel, d. Benj[amin], b. Feb. 20, 1727	1	82
Mehitabeel, d. Benjamin & Mehitabeel, d. Oct. 23, 1753	1	134
Mercy, d. Benjamin, b. Aug. 30, 1729	1	93
Rebecca, d. Benjamin, of New Haven, m. Samuel **BURWELL**, Jr., of Milford, Nov. 27, 1684, by The Gov.	1	19
Rebekah, d. Gershom, b. Dec. 28, 1730	1	92
Robert, his ch., d. [ ], 1821, ae. 3 y.	BP	45
Ruth, d. Sept. 7, 1784	SM	28
Samuel, s. Samuel, b. June 26, 1665	OL	20
BURKE, Ann, wid. of J., formerly Ann **SEARS**, d. [ ], 1822, at Jonas Hines'	BP	46
John, his 1ˢᵗ w. [ ], d. May 22, 1789, ae. 38	SM	39
BURLINGAME, [see under **BUCKINGHAM**]		
BURNHAM, -----, his ch., d. [ ], 1833	BP	69
BURNS, BURN, BYRNE, Abram, his ch., d. [ ], 1828	BP	58
Abram, his infant d. [ ], 1838	BP	79
Benjamin, drafted for Continental Army	1	58
Benjamin, d. [ ], 1806	BP	14
Charlotte, d. [ ], 1802, ae. 10 y.	BP	6
Daniel, Jr., d. July 29, 1796, ae. 20	SM	59
Daniel, his d. [ ], d. Dec. 24, 1802, ae. 10	SM	76
Daniel, d. [ ], 1811, ae. 66	BP	22
David, pd. £5 for not procuring men for Continental Army	1	55
David, his d. [ ], d. Oct. 30, 1777, ae. 1 y.	SM	14
David, his infant d. [ ], d. June 12, 1790	SM	42
David, Jr., d. July 27, 1793	SM	49
David, his w. [ ], d. Nov. 9, 1797, ae. 44	SM	62
David, d. [ ], 1830, ae. 77	BP	61
David, his wid. [ ], d. [ ], 1832	BP	67
James, d. [ ], 1794 (Absent)	SM	52
James, his w. [ ], d. [ ], 1833 (Written "James **BARN**")	BP	70
John, his ch., d. [ ], 1813	BP	32
John, his ch., d. [ ], 1822	BP	46
John, his s. [ ], d. [ ], 1835, ae. 17	BP	73
John, Jr., his ch., d. [ ], 1836	BP	74
Ralph, his ch., d. [ ], 1821	BP	45
Ralph, his other child twins, d. [ ], 1821	BP	45
Ralph, his child d. [ ], 1828, ae. 18 m.	BP	58
Ralph, his d. [ ], d. [ ], 1829, ae. 16	BP	60
Samuel, his infant, d. [ ], 1827	BP	56
-----, wid., d. [ ], 1840, ae. 93	BP	83
BURRILL, [see also **BURWELL**], -----, wid., m. Joseph **PECK**, Sept. 12, 1650, by Capt. Asa woods	LL	2
BURRIT, Susan, Mrs., d. [ ], 1833	BP	68

	Vol.	Page
BURTON, Richard, m. Hannah **TERRELL**, Mar. 6, 1723/4	1	73
-----, Mrs. a stranger, d. [ ], 1801	BP	3
-----, Mrs., d. Mar. 14, 1801	SM	72
BURWELL, BURWEL, [see also **BURRILL**], Abigail, d. Nathan, d. Sept. 3, 1703	1	41
Abigaill, d. Nathan, d. Sept. 3, 1703	OL	86
Abigaill, d. Sam[ue]ll [& Abigail], b. Dec. 6, 1727	1	92
Alice, w. John, adm. Church Oct. 4, [1640]; d. Dec. 19, 1666	OL	97
Alice, d. Nathan, b. Nov. 27, 1674	1	14
Alice, d. Nathan, b. Dec. 27, 1674	OL	28
Benedict, his marks for cattle, recorded Apr. 27, 1764	1	148
Benedict, his d. [ ], d. Aug. 28, 1779	SM	18
Benedict, his ch., d. [ ], 1813	BP	31
Daniel, his ch., d. [ ], 1806	BP	14
Deborah, w. Samuel, d. Oct. 10, 1706	1	43
Deborah, w. Sam[ue]ll, d. Oct. 10, 1706	OL	89
Elias, his ch., d. [ ], 1812, ae. 3 y.	BP	23
Elias, his ch., d. [ ], 1820	BP	42
Elias, his ch., d. [ ], 1820	BP	42
Elizabeth, d. John, bp. [1647, by Rev. Peter Prudden]	OL	102
Ephraim, s. John, bp. [1644, by Rev. Peter Prudden]	OL	101
Ephraim, m. Sarah **STREAM**, May 27, 1698, by Thomas Clark, J.P.	1	22
Ephraim, m. Sarah **STREAME**, May 27, 1698, by Thomas Clark, J.P.	OL	46
Ephraim, s. Ephraim, b. July 16, 1707	1	28
Ephraim, s. Ephraim, b. July 16, 1707	OL	61
Fitch, s. John & Mary, b. Sept. 21, 1783	1	170
Gere, d. [ ], 1835, ae. 79	BP	72
Jerah, his infant d. Dec. 28, 1783	SM	26
Jere, s. John & Mary, b. Oct. 25, 1776	1	170
Jno, d. [ ], 1649	ES	35
Jno W., his ch., d. [ ], 1806	BP	14
John, d. [ ], 1649	ES	16
John, hus. of Alice, adm. Church July 4, [1641]; d. Aug. 17, 1649	OL	98
John, m. Susannah **BALDWIN**, Jan. 2, 1717/18, by Major Eells, Asst. Witness John Fflower	1	66
John, s. John, b. Mar. 22, 1719	1	66
John, d. Aug. 20, 1721	1	68
John, d. Aug. 20, 1721	1	70
John, Jr., his s. [ ], d. Dec. 11, 1779	SM	18
John, had negro Jesse, d. June 30, 1780	SM	20
John, his negro boy d. Mar. 14, 1781	SM	21
John, d. Jan. 20, 1784	SM	27
John, his s. [ ], d. Dec. 20, 1784, ae. 1 y.	SM	28
John, had negro woman, d. Nov. 27, 1788	SM	37
John, his w. [ ], d. [ ], 1809	BP	19
John, d. [ ], 1830, ae. 80	BP	61
John W., his ch., d. [ ], 1802	BP	6
John W., another ch., of his, d. [ ], 1802	BP	6
John W., his d. [ ], d. Oct. 11, 1802	SM	76
John W., his d. [ ], d. Oct. 17, 1802, ae. 3 ½ years	SM	76
John Welch, s. John & Mary, b. Jan. 3, 1776	1	170

MILFORD VITAL RECORDS 47

	Vol.	Page
BURWELL, BURWEL, [see also BURRILL], (cont.)		
Joseph, s. Lieut. [ ], b. Sept. 20, 1682	1	18
Joseph, s. Lieut. Samuel, b. Sept. 20, 1682	OL	38
Martha, d. Ephraim [& Sarah], b. Feb. 21, 1702/3	OL	46
Martha, d. Ephraim, b. Feb. 21, 1703	1	22
Martha, d. Sam[ue]ll, d. Oct. 31, 1703	1	42
Martha, d. Samuel, Jr., d. Oct. The last day, 1703	OL	88
Martha, m. John BEARD, Jan. 30, 1728/9	1	84
Mary, d. John, b. Dec. 5, 1653	OL	7
Mary, d. John, b. Dec. 6, 1653	1	1
Mary, d. Samuel, b. Oct. 20, 1667	1	9
Mary, m. Joshua LOBDELL, Aug. 11, 1695, by Robert Treat, Gov.	1	24
Mary, m. Joshua LOBDELL, Aug. 11, 1695, by Rob[er]t Treat, Gov.	OL	50
Mary, d. Ephraim, b. Oct. 22, 1704	1	24
Mary, d. Ephraim, b. Oct. 22, 1704	OL	51
Mary, m. Samuel MERWIN, May 1, 1707, by Thomas Clarke, J.P.	1	28
Mary, m. Sam[ue]ll MARWIN, May 7, 1707, by Thomas Clark, J.P.	OL	60
Nathan, s. John, bp. [1646, by Rev. Peter Prudden]	OL	102
Nathan, s. Samuel, decd., m. Temperence BALDWIN, d. Richard, decd., Jan. 14, 1673, by Major Treat	1	13
Nathan, s. John, decd., m. Temperance BALDWIN, b. of Milford, Jan. 14, 1673, by Major Treat	OL	26
Nathan, d. [ ], 1836	BP	74
Polly, d. [ ], 1824	BP	50
Rebecca, d. Benjamin, of New Haven, m. Sam[ue]ll BURWELL, Jr., of Milford, Nov. 27, 1684, by The Governor	OL	41
Robert, his ch., d. [ ], 1828	BP	57
Robert, his w. [ ], d. [ ], 1828	BP	57
Robert, d. [ ], 1833, ae. 41	BP	69
Samuel, s. John, bp. [1640], by Rev. Peter Prudden	OL	100
Samuell, s. Samuel, b. June 26, 1665	1	9
Samuel, s. Samuel, b. Jan. 12, 1666	OL	22
Samuel, s. Samuel, b. Jan. 12, 1666/7	1	10
Samuel, Jr., of Milford, m. Rebecca BUNNELL, d. Benjamin, of New Haven, Nov. 27, 1684, by The Gov.	1	19
Sam[ue]ll, Jr., of Milford, m. Rebecca BURWELL*, d. Benjamin, of New Haven, Nov. 27, 1684, by The Governor *(Probably "BUNNELL")	OL	41
Sam[ue]ll, Capt., 1690	ES	40
Sam[ue]ll, Lieut., d. May 5, 1715	1	63
Samuel, of Milford, m. Abigail GOODYEAR, of New Haven, Jan. 12, 1726/7, by Sam[ue]ll Eells, Asst.	1	92
	1	92
Samuell, s. Sam[ue]ll [& Abigail], b. Dec. 12, 1729	SM	12
Samuel, d. Apr. [ ], 1777	SM	25
Sam[uel], his negro Crad, d. Jan. 26, 1783	SM	37
Samuel, his w. [ ], d. Sept. 9, 1788	BP	13
Samuel, Jr., d. [ ], 1806	BP	28
Samuel, his ch., d. [ ], 1815		

48   BARBOUR COLLECTION

	Vol.	Page
BURWELL, BURWEL, [see also **BURRILL**], (cont.)		
Samuel, d. [ ], 1816	BP	34
Samuel, his ch., d. [ ], 1825	BP	52
Sarah, d. Samuel, b. Apr. 6, 1663	1	9
Sarah, d. Ephraim, b. Apr. 6, 1699	1	22
Sarah, d. Ephraim [& Sarah], b. Apr. 6, 1699	OL	46
Sarah, m. Josiah **PLATT**, Jan. 8, 1706/7, by Samuel Eells, J.P.	1	27
Sarah, m. Josiah **PLATT**, Jan. 8, 1706/7, by Sam[ue]ll Eells, J.P.	OL	59
Stream, s. Ephraim, b. Apr. 11, 1701	1	22
Streame, s. Ephraim [& Sarah], b. Apr. 11, 1701	OL	46
Susannah, m. John **FOWLER**, Feb. 28, 1712/13, by Sam[ue]l Eells, Asst.	1	62
Susannah, wid., m. Stephen **MILES**, Feb. 11, 1724, by Sam[ue]ll Eells, Asst.	1	249
Susannah, [ ]	1	89
Thomas, his infant d. [ ], 1832	BP	66
Whitman, s. John & Mary, b. Mar. 14, 1781	1	170
Zachariah, m. Elizabeth **BALDWIN**, Nov. 18, 1663. "They removed to Newark, N.J., as appears by records of deed Leb. 4, Pge. 258"	1	5
Zachariah, m. Elizabeth **BALDWIN**, Nov. 18, 1663. Settled in Newark, N.J.	OL	15
-----, wid., d. Dec. 7, 1781	SM	22
BUSH, W[illia]m, d. [ ], 1820	BP	42
BUTLER, William, d. Dec. 27, 1792, ae. 1 ½ years	SM	48
BUTTERICK, BUTTRICK, BUTRICK, BUTTRIX, Anne, wid., d. July 26, 1799	BP	1
Asa, his ch., d. June 18, 1776	SM	6
Asa, d. Feb. 15, 1780	SM	19
-----, his ch. D. [ ], 1802	BP	5
BYANTON, Hannah, m. Abijah **BUCKINGHAM**, Jan. 11, 1759*, by Rev. Job Prudden. Recorded Sept. [ ] *(Probably an error. Conflicts with date of birth of first child)	1	151
BYRAN, W[illia]m, d. [ ], 1809, at North Carolina	BP	19
BYRNE, [see under **BURN**]		
B-----, Ed[ward], his w. [ ], d. [ ], 1840, in Poor House	BP	83
CACH (?), Susannah, d. Aug. 4, 1802	SM	75
CADY, Samuel, d. Oct. 7, 1795, at New York (non resident)	SM	57
-----, his ch. d. [ ], 1820	BP	42
-----, Mr., d. [ ], 1823	BP	49
CAFFINCH, Mary, d. John, bp. [1654, by Rev. Peter Prudden]; removed to New Haven Church	OL	105
CALLAHN, Robert, of Capt. Ann, d. Jan. [ ], 1777	SM	9
CAMBRIDGE, -----, d. Oct. 5, 1784	SM	28
CAMFIELD, [see under **CANFIELD**]		
CAMP, CAMPE, Abel, s. Samuel, s. Edward, b. Dec. 10, 1717	1	39
Abell, s. Enos, b. Jan. 21*, 1729 *(Perhaps Jan. 30)	1	89
Abel, d. Nov. 8, 1796, ae. 11	SM	60
Abigail, d. Nicholas, bp. [1647, by Rev. Peter Prudden]	OL	102
Abigail, d. Nicholas, b. Mar. 28, 1667	1	8
Abigail, d. Nicholas, b. Mar. 28, 1667	OL	19

	Vol.	Page

CAMP, CAMPE, (cont.)

	Vol.	Page
Abigail, d. Lieut. Samuel, b. Mar. 1, 1697	1	20
Abiga[i]l, d. Lieut. Sam[ue]ll [& Rebecca], b. Mar. 1, 1697	OL	44
Abigail, m. Timothy SMITH, Oct. 29, 1729, by Roger Newton, J.P.	1	84
Abigail, m. Joel NORTHROP, June 24, 1731, by Roger Newton, J.P.	1	98
Abigail, m. Joel NORTHROP, Oct. 12, 1756	1	136
Abigail, wid. had ch., d. [ ], 1832	BP	66
Alma, wid., her ch. d. [ ], 1832	BP	67
Amiel, [ch. of Gideon & Sarah Clark], b. June 20, 1761; recorded Apr. 17, 1777	1	166
Ammiel, d. Nov. 11, 1799, ae. 38	SM	68
Amos, s. Samuel, b. Feb. 12, 1692	1	21
Amos, s. Samuel, Sr., b. Feb. 12, 1692	OL	44
Amos, s. [ ], b. Nov. 15, 1733	1	96
Ann, d. Phinehas, b. Jan. 1, 1734/5	1	102
Bethiah, d. Samuel, Sr., b. Apr. 12, 1686	1	21
Bethiah, d. Sam[ue]ll, Sr., b. Apr. 12, 1686	OL	44
Caleb, s. Joseph, b. Feb. 14, 1704/5	1	25
Caleb, s. Joseph, b. Feb. 14, 1704/5	OL	51
David, s. Eleazer & Mary, b. Feb. 20, 1728/9	1	84
David, s. Eleazer [& Mary], b. Feb. 20, 1728/9	1	97
David, d. Feb. 19, 1798	SM	63
David, his s. [ ], d. July 4, 1802	SM	75
David, his ch., d. [ ], 1802	BP	5
David, his w. [ ], d. [ ], 1812	BP	24
David, his ch., d. [ ], 1812, ae. 3 y.	BP	24
David, d. [ ], 1821, ae. 42	BP	44
David, d. [ ], 1829, ae. 25	BP	59
David, m. Mahitabeel PECK, d. John [& Sarah], [ ]	1	133
Ebenezer, [s.] Samuel, Sr., b. Aug. 24, 1690	1	21
Ebenezer, s. Sam[ue]ll, Sr., b. Aug. 24, 1690	OL	44
Edward, see under Stephen CAMP	1	66
Edward, in 1671, destroyed the Indian Fort	ES	14
Edward, m. Mahitable SMITH, d. John, Sr., Jan. 15, 1673, by Major Treat	1	13
Edward, m. Mehitabeel SMITH, d. John, Sr., Jan. 15, 1673, by Major Treat	OL	26
Edward, s. John, Jr. [& Phebee], b. Jan. 12, 1711/12	OL	75
Edward, s. John, Jr., b. Jan. 12, 1712	1	35
Eleazer, m. Mary BOTCHFORD, Feb. 30*, 1728 *(Probably "May 30")	1	84
Eleazer, m. Mary BOTCHFORD, May 30, 1728, by Sam[ue]ll Gunn, J.P.	1	97
Elias, had negro woman, d. Mar. 18, 1782	SM	23
Elias, his ch., d. [ ], 1832	BP	67
Elias, d. [ ], 1835	BP	72
Elizabeth, d. Enos, b. Mar. 12, 1716. Written by P. R. Fleming, of Glasgow, Scotland (This entry in a different handwriting)	1	39
Elizabeth, d. Enos, b. Mar. 12, 1716/17	OL	84
Elizabeth, m. Benj[ami]n PLUMB, Mar. sometime, 1737, by		

	Vol.	Page

CAMP, CAMPE, (cont.)

	Vol.	Page
Newton, Asst.	1	113
Elizabeth, d. Nathaniel & Martha, b. Nov. 19, 1747	1	122
Elizabeth, wid., d. [ ], 1815	BP	29
Emily, d. [ ], 1831, ae. 15	BP	65
Enos, m. Martha **BALDWIN**, Sept. 28, 1710, by Joseph Treat, J.P.	1	32
Enos, m. Elizabeth **BALDWIN**, Sept. 28, 1710, by Joseph Treat, J.P.	OL	69
Enos, s. Enos, b. Feb. 1, 1714/15	1	37
Enos, s. Enos, b. Sept. 1, 1714/15	OL	79
Enos, adm. to Ch. 1733	ES	238
Enos, m. Elizabeth **CLARK**, June 19, 1744	1	118
Enos, d. June 20, 1768	1	155
Ephraim, s. Samuel, b. Sept. 1, 1702	1	21
Ephraim, s. Samuel, b. Sept. 17, 1702	OL	45
Eunice, wid., d. [ ], 1838	BP	80
Ezra, original member of 2nd Church formed in 1742	ES	87
Ezra, his s. [ ], d. July 12, 1787, ae. [ ]	SM	33
Ezra, his 1st w. [ ], d. July 19, 1790, ae. 27	SM	42
Gideon, m. Sarah **PRUDDEN**, Dec. 7, 1741	1	166
Gideon, [s. Gideon & Sarah Clark], b. Mar. 29, 1748	1	166
Hannah, d. Samuel, b. Jan. 31, 1677	1	17
Hannah, d. Samuel, b. Jan. 31, 1677	OL	34
Hannah, m. Thomas **SMITH**, Dec. 2, 1699, by Robert Treat, Dept. Gov.	1	22
Hannah, m. Thomas **SMITH**, Dec. 21, 1699, by Robert Treat, Dept. Gov.	OL	45
Hannah, m. Heth **PECK**, Feb. 26, 1729/30, by Sam[ue]ll Eells, Asst.	1	89
Heil, [s. Gideon & Sarah Clark], b. Dec. 7, 1751	1	166
Hezekiah, s. Lieut. Samuel, mason, b. Mar. 25, 1700	1	21
Hezekiah, s. Lieut. Sam[ue]ll, mason [& Rebecca], b. Mar. 25, 1700	OL	44
Hezekiah, m. Lydya **CLARK**, Mar. 1, 1721/2, by Rev. Sam[ue]ll Andrews	1	74
Hezekiah, s. Hezekiah & Lydia, b. June 2, 1723	1	74
Isaack, s. Enos, b. Feb. 24, 1720	1	67
Isaac, his ch., d. [ ], 1824	BP	51
Isaac, his ch., d. [ ], 1827	BP	56
Isaac, d. [ ], 1840, ae. 52	BP	83
Israel, s. Enos, b. Nov. 1, 1722	1	74
Joel, d. May 11, 1713	1	44
Joel, d. May 11, 1713	OL	91
Joel, s. Samuel, s. of Edward, b. May 25, 1715	1	39
John, [twin with Samuel], s. Nicholas, bp. [1645, by Rev. Peter Prudden]	OL	102
John, s. Nicholas, b. Dec. 15, 1657	1	2
John, twin with Sarah, s. of Nicholas, b. Sept. 14, 1662	1	5
John, twin with Sarah, s. Nicholas, b. Sept. 14, 1662	OL	14
John, s. William, b. Nov. 28, 1662	1	6
John, s. William, b. Nov. 28, 1662	OL	16
John, s. Samuel, b. Mar. 1, 1700	1	21
John, s. Sam[ue]ll, Sr., b. Mar. 1, 1700	OL	44

MILFORD VITAL RECORDS 51

	Vol.	Page
CAMP, CAMPE, (cont.)		
John, Jr., m. Phebe **CANFIELD**, July 5, 1709	1	34
John, Jr., m. Phebe **CANFIELD**, July 5, 1709, by Sam[ue]ll Eells, Asst.	OL	75
John, s. John, Jr., b. July 12, 1710	1	34
John, s. John, Jr. [& Phebee], b. July 12, 1710	OL	75
John, Dea., d. Aug. 21, 1731	1	92
John, Dea., d. Aug. 21, 1731	ES	238
John, Dea., d. [ ], 1731	ES	238
John, Jr., s. John, marks for cattle recorded June 6, 1739	1	107
Jonah, his ch., d. [ ], 1805	BP	11
Jonah, his ch., d. [ ], 1810, ae. 3 y.	BP	20
Jonah, d. [ ], 1839, ae. 56	BP	81
Jonathan, s. Samuel, Jr., b. Dec. 17, 1702	1	22
Jonathan, s. Sam[ue]ll, Jr., b. Dec. 17, 1702	OL	45
Joseph, s. Nicholas, d. Aug. 16, 1655	1	2
Joseph, s. Nicholas, d. Aug. 16, 1655	OL	9
Joseph, d. [ ], 1655	ES	35
Joseph, s. Eliphas, b. Dec. 15, 1657	OL	11
Joseph, s. Eleazer [& Mary], b. Apr. 7, 1631	1	97
Joseph, s. Nicholas, d. Aug. 16, 1755	ES	238
Josiah, d. Feb. 18, 1789, ae. 63	SM	39
Lemuel, s. Lieut. Samuel, b. Oct. 4, 1701	1	21
Lemuel, s. Lieut. Sam[ie]ll & [Rebecca], b. Oct. 4, 1701	OL	44
Lydia, d. Hezekiah & Lydia, b. Sept. 14, 1727	1	82
Mehetable, d. Samuel, b. Aug. 26, 1713	1	38
Mahitabeel, formerly w. David, d. of John & Sarah **PECK**, m. 2nd husband Lazarus **NORTHROP**, [ ] (See under Mahitabeel **PECK**)	1	133
Martha, d. Enos, b. July 28, 1712	1	34
Martha, d. Enos, b. July 28, 1712	OL	73
Martha, wid., d. Oct. 25, 1798	SM	64
Martha, d. Nath[anie]ll, b. [ ]	1	107
Mary, see under Marcy **EWINE**	1	8
Mary, d. Nicholas, b. July 12, 1660	1	4
Mary, d. Nicholas, b. July 12, 1660	OL	12
Mary, d. William, b. Mar. 22, 1663/4	1	6
Mary, d. William, b. Mar. 22, 1663 or 1664	OL	16
Mary, d. Samuel "Sometime now Mary **LAW**", m. Josiah **BALDWIN**, s. John, b. of Milford, June 25, 1666, by Mr. Fenn, Magestrte	OL	19
Mary, d. wid. Lane, m. Nathaniel **BRISCO**, Nov. 29, 1672, by John Clark, Commissioner	1	12
Mary, d. wid. Jane, m. Nathaniel **BISCO***, b. of Milford, Nov. 29, 1672, by John Clark, Com. *(**BRISCO**)	OL	25
Mary, m. Joseph **PECKE**, Jan. 27, 1678, by R[ober]t Treat, Dept. Gov.	1	16
Mary, m. Joseph **PECK**, Jan. 27, 1678, by The Dept. Gov.	OL	33
Mary, m. Samuel **CAMP**, Oct. 10, 1682, by Major Treat	1	18
Mary, m. Samuel **CAMP**, Oct. 10, 1682, by Major Treat	OL	38
Mary, d. Samuel, Sr., b. [ ] 21, 1684	1	19
Mary, d. Samuel, Sr., b. [ ] 21, 1684	OL	41

CAMP, CAMPE, (cont.)

	Vol.	Page
Mary, m. Thomas **CAMFIELD**, Jan. 3, 1705/6, by Capt. Eells	1	28
Mary, m. Thomas **CAMFIELD**, Jan. 3, 1705/6, by Capt. Eells	OL	60
Mary, m. Thomas **CANFIELD**, Jan. 3, 1705/6, by Sam[ue]ll Eells, J.P.	1	72
Mary, d. Samuel, mason, b. Jan. 4, 1706	1	28
Mary, d. Samuel, mason, b. Jan. 4, 1706	OL	59
Mary, Mrs., m. John **HARPIN**, Jan. 8, 1718, by Sam[ue]ll Eells, Asst.	1	67
Mary, m. Dr. [ ] **HARPEN**, July 8, 1718	ES	238
Mary, d. Nathaniell & Martha, b. Feb. 19, 1741/2	1	111
Mary, wid., d. [ ], 1805, ae. 85 y.	BP	12
Nathan, s. Samuel, b. Aug. 4, 1688	1	21
Nathan, s. Sam[ue]ll, Sr., b. Aug. [ ], 1688	OL	44
Nathan, s. Samuel, Sr., d. about Aug. 10, 1690	OL	86
Nathan, s. Samuel, Sr., d. Aug. 16, 1690	1	40
Nathan, s. Gideon & Sarah Clark, b. Apr. 7, 1743	1	166
Nathan, d. [ ], 1811	BP	22
Nathaniel, pd. £5 for not procuring men for Continental Army	1	55
Nath[anie]l, s. Nath[anie]l & Martha, b. July 30, 1739	1	108
Nathaniel, d. Feb. 1, 1780, ae. 78]	SM	19
Nathaniel, his infant s. [ ], d. Dec. 8, 1786	SM	32
Nathaniel, d. [ ], 1802	BP	6
Nathaniel, d. Dec. 1, 1802, ae. 61	SM	76
Newton, d. [ ], 1833, ae. 22	BP	70
Nicholas, adm. Church [Mar.] 12, [1643]	OL	98
Nicholas & w. Sarah had twin sons, b. Sept. 2, 1645; one d. 10 days after the mother's death (Sept. 6, 1645)	ES	35
Nicholas, [d.], 1706	ES	16
Nicholas, d. June 10, 1706	1	43
Nicholas, d. June 10, 1706	OL	88
Phinehas, s. Phinehas, b. Dec. 31, 1731	1	102
Phinehas, m. Rebeckah **CLARK**, Mar. 4, 1730/1	1	101
Rebecca, w. Dea. [ ], d. Mar. 28, 1710/11	1	43
Rebecca, w. Dea. [ ], d. Mar. 28, 1710/11	OL	89
Samuel, s. of Edward, see under Joel **CAMP** & Abel **CAMP**	1	39
Sam[ue]l, see under Stephen **CAMP**	1	66
Samuel, [twin with John], s. Nicholas, bp. [1645, by Rev. Peter Prudden]; d. at nurse Sister Fenns'	OL	102
Samuel, s. Nicholas, b. Sept. 15, 1655	1	2
Samuell, s. Nicholas, b. Sept. 15, 1655	OL	9
Samuel, of Milford, m. Hannah **BETTS**, of Norwalk, d. of Thomas, Nov. 13, 1672, by Mr. Olmsted, Comm. in Norwalk	1	12
Samuel, of Milford, m. Hannah **BETTS**, of Norwalk, d. Thomas, Nov. 13, 1672, by Mr. Omstead, Com.	OL	24
Samuel, s. Samuel, b. May 20, 1675	1	14
Samuel, s. Samuel, b. May 20, 1675	OL	29
Samuel, m. Mercy **SEWARD**, Jan. 6, 1681	1	18
Samuel, m. Mercy **SCOVELL**, Jan. 6, 1681	OL	38
Samuel, m. Mary **CAMP**, Oct. 10, 1682, by Major Treat	1	18
Samuel, m. Mary **CAMP**, Oct. 10, 1682, by Major Treat	OL	38
Samuel, Lieut., mason, m. Rebecca **CANFIELD**, Apr. 28, 1695,		

	Vol.	Page
CAMP, CAMPE, (cont.)		
by Robert Treat, Dept. Gov.	1	20
Sam[ue]ll, Lieut., mason, m. Rebecca **CANFIELD**, Apr. 28, 1696, by Rob[er]t Treat, Dept. Gov.	OL	44
Samuel, s. Samuel, mason, b. Nov. 17, 1704	1	25
Samuell, s. Samuell, Jr., mason, b. Nov. 17, 1704	OL	51
Samuel, Jr., m. Liddiah **UFFET**, Feb.1, 1704./5, by Thomas Clark, J.P.	OL	52
Samuel, s. Samuel, mason, b. Sept. 17, 1705	1	27
Samuel, s. Samuel, mason, b. Sept. 17, 1705	OL	59
Samuel, s. Edward, m. Dorothy **WETTEMORE**, July 17, 1712, by Samuel Eells, Asst.	1	33
Samuel, s. Edward, m. Dorothy **WETTEMORE**, July 17, 1712, by Samuell Eells, Asst.	OL	71
Samuel, of Newark, m. Joanna **LAMBERT**, wid. of Jesse, Nov. 24, 1726	1	49
Sam[ue]ll, [s. Gideon & Sarah Clark], b. Oct. 7, 1754	1	166
Samuel, his s. [ ], d. June 3, 1783, ae. 8 m.	SM	26
Samuel, his child d. Apr. 21, 1786	SM	31
Samuel, his infant s. [ ], d. Aug. 3, 1787	SM	34
Samuel, his d. [ ], d. Apr. 3, 1794, ae. 4 m.	SM	51
Samuel, d. [ ], 1826, ae. 72	BP	54
Samuel, d. [ ], 1832, at New Orleans	BP	67
Samuel, his wid. [ ], d. [ ], 1834	BP	72
Sarah, d. Nicholas, bp. [1643, by Rev. Peter Prudden]	OL	100
Sarah, w. Nicholas, adm. Church Aug. 4, [1644]; d. Sept. 6, 1645. First adult who died in this Town	OL	98
Sarah, w. Nicholas, d. Sept. 6, 1645, in Child birth	ES	35
Sarah, twin with John, d. of Nicholas, b. Sept. 14, 1662	1	5
Sarah, twin with John, d. Nicholas, b. Sept. 14, 1662	OL	14
Sarah, d. William, b. Nov. 11, 1666	1	7
Sarah, d. Wil[l]iam, b. Nov. 18, [16]66	OL	18
Sarah, d. Samuel, b. about Nov. 5, 1695	1	21
Sarah, d. Sam[ue]ll, Sr., b. about Nov. 5, 1695	OL	44
Sarah, wid., d. Dec. 21, 1802, ae. 83	SM	76
Sarah, wid., d. [ ], 1802, very aged	BP	6
Sarah, wid. Of Elias, d. [ ], 1805	BP	11
Stephen, s. Sam[ue]ll, s. of Edward, b. Feb. 4, 1719/20	1	66
Tararah (?), s. Gideon & Sarah Clark, b. June 1, 1745	1	166
Thomas, Jr., m. Liddiah **UFFUT**, Feb. 1, 1704/5, by Thomas Clark, J.P.	1	25
Timothy, s. Samuel, b. Apr. 1, 1701	1	21
Timothy, s. Sam[ue]ll, Jr., b. Apr. 1, 1701	OL	45
William, of Milford, m. Mary **SMITH**, of New Haven, Jan. 29, 1661, by Mr. Gilbert, Dept. Gov. of New Haven	1	6
William, of Milford, m. Mary **SMITH**, of New Haven, Jan. 29, 1661, by Mr. Gilbert, Dept. Gov. of New Haven	OL	16
William, d. [ ], 1839, ae. 23	BP	82
Zaccheas, s. Sam[ue]ll, b. Mar. 10, [ ], d. same day	1	69
-----, wid. Of Chestnut Hill, New Haven, m. John **LANE**, widower, of Milford, Apr. 4, 1662, by Robert Treat, Magistrate	1	4
-----, wid. Of Chestnut Hill, in New Town Parish, m. John **LANE**,		

BARBOUR COLLECTION

	Vol.	Page
CAMP, CAMPE, (cont.)		
widower, of Milford, Apr. 4, 1660, by Mr. Treat, Magestrate	OL	12
——, wid., d. July 29, 1779, ae. 74	SM	18
——, wid., d. Sept. [ ], 1791, ae. 91	SM	46
——, wid. had negro Edward, d. Aug. 20, 1792	SM	48
——, Mrs., d. [ ], 1822, ae. 70	BP	46
CAMPFIELD, [see under **CANFIELD**]		
CANFIELD, CAMFIELD, CAMPFIELD, CAFFIELD, Abigail, d.		
Oct. 6, 1787, ae. 56	SM	34
Allice, m. Josiah BASSIT, Apr. 25, 1717	1	66
Ann, d. Thomas & Mary, b. Apr. 26, 1728	1	84
Anne, wid., d. Sept. 16, 1787, ae. 77	SM	34
Azariah, m. Mercy BALDWIN, Feb. 26, 1719/20, by Major Sam[ue]ll Eells, Asst.	1	75
Azariah, s. Azariah, b. Nov. 25, 1720	1	75
David, d. Jeremiah, Jr., b. Mar. 7, 1725/6	1	81
David, m. Mary NORTHROP, Oct. 3, 1745, by Rev. Sam[ue]ll Whittlesey	1	120
Elizabeth, d. Thomas, b. Feb. 14, 1659	OL	12
Elizabeth, d. Thomas, b. Feb. 14, 1659/60	1	3
Elizabeth, m. Theophilus BALDWIN, Feb. 8, 1682, by Major Treat	1	18
Elizabeth, m. Theophilus BALDWIN, Feb. 8, 1682, by Major Treat	OL	38
Gideon, s. Tho[ma]s, b. June 4, 1717	1	72
Gould, d. [ ], 1836	BP	75
Hannah, d. Thomas, b. Nov. 20, 1667	1	8
Hannah, d. Tho[ma]s, b. Aug. 1, 1714	1	72
Israel, s. Thomas, b. Mar. 24, 1684	1	21
Israel, s. Thomas, b. Mar. 24, 1684/5	OL	42
Jeremiah, m. Judah MALLERY, July 24, 1711, by Jonathan Law, J.P.	1	39
Jeremiah, m. Judah MALLORY, July 24, 1711, by Jon[a]th[an Law, J.P.	OL	85
Jeremiah, s. Jeremiah, b. June 17, 1712	1	34
Jeremiah, s. Jeremiah, Jr., b. June 17, 1712	OL	74
Joel, s. Tho[ma]s, b. Feb. 7, 1711/12	1	72
John, s. Tho[ma]s & Mary, b. Apr. 4, 1725	1	81
Mary, d. Thomas, b. Jan. 1, 1656/7	1	3
Mary, d. Thomas, b. Jan. 1, 1656/7	OL	10
Mary, d. Thomas, b. Apr.24, 1709	1	31
Mary, d. Thomas, b. Apr. 24, 1709	OL	67
Mary, d. Thomas, b. May 24, 1709	1	72
Mary, d. Jeremiah & Judah, b. June 30, 1719	1	69
Mary, m. Jacob COLLINS, Nov. 2, 1743, by Rev. Samuel Whettlesey	1	114
Mary, d. David [& Mary], b. Oct. 31, 1746	1	120
Mehetable, d. Thomas, b. July 2, 1671	1	11
Mehitable, d. Thomas, b. July 2, 1671	OL	23
Mehitabeel, d. Jeremiah, b. June 19, 1729	1	86
Phebe, d. Thomas, bp. [1656, by Rev. Peter Prudden]	OL	105
Phebe, d. Thomas, m. John SMITH, s. John, Sr., Jan. 23, 1672, by John Clark, Com.	OL	25

	Vol.	Page
CANFIELD, CAMFIELD, CAMPFIELD, CAFFIELD, (cont.)		
Phebe, d. Tho[ma]s, m. John SMITH, s. John, Jan. 23, 1672/3, by John Clarke, Commissioner	1	12
Phebe, m. John CAMP, Jr., July 5, 1709	1	34
Phebee, m. John CAMP, Jr., July 5, 1709, by Sam[ue]ll Eells, Asst.	OL	75
Phebe, d. Jeremiah, b. Jan. 27, 1715/16	1	37
Phebe, d. Jeremiah, Jr., b. Jan. 27, 1715/16	OL	81
Phebe, m. Ebenezer SMITH, Jr., Aug. 10, 1742, by Rev. Sam[ue]ll Whittlesey	1	118
Rebecca, d. Thomas, Jr., b. Jan. 28, 1682	1	19
Rebecca, d. Thomas, Jr., b. Jan. 28, 1682	OL	40
Rebecca, m. Lieut. Samuel CAMP, mason, Apr. 28, 1695, by Robert Treat, Dept. Gov.	1	20
Rebecca, m. Lieut. Sam[ue]ll CAMP, mason, Apr. 28, 1696, by Rob[er]t Treat, Dept. Gov.	OL	44
Sarah, d. Thomas, bp. [1656, by Rev. Peter Prudden]	OL	105
Sarah, d. Thomas, b. Nov. 20, 1667	OL	19
Sarah, m. Josiah PLATT, Dec. 2, 1669, by John Clerk, Commissioner	1	9
Sarah, m. Josiah PLATT, b. of Milford, Dec. 2, 1669, by John Clark, Com.	OL	22
Thomas, s. Thomas, b. Oct. 14, 1654	1	2
Thomas, s. Thomas, b. Oct. 14, 1654	OL	8
Thomas, s. Thomas, bp. [1656, by Rev. Peter Prudden]	OL	105
Thomas, adm. Church Mar. 1, 1657, by Mr. Prudden	OL	99
Thomas, m. Rebecca ADKINSON, Feb. 26, 1679, by Major Treat, Dept. Gov.	OL	36
Thomas, s. Thomas, Jr., b. Jan. 5, 1680	OL	36
Tho[ma]s, Came to Milford, 1648; d. 1689	ES	176
Thomas, s. Jeremiah, b. Sept. 16, 1704	1	24
Thomas, s. Jeremiah, b. Sept. 16, 1704	OL	49
Thomas, m. Mary CAMP, Jan. 3, 1705/6, by Capt. Eells	1	28
Thomas, m. Mary CAMP, Jan. 3, 1705/6, by Capt. Eells	OL	60
Thomas, m. Mary CAMP, Jan. 3, 1705/6, by Sam[ue]ll Eells, J.P.	1	72
Thomas, s. Thomas, b. Dec. 28, 1706	1	28
Thomas, s. Thomas [& Mary], b. Dec. 28, 1706	OL	60
Tho[ma]s, s. Thomas, b. Dec. 28, 1706	1	72
Thomas, s. Tho[mas], [bp.] 1707	ES	238
Tho[ma]s, s. Thomas, d. May 3, 1712	1	72
Tho[mas], b. July 7, 1720	ES	238
Tho[ma]s, s. Thomas, b. Aug. 6, 1720	1	72
Tho[mas], Jr., b. [ ], 1720	ES	238
Zerviah, m. Daniel TERRELL, Dec. 12, 1716, by Rev. Sam[ue]ll Andrews	1	75
CARBY, Sarah, m. Sam[ue]ll BALDWIN, Apr. 9, 1712, by Sam[ue]ll Eells, Asst.	OL	74
CAREBEE, [see also LARRABEE], Jabez, s. Cubitt CAREBEE alias FREEMAN, b. Aug. 21, 1710	1	32
Jabez, s. Cubitt, alias FFREEMAN, b. Aug. 21, 1710	OL	68
CARLOS*, Mary, m. Samuel Coley, Oct. 21, 1669, by John Clark, Commissioner *(Perhaps "**CURTIS**")	1	9

	Vol.	Page
CARR, Demaris, m. Zachariah **WHITMAN**, Mar. 18, 1705, by Major Johnson	1	27
Damaris, m. Zachariah **WHITTMAN**, Mar. 18, 1705/6, byMajor Johnson	OL	56
CARRINGTON, Abigail*, his w. [ ], d. [ ], 1819 *(Probably "Abijah")	BP	39
Abijah, s. Elias, [ ]	1	162
Abraham, d. [ ], 1783, (Was not in Milford at time of death)	SM	26
Edward, Dr. his negro girl, d. July 23, 1787	SM	34
Edward, Dr. his negro boy, d. Nov. 4, 1788	SM	37
Edward, Dr. had negro girl, d. Jan. 14, 1789	SM	39
Edward, Dr., d. Sept. 23, 1795	SM	55
Edward, Dr., m. Susannah **WHETTLESEY**, d. Rev. Samuel & Susannah, [ ]	ES	238
Elias, Dr., m. Easther **NORTHROP**, d. Ephraim, Feb. 23, 1763. Witnesses Ephraim Northrop, Laraus Northrop	1	162
Elias, s. Elias & Easther, b. Feb. 19, 1764	1	162
Elias, Dr., d. Aug. 6, 1800, ae. 65	SM	69
Elias, his w. [ ], d. Feb. 12, 1801	SM	71
Elias, his w. [ ], d. [ ], 1801	BP	3
Elias, d. [ ], 1829	BP	60
Elizabeth, d. Jno, of New Haven, m. Stephen **HINE**, Jr., of Milford, Jan. 26, 1748/9, by Rev. Benjamin Woodbridge, of Amity	1	125
Ephraim, s. Elias & Esther, b. Sept. 23, 1768. (He was a loyalist in the Revolutionary War and at the close went to Nova Scotia)	1	162
Esther, d. Elias & Esther, b. Mar. 1, 1766	1	162
John, s. Elias & Esther, b. Mar. 14, 1772; d. Sept. 20, 1773	1	162
[John], [s. Elias & Esther, b.] He was a physician	1	162
Julia, d. Elias, m. Miles **MERWIN**, [ ]	1	162
Sam[ue]ll, s. Elias & Esther, b. June 7, 1767. "He left the morning after his marriage and was never seen again in Milford. None knew why he went or where he went except his brother Abijah."	1	162
Sarah, d. Elias & Esther, b. Feb. 27, 1770; m. [ ] **FOSTER**, [ ]	1	162
Susan, wid., d. [ ], 1801	BP	3
Susanna, wid., d. Jan. 11, 1801, ae. 54	SM	71
-----, Dr. his child d. [ ], 1810, ae. a few days	BP	20
-----, Dr., d. [ ], 1817	BP	36
-----, wid. [ ], d. [ ], 1840	BP	83
CARY, Elizabeth, of Bristoll, Mass., m. Gamaleel **CLARK**, of Milford, Dec. 25, 1740, by [ ] Howland, J.P.	1	118
Elizabeth, m. Gamaleel **CLARK**, Dec. 25, 1740	1	128
Eliza[eth] of Bristol, Mass., m. Gamaleel **CLARK**, [ ], 1740	ES	238
CASSING, Sarah, d. John, b. July 3, 1654. John Cassing moved to Guilford	OL	8
CEASER, Tim, negro his child d. [ ], 1804	BP	10
Timothy, had woman d. July 26, 1799	SM	67

	Vol.	Page
CEASER, (cont.)		
Timothy, his s. [ ], d. Nov. 19, 1804, ae. 19	SM	81
CEBIAS, -----, had negro Tony, d. Jan. 26, 1776	SM	5
CEBRA, James, drafted for Continental Army	1	58
William, d. Aug. 10, 1776, ae. 8 m.	SM	7
-----, Mrs. of New York, d. [ ], 1795 (non resident)	SM	57
[CHAPIN], CHEAPIN, Sarah, d. Joseph*, b. Mar. 15, 1667/8		
(*Overwritten to read "Japhet")	1	8
Sarah, d. Japhet, b. Mar. 15, 1667/8	OL	20
Thomas, s. Japhet, b. May 20, 1671	1	11
Thomas, s. Japhet, b. May 20, 1671	OL	23
CHARLES, Anna, d. William [& Thankfull], b. May 8, 1745	1	119
Mary, d. Will[ia]m & Thankfull, b. [ ] 30, 1747	1	123
Pennelope, d. William & Thankfull, b. Dec. 14, 1740	1	119
Thankfull, w. William, d. Nov. 19, 1747	1	123
William, m. Thankfull ASHBAND, d. Joseph, Apr. 18, 1739, by		
Roger Newton, Asst.	1	119
William, s. William [& Thankfull], b. Dec. 7, 1742	1	119
CHATFIELD, Elnathan, of Derby, m Hannah NORTHROP, of		
Milford, Sept. 12, 1754, by Rev. Benjamin Woodbridge, of		
Amity	1	135
Isaac, s. Elnathan & Hannah, b. Sept. 1, 1762	1	146
Joel, s. Elnathan & Hannah, b. Feb. 21, 1757	1	138
Rebeckah, d. Elnathan & Hannah, b. July 28, 1755	1	135
Rebeckah, m. Ramond SANFORD, Dec. 21, 1773, by Richard		
Mansfield, Missionary of Derby	1	165
Sarah, d. Elnathan & Hannah, b. Jan. 22, 1771	1	159
CHEAPIN, [see under CHAPIN]		
CHERRY, Pomp, drafted for Continental Army	1	58
CHURCH, Samson, drafted for Continental Army	1	57
CHURCHILL, Edward, d. Oct. 11, 1776, ae. 23	SM	8
CLARK, CLARKE, Abigail, d. George, Jr., bp. [1653, by Rev. Peter		
Prudden]	OL	104
Abigail, d. George, Jr., b. Jan. 9, 1653/4	1	1
Abigaile, d. George, Jr., b. Jan. 29, 1655	OL	7
Abigail, d. Georg[e], Jr., b. Apr. 1, 1680	OL	36
Abigail, d. George, 3rd, b. Oct. 17, 1706, d. Nov. 17, following	1	27
Abigail, d. George, 3rd, b. Oct. 17, 1706; d. Nov. 17, following	OL	57
Abigail, d. George, 2nd, b. Jan. 4, 1712	1	37
Abigail, d. George, 2nd [& Sarah], b. Jan. 4, 1712/13	OL	81
Abigail, m. Caleb SMITH, [ ] 26, 1728, by Sam[ue]ll Gunn,		
J.P.	1	110
Abigaill, d. Nathan & Abigaill, b. July 9, 1748	1	125
Abigail, d. Hezekiah, b. Jan. 2, 1755	1	134
Abigail, wid., d. [ ], 1805	BP	11
Abigail, Miss, d. [ ], 1815, ae. 22 y.	BP	29
Abigail, wid., d. [ ], 1833, ae. 79	BP	69
Abraham, Jr., d. Dec. 16, 1793, ae. [ ]	SM	50
Abraham, his child d. May 11, 1799, [ae.] 1 y. 10 m.	BP	1
Abraham, his s. [ ], d. May 12, 1799	SM	66
Abraham, d. [ ], 1836	BP	75
Alpheas, his w. [ ], d. [ ], 1821, North Milford	BP	44

CLARK, CLARKE, (cont.)

	Vol.	Page
Alphono, [s. Sheldon & Martha Anne], b. [ ], 1842	1	52
Amos, drafted for Continental Army	1	57
Amos, s. John, 3rd & Mable, b. Nov. 25, 1752	1	141
Amos, s. Joseph & Mary, b. Apr. 2, 1757	1	148
Amos, his s. [ ], d. Mar. 30, 1790	SM	41
Amos, his s. [ ], d. Oct. 25, 1795	SM	56
Amos, his d. [ ], d. Aug. 18, 1800	SM	69
Amos, his ch., d. [ ], 1803	BP	8
Amos, [a child], d. Oct. 31, 1803	SM	78
Amos, his child d. [ ], 1807, ae. 11 y.	BP	15
Amos, his w. [ ], d. [ ], 1832, ae. 66	BP	68
Amos, d. [ ], 1839, ae. 33	BP	82
Amy, d. Oct. 31, 1799, ae. 18	SM	68
Amy, d. of Thomas, a farmer, of Milford, m. Jesse Peck LAMBERT, s. Jesse & Anne, [ ]; moved to Woodbury; d. July 30, 1852, ae. 79	1	50
Andrew, pd. £5 for not procuring men for Continental Army	1	55
Andrew, s. Joseph & Mary, b. Oct. 12, 1739	1	108
Andrew, s. Joseph, Jr., b. Oct. 12, 1739	1	114
Andrew, s. Joseph & Mary, b. Oct. 12, 1739	1	147
Andrew, s. Andrew & Anne, b. Apr. 21, 1783	1	171
Andrew, Jr., d. Nov. 5, 1788	SM	37
Ann, d. Thomas, b. Oct. 9, 1707	1	31
Ann, d. Thomas, b. Oct. 9, 1707	OL	67
Ann, d. Thomas, d. May 29, 1708	1	43
Ann, d. Thom[a]s, d. May 29, 1708	OL	89
Ann, d. Samuel, merchant, b. June 30, 1709	1	32
Ann, d. Sam[ue]ll, merchant, b. June last day, 1709	OL	68
Anna, wid., d. [ ], 1820, N. Milford	BP	41
Anne Treat, d. Andrew & Anne, b. Aug. 27, 1785	1	171
Anon, his infant d. [ ], 1835	BP	72
Assena, d. David, b. Nov. 3, 1754	1	134
Benjamin, s. John, Jr. & Rebeckah, b. Jan. 9, 1738	1	143
Benjamin, Jr., his d. [ ], d. Feb. 20, 1803	SM	77
Benjamin, Jr., his child d. [ ], 1803	BP	7
Bethuell, s. Joseph & Mary, b. Oct. 27, 1750; d. Apr. 20, 1751	1	147
Betsey, d. Mar. 7, 1795 (non resident)	SM	57
Billing, d. Jan. 13, 1789, ae. 63	SM	39
Chancy, s. John, 3rd & Mable, b. Mar. 23, 1751	1	141
Daniel, s. Samuel, of Milford, m. Mary Emeline (Lambert) BALDWIN, [ ]; her 3d husband	1	52
Daniel, s. Joseph, b. Feb. 9, 1715/16	1	37
Daniel, s. Joseph, s. of Joseph, b. Feb. 9, 1715/16	OL	80
Daniel, Dea., d. Mar. 24, 1787, ae. 71	SM	33
David, m. Hannah PECK, Jan. 15, 1741/2	1	121
David, s. David [& Hannah], b. Sept. 29, 1742	1	121
David, s. Jos[eph], b. Mar. 21, 1744	1	114
David, s. Joseph & Mary, b. Mar. 21, 1744	1	147
David, Jr., m. Hannah JOHNSON, Oct. 4, 1762. Witnesses, Hezekiah Clark, Phinehas Peck	1	148
David, his s. [ ], d. May 11, 1781, ae. 27	SM	21
David, his infant s. [ ], d. June 7, 1789	SM	40

CLARK, CLARKE, (cont.)

	Vol.	Page
David, his infant s. [ ], d. Dec. 21, 1791	SM	47
David, his d. [ ], d. Sept. 4, 1798, ae. 5 m.	SM	64
David, his s. [ ], d. [ ], 1802, ae. 10 y.	BP	6
David, his s. [ ], d. Oct. 30, 1802, ae. 10	SM	76
David, his w. [ ], d. [ ], 1812	BP	23
David, his child d. [ ], 1815	BP	29
David, his child d. [ ], 1830	BP	62
David, d. [ ], 1831, ae. 80	BP	64
David, of Milford, [ ]	1	122
Deborah, d. George, 3rd, b. Jan. 14, 1703/4	1	27
Deborah, d. George, 3rd, b. Jan. 14, 1703/4	OL	57
Deborah, m. Phinehas PECK, Feb. 18, 1745/6, by Rev. David Humphrey, of Derby	1	120
Deborah, wid., d. [ ], 1808, ae. 90	BP	17
Dennis, d. Lazarus & Dennis, b. Dec. 2, 1780	1	169
Edmund, s. Jos[eph], Jr., b. Oct. 12, 1741	1	114
Edmond, s. Joseph & Mary, b. Oct. 12, 1741	1	147
Edmund, d. Oct. 22, 1795 (non resident)	SM	57
Elias, his d. [ ], d. July 18, 1780	SM	20
Elias, his son Capt., 1787	ES	41
Elias, had negro d. Jan. 31, 1802, ae. 84	SM	74
Elias, d. [ ], 1817, N. Milford	BP	37
Elijah, drafted for Continental Army	1	58
Elijah, Priv., member of Capt. Samuel Peck's Co., Milford 1776	1	54
Elisha, Corp., member of Capt. Samuel Peck's Co., Milford, 1776	1	54
Elisha, his s. [ ], d. Dec. 21, 1788 (twin infants)	SM	37
Elisha, his s. [ ], d. Dec. 27, 1796	SM	60
Elisha, his child d. [ ], 1801	BP	3
Elisha, his infant d. [ ], d. Jan. 28, 1801, ae. 1 y.	SM	71
Elisha, Jr., his other child (twins), d. [ ], 1811	BP	23
Elisha, Jr., his child d. [ ], 1811	BP	23
Elisha, his child d. [ ], 1812, ae. 2 y.	BP	24
Elisha, d. [ ], 1840, ae. 85	BP	83
Elizabeth, d. George, Jr., bp. [1655, by Rev. Peter Prudden]	OL	105
Elizabeth, d. George, 2nd, b. Feb. 2, 1707/8	1	37
Elizabeth, d. George, 2nd [& Sarah], b. Feb. 2, 1707/8	OL	81
Elizabeth, d. Nathan, b. Mar. 21, 1719	1	74
Elizabeth, m. Joseph ROGERS, Jr., b. of Milford, May [ ], 1740, by Sam[ue]ll Gunn, J.P.	1	112
Elizabeth, m. Enos CAMP, June 19, 1744	1	118
Elizabeth, d. Joseph & Mary, b. Mar. 16, 1752	1	147
Elizabeth, wid., d. May 29, 1777	SM	13
Enoch, his d. [ ], d. Aug. 12, 1777	SM	13
Enoch, his s. [ ], d. Feb. 4, 1784	SM	27
Enoch, his d. [ ], d. Feb. 16, 1788	SM	36
Enoch, his w. [ ], d. July 29, 1797, ae. 51	SM	61
Enoch, Jr., his w. [ ], d. Oct. 7, 1801	SM	73
Enoch, Jr., his w. [ ], d. [ ], 1801	BP	4
Enoch, d. [ ], 1807	BP	16
Enoch, d. [ ], 1811	BP	22
Ester, d. Geo[rge], farmer, b. [ ], 1647	ES	238
Esther, d. Oct. 20, 1661	ES	238

	Vol.	Page
CLARK, CLARKE, (cont.)		
Ezra, his child d. [ ], 1825	BP	52
Gamaleel, [s. Sa[mue]l, Jr.], [bp.], 1712	ES	238
Gamaleel, of Milford, m. Elizabeth **CARY**, of Bristoll, Mass., Dec. 25, 1740, by [ ] Howland, J.P.	1	118
Gamaleel, m. Elizabeth **CARY**, Dec. 25, 1740	1	128
Gamaleel, m. Elizab'eth] **CARY**, of Bristol, Mass., [ ], 1740	ES	238
Gamaleel, s. Gamaleel, b. July 9, 1744	1	129
Geo[rge], Dea., 1645	ES	238
Geo[rge], s. Geo[rge], b. [ ], 1648	ES	238
George, s. Corp. Thomas, b. Aug. 31, 1673	1	13
George, s. Corp. Thomas, b. Aug. the last day, 1673	OL	26
George, drafted for Continental Army	1	58
George, Sr., adm. Church Feb. 21, [1641]; d. Aug. [ ], 1690	OL	98
George, Sr., adm. Church Mar. 31, [1644]; d. June 18, 1690	OL	98
George, s. George, Jr., bp. [1648, by Rev. Peter Prudden]	OL	103
George, in 1671, destroyed the Indian Fort	ES	14
George, [s. Tho[mas & Hannah], b. [ ], 1673	ES	184
George, s. Tho[mas], [bp.], 1673	ES	238
George, s. George, Jr., b. Apr. 3, 1682	1	18
George, s. George, Jr., b. Apr. 3, 1682	OL	38
Geo[rge], carpenter, d. Ja[n] 16, 1690	ES	238
George, Sr., carpenter, d. [ ], 1690	ES	16
Geo[rge], Jr., farmer, d. Aug. [ ], 1690	ES	238
George, Jr., Dea., farmer, [d.], 1690	ES	16
George, 2nd, m. Sarah **BUCKINGHAM**, Jan. 3, 1705/6, by Robert Treat, Dept. Gov.	1	37
George, 2nd, m. Sarah **BUCKINGHAM**, Jan. 3, 1705/6, by Robert Treat, Dept. Gov.	OL	81
George, s. George, 2nd [& Sarah], b. July 1, 1710; d. 18th of the same month	OL	81
George, s. George, 2nd, b. July 2, 1710; d. same month 18th	1	37
George, s. George, 2nd, b. Sept. 28, 1711; d. Nov. 26, following	1	37
George, s. George, 2nd [& Sarah], b. Sept. 28, 1711; d. Nov. 26, following	OL	81
George, s. George, 3rd & Abigail, b. May 4, 1726	1	134
George, original member of 2nd Church formed in 1742	ES	87
George, Jr., Elder, original member of 2nd Church formed in 1742	ES	87
George, s. Job, b. Sept. 25, 1755	1	146
George, d. [ ], 1832	BP	66
George L., [s. Sheldon & Martha Anne], b. Sept. 24, 1833* *(Date conflicts with date of parents' marriage)	1	52
Hannah, d. George, Sr., bp. [1640], by Rev. Peter Prudden	OL	100
Hannah, m. John **PLATT**, June 6, 1660, by Robert Treat, Magistrate	1	4
Hannah, d. Thomas, b. Mar. 20, 1679	OL	35
Hannah, d. Thomas, b. Mar. 20, 1679/80	1	18
Hannah, w. Thomas, d. Nov. 4, 1703	1	41
Hannah, w. Thomas, d. Nov. 4, 1703	OL	87
Hannah, d. Joseph, b. Jan. 4, 1705	1	27
Hannah, d. Joseph, b. Jan. 4, 1705	OL	56
Hannah, m. Samuel **PRUDDEN**, Dec. 20, 1705, by Robert Treat,		

	Vol.	Page
CLARK, CLARKE, (cont.)		
Dept. Gov.	1	26
Hannah, m. Samuell **PRUDDEN**, Dec. 20, 1705, by Rob[er]t Treat, Dept. Gov.	OL	55
Hannah, m. Sam[ue]l **BALDWIN**, s. Samuel, s. of Peter, [ ] 1705	ES	184
Hannah, m. Jonathan **FOWLER**, Jan. 9, 1728/9, by Sam[ue]ll Eells, Asst.	1	89
Hannah, d. Joseph, Jr., b. Mar. 7, 1734	1	103
Hannah, d. Joseph [& Mary], b. May 22, 1759	1	148
Hester, d. George, Jr., d. Oct. 19, 1661	1	4
Hester, d. Benony, Jr., d. Oct. 19, 1661	OL	14
Hezekiah, of Milford, m. Mary **PECK**, of Newtown, Jan. 20, 1746/7, by Rev. David Judson	1	122
Hezekiah, s. Hezekiah, b. Aug. 13, 1749	1	126
Hiel, his s. [ ], d. May 19, 1779	SM	17
Heil, d. Jan. 9, 1791, ae. 37	SM	45
Isaac, s. Tho[ma]s & Susannah, b. Feb. 21, 1726/7	1	81
Isaac, [s. Thomas & Susanna], b. [ ], 1727	ES	238
Isaac, s. Joseph & Mary, b. Aug. 27, 1746	1	147
Esaac, Capt. His 2nd w. [ ], d. Mar. 11, 1786	SM	31
Isaac, Capt. D. July 12, 1787, ae. 61	SM	33
Isaac, Capt., d. 1787, ae. 61	ES	41
Isaac, his infant d. [ ], d. Nov. 8, 1790	SM	43
Isaac, his w. [ ], d. Dec. 29, 1800, ae. 42	SM	70
James, s. John, Jr., b. June 19, 1731; d. same day	1	103
James, Dr. his s. [ ], d. Sept. 6, 1779, ae. 4 m.	SM	18
Jane, d. [ ], 1833, ae. 16	BP	69
Jane, wid., d. [ ], 1835, ae. 80	BP	72
Jared, s. Dea. Thomas, b. Jan. 28, 1718/19	1	69
Jared, d. May 21, 1789, ae. 70	SM	39
Jehiel, s. John, 3rd & Mabel, b. Jan. 23, 1756	1	142
Jeheel, Priv. member of Capt. Samuel Peck's Co., Milford, 1776	1	54
Jennie Maria, d. Sept. 8, 1787, ae. 10	SM	34
Jeremiah, s. Lazarus & Dennis, b. May 10, 1778	1	168
Jerushah, m. Thomas **BALDWIN**, Jan. 17, 1711/12, by Samuel Eells, Asst. John Fowler, Susannah Fowler, Witnesses	1	63
Job, m. Jane **NORTHROP**, b. of Milford, Sept. 28, 1749, by Rev. Job Prudden	1	126
Job, s. Job, b. Dec. 22, 1751	1	128
Job, [twin with Joseph], s. [Job], b. Feb. 11, 1758	1	146
Job, Priv., member of Capt. Samuel Peck's Co., Milford 1776	1	54
Job, heard of death Feb. 5, 1780	SM	19
John, 2nd, pd. £5 for not procuring men for Continental Army	1	55
John, s. George, Jr., bp. [1652, by Rev. Peter Prudden]	OL	104
John, s. Thomas, b. Dec. 31, 1671	1	11
John, s. Thomas, b. Dec. 31, 1671	OL	24
John, [s. Tho[mas] & Hannah], b. [ ], 1671	ES	184
John, s. Thomas, d. Apr. 10, 1704	1	42
John, s. Tho[ma]s, d. Apr. 10, 1704	OL	87
John, s. Sa[mue]l, Jr. [ ], 1709	ES	238
John, s. Samuel, merchant, b. June 6, 1711	1	33
John, s. Sam[ue]ll, merchant, b. June 6, 1711	OL	71

	Vol.	Page

CLARK, CLARKE, (cont.)

	Vol.	Page
John, m. Rebeckah **PRIME**, Feb. 6, 1723, by Capt. Sam[ue]l Clark, J.P.	1	75
John, s. John, Jr., b. Jan. 15, 1726	1	103
John, 3rd, m. Mabel **LINES**, Dec. 31, 1747, by [ ]	1	141
John, d. June 8, 1794	SM	53
John, his child d. [ ], 1815	BP	28
John, his w. [ ], d. [ ], 1818, ae. 35	BP	38
John, Rev., his w. [ ], d. [ ], 1828, ae. 53	BP	58
John, his child d. [ ], 1829	BP	60
Jonah, d. [ ], 1802	BP	5
Jonah, d. June 30, 1802, ae. 37	SM	75
Jonathan, pd. £5 for not procuring men for Continental Army	1	55
Jon[a]th[an], s. Dea. Thomas, b. Mar. [ ], 1717; d. Apr. 9, 1717	1	69
Jon[a]th[an], s. Dea. Tho[mas], b. [ ], 1717	ES	238
Jonathan, Jr., his child d. Apr. 10, 1801, ae. 4 y.	SM	72
Jonathan, d. [ ], 1808, ae. 60	BP	17
Joseph, s. Thomas, b. Mar. 4, 1676	OL	31
Joseph, s. Thomas, b. Mar. 4, 1676/7	1	15
Joseph, s. Joseph, b. Oct. 9, 1708	1	30
Joseph, s. Joseph, b. Oct. 9, 1708	OL	65
Joseph, s. Tho[mas], Jr. [ ], 1717	ES	238
Joseph, Capt., Justice in 1722	ES	238
Joseph, adm. to Ch. 1730	ES	238
Joseph, s. Joseph & Mary, b. Jan. 9, 1737/8	1	107
Joseph, s. Dea. Joseph, m. Mary **SANFORD**, d. Capt. Andrew, Apr. [ ], 1737	1	106
Joseph, s. Dea. Joseph, m. Mary **SANFORD**, [ ], 1737	ES	238
Joseph, Jr., m. Mary **SANFORD**, Apr. 20, 1738	1	147
Joseph, [s. Joseph & Mary], b. [ ], 1738	ES	238
Joseph, 3rd, [s. Joseph, Jr. & Mary], b. Jan. 9, 1739	1	147
Joseph, [twin with Job], s. [Job], b. Feb. 11, 1758	1	146
Joseph, 3rd, s. [Joseph, Jr. & Mary], d. Aug. 19, 1758	1	147
Joseph, Jr., s. Joseph & Mary, b. June 27, 1761	1	148
Joseph, Jr., his child d. [ ], 1807	BP	16
Joseph, Jr., his twin child d. [ ], 1807	BP	16
Joseph, d. [ ], 1831, ae. 63	BP	65
Joseph, see Daniel **CLARK**	OL	80
Joseph C., Jr., d. [ ], 1831, ae. 44	BP	64
Joseph Camp, his s. [ ], d. Mar. 7, 1787	SM	33
Keziah, m. John **BUCKINGHAM**, Mar. 25, 1731, by Roger Newton, J.P.	1	96
Lazarus, s. David [& Hannah], b. Dec. 23, 1745	1	121
Lazarus, m. Dennis **BRADLEY**, Dec. 18, 1771, by Rev. Benj[amin] Woodbridge, of Amity. Witnesses Andrew Bradley, David Clark	1	168
Lazarus, s. Lazarus & Dennis, b. Nov. 18, 1773	1	168
Levy, s. Job & Jane, b. Aug. 12, 1753	1	134
Lewis, d. [ ], 1833	BP	69
Lewis, his child d. [ ], 1837, ae. 18 m.	BP	77
Lucy, wid., d. [ ], 1821, ae. 74	BP	45
Luke, his infant child d. [ ], 1815, at N. Milford	BP	30
Liddiah, m. Thomas **OVIATT**, June 7, 1705, by Samuel Eells,		

	Vol.	Page
CLARK, CLARKE, (cont.)		
J.P. (Lydia)	1	26
Liddiah, m. Thomas **OVIATT**, June 7, 1705, by Sam[ue]ll Eells, J.P.	OL	55
Lydya, m. Hezekiah **CAMP**, Mar. 1, 1721/2, by Rev. Sam[ue]ll Andrews	1	74
Lydia, d. John, Jr., b. June 15, 1729	1	103
Lydiah, d. John, 3rd & Mable, b. Aug. 26, 1749	1	141
Mabel, d. John, 3rd & Mabel, b. Oct. 8, 1754	1	142
Martha, d. Thomas, b. Jan. 15, 1705	1	31
Martha, d. Thomas, b. Jan. 15, 1705	OL	67
Martha, m. Samuel **PECK**, May 5, 1714, by Major Eells, Asst.	1	36
Martha, m. Samuel **PECK**, May 5, 1714, by Major E[e]lls, Asst.	1	36
Martha, m. Sam[ue]ll **PECK**, May 5, 1714, by Major Eells, Asst.	OL	77
Martha, d. Nathan, b. May 31, 1722	1	74
Mary, w. [George, Sr.], adm. Church Apr. 2, [1644]; d. Sept. 22, 1689	OL	98
Mary, d. George, Jr., bp. [1650, by Rev. Peter Prudden]	OL	104
Mary, d. George, farmer, m. Samuel **CLARK**, s. Dea. George, Dec. 21, 1673, by Major Rob[er]t Treat	1	13
Mary, d. George, farmer, m. Samuel **CLARK**, s. Dea. George, b. of Milford, Dec. 26, 1673, by Maj. Robert Treat	OL	26
Mary, [w. George], d. Sept. 22, 1689	ES	238
Mary, d. George, 3rd, b. Nov. 1, 1701	OL	57
Mary, d. Joseph, b. Mar. 24, 1703/4	1	23
Mary, d. Joseph, b. Mar. 24, 1703/4	OL	49
Mary, d. George, 3rd, b. Nov. 1, 1705	1	27
Mary, m. John **PRUDDEN**, Jan. 9, 1706/7, by Lieut. Gov. Treat	1	27
Mary, m. John **PRUDDEN**, Jan. 9, 1706/7, by Lieut. Gov. Treat	OL	58
Mary, m. Joseph **SMITH**, July 7, 1720, by Samuel Eells, Asst.	1	67
Mary, m. Joseph **SMITH**, s. Sergt. John, July 7, 1720, by Sam[ue]ll Eells, Asst.	1	89
Mary, d. Hez[ekiah] & Mary, b. Dec. 3, 1747	1	122
Mary, d. Joseph & Mary, b. Sept. 8, 1748	1	147
Mary, wid., d. May 8, 1780	SM	19
Mary, wid., d. [ ], 1802	BP	6
Mary, wid., d. Oct. 15, 1802, ae. 87	SM	76
Mary, d. [ ], 1828, ae. 70	BP	57
Mary, wid., d. [ ], 1833, ae. 72	BP	69
Mehetable, d. Samuel, b. Nov. 5, 1701; d. 19th of said month	1	20
Mehittabell, d. Sam[ue]ll, b. Nov. 6, 1701; d. 19th of said month	OL	43
Mehetable, d. Samuel, b. Oct. 2, 1702	1	20
Mehittabel, d. Sam[ue]ll, b. Oct. 2, 1702	OL	43
Mehetable, m. Richard **BRYAN**, Oct. 20, 1720, by Sam[ue]ll Eells, Asst.	1	68
Mehitabel, w. Capt. Sam[ue]ll, d. Dec. 16, 1721	1	69
Mercy, d. Hezekiah, b. [ ]	1	134
Meriann, m. John **PLATT**, b. of Milford, June 6, 1660, by Mr. Treat, Magestrate; Settled in Norwalk	OL	12
	BP	44
Merrett, d. [ ], 1821, ae. 24	1	142
Molle, d. John, 3rd & Mable, b. Nov. 9, 1757	1	128
Moses, s. Hezekiah, b. May 23, 1751		

CLARK, CLARKE, (cont.)

	Vol.	Page
Nancy, d. [ ], 1823, ae. 17	BP	48
Nathan, m. Elizabeth **FOWLER**, June 29, 1710, by Sam[ue]ll Eells, J.P.	1	74
Nathan, s. Nathan, b. Dec. 25, 1714	1	74
Nathan, s. Nathan & Abigaill, b. Aug. 3, 1746	1	125
Nathan, Capt., 1763	ES	41
Nathan, Capt. His w. [ ], d. Mar. 19, 1781	SM	21
Nathan, Capt., d. Feb. 26, 1783, ae. 68	SM	25
Nathan, Capt., d. [ ], 1807	BP	15
Nathan, Capt. His wid. [ ], d. [ ], 1812, ae. 77 y.	BP	24
Nathan, his w. [ ], d. [ ], 1830, ae. 50	BP	63
Nathan, m. Abigail **FLETCHER**, d. Newton, [ ]	ES	238
Nehemiah, d. Jan. 3, 1805, ae. 58	SM	82
Nehemiah, d. [ ], 1805	BP	10
Neh[emiah], Capt., d. [*], 1820, N. Milford		
*(Jan. 17 hand printed in original manuscript)	BP	41
Neh[emiah], Capt. his w. [ ], d. [ ], 1820, N. Milford	BP	41
Oliver, s. Samuel, Jr., b. July 6, 1704	1	25
Oliver, s. Sam[ue]ll, Jr., b. July 6, 1704	OL	51
Oliver, s. Capt. Sam[ue]ll, d. June 31, 1724	1	75
Oliver, s. Job, b. Dec. 11, 1759	1	146
Oliver, Capt., d. [ ], 1829, ae. 59	BP	59
Oliver, his infant d. [ ], 1832	BP	66
Oliver, his child d. [ ], 1839	BP	82
Oliver Allen, s. Gamaleel, b. Dec. 16, 1747	1	129
Peg, negro d. [ ], 1813	BP	31
Phebe, d. Mar. 11, 1792 (Absentee)	SM	48
Philene, d. John, 3rd & Mabel, b. Nov. 5, 1760	1	143
Primus, negro d. Mar. 20, 1804	SM	79
Rebecca, d. George, Jr., bp. [1645, by Rev. Peter Prudden]	OL	102
Rebecca, d. Thomas, b. Oct. 1, 1704	1	25
Rebbeckah, d. Thomas, Jr., b. Oct. 4, 1704	OL	51
Rebeckah, d. John, Jr., b. Nov. 19, 1724	1	103
Rebeckah, m. Phinehas **CAMP**, Mar. 4, 1730/1	1	101
Rebecca, wid., d. Aug. 7, 1778, ae. 74	SM	15
Rebecca, Mrs., d. [ ], 1817, ae. about 78	BP	37
Ruth, d. George, bp. [1641, by Rev. Peter Prudden]	OL	100
Sally, d. [ ], 1822, ae. 39	BP	47
Samuel, s. Dea. George, Sr., bp. [1645, by Rev. Peter Prudden]	OL	102
Sam[ue]l, s. Geo[rge], carpenter, b. [ ], 1645	ES	238
Samuel, s. Thomas, b. Aug. 4, 1666	1	8
Samuel, s. Thomas, b. Aug. 4, 1666	OL	19
Sam[uel], [s. Tho[mas] & Hannah], b. [ ], 1666	ES	184
Sam[ue]ll, in 1671, destroyed the Indian Fort	ES	14
Samuel, s. Dea. George, m. Mary **CLARK**, d. George, farmer, Dec. 21, 1673, by Major Rob[er]t Treat	1	13
Samuel, s. Dea. George, m. Mary **CLARK**, d. George, farmer, b. of Milford, Dec. 26, 1673, by Maj. Robert Treat	OL	26
Samuel, Capt., d. May 28, 1725	1	77
S[a]m[uel], Capt., d. May 28, 1725	ES	238
Sam[ue]l, Capt., d. [ ], 1725	ES	238

	Vol.	Page
CLARK, CLARKE, (cont.)		
Sam[ue]ll, Capt., 1720; d. 1728	ES	40
Samuel, Capt., d. Apr. 6, 1777	SM	12
Sam[ue]ll, Col., d. 1777	ES	41
Samuel, of Oister River, d. Mar. 25, 1778	SM	15
Samuel, Capt. of Oister River, d. Nov. 18, 1778	SM	16
Samuel, his child, d. Jan. 24, 1785	SM	29
Samuel, his s. [ ], d. Jan. 29, 1786	SM	31
Samuel, d. [ ], 1794	SM	53
Samuel, had negro woman d. Dec. 11, 1803, ae. 66	SM	78
Samuel, widower, his d. [ ], d. [ ], 1826	BP	54
Samuel, 3rd, d. [ ], 1826, ae. 40	BP	55
Samuel, d. [ ], 1831, ae. 24	BP	65
Samuel, d. [ ], 1834, ae. 84	BP	71
Samuel, 3rd, his s. [ ], d. [ ], 1836, ae. 7 y.	BP	74
Samuel B., d. [ ], 1824	BP	51
Sarah, d. George, Sr., m. Hon Jonathan LAW, s. Jonathan, [ ]	ES	130
Sarah, w. George, Jr., adm. Church Nov. 22, [1640]; d. July 19, 1689	OL	98
Sarah, d. George, Jr., bp. [1643, by Rev. Peter Prudden]	OL	101
Sarah, d. Geo[rge], Jr., b. [ ], 1643	ES	238
Sarah, d. George, Sr., carpenter, bp. [1643, by Rev. Peter Prudden]	OL	101
Sarah, of Milford, m. Reinold MARVIN, of Cebrook (Saybrook), Nov. 27, 1663, by Benjamin Ffenn, Magistrate	1	6
Sarah, of Milford, m. Ronold MARVIN, of Saybrook (?), Nov. 27, 1663, by Benjamin Fenn, Magestrate	OL	16
Sarah, d. Thomas, b. Mar. 4, 1663/4	1	6
Sarah, d. Thomas, b. Mar. 4, 1663 or 1664	OL	17
Sarah, of Milford, d. of George, Sr., m. Jonathan LAWE, of Stamford, s. Richard, June 1, 1664, by Benj[amin] Ffenn, Magistrate	1	6
Sarah, of Milford, d. George CLARK, Sr., m. Jonathan LAWE, of Stamford, June 1, 1664, by Benjamin Fenn, Magesrate	OL	16
Sarah, d. Georg[e], Jr., b. June 21, 1678	OL	36
Sarah, m. Samuel BEARD, July 8, 1696, by Thomas Clark, J.P.	1	25
Sarah, m. Samuel BEARD, July 8, 1696, by Thomas Clark, J.P.	OL	52
Sarah, w. [George, Jr.], d. July 19, 1698	ES	238
Sarah, d. George, 2nd, b. Oct. 24, 1706	1	37
Sarah, d. George, 2nd, [& Sarah], b. Oct. 24, 1706	OL	81
Sarah, d. Capt. Sam[ue]ll, d. May [ ], 1724	1	75
Sarah, d. John, Jr. & Rebeckah, b. Feb. 10, 1742/3	1	143
Sarah, d. Joseph & Mary, b. Apr. 30, 1754	1	147
Sarah, d. Nath[anie]ll Cary, b. Apr. 25, 1776	1	166
Sarah, wid., d. June 18, 1783, ae. 69	SM	26
Sheldon, 2d s. of Isaac, m. Martha Anne LAMBERT, [d. Edward A. & Martha], Nov. 24, 1838	1	52
Silence, m. Sam[ue]l BUCKINGHAM, May 20, 1714, by Rev. Sam[ue]l Andrews	1	64
Susan C., wid., d. [ ], 1831, ae. 51	BP	65
Thomas, s. George, Sr., m. Hannah GILBERT, d. William, of New Haven, decd., May 20, 1663, by Robert Treat	1	5

CLARK, CLARKE, (cont.)

	Vol.	Page
Thomas, s. George, Jr., m. Hannah **GILBERT**, d. Will., of New Haven, decd., May 20, 1663, by Rob[ert] Treat	OL	15
Tho[mas], s. Geo[rge], Sr., m. Hannah **GILBERT**, d. Dept. Gov. Nath[aniel], [ ], 1663	ES	184
Thomas, s. Thomas, b. Jan. 22, 1668	1	9
Thomas, s. Thomas, b. Jan. 22, 1668	OL	21
Thomas, [s. Tho[mas] & Hannah], b. [ ], 1668	ES	184
Tho[ma]s, s. Sa[mue]l, Jr., bp. 1700	ES	238
Thomas, m. Martha [ ], Nov. 22, 1703, by Thomas Hart, J.P.	1	23
Thomas, Jr., m. Martha [ ], Nov. 22, 1703, by Thomas Hart, J.P.	OL	48
Thomas, s. Thomas, b. Mar. 22, 1708/9	1	31
Thomas, s. Thomas, b. Mar. 22, 1708/9	OL	67
Tho[ma]s, s. Tho[ma]s, Bp. 1709	ES	238
Thomas, s. George, 2nd, b. Aug. 29, 1715	1	37
Thomas, s. George, 2nd, b. Aug. 29, 1715	OL	80
Thomas, d. Oct. 23, 1719	1	66
Thomas, d. Oct. 23, 1719	ES	238
Thomas, s. Capt. Sam[ue]l, m. Susannah **WOODRUFF**, Dec. 15, 1725, by Sam[ue]ll Eells, Asst.	1	81
Tho[mas], s. Capt. Sam[ue]l, m. Susanna **WOODRUFF**, [ ], 1725	ES	238
Tho[ma]s, Sr & w. Susan, adm. To Ch. 1730	ES	238
Tho[ma]s, Capt. 1750	ES	41
Thomas, Dea., his w. [ ], d. June 1, 1787	SM	33
Thomas, Jr., d. June 11, 1795, ae. 61	SM	55
Thomas, d. [ ], 1801	BP	4
Thomas, Dea., d. Apr. 12, 1801, ae. 92	SM	72
Thomas, his child d. [ ], 1830	BP	62
Treat, his w. [ ], d. Mar. 5, 1805, ae. 25	SM	82
Treat, his w. [ ], d. [ ], 1805	BP	10
Treat, d. [ ], 1830, ae. 65	BP	61
William, his w. [ ], d. Apr. 19, 1781, ae. 44	SM	21
W[illia]m, Capt., d. Aug. 3, 1792	SM	48
William, his twin s. [ ], d. Oct. 9, 1797, ae. 7 w.	SM	62
W[illia]m, his child d. [ ], 1799, ae. 13 y.	BP	2
William, d. [ ], 1838, ae. 81	BP	79
-----, wid. [ ], 1687	ES	238
-----, Dr. had negro, d. Apr. 5, 1777	SM	12
-----, had negro woman, d. [ ], 1802	BP	5
-----, wid., had negro Catie, d. [ ], 1803	BP	8
CLEMENS, Isaac, d. [ ], 1806	BP	13
Jno, of Middleborough, d. Jan. [ ], 1777	SM	10
CLINTON, Abigaill, d. Lawrence & Abigail, b. Aug. 24, 1751	1	129
Lawrence, m. Abigaill **NORTHROP**, May 20, 1741, by Rev. Benjamin Woodbridge	1	120
Margett, of West Haven, m. Joseph **STILSON**, of Milford, Nov. 20, 1747, by Rev. Benjamin Woodbridge, of Amity	1	126
Samuel, s. Lawrence, b. July 22, 1754	1	134
Samuel, his d. [ ], d. Oct. 11, 1779	SM	18
Sarah, d. Lawrence, b. Aug. 10, 1747	1	123

MILFORD VITAL RECORDS 67

	Vol.	Page
CLINTON, (cont.)		
Simeon, s. Lawrence, b. Feb. 9, 1748/9	1	126
CLUETT, Aletta Emma, of New York, m. Henry Bills **LAMBERT**, 2d s. David & Susannah, [ ]	1	53
COCHRAN, CONKRAN, James, d. [Feb.], 1803, at Seaboard Peck	SM	77
-----, Mr., d. [ ], 1803, at Sea, in Capt. Peck's vessel	BP	7
COGGESHALL, Charles, Capt., d. [ ], 1820, at Sea	BP	43
Elizabeth, d. Freegift [& Martha], b. Jan. 28, 1727/8	1	115
Eunice, wid., d. [ ], 1836, ae. 75	BP	74
F., Capt. had child d. [ ], 1802	BP	5
F., his child d. [ ], 1806	BP	13
F., Capt. his d. [ ], d. [ ], 1822	BP	48
Francis, s. William & Eunice, b. Feb. 13, 1797	1	174
Freegift, m. Martha **NETTLETON**, Jan. 28, 1725/6, by Sam[ue]ll Eells, Asst.	1	115
Freegift, m. Martha **NETTLETON**, [ ], 1726	ES	238
Freegift, his s. [ ], d. Mar. 6, 1802	SM	74
Freegift, Jr., Capt., d. [ ], 1828	BP	57
George, Capt. his chld d. [ ], 1837	BP	77
Hatty, d. [ ], 1833, at New Haven, bd. in Milford	BP	70
John, d. Nov. [ ], 1780, ae. 10	SM	20
John, d. [ ], 1780	ES	165
James, s. W[illia]m & Eunice, b. Feb. 25, 1795	1	174
Mabel, wid., d. May 20, 1777, ae. 42	SM	13
Martha, d. Freegift [& Martha], b. June 25, 1730	1	115
Robert, d. [ ], 1810	BP	21
Sarah, wid. her child d. [ ], 1830	BP	62
Thomas, his child d. [ ], 1827	BP	56
Thomas, d. [ ], 1832, ae. 32	BP	66
William, s. Freegift [& Martha], b. Nov. 9, 1732	1	115
William, m. Eunice **MALLETT**, Mar. 9, 1779, by Samuel Walas	1	139
William, his d. [ ], d. Oct. 30, 1791	SM	46
William, had negro boy d. Jan. 1, 1794	SM	51
William, had negro girl, d. Nov. [ ], 1798	SM	65
William, Capt., d. Oct. 29, 1800, ae. 42	SM	70
W[illia]m, Capt., d. [ ], 1810, at Sea	BP	21
-----, Mrs. Negro her child d. [ ], 1811	BP	22
COLEMAN, Josiah, of Sharon, d. Jan. [ ], 1777	SM	10
COLBRAITH, COLLBREATH, COLBREATH, Humphrey, d. June 2, 1791, ae. 88	SM	45
-----, Mr., d. [ ], 1809	BP	19
-----, Mrs., d. [ ], 1814	BP	27
COLLES, [see also **COLLINS** & **COOLEY**], Isaac, his d. [ ], d. Sept. 24, 1795	SM	55
COLLINS, COLINS, COLLIN, COLLINGE, COLLINGS, [see also **COLLES**], Amos, d. Feb. [ ], 1778	SM	15
Daniel, m. Ruth **WILKINSON**, Dec. 7, 1699, by Robert Treat, Dept. Gov.	1	22
Daniel, m. Ruth **WILKINSON**, Dec. 7, 1699, by Rob[er]t Treat, Dept. Gov.	OL	46
Daniel, s. Daniel, b. Dec. 9, 1700	1	22
Daniel, s. Daniell [& Ruth], b. Dec. 9, 1700	OL	46

	Vol.	Page
COLLINS, COLINS, COLLIN, COLLINGE, COLLINGS, [see also **COLLES**], (cont.)		
Daniel, d. [ ], ae. about 35 y.	ES	165
David, d. Aug. 9, 1776, ae. 9	SM	7
Edward, s. Daniel, b. Sept. 17, 1702; d. Feb. [ ], 1702/3	1	22
Edward, s. Daniell [& Ruth], b. Sept. 17, 1702; d. Feb. [ ], 1702/3	OL	46
Edward, s. Daniell [& Ruth], b. Sept. 17, 1702	OL	46
Jacob, m. Mary **CANFIELD**, Nov. 2, 1743, by Rev. Samuel Whettlsey	1	114
John, s. Daniell, Jr., b. May 13, 1727	1	91
John, Capt., m. Hannah **MERWIN**, d. John & Hannah, Oct. 29, 1730, by Sam[ue]ll Eells, Asst.	1	94
John, s. John [& Hannah], b. July 4, 1732	1	94
John, Jr., d. [ ], 1802	BP	6
John, Jr., d. Sept. 27, 1802, ae. 56	SM	75
John, d. [ ], 1805, ae. 79	BP	12
Joseph, d. Apr. 25, 1782	SM	23
Joseph, d. [ ]	ES	165
Mary, wid., d. [ ], 1811	BP	21
Nathan, s. Daniel, b. Nov. 25, 1703	1	24
Nathan, s. Daniell, b. Nov. 25, 1703	OL	49
Sarah, d. John, b. July 3, 1654	1	1
Sarah, m. Lieut. Ebenezer **SMITH**, Jan. 3, 1710, by Samuel Eells, Asst.	1	32
Sarah, m. Ebenezer **SMITH**, Lieut., Jan. 3, 1710/11, by Sam[ue]ll Eells, Asst.	OL	70
Sarah, m. Nathan **BLOTCHFORD**, Oct. 6, 1737, by Roger Newton, Asst.	1	104
Sarah, wid., d. Apr. 28, 1790, ae. 82	SM	41
Simeon, sailor, d. [ ], 1829	BP	60
COOLEY, COLEY, [see also **COLLES**, Abilene, d. Samuel, bp. [1643, by Rev. Peter Prudden]	OL	100
Anne, w. Samuel, adm. Church Feb. 14, 1641; d. Oct. 3, 1659	OL	98
Hannah, d. Samuel, b. Oct. 10, 1654	1	2
Hannah, d. Samuel, b. Oct. 10, 1654 (Perhaps "Lemuel")	OL	8
Hannah, d. Samuel, bp. [1654, by Rev. Peter Prudden]	OL	105
Hannah, d. Samuel, Sr., m. Joseph **GUERNSEY**, Apr. 10, 1673, by John Clarke, Commissioner	1	12
Hannah, d. Samuel, Sr., m. Joseph **GARNSEY**, Apr. 10, 1673, by John Clark, Com.	OL	25
Mary, d. Samuel, bp. [1651, by Rev. Peter Prudden]	OL	104
Mary, d. Samuel, b. Jan. 4, 1684	1	19
Mary, d. Sam[ue]ll, b. Jan. 14, 1684	OL	41
Peter, s. Samuel, bp. [1641], by Rev. Peter Prudden	OL	100
Richard, of Penn., d. Jan. [ ], 1777	SM	10
Samuel, adm. Church Oct. 25, [1640]	OL	97
Samuel, s. Samuel, bp. [1654, by Rev. Peter Prudden]	OL	102
Samuel, m. Mary **CARLES***, Oct. 21, 1669, by John Clark, Commissioner *(Perhaps "CURTIS")	1	9
Samuell, Jr., m. Mary **CURTIS**, b. of Milford, Oct. 21, 1669, by John Clark, Com.	OL	22

MILFORD VITAL RECORDS 69

	Vol.	Page
COOLEY, COLEY, [see also **COLLES,** (cont.)]		
Samuel, d. [ ], 1684 (One of the first planters)	ES	16
Samuel, s. Thomas, d. Feb. 6, 1703/4	1	41
Samuel, s. Thomas, d. Feb. 6, 1703/4	OL	86
Sarah, d. Samuel, bp. [1648, by Rev. Peter Prudden]	OL	103
Thomas, s. Samuel, b. Apr. 20, 1657	1	3
Thomas, s. Samuel, b. Apr. 20, 1657	OL	10
CORNWALL, -----, Mrs., d. [ ], 1824	BP	51
-----, his child d. [ ], 1826	BP	55
COTTON, Harriet, m. as 2d w. Henry **LAMBERT,** [s. Jesse Peck & Amy], [ ]	1	51
COWELL, Rebeckah, d. Joshiah, b. Feb. 8, 1747/8	1	123
CRANE, Sarah, m. Joseph **WHEELER,** Jr., Mar. 27, 1707, by Samuel Andrews	1	28
Sarah, m. Joseph **WHEELER,** Jr., Mar. 27, 1707, by Sam[ue]ll Andrews	OL	60
CRITTENDEN, CRETTINDEN, Charles G., s. John & Eunice, b. Mar. 1 1809	1	173
Samuel, Priv. Member of Capt. Samuel Peck's Co., Milford 1776	1	54
-----, his child d. [ ], 1817	BP	37
CRUICKSHANKS, George, member of Canadian Legislature, m. Sarah Susannah **LAMBERT,** [d. David & Susannah], [ ]; lived in York, Upper Canada	1	53
CUBITT, -----, Indian, m. E. M., Nov. 11, 1709	1	30
CURTIS, Charles, m. Emily Anne [**LAMBERT,** twin with Harriet, d. Jesse Peck & Amy], [ ]; moved to Ohio	1	51
Mary, m. Samuell **COLEY,** Jr., b. of Milford, Oct. 21, 1669, by John Clark, Com.	OL	22
Mary, see also Mary **CARLOS**		
Samuel, Capt. had infant d. [ ], d. July 4, 1796	SM	59
Samuel, Capt., d. Oct. 1, 1796 (Heard of death)	SM	60
Samuel, d. [ ], 1816, at Cuba	BP	34
Sarah, wid., d. [ ], 1815	BP	29
Sarah, wid., d. [ ], 1820, ae. 56	BP	41
-----, Mrs. at the Gulf, d. [ ], 1815	BP	30
CUSH, Eunice, d. Dec. 12, 1800	SM	70
Hoden, his d. [ ], d. Mar. 22, 1801, ae. 1 y. 3 m.	SM	72
Susannah, hers. [ ], d. May 16, 1782	SM	23
Su, negro, d. [ ], 1802	BP	5
DALISON, [see also **DAVIDSON**], Gilbert, came to Milford [ ]	ES	176
DANIELS, John, his child d. [ ], 1801	BP	3
John, Capt. His w. [ ], d. [ ], 1833	BP	68
John L., his s. [ ], d. May 19, 1801	SM	72
Patty, d. [ ], 1830, ae. 30	BP	61
Samuel, d. [ ], 1806	BP	13
Sarah, d. Feb. 12, 1783	SM	25
-----, wid., d. [ ], 1810	BP	20
-----, Capt. d. [ ], 1839	BP	81
DAVIDSON, [see also **DALISON**], Andrew, s. James & Elizabeth, b. Apr. 16, 1741	1	111
Anna, wid., d. [ ], 1826, ae. 85	BP	55
Anne, wid., d. May 24, 1798	SM	63

	Vol.	Page
DAVIDSON, [see also **DALISON**], (cont.)		
Betsey, d. [ ], 1802, ae. 18	BP	6
Betsey, d. Sept. 10, 1802	SM	75
Elizabeth, wid., d. Oct. 9, 1794, ae. 82	SM	52
H(?), Capt. his child d. [ ], 1829, ae. 1	BP	59
Howe, m. Polly **DICKINSON**, d. Sylvanus & Mary, [ ]	1	178
Isaac, drafted for Continental Army	1	57
Isaac, d. [ ], 1840, ae. 32	BP	83
James, m. Mrs. Elizabeth **TREAT**, Sept. 2, 1736, by Roger Newton, Asst.	1	104
James, s. James & Elizabeth, b. Aug. 24, 1737	1	105
James, Jr., his s. [ ], d. Sept. 9, 1798, ae. 10 m.	SM	64
James, Capt., d. [ ], 1826, ae. 88	BP	55
James, d. [ ], 1840	BP	84
John, s. James & Elizabeth, b. Dec. 15, 1739	1	111
Joseph, s. James & Elizabeth, b. Jan. 8, 1742/3	1	113
Joseph, d. Mar. 25, 1796, ae. 53	SM	58
Joseph, his child d. [ ], 1810	BP	20
Joseph, his child d. [ ], 1811	BP	22
Joseph, his child d. [ ], 1818, blind	BP	38
Mark, d. [ ], 1836, ae. 26	BP	61
Miles, his child d. [ ], 1828	BP	58
N., Capt. his child d. [ ], 1816	BP	35
Patrick, d. [ ], 1803, abroad at Seat	BP	7
Patrick, d. Jan. [ ], 1803	SM	77
Richard, s. James & Elizabeth, b. May 10, 1746	1	119
William, his 1ˢᵗ w. [ ], d. May 15, 1776, ae. 23	SM	6
William, his 2ⁿᵈ w. [ ], d. Nov. 17, 1780	SM	20
William, Jr., his child d. [ ], 1808	BP	18
William, Capt., d. [ ], 1811	BP	22
William, Capt., d. [ ], 1814, ae. 67	BP	26
DEAL, DEALE, Charles, came to Milford, 1656; d. 1685	ES	176
Charles, m. Pitty [ ], July 3, 1672, by John Clarke, Commissioner	1	12
Charles, m. Pitty **BOTS**, b. of Milford, July 3, 1672, by John Clark, Com.	OL	24
DEAN, Sarah, w. Robert, d. Jan. 17, 1703	1	41
Sarah, w. Robert, d. Jan. 17, 1703	OL	87
DEFOREST, Benjamin, m. Rachel **LAMBERT**, [d. David & Lurania], [ ]	1	53
Margaret, d. of Philo, m. Henry [**LAMBERT**], [s. Jesse Peck & Amy], [ ]	1	51
DELAMBERT, [see under **LAMBERT**]		
DELAVAN, DELEVEN, John, Jr., d. [ ], 1813, ae. 18	BP	31
John, his child d. [ ], 1815	BP	29
John, his d. [ ], d. Sept. 6, 1794, ae. 1 y.	SM	52
-----, his infant child d. [ ], 1829	BP	60
DENISON, Esther, d. Robert, b. Aug. 24, 1658	OL	11
Hannah, d. Robert, b. Mar. 19, 1661/2	1	5
Hannah, d. Robert, b. Mar. 19, 1661/2	OL	14
Hester, d. Robert, b. Aug. 24, 1658	1	3
Robert, came to Milford, 1645	ES	176

MILFORD VITAL RECORDS 71

	Vol.	Page
DENISON, (cont.)		
Samuel, s. Robert, b. June 14, 1656	1	3
Samuel, s. Robert, b. June 14, 1656	OL	10
DEWITT, DEWITTS, Abigail, wid., d. Mar. 23, 1776, ae. 34	SM	5
Abraham, had negro girl d. Sept. 9, 1790	SM	42
Abraham, his 1st w. [ ], d. Sept. 30, 1790, ae. 20	SM	43
Abraham, his infant s. [ ], d. Sept. 2, 1794	SM	52
A[braham] J. H., m. Martha **POND**, Jan. 3, 1790, by Rev. Will-[ia]m Lockwood	1	175
Abraham J. H., of Milford, m. Martha **BELDEN**, of Wethersfield, Aug. 22, 1792, by Rev. John Marsh, in Wethersfield	1	175
Abram H., d. [ ], 1820	BP	42
Albert, d. [ ], 1820, at the South	BP	42
Charles P., s. Abraham J. H. & Martha, b. July 5, 1799	1	175
Charlotte S., d. Abraham J. H. & Martha, b. Oct. 24, 1809	1	175
Garrett, his 1st w. [ ], d. Mar. 27, 1790, ae. 26	SM	41
Garrett, Jr., his s. [ ], d. Aug. 15, 1792, ae. 2 y.	SM	48
Garrett, d. Feb. 23, 1793, ae. 58	SM	49
Garrill J. H., s. Abraham J. H. & Martha, b. Aug. 24, 1793	1	175
Henry A., s. Abraham J. H. & Martha, b. Sept. 27, 1797	1	175
James L., s. Abraham J. H. & Martha, b. Mar. 24, 1803	1	175
John, Heard of death at Sea, Nov. 5, 1798	SM	65
Margaret, wid., d. Jan. 10, 1794, ae. 51	SM	51
Margaret, d. [ ], 1826, ae. 15	BP	54
Martha, w. Abraham J. H., d. Sept. 30, 1790	1	175
Martha P., d. Abraham J. H. & Martha, b. Sept. 18, 1790	1	175
Mary, from St. Croix, d. [ ], 1819, [ae.] 17	BP	39
Mary B., d. Abraham J. H. & Martha, b. May 8, 1801	1	175
Peter, heard of death at Sea, June 4, 1798	SM	64
Simeon B., s. Abraham J. H. & Martha, b. Oct. 18, 1795	1	175
William, s. Abraham J. H. & Martha, b. Aug. 30, 1794; d. Sept. 2, 1794	1	175
W[illia]m, d. Oct. 6, 1798, in New York of fever. Another record said "Fate unknown"	SM	64
William, s. Abraham J. H. & Martha, b. Jan. 24, 1805	1	175
-----, Mrs. had negro boy d. Mar. 9, 1776	SM	5
-----, Mr. his negro Jube, d. July 30, 1777	SM	13
-----, Mr. his negro man, d. Oct. [ ], 1795	SM	56
DICKERMAN, Isaac, Lieut., member of Capt. Samuel Peck's Co., Milford, 1776	1	54
DICKINSON, Catharine, twin with Isaac, d. [Sylvanus & Mary], b. June 17, 1785	1	178
Elizabeth, [d. Sylvanus & Mary], b. Mar. 26, 1795; m. John **BULL**, [ ]	1	178
Henry, [s. Sylvanus & Mary], b. Dec. 11, 1788; d. [ ], 1808, at Alexandria	1	178
Henry, d. [ ], 1813, at Alexandria	BP	31
Isaac, twin with Catharine, s. [Sylvanus & Mary], b. June 17, 1785	1	178
Isaac, Capt., d. [ ], 1838	BP	79
Polly, [d. Sylvanus & Mary], b. June 22, 1791; m. Howe **DAVIDSON**, [ ]	1	178
Samuel, Priv., member of Capt. Samuel Peck's Co., Milford 1776	1	54
Samuel, his w. [ ], d. [ ], 1832, ae. [ ]	BP	68

	Vol.	Page
DICKINSON, (cont.)		
Samuel, drafted for Continental Army	1	58
Samuel W., [s. Sylvanus & Mary], b. Apr. 10, 1793	1	178
Satitia, [d. Sylvanus & Mary], b. Mar. 6, 1799; (never married)	1	178
Susan, d. [Sylvanus & Mary], b. May 26, 1783	1	178
Sylvanus, m. Mary **MILES**, June 18, 1782	1	178
Silvanus, his d. [ ], d. May 22, 1796, ae. 1 w.	SM	58
Sylvanus, had negro Harry, d. Feb. 22, 1799	SM	66
Silvanus, d. [ ], 1832, ae. 78	BP	67
Townsend, [s. Sylvanus & Mary], b. July 22, 1800	1	178
William, [s. Sylvanus & Mary], b. June 24, 1787; d. at Sea	1	178
William, d. [ ], 1804 at Sea	BP	9
William, d. Aug. [ ], 1804 (drowned at Sea aboard Capt. Ferrin Turner's Vessel)	SM	80
DISBOROUGH, Abigail, m. William **GOLD**, Nov. 28, 1706	1	27
Abigail, m. William **GOLD**, Nov. 28, 1706	OL	59
DOOE, Jack, Town poor, d. [ ], 1821	BP	44
DOUGLASS, -----, Col. see under Capt. Samuel **PECK**	1	179
DOWN, DOWNS, DOWNES, Abigail, d. Daniel, b. Jan. 19, 1718/19	1	44
Abigail, d. Daniel, b. Jan. 19, 1718/19	OL	85
Abigail, m. Thomas **HITCHCOCK**, Dec. 24, 1741, by Roger Newton, Asst.	1	120
Ann, d. John, b. Nov. 27, 1734	1	102
Deborah, d. Daniel, b. Jan. 21, 1716/17	1	39
Deborah, d. Dan[ie]ll, b. Jan. 21, 1716/17	OL	84
Deborah, m. John **TIBBALLS**, b. of Milford, Jan. 22, 1748, by Rev. Job Prudden	1	132
Deliverance, had ch., John, b. July 18, 1704, Mary, b. Dec. 25, 1708, Elizabeth, b. Mar. 4, 1709/10	1	89
Elijah, s. Jonathan & Sarah, b. Nov. 15, 1758	1	140
Elizabeth, [d. Deliverance], b. Mar. 4, 1709/10	1	89
Elizabeth, m. Samuel **TERRELL**, Jr., Oct. 9, 1739	1	126
Elizabeth, d. John, b. Feb. 1, 1742	1	114
Hannah, wid., d. [ ], 1819	BP	40
James, his child d. [ ], 1815	BP	28
John, s. Deliverance, b. July 18, 1704	1	89
John, m. Ann **HINE**, May 24, 1733, by Rev. Samuel Andrews	1	98
John, member of 2nd Church formed in 1742	ES	87
John, s. John, b. June 5, 1745	1	114
John, Jr., m. Hannah **STONE**, Dec. 14, 1769, by Rev. Job Prudden, Witnesses, Samuel Fenn, Jane Treat, Donald Treat, Fitch Welch	1	165
John, s. John, Jr. & Hannah, b. Dec. 20, 1770	1	165
John, s. John, Jr. & Hannah, d. Sept. 19, 1773	1	165
John, his w. [ ], d. Jan. 17, 1795, ae. 85	SM	54
John, d. Jan. 11, 1799, ae. 95	BP	1
John, d. Jan. 12, 1799, ae. 95	SM	66
John(?), his child d. [ ], 1805, ae. 2 y.	BP	12
John, d. [ ], 1819, ae. about 70	BP	39
Lucretia, d. John, Jr. & Hannah, b. Sept. 6, 1773	1	165
Mary, d. Deliverance, b. Dec. 25, 1708	1	89
Mary, d. Jonathan & Sarah, b. Feb. 21, 1756	1	140

	Vol.	Page
DOWN, DOWNS, DOWNES, (cont.)		
Rebecca, d. Deliverance, b. Jan. 7, 1699/1700	1	23
Rebeckah, d. Deliverance, b. Jan. 7, 1699/1700	OL	47
Rebeckah, d. John & Ann, b. Dec. 6, 1746	1	121
Robert, tobacco planter came to Milford, 1660	ES	176
Samuel, s. Jonathan & Sary, b. Oct. 12, 1749	1	140
Samuel, s. John, Jr. & Hannah, b. May 4, 1772	1	165
Thomas, s. Jonathan & Sary, b. Mar. 17, 1753	1	140
DRAKE, Richard of Mass., d. Jan. [ ], 1777	SM	10
DRIVER, -----, his child d. [ ], 1830	BP	62
-----, his child d. [ ], 1836	BP	74
DUNNING, John, m. Sarah **LAMBERT**, d. Jesse & Deborah, [ ], Settled in Norwalk, Conn.	1	49
DURAND, Andrew, his w. [ ], d. Feb. 15, 1778, ae. 78	SM	15
Andrew, d. Oct. 14, 1791, ae. 89	SM	46
Charlotte, d. William, d. Oct. 19, 1798	SM	64
Charlotte, d. [ ], 1834, ae. 34	BP	71
Delia, d. [ ], 1839	BP	81
Fidelia, her child d. [ ], 1837, ae. 2	BP	78
Fisk, his infant s. [ ], d. May 29, 1793	SM	49
John, his s. [ ], d. July 5, 1776	SM	6
John, d. Jan. 20, 1780, ae. 45	SM	19
John, d. [ ], 1830	BP	61
Lucy, d. [ ], 1836, ae. 24	BP	76
Lucy Belden, d. William & Nancy B., b. Feb. 11, 1813	1	178
Mason, s. William, d. Sept. 16, 1794, ae. 1	SM	52
Merrett, d. Sept. 19, 1795	SM	55
S. B., his infant child d. [ ], 1829	BP	59
Samuel, his w. [ ], d. Mar. 6, 1798	SM	63
Samuel, his w. [ ], d. [ ], 1825	BP	52
Samuel, d. [ ], 1829, ae. 90	BP	59
Samuel, d. [ ], 1838	BP	79
Samuel B., his child d. [ ], 1831, ae. 2 y.	BP	64
Samuel B., his child d. [ ], 1833	BP	69
Samuel B., d. [ ], 1836, ae. 34, at New Haven	BP	76
William, his twin sons, d. June 13, 1796, ae. 1 d.	SM	59
William, his s. [ ], d. Sept. 24, 1800	SM	70
William Mason, s. William & Nancy B., b. May 10, 1814	1	178
-----, d. [ ], 1826, ae. 20	BP	55
-----, Mrs., d. [ ], 1828, ae. 96	BP	57
EABROOK*, Samuel, of East Haddam, d. Oct. 26, 1776, ae. 25 *(**EASTBROOK?**)	SM	8
EAST, Solomon, s. William, bp. [1643, by Rev. Peter Prudden]	OL	101
William, adm. Church May 8, [1640]; d. Aug. 27, 1661	OL	97
William, m. Mrs. Mary **PLUMB**, Mar. 16, 1675/6, by Capt. Thomas Topping	1	15
William, m. Mrs. Mary **PLUMBE**, Mar. 16, 1675/6, by Capt. Tho[ma]s Tapping	OL	30
William, cast out after Mr. Prudden's death and restored Aug. 17, 1660, d. [ ], 1781	ES	16
EELLS, EELL, ELLES, [see also **ELLIS**], Anna, d. John, b. May 1, 1729	1	86

	Vol.	Page
EELLS, EELL, ELLES, [see also **ELLIS**], (cont.)		
Charles, his child d. [ ], 1831, ae. 3 y.	BP	64
Daniel, d. Dec. 7, 1777	SM	14
Deborah, w. Sam[ue]l, adm. to Ch. 1730	ES	238
Deborah, [d. Samuel & Deborah], [ ], Feb. 8, 1733	ES	238
Esther, [d. Sam[ue]l, Jr., b. [ ], 1699	ES	238
Esther, [d. Samuel], bp. 1699	ES	238
Esther, d. [ ], 1807	BP	16
Eunice, d. Nov. 30, 1785	SM	30
Gamaleel, s. Sam[uel], [ ], 1712	ES	238
Harvey, his child d. [ ], 1838	BP	80
John, d. Ju[ ] 19, 1664, ae. 10 d.	ES	238
John, 2nd d. [Samuel & An[n]a], b. July 3, 1665; d. 13th of same month	1	7
John, s. [Samuel & Anna], b. July 3, [16]65, d. July 13, [16]65	OL	18
John, came to Milford, 1668	ES	177
John, [s. Sam[ue]l], bp. [ ], 1670	ES	238
John, Rev. 3rd s. Col. Samuel, b. [ ], 1703	ES	126
John, s. Capt. Sam[ue]l, bp. 1703; adm. To 1st ch.; removed to Canaan, Minister	ES	238
John, m. Anna **BEARD**, Jan. 11, 1727/8, by Sam[ue]ll Eells, Asst.	1	86
John, m. Anna **BEARD**, Jan. 11, 1728	ES	238
John, m. Ann **BEARD**, [ ], 1728	ES	238
Lent, s. Sam[ue]l, Jr., [ ], 1736	ES	238
Mary, d. Samuel, b. Feb. 18, 1670/1	1	10
Mary, d. Samuel, b. Feb. 18, 1670	OL	23
Nathan, his child d. [ ], 1833	BP	70
Nathaniel, s. Samuel, b. Nov. 26, 1677	1	16
Nathaniel, s. Sam[ue]ll, b. Nov. 26, 1677	OL	32
Nath[anie]l, s. Lieut. Sam[ue]l B., bp. [ ], 1677	ES	238
Nathaniel, s. Col. Sam[ue]l, b. [ ], 1705	ES	238
Nathaniel, [s. Samuel & Deborah], [ ], 1705	ES	238
Robert, s. Samuel, b. Nov. 14, 1672; d. Jan. 16, [16]73 (see Church Records)	1	12
Robert, s. Sam[ue]ll, b. Dec. 14, 1672	OL	25
Robert, s. Samuel, b. June 25, 1675; bd. Jan. 28, [16]76 [Church Record]	1	15
Robert, s. Sam[ue]ll, b. June 25, 1675	OL	29
Samuel, of Milford, m. Ana **LENTHALL**, Aug. 1, 1663, by Capt. Marshall, Commissioner at Lynn	1	7
Samuel, m. Anna **LOUTHALL**, Aug. 5, [16]63, by Capt. Marshall, Com. At Lin* *(Lynn)	OL	18
Samuel, 1st s. [Samuel & An[n]a], b. June 1, 1664; d. July 16, 1665	1	7
Samuel, s. Samuel [& Anna], b. June 1, [16]64	OL	18
Samuel, s. [Samuel & Anna], d. July 16, [16]65	OL	18
Samuel, s. [Samuel], b. Sept. 2, 1666	1	7
Samuel, s. [Samuel & Anna], b. Sept. 2, [16]66	OL	18
Samuel, came to Milford, 1668	ES	177
Samuel, Col. eldest s. Capt. Samuel, b. Sept. 2, 1670; d. 1714	ES	132
Sam[ue]l, s. Sam[ue]l, bp. [ ], 1670	ES	238
Sam[ue]l, Jr., adm. to 1st Ch. 1698	ES	238
Sam[ue]l, s. Sam[ue]l, Jr., b. Oct. [ ], 1698	ES	238

	Vol.	Page
EELLS, EELL, ELLES, [see also ELLIS], (cont.)		
Sam[ue]l, s. Sam[ue]l, bp. 1698	ES	238
Sam[ue]l, Capt., 1680; d. [ ], 1725	ES	40
Samuel, Capt., d. 1725	ES	132
Sam[ue]l, Capt., d. May 25, 1725 (Perhaps f. of Sam[ue]l Eells, Asst.)	ES	238
Sam[ue]l, Jr., Col., 1740	ES	40
Samuel, Jr., his w. [ ], d. Feb. 9, 1778	SM	15
Samuel, 3rd, his d. [ ], d. Jan. 19, 1789	SM	39
Samuel, Cornet, d. Jan. 24, 1789, ae. 98	SM	39
Samuel, Jr., his s. [ ], d. Jan. 18, 1796, ae. 2 y.	SM	58
Samuel, his w. [ ], d. Jan. 19, 1796	SM	58
Samuel, d. Apr. 8, 1804	SM	79
Samuell, d. [ ], 1835	BP	73
Samuel, drafted for Continental Army	1	58
-----, Lieut., his d. [ ], d. Dec. 17, 1776	SM	8
-----, Mr. of Barkhamsead, d. [, 1813]	BP	33
-----, wid., d. [ ], 1839	BP	81
ELIOT, ELLIOTT, Ann, m. Jonathan LAW, Dec. 20, 1698	1	27
Ann, m. Gov. Jonathan LAW, D[ec.] 20, 1698; d. Nov. 16, 1703	ES	130
Ann, m. Jonathan LAW, Dec. 20, 1698; d. Nov. 16, 1703	OL	56
Simeon, of Mass., d. Jan. [ ], 1777	SM	9
ELLIS, EELLIS, [see also EELLS], Anna, d. [ ], 1829	BP	59
Sibel, wid., d. July 8, 1799, ae. 44	SM	67
Sybyl, wid., d. July 18, 1799, ae. 44	BP	1
William, d. June 18, 1787, ae. 29	SM	33
-----, Mr., d. [ ], 1804	BP	8
EVANS, EVINS, Evan, his w. [ ], d. May 23, 1791, ae. 71	SM	45
Evan, d. Sept. 1, 1804	SM	81
Evan, d. [ ], 1804	BP	9
Evin, (Welch) drafted for Continental Army	1	58
EVERET, Samuel, of Attleborough, d. Jan. [ ], 1777	SM	10
EWINE(?), Marcy*, d. of Edward Camp, of New Haven, m. Josiah BALDWIN, s. John, June 25, 1667, by Mr. Ffenn *(Mary LAW)	1	8
FAIRCHILD, Ruth, wid., d. July 14, 1789, ae. 78	SM	40
FARLAND, -----, Mrs., d. [ ], 1806	BP	13
FARMAN, [see also FARNUM], Tho[mas], came to Milford, 1658	ES	177
FARNUM, [see also FARMAN], Daniel, of Windham, d. Jan. [ ], 1777	SM	9
FARRAND, FERRAND, FFERRAND, FFARRAND, Anna, d. Nathaniel, b. July 25, 1706; d. Aug. 24, 1706	1	27
Anna, d. Nathan[ie]l, Jr., b. July 25, 1706; d. Aug. 24, 1706	OL	58
Anna, w. Samuel, d. July 21, 1709	1	43
Daniel, s. Nathaniel, b. July 2, 1683	1	19
Daniel, s. Nathaniel, Jr., b. July 6, 1783 [probably 1683]	OL	40
Deborah, d. Nathaniel, Jr., b. Dec. 22, 1676	1	15
Deborah, d. Nathaniell, Jr., b. Dec. 22, 1676	OL	31
Elizabeth, d. Nathaniel, m. Walter SMITH, Sept. 26, 1676, by Capt. Tapping	1	15
Esther, wid., d. June 12, 1788	SM	36
Hannah, d. Nathaniel, Sr., m. Thomas THORNTEN, Aug. 5,		

	Vol.	Page
FARRAND, FERRAND, FFERRAND, FFARRAND, (cont.)		
1674, by Major Robert Treat	1	14
Hannah, d. Nathan, Sr., m Thomas **THRONTON**, Aug. 5, 1674, by Major Treat	OL	27
Hannah, w. Sam[ue]ll, d. July 21, 1709	OL	89
Na-----, came to Milford, 1645	ES	177
Nathaniel, s. Nathaniel, Jr., b. May 15, 1679	1	17
Nathaniel, s. Nathaniel, Jr., b. May 15, 1679	OL	35
Nathaniel, Jr., s. Nathaniel, b. Apr. 1, 1705	1	27
Nathan[ie]ll, s. Nathan[ie]ll, Jr., b. Apr. 1, 1705	OL	58
Nathaniel, Jr., [ ], 1734	ES	238
Nath[anie]l, Capt., 1750	ES	41
Samuel, s. Nathaniel, Jr., b. Mar. 15, 1680/1	OL	37
Sarah, d. Samuel, b. July 13, 1709	1	31
Sarah, d. Sam[ue]ll, b. July 13, 1709	OL	67
FENN, FFENN, FFENNE, Aaron, [s. James], bp. 1709	ES	238
A[a]ron, s. James, Jr. & Sarah, b. Nov. 20, 1746	1	124
Aaron, d. Oct. 14, 1778, ae. 70	SM	16
Aaron, d. [ ], 1833, ae. 81	BP	70
Aaron William, s. Maj. W[illia]m, d. [ ], 1813, ae. 13	BP	25
Abigail, d. Joseph, b. Oct. 5, 1717	1	68
Abigail, m. Joel **BALDWIN**, Dec. 26, 1734, by Sam[ue]ll Eells, Asst.	1	106
Ann, wid., d. [ ], 1828, ae. 60	BP	57
Benjamin, s. Benjamin, bp. [1640], by Rev. Peter Prudden	OL	100
Benjamin, s. Benjamin, m. Mehittable **GUNN**, d. Jasper, b. of Milford, Dec. 20, 1660, by Robert Treat, Magestrate	OL	13
Benjamin, s. Benjamin, m. Mehetable **GUNN**, d. of Jasper, Dec. 21, 1660, by Robert Treat, Magistrate	1	4
Benjamin, Sr., m. Mrs. Susannah **WOOD***, Mar. 12, 1663 *(WARD)	1	14
Benjamin, Sr., m. Mrs. Susanna **WARD**, Mar. 12, 1663	OL	28
Benj[ami]n, m. 2nd w. Susanna **WARD**, Mar. 12, 1663	ES	180
Benjamin, adm. Church Sept. 20, [1640]; dismissed to Boston, Feb. 6, 1669	OL	97
Benjamin, dismissed to Boston 1669/70, d. [ ], 1672, (One of the first planters)	ES	16
Benjamin, bp. 1692	ES	238
Benj[amin], adm. to 1st Ch. 1693	ES	238
Benj[amin], s. James, bp. 1706	ES	238
Benj[amin], Col., 1737	ES	40
Benjamin, m. Mary **PECK**, Nov. 4, 1741	1	117
Benj[amin], m. Mary **PECK**, Nov. 4, 1741	ES	238
Benj[amin], Jr., original member of 2nd Church formed in 1742	ES	87
Benj[amin], Elder, original member of 2nd Church formed in 1742	ES	87
Beniaman, s. Beniaman & Mary, b. July 30, 1742	1	117
Benj[amin], Jr., [s. Benjamin & Mary], b. July 30, 1742	ES	238
Benj[amin], Col., d. July 10, 1770	ES	94
Benj[ami]n, Jr., his d. [ ], d. Oct. 6, 1776, ae. 16	SM	7
Benjamin, Priv., member of Capt. Samuel Peck's Col, Milford, 1776	1	54

	Vol.	Page

FENN, FFENN, FFENNE, (cont.)

	Vol.	Page
Benjamin, Col., d. Feb. 20, 1778, ae. 58	SM	15
Benj[amin], Capt., 1773; Col. [ ]; d. 1778	ES	41
Benjamin, Lieut., d. Oct. 28, 1780, ae. 38	SM	20
Ben[jamin], his child d. [ ], 1813	BP	31
Benj[amin], his other child d. [ ], 1813	BP	31
Dan, his w. [ ], d. May 9, 1784, ae. 27	SM	27
Dan, d. Feb. 23, 1789, ae. 36	SM	39
Dan, his w. [ ], d. [ ], 1833	BP	68
E. T., his infant d. [ ], 1836	BP	75
Eliakim J., his child d. [ ], 1830	BP	63
Hannah, d. Benjamin, Jr. [ ], 1716	ES	238
Hannah, d. [James], bp. 1716	ES	238
Hannah, w. Dea. Benj[amin], d. June [ ], 1742	ES	238
Hannah, w. Dea. Benjamin, d. June 16, 1743	1	116
Hannah, w. Dea. Benj[ami]n, d. [ ], 1743	ES	238
Isaac, Jr., d. [ ], 1812	BP	24
Isaac, d. [ ], 1824	BP	51
James, s. Benjamin, b. May 14, 1672	1	12
James, s. Benjamin & Susanna, b. May 14, 1672	OL	24
James, adm. to 1ˢᵗ Ch. 1703	ES	238
James, 3ʳᵈ, s. James & Sarah, b. Sept. 6, 1739	1	124
James, Jr., d. Dec. 26, 1746	1	124
James, his w. [ ], d. June 7, 1790, ae. 48	SM	42
James, d. [ ], 1832, ae. 93	BP	67
Johanna, m. John **STONE**, Oct. 2, 1740, by Sam[ue]ll Eells, Asst.; d. May 19, 1741	1	123
Joanna, d. James, Jr. & Sarah, b. July 17, 1741	1	124
Joanna, d. [ ], 1818, ae. 76	BP	38
John, Jr., d. Nov. 27, 1777, ae. 27	SM	14
John, d. Sept. 4, 1793, ae. 79	SM	50
John, his child d. [ ], 1829	BP	60
Joseph, s. Benjamin, bp. [1642, by Rev. Peter Prudden]	OL	100
Joseph, m. Abigail [ ], Dec. 26, 1716, by Jonathan Law, J.P.	1	38
Joseph, m. Abigail [ ], Dec. 26, 1716, by Jon[a]th[an] Law, J.P.	OL	83
Joseph, s. Joseph, b. Nov. 30, 1719	1	68
Joseph, Jr., original member of 2ⁿᵈ Church formed in 1742	ES	87
Joseph, member of 2ⁿᵈ Church formed in 1742	ES	87
Maj. [ ], Capt., 1793	ES	41
Martha, d. Benjamin, bp. [1650, by Rev. Peter Prudden]	OL	103
Martha, m. [ ] **NEWTON**, s. Rev. R[ ], Mar. 12, 1669	ES	180
Martha, d. Benjamin, m. Lemuel **NEWTON**, s. Roger, Pastor, Mar. 14, 1668/9, by John Clerk, Commissioner	1	9
Martha, d. Benjamin, Asst., m. Samuel **NEWTON**, s. Rev. Roger, b. of Milford, Mar. 14, 1668/9, by William East, Com.	OL	22
Mary, d. Benjamin, bp. [1647, by Rev. Peter Prudden]	OL	102
Mary, m. John **HINE**, July 4, 1684, by Capt. Samuel Eells, Commissioner	1	19
Mary, m. John **HINE**, July 4, 1684, by Capt. Sam[ue]ll Eells, Com.	OL	41

FENN, FFENN, FFENNE, (cont.)

	Vol.	Page
Mary, wid., d. [ ], 1804, ae. 86 y.	BP	9
Mary, wid., d. May 2, 1804	SM	80
Mehitabel, d. Lieut. [Benjamin], adm. to Ch. 1719	ES	238
Mehetabeel, m. Joseph PLATT, Jr., June 16, 1720, by Sam[ue]ll Eells, Asst.	1	76
Nathan, his d. [ ], d. [ ], 1820	BP	42
Nathan, his w. [ ], d. [ ], 1820	BP	42
Nathan, his child d. [ ], 1838, in New Haven	BP	80
Nathan, d. [ ], 1840	BP	84
Park, his d. [ ], d. Mar. 11, 1796	SM	58
Samuel, s. Benjamin, Magistrate, b. Mar. 4, 1666	1	7
Samuel, s. Benjamin (Magestrate), b. Mar. 4, 1666	OL	18
Samuel, s. Benjamin & Susanna, b. Sept. 4, 1667	1	8
Samuel, s. Beniamin & Susanna, b. Sept. 4, 1667	OL	19
Samuel, s. Benjamin, b. July 11, 1671	1	11
Samuel, s. Benjamin, b. July 11, 1671	OL	23
Sam[ue]ll, s. James, Jr. & Sarah, b. Apr. 11, 1743	1	124
Samuel, his w. [ ], d. Dec. 1, 1801	SM	73
Sarah, d. Benjamin, bp. [1645, by Rev. Peter Prudden]	OL	101
Sarah, w. Benjamin, adm. Church Sept. 20, [1640]; d. Apr. 29, 1663	OL	97
Sarah, bp. 1692	ES	238
Sarah, w. Benj[amin] adm. to Ch. 1693	ES	238
Sarah, d. Joseph, b. Apr. 23, 1724	1	73
Sarah, m. Sam[ue]ll MERCHANT, b. of Milford, Aug. 29, 1739, by Roger Newton, Asst.	1	109
Sarah, m. Nathan PLATT, June 30, 1757, by Rev. Sam[ue]ll Whittlesey	1	137
Sarah, d. [ ], 1810, ae. 43 y.	BP	20
Susannah, d. Benjamin & Susannah, b. May 4, 1669	1	14
Susannah, d. Benjamin & Susannah, b. May 4, 1669	OL	28
Susana, wid., d. Feb. 13, 1799, ae. 72	BP	1
Susanna, wid., d. Feb. 13, 1799	SM	66
Susanna, d. [ ], 1808	BP	17
W[illia]m, his child d. [ ], 1805	BP	12
W[illia]m, Col. his child d. [ ], 1815, ae. 3 y.	BP	29

FISH, [see also FISK], Benj[amin], s. John, bp. 1695   ES   238
   Phinehas, bp. 1682   ES   238

FISK, FISKE, FFISKE, [see also FISH], Ebenezer, adm. to Ch. 1719   ES   238

Hannah, m. Jeremiah PECK, Aug. 20, 1713, by Samuel Eells, Asst.	1	38
Hannah, m. Jeremiah PECK, Aug. 20, 1713, by Sam[ue]ll Eells, Asst.	OL	80
John, m. Hannah BALDWIN, Jan. 17, 1681, by Major Treat	OL	37
John, Dr., came to Milford, 1690	ES	177
John, dismissed from 1st Ch. In Wenham, 1694	ES	238
John, [dismissed from 1st Ch. In Wenham], 1704	ES	238
John, adm. to Ch. 1719	ES	238
Mehitabeel, m. Richard PLATT, Jr., Mar. 1, 1736/7, by Roger Newton, Asst.	1	105
Phinehas, s. John, b. Dec. 2, 1682	OL	39
Phinehas, s. John, b. Dec. 4, 1682	1	19

	Vol.	Page

FISK, FISKE, FFISKE, [see also **FISH**], (cont.)

Phinehas, adm. to Ch. 1705	ES	238

FITCH, FFITCH, Samuel, m. Mrs. Sarah **BRYAN**, Oct. 23, 1678, by

Major Robert Treat, D.G.	1	16
Samuell, m. Mrs. Sarah **BRYAN**, Oct. 23, 1678, by Major Robert Treat, D.G.	OL	33
Sarah, Mrs., m. Zachariah **WHITMAN**, Jan. 6, 1702/3, by Robert Treat, Dept. Gov.	1	26
Sarah, Mrs., m. Zachariah **WHITMAN**, Jan. 6, 1702/3, by Robert Treat, Dept. Gov.	OL	55

FLETCHER, FFLETCHER, Abigail, d. John, bp. [1652, by Rev.

Peter Prudden]	OL	104
Abigail, d. Newton, m. Nathan **CLARK**, [ ]	ES	238
Elizabeth, d. John, bp. [1645, by Rev. Peter Prudden]	OL	102
Elizabeth, m. Elnathan **BOTSFORD**, Dec. 12, 1664, by Benj[amin] Ffenn	1	6
Elizabeth, m. Elnathan **BOXFORD**, b. of Milford, Dec. 12, 1666	OL	17
Hannah, d. John, bp. [1643, by Rev. Peter Prudden]	OL	101
John, adm. Church Nov. 14, [1641]; d. Apr. 18, 1662	OL	98
Mary, w. John, adm. Church Dec. 19, [1641]; d. [ ] at Farmington	OL	98
Rebecca, d. of John, of Milford, m. Andrew **WARNER**, of Hartford, Oct. 10, 1653, by William Fowler, J.P.	1	1
Rebeckah, d. John, of Milford, m. Andrew **WARNER**, of Stratford*, Dec. 10, 1653, by Mr. Ffowler, Magestrate *(Hartford?)	OL	7
Rebecka, see Rebecka **WARNER**	OL	99
Sam[ue]l, d. [ ], 1649, ae. 6 wks	ES	35
Samuel, s. John, bp. [1649, by Rev. Peter Prudden]; d. at the age of 6 wks.	OL	103
Samuel, [bd.] Sept. 2, 1649, ae. 6 wks.	ES	238
Sam[ue]l, s. Jno, d. Sept. 2, 1649, ae. 6 wks.	ES	238
Sarah, d. John, bp. [1641, by Rev. Peter Prudden]	OL	100

FOOT, John, d. [   ], 1833   BP   70

FORD, FORDE, FFORD, FFORDE, Amos, d. [   ], 1835, ae.

70	BP	73
Ann*, m. Henry **PECK**, Feb. 8, 1722/3, by Sam[ue]ll Eells, Asst. *(Note in pencil "parents of wife of Jesse **LAMBERT**")	1	72
Anna, d. Oct. 3, 1776, ae. 4	SM	7
B, Capt. his child d. [ ], 1815, ae. 14 m.	BP	28
Catharine Miles, d. [ ], 1838, ae. 18	BP	80
Eben[eze]r, b. Aug. 26, 1734	1	113
Elizabeth, d. Thomas, bp., [1654, by Rev. Peter Prudden]	OL	104
Elizabeth, wid., m. Eleazer **ROGGERS**, Mar. 27, 1663	1	5
Elizabeth, wid., m. Eleazer **ROGGERS**, Mar. 27, 1663, by Benjamin Ffenn	OL	15
Elizabeth, m. Nathan **BALDWIN**, June 24, 1715, by Major Eells, Asst.	1	36
Elizabeth, m. Nathan **BALDWIN**, June 24, 1715, by Major Eells, Asst.	1	36
Elizabeth, m. Nathan **BALDWIN**, June 24, 1715, by Major Eells, Asst.	OL	77

	Vol.	Page
FORD, FORDE, FFORD, FFORDE, (cont.)		
Hezekiah, d. Oct. 10, 1776, ae. 23	SM	7
Hezekiah, d. [ ], 1823, ae. 26	BP	48
Isaac, Priv., member of Capt. Samuel Peck's Co., Milford, 1776	1	54
John, Jr., pd. £5 for not procuring men for Continental Army	1	55
John, s. Thomas, b. Nov. 14, 1654	1	2
John, s. Thom[as], b. Nov. 14, 1654	OL	8
John, s. John, bp. [1654, by Rev. Peter Prudden	OL	105
John, his child d. June [ ], 1779	SM	17
John, his infant s. [ ], d. Dec. 1, 1786	SM	32
John, d. [ ], 1810, ae. 69 y.	BP	20
John, his w. [ ], d. [ ], 1829, ae. 68	BP	59
John, d. [ ], 1835, ae. 76	BP	73
Lydia, d. Thomas, b. Mar. 16, 1661	1	4
Lidya, d. Thomas, b. Mar. 16, 1660/1	OL	13
Lidia, m. John **NEWTON**, Apr. 14, 1680, by Major Treat, Dept. Gov.	1	18
Lidia, m. John **NEWTON**, Apr. 14, 1680, by Major Robert Treat, Dept. Gov.	OL	35
Mary, d. Thomas, b. Dec. 24, 1658	OL	11
Mary, d. Thomas, b. Dec. 27, 1658	1	3
Mary, d. Jan. 17, 1739	1	113
Ruth, d. John, b. Mar. 17, 1707	1	31
Ruth, d. John, b. Mar. 17, 1707	OL	67
S. B., Dea. his w. [ ], d. [ ], 1838, ae. 48	BP	79
Samuel, his infant child d. [ ], 1818	BP	38
Sibel, d. Oct. 16, 1776, ae. 13	SM	8
Sybyl, wid., d. [ ], 1815, ae. 75	BP	30
Tho[mas], came to Milford, 1646	ES	177
Thomas, adm. Church May 7, [1653]; d. May 15, 1665	OL	99
Thomas, s. Thomas, b. Feb. 14, 1656	1	3
Thomas, s. Thom[as], b. Feb. 14, 1656	OL	9
Thomas, b. Oct. 29, 1740/1	1	113
Thomas, his s. [ ], d. June 20, 1794, ae. 3 y.	SM	51
Thomas, d. [ ], 1837	BP	77
-----, Col. his infant child d. [ ], 1820	BP	42
FORDHAM, -----, Mr., m. Elizabeth **BENNING**, [ ]	OL	98
-----, m. Eliz[abeth] **BENNING**, [ ]	ES	238
FOSTER, David, his infant s. [ ], d. Feb. 19, 1801	SM	71
Isaac(?), his twin s. & d. [ ], d. Dec. 8, 1794	SM	53
Luke, d. [ ], 1808, at Sea	BP	17
Martha, d. Nov. 25, 1785	SM	30
-----, Capt. his child d. [ ], 1801	BP	3
-----, m. Sarah **CARRINGTON**, d. Elias & Esther, [ ]	1	162
FOWLER, FFOWLER, FOWER, Abigail, d. William, Jr., b. Nov. 27, 1660	1	4
Abigail, d. William, Jr., b. Nov. 27, 1660	OL	13
Ann Harpin, [d. William Harpin & Sarah], b. Mar. 21, 1813	1	59
Charlotte, d. [William Harpin & Sarah], b. June 9, 1810	1	59
Clark, 2d s. Josiah, of No. Milford, m. Hetty Matilda (**LAMBERT**), [d. John & Esther], [ ] 1836, after 12 years' courtship	1	52
Deborah, d. Capt. W[illia]m, decd., m. Jesse **LAMBERT**, May 10,		

	Vol.	Page
FOWLER, FFOWLER, FOWER, (cont.)		
1683	1	24
Elizabeth, m. Nathan **CLARK**, June 29, 1710, by Sam[ue]ll Eells, J.P.	1	74
Eunice, d. William, Jr. & Eunice, b. Mar. 4, 1726	1	85
Eunicem m. Stephen **BALDWIN**, Sept. 15, 1730, by Roger Newton, J.P.	1	87
Eunice, m. Solomon **WHITEMORE**, June 14, 1749, by Jno Fowler, J.P.	1	131
Frances Susan, [d. John William & Jane (**HYDE**)], b. Jan. 25, 1856	1	59
Franklin Hamilton, s. John W[illiam] & Jane (**HYDE**), b. Feb. 19, 1841	1	59
Hannah, d. Sergt. William, m. Daniel **BUCKINGHAM**, Nov. 21, 1661, by Matthew Gilbert, Dept. Gov.	1	4
Hannah, m. Ebenezer **SMITH**, Jan. 9, 1719, by Major Eells, Asst.	1	78
Hannah, d. Jonathan, b. Nov. 27, 1729	1	89
Hannah, wid., d. Apr. 3, 1790, ae. 85	SM	41
Harpin, his child d. [ ], 1805	BP	11
Harriet Cannon, [d. John William & Jane (**HYDE**), b. [ ]	1	59
Jane Amanda, [d. John William & Jane (**HYDE**)], b. [ ]	1	59
John, in 1671, destroyed the Indian Fort	ES	14
John, s. Sarah, bp. 1690	ES	238
John, m. Susannah **BURWEL**, Feb. 28, 1712/13, by Sam[ue]ll Eells, Asst.	1	62
John, s. John & Susannah, b. Feb. 7, 1717/18	1	63
John, Jr., m. Mary **NEWTON**, Dec. 9, 1742, by John Fowler, J.P.	1	137
Jno, Jr., m. Mary **NEWTON**, Dec. 9, 1742	ES	238
John, Capt., 1743	ES	40
John, 4[th], s. John & Mary, b. Aug. 21, 1748	1	137
John, Capt., d. Aug. 30, 1756	1	158
John, Capt., d. Aug. 30, 1756	ES	238
John, Sr., Capt., d. Aug. 30, 1756	ES	238
John, Capt., d. Aug. 30, 1756; had s. Town Clerk as late as 1774	ES	238
John, Jr., m. Mary Ann **HARPIN**, Oct. 22, 1767, by Rev. Sam[ue]ll Whittlesey	1	162
John, Jr., m. Mary Ann **HARPIN**, Oct. 22, 1767. Witnesses, John Fowler, Susanna Fowler	1	164
John, s. John & Mary Ann, b. Oct. 7, 1769	1	162
John, s. John & Mary Ann, b. Oct. 7, 1769	1	164
John, d. May 14, 1781, ae. 63	SM	21
John, his youngest child d. Oct. 10, 1784, ae. 4 y.	SM	28
John, Lieut., d. Aug. 17, 1787, ae. 39	SM	34
John, his infant s. [ ], d. June 6, 1789	SM	40
John, d. Oct. 13, 1790, ae. 21	SM	43
John, d. Oct. 25, 1802	SM	76
John, his child d. [ ], 1809, ae. 5 d.	BP	19
John William, s. [William Harpin & Sarah], b. Aug. 5, 1807	1	59
John William, only s. [William Harpin & Sarah], b. Aug. 5, 1807; m. Jane **HYDE**, of Bridgeport, d. Richard Henry, Aug. 10, 1837	1	59
John William, 2nd. s. [John William & Jane (**HYDE**)], b. Mar. 13,		

	Vol.	Page
FOWLER, FFOWLER, FOWER, (cont.)		
1843; d. Jan. 4, 1844	1	59
Jonathan, in 1671, destroyed the Indian Fort	ES	14
Jonathan, s. William, b. Oct. 27, 1704	1	25
Jonathan, s. William, b. Oct. 27, 1704	OL	52
Jonathan, m. Hannah **CLARK**, Jan. 9, 1728/9, by Sam[ue]ll Eells, Asst.	1	89
Jonathan, s. Jonathan & Hannah, b. Aug. 10, 1735	1	130
Jonathan, d. Sept. 21, 1789, ae. 55	SM	40
Joseph, his infant s. [ ], d. Dec. 21, 1799	SM	68
Joseph, his infant child d. [ ], 1799	BP	2
Joseph, his infant, d. [ ], 1802	BP	6
Joseph, his child d. [ ], 1811	BP	21
Joseph, his w. [ ], d. [ ], 1812, ae. 19 y.	BP	24
Joseph, his infant child d. [ ], 1824	BP	50
Joseph, Jr., d. [ ], 1825	BP	52
Joseph, his w. [ ], d. [ ], 1826	BP	55
Josiah, his child d. [ ], 1813	BP	25
Lucille Augusta, d. [John William & Jane (**HYDE**)], b. Apr. 2, 1845	1	59
M. A., had negro Sherman, d. Oct. 23, 1790	SM	43
Marcy, d. Lieut. William, b. Apr. 1, 1669	1	10
Margaret, d. William, b. Oct. 4, 1698	1	25
Marg[ar]et, d. William, b. Oct. 4, 1698	OL	52
Margarett, d. John & Susannah, b. June 8, 1715	1	63
Mark, 3rd s. John & Mary, b. Nov. 10, 1782	1	59
Martha, [d. William Harpin & Sarah], b. May 16, 1799	1	59
Mary, w. John, d. Mar. 28, 1774	1	164
Mary, d. Feb. 2, 1792, ae. 24	SM	47
Mary, d. William Harpin & Sarah, b. Sept. 16, 1797	1	59
Mary, mother of Deborah and w. of William, was d. of Edmund & Anne **TAPP** and sister of Jane (**TAPP**) **TREAT**	1	48
Mary Ann, wid., d. Nov. 24, 1798	SM	65
Mary Jane, [d. John William & Jane (**HYDE**)], b. June 10, 1846	1	59
Mercy, d. Lieut. [ ], b. Apr. 1, 1669; m. John **BETTS**, of Lebanon, [ ]	OL	22
Nathan, s. Jonathan & Hannah, b. July 22, 1741	1	130
Nathan, his w. [ ], d. Sept. 2, 1798	SM	64
Nathan, Jr., his child d. [ ], 1799, ae. 3 y. 7 m.	BP	2
Nathan, Jr., his s. [ ], d. Sept. 3, 1799, ae. 3 ½ y.	SM	67
Nathan, d. [ ], 1818	BP	38
Nathan, his w. [ ], d. [ ], 1818	BP	38
Nathan, his w. [ ], d. [ ], 1819	BP	39
Sarah, d. Sergt. William, m. Daniell **BUCKINGHAM**, b. of Milford, Nov. 21, 1661, by Matthew Gilbert, Dept. Gov.	OL	14
Sarah, d. Lieut. [ ], m. John **SMITH**, blacksmith, July 19, 1665, by Mr. Ffenn, Magistrate	1	7
Sarah, d. Lieut. William, m. John **SMITH**, blacksmith, b. of Milford, July 19, 1665, by Mr. Ffenn, Magestrate	OL	18
Sarah, d. John & Susannah, b. Aug. 1, 1723	1	74
Sarah, m. Richard **BRYAN**, Jr., Jan. 13, 1742. Witnesses John Fowler, Mary Fowler	1	158
Sarah, m. Richard **BRYAN**, July 13, 1742	ES	238

MILFORD VITAL RECORDS 83

	Vol.	Page
FOWLER, FFOWLER, FOWER, (cont.)		
Sarah, [d. William Harpin & Sarah], b. Apr. 28, 1804	1	59
Sarah, see Sarah NEWTON	1	74
Stephen, s. John & Mary, b. Mar. 9, 1752; d. same day	1	137
Susan, [d. William Harpin & Sarah], b. Aug. 23, 1802	1	59
Susan Ann, d. [ ], 1820	BP	42
Susannah, d. John & Susannah, b. Dec. 8, 1712. Was drowned Sept. 13, 1727, off Milford harbor now Tomilstone, bd. in H. Fowler's lot	1	62
Susanna, w. John, d. Mar. 18, 1744	1	158
Susannah, d. John & Mary, b. Aug. 12, 1744	1	137
William, agent of the 1st purchase	ES	1
William, original member of First Church gathered at New Haven Aug. 22, 1639	ES	57
William, d. Dec. [ ], 1660 (One of the first planters)	ES	16
William, Sr., d. Jan. 21, 1660/1	OL	13
William, Sr., d. Jan. 25, 1660/1	1	4
William, d. July* 25, 1660/1 *(Jan.)	OL	97
William, s. Lieut William, b. [ ], 1664	1	6
William, Lieut. Widower, m. Elizabeth BALDWIN, wid., Nov. 1, 1670, by John Clarke, Commissioner	1	10
William, Lieut., widower, m. Elizabeth BALDWIN, wid., Nov. 15, 1670, by John Clark, Com.	OL	23
William, 2d, Capt., 1677	ES	40
William, s. William, b. Mar. 14, 1700	1	25
William, s. William, b. Mar. 17, 1700	OL	52
William, Jr., m. Eunice HAYS, Apr. 1, 1724, by Sam[ue]ll Clark, J.P.	1	85
William, Jr., d. Mar. 7, 1727	1	85
William, s. Jonathan & Hannah, b. July 22, 1732	1	130
William, Jr., d. Dec. 8, 1785	SM	30
William, d. [ ], 1809, at N. Milford	BP	18
William, Capt., s. William, [m.] Mary TAPP, d. Edmund & Anne, [ ]	1	48
William Harpin, 2nd s. John & Mary, b. Oct. 29, 1775; m. Sally POND, 2nd d. Capt. Charles & Martha (MILES), Dec. 18, 1796	1	59
-----, wid., d. [ ], 1660	ES	238
-----, Mrs., d. [ ], 1808, at North Milford	BP	17
FRANKLIN, -----, his w. [ ], d. [ ], 1830	BP	63
FREEMAN, FFREEMAN, Cubitt, see Jabez CAREBEE	OL	68
Hannah, w. Stephen & d. Capt. ASTWOOD, adm. Church Sept. 17, [1653], by Mr. Prudden	OL	99
Hannah, b. Feb. the last, 1655	1	2
Hannah, d. Stephen, b. Feb. the last, 1655	OL	9
Hannah, d. Stephen, bp. [1656, by Rev. Peter Prudden]	OL	105
Hannah*, [wid. 1659 and 1662]; was d. of John ASTWOOD *(Written "Hannah FAIRMAN")	ES	238
Jabez, see Jabez CAREBEE	1	32
John, s. Stephen, b. Oct. 13, 1654	1	2
John, s. Stephen, b. Oct. 13, 1654	OL	8
John, s. John*, d. Dec. 24, 1654 *(Stephen(?)	1	2

	Vol.	Page
FREEMAN, FFREEMAN, (cont.)		
John, s. Stephen, d. Dec. 24, 1654	OL	8
John, s. Stephen, bp. [1654, by Rev. Peter Prudden]	OL	105
Mary, d. Stephen, b. Nov. 15, 1658	1	3
Mary, d. Stephen, b. Nov. 15, 1658	OL	11
Samuel, s. Stephen, b. Dec. 1, 1662	1	5
Samuell, s. Stephen, b. Dec. 1, 1662	OL	15
Stephen, adm. Church Feb. 25, [1648]	OL	99
Step[ ], came to Milford, 1658	ES	177
Steven, s. Steven, b. Feb. 7, 1660 (d.?)	OL	13
Stephen, s. Stephen, b. Feb. 20, 1660/1	1	4
Stephen, s. Stephen, d. Apr. 1, 1661	1	4
Steven, s. Steven, [b.] Apr. 1, 1661	OL	13
FRENCH, FFRENCH, Andrew, Dr., his child d. [ ], 1833, ae. 5	BP	68
Anna, d. Francis, of Derby, m. Thomas **WHEELER**, of Milford, June 1, 1685	1	21
Anna, d. Francis, of Derby, m. Thomas **WHEELER**, of Milford, June 1, 1685, at the house	OL	42
Bill, d. Feb. 9, 1799 (A French resident)	BP	1
Elizabeth Dudley, d. Jeremiah & Elizabeth, b. May 9, 1832	1	178
Ffrancis, of Pagasset (Derby), m. Lydia **BUNNELL**, of Milford, Apr. 10, 1661	1	4
Francis, of Paganick, m. Lydia **BUNNELL**, of Milford, Apr. 10, 1661	OL	14
Martha Maria, d. Jeremiah & Elizabeth P., d. Mar. 26, 1831, ae. 5 y.	1	178
Mary, d. of Frances, of Derby, m. Silvanus **BALDWIN**, Apr. 18, 1734, by Rev. Daniel Humpheres, of Derby	1	99
-----, his child d. [ ], 1831	BP	64
FRINK, -----, Mr. a stranger at Kelsey's, d. [ ], 1833	BP	70
FRISBY, Benjamin, of Harwinton, d. Jan. [ ], 1777	SM	9
FULLER, David, 3rd pastor of 2nd Church, Nov. 17, 1784; dismissed Dec. [ ], 1802	ES	93
GABRIEL, Anthony, s. Peter & Sarah, b. Dec. 15, 1772	1	166
Henry, s. Peter & Sarah, b. May 25, 1766	1	154
Henry, his w. [ ], d. [ ], 1807	BP	15
Henry, his child d. [ ], 1815, ae. 2 y.	BP	29
Peter, s. Peter & Sarah, b. Nov. 17, 1768	1	166
Peter, Priv., member of Capt. Samuel Peck's Co., Milford, 1776	1	54
Peter, his child d. [ ], 1802	BP	5
Peter, Jr., his s. [ ], d. Sept. 1, 1802	SM	75
Peter, d. [ ], 1811	BP	23
GALPIN, Hannah, of Middletown, m. Samuel **HIGBY**, Nov. 13, 1783, by Rev. Nathan Fenn. Removed to Milford, May 4, 1784	1	176
Sarah, d. Moses, b. July 23, 1770; m. Nehemiah **LAMBERT**, s. Jesse & Anne, [ ]	1	50
-----, Mr. from Berlin, d. [ ], 1816, ae. 36	BP	34
GARDINER, Daniel, heard of death in North Carolina, Aug. 7, 1799	SM	67
Daniel, d. [July], 1799, abroad	BP	1
GARNSEY, [see under **GUERNSEY**]		
GIBB, GIBBS, Edward, had Phillis, d. Nov. 8, 1785; drowned in Derby		

	Vol.	Page
GIBB, GIBBS, (cont.)		
And buried in Milford	SM	30
Esther, d. Thomas [& Esther], b. July 23, 1732	1	95
Eunice, Mrs., d. [ ], 1826, ae. 88	BP	55
Hannah, wid., d. July 15, 1779	SM	18
John, pd. £5 for not procuring men for Continental Army	1	55
John, s. Thomas & Esther, b. June 28, 1730	1	95
John, Jr., his infant d. [ ], d. June 29, 1788	SM	37
John, Jr., his w. [ ], d. Oct. 18, 1788	SM	37
John, Jr., d. [ ], 1790, at Sea	SM	43
John, Capt., d. [ ], 1809	BP	18
Lucy, of Derby, d. [ ], 1794	SM	53
Polly, of Derby, d. [ ], 1794	SM	53
Thomas, m. Mrs. Esther **BRYAN**, Aug. 20, 1729, by Sam[ue]ll Eells, Asst.	1	95
Tho[mas], m. Esther **BRYAN**, Aug. [ ], 1729	ES	238
-----, Mrs. had a Frenchman d. Mar. 3, 1776	SM	5
GIBSON, GIPSON, Abigaill, d. David & Abigaill, b. Sept. 1, 1726	1	90
Ann, d. David & Abigail, b. Aug. 2, 1732	1	93
David, m. Abigail **BRIMSMEAD**, Aug. [ ], 1724, by Major Sam[ue]ll Eells, Asst.	1	75
David, m. Abigail **BRIMSMEAD**, d. John & Abigail, Aug. 20, 1724, by Samuell Eells, Asst.	1	90
David, s. David & Abigaill, b. Feb. 26, 1728/9	1	90
Mary, d. David & Abigaill, b. Nov. 30, 1740	1	110
Sarah, wid., d. Dec. [ ], 1777	SM	14
William, d. Sept. 18, 1703	1	40
William, d. Sept. 18, 1703	OL	86
William, s. David & Abigaill, b. Feb. 13, 1735/6	1	103
GILBERT, Hannah, d. of William, of New Haven, decd., m. Thomas **CLARKE**, s. of George, Sr., May 20, 1663, by Robert Treat	1	5
Hannah, d. Will., of New Haven, decd., m. Thomas **CLARK**, s. George, Jr., May 20, 1663, by Rob[ert] Treat	OL	15
Hannah, d. Dept. Gov. Nath[aniel], m. Tho[mas] **CLARK**, s. Geo[rge] Sr., [ ], 1663	ES	184
-----, came to Milford, 1660	ES	177
GILKEY, Peter, Priv., member of Capt. Samuel Peck's Co., Milford 1776	1	54
GILLETT, GILIT, GILLETT, GILLIT, GILLITT, JELLET, Abell, s. Will[ia]m, b. Jan. 21, 1728/9	1	85
Abraham, s. Eliphal, b. Nov. 12, 1705	1	27
Abraham, s. Eliphall, b. Nov. 12, 1705	OL	59
Agnes, d. Eliphal, b. Mar. 19, 1715/16	1	37
Agnis, d. Eliphal, b. Mar. 19, 1715/16	OL	81
Ben, his w. [ ], d. [ ], 1822	BP	47
Benjamin, his infant child d. Jan. 23, 1796	SM	58
Benjamin, his child d. July 22, 1799	BP	1
Benjamin, his infant s. [ ], d. July 22, 1799	SM	67
Bryan, heard of death at Sea, May 28, 1798	SM	63
Elphal, s. Elipal, b. Mar. 22, 1719	1	65
Elisha, s. Will[ia]m, b. Aug. 17, 1733	1	96

	Vol.	Page
GILLETT, GILIT, GILLETT, GILLIT, GILLITT, JELLET, (cont.),		
Elizabeth, d. Will[ia]m & Elizabeth, b. Nov. 5, 1723	1	74
Francis, [child of Jeremiah & Francis], b. Dec. 16, 1725	1	85
Frances, m. Stephen MILES, May 1, 1734, by Sam[ue]ll Gunn, J.P.	1	99
Hannah, d. Eliphal, b. Oct. 26, 1710	1	32
Hannah, d. Eliphall, b. Oct. 26, 1710	OL	68
Hannah, d. Dec. 5, 1776, at the house of Ezra Merchant	SM	8
Jeremiah, m. Francis BRYAN, July 16, 1725, by Sam[uell Eells, Asst.	1	85
Jeremiah, d. Dec. 24, 1732	1	106
Jeremiah, s. Ephraim, b. Dec. 18, 1734	1	102
John, his d. [ ], d. Apr. 26, 1776	SM	5
John, Jr., his s. [ ], d. Aug. 1, 1789	SM	40
John, drafted for Continental Army	1	58
John William, Priv., member of Capt. Samuel Peck's Co., Milford 1776	1	54
John William, d. Oct. 22, 1786, ae. 33	SM	31
Jonathan, s. Eliphall, b. Sept. 16, 1703	1	22
Jonathan, s. Eliphall, b. Sept. 16, 1703	OL	46
Jon[a]th[an], s. Ephraim, b. Feb. 17, 1737	1	106
Joseph, d. May 17, 1783, ae. 1 ½ y.	SM	25
Mary, d. Eliphal & Mary (WHEELER), b. 1695; m. Jesse LAMBERT, Jr., Dec. 6, 1716, by Jonathan Law; d. June 6, 1776	1	49
Mary, d. Eliphal, b. [ ], 1695; m. Jesse LAMBERT, Dec. 6, 1716, by Jonathan Law	1	106
Mary, d. Eliphal & Mary (WHEELER), m. Jesse LAMBERT, Dec. 6, 1716, by Jonathan Law	1	39
Mary, m. Jesse LAMBERT, Dec. 6, 1716, by Jon[a]th[an] Law	OL	85
Mary, d. Jeremiah, b. Apr. 6, 1729	1	85
Mary, wid., d. [ ], 1829	BP	59
Rachel, d. Eliphal, b. Feb. 17, 1707/8	1	29
Rachel, d. Elipal, b. Feb. 17, 1707/8	OL	63
Sarah, m. Joseph SUMMERS, of Milford, Mar. 4, 1729/30, by Roger Newton, J.P.	1	90
Sarah, d. Jeremiah, b. Jan. 30, 1731/2	1	106
William, m. Elizabeth WELCH, Nov. 14, 1722, by Sam[ue]ll Clark, J.P.	1	74
William, d. June 5, 1780	SM	20
William, s. John W., d. [ ], 1800, supposed to have been lost at Sea	SM	71
William, s. D[ ], d. [ ], 1800, supposed to have been lost at Sea	SM	71
Zebulon, Dr., d. [ ], 1810, ae. 73	BP	20
GIPSON, [see under GIBSON]		
GLENNEY, GLENNY, Charlotte, d. William & Mary, b. Sept. 14, 1787	1	176
Daniel S., d. [ ], 1819	BP	39
Daniel S[ackett], s. William & Mary, b. Mar. 3, 1794	1	176
Jonas, s. William & Mary, b. Apr. 11, 1799	1	176

	Vol.	Page
GLENNEY, GLENNY, (cont.)		
Jonas, d. [ ], 1817, at Sea	BP	36
Maria, d. William & Mary, b. June 15, 1786	1	176
W., had negro man d. [ ], 1808	BP	17
William, s. William & Mary, b. Feb. 28, 1792	1	176
W[illia]m, Capt., heard of his death at Sea, Dec. 17, 1800	SM	70
W[illia]m, his child d. [ ], 1813	BP	31
-----, Capt. Had stranger colored d. at his house, [ ], 1832	BP	66
GLOVER, GLOVE, Elizabeth, had s. Samuel **LOVEMAN**, b. June 14, 1741	1	112
-----, his infant d. [ ], 1836	BP	75
GOLD, Ann, d. William, b. May 4, 1710	1	31
Ann, d. William, b. May 4, 1710	OL	68
Job, s. William, b. Jan. 10, 1711/12	1	34
Job, s. William, b. Jan. 10, 1711/12	OL	73
William, m. Abigail **DISBOROUGH**, Nov. 28, 1706	1	27
William, m. Abigail **DISBOROUGH**, Nov. 28, 1706	OL	59
William, s. William, b. Nov. 4, 1707	1	29
William, s. William, b. Nov. 4, 1707	OL	63
William, m. Mary **ATKINS**, Apr. 12, 1716, by Jonathan Law, J.P.	1	37
William, m. [ ] **ADKINS**, Apr. 12, 1716, by Jon[a]th[an] Law, J.P.	OL	80
GOLDSMITH, A. & James Rich, had s. [ ], d. June 21, 1796	SM	59
Gilbert, his d. [ ], d. Jan. 12, 1788	SM	36
Gillett, his d. [ ], d. Apr. 10, 1788	SM	36
Gillett, d. Apr. 7, 1793, at Sea (Heard of death)	SM	49
James, pd. £5 for not procuring men for Continental Army	1	55
James, drafted for Continental Army	1	57
James, d. [ ], ae. about 20 y.	ES	165
James, his 1st w. [ ], d. Oct. [ ], 1787 (Entry crossed out)	SM	34
James, his 1st w. [ ], d. Nov. 5, 1787	SM	35
James, Jr., his infant s. [ ], d. Feb. 20, 1793	SM	49
James, d. Dec. 8, 1795	SM	56
Joseph, drafted for Continental Army	1	58
William, his 2nd d. [ ], d. Oct. 18, 1785	SM	30
William, his s. [ ], d. July 9, 1787, ae. 3 m.	SM	33
William, d. July 26, 1799	BP	2
William, d. Aug. 12, 1799	SM	67
W[illia]m, his child d. [ ], 1824	BP	51
William, his child d. [ ], 1825	BP	53
William, drafted for Continental Army	1	57
William, d. [ ]	ES	165
-----, Jr., his child d. [ ], 1806, ae. 7 y.	BP	14
GOODWIN, GOODIN, Mary, m. Josiah **TERRELL**, Jan. 1, 1723/4, by Sam[ue]ll Eells, Asst.	1	73
Rejoyce, m. Hezekiah **RUE**, Mar. 12, 1718/19, by Jonathan Law, Asst.	1	67
Ruth, d. Thomas, b. Sept. 2, 1662	1	5
Ruth, d. Thomas, b. Sept. 2, 1662	OL	15
Thomas, m. Ruth **ROGERS**, d. of John, Nov. 9, 1661, by Mr.		

	Vol.	Page
GOODWIN, GOODIN, (cont.)		
Ffenn, Magistrate	1	4
Thomas, m. Ruth **ROGERS**, d. John, b. of Milford, Nov. 9, 1661, by Benjamin Fenn, Magestrate	OL	14
GOODYEAR, Abigail, of New Haven, m. Samuel **BURWELL,** of Milford, Jan. 12, 1726/7, by Sam[ue]ll Eells, Asst.	1	92
Esther, m. Ebenezer **BRYAN,** July 15, 1713, by John Allen, Asst.	1	77
Louis, d. of Stephen, of Hamden, a descendant of Stephen **GOODYEAR,** of New Haven, m. Jeremiah Bull **LAMBERT,** [s. Edward A. & Martha], Oct. 29, 1834; moved to Bath, Ohio, in spring of 1837	1	52
Stephen, see under Louis **GOODYEAR**	1	52
Theophilus, Priv., member of Capt. Samuel Peck's Co., Milford 1776	1	54
GOULD, Nath[an], came to Milford, 1646	ES	177
Samuel, s. William, b. Mar. 15, 1716/17	1	39
Sam[ue]ll, s. William, b. Mar. 15, 1716/17	OL	84
GRANNIS, David, Priv., member of Capt. Samuel Peck's Co., Milford 1776	1	54
GRAVES, -----, Mr., d. [, 1813]	BP	33
GRAY, Hugh, m. Mrs. [ ] **TIBBALLS,** [ ], by Robert Treat, Justice	1	20
Hugh, m. Mrs. Sibella **BRYAN,** [ ], by Robert Treat, Dept. Gov.	OL	43
William, his s. [ ], d. Jan. 6, 1790, ae. 2 y.	SM	41
GREEN, GREENE, Eli, his child d. [ ], 1801	BP	3
Eli, his s. [ ], d. Jan. 15, 1801, ae. 1 y.	SM	71
Eli, his d. [ ], d. Oct. 29, 1804	SM	81
Eli, his child d. [ ], 1804, ae. 8 y.	BP	9
Eli, Jr., d. [ ], 1816	BP	35
Elias, Mrs. her child d. [ ], 1817 (blind)	BP	37
Isaac, d. June 22, 1790, ae. 63	SM	42
John Still, d. Apr. 15, 1782, ae. 21	SM	23
Jonas, Capt., d. June 23, 1789, ae. 58	SM	40
Joseph, his w. [ ], d. July 5, 1781, ae. 47	SM	21
Joseph, his child d. [ ], 1805	BP	11
Joseph, Capt., d. [ ], 1821, Kentucky	BP	45
Joseph, pd. £5 for not procuring men for Continental Army	1	55
Martha, m. Daniel **SOCKETT,** June 16, 1763, by Samuel Wales	1	164
Mary, d. [ ], 1816, ae. 14	BP	35
Sally, d. [ ], 1816, ae. 23	BP	35
Samuel, d. Apr. 28, 1777; killed in battle at Danbury	SM	12
Samuel, his d. [ ], d. Nov. 17, 1804	SM	81
Samuel, Capt. his child d. [ ], 1809	BP	18
Samuel, drafted for Continental Army	1	57
Sarah, wid., d. Dec. 16, 1804	SM	81
Sarah, wid., d. [ ], 1804	BP	10
-----, Capt. his Indian boy d. Oct. 15, 1776	SM	8
-----, Mrs., d. [ ], 1805	BP	12
-----, wid., d. [ ], 1838	BP	79
GREGORY, Elisha, of Mass., d. Jan. [ ], 1777	SM	10
GUERNSEY, GARNSEY, Abigail, d. Jon[a]th[an], b. Oct. 29, 1726	1	83

	Vol.	Page
GUERNSEY, GARNSEY, (cont.)		
Hannah, d. Joseph, b. Mar. 4, 1677/8	1	17
Hannah, d. Joseph, b. Mar. 4, 1677/8	OL	34
John, [twin with Peter], s. Joseph, Jr., b. Apr. 6, 1709	1	30
John, [twin with Peter], s. Joseph, Jr., b. Apr. 6, 1709	OL	65
Jonathan, m. Abigail **NORTHROP**, Jan. 6, 1724/5, by Sam[ue]ll Eells, Asst.	1	77
Jonathan, s. Jon[a]th[an], b. Feb. 28, 1728/9	1	83
Jonathan, s. Jon[a]th[an] & Abigail, b. Feb. 28, 1728/9	1	87
Joseph, m. Hannah **COLEY**, d. Samuel, Sr., Apr. 10, 1673, by John Clarke, Commissioner	1	12
Joseph, m. Hannah **COLEY**, d. Samuel, Sr., Apr. 10, 1673, by John Clark, Com.	OL	25
Joseph, s. Joseph, b. Jan. 13, 1674	1	14
Joseph, s. Joseph, b. Jan. 13, 1674	OL	28
Joseph, came to Milford, [ ]	ES	177
Mary, d. Joseph, b. May 1, [ ]	OL	37
Peter, [twin with John], s. Joseph, Jr., b. Apr. 6, 1709	1	30
Peter, [twin with John], s. Joseph, Jr., b. Apr. 6, 1709	OL	65
Peter, m. Ann **GUNN**, d. Nath[anie]ll, Dec. 9, 1731, by Samuel Gunn, J.P.	1	94
Peter, s. Peter & Ann, b. July 31, 1732	1	94
Peter, s. Peter & Ann, d. Mar. 22, 1733	1	96
-----, m. Ann **GUNN**, d. Nathan[ie]l, [ ]	OL	84
GUNN, GUN, Abel, s. Jasper, bp. [1643, by Rev. Peter Prudden]	OL	101
Abel, s. Joshua, m. Mary **SMITH**, d. John, b. of Milford, Oct. 29, 1666, by Mr. Ffenn, Magestrate	OL	19
Abel, s. Jasper, m. Mary **SMITH**, d. John, Oct. 29, 1667, by Mr. Ffenn, Magistrate	1	8
Abell, s. Jobamah, b. May 5, 1680	OL	36
Abigail, d. Ens. Samuel, b. Mar. 29, 1699	1	32
Abigail, d. Ens. Sam[ue]ll [& Mercy], b. Mar. 29, 1699	OL	69
Abner, s. Nathaniel, b. Aug. 2, 1719	1	66
Abner, formerly of Milford, now of New Milford, d. 1778	SM	16
Abner, wid., d. May 31, 1795, at New Milford (non resident)	SM	57
Ann, d. Nathaniel, b. Aug. 25, 1712	1	39
Ann, d. Nathan[ie]l, b. Aug. 25, 1712; m. [ ] [**GARNSEY**, [ ]	OL	84
Ann, d. Nath[anie]ll, m. Peter **GARNSEY**, Dec. 9, 1731, by Samuel Gunn, J.P.	1	94
Ann, d. Stephen [& Susannah], b. Dec. 28, 1758; d. Feb. 14, 1842	1	152
Ann, d. Stephen, m. Jeremiah **BULL**, s. Jabez Benedict & Naomi], Aug. 30, 1780	1	45
Anna, wid., d. May 24, 1787, ae. 96	SM	33
Anne, m. Jeremiah **BULL**, Aug. 30, 1780, by Rev. Samuel Wales	1	152
Christian, d. Jobamah, b. Aug. 3, 1677	1	16
Christian, d. Jobamah, b. Aug. 3, 1677	OL	31
Christian, m. Haney **BOTCHFORD**, Nov. 12, 1700, by Rob[er]t Treat, Dept. Gov.	OL	45
Christiania, m. Henry **BOTCHFORD**, Nov. 12, 1700, by Robert Treat, Dept. Gov.	1	21

	Vol.	Page
GUNN, GUN, (cont.)		
Daniel, s. Jasper, bp. [1645, by Rev. Peter Prudden]	OL	102
Elizabeth, d. Jobamah, b. Apr. 5, 1672	1	11
Elizabeth, d. Jobamah, b. Apr. 5, 1672	OL	24
George, d. [ ], 1829, ae. 21	BP	60
Isaac, d. Jan. 25, 1776, ae. 30	SM	5
Isaac, d. [ ], 1830	BP	62
Isaiah, s. Ens. Samuel, b. May 14, 1710	1	32
Isaiah, s. Ens. Sam[ue]ll, b. May 14, 1710; did not marry	OL	69
Jasper, 1st physician of Milford	ES	32
Jasper, physician, adm. Church Apr. 25, [1641]; d. Jan. 12, 1670	OL	98
Jasper, [d.] Aug. [ ], 1670	ES	16
Jobamah, s. Jasper, m. Sarah S. **LANE**, d. John, Oct. 30, 1663	1	6
Jobamah, s. Jasper, m. Sarah **LANE**, d. John, b. of Milford, Oct. 30, 1663	OL	15
John, d. July 7, 1776, ae. 36	SM	6
John, d. [ ], 1823, ae. 23	BP	49
Lazarus, s. Ens. Samuel, b. Oct. 14, 1707	1	32
Lazarus, s. Ens. Sam[ue]ll, b. Oct. 14, 1707; did not marry	OL	69
Mary, w. Jasper, adm. Church Apr. 25, [1641]; dismissed to Church of Hatfield	OL	98
Mary, d. Ens. Samuel, b. May 7, 1713	1	34
Mary, d. Ens. Sam[ue]ll, b. May 7, 1713	OL	73
Mary, m. Amos **NORTHROP**, Jan. 6, 1714, by Sam[ue]l Eells, Asst.	1	62
Mary, wid., d. Jan. 28, 1789	SM	39
Mehitabel, d. Jasper, bp. [1641, by Rev. Peter Prudden]	OL	100
Mehittable, d. Jasper, m. Benjamin **FFENN**, s. Benjamin, b. of Milford, Dec. 20, 1660, by Robert Treat, Magestrate	OL	13
Mehetable, d. of Jasper, m. Benjamin **FFENN**, s. of Benjamin, Dec. 21, 1660, by Robert Treat, Magistrate	1	4
Nathan, s. Nathaniel, b. Nov. 28, 1716	1	39
Nathan, s. Nathaniel, b. Nov. 28, 1716; settled in New Milford	OL	84
Nathaniel, s. Jobamah, b. July 21, 1682	1	21
Nathaniel, s. Jobamah, b. July 27, 1682	OL	42
Nathaniel, m. Ann **HINE**, May 31, 1711, by Samuel Andrews, Clerk	1	33
Nathaniel, m. Ann **HINE**, May last day, 1711, by Samuel Andrews, Clerk	OL	70
Samuel, s. Jobamah, b. Jan. 15, 1669	1	10
Samuel, s. Jobamah, b. Jan. 15, 1669	OL	22
Samuel, m. Mercy **SMITH**, Nov. 11, 1697	OL	69
Samuel, m. Mercy **SMITH**, Nov. 11, 1698	1	32
Samuel, s. Ens. Samuel, b. Aug. 25, 1701	1	32
Samuell, s. Ens. Sam[ue]ll [& Mercy], b. Aug. 25, 1701	OL	69
Samuel, his s. [ ], d. Nov. 5, 1804	SM	81
Samuel, his child d. [ ], 1804	BP	9
Samuel, Capt., his child d. [ ], 1804	BP	10
Samuel B., d. [ ], 1838, ae. 70	BP	79
Sarah, d. Jeremiah, b. Mar. 30, 1674	1	13
Sarah, d. Jobamah, b. Mar. 30, 1674	OL	26
Sarah, d. Ens. Samuel, b. Feb. 12, 1704/5	1	32
Sarah, d. Ens. Sam[ue]ll, b. Feb. 12, 1704/5; m. Ephraim		

	Vol.	Page
GUNN, GUN, (cont.)		
NORTHROP, s. W[illia]m N. [ ]	OL	69
Sarah, d. Samuel, m. Ephraim NORTHROP, Nov. 26, 1730	1	46
Sarah, m. Ephraim NORTHROP, Nov. 26, 1730, by Sam[ue]ll Gunn, J.P.	1	97
Stephen, s. Nathaniel, b. Nov. 18, 1725	1	79
Stephen, m. Susannah OVIATT, Nov. 28, 1757, by Roger Newton, Asst.	1	152
Stephen, [s. Stephen & Susannah], b. May [ ], 1768	1	152
Stephen, his w. [ ], d. Nov. 30, 1780, ae. 52	SM	20
Stephen, chosen Dea. Aug. 31, 1786	ES	238
Stephen, d. [ ], 1812, ae. 87	BP	24
Stephen, his w. [ ], d. [ ], 1826	BP	54
Stephen, his infant d. [ ], 1827	BP	56
Stephen, d. [ ], 1829, ae. 63	BP	60
Stephen, pd. £5 for not procuring men for Continental Army	1	55
Susannah, [d. Stephen & Susannah], b. July 14, 1764	1	152
Susanna, wid., d. [ ], 1831, ae. 80	BP	64
-----, Mrs., d. [ ], 1820, ae. 83	BP	41
HALL, Eunice, of Wallingford, m. Samuel ANDREW, Jr., of Milford, Dec. 9, 1719, by Capt. John Hall, of Wallingford, J.P.	1	69
Eunice, of Wallingford, m. Samuel ANDREW, Jr. [s. Rev. Samuel], Dec. 9, 1719	ES	238
HAMLIN, Jonathan, d. Sept. 19, 1786, ae. 16	SM	31
HAND, James, s. John, of The Isle of Wight, bp. [1647, by Rev. Peter Prudden]; brought up by Brother Brooks	OL	102
HARPIN, HARPIEN, HARPINE, HERPIN, Ann, d. Dr. John, b. May 19, 1724	1	78
Charlotte, d. John, Jr. & Mary, b. Jan. 18, 1762	1	145
Elizabeth, d. Dr. John & Mary, b. Dec. 25, 1728	1	94
Elizabeth, Mrs., m. Samuel ANDREWS, Nov. 3, 1748, by Jonathan Law, Gov.	1	127
Elizabeth, Mrs., m. Sam[ue]ll HARPIN*, Nov. 3, 1748 *(Probably "ANDREWS")	ES	238
Esther, d. Dr. John [& Mary], b. Nov. 16, 1730	1	94
Frances, d. John, b. Feb. 18, 1765	1	145
Frances, d. John & Mary, b. Feb. 18, 1765	1	150
Harriet, d. John, Jr. & Mary, b. Dec. 17, 1759	1	145
Harriet, see Harriet MERCHANT	1	174
Jno, Jr., adm. to Ch. 1741	ES	238
Jno, m. Mary REED, of Fairfield, [ ], 174[ ]	ES	238
John, m. Mrs. Mary CAMP, Jan. 8, 1718, by Sam[ue]ll Eells, Asst.	1	67
John, s. Dr. John, b. July 6, 1721; d. Aug. 16, 1721	1	68
John, s. Dr. John & Mary, b. Apr. 22, 1722	1	69
John, Dr. his marks for cattle recorded Apr. 6, 1743	1	114
John, Jr., of Milford, m. Mrs. Mary REED, of Fairfield, Sept. 4, 1745, by Jno Reed, J.P.	1	123
John, his w. [ ], d. Dec. 27, 1781	SM	22
John, d. Feb. 1, 1791, ae. 69	SM	45
John Anthony, s. Jno, Jr. & Mary, b. May 21, 1747	1	123
John Anthony, s. John, Jr., b. Apr. 5, 1751	1	145

	Vol.	Page
HARPIN, HARPIEN, HARPINE, HERPIN, (cont.)		
John Still Anthony, s. John, Jr., b. Apr. 5, 1751	1	128
Mary, d. Dr. John [& Mary], b. Aug. 2, 1719	1	67
Mary, adm. to Ch. 1741	ES	238
Mary, d. John & Mary, b. Jan. 12, 1753	1	145
Mary, wid., d. Apr. 4, 1780	SM	19
Mary Ann, d. John, Jr. & Mary, b. Mar. 3, 1748/9	1	125
Mary Ann, m. John **FOWLER**, Jr., Oct. 22, 1767, by Rev. Sam[ue]ll Whittlesey	1	162
Mary Ann, m. John **FOWLER**, Jr., Oct. 22, 1767. Witnesses, John Fowler, Susanna Fowler	1	164
Nathaniell, s. Dr. John, b. May 28, 1726; d. [ ] 1, 1727	1	94
Ruth, d. John & Mary, b. Dec. 4, 1754	1	145
Sam[ue]l, m. Mrs. Elizabeth **HARPIN**, Nov. 3, 1748	ES	238
Susanna, wid., d. [ ], 1802	BP	5
William Read, s. John, Jr. & Mary, b. Jan. 25, 1757	1	145
-----, Dr., m. Mary **CAMP**, July 8, 1718	ES	238
-----, wid., d. May 10, 1802	SM	74
HARRIMAN, John, s. John, b. Feb. 20, 1673	1	13
John, s. John, b. Feb. 21, 1673	OL	26
HARRIS, -----, Mr. his child d. [ ], 1816, ae. 3 y.	BP	34
HART, Abel, of Farmington, d. Jan. [ ], 1777	SM	9
-----, Mr., d. [, 1813]	BP	33
HARVEY, Edmund, adm. Church Sept. 13, [1640]; d. May 22, 1648, at Fairfield	OL	97
Josiah, s. Edmund, bp. [1640], by Rev. Peter Prudden	OL	100
Martha, w. Edmund, adm. Church June 20, [1641]	OL	98
HATCH, Nathan, d. [ ], 1778	SM	16
HATCHET, David, d. Mar. [ ], 1795 (non resident)	SM	57
Kate, d. [ ], 1819, ae. 35, North Milford	BP	40
HATLEY, HATLY, Philip, dismissed to 1st Ch. in London 1640	ES	16
Philip, adm. Church May 9, [1641]; dismissed to Coleman St. Church London, pastor Tho[ma]s Goodwin, by vote Aug. 19, 1649	OL	98
Philip, removed to London, 1648	ES	17
HAUGHTON, Sarah, m. Benjamin **SMITH**, Feb. 9, 1682, by Major Treat	1	18
Sarah, m. Benjamin **SMITH**, Feb. 9, 1682, by Major Treat	OL	38
HAWES, Bethyah, m. Obed **SEWARD**, Oct. 31, 1660	1	4
Bethiah, m. Obed **SEWARD**, Oct. 31, 1661, by Robert Treat, Magestrate	OL	13
HAWLEY, John, Sergt., member of Capt. Samuel Peck's Co., Milford, 1776	1	54
Nathan, Priv., member of Capt. Samuel Peck's Co., Milford, 1776	1	54
HAYES, HAYS, Eunice, m. William **FOWLER**, Jr., Apr. 1, 1724, by Sam[ue]ll Clark, J.P.	1	85
Robert, s. Sergt. Thomas, b. Sept. 30, 1679	1	17
Robert, s. Sergt. Thomas, b. Sept. 30, 1679	OL	33
Tho[mas], came to Milford, 1645	ES	177
Thomas, m. Elizabeth **PECK**, d. Joseph, Dec. 29, 1677, by Major Treat	OL	32
	ES	238
HAYNES, Isabell, m. Miles **MERWIN**, [ ]		

MILFORD VITAL RECORDS 93

	Vol.	Page
HEARTGROW, Mary, d. Mar. 25, 1799	SM	66
HEATH, John, drafted for Continental Army	1	57
HECOCK, [see also **HITCHCOCK**], Aaron, d. [ ], 1838	BP	79
-----, Mrs., d. [ ], 1832, ae. 74	BP	66
HEMMINGWAY, Eunice, d. of Isaac, of Woodbridge, m. as 3d w., Benjamin Lott **LAMBERT**, Sept. 8, 1817	1	53
HEPBURN, HEPBERN, HEPBOURNE, HOPBURN, David, d. Sept. 17, 1709, ae. 25 (sailor)	SM	43
Elliot, d. [ ], 1823, ae. 18	BP	49
J., at his house had young woman d. [ ], 1830	BP	62
Joel, s. Peter & Susannah, b. Nov. 11, 1757	1	139
John, his child d. [ ], 1812, ae. 2 y.	BP	24
John, d. [ ], 1822, at Sea	BP	47
John, his w. [ ], d. [ ], 1823	BP	49
John, his w. [ ], d. [ ], 1828, ae. 55	BP	58
Lewis, d. [ ], 1819, New York	BP	39
Mary, wid., d. [ ], 1820, ae. 80	BP	42
Nathaniel, his d. [ ], d. Sept. 12, 1797, ae. 1 y.	SM	62
Nathaniel, his d. [ ], d. Oct. 26, 1802	SM	76
Nathaniel, his child d. [ ], 1802	BP	6
Peter, m. Susannah **BALDWIN**, Dec. 16, 1753, by Nathan Baldwin, J.P.	1	139
Peter, d. Nov. [ ], 1780	SM	20
Peter, Capt., d. [ ], 1816, ae. 84	BP	35
Peter, drafted for Continental Army	1	57
Peter Clark, s. Peter & Susannah, b. Oct. 28, 1755	1	139
Richard, his child d. [ ], 1808	BP	18
Thomas, d. [ ], 1803	BP	8
-----, d. [ ], 1826, ae. 60	BP	54
-----, wid., her child d. [ ], 1830, ae. 9	BP	62
HERRIMAN, John, of New Haven, m. Hannah **BRYAN**, d. Richard, Nov. 20, 1672, by John Clarke, Commissioner	1	12
John, of New Haven, m. Hannah **BRYANT**, d. Richard, of Milford, Nov. 20, 1672, by John Clark, Com.	OL	25
HERVEY, Elizabeth, m. Thomas **BEAZLEY**, May 20, 1649/50, by Capt. Asa Woods* *(Capt. Astwood)	LL	2
HEWEY, E., removed to Fairfield, 1654	ES	17
Edmund, d. May 22, 1648, at Fairfield	ES	16
Edmund, d. [ ], 1648, at Fairfield	ES	35
HIAT, [see under **HYATT**]		
HIGBY, Abigail R., d. Samuel & Hannah, b. Jan. 13, 1797	1	176
Benjamin, s. Samuel & Hannah, b. July 11, 1804	1	176
Betsey, d. Samuel & Hannah, b. July 20, 1784	1	176
Hannah, d. Samuel & Hannah, b. May 16, 1786	1	176
Hervey, s. Samuel & Hannah, b. Jan. 27, 1801	1	176
Isaac R., twin with Samuel G., s. Samuel & Hannah, b. Mar. 17, 1791	1	176
Isaac R., s. Samuel & Hannah, d. June 10, 1816	1	176
J. Riley, d. [ ], 1816, ae. 24	BP	34
Lucy, [d. Samuel & Hannah], b. Apr. 27, 1794	1	176
Roxcy, d. Samuel & Hannah, b. Sept. 1, 1788	1	176
Samuel, m. Hannah **GALPIN**, of Middletown, Nov. 13, 1783, by		

	Vol.	Page
HIGBY, (cont.)		
Rev. Nathan Fenn. Removed to Milford, May 4, 1784	1	176
Samuel G., twin with Isaac R., s. Samuel & Hannah, b. Mar. 17, 1791	1	176
-----, Mr. his infant d. June 5, 1799	BP	1
-----, Mr. his s. [ ], d. June 5, 1799	SM	67
HIGGINS, Fitch, d. Apr. 23, 1783, ae. 2 y.	SM	25
Timothy, his twin s. [ ], d. Dec. 2, 1798	SM	65
HILL, -----, his child d. [ ], 1832	BP	67
HINE, A. M., d. Sam[ue]ll, Sr., b. Feb. 19, 1710/11	OL	69
A[a]ron, s. John, Jr. [& Mehitabeel], b. Mar. 26, 1732	1	101
Aaron, his w. [ ], d. Feb. 9, 1799, ae. 59	BP	1
Aaron, his w. [ ], d. Feb. 9, 1799	SM	66
Aaron, Sr., his child d. [ ], 1807	BP	16
Aaron, his child d. [ ], 1813	BP	31
Aaron, his child d. [ ], 1813	BP	31
Aaron, d. [ ], 1813, in Milford (North)	BP	31
Abel, d. [ ], 1805, ae. 28 y.	BP	10
Abel K., his infant, d. [ ], 1836	BP	74
Abigail, d. Thomas, b. May 25, 1702	1	22
Abigail, d. Thomas, b. May 25, 1702	OL	46
Abigail, m. George **TERRELL**, Aug. [ ], 1722, by Sam[ue]ll Clarke, J.P.	1	70
Abraham, s. John, Jr. [& Mehitabeel], b. May 26, 1728	1	101
Abraham, his s. [ ], d. Mar. 17, 1788, ae. 4 y.	SM	36
Abraham, Jr., his s. [ ], d. Apr. 4, 1799	SM	66
Abram, d. [ ], 1810, ae. 82	BP	21
Abram, Jr., d. [ ], 1813, ae. 18	BP	31
Alexander, s. Stephen, b. Feb. 10, 1698/9	1	23
Alexander, s. Stephen, b. Feb. 10, 1698/9	OL	47
Alexander, s. Allexander, b. Mar. 23, 1724/5	1	77
Allexander, of Milford, m. Mary **LINES**, of New Haven, May 21, 1725, by Ebenezer Joyson, J.P.	1	77
Alice, d. Thomas, b. Oct. 5, 1666	1	7
Ales, d. Thomas, b. Oct. 5, 1666	OL	17
Ealis*, d. Thomas, b. Dec. 16, 1667 *(Alice)	1	8
Ales, d. Thomas, b. Dec. 16, 1667	OL	20
Ambrose, of Milford, m. Sarah **RAPIER**, of Boston, Feb. 6, 1717, by Samuel Fowler, Asst., in Boston	1	66
Ambrose, s. Ambrose, b. Jan. 30, 1718/19	1	66
Amos, s. Allexander, b. July 10, 1727	1	82
Amos, s. Charles, b. July 29, 1754	1	150
Ann, d. Samuel, Sr., b. Feb. 19, 1710/11	1	32
Ann, m. Nathaniel **GUNN**, May 31, 1711, by Samuel Andrews Clerk	1	33
Ann, m. Nathaniel **GUN[N]**, May last day, 1711, by Samuel Andrews, Clerk	OL	70
Ann, m. John **DOWN**, May 24, 1733, by Rev. Samuel Andrews	1	98
Anne, d. Charles, b. July 24, 1761	1	150
Benjamin, s. John & Elizabeth, b. Oct. 9, 1719	1	70
Bettie, d. Allexander, b. Sept. 14, 1737	1	104
Dan, s. Allexander, b. May 7, 1734	1	102
Dan, of Milford, m. Ruth **ALLEN**, d. Sam[ue]ll, of New Haven,		

	Vol.	Page
HINE, (cont.)		
Feb. 18, 1756, by Rev. Benjamin Woodbridge, of Amity	1	135
Daniel, s. Samuel, b. Dec. 31, 1707	1	29
Daniel, s. Samuel, b. Dec. last day, 1707	OL	62
Daniel, his child d. [ ], 1836	BP	74
Daniel, his child d. [ ], 1837	BP	77
David, s. George, b. Oct. 24, 1745	1	121
Ebene[ze]r, s. Sam[ue]ll, Jr., b. Sept. 21, 1746	1	121
Edw[ ], of Southbury, m. Charlotte H. **[LAMBERT]**, [d. Benjamin Lott & Eunice], [ ]	1	53
Elijah, s. Joseph, Jr.*, b. Jan. 5, 1734/5 *(Should it not be "John, Jr."?)	1	101
Eliphall, d. George, b. Mar. 8, 1746/7	1	121
Elizabeth, d. Stephen, b. Dec. 14, 1693	1	23
Elizabeth, d. Stephen, b. Dec. 14, 1693	OL	47
Elizabeth, d. Samuel, Jr., b. Nov. 17, 1712	1	34
Elias[be]th, d. Sam[ue]ll, Jr., b. Nov. 17, 1712	OL	73
Elizabeth, w. John, Jr., d. July [ ], 1723	1	101
Elizabeth, m. Edward **BALDWIN**, Dec. 6, 1733, by Sam[ue]ll Eells, Asst.	1	119
Elizabeth, d. Sam[ue]ll, Jr. & Rebeckah, b. Feb. 14, 1741/2	1	121
Enoch, s. Charles, b. Apr. 23, 1764	1	150
Esther, d. Thomas, b. June 20, 1695	1	22
Esther, d. Thomas, b. June 20, 1695	OL	46
George, see under George **HINNE**	1	5
George, s. of Thomas **HINDE**, b. June 22, 1662	1	5
George, s. Thomas, b. June 22, 1662	OL	14
George, s. Thomas, b. June 29, 1673	1	12
George, s. Thomas, b. June 29, 1673	OL	26
George, s. Samuel, b. Mar. 17, 1703/4	1	25
George, s. Sam[ue]ll, b. Mar. 17, 1793/4* *[1703/4]	OL	51
George, m. [ ] **MORRIS**, May 10, 1744, by Rev. Sam[ue]ll Whittlesey	1	121
Hannah, d. Thomas, b. Dec. 22, 1695* *(1697)	1	22
Hannah, d. Thomas, b. Dec. 22, 1697	OL	46
Hannah, d. Mar. 31, 1795, ae. 5	SM	54
Isaac, s. John, Jr. [& Mehitabeel], b. Sept. 1, 1730	1	101
Isaac, m. Ann **BRISTOLL**, Jan. 12, 1757, by Rev. Job. Prudden	1	141
Isaac, his w. [ ], d. [ ], 1838	BP	80
James, d. [ ], 1813, at Sea	BP	32
Jared, s. Josiah & Mehitabeel, b. Apr. 14, 1734	1	99
Jared, d. Apr. [ ], 1777	SM	12
Joel, s. Charles, b. Jan. 30, 1752	1	150
Joel, his d. [ ], d. Jan. 23, 1778, ae. 3 m.	SM	15
Joel, his child d. [ ], 1817	BP	36
Joel, d. [ ], 1819, ae. 83	BP	39
Joel, his wid., d. [ ], 1825	BP	52
Joel, d. [ ], 1832, ae. 50	BP	68
John, came to Milford, 1640	ES	177
John, s. Thomas, b. Mar. 17, 1656	1	3
John, s. Thomas, b. Mar. 17, 1656	OL	9
John, m. Mary **FENN**, July 4, 1684, by Capt. Samuel Eells, Commissioner	1	19

	Vol.	Page
HINE, (cont.)		
John, m. Mary FENN, July 4, 1684, by Capt. Sam[ue]ll Eells, Com.	OL	41
John, m. Elizabeth BALDWIN, May 3, 1716	1	39
John, m. Elizabeth BALDWIN, May 3, 1716	OL	84
John, Jr., of Milford, m. Mehitabeel WATERS, of Stratford, Dec. 31, 1725, by Sam[ue]ll Clark, J.P.	1	101
John, Sergt., d. Apr. 1, 1739	1	108
John, d. Feb. 26, 1777, ae. 92	SM	11
John, Jr., his w. [ ], d. May 2, 1783	SM	25
John, d. Mar. 16, 1784	SM	27
John, d. [ ], 1812, in the Army	BP	24
John, his grandson d. [ ], 1816. "Killed in a mill at North Milford"	BP	35
John, his w. [ ], d. [ ], 1817	BP	37
John, his child d. [ ], 1834, ae. 2	BP	72
Jonah, d. [ ], 1813	BP	25
Jonas, his w. [ ], d. [ ], 1838, ae. 54	BP	80
Jonathan, s. John & Elizabeth, b. Sept. 17, 1722	1	70
Joseph, s. John, Jr. [& Mehitabeel], b. Oct. 18, 1726	1	101
Joseph, s. John, d. Apr. 27, 1746	1	115
Joseph, d. Apr. [ ], 1799, at Sea	SM	68
Josiah, s. Samuel, b. Jan. 21, 1709/10	1	31
Josiah, s. Sam[ue]ll, Jr., b. Jan. 21, 1709/10	OL	66
Josiah, s. Sam[ue]ll & Elizabeth, m. Mehitabeel NORTHROP, Aug. 23, 1733, by Roger Newton, J.P.	1	99
Loes, d. Isaac & Ann, b. Jan. 14, 1758	1	141
Loes, d. Charles, b. Nov. 1, 1758	1	150
Lidiah, d. Thomas, b. Jan. 3, 1699	1	22
Lediah, d. Thomas, b. Jan. 3, 1699	OL	46
Lydia, d. Charles, b. Sept. 25, 1756	1	150
Mary, d. Allexander, b. Dec. 14, 1729	1	84
Mary, d. Allexander, b. Dec. 17, 1729	1	87
Mary, d. Oct. 7, 1776, ae. 89	SM	7
Mary, wid., d. Oct. 31, 1793, ae. 84	SM	50
Mehitabeel, d. Jno & Mehitabeel, b. Mar. 8, 1740/1	1	115
Minerva, d. [ ], 1821, ae. 13	BP	44
Moses, s. Stephen, b. Dec. 9, 1751	1	129
Nancy, d. [ ], 1832, ae. 24	BP	68
Nathan, s. Thomas, Jr., b. Apr. 22, 1732	1	93
Nathan, his child d. [ ], 1807	BP	15
Nathan, his w. [ ], d. [ ], 1837	BP	77
Nathan, d. [ ], 1838, ae. 71	BP	80
Philena, d. Stephen, Jr., b. July 30, 1749	1	129
Polly, her infant d. [ ], d. Aug. 8, 1794	SM	51
Rebecca, d. Thomas, Jr., b. Sept. 18, 1679	OL	36
Rebeckah, d. Samuel, Jr. & Rebeckah, b. Apr. 9, 1739	1	121
Richard, d. [ ], 1813, at Sea	BP	32
Samuell, s. Thomas, b. Jan. 26, 1659	OL	12
Samuel, s. Thomas, b. Jan. 26, 1659/60	1	3
Samuel, Jr., m. Elizabeth TIBBALLS, June 9, 1709, by Joseph Treat, J.P.	1	31
Samuel, Jr., m. Elizabeth TIBBALLS, June 9, 1709, by Ja[me[s		

	Vol.	Page

HINE, (cont.)

Treat, J.P.	OL	66
Samuel, s. Samuel, b. May 3, 1717	1	38
Sam[ue]ll, s. Sam[ue]ll, Jr., b. May 3, 1717	OL	82
Sam[ue]ll, 3rd, m. Rebeckah OVIATT, Aug. 9, 1739, by Sam[ue]ll Eells, Asst.	1	120
Sam[ue]ll, s. Sam[ue]ll, Jr. & Rebeckah, b. Nov. 9, 1743	1	121
Samuel, his w. [ ], d. Aug. 11, 1777	SM	13
Samuel, Jr., d. Mar. 28, 1800, at Derby	SM	69
Samuel, his w. [ ], d. [ ], 1829	BP	59
Samuel, d. [ ], 1833, ae. 91	BP	69
Stephen, s. Thomas, b. Oct. 25, 1663	1	5
Stephen, s. Thomas, b. Oct. 25, 1663	OL	15
Stephen, s. Stephen, b. May 22, 1695	1	23
Stephen, s. Stephen, b. May 22, 1695	OL	47
Stephen, d. [ ], 1836, ae. 69	BP	76
Stephen, Jr., of Milford, m. Elizabeth CARRINTON, d. Jno, of New Haven, Jan. 26, 1748/9, by Rev. Benjamin Woodbridge, of Amity	1	125
Susannah, m. John OVIATT, Jan. 16, 1723/4, by Sam[ue]ll Eells, Asst.	1	73
Tho[mas], came to Milford, 1645	ES	177
Thomas, s. Thomas, b. Oct. the last, 1653	1	1
Thomas, s. Thomas, b. Oct. the last, 1653	OL	7
Thomas, had s. [ ], b. Dec. 3, 1657	1	3
Thomas, his s. [ ], b. Dec. 3, 1657	OL	10
Thomas, Jr., m. Rebecca HIAT, of Stamford, Nov. 13, 1678, by Major Treat, Dept. Gov.	1	16
Thomas, Jr., m. Rebecca HIAT, of Stamford, Nov. 13, 1678, by Major Treat, Dept. Gov.	OL	33
Thomas, of Milford, m. Hannah BRISTOLL, Nov. 9, 1684, by John Nash, Asst.	1	19
Thomas, m. Hannah BRISTOLL, Nov. 9, 1684, by Jno Nash, Asst.	OL	41
Thomas, d. [ ], 1697	ES	238
Thomas, Jr., m. Mary HOLLINWORTH, Jan. 7, 1730/1, by Sam[ue]ll Gunn, J.P.	1	88
Thomas, d. June 3, 1776, ae. 69	SM	6
Titus, drafted for Continental Army	1	57
Titus, s. Sam[ue]ll, Jr. & Rebeckah, b. Feb. 9, 1744	1	121
Titus, his child d. Feb. 6, 1776	SM	5
Titus, Priv., member of Capt. Samuel Peck's Co., Milford 1776	1	54
Titus, d. [ ], 1822	BP	46
William, s. Thomas, b. Aug. 15, 1670	1	10
William, s. Thomas, b. Aug. [ ], 1670	OL	22
William, m. Abigail HOLLINWORTH, Apr. 20, 1727, by Roger Newton, J.P.	1	81
Wyllys, d. sometime past, 1826	BP	54
-----, wid., d. [ ], 1813, ae. 66	BP	25
-----, wid. her child d. [ ], 1815	BP	28
-----, Mr. his child d. [ ], 1819, N. Milford	BP	40
-----, Mrs., d. [ ], 1827	BP	56
-----, d. [ ], at New Haven	ES	165

98   BARBOUR COLLECTION

	Vol.	Page
HINMAN, Jane, d. of Benjamin J., of Southbury, m. as 2d w., David D. [LAMBERT], [s. Benjamin Lott & Eunice], [ ]	1	53
HITCHCOCK, [see also HECOCK], Abel, of Amity, drafted for Continental Army	1	57
Able, s. Thomas, b. May 2, 1751	1	134
Daniel, s. Tho[ma]s & Abigaill, b. May 10, 1745	1	120
David, s. Tho[ma]s & Abigaill, b. May 11, 1745	1	120
Ebenezer, Priv., member of Capt. Samuel Peck's Co., Milford 1776	1	54
J., Capt., his w. [ ], d. [ ], 1827	BP	56
Jared, of Amity, drafted for Continental Army	1	57
Jared, s. Thomas & Abigail, b. June 4, 1759	1	142
Mary, d. Thomas, b. Sept. 14, 1753	1	134
Sarah, d. Thomas & Abigaill, b. Dec. 2, 1742	1	120
Thomas, m. Abigail **DOWNS**, Dec. 24, 1741, by Roger Newton, Asst.	1	120
HODGE, HODGES, Benjamin, his s. [ ], d. May 5, 1795	SM	55
David, drafted for Continental Army	1	57
David, his d. [ ], d. Nov. 13, 1776, ae. 32	SM	8
David, his s. [ ], d. Mar. 31, 1790, ae. 1 y.	SM	41
David, his s. [ ], d. May 26, 1791, ae. 2 y.	SM	45
Jesse, his w. [ ], d. [ ], 1807	BP	15
Julia, d. July 24, 1793, ae. 9 y. 5 m.	SM	49
Patty, d. [ ], 1813, at N. Milford	BP	25
HOLBROOK, HOLEBROOK, Abell, m. Hannah **MARWIN**, d. Miles, Dec. 17, 1683	OL	40
Abell, m. Hannah **MARWIN**, d. Miles, Dec. 20, 1683	1	19
Abigail, m. Sam[ue]ll **SANFORD**, b. of Milford, May 11, 1721, by Rev. Sam[ue]l Andrews	1	70
Goodman, weaver, came to Milford, 1658	ES	177
Israel, m. Mary **WELSH**, Nov. 20, 1677, by Major Treat	1	18
Israel, m. Mary **WELSH**, Dec. 20, 1677, by Major Treat	OL	35
Mary, d. Richard, m. Ebenezer **WHEELER**, Sept. 8, 1675, by Alexander Bryan, Asst.	1	14
Mary, d. Richard, m. Ephraim **WHEELER**, Sept. 8, 1675, by Alexander Bryan, Asst.	OL	29
Mary, d. Israel, b. Apr. 7, 1679	1	18
Mary, d. Israel, b. Apr. 7, 1679	OL	35
Mary, wid., m. John **MARVIN**, Apr. 12, 1683	1	21
Mary, wid., m. John **MARVIN**, Apr. 12, 1683	OL	42
Mary, m. Stephen **MILES**, [ ], 1697, by Tho[ma]s Clark, J.P., Witnesses Miles Merwin, Hannah Merwin	1	72
Patience, d. Richard, b. Dec. 19, 1658	1	3
Patience, d. Richard, b. Dec. 19, 1658	OL	11
Patience, m. Joseph **WHEELER**, June [ ], 1678, by Major Treat	1	17
Patience, m. Joseph **WHEELER**, June [ ], 1678, by Major Treat	OL	35
Peletiah, s. Richard, b. Apr. 1, 1661	1	4
Pelatiah, s. Richard, b. Apr. 1, 1661	1	5
Pelatiah, s. Richard, b. Apr. 5, 1661	OL	14
Pelatiah, s. Richard, b. Apr. 6, 1661	OL	14

	Vol.	Page
HOLBROOK, HOLEBROOK, (cont.)		
Rich[ard], came to Milford, 1660; d. 1670	ES	177
HOLDEN, Richard, of No. 4, d. Jan. 24, 1777	SM	11
HOLLINGWORTH, HOLLINWORTH, Abigail, m. John **BEARD**, Mar. 15, 1704/5, by Thomas Clark, J.P.	1	25
Abigail, m. John **BEARD**, Mar. 15, 1704/5, by Thomas Clark, J.P.	OL	53
Abigail, m. William **HINE**, Apr. 20, 1727, by Roger Newton, J.P.	1	81
Mary, m. Thomas **HINE**, Jr., Jan. 7, 1730/1, by Sam[ue]ll Gunn, J.P.	1	88
Richard, m. Ann **BALDWIN**, b. of Milford, June 16, 1755, by Sam[ue]ll Eells, Asst.	1	117
HOLT, Mary, see Mary **(HOLT) ASHBAND**	1	127
HOOKER, Anne, d. Jan. 6, 1793, ae. 27	SM	49
Deborah, wid., d. [ ], 1828	BP	58
James, d. Apr. [ ], 1803, at Sea	SM	77
John, his d. [ ], d. Aug. 12, 1782	SM	23
John, d. [ ], 1794	SM	53
John, drafted for Continental Army	1	57
-----, Mr., d. [, 1813]	BP	33
HOPKINS, Elisha, formerly of Milford, d. Apr. 20, 1777	SM	12
HOTCHKISS, HOTCHKINN, Abraham, Priv., member of Capt. Samuel Peck's Co., Milford 1776	1	54
Loes, d. Joseph & Elizabeth, b. June 8, 1761	1	144
Mary, of Groton, m. John **PLUMM**, Jr., of Milford, Nov. [ ], 1747, by Joshua Hemstead, J.P.	1	129
HOUGHTON, Rich[ard], came to Milford, [ ]	ES	177
HOW, Samuel, his 1ˢᵗ w. [ ], d. Sept. 14, 1796	SM	59
HUBBARD, HUBBERT, Abigail, d. George, bp. [1644, by Rev. Peter Prudden]	OL	101
Daniel, s. George, bp. [1644, by Rev. Peter Prudden]	OL	101
G., removed to Guilford, 1650	ES	17
George, adm. Church Jan. 15, 1643; dismissed to Guilford, Oct. 6, 1650	OL	98
George, [d.]	ES	16
Hannah, d. George, bp. [1644, by Rev. Peter Prudden]	OL	101
John, m. Sarah **TERRELL**, Nov. 4, 1707/8 [sic], by Capt. Eells, J.P.	1	30
John, m. Sarah **TERRELL**, Nov. 4, 1707/8, by Capt. Eells, J.P.	OL	65
Mary, w. George, adm. Church Aug. 4, [1644]	OL	98
Sarah, wid., d. of John **TERRELL**, m. Lewis **WILKINSON**, Dec. 4, 1722, by Jon[a]th[an] Law, Asst.	1	70
-----, d. Rev. Mr. [ ], m. Rev. Sam[ue]l Whittlesey, Jr., s. Rev. Samuel, [ ]	ES	121
-----, d. Dr. [ ], of New Haven, m. Samuel **WHITTLESEY**, Jr., physician and Town Clerk, [ ]; m. 2ⁿᵈ h.	ES	238
Rev. Mr. **LEWIS**, of Rocky Hill, [ ]	BP	13
HULL, Hannah, her child d. [ ], 1806	SM	61
HUMISTON, Amos, of Litchfield, d. June 21, 1797, ae. 48		
HUMPHREY, Sarah, of Derby, m. as 2d w. Benjamin Lott **LAMBERT**, Feb. 1, 1816; d. Dec. 8, 1816	1	53

	Vol.	Page
HUMPHREYVILLE, Abigaill, of New Haven, m. Samuel BALDWIN, Jr., s. of Samuel, of Milford, Jan. 8, 1753, by Rev. Benjamin Woodbridge, of Amity	1	131
Rebeckah, of N.H., m. Stephen MILES, of Milford, Dec. 6, 1751, by Jno Fowler, J.P.	1	128
HUNT, Sarah, m. Gideon BUCKINGHAM, Feb. 3, 1703, by Robert Treat, Dept. Gov.	1	22
Sarah, m. Gideon BUCKINGHAM, Feb. 3, 1703/4, by Rob[er]t Treat, Dept. Gov.	OL	47
[HYATT], HYAT, HIAT, Rebecca, of Stamford, m. Thomas HINE, Jr., Nov. 13, 1678, by Major Treat, D.G.	1	16
Rebecca, of Stamford, m. Thomas HINE, Jr., Nov. 13, 1678, by Major Treat, Dept. Gov.	OL	33
HYDE, Jane, of Bridgeport, d. Richard Henry, b. Jan. 4, 1817; m. John William FOWLER, only s. William Harpin & Sarah, Aug. 10, 1837	1	59
IMMANUEL, Ann, d. Mar. 23, 1791	SM	45
INGERSOLL, Clement, Mrs., d. [ ], 1817	BP	36
David, [s. Jonath[an], [ ], 1719	ES	238
David, [s. Jonath[an], [ ], 1722	ES	238
David, s. David & Mehitabeel, b. Dec. 11, 1740	1	110
David, b. [ ], 1740	ES	238
David, m. Clement TREAT, Mar. 9, 1768, by Rev. Samuel Whittlesey. Witnesses, Stephen Treat, Rebeckah Powell, Susannah Fowler, Susanna Whittlesey	1	164
David, [adm. to Ch.] 1771	ES	238
David, [Sr.], d. July 10, 1774	1	164
David, Town Clerk, d. Aug. 24, 1774	ES	238
David, d. [ ], 1820, at the South	BP	43
David B., d. [ ], 1838, ae. 66	BP	79
David Bryan, s. David & Clement, b. Aug. 16, 1771	1	164
George R., his infant child d. [ ], 1829	BP	59
George R., his other child d. [ ], 1829	BP	59
Jared, s. Jonath[an], bp. 1721	ES	238
Jere[mia]h, adm. to Ch. 1712	ES	238
Jonathan, s. David & Clement, b. Oct. 24, 1773	1	164
Martha Ann, d. [ ], 1822, ae. 13	BP	46
Mary, d. Jonath[an], [ ], 171[ ]	ES	238
M[e]hetable, d. David & Clement, b. Oct. 25, 1768	1	164
Mehetable, wid., d. June 7, 1798, ae. 77	SM	64
-----, wid. had negro woman d. Sept. 19, 1789	SM	40
ISBELL, ISBEL, ISBALL, Chauncey, s. Israel & Sarah, b. July 10, 1752	1	131
Chancy, d. Apr. [ ], 1777; killed in battle at Danbury	SM	12
David, his child d. [ ], 1822	BP	46
Huldah, her child d. [ ], 1805	BP	11
Israel, m. Sarah TIBBALLS, Apr. 18, 1750, by Rev. Samuel Whittlesey	1	126
Israel, s. Israel & Sarah, b. Dec. 9, 1750	1	128
Israel, his 1st w. [ ], d. Feb. 19, 1791	SM	45
Israel, his d. [ ], d. Apr. 27, 1791	SM	45
Israel, d. [ ], 181	BP	26

MILFORD VITAL RECORDS 101

	Vol.	Page
ISBELL, ISBEL, ISBALL, (cont.)		
Job, s. Israel & Sarah, b. Oct. 13, 1755	1	135
Lavinia, d. [ ], 1837, ae. 22	BP	78
Polly, d. Feb. 10, 1795, ae. 14	SM	54
Sarah, d. Israel & Sarah, b. Feb. 16, 1757	1	137
Sarah, wid., d. Oct. 29, 1799, ae. 68	SM	68
Sarah, wid. D. [ ], 1799	BP	2
IVES, Allen, Sergt., member of Capt. Samuel Peck's Co., Milford, 1776	1	54
Joel, Priv., member of Capt. Samuel Peck's Co., Milford 1776	1	54
JACKSON, John, drafted for Continental Army	1	58
Solomon, of Middleborough, d. Jan. [ ], 1777	SM	10
-----, Mrs. her child at Poor House d. [ ], 1831	BP	64
JAMES, Jeffrey, colored, d. [ ], 1827, ae. 80	BP	56
Jeffray, drafted for Continental Army	1	58
Timoty, d. June 9, 1802, ae. 62	SM	75
JARVIS, James, d. [ ], 1813, at Sea	BP	32
JAY, Walter, came to Milford, 1657	ES	177
JAYNER, Isabel, adm. Church Nov. 29, [1640]; since m. Miles **MOORE**, [ ]; cast out of Church	OL	98
JEFFREY, JEFFRERES, JEFFRIES, Pomp, infant d. Dec. 6, 1804	SM	81
Pomp, his child, d. [ ], 1822	BP	47
Sal, wid. Pomp, negro, d. [ ], 1833	BP	69
Thomas, negro, his w. [ ], d. [ ], 1821	BP	44
Thomas, colored, his w. [ ], d. [ ], 1831	BP	64
Thomas, negro d. [ ], 1840	BP	83
JELLET, [see under **GILLETT**]		
JENNINGS, JENNING, JENINS, Beela, of Fairfield, m. Sam[ue]ll **TREAT**, Jr., Oct. 26, 1742	ES	238
B[e]ula[h], of Fairfield, m. Samuel **TREAT**, Jr., of Milford, Oct. 26, 1743, by Sam[ue]ll Whittlesey, Jr.	1	122
Hannah, m. Samuel **PECK**, Aug. 18, 1735, by Edmund Lewis, Asst.	1	105
-----, Mrs., d. [ ], 1820, ae. 82	BP	41
JIRDHAM, -----, came to Milford, [ ]	ES	177
JOHNSON, Elisha, s. Elisha & Mary, b. May 14, 1775	1	167
Elisha, s. Elisha, b. June 15, 1775	1	165
Elizabeth, of Stratford, m. James **PRITCHARD**, of Milford, Dec. 25, 1721, by Joseph Curtiss, Asst.	1	88
Hannah, m. David **CLARK**, Jr., Oct. 4, 1762. Witnesses, Hezekiah Clark, Phinehas Peck	1	148
Phebe, heard of death Aug. 10, 1777 (formerly of Milford)	SM	13
Philemon, drafted for Continental Army	1	57
Phineas, drafted for Continental Army	1	58
Rebecca, wid., d. Aug. 7, 1795, at New Haven (non resident)	SM	57
Sarah, m. Daniel **SMITH**, Jan. 17, 1737/8, by Is[aa]c Dickerman, J.P.	1	105
Sarah, d. Seth & Hannah, b. Mar. 1, 1740	1	138
Sherman, fourth pastor of 2nd Church, Feb. 6, 1805; d. May 21, 1806	ES	93
Sherman, Rev., d. [ ], 1806, ae. 30	BP	13
Thankfull, of Stratford, m. Noah **BALDWIN**, of Milford, Mar. 27		

	Vol.	Page

JOHNSON, (cont.)
    1733, by Rev. Hez[ekiah] Gold, of Stratford — 1, 98
    Zerviah, of Derby, m. Timothy **BALDWIN**, of Milford, July 22, 1719, by Sam[ue]ll Bishop, J.P. — 1, 79
    -----, Mrs., d. [   ], 1809, at North Milford — BP, 19

JONES, Benjamin, m. Hannah **SPENCER**, May 2, 1661, by Robert Treat — 1, 5
    Benjamin, m. Hannah **SPENCER**, May 2, 1661, by Rob[ert] Treat — OL, 15
    Benjamin, s. Benjamin, b. June the last day, 1662 — 1, 5
    Hannah, wid., d. [   ], 1835, at Bethany, ae. 86 — BP, 73
    Isaac, his d. [   ], d. Dec. 22, 1783 — SM, 26
    Isaac, his w. [   ], d. [   ], 1806 — BP, 14
    Isaac, d. [   ], 1823 — BP, 48
    James, d. [   ], 1802, abroad at Sea — BP, 5
    John, his w. [   ], d. [   ], 1838, ae. 72 — BP, 79
    Nathan, his infant s. [   ], d. May 18, 1795 — SM, 55
    Rebecca, m. Benjamin **PERTHET***, Nov. 14, 1683, by Samuel Eells, Commissioner   *(**PRITCHARD**) — 1, 19
    Rebecca, m. Benjamin **PRITCHET***, Nov. 14, 1683, by Samuel Eells, Com.   *(**PRITCHARD** hand printed above surname in original manuscript) — OL, 40
    Samuell (?), d. [   ], 1805, drowned at Sea — BP, 11
    -----, his w. [   ], d. [   ], 1836 — BP, 75

KELLOG[G], Mary, d. Daniel, of Norwalk, m. Joseph **PLAT[T]**, May 5, 1680, by Lieut. Olmstead — OL, 36

KELSEY, -----, his child d. [   ], 1827 — BP, 56

KENT, Elisha, adm. to Ch. 1732 — ES, 238

KEITH, KIETH, John, his w. [   ], d. [   ], 1807 — BP, 15
    John B., d. [   ], 1811, at New Haven — BP, 22
    -----, killed by husband, 1804 — ES, 134
    -----, his d. [   ], had child d. [   ], 1833 — BP, 68

KILLUM, Daniell, s. Daniel & Mary, b. Feb. 13, 1732/3 — 1, 108
    Elleanor, d. Daniel & Mary, b. Apr. 27, 1729 — 1, 108
    John, s. Daniel & Mary, b. Oct. 6, 1730 — 1, 108
    Katharine, d. Daniel & Mary, b. May 20, 1739 — 1, 108
    Moses, s. Daniel & Mary, b. Sept. 29, 1736 — 1, 108
    Rhoda, d. Daniel & Mary, b. May 27, 1727 — 1, 108
    Susannah, d. Daniel, b. July 27, 1738 — 1, 107
    Thomas, s. Daniel & Mary, b. Jan. 9*, 1734   *(Followed by "Jan. 1") — 1, 108

KING, Robert, his s. [   ], d. Oct. 17, 1801, ae. 1 y. — SM, 73
    -----, Mr. his child d. [   ], 1801 — BP, 4

KNEELAND, -----, Rev. Dr., d. May [   ], 1777 — SM, 12

LADD, [see under **LUD**]

LAGLEY, Charity, m. Moses **STILSON**, Mar. 17, 1704/5, by Samuel Eells, J.P. — 1, 25

LAMBERT, LAMBER, DELAMBERT, LAMBERTINI, Abigail, [d. Jesse & Anne], b. Mar. 22, 1759; m. John **SMITH**, [   ]; d. Jan. 18, 1836 — 1, 50
    Alfred, [s. Edward R. & Eliza], b. Sept. 2, 1854 — 1, 47
    Alfred, [s. Edward Rodolphus & Eliza], b. Sept. 2, 1854 — 1, 52

MILFORD VITAL RECORDS 103

	Vol.	Page
LAMBERT, LAMBER, DELAMBERT, LAMBERTINI, (cont.)		
Amy, wid. of Jesse Peck **LAMBERT**, d. July 30, 1852, ae. 79	1	50
Anna, w. Benjamin Lott, d. Jan. 22, 1815	1	53
Anna T., [d. Benjamin Lott & Anna], b. Sept. 19, 1813; m. Edwin **WOODRUFF**, May 14, 1837; moved to Tallmadge, Ohio	1	53
Anne, [d. Jesse & Anne], b. Jan. 7, 1748; m. Nathan **BRISTOL**, of Milford, Feb. 3, 1777	1	50
Anne, twin with Sarah, [d. Frederic & Sally], b. July 30, 1799; m. Charles **BLOSS**, [ ]	1	50
Anne, wid. Jesse, eldest s. of Jesse & Mary, d. July 3, 1809, ae. 84	1	50
Anne, [d. Edward R. & Eliza], b. Jan. 10, 1838	1	47
Anne, [d. Edward Rodolphus & Eliza], b. Jan. 10, 1838	1	52
Annette Louisa, [d. Benjamin Lott & Susan], b. Aug. 11, [18]55	1	53
Benjamin, his child d. [ ], 1812	BP	23
Benj[amin], his w. [ ], d. [ ], 1815, N. Milford	BP	28
Benj[amin], his 2nd w. [ ], d. [ ], 1816	BP	35
Benjamin Lott, [s. David & Martha], b. Sept. 20, 1782	1	51
Benjamin Lott, 7th s. of David & Martha, m. 1st w. Anna **TOMLINSON**, d. David, of Milford, Mar. 27, 1811; m. 2d w. Sarah **HUMPHREY**, of Derby, Feb. 1, 1816; m. 3d w. Eunice **HEMMINGWAY**, d. of Isaac, of Woodbridge, Sept. 8, 1817	1	53
Benjamin Lott, d. Oct. 11, 1825	1	53
Benjamin Lott, [s. Benjamin Lott & Eunice], b. Dec. 21, 1825; m. Mary **BARNES**, d. of Anson B., of N.H., Nov. 4, 184[ ]; m. 2d w. Susan **TREAT**, d. of Jonah, of Orange, June 23, 1848	1	53
Benjamin Lott, twin with Celia Jane, [s. David D. & Jane], b. Feb. 18, 1856	1	53
Benjamin Richard, [s. John & Esther], b. June 30, 1819; d. in infancy	1	52
Cardinal, elected Bishop of Rome Aug. 27, 1730; related to Earl of Cavan's family, Ireland, who descend from Rudolph **DELAMBERT**, the first of the name in English History	1	48
Celia B., w. David D., d. Sept. 7, 1849	1	53
Celia Jane, twin with Benjamin Lott, [d. David D. & Jane], b. Feb. 18, 1856	1	53
Charlotte, [d. Enoch & Azubah], b. June 10, 1823	1	52
Charlotte, [d. Willis & Eliza], b. [ ], 1832	1	51
Charlotte, [d. Frederic & Sally], [b.]	1	50
Charlotte H., [d. Benjamin Lott & Eunice], b. Nov. 8, 1818; m. Edw[ ] **HINE**, of Southbury	1	53
Clarissa, [d. Frederic & Sally], b. Aug. 25, 1801; m. Nicholas **MORSE**, [ ]	1	50
Dan[ie]l Webster, [s. Harvey & Jennet], b. [ ]	1	51
David, m. Martha **NORTHROP**, [d. Ephraim & Sarah], [ ]	1	97
David, s. Jesse, from England in 1680, m. Lurania **BILLS**, of Lebanon, d. John & Mercy (**FOWLER**), Feb. 1, 1727; moved to Norwalk; settled on land now lying in Wilton, which he so named when Wilton was incorporated	1	53
David, s. Jesse, b. June 5, 1700	1	26
David, [s. Jesse & Deborah], b. [ ], 1700	1	49

	Vol.	Page
LAMBERT, LAMBER, DELAMBERT, LAMBERTINI, (cont.)		
David, s. Jesse & Deborah, b. June 5, 1700; m. Lavinia **BILL**, of Lebanon, d. John, July 1, 1727; settled in Norwalk; d. [ ], 1782	OL	54
David, s. Jesse, received land from his father as recorded in Lib. 4, p. 340, Milford Land Records, on Mar. 18, 1717/8; moved to Norwalk	1	49
David, [s. Jesse & Mary], b. Dec. 2, 1731	1	49
David, s. Jesse [& Mary], b. Dec. 2, 1731; m. Martha **NORTHROP**, d. Eph[rai]m, [ ], 1755; d. Nov. 8, 1815	1	106
David, [s. David & Lurania], b. [ ], 1739; graduated at Yale in 1761	1	53
David, 3d s. Jesse [& Mary], m. Martha **NORTHROP**, d. Ephraim & Sarah (**GUNN**), Mar. 8, 1757; d. Nov. 8, 1815, ae. 84	1	51
David, [s. David & Martha], b. Dec. 29, 1757; settled in Sharon, Conn.	1	51
David, only s. of David & Lurania, m. Susannah **ROGERS**, d. Dr. Uriah, of Norwalk, Dec. 17, 1769; d. Mar. 4, 1815, in Wilton	1	53
David, Jr., Priv., member of Capt. Samuel Peck's Co., Milford, 1776	1	54
David, [s. David & Louis], b. Mar. 23, 1799; d. unmarried in 1840	1	52
David, 1ˢᵗ s. David & Martha, m. Louis **PRINDLE**, d. Stephen, Esq., [ ]; moved to Sharon, Conn., in spring of 1806; d. Mar. [ ], 1837	1	52
David, d. [ ], 1815	BP	30
David, his w. [ ], d. [ ], 1815, North Milford	BP	30
David, [s. Henry Bills & Aletta Emma], b. [ ], 1817; graduated at Washington College, Hartford, Conn., in 1836; m. [ ]	1	53
David D., [s. Benjamin Lott & Anna], b. Mar. 27, 1812; d. in infancy	1	53
David D., [s. Benjamin Lott & Eunice, b.], Sept. 21, 1820; m. Celia B. **BLAKE**, d. of Allen B., of Winchester, Conn., Aug. 24, [ ]; m. 2d w. Jane **HINMAN**, d. of Benjamin J., of Southbury, Ct.	1	53
David Edward, [s. Enoch & Azubah], b. Mar. 20, 1832	1	52
David Jesse, [s. John & Esther], b. Oct. 17, 1815; d. in infancy	1	52
David Rogers, [s. David & Susannah], b. Dec. 8, 1772; merchant in New York; killed June 3, 1825 in New York by a blow from a ruffian	1	53
Deborah, [d. Jesse & Deborah], b. [ ], 1695, d. [ ], unmarried	1	49
E. R., in 1840, sent to Pension Bureau, Wash., roll of Capt. Samuel Peck's Co., of Milford, 1776	1	54
Edward, his child d. [ ], 1811, ae. 2 y.	BP	22
Edward, d. Feb. 15, 1831, ae. 57	BP	64
Edward A., s. David, m. Anne **BULL**, d. Jeremiah & Ann, Jan. 16, 1806	1	45
Edward A., 4ᵗʰ s. David, m. Anna **BULL**, d. Jeremiah & Anne,		

	Vol.	Page

LAMBERT, LAMBER, DELAMBERT, LAMBERTINI, (cont.)

	Vol.	Page
Edward Allen, [s. David & Martha], b. Aug. 3, 1780	1	51
Edward Allyn, 6th s. David & Martha, m. Anne **BULL**, only child of Jeremiah & Anne (**GUNN**), Jan. 16, 1806, by Bezaleel Pinnio; d. Feb.15, 1831, ae. 51	1	52
Edward R., eldest s. Edward A. & Anne, b. Mar. 20, 1808; m. Eliza **BOOTH**, d. John & Dencie, of Wallingford, Jan. 1, 1833, by Dr. Harry Croswell	1	47
Edward Richard, [s. Edward Rodolphus & Eliza], [b.] Feb. 10, 1834	1	52
Edward Richard, [s. Edward R. & Eliza], b. Feb. 10, 1834	1	47
Edward Rodolphus, [s. Edward A. & Anne], b. Mar. 20, 1808; m. Eliza **BOOTHE**, d. John, of Wallingford, Ct., Jan. 1, 1833, in Trinity Church, New Haven by Dr. Crosswell	1	52
Eliza Booth, [d. Edward R. & Eliza], b. Jan. 1, 1836; d. Aug. 6, 1838	1	47
Eliza Boothe, [d. Edward Rodolphus & Eliza], b. Jan. 1, 1836]; d. Aug. 6, 1838	1	52
Eliza Booth, d. E. R., d. [ ], 1838, ae. 1 y. 1 m.	BP	79
Elizabeth, [d. Jesse & Deborah], b. [ ], 1697; m. Joseph **BIRCHARD**, [ ]. Settled in Norwalk, Conn.	1	49
Elizabeth, [d. David & Lurania], b. Feb. 17, 1728; m. [ ] **LOCKWOOD**	1	53
Elizabeth, [d. David & Susannah], b. Feb. 3, 1771; d. unmarried	1	53
Elizabeth, [d. Edward R. & Eliza], b. June 22, 1846	1	47
Elizabeth, [d. Edward Rodolphus & Eliza], b. June 22, 1846	1	52
Elizabeth, [d. David & Louis], b. [ ]	1	52
Elizabeth Jane, [d. Willis & Eliza], b. [ ], 1824	1	51
Elizabeth Marietta, [d. John & Esther], b. Sept. 12, 1804; d. Mar. 1, 1816	1	52
Elizabeth Marietta, [d. John & Esther], b. June 30, 1816; d. Apr. 19, 1834	1	52
Emily Anne, [twin with Harriet, d. Jesse Peck & Amy], b. [ ], 1811; m. Charles **CURTIS**, [ ]; moved to Ohio, and d. soon after; no children	1	51
Emma Louisa, [d. Henry Bills & Aletta Emma], b. [ ], 1808; d. [ ], 1835	1	53
Enoch, [s. David & Louis], b. Sept. 10, 1789; m. Azubah, d. Capt. **RICHARDS**, of West Haven, Ct.	1	52
Ephraim, [s. David & Louis], [b. 1791?]	1	52
Ephraim Northrop, [s. David & Martha], b. Jan. 3, 1760; never married; soldier in Revolution; d. [ ], 1829	1	51
Esther, [d. David & Susannah], b. Apr. 14, 1780	1	53
Esther Maria, [d. John & Esther], b. Nov. 23, 1802; d. Jan. 7, 1811	1	52
Esther Maria, [d. John & Esther], b. Jan. 20, 1811; m. Austin **TREAT**, s. Joseph, of No. Milford, [ ], 1830	1	52
Frances, [child of Harvey & Jennet], [b.]	1	51
Frederic, [s. Jesse & Anne, b.] Oct. 29, 1794; m. Sally **POTTER**, who lived with Harvey **STEELE**, of Ontario County, N.Y. [ ]; they settled in the town of Friendship, Alleghany County, N.Y.	1	50

	Vol.	Page

LAMBERT, LAMBER, DELAMBERT, LAMBERTINI, (cont.)

George Benjamin, [s. Enoch & Azubah], b. July 22, 1825	1	52
George DeForest, [s. Henry & Margaret], b. [ ], 1833	1	51
George William, [s. Henry Bills & Aletta Emma], b. [ ], 1812; d. [ ], 1832	1	53
Hannah, [d. Jesse & Mary], b. Aug. 18, 1734; m. John **WOODRUFF**, Mar. 13, 1757; settled in Watertown, Conn.; d. Feb. 22, 1813	1	49
Hannah, d. Jesse [& Mary], b. Apr. 18, 1734; m. John **WOODRUFF**, [ ]; moved to Watertown, Conn.; d. Feb. 22, 1823	1	106
Hannah, [d. Jesse & Anne], b. Aug. 22, 1756; m. Joseph **PECK**, of Milford, Feb. 16, 1778	1	50
Harriet, [twin with Emily Anne, d. Jesse Peck & Amy], b. [ ], 1811; m. Seth **STRONG**, of Woodbury, [ ], 1831	1	51
Harriet, [d. Willis & Eliza], b. [ ], 1835; d. Apr. [ ], 1837	1	51
Harvey, [d. Frederic & Sally], [b.]	1	50
Harvey, [s. Jesse Peck & Amy], b. Mar. [ ], 1804; m. Jennet **LEAVENWORTH**, [ ]; moved to Mt. Vernon, Knox County, Ohio	1	51
Helen, [d. Edward R. & Eliza], b. Jan. 10, 1843; d. Sept. 15, 1844	1	47
Helen, [d. Edward Rodolphus & Eliza], b. Jan. 10, 1843; d. Sept. 15, 1849	1	52
Henry, [s. Jesse Peck & Amy], m. 2d w. Harriet **COTTON**, [ ]	1	51
Henry, [s. Jesse Peck & Amy], b. [ ], 1807; m. Margaret **DEFOREST**, d. of Philo, [ ]	1	51
Henry A., [s. Edward R. & Eliza], b. Apr. 10, 1841	1	47
Henry A., [s. Henry & Margaret], b. [ ]	1	51
Henry Augustas, [s. Henry Bills & Aletta Emma], b. [ ], 1810; lawyer in New York City; m. 1st w.	1	53
Henry Augustus, [s. Edward Rodolphus & Eliza], b. Apr. 10, 1841	1	52
Henry Bills, [s. David & Susannah], b. Mar. 8, 1777	1	53
Henry Bills, 2d s. David & Susannah, m. Aletta Emma **CLUETT**, of New York, [ ]; d. Aug. [ ], 1840	1	53
Hetty Matilda, [d. John & Esther], b. May 1, 1809; m. Clark **FOWLER**, 2d s. of Josiah, of No. Milford, [ ], 1836, after 12 years' courtship	1	52
Hugh, [s Rodolph], had son William who married a gd. dau. of William, the First, and dau. of the Earl of Warren and Surry. From these are descended the Earl of Cavan, in Ireland, and all of the name in England	1	48
Jane, her s. [ ], d. Aug. 25, 1799	SM	67
Jane Olivia, [d. John & Esther], b. Jan. 11, 1823	1	52
Jeremiah Bull, [s. Edward A. & Martha], b. Oct. 29, 1814; m. Louis **GOODYEAR**, d. of Stephen, of Hamden, a descendant of Stephen **GOODYEAR**, of New Haven, Oct. 29, 1834; moved to Bath, Ohio, in spring of 1837	1	52
Jesse, British Navy Officer; came to Boston from England; in		

MILFORD VITAL RECORDS 107

	Vol.	Page
LAMBERT, LAMBER, DELAMBERT, LAMBERTINI, (cont.) a few days went on to New Haven and in 1680 to Milford; m. Deborah **FOWLER**, d. Capt. William & Mary, [ ], 1683	1	48
Jesse, m. Deborah **FOWLER**, d. Capt. W[illia]m, decd., May 10, 1683	1	24
Jesse, s. Jesse & Deborah, b. Apr. 20,1692	1	26
Jesse, s. Jesse & Deborah, b. [ ], 1692; d. Dec. 26, 1772	OL	53
Jesse, [s. Jesse & Deborah], b. [ ], 1692	1	49
Jesse, m. Mary **GILETT**, d. of Eliphal & Mary (**WHEELER**), Dec. 6, 1716, by Jonathan Law	1	39
Jesse, Jr., m. Mary **GILLET**, d. Eliphal & Mary (**WHEELER**), Dec. 6, 1716, by Jonathan Law; d. Dec. 26, 1773	1	49
Jesse, m. Mary **GILLITT**, Dec. 6, 1716, by Jon[a]th[an] Law	OL	85
Jesse, m. Mary **GILLITT**, d. Eliphal **GILLITT**, Dec. 6, 1716, by Jonathan Law	1	106
Jesse, d. [ ], 1718; will proved Dec. 4, 1718, New Haven Probate, Lib. 4, p. 512-3	1	49
Jesse, s. Jesse, received land from his father as recorded in Lib. 5, p. 340, Milford Land Records, on Mar. 18, 1717/8	1	49
Jesse, [s. Jesse & Mary], b. Oct. 28,1719	1	49
Jesse, s. Jesse [& Mary], b. Oct. 28, 1719; m. Ann **PECK**, d. Capt. Henry, Oct. 25, 1745	1	106
Jesse, original member of 2nd Church formed in 1742	ES	87
Jesse, m. Ann **PECK**, d. Henry [& Ann], Oct. 28, 1745	1	93
Jesse, eldest s. Jesse & Mary, m. Anne **PECK**, d. Capt. Henry **PECK**, Oct. 28, 1745; d. July 30, 1794, ae. 75; see Lib. 18, p. 314-19, Probate Records for settlement of estate	1	50
Jesse, [s. David & Martha], b. Mar. 24, 1762; d. in infancy	1	51
Jesse, [s. Jesse & Anne], b. May 2, 1765; d. May 12, 1765	1	50
Jesse, d. Dec. 26, 1773, in the 82nd y. of his age	1	164
Jesse, d. July 30, 1794, ae. 76	SM	51
Jesse, m. 2d w. Joanna **WATKINS**, wid. of Joseph, of Stratford, & d. of Samuel **BUCKINGHAM**, [ ]	1	49
Jesse Peck, [s. Jesse & Anne], b. Sept. 5, 1769; d. Oct. 21, 1836	1	50
Jesse Peck, s. Jesse & Anne, m. Amy **CLARK**, d. of Thomas, a farmer, of Milford, [ ]; moved to woodbury; d. Oct. 21, 1836	1	50
Joanna, wid. of Jesse, m. 3d h. Samuel **CAMP**, of Newark, Nov. 24, 1726	1	49
John, [s. David & Martha], b. Nov. 26, 1770	1	51
John, [s. John & Esther], b. Aug. 5, [1799]; d. Aug. 26, 1799	1	52
John, his child d. [ ], 1811, ae. 8 y., at N. Milford	BP	21
John, his child d. [ ], 1817, N. Milford	BP	36
John, his child d. [ ], 1819, N. Milford	BP	40
John, [s. Enoch & Azubah], b. Feb. 22, 1821	1	52
John, 5th s. David & Martha, m. Esther **WOODRUFF**, d. Matthew & Esther (**BULL**), of No. Milford, Jan. 3, 1799; d. Jan. 17, 1852, ae. 82	1	52
John, s. David, m. Esther **WOODRUFF**, [ ]	1	152
John James, [s. David & Susannah], b. June 18, 1787; m. Eliza **BETTS**, of Wilton, [ ], had one son who died in		

	Vol.	Page

LAMBERT, LAMBER, DELAMBERT, LAMBERTINI, (cont.)

	Vol.	Page
infancy	1	53
John Lott, [s. John & Esther], b. Mar. 10, 1801; d. unmarried Mar. 25, 1860	1	52
Julia, [d. Jesse Peck & Amy], b. Dec. 30, 1798; m. Anthony C. **STRONG**, Esq., of Woodbury, [ ]	1	51
Julia, [d. Edward R. & Eliza], b. Aug. 22, 1852	1	47
Julia, [d. Edward Rodolphus & Eliza], b. Aug. 22, 1852; d. June 21, 1853	1	52
Julia, [d. Harvey & Jennet], [b.]	1	51
Julia Maria, [d. David & Susannah], b. Apr. 5, 1792	1	53
Julius Nehemiah, [s. Treat & Charlotte], b. May 25, 1827; d. May 25, 1828	1	50
Julius Treat, [s. Treat & Charlotte], b. July 29, 1829	1	50
Louis, [d. David & Louis], b. [, 1793?]; [probably d. in infancy]	1	52
Louis, [d. David & Louis], b. [, 1795?]; m. Geo[rge] **WHITE**, Esq., [ ]	1	52
Louisa B., [d. Benjamin Lott & Eunice], b. Mar. 31, 1823; m. Frederic Bryan **PLATT**, of Orange, [ ]	1	53
Lurania, [d. Jesse & Anne], b. Mar. 9, 1754	1	50
Lurania, [d. David & Susannah], b. Jan. 22, 1775	1	53
Mabel, [d. David & Martha], b. June 17, 1774	1	51
Mabel, [d. Edward R. & Eliza], b. Jan. 10, 1845; d. Jan. 12, 1845	1	47
Mabel, [d. Edward Rodolphus & Eliza], b. Jan. 10, 1845; d. Jan. 12, following	1	52
Mabel Louisa, [d. John & Esther], b. Jan. 25, 1814; m. Homer **SWIFT**, of New Lebanon, N.Y., Apr. 14, 1839; settled at Oyster River, Milford	1	52
Margaret, [d. Henry & Harriet], b. [ ]	1	51
Margaret, w. Henry, d. Nov. 20,1852	1	51
Martha, d. Jesse, b. Oct. 14, 1686	1	26
Martha, [d. Jesse & Deborah], b. [ ], 1686; d. Oct. 28, 1703, in her 20th* year *(Probably "17th y.")	1	49
Martha, [d. Jesse & Mary], b. Jan. 28, 1721; m. Benjamin **PRITCHARD**, descendant of Roger **PRITCHARD**, of Springfield, Mass., May 23, 1753	1	49
Martha, d. Jesse [& Mary], b. Jan. 28, 1721; m. Benjamin **PRITCHARD**, [ ]	1	106
Martha, w. David, d. Oct. 27, 1815, ae. 78	1	46
Martha, w. David, d. Oct. 27, 1815, ae. 78	1	51
Martha, [d. David & Louis], b. [ ]; d. [ ]	1	52
Martha Anne, [d. Edward A. & Martha], [b.] May 13, 1809; d. Aug. 2, 1811	1	52
Martha Anne, [d. Edward A. & Martha], b. Mar. 10, 1813; m. Sheldon **CLARK**, 2d s. of Isaac, Nov. 24, 1838	1	52
Mary, d. Jesse & Mary, b. Oct. 10, 1717; m. John **SANFORD**, Sept. 14, 1719* *(Should be 1743. See p. 49)	1	106
Mary, d. Jesse & Mary, b. Oct. 10, 1717; m. John **SANFORD**, Sept. 14, 1743	1	49
Mary, m. John **SANFORD**, Sept.14, 1743, by Roger Newton, Asst.	1	117

	Vol.	Page
LAMBERT, LAMBER, DELAMBERT, LAMBERTINI, (cont.)		
Mary, [d. Jesse & Anne], b. Sept. 27, 1746; d. Dec. 31, 1765	1	50
Mary, wid. of Jesse, Jr., d. June 6, 1776	1	49
Mary, wid., d. June 6, 1776, ae. 79	SM	6
Mary, [d. David & Martha], b. Feb. 3, 1766; m. Thomas **SMITH**, [ ]; had 6 children; d. [ ], 1810	1	51
Mary, w. Benjamin Lott, d. Aug. 20, 1847	1	53
Mary Emeline, [d. John & Esther], b. Nov. 30, 1806; m. 1ˢᵗ h. Mark **WILCOX**, Apr. 15, 1849; m. 2d h. Amos **BALDWIN**, [ ], m. 3d h. Daniel **CLARK**, s. of Samuel of Milford; lived in Middlebury	1	52
Meade, [s. Harvey & Jennet], [b.]	1	51
Mehetable, [d. Jesse & Anne], b. Jan. 21, 1752; m. Samuel **TIBBALLS**, [ ]; d. Mar. 2, 1774	1	50
Nancy, [d. Jesse Peck & Amy], b. Nov. 18, 1795; m. Asahel **MITCHELL**, of Woodbury, [ ]	1	51
Nathan Clark, [s. Willis & Eliza], b. [ ], 1837	1	51
Nehemiah, [s. Jesse & Anne], b. May 2, 1763; d. Apr. 21, 1767	1	50
Nehemiah, [s. Jesse & Anne], b. Oct. 21, 1766; d. Mar. 26, 1825	1	50
Nehemiah, s. Jesse & Anne, went to Bethlehem, Conn., when 20 y. old; m. Sarah **GALPIN**, d. Moses, [ ]]; d. Mar. 26, 1825	1	50
Rachel, d. Jesse & Deborah, b. [ ], 1684; m. Samuel **SMITH**, Dec. 30, 1703	1	49
Rachel, m. Samuel **SMITH**, Dec. 31, 1703, by Thomas Clark, J.P.	1	25
Rachell, m. Samuel **SMITH**, Dec. 30, 1703, by Thomas Clark, J.P.	OL	52
Rachel, d. Jesse [& Mary], b. Feb. 1, 1728/9; m. Henry **PECK**, [ ]; settled in Newtown, Conn.	1	106
Rachel, [d. David & Lurania], b. [ ], 1730; m. Benjamin **DEFOREST**, [ ]	1	53
Rachal, [d. Jesse & Mary], b. Feb. 15, 1728; m. Hannah* **PECK**, May 15, 1751; settled in Brookfield, Conn. *(Should be Henry)	1	49
Rachel, [m. Henry **PECK**, s. Henry. Settled in Brookfield, Conn.] (Written in pencil)	1	77
Richard, [s. Jesse & Deborah], b. [ ], 1688; d. before his father but was living as appears by Lib. 2ⁿᵈ of New Haven County Court Records, in 1707	1	49
Richard, [s. Jesse & Mary], b. June 8, 1725; m. Ann **MANUELL**, wid. of Angelo(?), [ ], 1666; d. Apr. 25, 1777, ae. 52; left no children	1	49
Richard, s. Jesse [& Mary], b. June 8, 1725; m. Ann **MANUEL**, [ ]; d. Apr. 25, 1777; had no children	1	106
Richard, d. Apr. 25, 1777, ae. 50	SM	12
Richard Lott, [s. David & Martha], b. Nov. 3, 178; engaged in mercantile business in West Indies and was lot on his second passage out in 1791	1	51
Rodolph, went to England from Normandy with William, the Conqueror, as his armor bearer. The family had been in Normandy since the subversion of the Kingdom of		

	Vol.	Page
LAMBERT, LAMBER, DELAMBERT, LAMBERTINI, (cont.)		
Lombardy, Italy. Originally spelled "Lombard"	1	48
Roger, first cousin of Jesse **LAMBERT**, settled in New Jersey before Sept. 25, 1684	1	48
Roger, [s. Edward R. & Eliza], b. July 18, 1849; d. July 18, 1849	1	47
Samuel Fitch, [s. David & Susannah], b. Dec. 21,1784	1	53
Sarah, [d. Jesse & Deborah], [b.] [ ], 1690; m. John **DUNNING,** [ ]; settled in Norwalk, Conn.	1	49
Sarah, [d. Jesse & Anne], b. [ ], 1750; m. Stephen **TREAT**, of Milford, Dec. 25, 1785	1	50
Sarah, [d. David & Martha], b. Oct. 28, 1763; d. Aug. [ ], 1817	1	51
Sarah, twin with Anne, [d. Frederic & Sally], b. July 30, 1799; m. Noble **ALLEN**	1	50
Sarah, 2d w.of Benjamin Lott **LAMBERT**, d. Dec. 8, 1816	1	53
Sarah, [d. Jeremiah Bull & Louis], [b.] Apr. 6, 1843	1	52
Sarah, [d. David & Louis], b. [ ]	1	52
Sarah H., [d. Benjamin Lott & Sarah], b. Nov. 11, 1816; m. Sherman **PETTEBONE**, of Burlington, Ct., May 20, 1835; moved to Tallmadge, Ohio	1	53
Sarah Susannah, [d. David & Susannah], b. June 26, 1782; m. George **CRUICKSHANKS**, member of Canadian Legislature and lived in York, Upper Canada	1	53
Sidney Smith, [s. Jeremiah Bull & Louis], b. Sept. 5, 1839	1	52
Susannah, w. David, d. [ ], 1828	1	53
Treat, [s. Nehemiah & Sarah], b. July 8, 1791; settled in Canton (Cherry Brook Soc.), Conn.; m. Charlotte **BARBER**, d. Azariah, [ ]	1	50
Treat, [s. Jesse Peck & Amy], b. Dec. 17, 1796; m. Jennet **MINOR**, Feb. 23, 1841	1	51
Wilbur Cotton, [s. Henry & Harriet], b. [ ]	1	51
William, s. Hugh, married a gd. dau. of William, the First, and dau. of the Earl of Warren and Surry. From these are descended the Earl of Cavan, in Ireland and all of the name in England	1	48
Willis, [s. Jesse Peck & Amy], b. July 4, 1801; m. Eliza **MINOR**, d. of Matthew, [ ], 1823	1	51
Willis Peck, [s. Willis & Eliza], b. [ ], 1828; d. Nov. [ ], 1833	1	51
-----, Miss, d. [ ], 1817, North Milford	BP	37
-----, first child of Treat & Charlotte, b. Oct. 24, 1825; d. in infancy	1	50
-----, s. [Edward Rodolphus & Eliza], d. [ ], 1849	1	52
-----, of Virginia, m. Jabez **BULL**, s. Fame, [ ]; settled in Florida	1	45
LANE, Isaac, s. John, bp. [1641, by Rev. Peter Prudden]	OL	100
John, wid. Of Milford, m. wid. [**CAMP**, of Chestnut Hill, in New Town Parish, Apr. 4, 1660, by Mr. Treat, Magestrate	OL	12
John, widower of Milford, m. wid. [ ] **CAMP**, of Chestnut Hill, New Haven, Apr. 4, 1662, by Robert Treat, Magistrate	1	4
John, [d.], 1669	ES	16

	Vol	Page
LANE, (cont.)		
Sarah, w. John, adm. Church June 27, [1641]	OL	98
Sarah, d. John, bp. [1642, by Rev. Peter Prudden]	OL	100
Sarah, d. John, m. Jobamah **GUNN**, s. Jasper, b. of Milford, Oct. 30, 1663	OL	15
Sarah S., d. John, m. Jobamah **GUNN**, s. Jasper, Oct. 30, 1663	1	6
LARNED, Samuel, s. Isaac, of Mass. Bay, m. Rebeckah **SANFORD**, Sept. 7, 1731, by Samuel Gunn, J.P.	1	92
LAROES, William, d. Feb. [ ], 1799	SM	66
[LARRABEE], LAREABEE, [see also **CAREBEE**, W[illia]m, Capt., d. Sept. 14, 1794 (Heard of death at Martineco)	SM	52
LATIN(?), B. W., d. [ ], 1833	BP	69
LAW, LAWE, Abigail, w. Jonathan, d. Dec. 14, 1705	1	42
Abigail, [w.] Jonathan, d. Dec. 14, 1705	OL	56
Abigail, w. Jonathan, d. Dec. 14, 1705	OL	88
Abigail, [d. Gov. Jonathan], d. Dec. 14, 1705	ES	130
Abigail, d. Jon[a]th[an], b. Mar. 12, 1708/9	OL	65
Abigail, d. Jonathan, b. Mar. 12, 1708/9	1	30
Abigail, [bp.] 1709	ES	238
Abigail, w. Jon[a]th[an], d. Sept.25,1724	1	75
Abigail, [w.] Gov. Jonathan **LAW**, d. Sept.25,1724	ES	130
Abigail, w. Jon[atha]n, d. Sept. 25, 1724	ES	238
Abigail, w. Jon[athan], d. [ ], 1724	ES	238
Ann, d. Jonathan, b. Aug. [ ], 1702	1	27
Ann, d. Jonathan [& Ann], b. Aug. [ ], 1702	OL	56
Ann, bp. 1702	ES	238
Ann, w. Jonathan, d. Nov. 16, 1703	1	42
Ann, w. Jonathan, d. Nov.16, 1703	OL	88
Benedict, m. Sarah **BRYAN**, Jan. 4, 1770. Witnesses David Bryan, Susanna Fowler	1	160
Benedict, d. [ ], 1819, N. Milford	BP	40
Benj[amin]* A., his 1ˢᵗ w. [ ], d. Nov. 30, 1785 *(Benedict hand printed in original manuscript)	SM	30
Jabel, [s. Jonathan, Jr.], [b.] [ ], 1706	ES	238
Jahleel, s. Jonathan, Jr., d. Aug. 2, 1701	1	40
Jahleel, s. Jonathan, d. Aug. 2,1701	1	42
Jahiel, s. Jonathan, d. Aug. 2, 1701	OL	86
Jahleel, s. Jonathan, d. Aug. 16,1701	OL	88
Jahleel, s. Jonathan, b. Feb. 15, 1706/7	1	28
Jahleel, s. Jonathan, b. Feb. 15, 1706/7	OL	61
Jahleel, [bp.] 1707	ES	238
Jehiel, [s. Hon. Jonathan], settled in Cheshire	ES	130
Jno, came to Milford [with] wife Sarah **CLARK**, 1668	ES	177
John, [bp.] 1735	ES	238
John, d. [ ], 1816, at N. Milford	BP	35
John, [s. Hon. Jonathan], d. in Army	ES	130
Jonathan, of Stamford, s. Richard, m. Sarah **CLARKE**, of Milford, d. of George, Sr., June 1, 1664,by Benj[amin] Ffenn, Magistrate	1	6
Jonathan, of Stamford, m. Sarah **CLARK**, of Milford, d. George, Sr., June 1, 1664, by Benjamin **FENN**, Magestrate	OL	16
Jonathan, s. Jonathan & Sarah (**CLARK**), b. Aug. 6, 1674 [Gov.		

	Vol.	Page
LAW, LAWE, (cont.)		
of Conn. 1742-51, 9 y.]	1	14
Jonathan, s. Jonathan, b. Aug. 7, 1674 (Governor Law, 1740)	OL	27
Jonathan, Hon.s. Jonathan & Sarah (**CLARK**), b. Aug. 6, 1674; d. Nov. 6, 1750, ae. 74	ES	130
Jonathan, m. Ann **ELLIOTT**, Dec. 20, 1698	1	27
Jonathan, m. Ann **ELLIOTT**, Dec. 20, 1698	OL	56
Jonathan, Gov., m. Ann **ELLIOTT**, D[ec.] 20, 1698	ES	130
Jon[athan], Jr., adm. to 1ˢᵗ Ch. 1998	ES	238
Jonathan, m. Abigail **ARNOLD**, Feb. 14, 1704/5	OL	56
Jonathan, s. Jonathan, Jr., b. Dec. 5, 1705	1	26
Jon[athan], s. [Jonathan, Jr.], bp. 1705	ES	238
Jonathan, Gov., m. Abigail **ARNOLD**, Feb. 14, 1705	ES	130
Jonathan, s. Jonath[an], Jr., b. Nov. [ ], 1705	ES	238
Jonathan, s. Jona[tha]n, Jr., b. Dec. 5, 1705	OL	55
Jonathan, m. Abigail **ANDREW**, Aug. 1, 1706, by Lieut. Gov. Treat	1	27
Jonathan, m. Abigail **ANDREWS**, Aug. 1, 1706, by Lieut. Gov. Treat	OL	56
Jonathan, Gov. M. Abigail **ANDREWS**, Aug. 2, 1706	ES	130
Jonathan, Sr., d. Jan. 9, 1711/12, in the 75ᵗʰ or 76ᵗʰ y. of his age	1	40
Jon[a]th[an], s. Richard, of Stamford, d. Jan. 9, 1711/12, in the 75ᵗʰ or 76ᵗʰ y. of his age	OL	90
Jon[a]th[an], Sr., d. Jan. 9, 1712	ES	238
Jon[a]th[an], d. Sept. 25, 1724	ES	238
Jonathan, Gov., m. Sarah **ALLEN**, of Fairfield, [ ], 1725	ES	130
Jonathan, Gov., m. Eunice **ANDREWS**, wid. Sam[ue]l, Jr., 1730	ES	130
Jonathan, Jr., m. Mrs. Eunice **ANDREWS**, b. of Milford, Jan. 11, 1736/7, by Jon[a]th[an] Law, Dept. Gov.	1	104
Jon[atha]n, was Dept. Gov. 1736	ES	238
Jonathan, s. Benedict [& Sarah], b. Aug. 6, 1771	1	160
Jonathan, d. Sept. 24, 1790, ae. 85	SM	43
Jonathan, d. [ ], 1803	BP	7
Jonathan, d. July [ ], 1803, in New London	SM	78
Jonathan, [s. Hon. Jonathan,]	ES	130
Mary, "sometime d. of Samuel **CAMP**, m. Josiah **BALDWIN**, s. John, b. of Milford, June 25, 1666, by Mr. Fenn, Magestrate	OL	19
Richard, s. Jonathan, b. July 8, 1713	1	34
Richard, s. Jon[a]th[an], b. July 8, 1713	OL	74
Richard, s. Jonathan, d. Sept. 12, 1713	1	44
Richard, s. Jonathan, d. Sept. 12, 1713	OL	91
Richard, s. [Hon. Jonathan], b. Mar. [ ], 1732; d. [ ], Mayor of New London	ES	130
Richard, [bp.] 1732	ES	238
Samuel, s. Jonathan, Jr., b. May 27, 1711	1	32
Samuel, s. Jonathan, Jr., b. May 27, 1711	OL	70
Sam[ue]l, [bp.] 1711	ES	238
Sam[ue]l, s. Jonath[an], [ ], 1717	ES	238
Samuel, d. Feb. 3, 1780, ae. 69	SM	19
Samuel, [s. Hon. Johnathan] lived with his brother Jonathan	ES	130
Sarah, d. Jonathan, b. Aug. 19, 1701	1	27
Sarah, d. Jonathan [& Ann], b. Aug. 19, 1701	OL	56

	Vol.	Page
LAW, LAWE, (cont.)		
Sarah, bp. 1701	ES	238
Sarah, w. Jonathan, d. Feb. 15, 1705/6	1	43
Sarah, w. Jon[a]th[an], Sr., d. Feb. 15, 1705/6	OL	88
Sarah, d. Jonathan, d. June 18, 1717, in the 16th y. of her age	1	44
Sarah, d. Jon[a]th[an], d. June 18, 1717, in the 16th y. of her age	OL	91
Sarah, of Fairfield, [w. Jonathan], d. [ ], 1726	ES	238
Sarah, w. Jno, Dept. Gov., dismissed from Fairfield, adm. here; d. Jan. 17, 1727	ES	238
Sarah, [bp.] 1730	ES	238
Willis, d. [ ], 1819, ae. 20	BP	39
-----, his d. [ ], d. Sept. 14,1776, ae. 3	SM	7
-----, Gov., m. Abigail ANDREWS, oldest child of Rev. Samuel, [ ]	ES	118
-----, Gov. m. Eunice ANDREWS, wid. of Samuel, [ ]	ES	118
LAWRENCE, LARRANCE, John, Capt. heard of death at Sea, Nov. 15, 1782	SM	24
Martha, w. Thomas, adm. Church Feb. 11, [1645]; dismissed to Stamford	OL	98
Martha, d. Thomas, bp. [1646, by Rev. Peter Prudden]	OL	102
Mary, m. Zachariah ROBERTS, Feb. 8, 1676/7, by Major Treat	1	16
Mary, m. Zachariah ROBERTS, Feb. 8, 1676/7, by Major Treat	OL	32
Thomas, adm. Church Dec. 4, [1642]	OL	98
Thomas, d. Mar. 18, 1648	ES	16
Thomas, d. [ ], 1648	ES	35
Thomas, s. Thomas, b. after the death of his father, bp. {1648, by Rev. Peter Prudden]	OL	103
William, s. William, b. Nov. 3, 1657	1	3
William, s. Will[iam], b. Nov. 3, 1657	OL	10
LAWSON, Hannah, d. Apr. 28,1778, ae. 49	SM	15
LEAVENWORTH, Jennet, m. Harvey LAMBERT, [s. Jesse Peck & Amy], [ ], moved to Mt. Vernon, Knox County, Ohio	1	51
LEE, Hezekiah, of Harwinton, d. Jan. [ ], 1777	SM	10
LEECE, Sarah, d. Sept. 20, 1778, ae. 81	SM	16
LEET, Sarah, m. Thomas Newton, Jr., Jan. 13, 1729	ES	238
Sarah, m. Thomas NEWTON, Jr., Jan. 13, 1729/30, by Sam[ue]ll Eells, Asst.	1	84
LENTHALL, [see also LOUTHALL], Ana, m. Samuel EELLS, of Milford, Aug. 1, 1663, by Capt. Marshall, Commissioner at Lynn	1	7
LEWIS, LEWES, Ann, wid., d. Dec. 18,1793	SM	50
Elerington, d. Elisha & Ann, b. May 22, 1756	1	149
Elisha, drafted for Continental Army	1	58
Elisha Arnold, s. Elisha & Ann, b. June 18, 1760	1	149
John, s. Walter [& Sarah], b. June 15, 1729	1	90
Sarah, formerly Sarah PECK, d. Feb. [ ], 1795 (non resident)	SM	57
Sarah, wid., d. Aug. 8, 1779, ae. 81	SM	18
Sarah Walters, Miss d. [ ], 1813, ae. 82	BP	25
Walter, m. Sarah BASSETT, Nov. [ ], 1728, by Sam[ue]ll Eells, Asst.	1	90
-----, Rev. m. wid. [ ] of Rev. Samuel WHITTLESEY,		

	Vol.	Page

LEWIS, LEWES, (cont.)
    Jr., [   ]   ES   121

LINES, Abel, Priv., member of Capt. Samuel Peck's Co., Milford
1776   1   54
    Mabel, m. John **CLARK**, 3rd, Dec. 31, 1747, by [   ]   1   141
    Mary, of New Haven, m. Allexander **HINE**, of Milford, May 21,
1725, by Ebenezer Joyson, J.P.   1   77

LOBDELL, LOBDILL, LODDELL, Ebenezer, s. Joshua, b. Feb. 24,
1707/8   1   30
    Ebenezer, s. Joshuah, b. Feb. 24, 1707/8   OL   64
    Joshua, m. Mary **BURWELL**, Aug. 11, 1695, by Robert Treat,
Gov.   1   24
    Joshua, m. Mary **BURWELL**, Aug. 11, 1695, by Rob[er]t Treat,
Gov.   OL   50
    Joshua, s. Joshua, b. Mar. 16, 1703/4   1   24
    Joshua, s. Joshua, b. Mar. 16, 1703/4   OL   50
    Mary, d. Joshua, b. Oct. 31, 1704   1   30
    Mary, d. Joshuah, b. Oct. 31, 1704   OL   64
    Samuell, s. Joshua, b. Feb. 2, 1699   OL   50
    Samuel, s. Joshua, b. Feb. 2, 1699/1700   1   24
    Sarah, d. Joshua, b. Feb. 1, 1702/3   1   24
    Sarah, d. Joshua, b. Feb. 1, 1702/3   OL   50
    Simon, came to Milford, 1645   ES   177
    Susannah, d. Joshua, b. Feb. 27, 1709/10   1   31
    Susannah, d. Joshuah, b. Feb. 27, 1709/10   OL   67

LOCKWOOD, William, succeeded to ministry of First Church, Mar.
17, 1784; dismissed Apr. 28, 1796   ES   57
    -----, m. Elizabeth **LAMBERT**, [d. David & Lurania], [   ]   1   53

LONGSTAFFE, Hannah, m. John **WILKINSON**, Jan. [   ], 1717/18,
by Samuel Eells, Asst.   1   64

LOUDEN, Catharine, d. [   ], 1834   BP   71
    Peter, his child d. [   ], 1809   BP   19
    Peter, d. [   ], 1816, ae. [   ]   BP   34

LOUNSBURY, Jairus, Priv., member of Capt. Samuel Peck's Co., Milford, 1776   1   54
    Linus, Priv. member of Capt. Samuel Peck's Co., Milford, 1776   1   54

LOUTHALL, [see also **LENTHALL**], Anna, m. Samuel Eells, Aug.
5, [16]63, by Capt. Marshall, Com. at Lin   OL   18

LOVEKIN, Samuel, d. Jan. [   ], 1777   SM   9

LOVEMAN, [see also **LOVEWELL**], Eleazer, of Rocky Hill, d.
Jan. [   ], 1777   SM   10
    Samuel, s. Elizabeth **GLOVE**, b. June 14, 1741   1   112

LOVEWELL, [see also **LOVEMAN**], Ebenezer, s. Sam[ue]ll, b.
Sept. 7, 1741   1   112

LUCE, Mary Ann, d. [   ], 1814   ES   160

LUD*, Asa, of Haverill, d. Jan. [   ], 1777   *(Perhaps "LAD[D]")   SM   9

LYON, H., removed to Fairfield, 1654   ES   17
    Henry, [d.   ]   ES   18
    Henry, adm. Church Feb. 25, [1648], dismissed to Fairfield
Church   OL   99

LYRAN, LYRON, Hagar, negro, d. Oct. 11, 1795   SM   56
    Jeffrey, d. Oct. 13, 1793, ae. 67   SM   50

MILFORD VITAL RECORDS

	Vol.	Page
MCFEE, Angus, Priv., member of Capt. Samuel Peck's Co., Milford 1776	1	54
Angus, drafted for Continental Army	1	58
MACGREGOR, -----, his child d. [ ], 1839	BP	81
MCKANE, John, for Jeremiah SMITH, drafted for Continental Army	1	58
MCLOUD, John, Priv., member of Capt. Samuel Peck's Co., Milford, 1776	1	54
MADISON, Tho[ma]s, of New London, d. Jan. [ ], 1777	SM	10
MALLETT, A., Capt. his child d. [ ], 1831	BP	65
Alfred, his child d. [ ], 1828, ae. 2 y.	BP	58
Alice, m. Maj. David **BALDWIN**, [ ], 1764.	ES	
Eunice, m. William **COGGESHALL**, Mar. 9, 1779, by Samuel Walas	1	139
Isaac, d. [ ], 1802	BP	6
Isaac, d. [ ], 1802 at Sea	SM	74
John, his s. [ ], d. Dec. 29, 1797	SM	62
John, had infant s. [ ], d. Dec. 16, 1800	SM	70
John, his w. [ ], d. [ ], 1834, ae. 60	BP	72
John, d. [ ], 1834; (crossed)	BP	72
John, d. [ ], 1835	BP	72
Lewis, Priv., member of Capt. Samuel Peck's Co., Milford 1776	1	54
Lewis, his w. [ ], d. Oct. 19, 1789, ae. 78	SM	40
Lewis, d. Sept. 7, 1790, ae. 82	SM	42
Louis*, his w. [ ], d. May 27, 1802, ae. 68 *(Lewis)	SM	74
Louis, his w. [ ], d. [ ], 1802	BP	5
Lewis, d. [ ], 1804	BP	8
Lewis, d. Apr. 3, 1804	SM	79
Luke, his infant, d. [ ], 1833	BP	70
Maria, d. [ ], 1810, ae. 18	BP	20
Miles, his child d. [ ], 1810	BP	21
Miles, his s. [ ], d. [ ], 1817, N. Milford	BP	36
Peter, his w. [ ], d. [ ], 1828, ae. 55	BP	58
Stephen, d. [ ], 1800, supposed to be lost at Sea	SM	71
Stephen, s. Peter, d. [ ], 1815, ae. 14 y.	BP	29
-----, Capt. his child d. [ ], 1830	BP	62
-----, Capt. his child d. [ ], 1835	BP	73
MALLORY, MALARY, MALORY, A., wid., had negro Rose, d. Feb. 4, 1796	SM	58
Aaron, s. Moses [& Frances], b. Nov. 11, 1746	1	122
A[a]ron, s. Moses, b. Mar. 10, 1753	1	133
A[a]ron, s. Moses, b. Mar. 23, 1753	1	133
Amos, his d. [ ], d. May 15, 1801	SM	72
Amos, his child d. [ ], 1801	BP	3
Amos, his child d. [ ], 1805	BP	12
Amos, drafted for Continental Army	1	57
Ann, wid., d. Feb. 7, 1800, ae. 45	SM	69
Anne, wid., d. [ ], 1800, ae. 45	BP	2
Annes, d. Moses & Frances, b. Jan. 29, 1758	1	138
Benajah, his w. [ ], d. [ ], 1829	BP	59
Benajah, Capt., d. [ ], 1837	BP	77
Benjamin, s. Moses & Frances, b. Nov. 20, 1750	1	127
Benjamin, s. Moses, b. Dec. 22, 1765	1	149
Daniel, Capt., d. Sept. 10, 1795, at Carolina (Heard of death)	SM	55

	Vol.	Page
MALLORY,MALARY, MALORY, (cont.)		
David, s. Moses & Frances, b. Oct. 18, 1760	1	142
David, drafted for Continental Army	1	57
Francis, d. Moses, b. Sept. 29, 1748	1	125
Jasper, d. Aug. 8, 1785, ae. 29	SM	29
John, d. May 3, 1776, ae. 36	SM	6
Jonas, heard of death at Sea, Nov. 12, 1798	SM	65
Judah, m. Jeremiah **CANFIELD**, July 24, 1711, by Jonathan Law, J.P.	1	39
Judah, m. Jeremiah **CANFIELD**, July 24, 1711, by Jon[a]th[an] Law, J.P.	OL	85
Lorin, d. [ ], 1823	BP	49
Malthus(?), d. [ ], 1824	BP	50
Moses, m. Frances **OVIATT**, Aug. 19, 1744, by Rev. Jedadiah Mills, of Preston	1	122
Moses, s. Moses [& Frances], b. Feb. 22,1744/5	1	122
Moses, Priv., member of Capt. Samuel Peck's Co., Milford, 1776	1	54
Moses, d. Dec. 7, 1793, ae. 69	SM	50
Moses, his w. [ ], d. [ ], 1811, ae. 70	BP	21
Moses, d. [ ], 1826	BP	55
Munson, s. Abijah & Hannah, b. July 31, 1798	1	174
Rebeckah, d. Moses, b. June 12, 1755	1	134
Sam[ue]ll, s. Moses & Frances, b. Oct. 27, 1762	1	146
Samuel, his d. [ ], d. Oct. 27, 1790, ae. 43	SM	43
Samuel, his w. [ ], d. [ ], 1813	BP	25
Sam[ue]l, d. [ ], 1818,ae. 60	BP	38
-----, Mrs., d. [ ], 1808	BP	18
-----, wid., d. [ ], 1812	BP	23
MALTBY, MAULBEE, MALBE, John, m. Mary **BRYAN**, d. of Richard, merchant, Feb. 28, 1666, by Thomas Clark, Commissioner *(Written "John **MAULBE**")	1	8
John, merchant, m. Mary **BRYAN**, d. Richard, merchant, Feb. 28, 1666, by Mr. Clark, Com.	OL	19
Mary, d. John, merchant, b. Feb. 18, 1670	OL	23
Mary, d. John, merchant, b. Feb. 18, 1670/1	1	10
MANSFIELD, Samuel, d. Sept. 20, 1776	SM	7
Susannah, of New Haven, m. John **STONE**, of Milford, Jan. 14, 1741/2, by Jos[eph] Noyes	1	123
MANSILL, Joseph, of New Haven or Waterbury, d. Jan. [ ], 1777	SM	9
MANSON, [see also **MUNSON**], Daniel, d. [ ], 1827, ae. 83	BP	56
MANUELL, Ann, wid., of Angelo (?), m. Richard **LAMBERT**,, [s. Jesse & Mary], [ ], 1666	1	49
Ann, m. Richard **LAMBERT**, s. Jesse [& Mary], [ ], had no children	1	106
MARCHANT, [see under **MERCHANT**]		
MARDIKE, W[illia]m, his w. [ ], d. Jan. 16, 1785	SM	29
William, d. Oct. 8, 1794	SM	52
MARKS, MARCKS, Abram, his w. [ ], d. [ ], 1816	BP	34
Edward, his infant s. [ ], d. Oct. 26, 1788	SM	37
Hannah, m. Benjamin **PRITCHARD**, Jr., July 4, 1733, by Rev. Jon[a]th[an] Arnold	1	95
Mary, wid., d. [ ], 1812	BP	23

	Vol.	Page
MARKS, MARCKS, (cont.)		
Zachariah, d. Aug. 25, 1802, ae. 68	SM	75
Zachariah, d. [ ], 1802	BP	5
-----, Mr., d. [ ], [1811, not heard of at the time]	BP	24
MARSH, MASH, Dorothy, d. Jonathan, bp. [1653, by Rev. Peter Prudden]	OL	104
John, s. Jonathan, bp. [1654, by Rev. Peter Prudden]	OL	104
John, s. Jonathan, b. [ ], 1655	OL	7
Joh[a]th[an], s. John[a]th[an], b. Feb. [ ], 1653/4	1	1
Johnathan, s. Jonathan, b. Sept. 29, 1657	1	3
Jonathan, s. Jonathan, b. Sept. 29, 1657	OL	10
Mary, w. Jonathan, adm. Church Feb. 2, [1653]	OL	99
Mary, d. Jonathan, bp. [1653, by Rev. Peter Prudden]	OL	104
Sam[ue]ll, came to Milford, 1649	ES	178
Sarah, d. Jonathan, bp. [1653, by Rev. Peter Prudden]	OL	104
MARSHALL, Abigail, Miss d. [ ], 1837, ae. 25	BP	78
E., Mrs., d. [ ], 1819, ae. 80	BP	40
Jonathan, d. [ ], 1815, ae. 71	BP	28
Joseph, his w. [ ], d. Jan. 24, 1789, ae. 71	SM	39
Joseph, d. [ ], 1801	BP	3
Joseph, Jr., d. [ ], 1801	BP	3
Joseph, Sr., d. Feb. 17, 1801	SM	71
Joseph, schoolmaster, d. Apr. 20, 1801	SM	72
Joseph, d. [ ], 1818, ae. 40	BP	38
Lydia, of Derby, d. Dec. 30, 1785, ae. 32	SM	30
Sam[ue]ll Bryan, fifer, member of Capt. Samuel Peck's Co., Milford, 1776	1	54
Susanna, d. Aug. 26, 1776, ae. [ ]	SM	7
MARTIN, Joseph Plum, Priv., member of Capt. Samuel Peck's Co., Milford, 1776. After the War he settled in Prospect, Me.	1	54
Joseph Plumb, drafted for Continental Army	1	58
Susanna, her s. [ ], d. Dec. 30, 1789	SM	40
MARVIN, MERVIN, [see also **MERWIN**], Elizabeth, Mrs., m. Lieut. Joseph Treat, widower, Nov. 8, 1705, by Robert Treat, Dept. Gov.	1	26
Hannah, d. Miles, b. Nov. 15, 1667	1	8
Han[n]ah, d. Miles, b. Nov. 15, 1667	OL	19
Hannah, d. Miles, m. Abell **HOLBROOK**, Dec. 20, 1683	1	19
Han[n]ah, d. Sam[ue]ll, b. Jan. 14, 1701/2	OL	72
Hannah, d. John, b. Nov. 2, 1709	1	32
Jestinah, d. Samuel, b. Oct. 16, 1704	1	25
John, m. Mary **HOLBROOK**, wid., Apr. 12, 1683	1	21
John, s. John, b. Sept. 23, 1684	1	21
John, m. Elizabeth **BALDWIN**, Jan. 6, 1704/5, by Capt. Samuel Eells, J.P.	1	26
John, m. Hannah **PLATT**, Feb. 7, 1705/6, by Capt. Eells	1	26
John, s. John, b. Apr. 3, 1707	1	30
Martha, [twin with Mary], d. Miles, b. Jan. 23, 1665	OL	17
Martha, m. James **PRIME**, Sept. 20, 1685, by Capt. John Beard, Commissioner	1	21
Mary, [twin with Martha], d. Miles, b. Jan. 23, 1665	OL	17
Reinold, of Cebrook (Saybrook), m. Sarah **CLARKE**, of Milford,		

	Vol.	Page
MARVIN, MERVIN, [see also **MERWIN**], (cont.)		
Nov. 27, 1663, by Benjamin Ffenn, Magistrate	1	6
Ronold, of Saybrook, m. Sarah **CLARK**, of Milford, Nov. 27, 1663, by Benjamin Fenn, Magestrate	OL	16
Samuel, Sr., d. Jan. 12, 1705/6	1	26
Sarah, m. Zachariah **BALDWIN**, Aug. 25, 1708, by Thomas Clarke, J.P.	1	30
MARWIN, [see under **MERWIN**]		
MASH, [see under **MARSH**]		
MATHER, Samuel, son-in-law of [Gov. Robert], [ ]	ES	238
MATTHEWS, -----, Mrs., d. [ ], 1837	BP	78
MAYO, Elizabeth, m. Rev. Samuel **TREAT**, s. Gov. Robert, [ ]; had 11 children	ES	105
MECOCK, Tho[ma]s, came to Milford, 1658	ES	178
MELBOURNE, George, Sergt. of Salem, d. Jan. [ ], 1777	SM	9
MERCHANT, MARCHANT, Abraham, s. Joseph, b. Apr. 9, 1725	1	109
Abraham, d. Aug. 2, 1790, ae. 64	SM	42
Amos, s. Joseph, b. July 12, 1722	1	109
Amos, s. Samuel, b. Sept. 29, 1748	1	128
Amos, s. Samuel, d. Dec. 25, 1750	1	128
Esther, d. Sam[ue]ll, b. Jan. 21, 1744	1	128
Ezra, s. Joseph, b. Dec. 20, 1720	1	109
Harriet, divorced w. of Sam[ue]l & d. of John **HARPIN**, m. Henry **BULL**, Apr. 7, 1785, by Rev. David Fuller	1	174
Job, s. Joseph, b. Sept. 2, 1715	1	109
Job, Jr., a prisoner in New York, heard of his death, Jan. 20, 1777	SM	11
Job, his w. [ ], d. Sept. 1, 1785, ae. 63	SM	29
Job, d. Sept. 19, 1789	SM	40
Joseph, of Milford, m. Abigaill **WHEELER**, of Durham, Oct. 27, 1714, by Joseph Treat, J.P.	1	109
Joseph, d. Mar. 24, 1779. "Killed with a gun by D. Curtis"	SM	17
Samuell, s. Joseph, b. Nov. 1, 1718	1	109
Sam[ue]ll, m. Sarah Fenn, b. of Milford, Aug. 29, 1739, by Roger Newton, Asst.	1	109
Samuel, s. Sam[ue]ll, b. Mar. 1, 1742	1	128
Samuel, d. Oct. 9, 1793	SM	50
Sarah, d. Sam[ue]ll & Sarah, b. Aug. 16, 1740	1	110
Sibella, d. Samuel, b. Dec. 15, 1750	1	128
Stephen, d. Aug. 17, 1784, on Long Island	SM	28
Stephen, drafted for Continental Army	1	58
Susannah, d. Samuel, b. Mar. 3, 1746	1	128
Thomas, s. Joseph, b. June 9, 1727	1	109
-----, Mrs., d. [ ], 1804	BP	8
-----, wid., d. Jan. 14, 1804	SM	79
MERRETT, Timothy, his s. [ ], d. Sept. 16, 1777	SM	13
MERRIMAN, Abel, his child d. [ ], 1825	BP	52
Abel, colored his child d. [ ], 1833	BP	68
Peter, colored d. [ ], 1838, ae. 55	BP	80
MERWIN, MARWIN, MURWIN, [see also **MARVIN**], Abigail, wid., d. [ ], 1834, ae. 82	BP	72
Ann, d. Daniel, b. Nov. 30, 1712	1	35
Ann, d. Daniel [& Sarah], b. Nov. 30, 1712	OL	77

MERWIN, MARWIN, MURWIN, [see also MARVIN], (cont.)

	Vol.	Page
Ann, d. Daniel, b. Mar. 24, 1715/16	1	38
Ann, d. Dan[ie]ll, b. Mar. 24, 1715/16	OL	82
Ann, d. Miles, Jr. & Ann, b. Dec. 23, 1723	1	74
Ann, w. Miles, Jr., d. Dec. 31, 1723	1	74
Ann, m. Andrew **BALDWIN**, May 23, 1753, by Nathan Baldwin, J.P.	1	133
Anson, his infant child d. [ ], 1814	BP	26
Clemence, wid., d. Oct. 29, 1794, ae. 84	SM	52
Daniel, s. Miles, b. June 28, 1661	1	4
Daniel, m. Sarah **BOTCHFORD**, Nov. 30, 1710, by Joseph Treat, J.P.	1	35
Daniel, m. Sarah **BOTCHFORD**, Nov. last day, 1710, by Joseph Treat, J.P.	OL	76
Daniel, s. Daniel, b. Sept. 15, 1714	1	35
Daniel, s. Dan[ie]ll [& Sarah], b. Sept. 15, 1714	OL	77
Daniel, d. Dec. 19, 1798	SM	65
Daniel, his w. [ ], d. [ ], 1821	BP	45
David, s. John, Jr., b. Mar. 2, 1716	1	74
David, d. [ ], 1816	BP	34
David, d. [ ], 1832	BP	67
Deborah, d. Miles, b. Apr. 24, 1670	1	10
Deborah, d. Miles, b. Apr. 24, 1670	OL	22
Elizabeth, d. Miles, Jr., b. Jan. 10, 1683	1	19
Elizabeth, d. Miles, Jr., b. Jan. 10, 1683	OL	41
Elizabeth, Mrs. m. Lieut. Joseph **TREAT**, [b.] of Milford, Nov. 8, 1705, by Robert Treat, Dept. Gov.	OL	54
Elizabeth, d. John, Jr. [& Elizabeth], b. Apr. 11, 1732	1	98
Elizabeth, wid., d. [ ], 1833, ae. 96	BP	70
Eunice, wid., d. [ ], 1836	BP	75
Hannah, d. Miles, m. Abell **HOLBROOK**, Dec. 17, 1683	OL	40
Hannah, d. Samuel, b. Jan. 14, 1701/2	1	33
Hannah, d. John, Jr., b. Nov. 2, 1709	OL	70
Hannah, d. John & Hannah, m. Capt. John **COLLINS**, Oct. 29, 1730, by Sam[ue]ll Eells, Asst.	1	94
Homer, d. [ ], 1840, ae. 25	BP	84
Jack, negro, d. [ ], 1803, at Sea	BP	7
Jered, his w. [ ], d. [ ], 1839, ae. 25	BP	82
Jestinah, d. Samuell, b. Oct. 16, 1704	OL	51
John, m. wid. Mary **HOLBROOK**, Apr. 12, 1683	OL	42
John, s. Jno, b. Sept. 23, 1684	OL	42
John, m. Elizabeth **BALDWIN**, Jan. 6, 1704/5, by Capt. Sam[ue]ll Eells, J.P.	OL	53
John, m. Hannah **PLATT**, Feb. 7, 1705/6, by Capt. Eells	OL	56
John, s. John, Jr., b. Apr. 3, 1707	OL	65
John, d. Jan. 15, 1727/8	1	82
John, Jr., m. Elizabeth **NETTLETON**, b. of Milford, Dec. 2, 1730, by Sam[ue]ll Eells, Asst.	1	98
John, s. John, Jr., b. July 25, 1735	1	108
John, Jr., his s. [ ], d. Apr. 24, 1778	SM	15
John, his s. [ ], d. May 21, 1780	SM	19
John, his negro boy d. Mar. 9, 1781	SM	21

	Vol.	Page
MERWIN, MARWIN, MURWIN, [see also **MARVIN**], (cont.)		
John, d. Feb. 17, 1792, ae. 84	SM	47
John, 3rd, d. [ ], 1820, ae. 41	BP	41
John, Jr., d. [ ], 1822	BP	47
John, d. [ ], 1826, ae. 90	BP	54
Joseph, s. Jonathan, Jr., b. Feb. 2, 1711/12	1	33
Joseph, s. Jno, Jr., b. Feb. 2, 1711/12	OL	72
Joseph, d. Feb. 4, 1782	SM	23
Julia, Mrs., d. [ ], 1808, ae. 26	BP	18
Julia, d. Thom[as], d. [ ], 1820, ae. 16	BP	41
Lewis, d. [ ], 1822	BP	47
Margaret, of Oister River, d. Oct. 29, 1790	SM	44
Mark, his infand child d. [ ], 1819	BP	39
Mark, his w. [ ], d. [ ], 1835, ae. 39	BP	72
Martha, [twin with Mary], d. Miles, b. Jan. 23, 1665/6	1	7
Martha, m. James **PRIME**, Sept. 20, 1685, by Capt. John Beard, Com.	OL	42
Martha, d. [ ], 1830, ae. 18	BP	62
Mary, [twin with Martha], d. Miles, b. Jan. 23, 1665/6	1	7
Mary, w. John, d. Oct. 20, 1703	1	41
Mary, w. John, d. Oct. 20, 1703	OL	87
Mary, d. John, Jr., b. Sept. 22,1725	1	79
Mary, wid., d. Nov. 27, 1797, ae. 73	SM	62
Mary Miels, d. Miles & Mary, b. Mar. 10, 1734	1	100
Miles, s. Miles, b. Dec. 14, 1658	1	3
Miles, s. Miles, b. Dec. 14, 1658	OL	11
Miles, d. Apr. 23, 1697	1	40
Miles, Sr., d. Apr. 23, 1697	OL	86
Miles, tanner, came to Milford, 1665; d. 1697	ES	178
Miles, m. Anne **TREAT**, Sept. 25, 1718, by Rev. Samuel Andrews, Witnesses, John Fowler, Susannah Fowler	1	67
Miles, s. Miles [& Anne], b. Nov. 29, 1719	1	67
Miles, s. Daniel, b. Mar. 29, 1721	1	68
Miles, d. Sept. 18,1724, in the 66th y. of his age	1	76
Miles, of Milford, m. Mrs. Mary **ALLEN**, of New Haven, Nov. 11, 1730, by Sam[ue]ll Bishop, J.P. Witnesses Stephen Trowbridge, Joseph Miles	1	88
Miles, had negro Harry, d. Sept. 12, 1794	SM	52
Miles, Mrs. had negro Cyrus, d. [ ], 1807	BP	15
Miles, Jr., his child d. [ ], 1808	BP	17
Miles, d. [ ], 1820	BP	42
Miles, his w. [ ], d. [ ], 1829	BP	60
Miles, m. Julia **CARRINGTON**, d. Elias, [ ]	1	162
Miles, m. Isabell **HAYNES**, [ ]	ES	238
Peter, d. Apr. 2, 1801	SM	72
Samuell, s. Miles, b. Aug. 21, 1656	OL	10
Samuel, Sr., d. Jan. 12, 1705/6	OL	55
Samuel, m. Mary **BURWELL**, May 1, 1707, by Thomas Clarke, J.P.	1	28
Sam[ue]ll, m. Mary **BURWELL**, May 7, 1707, by Thomas Clark, J.P.	OL	60
Samuel, his w. [ ], d. Dec. 8, 1799, ae. 24	SM	68
Samuel, his w. [ ], d. [ ], 1799, ae. 24	BP	2

	Vol.	Page

MERWIN, MARWIN, MURWIN, [see also MARVIN], (cont.)

	Vol.	Page
Samuel, d. [ ], 1825, ae. 63	BP	53
Samuel, his w. [ ], d. [ ], 1831	BP	65
Sarah, w. Miles, d. Mar. 5, 1697/8	1	40
Sarah, w. Miles, Sr., d. Mar. 5, 1697/8	OL	86
Sarah, m. Zachariah **BALDWIN**, Aug. 25, 1708, by Thomas Clark, J.P.	OL	64
Sarah, d. John, b. Apr. 15, 1714	1	35
Sarah, d. John, b. Apr. 15, 1714	OL	77
Sarah, d. Daniel, b. June 10, 1718	1	38
Sarah, d. Daniel, b. June 10, 1718	OL	82
Stephen, s. Miles, Jr., b. Oct. 22, 1722; d. Dec. 23, 1722	1	72
Susannah, Mrs., d. [ ], 1825	BP	52
Tho[ma]s, his other d. [ ], d. [ ], 1820	BP	41
W[illia]m, his child d. [ ], 1823	BP	48
-----, wid. had negro Tanier, d. Nov. 13, 1776	SM	8
MEVERICK (?), -----, Mrs., d. [ ], 1824	BP	51

MIELS, [see under **MILES**]

MILES, MIELS, Bethiah, m. Josiah **TIBBALLS**, Jr., Oct. 24, 1705,

	Vol.	Page
by Samuel Eells, J.P.	1	30
Bethiah, m. Josiah **TIBBALLS**, Jr., Oct. 24, 1705, by Sam[ue]ll Eells, J.P.	OL	64
Dan, Capt. his child d. [ ], 1810	BP	21
Dan, Capt. D. [ ], 1813, at Sea	BP	32
Daniel, s. John & Martha, b. Oct. 11, 1747	1	155
Daniel, his d. [ ], d. Mar. 23, 1782	SM	23
Daniel, d. Feb. 1, 1786	SM	31
Daniel, his s. [ ], d. Nov. 10, 1791	SM	46
Daniel, his w. [ ], d. Nov. 1, 1799	SM	68
Daniel, Capt. his w. [ ], d. [ ], 1799	BP	2
Daniel, Jr., Capt., d. [ ], 1805	BP	11
Daniel, Capt., d. [ ], 1808	BP	17
David, s. Stephen, b. Dec. 21, 1731	1	94
David, s. John & Martha, b. May 20, 1745	1	155
David, his 1st w. [ ], d. Apr. 22, 1791	SM	45
David, d. Jan. 14, 1800, ae. 53	BP	2
David, d. Jan. 16, 1800, ae. 55	SM	69
David, his child d. [ ], 1822	BP	46
Isaac, s. Stephen & Susannah, b. May 8, 1728	1	249
Isaac, d. Nov. 15, 1780, ae. 56	SM	20
Isaac, Capt., d. Dec. [ ], 1800, supposed to be lost at Sea	SM	70
Jane, Mrs., d. [ ], 1824	BP	50
Jared, s. John & Martha, b. Sept. 3, 1750	1	155
Jared, in captivity, heard of death Apr. 18, 1780	SM	19
John, m. Martha **SMITH**, b. of Milford, Nov. 3, 1737, by Sam[ue]ll Eells, Asst.	1	107
John, s. John & Martha, b. Aug. 3, 1738	1	155
John, d. [ ], 1815, ae. 77	BP	30
Katharine, m. Nathaniel **SMITH**, Apr. 21, 1752, by Rev. Sam[ue]ll Whittlesey	1	133
Martha, b. [ ], 1704; m. Capt. Charles **POND**, [ ]; d. May 29, 1797	1	59
Martha, d. John & Martha, b. Apr. 26, 1740	1	155

	Vol.	Page
MILES, MIELS, (cont.)		
Martha, wid., d. Apr. 26, 1797	SM	61
Martha, wid., d. [ ], 1831, ae. 50	BP	64
Mary, d. Stephen, b. Feb. 17, 1734/5	1	102
Mary, m. Sylvanus **DICKINSON**, June 18, 1782	1	178
R., removed to New Haven, [ ]	ES	17
Rebeckah, d. Stephen [& Rebeckah], b. Oct. 21, 1751	1	128
Richard, d. [ ], (One of the first planters)	ES	16
Richard, adm. Church, Oct. 13, [1639], at New Haven	OL	97
Samuel, bp. Apr. 12, [1640], at New Haven, by Rev. Peter Prudden	OL	100
Sarah, Mrs., m. Rev. Jonathan **ARNOLD**, of West Haven, July 29, 1728, by Sam[ue]ll Eells, Asst.	1	82
Sarah, d. Daniel & Elizabeth, b. July 15, 1751	1	131
Stephen, m. Mary **HOLBROOK**, [ ], 1697, by Tho[ma]s Clark, J.P., Witnesses Miles Merwin, Hannah Merwin	1	72
Stephen, his eldest s. b. Jan. 20, 1701	1	71
Stephen, s. Stephen & Mary (**HOLBROOK**), b. Jan. 20, 1701	1	72
Stephen, m. Susannah **BURWELL**, wid., Feb. 11, 1724, by Sam[ue]ll Eells, Asst.	1	249
Stephen, s. Stephen & Susannah, b. Aug. 5, 1726	1	249
Stephen, m. Frances **GILLETT**, May 1, 1734, by Sam[ue]ll Gunn, J.P.	1	99
Stephen, of Milford, m. Rebeckah **HUMPHREYVILLE**, of New Haven, Dec. 6, 1751, by Jno Fowler, J.P.	1	128
Susan, d. [ ], 1840, ae. 26, at Alton, Ill.	BP	83
Susannah, d. Stephen, b. June 7, 1730/1	1	89
Susannah, w. Stephen, d. June 16, 1733	1	96
Susannah, d. Jan. 16, 1788, ae. 36	SM	36
Susanna A., d. Theophilus, d. Sept. 27, 1796, ae. 3 y.	SM	59
Theophilus, s. Samuel, b. Dec. 1, 1703	OL	48
Theophilus, s. Samuel, b. Dec. 10, 1703	1	23
Theo[philus], Capt., 1750	ES	41
Theo[philus], Col., d. [ ], 1767, ae. 63	ES	180
Theophilus, s. Theophilus, d. Oct. 2, 1796	SM	60
Theophilus, d. [ ], 1833	BP	70
Thorp, his 1ˢᵗ w. [ ], d. May 15, 1790, ae. 27	SM	42
Tyler, d. [ ], 1829, ae. 76	BP	60
-----, wid., d. [ ], 1825, ae. 86	BP	53
MILLER, MILLAR, Amos, his child d. [ ], 1803, ae. 7	BP	7
-----, Mr., his d. [ ], d. Apr. 8, 1803	SM	77
-----, his child d. [ ], 1834	BP	71
MILLS, Tyley, s. Daniell & Elizabeth, b. Apr. 27, 1755	1	135
MINOR, [see also **MINOT**], E., his infant d. [ ], 1820, ae. 3 d.	BP	41
Eastman, d. [ ], 1825	BP	52
Eliza, d. of Matthew, m. Willis [**LAMBERT**], [s. Jesse Peck & Amy], [ ], 1823	1	51
J. J., d. [ ], 1831, ae. 53	BP	64
Jennet, m. Treat [**LAMBERT**], [s. Jesse Peck & Amy], [ ]	1	51
MINOT, [see also **MINOR**], Richard, of Mass., d. Jan. [ ], 1777	SM	9
MITCHELL, Asahel, of Woodbury, m. Nancy **LAMBERT**, [d. Jesse Peck & Amy], [ ]	1	51

MILFORD VITAL RECORDS

	Vol.	Page
MITCHELL, (cont.)		
George, d. Dec. 6, 1786	SM	32
Justice, Rev. of New Canaan, m. [ ]	ES	128
Mehitable, d. [Sept.] 1777, at New Haven	SM	13
Ruth, wid., d. Oct. 14, 1799	SM	68
Whiting, s. George, b. Aug. 5, 1767	1	172
-----, wid., d. [ ], 1799	BP	2
MONRO, -----, Mr., d. [ ], 1830, ae. 56	BP	61
MOORE, Abel, s. Miles, bp. [1651, by Rev. Peter Prudden]	OL	104
Deborah, d. Miles, bp. [1647, by Rev. Peter Prudden]	OL	102
Elnathan, s. Miles, bp. [1644,by Rev. Peter Prudden]	OL	101
Elnathan, d. M[ ] 11, 1645, ae. 11 m.	ES	238
Elnathan, d. [ ], 1648, ae. 4 y.	ES	35
Elnathan, s. Miles, b. Oct. 14, 1655	1	2
Elnathan, s. Miles, b. Oct. 14, 1655	OL	9
Elnathan, s. Miles, bp. [1655, by Rev. Peter Prudden]. ("Crossed over in the original perhaps because his mother was excommunicated")	OL	105
Lydia, d. Miles, bp. [1649, by Rev. Peter Prudden]	OL	103
Mary, d. Miles, b. Feb. 5, 1653	OL	7
Mary, d. Miles, bp. [1653, by Rev. Peter Prudden]	OL	104
Mary, d. Miles, b. Jan. 1, 1653/4	1	1
Miles, m. Isabel **JAYNER**, [ ]	OL	98
Miles, adm. Church [ ], 1651	OL	99
Miles, came to Milford, 1666	ES	178
Miriam, d. Miles, bp. [1647, by Rev. Peter Prudden]	OL	102
MORRIS, David, Priv., member of Capt. Samuel Peck's Co., Milford 1776	1	54
David, heard of death (in captivity), Mar. 4, 1780	SM	19
Elisha, his child d. [ ], 1812	BP	24
Elisha, his w. [ ], d. [ ], 1821	BP	44
George, d. Mar. 10, 1776, ae. 45	SM	5
John, drafted for Continental Army	1	58
John, s. George & Eunice, b. Apr. 4, 1754	1	133
Joseph, d. Nov. 10, 1776, at Seabrook	SM	8
Joseph, d. Jan. 3, 1778	SM	15
Joseph, his w. [ ], d. [ ], 1805	BP	10
Mercy, d. Mar. [ ], 1778	SM	15
Newton J., his s. [ ], d. Sept. 12, 1789	SM	40
Newton John, his 1ˢᵗ w. [ ], d. Apr. 1, 1792, ae. 34	SM	47
Richard, his s. [ ], d. Apr. 29,1796	SM	58
Richard, d. [ ], 1825, ae. 63	BP	53
Thomas, formerly of Milford, d. May [ ], 1777	SM	12
W[illia]m, d. [ ], 1805	BP	12
-----, m. George **HINE**, May 10, 1744, by Rev. Sam[ue]ll Whittlesey	1	121
-----, wid., d. Sept. 9, 1781	SM	22
MORSE, Nicholas, m. Clarissa [**LAMBERT**, d. Frederic & Sally,]	1	50
MULET, Elioce, m. Maj. David **BALDWIN**, Feb. 2,1764. Witnesses: Lewes Mulet, Jr., Mary Mulet	1	156
MULFORD, -----, Capt., d. [ ], 1812, at N. Milford	BP	23
MUNSE, [see also **MUNSON**], Esther, of Derby, m. Gideon		

	Vol.	Page
MUNSE, [see also MUNSON], (cont.)		
NORTHROP, of Milford, Mar. 17, 1747/8, by Rev. Daniel Humphrey, of Derby	1	123
MUNSON, [see also MUNSE], Daniel, m. Mary SEARS, May 22, 1766, by Rev. Job Prudden. Witnesses; Job Fowler, Jr., Susannah Fowler, 2nd	1	168
Daniel, s. Daniel & Mary, b. Sept. 20, 1773	1	168
Daniel, Jr., his w. [ ], d. Jan. 3, 1797, ae. 22	SM	61
Elizabeth, d. Daniel & Mary, b. July 30, 1775	1	168
Frances, d. Daniel & Mary, b. Dec. 28, 1779	1	168
John, s. Daniel & Mary, b. Jan. 27, 1778	1	168
Lewis, his infant d. [ ], 1837	BP	77
Mary, d. Daniel & Mary, b. Aug. 11, 1771	1	168
Sarah, d. Daniel & Mary, b. Sept. 3, 1769	1	168
William, s. Daniel & Mary, b. Feb. 26, 1767	1	168
-----, wid., d. [ ], 1833	BP	68
-----, his infant d. [ ], 1839	BP	82
MURDOCK, -----, Mr., d. [ ], 1813	BP	33
MURWIN, [see under MERWIN]		
MYRECK, Polly, Indian, d. [ ], 1813	ES	14
M-----, E-----, m. [ ] CUBITT, Indian, Nov. 11, 1709	1	30
NETTLETON, Albert, his child d. [ ], 1837	BP	78
Amos, his child d. [ ], 1815, North Milford	BP	28
Benoni, s. Nathan, b. June 12, 1729; d. June 17, [1729]	1	85
Caleb, his w. [ ], d. Apr. 10, 1799	SM	66
Caleb, his w. [ ], d. May 12, 1799	BP	1
Caleb, his child d. [ ], 1807	BP	15
Caleb, his child d. [ ], 1808	BP	17
Caleb, d. [ ], 1839, ae. 82	BP	81
David, d. June 12, 1792, ae. 28	SM	48
David, d. [ ], 1827, ae. 35	BP	56
Eli, s. Nathan, & Sibella, b. Apr. 9, 1761	1	154
Elizabeth, d. Samuel, b. Oct. 6, 1686	1	24
Elizabeth, d. Samuell, b. Oct. 6, 1686	OL	50
Elizabeth, m. John MERWIN, Jr., b. of Milford, Dec. 2, 1730, by Sam[ue]ll Eells, Asst.	1	98
Hannah, d. Samuel, of Branford, m. Thom[as] UFFOT, s. of Thomas [ ], by Mr. Fenn, J.P.	1	3
Hannah, d. Samuel, of Branford, m. John UFFET, s. Thomas, of Milford, [ ], by Mr. Ffenne, Magestrate	OL	10
Harry, d. [ ], 1821 "Shot by J. Clark a lad"	BP	44
Isaac, d. Dec. 5, 1800	SM	70
Isaac, his child d. [ ], 1805	BP	11
Jean, wid., d. [ ], 1809	BP	18
John, s. Samuel, b. Sept. 18, 1689	1	24
John, s. Samuell, b. Sept. 18, 1689	OL	50
John, s. Nathan & Sibella, b. Jan. 9, 1765	1	154
Joseph, s. Samuel, b. Feb. 16, 1700	1	24
Joseph, s. Samuell, b. Feb. 16, 1700	OL	51
Joseph, his child d. [ ], 1829	BP	60
Joseph, his child d. [ ], 1835	BP	73
Joseph, his child d. [ ], 1837, ae. 18 m.	BP	77

	Vol.	Page
NETTLETON, (cont.)		
Levi, had s. [ ], d. Feb. 11, 1797, ae. 4 m.	SM	61
Levi, his s. [ ], d. Nov. 22, 1798	SM	65
Levi, his w. [ ], d. [ ],1828	BP	58
Lewis, d. [ ], 1829	BP	60
Martha, d. Samuel, b. Oct. 20, 1697	1	24
Martha, d. Sam[ue]ll, b. Oct. 27, 1697	OL	51
Martha, m. Freegift **COGGESHALL**, Jan. 28, 1725/6, by Sam[ue]ll Eells, Asst.	1	115
Martha, m. Freegift **COGGESHALL**, [ ], 1726	ES	238
Ma[r]tha, m. Justice **BALDWIN**, Nov. 26, 1771, by Rev. Sam[ue]ll Whittlesey	1	160
Mary, d. Silvanus & Mary, b. Oct. 1, 1732	1	93
N., Dea., his w. [ ], d. [ ], 1830, ae. 72	BP	62
Nathan, s. Samuel, b. Jan. 21, 1693/4	1	24
Nathan, s. Samuell, b. Jan. 21, 1693/4	OL	50
Nathan, m. Susannah **PLUM**, Jan. 14, 1724/5, by Sam[ue]ll Eells, Asst.	1	85
Nathan, m. Sybell **BUCKINGHAM**, Nov. 3, 1757, by Rev. Job Prudden	1	137
Nathan, s. Nathan & Sibbell, b. Feb. 10, 1759	1	140
Nathan, d. Sept. 23, 1782, ae. 49	SM	24
Nath[anie]ll, m. Martha **BALDWIN**, Feb. 8, 1681, by Major Treat	OL	38
S., Mrs., d. [ ], 1803, ae. 64	BP	7
S[a]m[uel], came to Milford, 1645	ES	178
Samuel, m. Martha **BALDWIN**, Feb. 8, 1681, by Maj. Treat	1	18
Samuel, s. Samuel, b. Dec. 16, 1691	1	24
Samuell, s. Samuell, b. Dec.16, 1691	OL	50
Samuel, s. Silvanus [& Mary], b. Dec. 18,1729	1	93
Samuel, d. Jan. 25, 1778, ae. 86	SM	15
Samuel, d. Sept. 28, 1803, ae. 74	SM	78
Samuel, d. [ ], 1803	BP	8
Silvanus, [see under Sylvanus]		
Susannah, d. Nathan, b. Apr. 26,1726	1	85
Silvanus, s. Samuel, b. Oct. 12, 1704	1	24
Silvanus, s. Sam[ue]ll, b. Oct. 12, 1704	OL	51
Silvanus, m. Mary **WHITTEMORE**, Apr. 24, 1729, by Sam[ue]ll Eells, Asst.	1	93
Sylvanus, d. May 6, 1780, ae. 76	SM	19
Sym[ ]m, his child d. [ ], 1833,ae. 25	BP	69
Thaddeus, his w. [ ], d. May 11, 1799	SM	66
Thad[d]eus, Jr., his d. [ ], d. Aug. 22, 1802	SM	75
Thaddeus, d. [ ], 1808	BP	17
Theophilus, s. Samuel, b. June 1, 1702	1	24
Theophilus, s. Sam[ue]ll, b. June 1, 1702	OL	51
Theophilus, s. Samuel, d. May 6, 1713	1	44
Theophilus, s. Sam[ue]ll, d. May 6, 1713	OL	91
Thomas, his w. [ ], d. May 10,1799	BP	1
Tho[ma]s, his child d. [ ], 1802	BP	5
W[illia]m, his infant child d. [ ], 1830	BP	61
W[illia]m, his w. [ ], d. [ ], 1830	BP	61
-----, wid., d. July 5, 1803	SM	78

	Vol.	Page
NEWHALL, Eleazer, of Milford, m. Elizabeth ROBERTS, of Milford, May 5, 1739, by Sam[ue]ll Eells, Asst.	1	108
NEWTON, Abie, [d. Ezekiel, Jr. & Abigail], b. Feb. [ ], 1722	ES	238
Abigail, Mrs. dismissed from Ch. in Guilford, 1696 & received here	ES	238
Abigail, d. Ezek[iel], bp. 1716	ES	238
Abigaill, d. Fletcher, m. Nathan PECK, May 5, 1845*, by Rev. Sam[ue]ll Whittlesey *(Probably 1745?)	1	125
Abigail, [d. Fletcher]	ES	238
Abner, s. Capt. Sam[ue]ll, b. May [ ], 1699; went to Durham	ES	238
Alice, d. Rev. Rog[er], [ ] Sept. 18, 1674	ES	238
Alice, [d. Rev. Roger,]	ES	116
Allis, [twin with Hannah], d. Fletcher, [ ], 1718	ES	238
Alice, d. Fletcher, bp. 1718	ES	238
Alice, d. Fletcher, [ ], 1738	ES	238
Alice, d. Fletcher & Hannah, d. Oct. 1,1777, ae. 62	SM	14
Ann, d. Tho[ma]s,b. Sept. 22, 1718	1	81
Ann, [d. Thomas & Mary], b. Oct. 22,1719	ES	238
Avice, [d. Ezekiel, Jr.], [ ], 1719	ES	238
Bette, d. Tho[ma]s, b. Feb. 5, 1715/16	1	81
Bettie, [d. Thomas & Mary], b. Feb. 5, 1716	ES	238
Bette, d. Tho[mas], [ ], 1717	ES	238
Christopher, s. [Ezekiel], bp. 1716	ES	238
Christopher, s. Ezekiel, Jr., b. Dec. [ ], 1716	ES	238
Christopher, Rev., d. [ ], 1787 (non resident)	SM	35
Christopher, Rev., s. Ezekiel & grandson of Rev. Roger, b. Dec. [ ], 1716; d. [ ], 1787	ES	121
Christopher, d. [Feb.], 1795, at Sea	SM	54
Christopher, his w. [ ], d. Sept. 6, 1795 (non resident)	SM	57
Comfort, d. Oct. 8,1799, ae. 30	SM	68
Comfort, d. [ ], 1799, ae. 30	BP	2
Elizabeth, [d. Fletcher], bp. 1724	ES	238
Eunice, d. Ezek[iel], bp. 1716	ES	238
Eunice, [d. Thomas, Jr. & Sarah], b. Apr. 9, 1732	ES	238
Eunice, d. Thomas, Jr., b. Apr. 9, 1733	1	93
Ezekiel, s. Richard, b. Dec. 19, 1659	1	2
Ezekiell, s. Roger, b. Dec. 19, 1659	OL	12
Ezekiel, s. wid. Lydia, bp. 1700	ES	238
Ezekiel, s. Lydia, bp. A[ug] 7, 1700	ES	238
Ezekiel, m. Abigail BRISCOE, May 21, 1711, by Rev. Grindal Rawson, of Mendam	1	35
Ezekiel, m. Abigail BRISCOE, May 21, 1711, by Rev. Grindall Rawson, of Mendam	OL	75
Ezekiel, s. Ezek[iel], bp. 1716	ES	238
Ezekiel, [s. Rev. Roger,]	ES	116
Fletcher, s. Roger, b. Jan. [ ], 1685	ES	238
Fletcher, s. Roger, grandson of Rev. [ ], bp. [ ], 1686	ES	238
Francis, came to Milford, 1660; d. 1665	ES	178
George, Col. S. of supposed Capt. Samuel & grandson of Rev. Roger, b. about 1684; d. Jan. 15, 1771, ae. 87. Distinguished on a military ex. to Long Island 1709/10; m. Susannah BRYAN, Apr. 10, 1712; had children, Roger, Susannah, Martha	ES	116

MILFORD VITAL RECORDS 127

	Vol.	Page
NEWTON, (cont.)		
Hannah, [d. Capt. Roger], b. [ ], 1715	ES	238
Hannah, d. Fletcher, bp. 1718	ES	238
Hannah, [twin with Allis], d. Fletcher, [ ], 1718	ES	238
Hannah, d. [Sergt. Sam[ue]l], [ ], 1727	ES	238
James, s. James & Rebeckah, b. Sept. 20, 1753	1	142
John, m. Lidia FORD, Apr. 14, 1680, by Major Treat, Dept. Gov.	1	18
John, m. Lidia FORD, Apr. 14, 1680, by Major Robert Treat, Dept. Gov.	OL	35
Joh, d. [ ], 1699	ES	238
John, s. Lydia, bp. A[ug] 7, 1700	ES	238
John, s. wid. Lydia, bp. 1700	ES	238
John, [s. Ezekiel, Jr.], [ ], 1725	ES	238
John, [s. Ezekiel, Jr. & Abigail], b. July [ ], 1726	ES	238
John, his negro Jeff, d. May 8, 1776	SM	6
John, 3rd, d. Oct. 4, 1776	SM	7
John, Jr., his w. [ ], d. Apr. 22, 1779	SM	17
John, d. Mar. 31, 1781, ae. 84	SM	21
John, Capt., d. [ ], 1795, at Crown Point (non resident)	SM	57
John, d. Dec. 21, 1797	SM	62
John, [s. Rev. Roger]	ES	116
Jonah, s. Samuel, b. Oct. 20, 1714	1	36
Jonah, s. Samuel, b. Oct. 20, 1714	1	36
Jonah, s. Sam[ue]ll, b. Oct. 20, 1714	OL	77
Jonah, Jr., d. Oct. [ ], 1794, ae. 18	SM	52
Jonah, Capt. his negro d. Aug. 20, 1803	SM	78
Jonah, Capt., d. [ ], 1816, ae. 72	BP	34
Jonah, Capt. His wid., d. [ ], 1818. "Drowned in the Housatonic"	BP	38
Joseph, s. Sam[ue]l, [ ], 171[ ]	ES	238
Joseph, s. Sam[ue]l, [ ], 1718	ES	238
Joseph, s. Thomas, Jr., b. Sept. 14, 1730	1	89
Joseph, [s. Thomas, Jr. & Sarah], b. Sept. 14, 1730	ES	238
Joseph, s. Tho[mas, Jr. [ ], 1730	ES	238
Joseph, d. [ ], 1807, ae. 57	BP	16
Lemuel, s. Roger, Pastor, m. Martha FFENN, d. Benjamin, Mar. 14, 1668/9, by John Clerk, Commissioner	1	9
Luriah, d. Ezekiel, Jr., [ ], 1718	ES	238
Luriah, [child of Ezekiel, Jr. & Abigail], b. Jan. [ ], 1718	ES	238
Lydia, had sons Ezekiel & John, bp. A[ug.] 7, 1700	ES	238
Martha, d. Samuel, b. July 14, 1671	1	11
Martha, d. Samuel, b. July 14, 1671	OL	23
Martha, [d. Capt. Roger], bp. 1729	ES	238
Martha, d. Capt. Roger & Susannah, b. Jan. 27, 1729/30	1	88
Martha, [d. Col. Roger & Susannah], b. J[ ] 27, 1730	ES	238
Martha, [d. Col. George & Susannah], [ ]	ES	116
Mary, d. Sam[ue]l N., bp.[ ], 1680	ES	238
Mary, d. Roger, b. Aug. [ ], 1687	ES	238
Mary, d. Roger, [ ], 1688	ES	238
Mary, w. Thomas, adm. to 1st Ch. 1705	ES	238
Mary, d. Tho[ma]s & Mary, b. Aug. 25, 1708/9	1	80
Mary, [d. Thomas & Mary], b. Feb. 9, 1709	ES	238
Mary, d. Thomas, [ ] Nov. 8, 1709	ES	238

128   BARBOUR COLLECTION

	Vol.	Page
NEWTON, (cont.)		
Mary, d. [Thomas], bp. 1709	ES	238
Mary, [d. Fletcher], bp. 1721	ES	238
Mary, m. John **FOWLER**, Jr., Dec. 9, 1742, by John Fowler, J.P.	1	137
Mary, m. Jno **FOWLER**, Jr., Dec. 9, 1742	ES	238
Mary, w. Thomas, d. Mar. 29, 1744	1	118
Mary, w. Thomas, d. Mar. 29, 1744	ES	238
Mary, w. Thomas, d. May 29, 1744	ES	238
Phebe, d. Samuel, b. Nov. 25, 1706	1	28
Phebe, d. Samuel, b. Nov. 25, 1706	OL	60
Phebe, d. Sam[ue]l, bp. 1709	ES	238
Phebe, [twin with Samuel], d. Sam[ue]l, b. [ ], 1711	ES	238
Phebe, m. Joseph **WOODRUFF**, Jan. 22, 1728/9, by Roger Newton, J.P.	1	92
Roger, Col., [ ]	ES	40
Roger, [s. Col. George & Susannah] [ ]	ES	116
Roger, [s. Rev. Roger,]	ES	116
Roger, s. Sam[ue]l N., bp. [ ]	ES	238
Roger, came to Milford, 1659	ES	178
Roger, Rev., d. July 7, 1683; had been pastor 22 ½ yrs.; his children were, Samuel, Ezekiel, John, Roger, Sarah & Alice; his w. [ ], d. Feb. 4, 1675	ES	116
Roger, [s. Sam[ue]l & grandson of Rev. Roger, b.], Mar. [ ], 1680	ES	238
Roger, 2d pastor of First Church Aug. 22, 1660, coming from Farmington; d. June 7, 1683	ES	57
Roger, adm. to 1st Ch. 1681; d. Apr. 19, 1690	ES	238
Roger, Capt., 1711	ES	40
Roger, Capt., m. Mrs. Susannah **BRYAN**, Apr. 10, 1712	1	34
Roger, Capt., m. Mrs. Susannah **BRYAN**, Apr. 10, 1712	OL	73
Roger, s. Capt. Roger, b. Mar. 14, 1712/13	1	35
Roger, s. Capt. Roger, b. Mar. 14, 1712/13	OL	75
Roger, s. Capt. Roger, bp. 1713	ES	238
Roger, Capt. adm. To Ch. 1713	ES	238
Roger, s. Capt. Roger, b. [ ], 1713	ES	238
Roger, Capt. had Pomphey, Indian m. Pitty, Indian, Jan. 6, 1727/8, by Roger Newton, J.P.	1	91
Roger, Col., d. Jan. 15, 1771	1	165
Samuel, s. Rev. Roger, m. Martha **FFENN**, d. Benjamin, Asst., b. of Milford, Mar. 14, 1668/9, by William East, Com.	OL	22
Samuel, s. Samuel, b. June 26, 1677	1	16
Samuel, s. Samuel, b. June 26, 1677	OL	31
Sam[uel], s. Sam[ue]l & grandson of Rev. R[oger], b. Ju[ ] 26, 1777; d. [ ], 1708	ES	238
Sam[ue]l, Capt., 1698	ES	40
Samuel, m. Phebe **PLATT**, Nov. 29, 1705, by Robert Treat, Dept. Gov.	1	26
Samuel, m. Phebe **PLATT**, Nov. 29, 1705, by Robert Treat, Dept. Gov.	OL	54
Samuel, s. Samuel, b. Aug. 1, 1710	1	31
Samuel, s. Samuel, b. Aug. 1, 1710	1	36
Samuel, s. Sam[ue]ll, b. Aug. 1, 1710	OL	68
Sam[ue]ll, s. Sam[ue]ll, b. Aug. 1, 1710	OL	77

MILFORD VITAL RECORDS

	Vol.	Page
NEWTON, (cont.)		
Sam[ue]l, adm. to 1ˢᵗ Ch. 1710	ES	238
Samuel, [twin with Phebe], s. Sam[ue]l, b. [ ], 1711	ES	238
Samuel, Sr., had two sons Samuel & Roger	ES	238
Samuel, s. [Rev. Roger], b. [ ]	ES	116
Sarah, d. Roger, b. Jan. 24, 1661	1	5
Sarah, d. Roger, b. Jan. 24, 1661	OL	14
Sarah, Mrs., m. John WILSON, July 4, 1683	1	19
Sarah, Mrs., m. John WILSON, July 4, 1683	OL	39
Sarah, Mrs., m. John WILSON, [ ], 1683	ES	185
Sarah, d. Samuel N., b. Sept. [ ], 1686	ES	238
Sarah, d. Sam[ue]l, [ ], 1686	ES	238
Sarah, d. Tho[ma]s & Mary, b. July 10, 1713	1	81
Sarah, [d. Thomas & Mary], b. July 10, 1713	ES	238
Sarah, [d. Ezekiel, Jr.], [ ], 1723	ES	238
Sarah, [d. Ezekiel, Jr. & Abigail], b. July [ ], 1723	ES	238
Sarah, Mrs. alias **FOWLER**, d. Aug. 5, 1723	1	74
Sarah, [d. Rev. Roger,]	ES	116
Susan, grand-daughter of Rev. R[oger], b. July 16, 1671	ES	238
Susan, d. [Thomas], bp. 1711	ES	238
Susan, d. [ ], 1809, ae. 22	BP	18
Susanna, d. Samuel, b. July 15, 1671, [1673?]	1	16
Susanna, d. Samuel, b. July 15, 1671	OL	31
Susanna, d. Tho[ma]s & Mary, b. Jan. 25, 1711/12	1	80
Susannah, [d. Capt. Roger], bp. 1715	ES	238
Susanna, d. Capt. Roger, b. Jan. 14, 1715/16	1	38
Susannah, d. Capt. Roger, b. Jan. 14, 1715/16	OL	83
Susannah, Mrs., m. Sam[ue]ll **WHITTLESEY**, Sept. 21, 1743, by Roger Newton, Asst.	1	151
Susannah, eldest d. of Col. Roger, m. Rev. Samuel **WHITTLE-SEY**, s. Rev. Samuel, Sept. 21, 1743. Had children Samuel, Susannah, Roger Newton, Sarah	ES	121
Susanna, Mrs., m. Rev. Sam[ue]ll **WHITTLESEY**, Sept. 21, 1743, by Roger Newton	1	153
Susannah, d. Col. Roger, m. Rev. Samuel **WHETTLESEY**, s. Rev. Samuel, of Wallingford, Sept. 21, 1743	ES	238
Susannah, m. Samuel **WHITTLESEY**, Sept. 21, 1743	ES	238
Susannah, m. Sam[uel] **WHITTLESEY**, Sept. 21, 1743	ES	238
Susannah, [d. Col. George & Susannah], [ ]	ES	116
Susanna, d. Rog[er], m. Ez[ ] **STONE**, [ ]	ES	238
Thomas, s. Samuel, b. Apr. 21, 1675	1	16
Thomas, s. Sam[ue]ll, b. Apr. 21, 1675	OL	29
Thomas, s. Samuel, b. Apr. 21, 1675	OL	31
Thomas, s. Samuel, b. Apr. 21, 1675; [d. Apr. 30, 1675]	1	14
Tho[mas], s. Sam[ue]l, bp. [ ], 1675	ES	238
Thomas, s. Rev. [ ], b. Apr. [ ], 1675; m. Mary **BALDWIN**, June 20, 1704	ES	238
Tho[mas], s. Lieut. [ ], b. [ ], 1697; d. 1698	ES	238
Thomas, m. Mary **BALDWIN**, June 20, 1704, by Thomas Clark, J.P.	1	79
Thomas, s. Tho[ma]s, b. Feb. 28, 1704/5; d. May 31, 1705	1	80
Thomas, adm. to 1ˢᵗ Ch. & bp. [ ], 1705	ES	238

	Vol.	Page
NEWTON, (cont.)		
Tho[mas], adm. to 1ˢᵗ Ch. 1705	ES	238
Thomas, s. Tho[ma]s, b. [ ], 1706	ES	238
Tho[ma]s, s. Tho[ma]s & Mary, b. Feb. 8, 1706/7	1	80
Thomas, Jr., [s. Thomas & Mary], b. Feb. 8, 1707; m. Sarah LEET, Jan. 13, 1729	ES	238
Tho[mas], s. Tho[mas], bp. 1707	ES	238
Thomas, Jr., m. Sarah LEET, Jan. 13, 1729/30, by Sam[ue]ll Eells, Asst.	1	84
-----, s. Rev. R[ ], m. Martha FENN, Mar. 12, 1669	ES	180
-----, [child of Sam[ue]l & grandson of Rev. Roger, b. May [ ], 1679]	ES	238
-----, [ ], 1716	ES	238
-----, Col. his sister m. Joseph WOODRUFF, [ ], 1720	ES	238
-----, w. Col. [ ], d. May 15, 1776	SM	6
-----, wid., d. Jan. 18, 1784	SM	27
-----, Capt. had negro Tim, d. Oct. 17, 1796, at Sea (Heard of death)	SM	60
-----, wid., d. [ ], 1826, ae. 78	BP	54
NICHOLS, Amos, s. Peter, negro, d. Mar. 11, 1800	SM	69
Peter, his s. [ ], d. June 8, 1801	SM	72
Peter, his w. [ ], d. Aug. 11, 1800	SM	69
Peter, negro his child d. [ ], 1811	BP	22
NORTHROP, NORTHROPP, A., Mrs. her child d. [ ], 1809	BP	19
Abel, his child d. Jan. 7, 1791	SM	45
Abel, d. May 13, 1803	SM	77
Abel, d. [ ], 1803	BP	7
Abel, his wid., d. [ ], 1825	BP	53
Abel, [s. Joseph & Ruth], b. [ ]	1	46
Abigail, d. Samuel, b. May 14, 1699	1	23
Abigall, d. Sergt. Sam[ue]ll, b. May 14, 1699	OL	48
Abigail, m. Jonathan GARNSEY, Jan. 6, 1724/5, by Sam[ue]ll Eells, Asst.	1	77
Abigail, d. Ephraim [& Sarah], b. Aug. 10, 1731	1	97
Abigail, [d. Ephraim], b. Aug. 10, 1731; d. Mar. 20, 1790	1	46
Abigail, d. Joel & Abigaill, b. Apr. 4, 1734	1	98
Abigaill, m. Lawrence CLINTON, May 20, 1741, by Rev. Benjamin Woodbridge	1	120
Abigail, d. Capt. Joel, of Milford, m. Richard SPERRY, Jr., of New Haven, Dec. 9, 1755, by Rev. Benjamin Woodbridge of Amity	1	134
Abigail, d. Joel & Abigail, b. Apr. 5, 1761	1	145
Abigail, d. Mar. 20, 1790, ae. 56	SM	41
Abigail Grace, d. Job & Violet, b. Oct. 19, 1770	1	159
Amos, m. Mary GUNN, Jan. 6, 1714, by Sam[ue]ll Eells, Asst.	1	62
Amos, m. Ann BALDWIN, Dec. 16, 1741, by Sam[ue]ll Gunn, J.P.	1	112
Amos, s. Amos & Ann, b. Dec. 19, 1742	1	113
Amos, his infant s. [ ], d. Oct. 7, 1799	SM	68
Amos, his child d. [ ], 1799	BP	2
Amos, his s. [ ], d. Oct. 24, 1800	SM	70
Amos, his child d. [ ], 1812, ae. 17 y.	BP	23

MILFORD VITAL RECORDS 131

	Vol.	Page
NORTHROP, NORTHROPP, (cont.)		
Andrew, [s. Joseph & Ruth], b. June 9, 1735/6	1	46
Andrew, s. Joseph [& Ruth], b. Jan. 9, 1735/6	1	103
Ann, [d. William], b. [ ], 1708	1	46
Anne, d. Joel, b. Jan. 8, 1764	1	148
Betsey, d. [ ], 1819, N. Milford	BP	39
Caleb, d. [ ], 1788	ES	165
Caleb, d. [ ], 1812	BP	23
Clement, his infant d. [ ], d. Apr. 22, 1790	SM	41
Clement, his 1ˢᵗ w. [ ], d. Apr. 20, 1791, ae. 35	SM	45
Clement, his 2ⁿᵈ w. [ ], d. Mar. 6, 1795, ae. 46	SM	54
Clement, d. [ ], 1810	BP	20
Daniel, [s. Joseph], b. Aug. 1, 1701	1	46
Daniel, s. Gideon & Easther, b. Nov. 20, 1757	1	140
Daniel, d. Oct. 22, 1788 (died absent)	SM	38
Daniel, d. [ ], 1788, at Derby	ES	165
David, s. David, b. Aug. 1, 1701	1	22
David, s. Daniell, b. Aug. 1, 1701	OL	47
David, s. Gideon & Easther, b. Nov. 12, 1750	1	140
Ebenezer, s. Daniel, b. May 8, 1698	1	22
Ebenezer, s. Daniell, b. May 18, 1698	OL	47
Elizabeth, d. Phinehas & Elizabeth, b. Jan. 17, 1732	1	96
Elizabeth, d. Gideon, b. Apr. 16, 1749	1	125
Eliza[bet]h, wid., d. [ ], 1814	BP	26
Ephraim, s. William, b. Jan. 2, 1696	OL	44
Ephraim, s. William, b. Jan. 4, 1696	1	20
Ephraim, farmer, [s. William], b. Jan. 4, 1696; m. Sarah, d. Samuel **GUNN**, Nov. 26, 1730; d. Oct. 10, 1767	1	46
Ephraim, m. Sarah **GUNN**, Nov. 26, 1730, by Sam[ue]ll Gunn, J.P.	1	97
Ephraim, [s. Ephraim], b. Apr. 26, 1733; d. at the North in the French War	1	46
Ephraim, s. Ephraim & Sarah, b. Apr. 26, 1733; d. [ ], 1752, in the Army at the North in the French War	1	97
Ephraim, his w. [ ], d. Nov. 1, 1780	SM	20
Ephraim, d. Oct. 10, 1787, ae. 91	SM	34
Ephraim, s. W[illia]m N., m. Sarah **GUNN**, d. Ens. Sam[ue]ll [ ]	OL	69
Easther, d. Gideon & Easther, b. Apr. 7, 1755	1	140
Easther, d. Ephraim, m. Dr. Elias **CARRINGTON**, Feb. 23, 1763. Witnesses Ephraim Northrop, Laraus Northrop	1	162
Esther, [d. Ephraim], b. [ ]; m. Elias **CARRINGTON**, M.D., [ ]	1	46
Esther, [d. Ephraim & Sarah], b. [ ]	1	97
Gideon, of Milford, m. Esther **MUNSE**, of Derby, Mar. 17, 1747/8, by Rev. Daniel Humphrey, of Derby	1	123
Gideon, s. Gideon & Easther, b. Nov. 7, 1752	1	140
Hannah, d. Samuel, b. Dec. 13, 1696	1	23
Hannah, d. Sergt. Sam[ue]ll, b. Dec. 13, 1696	OL	48
Hannah, d. William, b. Dec. 1, 1699	1	20
Hannah, d. William, b. Dec. 1, 1699	OL	44
Hannah, [d. William], b. Dec. 1, 1699	1	46
Hannah, m. Roger **PRITCHARD**, Mar. 8, 1715/16, by Joseph		

NORTHROP, NORTHROPP, (cont.)

	Vol.	Page
Treat, J.P.	1	66
Hannah, m. James **SMITH**, Jr., Mar. 20, 1727/8	1	97
Hannah, d. Joel & Ruth, b. Sept. 27, 1728	1	248
Hannah, of Milford, m. Elnathan **CHATFIELD**, of Derby, Sept. 12, 1754, by Rev. Benjami Woodbridge, of Amity	1	135
Heth, [s. Joseph & Ruth], b. [ ]	1	46
Heth, pd. £5 for not procuring men for Continental Army	1	55
Hezekiah, s. Joel, b. Apr. 26, 1766	1	149
Isaac, of Amity, drafted for Continental Army	1	57
Isaac, s. Job & Violet, b. Mar. 28, 1760	1	143
Jane, d. Amos, d. Apr. 28, 1730	1	86
Jaen, d. Amos, d. Apr. 28, 1730	1	95
Jaen, d. Joseph [& Ruth], b. May 14, 1732	1	103
Jane, m. Job **CLARK**, b. of Milford, Sept. 28, 1749, by Rev. Job Prudden	1	126
Jeremiah, s. Joseph, formerly of Springfield, Mass., now of Milford, b. Jan. 18, 1653	OL	7
Jeremiah, s. Joseph, bp. [1653, by Rev. Peter Prudden]	OL	104
Jeremiah, s. Joseph, b. Jan. 18, 1653/4	1	1
Jeremiah, [s. Joseph], b. Jan. 19, 1653/4	1	46
Joan, d. Amos, b. Mar. 13, 1718	1	62
Job, s. William, b. [ ], 1705; settled in New Milford	OL	44
Job, [s. William], b. [ ], 1705; settled in Newtown	1	46
Joel, s. Sergt. Samuel, b. Feb. 14, 1691	1	23
Joell, s. Sergt. Sam[ue]ll, b. Feb. 14, 1691	OL	48
Joel, m. Abigail **CAMP**, June 24, 1731, by Roger Newton, J.P.	1	98
Joel, s. Joel & Abigail, b. Apr. 26, 1732	1	98
Joel, m. Abigail **CAMP**, Oct. 12, 1756	1	136
Joel, s. Joel & Abigail, b. Feb. 23, 1758	1	138
John, s. Joseph, b. Sept. 7, 1656	1	3
John, s. William, b. June 17, 1703	1	20
John, s. William, b. June 17, 1703; settled in Ridgefield, Conn.	OL	44
John, [s. William], b. June 17, 1703; settled in Ridgefield	1	46
John, [s. Joseph & Ruth], b. May 14, 1732	1	46
John, [s. Joseph], b. Sept. 7, 1756	1	46
John, s. Joseph, b. Sept. 7, 1756	OL	9
John, s. Job & Violet, b. Apr. 1, 1775	1	166
Joseph, came to Milford in 1639 with the Watertown Co., via Wethersfield; his name appears on the Court Records of Springfield; d. 1699* *(Hand corrected to 1669 in original manuscript)	1	46
Joseph, adm. Church Mar. 27, [1642] d. Sept. 11, 1669	OL	98
Joseph, s. Joseph, bp. [1649, by Rev. Peter Prudden]	OL	103
Joseph, [s. Joseph, bp. July 17, 1649; d. June 1, 1700	1	46
Joseph, [d.] Sept. 11, 1669	ES	18
Joseph, in 1671, destroyed the Indian Fort	ES	14
Joseph, s. William, b. Feb. 6, 1698	1	20
Joseph, s. William, b. Feb. 6, 1698	OL	44
Joseph, [s. William], b. Feb. 6, 1698; was a shoemaker; m. Ruth **ALLEN**, June 10, 1725	1	46
Joseph, m. Susanna **ROBERTS**, Nov. 20, 1713, by Joseph Treat, J.P.	1	35

	Vol.	Page
NORTHROP, NORTHROPP, (cont.)		
Joseph, m. Susannah **ROBERTS**, Nov. 20, 1713, by Joseph Treat, J.P.	OL	76
Joseph, m. Ruth **ALLEN**, June 10, 1725, by Sam[ue]ll Eells, Asst.	1	103
Joseph, [s. Joseph & Ruth], b. Jan. 24, 1728/9	1	46
Joseph, s. Joseph [& Ruth], b. Jan. 24, 1728/9	1	103
Joseph, s. Job & Violet, b. July 29, 1766	1	154
Josiah, s. Zopher, b. Sept. 29, 1699	1	24
Josiah, s. Zopher, b. Sept. 29, 1699	OL	49
Josiah, member of 2nd Church formed in 1742	ES	87
Josiah, d. Feb. 4, 1788	SM	36
Lazarus, pd. £5 for not procuring men for Continental Army	1	55
Lazarus, [s. Ephraim & Sarah], b. June 8, 1735	1	97
Lazarus, s. Ephraim, b. June 8, 1735	1	103
Lazarus, [s. Ephraim], b. June 8, 173[5?]; d. Nov. 2, 1802	1	46
Lazarus, d. Nov. 2, 1802	SM	76
Lazarus, d. [ ], 1802	BP	6
Lazarus, m. Mahitabeel **CAMP**, w. of David & d. John & Sarah **PECK**, [ ]	1	133
Lydia, d. Sam[ue]ll, Jr., b. Oct. 25, 1749	1	125
Margaret, d. Samuel, b. Aug. 19, 1702	1	23
Marg[ar]et, d. Sergt. Sam[ue]ll, b. Aug. 19, 1702	OL	48
Margaret, d. Joel & Abigail, b. Apr. 22, 1771	1	157
Martha, [d. Ephraim & Sarah], b. [ ], 1737; m. David **LAMBERT**, [ ]	1	97
Martha, [d. Ephraim], b. July 21, 1737; m. David **LAMBERT**, d. Oct. 27, 1815, ae. 78	1	46
Martha, d. Eph[rai]m, m. David **LAMBERT**, s. Jesse [& Mary], [ ], 1755	1	106
Martha, d. Ephraim & Sarah (**GUNN**), m. David **LAMBERT**, 3d s. Jesse [& Mary], Mar. 8, 1757; d. Oct. 27, 1815, ae. 78	1	51
Mary, d. Joseph, decd., b. Jan. 6, 1669	OL	23
Mary, d. Joseph, b. Jan. 1, 1669/70	1	10
Mary, [d. Joseph], b. Jan. 1, 1670	1	46
Mary, d. Samuel, b. Sept. 13, 1694	1	23
Mary, d. Sergt. Sam[ue]ll, b. Sept. 13, 1694	OL	48
Mary, d. Zopher, b. Aug. 16, 1702	1	24
Mary, d. Zopher, b. Aug. 16, 1702	OL	49
Mary, d. Amos, b. Sept. 29, 1714	1	62
Mary, m. Josiah **TIBBALLS**, Jr., Apr. 4, 1717, by Sam[ue]l Eells, Asst.	1	62
Mary, [d. Joseph & Ruth], b. May 24, 1726	1	46
Mary, d. Joseph [& Ruth], b. May 24, 1726	1	103
Mary, m. Henry **PECK**, July 4, 1729, by Sam[ue]ll Gunn, J.P.	1	95
Mary, d. Joel [& Mary], b. Dec. 27, 1734	1	97
Mary, [d. Ephraim & Sarah], b. [ ], 1739; m. Joel **SMITH**, [ ]	1	97
Mary, m. David **CANFIELD**, Oct. 3, 1745, by Rev. Sam[ue]ll Whittlesey	1	120
Mary, d. Job & Violet, b. Mar. 2, 1762	1	144
Mary, [d. Ephraim], b. [ ]; m. Joel **SMITH**, [ ]	1	46

NORTHROP, NORTHROPP, (cont.)

	Vol.	Page
Mary Ann, d. Aug. 6, 1791, ae. 16	SM	46
Mehitabeel, m. Josiah **HINE**, s. Sam[ue]ll & Elizabeth, Aug. 23, 1733, by Roger Newton, J.P.	1	99
Mehitable, wid., d. [ ], 1833, ae. 80	BP	69
Mercy, d. Samuel, b. Sept. 7, 1715	1	37
Mercy, d. Sam[ue]ll, b. Sept. 7, 1715	OL	79
Moses, s. Joseph, bp. 1695	ES	238
Moses, d. [ ], 1807, ae. 77	BP	15
Philo, s. Job & Violet, b. Apr. 11, 1767	1	155
Phinehas, m. Elizabeth **BRINSMEAD**, Dec. 9, 1732, by Sam[ue]ll Gunn, J.P.	1	94
Rebeckah, d. Job & Violet, b. Oct. 30, 1768	1	155
Rebeckah, d. Job & Violet, b. Dec. 11, 1772	1	163
Ruth, d. Joel, b. Aug. 23, 1725	1	248
Ruth, [d. Joseph & Ruth], b. Mar. 15, 1730	1	46
Ruth, d. Joseph [& Ruth], b. Mar. 15, 1730	1	103
Ruth, w. Joel, d. Dec. 27, 1730	1	98
Ruth, m. Samuel **BRISCOE**, Dec. 11, 1746, by Rev. Benjamin Woodbridge, of Amity	1	120
Ruth, wid., d. Nov. 9, 1780	SM	20
Samuel, s. Joseph, bp. [1651, by Rev. Peter Prudden]	OL	104
Samuel, [s. Joseph], b. [ ], 1658	1	46
Samuel, m. Sarah **ANDREWS**, Feb. 25, 1713/14, by Jonathan Law, J.P.	1	35
Sam[ue]ll, m. Sarah **ANDREWS**, Feb. 25, 1713/14, by Jon[a]th[an] Law, J.P.	OL	75
Sam[ue]ll, s. Sam[ue]ll, b. June 24, 1718	1	66
Samuel, Jr., of Milford, m. Lydia **THOMAS**, of New Haven, June 10, 1746, by Isaac Dickerman, J.P.	1	125
Samuel, Sr., d. [ ] 26, 1748	1	124
Sam[ue]ll, b. Apr. 1, 1749; d. Apr. 15, [1749]	1	125
Samuel, s. Samuel & Lydia, b. Oct. 18, 1755	1	134
Sarah, d. David, b. July 28, 1702	1	22
Sarah, d. Daniell, b. July 28, 1702	OL	47
Sarah, d. Joel & Ruth, b. Mar. 20, 1727	1	248
Sarah, [wid. of Ephraim], d. Nov. 1, 1780	1	46
Thomas, s. William, b. Mar. 16, 1701	1	20
Thomas, tailor, [s. William], b. Mar. 16, 1701; settled in Newtown	1	46
Thomas, s. William, b. May 16, 1701; settled in New Town, Conn.	OL	44
Timothy, d. Nov. 16, 1777	SM	14
William, s. Joseph, b. June 2, 1666	1	8
William, s. Josiah, b. June 2, 1666	OL	19
William, [s. Joseph], b. June 2, 1666; m. Hannah **BALDWIN**(?)	1	46
William, s. William, b. Dec. 16, 1694	1	20
William, s. William, b. Dec. 16, 1694; settled in Greenfield Hill, Fairfield Co.	OL	44
William, farmer, [s. William], b. Dec. 16, 1694; settled in Greenfield, Town of Fairfield	1	46
William, d. [ ], 1803, at Sea, in Capt. Peck's vessel	BP	7
William, d. [ ], 1812	BP	23
William A., d. Feb. [ ], 1803, at Sea, board Peck	SM	77
Zopher, s. Joseph, b. June 21, 1661	1	4

	Vol.	Page
NORTHROP, NORTHROPP, (cont.)		
Zophar, [s. Joseph], b. June 21, 1661	1	46
Zopher, s. Joseph, b. June 25, 1661	OL	14
-----, wid. [ ], [1659 and 1662]	ES	238
-----, Capt. his w. [ ], d. [ ], 1801	BP	4
-----, Mrs., d. [ ], 1813, at New Haven	BP	26
NORTON, Elizabeth, d. John, of Hermingtown, m. John **PLUMB,** s. Robert, decd., Nov. 24, 1 668, by John Allyn, Magistrate	1	9
Elizabeth, d. John, of Farmington, m. John **PLUMB,** s. Robert, of Milford, decd., Nov. 24, 1668, by John Allene, Magestrate	OL	21
Samuel, s. James & Rebeckah, b. Nov. 25, 1743	1	118
NOTT, W[illia]m, Capt. his w. [ ], d. Dec. 14, 1778	SM	16
William, his w. [ ], d. Nov. 18, 1801	SM	73
-----, Capt., d. [ ], 1815, ae. 76	BP	29
NOYES, Mary, d. James, b. Oct. 9, 1666	OL	18
OATMAN, Pheebee, of Stratford, m. Phinehas **TERRELL,** of Milford, July 7, 1747, by Sam[ue]ll Adams, J.P.	1	125
O'KANE, O'KAINE, O'CAINE, [Anthony], his s. [ ], supposed to be dead, 1817	BP	36
Anthony, d. [ ], 1817, in West Indies	BP	36
Anthony, his w. [ ], d. [ ], 1826	BP	55
Francis, his child d. [ ], 1832, ae. 2 y.	BP	66
Francis, had another child d. [ ], 1832, ae. 4 y.	BP	66
Francis, his infant child d. [ ], 1833	BP	70
Notts Anthony, Frenchman, drafted for Continental Army	1	58
OLMSTEAD, ULMSTEAD, UMSTEAD, Betsey, had negro d. [ ], 1801	BP	3
David, his d. [ ], d. Sept. 16, 1804	SM	81
Prince, his d. [ ], d. Jan. 24, 1793, ae. 2 m.	SM	49
Prince, his d. [ ], d. June 23, 1801	SM	72
Prince, d. [ ], 1806	BP	14
-----, his child d. [ ], 1804	BP	9
OSBORNE, OSBORN, Hannah, d. Richard, m. John **BALDWIN,** s. Nathaniel, Nov. 19, 1663, by Robert Treat	1	5
Han[n]ah, d. Richard, m. John **BALDWIN,** s. Nathaniell, Nov. 19, 1663, by Rob[ert] Treat	OL	15
-----, wid., her child d. [ ], 1828, ae. 3	BP	58
O'TEAD, -----, his child s. [ ], d. [ ], 1819, N. Milford	BP	40
OVIATT, OUIATT, OVIT, OVITT, Abel, his w. [ ], d. [ ], 1832, ae. 54	BP	67
Abigail, d. Thomas, b. Aug. 17, 1674	1	14
Abigail, d. Tho[ma]s, b. Aug. 17, 1674	OL	27
Adam, his infant child, d. [ ], 1833	BP	69
Alex, his d. [ ], d. [ ], 1832, N. Haven	BP	68
Alexander, d. Jan. 31, 1776	SM	5
Alexander, his d. [ ], d. June 25, 1781, ae. 7 w.	SM	21
Alexander, d. Dec. [ ], 1795 (Heard sometime since of death at Sea)	SM	56
Alexander, his w. [ ], d. Sept. 25, 1804	SM	81
Alexander, d. [ ], 1810, ae. 73	BP	20
Amie, d. Thomas, b. Feb. 10, 1667	1	8
Ami, d. Thomas, b. Feb. 10, 1667	OL	19

OVIATT, OUIATT, OVIT, OVITT, (cont.)

	Vol.	Page
Amos, his w. [ ], d. [ ], 1820	BP	42
Amos, d. [ ], 1833	BP	70
Ann, d. Sam[ue]ll & Rodah, b. Oct. 14, 1761	1	145
Ann, d. Sam[ue]ll, b. Oct. 13, 1762	1	150
Benjamin, s. Sam[ue]ll, Jr., b. June 9, 1729	1	85
Charles, his d. [ ], d. Dec. 28, 1793, ae. 1 m.	SM	50
Charles, his s. [ ], d. Dec. 6, 1796, ae. 1 w.	SM	60
Charles, his child d. [ ], 1803	BP	8
Charles, his d. [ ], d. Oct. 2, 1803, s.b.	SM	78
Charles, his child d. [ ], 1813	BP	26
Charles, his w. [ ], d. [ ], 1813	BP	31
Charles, d. [ ], 1827, ae. 59	BP	56
Clara, d. [ ], 1808, ae. 13 y.	BP	18
Curtis, his infant d. [ ], 1832	BP	67
Daniell, s. Roger, b. Mar. 1, 1659/60	OL	12
Eben, d. [ ], 1829, ae. 73	BP	59
Ebenezer, Priv., member of Capt. Samuel Peck's Co., Milford 1776	1	54
Ebenezer, his s. a twin d. Sept. 11, 1791	SM	46
Ebenezer, Jr., d. [ ], 1816, ae. [ ]	BP	34
Easther, d. Thomas, b. Mar. 20, 1665	OL	19
Esther, d. Samuel, b. Oct. 10, 1703	1	23
Esther, d. Sam[ue]ll, b. Oct. 10, 1703	OL	47
Francis, d. Thomas, b. Nov. 1, 1669	1	10
Ffrances, d. Thomas, b. Nov. 1, 1669	OL	22
Francis, d. Sam[ue]ll, Jr., b. Jan. 17, 1725/6	1	79
Frances, m. Moses **MALORY**, Aug. 19,1744, by Rev. Jedadiah Mills, of Preston	1	122
Giles, b. Jan. 8, 1709; recorded Apr. 14, 1721	1	68
Harriet, d. [ ], 1815, ae. 15	BP	30
Hester, d. Thomas, b. Mar. 20, 1665	1	8
Huldah, w. Ira, d. [ ], 1833	BP	70
Isaac, Jr., pd. £5 for not procuring men for Continental Army	1	55
Isaac, pd. £5 for not procuring men for Continental Army	1	55
Isaac, Jr., his d. [ ], d. Jan. 2, 1792, ae. 3 y.	SM	47
Isaac, d. [ ], 1810	BP	20
Isaac, Jr., his infant child d. [ ], 1819	BP	39
Isaac, his w. [ ], d. [ ], 1833	BP	70
Isaac, d. [ ], 1840, ae. 80	BP	84
James, d. [ ], 1836, ae. 19	BP	75
John, s. Thomas, b. May 11, 1664	1	8
John, s. Thomas, b. May 11, 1664	OL	19
John, m. Susannah **HINE**, Jan. 16, 1723/4, by Sam[ue]ll Eells, Asst.	1	73
John, s. Sam[ue]ll & Rodah, b. June 17, 1753	1	142
John, formerly of Milford, d. May 4, 1777	SM	12
Lydia, wid., d. Jan. 29, 1778, ae. 78	SM	15
Mary, d. Samuel, b. Apr. 1, 1706	1	28
Mary, d. Sam[ue]ll, b. Apr. 1, 1706	OL	61
Merrett, his child d. [ ], 1840	BP	83
Morris, his w. [ ], d. [ ], 1834, ae. 33	BP	71
Nathan, his s. [ ], d. Jan. 5, 1792	SM	47

MILFORD VITAL RECORDS 137

	Vol.	Page
OVIATT, OUIATT, OVIT, OVITT, (cont.)		
Nathan, his d. [ ], d. Aug. 29, 1794	SM	51
Nathan, his w. [ ], d. [ ], 1824	BP	50
Nathan, his d. [ ], m. Thad PLUM, d. [ ], 1825, ae. 28	BP	52
Rebeckah, d. Sam[ue]ll & Rebeckah, b. Aug. 2, 1719	1	77
Rebeckah, m Sam[ue]ll HINE, 3rd, Aug. 9, 1739, by Sam[ue]ll Eells, Asst.	1	120
Samuel, s. Thomas, b. Nov. 24, 1672	1	12
Samuel, s. Thomas, b. Nov. 24, 1672	OL	25
Sam[ue]ll, m. Rebeckah **PRITCHARD**, Nov. 16, 1717, by Sam[ue]ll Eells	1	77
Sam[ue]ll, s. Sam[ue]ll & Rebeckah, b. Apr. 1, 1722	1	77
Sam[ue]l, member of 2nd Church formed in 1742	ES	87
Susannah, m. Stephen GUNN, Nov. 28, 1757, by Roger Newton, Asst.	1	152
Susy, d. [ ], 1838	BP	80
Thomas, s. Thomas, b. Aug. 30, 1677	1	16
Thomas, s. Thomas, b. Aug. 30, 1677	OL	32
Thomas, [d.], 1691	ES	16
Thomas, m. Liddiah CLARK, June 7, 1705, by Samuel Eells, Justice	1	26
Thomas, m. Liddiah CLARK, June 7, 1705, by Sam[ue]ll Eells, J.P.	OL	55
Thomas, s. Thomas, b. Apr. 28, 1706	1	29
Thomas, s. Thomas, b. Apr. 28, 1706	OL	62
Wheeler, his twin s. & d. [ ], d. Jan. 9, 1796	SM	58
Wheeler, his w. [ ], d. [ ], 1840	BP	84
William, drafted for Continental Army	1	58
William, s. Sam[ue]ll & Rodah, b. Oct. 12, 1755	1	142
W[illia]m(?), his d. [ ], d. [ ], 1825	BP	53
-----, Mr., d. [ ], 1804	BP	9
-----, Mr. his child d. [ ], 1809	BP	19
-----, Mr., d. [ ], 1817	BP	36
PAINE, Benjamin, Priv., member of Capt. Samuel Peck's Co., Milford 1776	1	54
Josiah, Capt., 1692; d. [ ], 1756	ES	40
PARDEE, PARDIE, Anne, d. Josiah, b. Mar. 16, 1771	1	171
Content, d. Josiah, b. Nov. 22, 1769	1	171
Jo, his child d. [ ], 1813	BP	32
John, Sr., d. [ ], 1822	BP	46
Joseph, Jr., his child d. [ ], 1804	BP	8
Joseph, d. Apr. 4, 1804, s.b.	SM	79
Joseph, Jr., his child d. [ ], 1815, North Milford	BP	28
Josiah, s. Josiah, b. Apr. 10, 1775	1	171
Josiah, d. Mar. 7, 1803, ae. 63	SM	77
Josiah, d. [ ], 1803, ae. 65	BP	7
Josiah, d. [ ], 1822	BP	46
Mabel, d. Josiah, b. Jan. 18, 1773	1	171
Mehitabeel, d. Josiah, b. Nov. 24, 1777	1	171
Rachel, w. Samuel, d. May 6, 1774	1	164
Rebecca, d. Josiah, b. Apr. 9, 1768	1	171
Sarah, d. Josiah, b. Oct. 7, 1766	1	171

	Vol.	Page
PARDEE, PARDIE, (cont.)		
Sarah, Mrs.,d. [ ], 1824	BP	51
-----, Mrs., d. [ ], 1828	BP	57
PARISH, W[illia]m, his infant d. [ ], 1831	BP	65
-----, his infant child d. [ ], 1828	BP	58
PARKER, James, his w. [ ], d. Oct. 11, 1777	SM	14
James, d. [ ], 1807	BP	15
Jeremiah, s. James & Mary, b. Jan. 8, 1758	1	139
Jeremiah, b. Jan. 8, 1758	ES	238
Jeremiah, Priv., member of Capt. Samuel Peck's Co., Milford, 1776	1	54
Jeremiah, his child d. Nov. 21, 1791	SM	47
Jeremiah, Jr., of N. Milford, d. [ ], 1812	BP	24
Jerry, d. [ ], 1813, ae. [ ]	BP	25
Joseph, s. James, b. June 16, 1735	1	102
-----, wid., d. [ ], 1809	BP	19
-----, Mrs., d. [ ], 1834, ae. 68	BP	71
PARKS, -----, his child d. [ ], 1832	BP	66
-----, Mr., d. [ ], 1833, ae. 72	BP	68
PARSONS, PERSONS, Mary, of Derby, m. John **SHEPHARD**, of Milford, May [ ], 1732, by John Riggs, J.P.	1	97
Nancy, d. Sept. 11, 1802, ae. 17	SM	75
Nancy, d. [ ], 1802, ae. 18	BP	6
Samuel, his child d. [ ], 1837, ae. 4	BP	78
PEACOCK, Deborah, d. John, bp. [1644, by Rev. Peter Prudden]	OL	101
J., removed to Stratford, 1661	ES	17
Jayer, w. John, adm. Church Dec. 26, [1641]; dismissed to Stratford Dec. 7, 1651	OL	98
John, d. [ ]. (One of the first planters)	ES	16
John, s. John, bp. [1641, by Rev. Peter Prudden]	OL	100
John, s. John, bp. [1643, by Rev. Peter Prudden]	OL	101
PEARTREE, John, had negro Prince, d. Jan. 3, 1789	SM	39
PEAS[E], Benjamin, d. Jan. [ ], 1777	SM	10
PECK, Abigail, d. Ens. Joseph, b. Sept. 25, 1701	1	23
Abigail, d. Ens. Joseph, b. Sept. 25, 1701	OL	47
Abigail, d. Joseph, Jr., b. June 24, 1709	1	30
Abigail, d. Joseph, Jr., b. June 24, 1709	OL	66
Abigail, d. [ ], 1828, ae. 15	BP	57
Abraham, s. Capt. Benjamin & Amey, b. June 29, 1761	1	171
Abraham, his infant d. [ ], d. Aug. 17, 1788	SM	37
Abraham, his s. [ ], s.b. Oct. 29, 1790	SM	43
Abraham, his d. [ ], d. Nov. 13, 1791	SM	46
Abraham, his d. [ ], d. Dec. 20, 1792	SM	48
Abram, d. [ ], 1824	BP	50
Abram, his child d. [ ], 1829	BP	60
Allick, his child d. [ ], 1817, ae. 4 y. "Drowned in river near Fowler's Mill; fell through bridge"	BP	36
Amy, w. Jesse, d. July 30, 1852, ae. 79	1	50
Ann, d. Henry [& Ann], b. Aug. 15, 1725; m. Jesse **LAMBERT**, Oct. 28, 1745; d. July 3, 1809	1	93
Ann, w. Henry, d. Dec. 28, 1726	1	93
Ann, d. Capt. Henry, m. Jesse **LAMBERT**, s. Jesse [& Mary],		

	Vol.	Page
PECK, (cont.)		
Oct. 25, 1745	1	106
Anne, d. Benjamin & Sarah, b. Mar. 12, 1768	1	171
Anne, d. Capt. Henry, m. Jesse **LAMBERT**, eldest s. Jesse & Mary, Oct. 28, 1745; d. July 3, 1809. ae. 84	1	50
Anthony, hear of his death Aug. 27, 1797, at Martinique	SM	62
Benjamin, s. Henry [& Ann], b. Nov. 16, 1726	1	93
Benjamin, s. Benjamin & Amey, b. Apr. 24, 1764	1	171
Benjamin, Capt., d. Oct. 11, 1803	SM	78
Benjamin, Capt., d. [ ], 1803	BP	8
Benjamin, Jr., his child d. [ ], 1830	BP	61
Benjamin, d. [ ], 1838, ae. 72	BP	79
Charlotte, d. [ ], 1826, ae. 22	BP	55
Comfort, [twin with Content], d. Jeremiah, b. Apr. 1, 1734	1	102
Content, [twin with Comfort], d. Jeremiah, b. Apr. 1, 1734	1	102
Content, d. Jeremiah, Jr., b. May 30, 1747	1	122
Dan, his d. [ ], d. Nov. 22, 1800	SM	70
Dan, his s. [ ], d. Apr. 16, 1801	SM	72
Dan, his child d. [ ], 1801	BP	3
D. M., his w. [ ], d. [ ], 1827, ae. 32	BP	56
David, d. [ ], 1807	BP	16
David, his child d. [ ], 1838	BP	80
Elisha, his child d. [ ], 1836	BP	74
Elizabeth, d. Joseph, bp. [1651, by Rev. Peter Prudden]	OL	104
Elizabeth, d. Joseph, m. Sergt. Thomas **THAYER**, Oct. [Dec.] 29, 1677, by Major Treat	1	16
Elizabeth, d. Joseph, m. Thomas **HAYES**, Dec. 29, 1677, by Major Treat	OL	32
Elizabeth, of Newtown, m. Nathan **PRATT**, of Milford, June 5, 1740, by Rev. Elisha Kent	1	109
Ephraim, his child d. [ ], 1805	BP	11
Eph[rai]m, his w. [ ], d. [ ], 1806	BP	13
Ephraim, d. [ ], 1839, ae. 72	BP	81
Fenn, d. Nov. [ ], 1804, in Gaudeloupe	SM	81
Fenn, d. [ ], 1804	BP	10
Hannah, d. Jeremiah, b. May 6, 1716	1	38
Han[n]ah, d. Jeremiah [& Hannah], b. May 6, 1716	OL	80
Hannah, d. Heth & Hannah, b. July 5, 1733	1	96
Hannah, m. David **CLARK**, Jan. 15, 1741/2	1	121
Henry, m. Ann **FORD***, Feb. 8, 1722/3, by Sam[ue]ll Eells, Asst. *(Note in pencil "parents of wife of Jesse **LAMBERT**")	1	72
Henry, s. Henry, b. Dec. 7, 1723. (In pencil "m. Rachel **LAMBERT**. Settled in Brookfield, Conn.")	1	77
Henry, s. Henry, b. Dec. 7, 1723	1	239
Henry, m. Mary **NORTHROP**, July 4, 1729, by Sam[ue]ll Gunn, J.P.	1	95
Henry, Dea., original member of 2nd Church formed in 1742	ES	87
Henry, m. Rachel **LAMBERT**, d. Jesse [& Mary], [ ]. Settled in Newtown, Conn.	1	106
Henry*, m. Rachal **LAMBERT**, [child of Jesse & Mary], May 15, 1751; settled in Brookfield, Conn. *(Written "Hannah")	1	49

PECK, (cont.)

	Vol.	Page
Henry Curtis, [s. Capt. Cornelius], b. Oct. 19, 1829	1	178
Heth, s. Ens. Joseph, b. Oct. 3, 1703	1	23
Heth, s. Ens. Joseph, b. Oct. 3, 1703	OL	48
Heth, m. Hannah **CAMP**, Feb. 26, 1729/30, by Sam[ue]ll Eells, Asst.	1	89
Heth, s. Heth & Hannah, b. May 29, 1731	1	96
Hezekiah, Jr., d. [ ], 1809	BP	19
Hezekiah, his w. [ ], d. [Feb.], 1837, ae. 69	BP	78
Isaac, s. Jeremiah, Jr., b. Feb. 9, 1748/9	1	124
Isaac, d. [ ], 1822	BP	46
James, d. Dec. [ ], 1800, supposed to be lost at Sea	SM	70
Jeremiah, m. Hannah **FISK**, Aug. 20, 1713, by Samuel Eells, Asst.	1	38
Jeremiah, m. Hannah **FFISKE**, Aug. 20, 1713, by Sam[ue]ll Eells, Asst.	OL	80
Jeremiah, s. Jeremiah, b. Jan. 12, 1720/1	1	69
Jeremiah, Jr., Dea., original member of 2nd Church formed in 1742	ES	87
Jeremiah, s. Jeremiah, m. Frances **PLATT**, d. Joseph, Oct. 26, 1743, by Rev. Samuel Whittlesey. Witnesses, Jared Bull, Nath[anie]l Smith	1	117
Jeremiah, s. Jeremiah, Jr., b. Nov. 4, 1744	1	118
Jeremiah, s. John, s. of John, see under Sibella **PECK**	1	45
John, see under Sibella **PECK**	1	45
John, drafted for Continental Army	1	57
John, s. Joseph, b. Mar. 4, 1654	OL	8
John, s. Joseph, b. Mar. 4, 1654/5	1	2
John, s. Joseph, bp. [1655, by Rev. Peter Prudden]	OL	105
John, s. Joseph, b. Sept. 14, 1685	1	21
John, s. Joseph, Jr., b. Sept. 14, 1685	OL	42
John, s. Lieut. [ ], d. Nov. 27, 1709	1	43
John, s. Lieut. [ ], d. Nov. 27, 1709	OL	89
John, s. Jeremiah, b. Dec. 9, 1718	1	63
John, member of 2nd Church formed in 1742	ES	87
John, m. Sarah **PLATT**, Feb. 15, 1750/1, by Rev. Job Prudden	1	133
John, s. John, b. June 26, 1755	1	135
John, his w. [ ], d. June 21, 1783, ae. 62	SM	26
John, d. Oct. 21, 1790, ae. 72	SM	43
John, his infant d. [ ], d. Feb. 20, 1793	SM	49
John, his d. [ ], d. Oct. 21, 1795	SM	56
John, [s. Capt. Cornelius], b. Aug. 4, 1831	1	178
John, m. [ ]	1	133
Joseph, came to Milford, 1645	ES	178
Joseph, m. wid. [ ] **BURRILL**, Sept. 12, 1650, by Capt. Asa Woods	LL	2
Joseph, adm. Church May 8, 1652	OL	99
Joseph, s. Joseph, bp. [1653, by Rev. Peter Prudden]	OL	104
Joseph, m. Mary **CAMP**, Jan. 27, 1678, by R[ober]t Treat, Dept. Gov.	1	16
Joseph, m. Mary **CAMP**, Jan. 27, 1678, by Dept. Gov.	OL	33
Joseph, s. Joseph, Jr., b. Feb. 25, 1680	OL	37

	Vol.	Page
PECK, (cont.)		
Joseph, Sr., d. Feb. 26, 1700/1	1	40
Joseph, Sr., d. Feb. 26, 1700/1	OL	86
Joseph, Jr., m. Abigail **BALDWIN**, Jan. 14, 1706/7	1	27
Joseph, Jr., m. Abigail **BALDWIN**, Jan. 14, 1706/7	OL	59
Joseph, s. Joseph, Jr., b. Oct. 2, 1707	1	28
Joseph, s. Joseph, Jr., b. Oct. 2, 1707	OL	61
Joseph, s. John & Sarah, b. Aug. 26, 1757	1	139
Joseph, of Milford, m. Hannah **LAMBERT**, Feb. 16, 1778	1	50
Lucy, d. Jeremiah, b. Oct. 23, 1730	1	102
Martha, d. Samuel, b. Jan. 31, 1714/15	1	36
Martha, d. Sam[ue]ll, b. Jan. last day, 1714/15	OL	77
Mary, d. Joseph, b. Apr. 29, 1670	1	10
Mary, d. Joseph, b. Apr. 29, 1670	OL	22
Mary, d. Joseph, Jr., b. Dec. 15, 1682	1	18
Mary, d. Joseph, Jr., b. Dec. 15, 1682	OL	39
Mary, m. Timothy **BOTCHFORD**, Feb. 14, 1704/5, by Samuel Eells, J.P.	1	25
Mary, m. Timothy **BOTCHFORD**, Feb. 14, 1704/5, by Samuel Eells, J.P.	OL	52
Mary, d. Samuel, b. July 30, 1718	1	62
Mary, m. Benjamin **FENN**, Nov. 4, 1741	1	117
Mary, m. Benj[amin] **FENN**, Nov. 4, 1741	ES	238
Mary, of Newtown, m. Hezekiah **CLARK**, of Milford, Jan. 20, 1746/7, by Rev. David Judson	1	122
Mary Ann, [d. Capt. Cornelius], b. June 10, 1825	1	178
Mehitabeel, d. Henry, b. Oct. 3, 1735	1	102
Mahitabeel, d. John [& Sarah], b. Feb. 15, 1753; m. David **CAMP**, [ ]; m. 2nd h. Lazarus **NORTHROP**, [ ]	1	133
Michael, s. Sam[ue]ll & Hannah, b. Aug. 10, 1738	1	107
Michael, his s. [ ], s.b. Nov. 26, 1790	SM	44
Michael & w. Polly had s. [ ], s.b. Feb. 26, 1798	SM	63
Michael, d. [ ], 1829, ae. 90	BP	60
Michael, Capt. his w. [ ], d. [ ], 1840, ae. 60	BP	83
Moses, Priv., member of Capt. Samuel Peck's Co., Milford 1776	1	54
Nathan, m. Abigaill **NEWTON**, d. Fletcher, May 5, 1745*, by Rev. Sam[ue]ll Whittlesey *(Written "1845")	1	125
Nathaniel, s. Nath[anie]ll, b. Oct. 9, 1734	1	99
Phebe, d. Nathaniel, b. Feb. 22, 1732/3	1	95
Phinehas, s. Jeremiah, b. Apr. 10, 1723	1	102
Phinehas, m. Deborah **CLARK**, Feb. 18, 1745/6, by Rev. David Humphrey, of Derby	1	120
Phinehas, s. Phinehas [& Deborah], b. Jan. 1, 1746/7	1	120
S-----, Lieut. had negro Cyrus, d. Feb. 1, 1777	SM	11
S. Capt. his child d. [ ], 1801	BP	3
Samuel, m. Martha **CLARK**, May 5, 1714, by Major E[e]lls, Asst.	1	36
Samuel, m. Martha **CLARK**, May 5, 1714, by Major Eells, Asst.	1	36
Sam[ue]ll, m. Martha **CLARK**, May 5, 1714, by Major Eells, Asst.	OL	77
Samuel, s. Samuel, b. May 21, 1716	1	38

	Vol.	Page
PECK, (cont.)		
Sam[ue]ll, s. Sam[ue]ll, b. May 21, 1716	OL	83
Samuel, m. Hannah **JENNINGS**, Aug. 18, 1735, by Edmund Lewis, Asst.	1	105
Samuel, s. Sam[ue]ll & Hannah, b. Aug. 22, 1736	1	107
Sam[ue]ll, Jr., m. Mehitabeel **SMITH**, July 7, 1762, by Rev. Sam[ue]ll Whittlesey	1	144
Sam[ue]ll, Jr., m. Mehitabeel **SMITH**, July 7, 1762, by Sam[ue]ll Whittlesey	1	149
Samuel, Capt., of a Company in Milford, 1776	1	54
Samuel, Capt. his Co., was of Col. Douglass Reg., Gen. Wadsworth's Brigade. Date of enlistment June 20, 1776. Date of discharge, Dec. 28, 1776. Amount due for service £799-13. Wages of Capt. per mo. £8; wages of Lieut. per mo. £5-8; wages of Ens. per mo. £4 -	1	179
Samuel, Lieut. his w. [ ], d. Aug. 24, 1783, ae. 66	SM	26
Samuel, Lieut. his 2nd w. [ ], d. Nov. 14, 1796, ae. 73	SM	60
Samuel, his s. [ ], d. May 27, 1800	SM	69
Samuel, Jr., his s. [ ], d. June 3, 1801	SM	72
Samuel, Sr., d. Dec. 30, 1801, ae. 86	SM	73
Samuel, d. [ ], 1801	BP	4
Sam[ue]ll, Capt., his child d. [ ], 1810	BP	21
Samuel, Capt., d. [ ], 1822	BP	46
Samuel, Lieut., his wid., d. [ ], 1826	BP	54
Samuel, Capt. his Co., Wages of Sergt. £2-8; Capt. his Co., Wages of Corp. £2-4; Capt. his Co., Wages of Fife & Drummer £2-4; Capt. his Co., Wages of Privates £2	1	179
Samuel C., his child d. [ ], 1840, ae. 3 y.	BP	84
Sam[ue]ll Fiske, s. Phinehas, b. Mar. 25, 1750	1	127
Sarah, d. Jeremiah, b. May 25, 1726	1	102
Sarah, d. John [& Sarah], b. Oct. 15, 1751	1	133
Sarah, d. Capt. Benj[amin] & Sarah, b. Nov. 25, 1765	1	171
Sarah, wid., d. [ ], 1809	BP	19
Sarah, wid. her infant d. [ ], 1809	BP	19
Sarah, see Sarah **LEWIS**	SM	57
Sarah Frances, [d. Capt. Cornelius], b. July 1, 1827	1	178
Sibella, d. Jeremiah, b. June 24, 1728	1	102
Sibella, d. Jeremiah, s. of John, s. of John, m. Jirah [**BULL**], [s. Benjamin], [ ]	1	45
Simeon, s. Jeremiah, Jr., b. Aug. 19, 1752	1	131
-----, wid., d. [ ], 1818, ae. 94	BP	38
PELELEHEN, John, Dea. [d.] Apr. 18, 1662	ES	16
PENCE, James, drafted for Continental Army	1	58
PENDLETON, James, adm. Church, Oct. 13, [1639], at New Haven	OL	97
PENFOLD, -----, Mr. his other child d. [ ], 1813	BP	32
-----, his infant child d. [ ], 1813	BP	32
-----, Mrs. her infant child d. [ ], 1817	BP	36
PENNEO, [see under **PINNEO**]		
PERIT, PERRET, PERRIT, PERRITT, [see also **PETTIT**], Abigail, wid., d. June 27, 1794, in New Haven	SM	53
Job, d. [ ], 1794	SM	53
John, d. Feb. 8, 1795, at Philadelphia, ae. 57	SM	57

	Vol.	Page
PERIT, PERRET, PERRIT, PERRITT, [see also **PETTIT**], (cont.)		
Peter, m. Abigail **SHEPHARD**, Oct. 31, 1734, by Sam[ue]ll Eells, Asst.	1	101
Peter, m. Abig[ail] **SHEPARD**, [ ], 1734	ES	238
Peter, d. Apr. 8, 1791, ae. 84	SM	45
Peter, d. Sept. 24, 1803, ae. 68	SM	78
Peter, Capt., d. [ ], 1803	BP	8
Samuel, d. [ ], 1808, ae. 64	BP	17
-----, wid., d. [ ], 1805	BP	12
PERKINS, Samuel, Corp., member of Capt. Samuel Peck's Co., Milford, 1776	1	54
PERRET, [see under **PERIT**]		
PERRY, -----, Mr., d. [ ], 1807	BP	16
PERTHET, [see under **PRITCHARD**]		
PETER, PETERS, Hezekiah, his infant s. [ ], d. May 10, 1804	SM	80
John, drafted for Continental Army	1	57
Susanna, her s. [ ], d. Mar. 25, 1781	SM	21
PETTEBONE, Sherman, of Burlington, Ct., m. Sarah H. [**LAMBERT**, d. Benjamin Lott & Sarah], May 20, 1835; moved to Tallmadge, Ohio	1	53
PETTIT, PETTET, [see also **PERIT**], Martha, m.Jeremiah **BEARD**, May 26, 1697, by Tho[mas] Clarke, Justice	1	20
Mary, of Stratford, m. Jeremiah **BEARD**, May 26, 1697, by Thomas Clark, J.P.	OL	43
PHILLIPS, PHILIPS, D[anie]l, came to Milford, 1660	ES	178
John, d. Mar. 12, 1780, ae. 40	SM	19
Mary, wid., d. Dec. 9, 1782, ae. 40	SM	24
Samuel, s. David, b. May 30, 1670	1	7
Samuel, s. David, b. July 30, 1670	OL	17
Sarah, d. David, b. July 13, 1666	1	7
Sarah, d. David, b. July 13, 1666	OL	17
PIERCE, Samuel, his child d. [ ], 1807	BP	16
PINNEO, PENNEO, Bezeleel, succeeded to ministry of First Church Oct. 26, 1796	ES	57
Beza, his w. [ ], 1816, ae. 36	BP	35
PITKIN, Caleb, fifth pastor of 2nd Church, A[ ] 16, 1808; d. Oct. 22, 1816	ES	93
PLATT, PLAT, Abigail, m. Samuel **BRISCOE**, July 3, 1712, by Samuel Eells, Asst.	1	33
Abigail, m. Sam[ue]ll **BRISCOE**, July 3, 1712, by Sam[ue]ll Eells, Asst.	OL	71
Abigail, d. Josiah, Jr., b. Oct. 9, 1715	1	37
Abigail, d. Josiah, Jr., b. Oct. 9, 1715	OL	80
Abigail, d. Nathan, b. May 1, 1752; d. Oct. 10, 1752	1	131
Ann, d. Richard, b. Nov. 14, 1710	1	62
Ann*, m. Benj[ami]n **BULL**, Apr. 11, 1754, by Sam[ue]ll Whittlesey *(His 2d w.)	1	152
Asa, his negro child, d. Sept. 3, 1797	SM	62
Asa, his child d. [ ], 1808	BP	18
Benjamin, his d. [ ], d. Aug. 23, 1781, ae. 1 y.	SM	22
Benjamin, his d. [ ], d. Aug. 20, 1793, ae. 20	SM	49

PLATT, PLAT, (cont.)

		Vol.	Page
Benjamin, his w. [ ], d. June 1, 1804		SM	80
Benjamin, his w. [ ], d. [ ], 1804, ae. 41		BP	9
Benj[amin], d. [ ], 1808		BP	17
Clarissa, d. Jerah, d. Sept. 25, 1794		SM	52
David, d. [ ], 1806, ae. 54		BP	14
Ebenezer, d. Oct. 1, 1776, ae. 30		SM	7
Ebenezer, d. Aug. 13, 1790, ae. 75		SM	42
Elizabeth, d. Nathan, b. Jan. 7, 1745/6; d. Jan. 13, [1745/6]		1	126
Elizabeth, d. Nathan, b. Mar. 19, 1748/9		1	126
Elizabeth, w. Nathan, d. May 17, 1753		1	132
Epenetis, bp. July 2, [1640], the first at Milford, by Rev. Peter Prudden		OL	100
Epenetus, s. Joseph, b. May 17, 1696		1	17
Epenetus, s. Joseph, b. May 17, 1696		OL	33
Esther, d. Richard, b. Feb. 14, 1708		1	62
Fisk, his w. [ ], d. [ ], 1820		BP	41
Frances, d. Josiah, b. Feb. 23, 1717		1	38
Ffrances, d. Josiah, Jr., b. Feb. 23, 1717		OL	82
Frances, d. Joseph, m. Jeremiah **PECK**, s. Jeremiah, Oct. 26, 1743, by Rev. Samuel Whittlesey. Witnesses, Jared Bull, Nath[anie]l Smith		1	117
Frederic **BRYAN**, of Orange, m. Louisa B. [**LAMBERT**], [d. Benjamin Lott & Eunice], [ ]		1	53
Gideon, s. Lieut. [ ], bp. 1700		ES	238
Gideon, m. Mary **BUCKINGHAM**, Feb. 28, 1716, by Sam[ue]ll Eells, Asst.		1	83
Gideon, d. Gideon, [ ], 1733		ES	238
Gideon, Priv., member of Capt. Samuel Peck's Co., Milford, 1776		1	54
Gideon, his negro woman, d. Oct. 23, 1783		SM	26
Gideon, d. Sept. 24, 1796, ae. 62		SM	59
Grace, d. Sam[ue]ll, Jr. & Hannah, b. Aug. 11, 1750		1	128
Hannah, d. Richard, bp. [1643, by Rev. Peter Prudden]		OL	101
Hannah, m. John **MARVIN**, Feb. 7, 1705/6, by Capt. Eells		1	26
Hannah, m. John **MARVIN**, Feb. 7, 1705/6, by Capt. Eells		OL	56
Hannah, d. Sam[ue]ll, Jr. [& Hannah], b. May 21, 1743		1	115
Hannah, d. [ ], 1805		BP	10
Hannah, wid., d. [ ], 1809, ae. 77 y.		BP	19
Hester, d. Sam[ue]ll, Jr. [& Hannah], b. May 17, 1747		1	115
Isaac, s. Josiah, Jr., b. Apr. 29, 1711		1	36
Isaac, s. Josiah, Jr., b. Apr. 29, 1711 (mother was Sarah **BURWELL**)		OL	78
Isaac, m. Phebe **SMITH**, Mar. 12, 1739/40, by Rev. Sam[ue]ll Whittlesey		1	114
Isaac, Jr., his w. [ ], d. [ ], 1815		BP	29
Isaac, d. [ ], 1817, ae. 62		BP	36
James, his child d. Jan. [ ], 1779, ae. 1 y.		SM	17
John, m. Hannah **CLARK**, June 6, 1660, by Robert Treat, Magistrate		1	4
John, m. Meriann **CLARK**, b. of Milford, June 6, 1660, by Mr. Treat, Magestrate; settled in Norwalk		OL	12
John, m. Phebe **BRACE**, June 27, 1675, by Robert Treat, Dept.			

MILFORD VITAL RECORDS 145

	Vol.	Page
PLATT, PLAT, (cont.)		
Gov.	1	20
John, s. Josiah, b. Sept. 5, 1677	1	16
John, s. Josiah, b. Sept. 5, 1677	OL	32
John, m. Phebe **BRACE**, June 27, 1703, by Robert Treat, Dept. Gov.	OL	43
Jonah, his w. [ ], d. [ ], 1831	BP	64
Jonas, d. Apr. 11, 1786, ae. 63	SM	31
Joseph, s. Richard, bp. [1649, by Rev. Peter Prudden]	OL	103
Joseph, in 1671, destroyed the Indian Fort	ES	14
Joseph, m. Mary **KELLOG[G]**, d. Daniel, of Norwalk, May 5, 1680, by Lieut. Olmstead	OL	36
Joseph, s. Joseph, b. Feb. 4, 1683	1	19
Joseph, s. Joseph, b. Feb. 4, 1683	OL	39
Joseph, s. Joseph, b. Feb. 4, 1683	OL	41
Joseph, s. Joseph, b. Oct. 4, 1683	1	19
Joseph, m. Elizabeth **WOODBURY**, Jan. 19, 1701/2, by Rob[er]t Treat, Dept. Gov.	OL	49
Joseph, m. Elizabeth **WOODBURY**, Jan. 19, 1711/12, by Robert Treat, Dept. Gov.	1	23
Joseph, Jr., m. Mehetabeel **FENN**, June 16, 1720, by Sam[ue]ll Eells, Asst.	1	76
Joseph, s. Joseph, Jr., b. Nov. 13, 1724	1	76
Joseph, Dea., d. [ ], 1724	ES	238
Joseph, Sergt., d. Feb. 18, 1778, ae. 68	SM	15
Joseph, his negro woman Sabina, d. Dec. 11, 1782	SM	24
Joseph, chosen Dea. June 9, 1789	ES	238
Joseph, his child d. [ ], 1805	BP	10
Joseph, Capt., his w. [ ], d. [ ], 1819	BP	39
Joseph, Jr., Capt. His w. [ ], d. [ ], 1828	BP	57
Joseph, Capt. his w. [ ], d. [ ], 1831	BP	64
Joseph, Capt., d. [ ], 1833, ae. 79	BP	69
Josiah, s. Richard, bp. [1645, by Rev. Peter Prudden]	OL	102
Josiah, m. Sarah **CA[M]PFIELD**, Dec. 2, 1669, by John Clerk, Commissioner	1	9
Josiah, m. Sarah **CAMPFIELD**, b. of Milford, Dec. 2, 1669, by John Clark, Com.	OL	22
Josiah, s. Josiah, b. June 29, 1671	1	11
Josiah, s. Josiah, b. June 29, 1671	OL	23
Josiah, s. Josiah, b. Jan. 12, 1679	1	17
Josiah, s. Josiah, b. Jan. 12, 1679	OL	34
Josiah, m. Sarah **BURWELL**, Jan. 8, 1706/7, by Samuel Eells, J.P.	1	27
Josiah, m. Sarah **BURWELL**, Jan. 8, 1706/7, by Sam[ue]l Eells, J.P.	OL	59
Josiah, s. Josiah, Jr., b. Oct. 13, 1707	1	36
Josiah, s. Josiah, Jr., b. Oct. 13, 1707 (mother was Sarah **BURWELL**)	OL	78
Josiah, Dea., d. Jan. 1, 1724	1	76
Josiah, Dea., d. Jan. 1, 1724	ES	238
Josiah, adm. to Ch. 1736	ES	238
Mary, w. Richard, adm. Church Aug. 15, [1641]; bp. Mar. 24,		

	Vol.	Page
PLATT, PLAT, (cont.)		
1675/6	OL	98
Mary, d. Josiah, b. Nov. 13, 1675	1	15
Mary, d. Josiah, b. Nov. 13, 1675	OL	29
Mary, d. Josiah, b. Feb. 31, [sic], 1681	OL	37
Mary, m. John **WOODRUFFE**, Dec. 22,1698, by Robert Treat, Gov.	1	20
Mary, m. John **WOODRUFFE**, Dec. 22,1698, by Robert Treat, Gov.	OL	43
Mary, d. Richard, b. Sept. 4, 1713	1	62
Mary, d. Gideon & Mary, b. Jan. 18, 1716/17	1	83
Mary, d. Sam[ue]ll, Jr. [& Hannah], b. Jan. 28, 1748/9	1	115
Mary, w. Nathan, d. July 18, 1756	1	135
Mary, w. Nathan, d. July 18, 1756	1	136
Mehetibeel, d. Richard & Mehetibeel, b. May 15, 1738	1	111
Mehetabel, wid., d. Feb. 11, 1784	SM	27
Nathan, s. Josiah, Jr., b. July 9, 1709	1	36
Nathan, s. Josiah, Jr., b. July 9, 1709 (mother was Sarah **BURWELL**)	OL	78
Nathan, s. Nathan, b. Oct. 19, 1741; d. Oct. 20, [1741]	1	126
Nathan, s. Nathan, b. Oct. 20, 1750	1	127
Nathan, of Milford, m. Mary **STILSON**, of New Town, Jan. 7, 1754, by Rev. Benjamin Woodbridge, of Amity	1	133
Nathan, m. Sarah **FENN**, June 30, 1757, by Rev. Sam[ue]ll Whittlesey	1	137
Nathan, of Milford, m. Ann **ALLING**, of East Haven, Sept. 21, 1771, by Noah Willeston	1	160
Nehemiah, d. July 9, 1776, ae. 35	SM	6
Phebe, d. John, b. Aug. 27, 1705	1	26
Phebe, d. John, b. Aug. 27, 1705	OL	54
Phebe, m. Samuel **NEWTON**, Nov. 29, 1705, by Robert Treat, Dept. Gov.	1	26
Phebe, m. Samuel **NEWTON**, Nov. 29, 1705, by Robert Treat, Dept. Gov.	OL	54
Phebe, wid., d. Sept. 12, 1779	SM	18
Richard, s. Josiah, b. [ ]	OL	38
Richard, adm. Church, Jan. 29, 1639/40, at New Haven	OL	97
Richard, d. [ ], 1671 (One of the first planters)	ES	16
Richard, s. Josiah, b. Aug. 9, 1682	1	18
Richard, m. Esther **BUCKINGHAM**, Nov. 7, 1706, by Capt. Eells	1	27
Richard, m. Esther **BUCKINGHAM**, Nov. 7, 1706, by Capt. Eells	OL	58
Richard, s. Richard, b. Feb. 2, 1714/15	1	62
Richard, Jr., m. Mehitabeel **FISKE**, Mar. 1, 1736/7, by Roger Newton, Asst.	1	105
Richard, s. Richard, Jr., b. Mar. 30, 1742	1	117
Richard, his negro d. Sept. 3, 1777	SM	13
Richard, his negro d. Apr. 26, 1779	SM	17
Richard, his child d. Nov. 5, 1779	SM	18
Richard, had negro Tony, d. Sept. 18, 1780	SM	20
Richard, his infant s. [ ], d. Sept. 17, 1791	SM	46

	Vol.	Page
PLATT, PLAT, (cont.)		
Richard, d. Jan. 11, 1799, ae. 56	BP	1
Richard, d. Jan. 11, 1799	SM	66
Samuel, s. Richard, b. Nov. 6, 1720	1	67
Samuel, Jr., m. Hannah **PRUDDEN**, May 13, 1742, by Roger Newton, Asst.	1	115
Samuel, s. Sam[ue]ll, Jr. [& Hannah], b. Oct. 22, 1744	1	115
Samuel, Dea. his 1st w. [　　　　], d. Nov. 8, 1786	SM	32
Sa[mue]ll, chosen Dea. 1787	ES	238
Samuel, Dea., d. Dec. 6, 1794	SM	53
Sarah, d. Josiah, b. Sept. 7, 1673	1	13
Sarah, d. Josiah, b. Sept. 7, 1673	OL	26
Sarah, d. Joseph, b. Mar. 28, 1702/3	1	41
Sarah, d. John, b. Mar. 5, 1703/4	1	23
Sarah, d. Josiah, Jr., b. Mar. 25, 1713	1	36
Sarah, d. Josiah, Jr., b. Mar. 25, 1713 (mother was Sarah **BURWELL**)	OL	78
Sarah, d. Joseph, Jr., b. Sept. 4, 1721	1	76
Sarah, m. Joseph **BEARD**, June 22, 1737, by Sam[ue]ll Eells, Asst.	1	113
Sarah, m. John **PECK**, Feb. 15, 1750/1, by Rev. Job Prudden	1	133
Sarah, d. Nathan & Sarah, b. June 2, 1758	1	143
Sarah, d. Nathan, d. June 30, 1762	1	144
Sarah, w. Nathan, d. Nov. 30, 1762	1	144
Stephen, once of Milford, his d. Hannah and two sons, d. [1776?]	SM	8
Sybyl, wid., d. [　　　　], 1829	BP	59
William, s. Jon[atha]n & Hannah, b. Oct. 2, 1797	1	173
William, his child d. [　　　　], 1828	BP	57
-----, Dea., d. [　　　　], 1806	BP	14
-----, Jr., Mr. his child, d. [　　　　], 1813	BP	31
-----, Capt. his w. [　　　], d. [　　　], 1815	BP	30
-----, wid., d. [　　　　], 1820, ae. 84	BP	42
-----, Capt. his w. [　　　], d. [　　　], 1823, ae. 63	BP	49
PLUMB, PLUMBE, PLUM, PLUME, PLUMM, Abigail, d. Rob[ert], d. [　　　　], 1660, ae. 10	ES	238
Abigail, d. John, Jr. & Mary, b. Nov. 16, 1748	1	129
Ann, d. Joseph & Susannah, m. Samuel **SANFORD**, s. Capt. Andrew & Hannah, Jan. 6, 1731/2, by Sam[ue]ll Gunn, J.P.	1	94
Benj[ami]n, m. Elizabeth **CAMP**, Mar. sometime, 1737, by Roger Newton, Asst.	1	113
Comfort, [d. Benjamin & Elizabeth], b. Jan. 24, 1737/8	1	113
Dorothy, m. Samuel **PRINDLE**, Jan. 1, 1699	1	29
Dorothy, m. Sam[ue]ll **PRINGLE**, Jan. 1, 1699, by Robert Treat, Dept. Gov.	OL	62
Elizabeth, d. John, b. Nov. 1, 1669	1	10
Elizabeth, d. John, b. Nov. 1, 1669	OL	22
Elizabeth, d. Joseph, b. Mar. 17, 1709/10	1	33
Elizabeth, d. Joseph, b. Mar. 17, 1709/10	OL	71
Elizabeth, d. John & Elizabeth, b. May 14, 1775	1	172
Ellen, d. John, b. Jan. 27, 1723/4; d. Feb. 7, 1723/4	1	73
Frances, m. John **SEERS**, b. of Milford, Mar. 3, 1740, by		

PLUMB, PLUMBE, PLUM, PLUME, PLUMM, (cont.)

	Vol.	Page
Sam[ue]ll Johnson, Missionary	1	132
Frances, [child of John & Elizabeth], b. Dec. 4, 1782	1	172
Freelove, d. John, b. Sept. 7, 1728	1	84
Freeman, s. John & Elizabeth, b. May 27, 1788	1	172
Isaac, s. John & Elizabeth, b. June 16, 1780	1	172
Isaac, d. [ ], 1804, at Sea	BP	9
Isaac, d. Aug. [ ], 1804 (Drowned at Sea Aboard Capt. Ferrin Turner's Vessel)	SM	80
Joel, s. John & Elizabeth, b. Nov. 5, 1777	1	172
Jno, came to Milford, [ ]	ES	178
John, s. Robert, bp. [1646, by Rev. Peter Prudden]	OL	102
John, s. of late Rob[ert], decd., b. July 10, 1655	OL	9
John, s. Robert, decd., m. Elizabeth **NORTON**, d. John, of Hermington, Nov. 24, 1668, by John Allyn, Magistrate	1	9
John, s. Robert, of Milford, decd., m. Elizabeth **NORTON**, d. of John, of Farmington, Nov. 24, 1668, by John Allene, Magestrate	OL	21
John, s. John, b. July 29, 1671	1	11
John, s. John, b. July 29, 1671	OL	23
John, m. Keziah **ALLEN**, Mar. 27, 1723, by Sam[ue]l Andrews, Rev.	1	73
John, s. John, Jr., b. July 7, 1726	1	81
John, Jr., of Milford, m. Mary **HOTCHKINN**, of Groton, Nov. [ ], 1747, by Joshuah Hemstead, J.P.	1	129
John, m. Elizabeth **SEARS**, Jan. 1, 1772. Witnesses Barnabus Woodrock, Daniel Manson	1	172
John, s. John & Elizabeth, b. Dec. 31, 1772	1	172
John, his child d. [ ], 1805	BP	10
John, Jr., his d. [ ], d. Apr. 25, 1805, ae. 3 y.	SM	82
John, his w. [ ], d. [ ], 1829, ae. 76	BP	59
John, Jr., his w. [ ], d. [ ], 1830, ae. 60	BP	63
John, d. [ ], 1833, ae. 82	BP	69
John Still, s. John, Jr. & Mary, b. June 4, 1752	1	129
Joseph, s. the late Robert, Sr., b. July 10, 1655	1	2
Joseph, s. Robert, bp. [1655, by Rev. Peter Prudden]	OL	105
Joseph, m. Elizabeth **BAILEY**, Dec. 5, 1709, by Jonathan Law, J.P.	1	31
Joseph, m. Elizabeth **BAILEY**, Dec. 5, 1709, by Jon[a]th[an] Law, J.P.	OL	67
Joseph, 3rd, his s. [ ], d. Jan. 18, 1789	SM	39
Joseph, Jr., his s. [ ], d. Aug. 19, 1791 (being one of three born last night)	SM	46
Joseph, Jr., his s. [ ], d. Mar. 6, 1792	SM	47
Keziah, d. John, b. Mar. 10, 1724/5	1	77
Lucinday, d. John [& Elizabeth], b. July 22, 1785	1	172
Lyman, his child d. [ ], 1837	BP	77
Lyman, his child d. [ ], 1838	BP	80
Mary, d. Robert, bp. [1644, by Rev. Peter Prudden]	OL	101
Mary, m. Matthew **WOEDEROUFFE***, June 16, 1668, by Mr. Ffeenn *(**WOODRUFF**)	1	9
Mary, m. Matthew **WOODS RAFFE***, [ ], 1668, by Mr.		

	Vol.	Page
PLUMB, PLUMBE, PLUM, PLUME, PLUMM, (cont.)		
Ffenn, Magestrate	OL	21
Mary, d. John, b. May 15, 1673	1	12
Mary, d. John, b. May 15, 1673	OL	25
Mary, Mrs., m. William **EAST**, Mar. 16, 1675/6, by Capt. Thomas Topping	1	15
Mary, Mrs., m. William **EAST**, Mar. 16, 1675/6, by Capt. Tho[ma]s Tapping	OL	30
Nancy, d. [ ], 1833, ae. 23	BP	70
Prudence, d. John, Jr. & Mary, b. July 17, 1750	1	129
Robert, adm. Church Aug. 4, [1644]; d. July 15, 1655	OL	98
Robert, s. Robert, bp. [1648, by Rev. Peter Prudden]	OL	103
Robert, d. May 12, 1655	1	2
Robert, d. July 13, 1655	OL	8
Robert, [d.], 1655	ES	18
Robert, d. [ ], 1655	ES	35
Robert, d. Dec. 4, 1703	1	41
Robert, d. Dec. 4, 1703/4	OL	87
Robert, m. Mary **BALDWIN**, [ ]	OL	98
Robert, d. [ ] 12, [ ]	OL	8
Ruth, Mrs. of Milford, m. John **WHEELER**, of Woodbury, July 3, 1706, by Samuel Eells, J.P.	1	27
Ruth, Mrs. of Milford, m. John **WHEELER**, of Woodbury, July 3, 1706, by Sam[ue]ll Eells, J.P.	OL	57
Samuel, s. Robert, bp. [1650, by Rev. Peter Prudden]	OL	103
Samuel, s. Robert, bp. [1652, by Rev. Peter Prudden]	OL	104
Samuel, his w. [ ], d. May 28, 1781, ae. 66	SM	21
Samuel, d. Mar. 17, 1795, ae. 84	SM	54
Samuel, d. [ ], 1806, ae. 17	ES	165
Samuel, d. [ ], 1809	BP	19
Sarah, d. Joseph, b. June 17, 1711	1	33
Sarah, d. Joseph, b. June 17, 1711	OL	71
Sarah, [d. John & Elizabeth], b. Dec. 27, 1790	1	172
Susannah, m. Nathan **NETTLETON**, Jan. 14, 1724/5, by Sam[ue]ll Eells, Asst.	11	85
Thad, his w. & d. of Nathan **OVIATT**, d. [ ], 1825, ae 28	BP	52
Thad, his infant d. [ ], 1825	BP	52
Wilson, his child d. [ ], 1836	BP	76
-----, wid., d. [ ], 1659/60	ES	238
-----, Mrs., heard of death Oct. 15, 1779	SM	18
POMEROY, POMROY, John, of Northampton, d. Jan. [ ], 1777	SM	9
Sarah, wid., d. May 9, 1783, ae. 45	SM	25
POMPEY, POMPHEY, ----- & Pittey, Indians, had d. Tamar, b. May 23, 1728 & Pittey, Indians, had s. Nimrod, b. Nov. 4, 1730	1	91
-----, d. May 21, 1777	SM	13
-----, his w. [ ], d. May 7, 1790	SM	41
POND, Adam, Capt., d. [ ], 1823	BP	49
Charles, Capt., b. [ ], 1744, in Milford, m. Martha **MILES**, [ ]; d. May 18, 1832	1	59
Charles, Capt. his w. [ ], d. May 29, 1797	SM	61
Charles, had negro s. of Eustatia, d. May 30, 1791	SM	45
Charles, Jr., d. [ ], 1828, ae. 18	BP	57

	Vol.	Page
POND, (cont.)		
Charles, Capt., d. [ ], 1832, ae. 88	BP	67
Elizabeth, wid., d. Feb. 19, 1804, ae. 59	SM	79
Elizabeth, Mrs., d. [ ], 1804	BP	8
Julia, d. July 22, 1776, ae. 2	SM	6
Lucy, d. Nov. 7, 1790, ae. 17	SM	43
Martha, m. A[braham] J. H. **DEWITT**, Jan. 3, 1790, by Rev. Will[ia]m Lockwood	1	175
Mary, d. Cha[rle]s H., d. [ ], 1836, ae. 18 in Missouri	BP	76
Peter, his w. [ ], d. Mar. 8, 1795, ae. 52	SM	54
Peter, d. [ ], 1807, ae. 67 y.	BP	15
Peter, Capt. his child d. [ ], 1810	BP	20
Peter, Capt., d. [ ], 1813, in West Indies	BP	31
Sally, 2nd d. Capt. Charles & Martha (**MILES**), b. June 2, 1774; m. William Harpin **FOWLER**, 2nd s. John & Mary, Dec. 18, 1796	1	59
Samuel, Capt. heard of death Aug. 3, 1777	SM	13
Sarah, wid., d. [ ], 1836	BP	75
Susan, d. [ ], 1813, ae. 17	BP	25
Zachariah, pd. £5 for not procuring men for Continental Army	1	55
Zachariah, d. Apr. 13, 1782	ES	160
Zacheus, d. Apr. 13, 1782, ae. 40	SM	23
-----, wid. her d. [ ], d. Sept. 25, 1777	SM	13
-----, Capt. had negro Cato, d. Nov. 30, 1793	SM	50
PORTER, David, d. [ ], 1837, ae. 16	BP	78
Hannah, d. Mar. 26, 1805	SM	82
Hezekiah, his child d. [ ], 1804	BP	9
Hezekiah, his infant child d. [ ], 1828	BP	57
Hezekiah, his w. [ ], d. [ ], 1838, ae. 53	BP	80
Hanna, d. [ ], 1813	BP	25
-----, Mrs., d. [ ], 1805	BP	10
-----, Mrs., d. [ ], 1820, ae. 84	BP	41
-----, Came to Milford, [ ]	ES	178
POTTER, Sally, who lived with Harvey **STEELE**, of Ontario County, N.Y., m. Frederic **LAMBERT**, [s. Jesse & Anne], [ ]; they settled in the town of Friendship, Alleghany County, N.Y.	1	50
Simeon, d. May 7, 1650	LL	1
POWELL, John, his s. [ ], d. Mar. 10, 1783, s.b.	SM	25
PRACHET, [see under **PRITCHARD**]		
PRATT, Mary, d. Joseph, b. May 6, 1704	1	23
Mary, d. Joseph, b. May 6, 1704	OL	49
Nathan, of Milford, m. Elizabeth **PECK**, of Newtown, June 5, 1740, by Rev. Elisha Kent	1	109
Sarah, d. Joseph, b. Mar. 28, 1702/3	OL	87
Sarah, d. John, b. Mar. 5, 1703/4	OL	49
PRIME, James, Came to Milford, 1644	ES	178
James, m. Martha **MARWIN**, Sept. 20, 1685, by Capt. John Beard, Com.	OL	42
James, m. Marthan **MARVIN**, Sept. 20, 1685, by Capt. John Beard, Commissioner	1	21
Rebecca, m. Walter **SMITH**, Apr. 1, 1677	1	16

	Vol.	Page
PRIME, (cont.)		
Rebecka, m. Walter **SMITH**, Apr. 1, 1677	OL	33
Rebeckah, m. John **CLARK**, Feb. 6, 1723, by Capt. Sam[ue]l Clark, J.P.	1	75
PRINCE, PRINCEE, Curtis, his w. [ ], d. [ ], 1829	BP	59
Curtis, his child d. [ ], 1832	BP	66
David, had negro William, d. Jan. 18, 1797	SM	61
David, his w. [ ], d. [ ], 1810	BP	20
David, his w. [ ], d. [ ], 1826	BP	55
David, d. [ ], 1827, ae. about 80	BP	56
David, d. [ ], 1828	BP	57
Deborah, m. Samuel **PRINCE**, Jan. 14, 1704/5, by Thomas Clark, J.P.	1	25
Deborah, m. Samuel **PRINCE**, Jan. 14, 1704/5, by Thomas Clark, J.P.	OL	52
Job, his infant child d. [ ], 1817	BP	36
Job, his child d. [ ], 1824	BP	50
Joseph, his child d. [ ], 1812	BP	24
Josiah, s. Josiah, b. Nov. 3, 1714	1	38
Josiah, s. Josiah, b. Nov. 3, 1714	OL	83
Josiah, Capt., d. Dec. 22, 1729	1	86
Josiah, Capt., d. [ ], 1729	ES	238
Nathan, his s. [ ], d. June 27, 1779	SM	17
Nathan, d. May 1, 1780	SM	19
Nathan, d. [ ], 1825	BP	53
Nelson, his child d. [ ], 1829	BP	81
Rebecca, d. Josiah, b. Oct. 2, 1716	1	38
Rebeckah, d. Josiah, b. Oct. 2, 1716	OL	83
Sal, her child d. [ ], 1811	BP	22
Samuel, m. Deborah **PRINCE**, Jan. 14, 1704/5, by Thomas Clark, J.P.	1	25
Samuel, m. Deborah **PRINCE**, Jan. 14, 1704/5, by Thomas Clark, J.P.	OL	52
Sarah, d. Oct. 1, 1750	1	130
-----, his d. [ ], d. [ ], 1809	BP	19
-----, Mrs., d. [ ], 1840, at Poor House	BP	83
PRINDLE, PRINGLE, Elizabeth, d. Samuel, b. Oct. 27, 1700	1	26
Elizabeth, d. Samuel, b. Oct. 27, 1700	OL	53
Ephraim, s. Ebenezer, b. Apr. 19, 1707	1	28
Ephraim, s. Ebenezer, b. Apr. 19, 1707	OL	60
Jehasaphat, s. Ebenezer, b. July 12, 1709	OL	66
Jno, Came to Milford, 1645	ES	178
John, s. Samuel, b. Sept. 12, 1704	1	26
John, s. Samuel, b. Sept. 12, 1704	OL	54
Jonathan, s. Eleazer, b. July 1, 1704	1	25
Jonathan, s. Eleazer, b. July 1, 1704	OL	52
Louis, d. Stephen, Esq., m. David **LAMBERT**, 1ˢᵗ s. David & Martha, [ ]; moved to Sharon, Conn.	1	52
Nathan, s. Ebenezer, b. Apr. 7, 1704	1	23
Nathan, s. Ebenezer, b. Apr. 7, 1704	OL	48
Samuel, m. Dorothy **PLUM**, Jan. 1, 1699	1	29
Sam[ue]ll, m. Dorothy **PLUM**, Jan. 1, 1699, by Robert Treat,		

	Vol.	Page
PRINDLE, PRINGLE, (cont.)		
Dept. Gov.	OL	62
Samuel, s. Samuel, b. Sept. 23, 1702	1	26
Samuel, s. Samuel, b. Sept. 23, 1702	OL	54
PRITCHARD, PERTHET, PRACHET, PRITCHET, PRITCHETT, Abigail, d. Roger & Sarah, b. Mar. 15, 1733/4	1	105
Abraham, s. Roger & Sarah, b. Oct. 12, 1737	1	105
Benjamin, s. Roger, b. Jan. the last, 1657	1	3
Benjamin, s. Roger, b. Jan. the last, 1657	OL	11
Benjamin, m. Rebecca **JONES**, Nov. 14, 1683, by Samuel Eells, Commissioner	1	19
Benjamin, m. Rebecca **JONES**, Nov. 14, 1683, by Samuel Eells, Com.	OL	40
Benjamin, Jr., m. Mary **ANDREWS**, Jan. 20, 1712/13, by Samuel Eells, Asst.	1	91
Benjamin, Jr., m. Hannah **MARKS**, July 4, 1733, by Rev. Jon[a]th[an Arnold	1	95
Benjamin, descendant of Roger **PRITCHARD**, of Springfield, Mass., m. Martha **LAMBERT**, d. Jesse & Mary, May 23, 1753	1	49
Benjamin, d. Mar. 30, 1782, ae. 66	SM	23
Benjamin, m. Martha **LAMBERT**, d. Jesse [& Mary], [ ]	1	106
Desire, d. Benj[ami]n, Jr., b. July 7, 1734	1	104
Elizabeth, d. James & Elizabeth, b. Mar. 12, 1726/7	1	88
Esther, d. Benj[ami]n, Jr., b. Nov. 9, 1735	1	104
George, s. James [& Elizabeth], b. Oct. 5, 1724	1	88
Hannah, d. Roger, b. Oct. 2, 1718	1	66
Isaac, s. James, b. Sept. 20, 1729	1	88
James, of Milford, m. Elizabeth **JOHNSON**, of Stratford, Dec. 25, 1721, by Joseph Curtiss, Asst.	1	88
James, s. James & Elizabeth, b. Jan. 31, 1722/3	1	88
Joseph, s. Roger, b. Oct. 2, 1654	1	1
Joseph, s. Roger, b. Oct. 9, 1654; was killed in battle. Probate records. Inventory dated June 13, 1676	OL	8
Joseph, s. Roger, bp. [1654, by Rev. Peter Prudden]	OL	105
Martha, wid., d. Mar. 4, 1804, ae. 81	SM	79
Matty, d. [ ], 1812	BP	23
Nathaniel, his w. [ ], d. Aug. 25, 1781, ae. 63	SM	22
Nathaniel, d. Feb. 3, 1792, ae. 71	SM	47
Phebe, d. Roger & Sarah, b. Apr. 16, 1731	1	105
Rebeckah, m. Sam[ue]ll **OVIATT**, Nov. 16, 1717, by Sam[ue]ll Eells	1	77
Roger, Came to Milford, 1653	ES	178
Roger, adm. Church May 28, [1653]	OL	99
Roger, lately of Springfield, Mass., m. Elizabeth **SLOUGH**, of Milford, Dec. 18, 1653, by William Fowler, J.P.	1	1
Roger, lately of Springfield, m. Elizabeth **SLOUGH**, of Milford, Dec. 18, 1653, by Mr. Fowler, Mag.	OL	7
Roger, m. Hannah **NORTHROP**, Mar. 8, 1715/16, by Joseph Treat, J.P.	1	66
Roger, s. Roger, b. Dec. 25, 1716	1	66

MILFORD VITAL RECORDS 153

	Vol.	Page
PRITCHARD, PERTHET, PRACHET, PRITCHET, PRITCHETT, (cont.)		
Sibella, d. Roger & Sarah, b. Jan. 9, 1736/7; d. Dec. 23, 1737	1	105
-----, Mrs., d. [ ], 1804, ae. 81	BP	8
-----, Mrs., d. [ ], 1834	BP	71
-----, Mr., d. [ ], 1837	BP	78
PRITCHET, PRITCHETT, [see under **PRITCHARD**]		
PRUDDEN, PRUDEN, Abigail, d. Peter, bp. [1647, by Rev. Peter Prudden]	OL	102
Abigail, [d. Rev. Peter & Johannah], b. Dec. [[[]], 1647; m. Joseph **WALTER,** [ ], 1667	ES	104
Abigail, [d. Peter], b. D[ec.] [ ], 1647; m. Joseph **WALTERS,** [ ], 1667	ES	182
Abigail, d. Peter, decd., m. Joseph **WALKER,** Nov. 14, 1667, by Mr. Ffenn, Magistrate	1	9
Abigail, d. Peter, decd., m. Joseph **WALTER,** Nov. 14, 1667, by Mr. Ffenn, Magestrate	OL	21
Ann, d. Samuel, d. Jan. 26, 1788, ae. 4 y.	SM	36
Elizabeth, [d. Rev. Peter & Johannah], b. [May] [ ], 1642	ES	104
Elizabeth, d. James bp. [1643, by Rev. Peter Prudden]	OL	100
Elizabeth, [twin with Sam[ue]ll, d. Peter], b. Feb. [ ], 1643	ES	182
Elizabeth, d. James, adm. church Sept. 8, [1644]. Since m. W[illia]m **STOUGH**	OL	98
Enoch, d. Feb. 2, 1802, ae. 82	SM	74
Enoch, d. [ ], 1802, ae. 84	BP	5
Enoch, s. John, [ ]	ES	238
Eunice Newton, d. Aug. 3, 1784, ae. 2 y.	SM	28
Fletcher, s. Jno, Jr. & Hannah, [ ], 1738	ES	238
Fletcher, Col., 1785	ES	41
Grace, d. Sam[ue]ll & Hannah, b. Oct. 20, 1730	1	111
Hannah, d. Peter, bp. [1640], by Rev. Peter Prudden	OL	100
Hannah, m. Samuel **PLATT,** Jr., May 13, 1742, by Roger Newton, Asst.	1	115
Hannah, wid., d. Oct. 6, 1790, ae. 73	SM	43
James, d. Aug. [ ], 1648 (One of the first planters)	ES	16
James, brother of the pastor [Peter], [d.], 1648	ES	35
James, Planter in 1648 (He left one daughter, who m. W[illia]m **STOW,** [ ]	ES	238
Job, [s. John & Mary], [bp.], 1715	ES	238
Job, Rev. s. John, 3rd s. of Rev. Samuel, who was eldest s. of Rev. Peter, b. Aug. [ ], 1715; m. Esther **SHERMAN** of New Haven, Aug. 22, 1756; d. June 24, 1774, ae. 59	ES	127
Job, s. John, [ ], 1715	ES	238
Job, m. Esther **SHERMAN,** of New Haven, Aug. 22, 1750	ES	238
Job, Rev. of Milford, m. Esther **SHERMAN,** of New Haven, Aug. 22, 1750/1, by Rev. Eathan Birdseye, of West Haven	1	128
Job, first pastor of 2nd Church in 1747; d. June 24, 1774	ES	93
Joanna, w. Peter, adm. Church, Dec. 8, [1639], at New Haven, m. Capt. [ ] **WILLETT,** of Plimouth, Sept. 19, 1672	OL	97
Johanna, [d. Rev. Peter & Johannah], b. Aug. [ ], 1640; m. Capt. [ ] **WILLETT,** of Plimouth, Sept. 19, 1671	ES	104
Joanna, [d. Peter], b. 1640; m. Capt. **WILLETT,** of Plymouth,		

	Vol.	Page
PRUDDEN, PRUDEN, (cont.)		
Sept. 1671. "A note states this is incorrect; it was the widow who m. the Capt."	ES	182
Johannah, wid. of Peter, m. Capt. [ ] **WILLETT**, of Plymouth, Sept. 19, 1671, by Benjamin Ffenne, Asst.	1	11
Johannah, Mrs. of Milford, m. Capt. [ ] **WILLET**, of Plimouth, Sept. 19, 1671, by Benjamin Ffenn, Asst.	OL	24
Joanna, d. Samuel, b. May 1, 1676	1	15
Joanna, d. Sam[ue]ll, b. May 1, 1676	OL	31
Joanna, d. Sam[ue]ll, of N[ew] J[ersey], bp. 1676	ES	238
Johannah (**BOICE**), wid. Rev. Peter, m. James **BISHOP**, in the winter of 1683	ES	101
John, s. Peter, bp. [1645, by Rev. Peter Prudden]	OL	102
John, [s. Peter], b. N[ov.] [ ], 1645	ES	182
John, s. John, bp. 1676	ES	238
John, adm. to 1ˢᵗ Ch. 1676	ES	238
John, s. Sam[ue]ll, [ ], 1680	ES	238
John, m. Mary **CLARK**, Jan. 9, 1706/7, by Lieut. Gov. Treat	1	27
John, m. Mary **CLARK**, Jan. 9, 1706/7, by Lieut. Gov. Treat	OL	58
John, s. John, [ ] June [ ], 1711	ES	238
John, s. John & Mary, bp. 1711	ES	238
John, [s. Rev. Peter & Johannah], b. Nov. [ ], 1645; d. [Dec. 11, 1725, ae. 80]	ES	104
John & w. Hannah, adm. to Ch. 1738	ES	238
John had Rose, d. Sept. 3, 1786	SM	31
John, d. Sept. 3, 1786, ae. 79	SM	31
Jonath[an], [s. John & Mary], [bp.] 1722	ES	238
Jonathan at his house, a man of Southbury, d. Oct. 27, 1796, supposed to be about 60	SM	60
Jonathan, d. [ ], 1806, ae. 82	BP	13
Jon[atha]n, his w. [ ], d. [ ], 1819, N. Milford	BP	40
Joseph, s. John, b. June 21, 1712	1	33
Joseph, s. John, b. June 21, 1712	OL	71
Joseph, [s. John & Mary], [bp.] 1712	ES	238
Joseph, s. John, [ ], 1712	ES	238
Joseph, s. Sam[ue]ll, b. Mar. 14, 1744/5	1	115
Joseph, d. Jan. 1, 1795, ae. 82	SM	54
Joseph, his child d. [ ], 1813, at North Milford	BP	25
Jos[eph], his w. [ ], d. Jan. 6, 1813, at N. Milford	BP	25
Mary, d. Peter, bp. [1641, by Rev. Peter Prudden]	OL	100
Mary, d. [Rev. Peter & Johannah], b. July [ ], 1641	ES	104
Mary, [d. Peter], b. Jan. [ ], 1641	ES	182
Mary, d. [John & Mary], [bp.] 1728	ES	238
Mary, Maj. (?)*, d. John, m. Ephraim **STRONG**, Jr. [ ], 1746, by Rev. John Smith, at White Plains *(Probably Maj. John)	ES	238
Mary, d. of John, m. Ephraim **STRONG**, b. of Milford, [ ], 1746, by Rev. Mr. Smith. This certificate sworn to Sept. 4, 1770, by Mehetabel Smith, w. of Rev. Mr. Smith & his d. Elizabeth now of White Plains	1	156
Mary, d. John, m. Ephraim **STRONG**, b. of Milford, in the Spring 1746, by Rev. Mr. Smith. Sworn to by his w. Mehitabel Smith & his d. Elizabeth Smith, May 24, 1771 before		

	Vol.	Page
PRUDDEN, PRUDEN, (cont.)		
Abram Hatfield, J.P.	1	159
Mary, wid., d. May 9, 1777, ae. 89	SM	13
Mildred, d. Peter, bp. [1653, by Rev. Peter Prudden]	OL	104
Mildred, [d. Peter], b. Mar. 1653; m. Silva **BALDWIN**, [ ]; d. Jan. 6, 1712	ES	182
Mildred, [d. Rev. Peter & Johannah], b. Mar. [ ], 1653; m. Lieut. Silvanus **BALDWIN**, Sept. 19, 1671; d. July 6, 1712	ES	104
Mildred, m. Silvanus **BALDWIN**, b. of Milford, Sept. 20, 1671, by Benjamin Ffenn, Asst.	OL	24
Mildred, m. Silvanus **BALDWIN**, Sept. 12, [ ], by Benj[amin] Ffenne, Asst.	1	11
Nehemiah, Rev. s. John & nephew of Rev. Job, b. [ ]; d. Sept. 7, 1815, ae. 66, in Enfield. He left a wid. who was a sister of his 1ᵗ w., son, 2 daughters	ES	128
Peter, Rev., b. 1620(?), in Yorkshire, Eng.; m. Johannah **BOICE**, about 1637; came to Amrica, 1637; had nine children; d. July 1656	ES	101
Peter, ordained Apr. 11, 1640, at New Haven, by Zachariah Whitman, William Fowler, Edmund Zapp. Moderater Zachariah Whitman	OL	97
Peter, d. [ ], 1652, ae. 15 d.	ES	35
Peter, s. Peter, bp. [1652, by Rev. Peter Prudden]; d. [ ]	OL	104
Peter, Jr., d. June 10, 1652, ae. 15 d.	ES	238
Peter, d. [ ], 1656 (One of the first planters)	ES	16
Peter, Rev., pastor of First Church, d. July [ ], 1656	ES	57
Peter, d. July [ ], 1656	OL	97
Peter, s. Samuel, b. July 28, 1671	1	11
Peter, s. Samuel, b. July 28, 1671	OL	23
Peter, s. Sam[ue]l, bp. May 23, 1672	ES	238
Peter, s. Sam[uel], b. M[ ], [ ], 1672	ES	238
Peter, d. May 17, 1705	OL	88
Peter, d. May 19, 1705	1	26
Peter, his w. d. May 19, 1705	1	42
Peter, d. May 19, 1705	OL	55
Peter, d. Feb. 13, 1777, ae. 68	SM	11
Peter, [s. Rev. Peter & Johannah], b. [ ], lived 15 d.	ES	104
Peter, [s. Peter], b. [ ]	ES	182
Peter, Rev., m. Joanna **BISHOP**, [ ]	ES	238
Samuel, [s. Rev. Peter & Johannah], b. Feb. [ ], 1643	ES	104
Sam[ue]ll, twin with Elizabeth, s. Peter], b. Feb. [ ], 1643; m. [ ]	ES	182
Samuel, s. Peter, bp. [1643, by Rev. Peter Prudden]	OL	101
Samuel, s. Samuel, b. Aug. 14, 1673	1	13
Samuel, s. Samuel, b. Aug. 14, 1673	OL	26
Sam[ue]l, s. Samuel, b. Oct. [ ], 1673	ES	238
Sam[ue]l, s. Sam[ue]l, bp. 1673	ES	238
Samuel, s. Samuel, b. June 26, 1677	ES	238
Samuel, d. [ ], 1684	ES	238
Samuel, m. Hannah **CLARK**, Dec. 20, 1705, by Robert Treat, Dept. Gov.	1	26
Samuell, m. Hannah **CLARK**, Dec. 20, 1705, by Rob[er]t Treat, Dept. Gov.	OL	55

	Vol.	Page
PRUDDEN, PRUDEN, (cont.)		
Sam[ue]ll, s. Sam[ue]ll & Hannah, b. Oct. 26, 1707	1	105
Sam[ue]ll, s. Sam[ue]ll & Hannah, b. [ ], 1707	ES	238
Sam[ue]ll, Jr., m. Sara **BEARD**, b. of Milford, Feb. 25, 1741/2, by Rev. Sam[ue]ll [ ]	1	112
Samuel, s. Sa[mue]ll & Sary, b. June 3, 1743	ES	238
Sam[ue]ll, s. Sam[ue]ll & Sary, b. June 5, 1743	1	117
Sam[ue]ll, s. Sam[uel] & Sarah, b. [ ], 1743	ES	238
Samuel, his w. [ ], d. May 15, 1794, ae. 35	SM	51
Samuel, his 2nd w. [ ], d. Dec. [ ], 1800, ae. 36	SM	70
Samuel, d. [ ], 1819, ae. 75	BP	39
Samuel, d. [ ], 1832, ae. 47, N. Milford	BP	67
Sam[uel], s. P[eter], adm. to 1st Ch. [ ]	ES	238
Sarah, d. Peter, b. May 9, 1650	LL	2
Sarah, d. Peter, bp. [1650, by Rev. Peter Prudden]	OL	103
Sarah, d. [Rev. Peter & Johannah], b. May [ ], 1650; m. Gideon **ALLEN**, [ ]	ES	104
Sarah, [d. Peter], b. May [ ], 1650; m. G[ ] **ALLEN**, [ ]	ES	102
Sarah, m. Gideon **CAMP**, Dec. 7, 1741	1	166
Sarah, d. Samuell & Sarah, b. July 23, 1746	1	115
Sarah, d. Samuel, d. Jan. 26, 1788, ae. 6 y.	SM	36
Sarah, wid., d. July 27, 1788	SM	37
Sibel, d. [John & Mary], [bp.] 1733	ES	238
T-----, had negro Morroco, d. Jan. 21, 1777	SM	11
Toney(?), drafted for Continental Army	1	58
Walter, his child d. [ ], 1820	BP	42
-----, Mr., d. [ ], 1656	ES	34
-----, wid., d. Mar. 19, 1660	ES	238
-----, had negro Pluto, d. [ ], 1815, ae. 71	BP	29
-----, Dea. his w. [ ], d. [ ], 1819, N. Milford	BP	40
-----, d. James, m. W[illia]m **STOW**, [ ]	ES	238
PRUEBY(?), Nathaniel, bp. Apr. 13, 1673	1	12
PURDY, PURDIE, Isaac, d. Oct. 1, 1777, ae. 23, killed in battle	SM	14
Philene, m. Isaac **BALDWIN**, Dec. 24, 1766, by Benjamin Woodbridge	1	163
RALSTON, James, of [Long Island], d. Sept. 25, 1779	SM	18
RAPIER, Sarah, of Boston, m. Ambrose **HINE**, of Milford, Feb. 6, 1717, by Samuel Fowler, Asst., in Boston	1	66
REED, READ, Mary, Mrs. of Fairfield, m. John **HERPIN**, Jr., of Milford, Sept. 4, 1745, by Jno Reed, J.P.	1	123
Mary, of Fairfield, m. Jno **HARPIN**, [ ], 174[ ]	ES	238
Tho[mas], came to Milford, 1647	ES	178
RHODES, John, d. [ ], 1810, ae. 70	BP	20
John, Jr., his child d. [ ], 1810	BP	20
Sarah, w. John, d. Jan. 8, 1795	SM	54
RICH, James & A[ ] **GOLDSMITH** had s. [ ], d. June 21, 1796	SM	59
RICHARDS, Azubah, d. Capt., of West Haven, Ct., m. Enoch **LAMBERT**, [s. David & Louis], [ ]	1	52
RICHMOND, William, d. [ ], 1836	BP	75
RIGGS, Edward, came to Milford, [ ]	ES	178

MILFORD VITAL RECORDS 157

	Vol.	Page
RIGGS, (cont.)		
Elizabeth, d. Samuel, of Pagaset, b. June 13, 1668	OL	21
Elizabeth, d. Samuel, of Pagusset, b. Jan. 13, 1668/9	1	9
Samuel, of Pagussie, m. Sarah **BALDWIN**, d. of wid. Elizabeth June 14, 1667, by Samuell Shearman, Magistrate	1	8
Samuel, of Pagosis, m. Sarah **BALDWIN**, d. Elizabeth (wid.), of Milford, June 14, 1667, by Samuel Sherman, Magestrate	OL	20
Samuel, s. Samuel, of Pagaset, b. Jan. 9, 1670	OL	23
Samuel, s. Samuel, of Pagussa, b. Jan. 9, 1670/1	1	10
RILEY, RIELLEY, James, his s. [ ], d. Nov. 17, 1794,ae. 2 w.	SM	53
James, his s. [ ], d. Sept. 11,1801	SM	73
-----, Capt. his child d. [ ], 1801	BP	4
RIVINGTON, -----, Mrs. of New York, d. [ ], 1795 (non resident)	SM	57
ROACH, Thankfull, of Milford, m. Jeremiah **BLANGE**, of North Lyme, July 31, 1739, by Rev. Sam[ue]ll Whittlesey, Jr.	1	108
ROBBINS, -----, Mr., d. [, 1813]	BP	33
ROBERTS, Alice, d. William, b. Aug. 12, 1666	1	7
Ales, d. William, b. Aug. 12, 1666	OL	17
Elizabeth, of Milford, m. Eleazer **NEWHALL**, of Milford, May 5, 1739, by Sam[ue]ll Eells, Asst.	1	108
Frederick, d. [ ], 1825	BP	53
Hezekiah, s. Zachariah, b. Oct. 15, 1685	1	21
Hezekiah, s. Zachariah, b. Oct. 15, 1685	OL	42
Joanna, w. William, adm. Church May 8, [1653]; d. May 30, 1693	OL	99
Johannah, d. William, b. June 26, 1657	1	3
Joannah, d. William, b. June 26, 1657	OL	10
Lidiah, d. William, b. Aug. 27, 1672	1	12
Lidiah, d. William, b. Aug. 27, 1672	OL	24
Phebe, s. William, b. Oct. 6, 1659	1	3
Phebe, d. William, b. Nov. 6, 1659	OL	11
Phebe, d. William, b. Mar. 13, 1660	OL	13
Phebe, d. William, b. Mar. 13, 1661	1	4
Sam[uel], d. [ ], 1811, drowned at N. Milford	BP	23
Sarah, d. William, bp. [1653, by Rev. Peter Prudden]	OL	104
Susanna, m. Joseph **NORTHROP**, Nov. 20, 1713, by Joseph Treat, J.P.	1	35
Susannah, m. Joseph **NORTHROP**, Nov. 20, 1713, by Joseph Treat, J.P.	OL	76
W[illia]m, came to Milford, 1645; d. 1689	ES	178
William, s. William, b. Aug. 24, 1663	1	5
William, s. Zachariah, b. Oct. 4, 1683	1	19
William, s. Zachariah, b. Oct. 4, 1683	OL	39
Zachariah, s. William, bp. [1653, by Rev. Peter Prudden]	OL	104
Zachariah, m. Mary **LARRANCE**, Feb. 8, 1676/7, by Major Treat	1	16
Zachariah, m. Mary **LAWRENCE**, Feb. 8, 1677, by Major Treat (1676/7)	OL	32
Zachariah, s. Zachariah, b. Mar. 7, 1677/8	1	16
Zachariah, s. Zachariah, b. Mar. 7, 1677/8	OL	32
ROBINSON, -----, Dr. of New York, d. July 12, 1776, at Dr. Clarks, ae. 48	SM	6

	Vol.	Page
ROBINSON, (cont.)		
-----, Mrs. of New York, d. [ ], 1795 (non resident)	SM	57
ROE, John his w. [ ], negro, d. Jan. [ ], 1803, at Seaboard Turner	SM	77
ROGERS, ROGGERS, Abigail, d. John, b. June 20, 1654	1	1
Abigail, d. John, b. June 20, 1654	OL	8
Abigail, d. John, bp. [1654, by Rev. Peter Prudden]	OL	105
Bathshuba, d. James, bp. [1650, by Rev. Peter Prudden]	OL	104
Eleazer, s. John, bp. [1642, by Rev. Peter Prudden]	OL	100
Eleazer, m. Elizabeth **FFORDE,** wid., Mar. 27, 1663	1	5
Eleazer, m. Elizabeth **FORD,** wid., Mar. 27, 1663, by Benjamin Ffenn	OL	15
Elizabeth, w. James, adm. Church Feb. 11, [1645]	OL	98
Elizabeth, d. Joseph, b. Dec. 10, 1703	OL	50
Elizabeth, d. Joseph, b. Dec. 11, 1703	1	24
Elizabeth, m. Nathan **BALDWIN,** July 31, 1712, by Samuel Eells, J.P.	1	34
Elizabeth, m. Nathan **BALDWIN,** July 31, 1712, by Sam[ue]ll Eells, Asst.	OL	74
Elizabeth, d. Joseph, Jr. [& Elizabeth], b. Feb. 4, 1740/1	1	112
Esther, wid., d. Feb. 1, 1777	SM	11
Hannah, d. John, bp. [1647, by Rev. Peter Prudden]	OL	102
Hannah, d. Eleazer, b. June 10, 1663	1	6
Han[n]ah, d. Eleazer, b. June 10, 1663	OL	15
Jabez, s. John, bp. [1649, by Rev. Peter Prudden]	OL	103
Jeffer, d. Mar. [ ], 1777	SM	12
Jeffrey, drafted for Continental Army	1	58
Jeremiah, his d. [ ], d. Sept. 20, 1776	SM	7
John, adm. Church May 28, [1642]	OL	98
John, s. John, bp. [1644, by Rev. Peter Prudden]	OL	101
John, s. James, bp. [1648, by Rev. Peter Prudden]	OL	103
John, [d.] 1684	ES	16
Jonathan, s. James, b. Dec. the last, 1655; the family moved to New London	OL	9
Jonathan, s. James, b. Dec. the last, 1655	1	2
Jonathan, s. James, bp. [1655, by Rev. Peter Prudden]	OL	105
Jonathan, d. [ ], 1821, North Milford	BP	44
Joseph, s. James, bp. [1646, by Rev. Peter Prudden]	OL	102
Joseph, s. Eleazer, b. Sept. 12, 1671	1	11
Joseph, s. Eleazer, b. Sept. 12, 1671	OL	24
Joseph, s. Joseph, b. Aug. 30, 1706	1	27
Joseph, s. Joseph, b. Aug. 30, 1706	1	29
Joseph, s. Joseph, b. Aug. 30, 1706	OL	58
Joseph, s. Joseph, b. Aug. 30, 1706	OL	63
Joseph, Lieut. had negro Tonee & Ann, Indian, married, sometime in Mar. 1731/2 by Roger Newton, J.P.	1	107
Joseph, Jr., m. Elizabeth **CLARK,** b. of Milford, May [ ], 1740, by Sam[ue]ll Gunn, J.P.	1	112
Joseph, s. Joseph, Jr. [& Elizabeth], b. June 17, 1742	1	112
Joseph, his w. [ ], d. Jan. 30, 1779	SM	17
Joseph, Jr., his s. [ ], d. Jan. 15, 1781	SM	21
Joseph, Jr., his child d. Sept. 2, 1781	SM	22
Joseph, Jr., his child d. [ ], d. June 21, 1782	SM	23

	Vol.	Page
ROGERS, ROGGERS, (cont.)		
Joseph, his d. [ ], d. May 7, 1783	SM	25
Joseph, d. Feb. 2, 1784	SM	27
Joseph, his infant d. [ ], d. Jan. 5, 1790	SM	41
Joseph, d. [ ], 1824, ae. 71	BP	50
Joseph, his wid. [ ], d. [ ], 1830, ae. 65	BP	61
Josiah, his w. [ ], d. Sept. 26, 1799	SM	67
Josiah, Capt., d. [ ], 1813	BP	25
Mary, d. Samuel, b. Oct. 9, 1666	1	7
Richard, d. [ ], 1815, ae. 13(?), at the South	BP	30
Ruth, d. John, bp. [1642, by Rev. Peter Prudden]	OL	100
Ruth, w. John, adm. Church Nov. 3, [1644]	OL	98
Ruth, d. of John, m. Thomas **GOODIN**, Nov. 9, 1661, by Mr. Ffenn, Magistrate	1	4
Ruth, d. John, m. Thomas **GOODIN**, b. of Milford, Nov. 9, 1661, by Benjamin Fenn, Magestrate	OL	14
Ruth, m. Sam[ue]ll **TIBBALLS**, July 3, 1718, by Major Sam[ue]ll Eells, Asst. Witnesses, Jon[a]th[an] Baldwin, Jr., Mary Baldwin	1	71
Samuel, s. Eleazer, b. Mar. 14, 1667/8	1	9
Samuel, s. Eleazer, b. May 14, 1668	OL	20
Sarah, d. Eleazer, b. Oct. 5, 1665	1	6
Sarah, d. Eliezer, b. Oct. 5, 1665	OL	17
Sharper, drafted for Continental Army	1	58
Susannah, d. of Dr. Uriah, of Norwalk, m. David **LAMBERT**, only s. of David & Lurania, Dec. 17, 1769; d. [ ], 1828	1	53
-----, Capt. his w. [ ], d. [ ], 1799, ae. 23	BP	2
ROODE, [see also **RUDE**], John, his child d. [ ], 1837	BP	78
ROULAN, ROULLAN, RULLAN, Ann, d. William, b. Apr. 3, 1717	1	64
John, s. William, b. Jan. 20, 1718/19	1	64
Stephen, s. William, b. July 19, 1714/15	1	64
William, m. Mrs. Mary **VALLOW**, Sept. 23, 1714, by Rev. Samuel Andrews	1	64
William, b. Dec. 6, 1720; d. Feb. 21, 1720/1	1	67
RUDE, [see also **ROODE**], -----, his infant child d. [ ], 1837	BP	78
RUE, Ebiather, s. Hezekiah, b. Sept. 21, 1725	1	78
Hannah, d. Hezekiah, b. Jan. 13, 1718/19	1	75
Hannah, d. Hezekiah, d. Feb. 16, 1718/19	1	75
Hannah, d. Hezekiah, b. Aug. 7, 1723	1	75
Hezekiah, m. Rejoyce **GOODWIN**, Mar. 12, 1718/19, by Jonathan Law, Asst.	1	67
John, s. Hezekiah, b. Feb. 21,1719/20	1	75
Mehetabeel, d. Hezekiah, b. May 4, 1728	1	83
RULLAN, [see under **ROULAN**]		
RUSSELL, William, drafted for Continental Army	1	58
SACKETT, SACKET, SOCKETT, Daniel, m. Marth **GREEN**, June 16, 1763, by Samuel Wales	1	164
Daniel, had negro boy d. Apr. 8, 1789	SM	39
Daniel, d. [ ], 1830, ae. 17	BP	61
-----, Col., d. [ ], 1822	BP	46
SALISBURY, SALSBURY, P., had another child d. [ ], 1804	BP	8
Philip, his d. [ ], d. July 21, 1801	SM	72

	Vol.	Page
SALISBURY, SALSBURY, (cont.)		
Philip, his s. [ ], d. Dec. 13, 1802	SM	76
Philip, his child d. [ ], 1802	BP	6
Philip, infant d. Jan. 10, 1804	SM	79
Philip, his s. [ ], d. Mar. 5, 1804	SM	79
Philip, his child d. [ ], 1804	BP	8
SAMSON, Wi[lham], s. Lieut. Wiham, b. [ ], 1664	OL	17
SANFORD, SANDFORD, SANEFORD, SAMFFORD,		
STAMFORD, Abigail, d. Samuel, Sr., b. Oct. 14, 1714	1	35
Abigail, d. Sam[ue]ll, Sr., b. Oct. 14, 1714	OL	76
Abigail, d. Samuel, Jr. & Abigail, b. Feb. 11, 1740/1	1	110
Andrew, Jr., m. Mary **BOTSFORD,** d. Henry, Jan. 8, 1667, by Mr. Ffenn, Magistrate	1	8
Andrew, Jr., m. Mary **BOTSFORD,** d. Henry, b. of Milford, Jan. 8, 1667, by Mr. Ffenn, Magestrate	OL	20
Andrew, had s. [ ], b. Mar. 30, 1673	1	12
Andrew, his s. [ ], b. Mar. 30, 1673	OL	25
Andrew, s. Andrew, Jr., b. July 13, 1673	1	13
Andrew, s. Andrew, Jr., b. July 13, 1673	OL	26
Andrew, Jr., original member of 2nd Church formed in 1742	ES	87
Comfort, d. Nathan & Abigail, b. Jan. 31, 1756	1	135
Dan, his child d. [ ], 1834, ae. 2 y.	BP	71
David, s. Samuel, b. Sept. 8, 1709	1	30
David, s. Sam[ue]ll, b. Sept. 8, 1709	OL	66
David, Priv. member of Capt. Samuel Peck's Co., Milford, 1776	1	54
David, d. Nov. [ ], 1780, in the Army	SM	20
David, d. [ ], 1820, at Sea	BP	43
Ebenezer, [twin with Nathaniel], s. Nathaniel, b. Mar. 10, 1710/11	1	33
Ebenezer, [twin with Nathaniel], s. Nathaniel, b. Mar. 10, 1710/11	OL	72
Elihu, m. Hannah **SANFORD,** June 28, 1758, by Rev. Job Prudden	1	141
Elihu, s. Elihu & Hannah, b. Apr. 26, 1759	1	141
Elijah, his child d. [ ], 1805	BP	11
Elijah, his child d. [ ], 1808	BP	18
Elijah, his child d. [ ], 1815	BP	28
Eliphalet, his child d. [ ], 1811, ae. 7 y.	BP	22
Eliphalet, d. [ ], 1837	BP	78
Elisha, had d. [ ], who had child d. [ ], 1806	BP	14
Elizabeth, d. Thomas, bp. [1648, by Rev. Peter Prudden]	OL	103
Elizabeth, d. Thomas, of Milford, m. Obadiah **ALLEYNE,** of Mattabeseak, Oct. 21, 1669, by John Clarke, Commissioner	1	10
Elizabeth, d. Thomas, of Milford, m. Obadiah **ALYNE,** of Mettabeseck, [ ], 1669, by John Clark, Com.	OL	22
Elizabeth, d. Andrew, Jr., b. Mar. 5, 1674/5	1	14
Elizabeth, d. Andrew, Jr., b. Mar. 5, 1674/5	OL	29
Elizabeth, d. Samuel, b. Dec. 13, 1716	1	38
Elizabeth, d. Samuel, b. Dec. 13, 1716	OL	80
Ephraim, s. Thomas, bp. [1646, by Rev. Peter Prudden]	OL	102
Ephraim, s. Ephraim, b. May 11, 1677	1	16
Ephraim, s. Ephraim, b. May 11, 1677	OL	32
Esther, d. Samuel, b. Nov. 9, 1711	1	39
Esther, d. Sam[ue]ll, b. Nov. 9, 1711	OL	85
Esther, d. Andrew, Jr., b. May 6, 1677	1	16

	Vol.	Page
SANFORD, SANDFORD, SANEFORD, SAMFFORD, STAMFORD, (cont.)		
Esther, d. Andrew, Jr., b. May 6, 1677	OL	31
Ezekiel, s. Andrew, Jr., b. July 11, 1683	1	19
Ezekiel, s. Andrew, Jr., b. July 11, 1683	OL	39
George, d. [ ], 1835, at New York	BP	72
Gideon, s. Samuel, Jr., b. Jan. 10, 1734/5	1	101
Han[n]ah, d. Andrew, b. Feb. 19, 1669	OL	22
Hannah, d. Andrew, b. Feb. 19, 1669/70	1	10
Hannah, d. Samuel, b. Feb. 2, 1675	1	15
Hannah, d. Sam[ue]ll, b. Feb. 2, 1675	OL	29
Hannah, d. Sam[ue]ll, b. Mar. 12, 1728/9	1	84
Hannah, d. Samuel & Ann, b. Apr. 30, 1733	1	96
Hannah, m. Elihu **SANFORD**, June 28, 1758, by Rev. Job Prudden	1	141
Hannah, d. Elisha, d. July 26, 1788 (died absent)	SM	38
Henry, s. Nathan, b. Jan. 22, 1752	1	129
Isaac, s. Sam[ue]ll, Jr., b. Nov. 24, 1731	1	91
Isaac, d. Sept. 16, 1795	SM	55
Jehosaphat, s. Samuel, b. July 12, 1709	1	30
Joel, s. Nathan & Abigail, b. Dec. 22, 1754	1	134
John, m. Mary **LAMBERT**, d. Jesse & Mary, Sept. 14, 1719* *(Probably "1743", see Page 49)	1	106
John, original member of 2nd Church formed in 1742	ES	87
John, m. Mary **LAMBERT**, Sept. 14, 1743, by Roger Newton, Asst.	1	117
John, his 2nd w. [ ], d. June 15, 1789, ae. 62	SM	40
John, d. Dec. 29, 1799, ae. 80	SM	68
John, d. [ ], 1799	BP	2
John, m. Mary **LAMBERT**, d. Jesse & Mary, [ ]	1	49
Jonathan, s. Samuel, b. July 13, 1704	1	25
Jonathan, s. Samuel, b. July 13, 1704	OL	51
Jonathan, s. Sam[ue]ll, Jr., b. Dec. 14, 1736	1	104
Julia, d. [ ], 1831, at North Haven	BP	65
Margaret, wid., d. June 28, 1781, ae. 67	SM	21
Martha, wid., d. May 23, 1802	SM	74
Mary, d. Thomas, bp. [1641, by Rev. Peter Prudden]	OL	100
Mary, d. Andrew, b. Nov. 16, 1668	1	9
Mary, d. Andrew, Jr., b. Nov. 16, 1668	OL	21
Mary, d. Andrew, Jr., b. July 1, 1679	1	17
Mary, d. wid. Hannah, d. Feb. 2, 1703	1	41
Mary, d. wid. Hannah, d. Feb. 2, 1703	OL	87
Mary, d. Capt. Andrew, m. Joseph **CLARK**, s. Dea. Joseph, Apr. [ ], 1737	1	106
Mary, m. Joseph **CLARK**, s. Dea. Joseph, [ ], 1737	ES	238
Mary, m. Joseph **CLARK**, Jr., Apr. 20, 1738	1	147
Mary, d. Feb. 3, 1777 (Written "Mary **BANFORD**")	SM	11
Mercy, d. Andrew, Jr., b. July 1, 1679	OL	34
Moses, s. Sam[ue]ll, b. Dec. [ ], 1726	1	83
Nathan, s. Sam[ue]ll & Abigail (**HOLBROOK**), b. May 26, 1722	1	70
Nathan, m. Abigail **TIBBALLS**, d. of Eben[eze]r, June 13, 1748,		

BARBOUR COLLECTION

	Vol.	Page
SANFORD, SANDFORD, SANEFORD, SAMFFORD, STAMFORD, (cont.)		
by Nathan Baldwin, J.P.	1	124
Nathan, s. Nathan & Abigail, b. Mar. 7, 1748/9	1	124
Nathaniel, s. Ephraim, b. Oct. 10, 1682	1	18
Nathaniell, s. Ephraim, b. Oct. 10, 1682	OL	39
Nathaniel, [twin with Ebenezer], s. Nathaniel, b. Mar. 10, 1710/11	1	33
Nathaniel, [twin with Ebenezer], s. Nathaniel, b. Mar. 10, 1710/11	OL	72
Ramond, m. Rebeckah **CHATFIELD**, Dec. 21, 1773, by Richard Mansfield, Missionary of Derby	1	165
Raymond, d. [ ], 1793, at Sea	SM	50
Rebeckah, m. Samuel **LARNED**, s. Isaac, of Mass. Bay, Sept. 7, 1731, by Samuel Gunn, J.P.	1	92
Samuel, s. Thomas, bp. [1643, by Rev. Peter Prudden]	OL	100
Samuel, s. Ephraim, b. Jan. 26, 1672	1	12
Samuel, s. Ephraim, b. Jan. 26, 1672	OL	25
Samuel, s. Andrew, b. Mar. 17, 1671/2	1	11
Samuell, s. Andrew, Jr., b. Mar. 17, 1671/72	OL	24
Samuel, s. Ephraim, b. Mar. 9, 1673/4	1	13
Samuell, s. Ephraim, b. Mar. 9, 1673/4	OL	26
Samuel, s. Andrew, b. Jan. 27, 1674	1	14
Samuel, s. Andrew, Sr., b. Jan. 27, 1674	OL	28
Samuel, s. Thomas, m. Hannah **BRIMSON***, d. Richard, of Farmington, Aug. 16, 1674, by Major Treat *(**BRUNSON**)	1	13
Samuell, s. Thomas, of Milford, m. Hannah **BRINCON***, d. Richard, of Farmington, Apr. 16, 1674, by Major Treat *(**BRUNSON**)	OL	27
Samuel, s. Samuel, b. Mar. 12, 1678/9	1	18
Samuel, s. Samuell, b. Mar. 12, 1679/80	OL	35
Samuel, s. Smauel, Jr., b. Apr. 1, 1704	1	24
Samuel, s. Samuel, Jr., b. Apr. 1, 1704	OL	49
Sam[ue]ll, m. Abigail **HOLBROOK**, b. of Milford, May 11, 1721, by Rev. Sam[ue]l Andrews	1	70
Samuel, s. Capt. Andrew & Hannah, m. Ann **PLUMBE**, d. Joseph & Susannah, Jan. 6, 1731/2, by Sam[ue]ll Gunn, J.P.	1	94
Sam[uel], Jr. member of 2nd Church formed in 1742	ES	87
Samuel, 3d, original member of 2nd Church formed in 1742	ES	87
Sam[ue]l, Jr., original member of 2nd Church formed in 1742	ES	87
Samuel, d. May 3, 1781, ae. 83	SM	21
Samuel, d. Mar. 17, 1804	SM	79
Sam[ue]l, Capt., d. [ ]	ES	165
Sarah, w. Thomas, adm. Church Dec. 15, [1642]	OL	98
Sarah, d. Thomas, m. Richard **SHUTTE**, seaman, Aug. 14, 1656, by Mr. Fenn, J.P.	1	3
Sarah, d. Thomas, m. Richard **SHUTE**, seaman, Aug. 14, 1656, by Mr. Ffenn, Magestrate	OL	10
Sarah, d. Andrew, b. Apr. 7, 1677	1	15
Sarah, d. Andrew, Sr., b. Apr. 7, 1677	OL	31
Sarah, d. Samuel, b. July 10, 1682	1	18
Sarah, d. Sam[ue]ll, b. July 10, 1682	OL	38
Sarah, m. Joseph **BEARD**, Apr. 10, 1703, by Robert Treat, Dept. Gov.	1	22

	Vol.	Page
SANFORD, SANDFORD, SANEFORD, SAMFFORD, STAMFORD, (cont.)		
Sarah, m. Joseph **BEARD**, Apr. 10, 1703, by Rob[ert] Treat, Dept. Gov.	OL	45
Sarah, d. Sam[ue]ll, Jr., b. Sept. 27, 1724	1	75
Sarah, d. Jan. 9, 1798	SM	63
Sarah, Mrs., d. [ ], 1802	BP	5
Stephen, s. Samuel, b. Nov. 20, 1706	1	27
Stephen, s. Sam[ue]ll, b. Nov. 20, 1706	OL	58
Strong, s. Elihu & Hannah, b. Oct. 5, 1760	1	143
Thomas, adm. Church Jan. 9, 1642	OL	98
Thomas, s. Thomas, bp. [1644, by Rev. Peter Prudden]	OL	101
Thomas, s. Samuel, b. Sept. 29, 1678; d. Mar. 3 following	1	17
Thomas, s. Samuell, b. Sept. 29, 1678; d. Mar. 3, following	OL	35
Thomas, s. Ephraim, b. Jan. 29, 1679	1	17
Thomas, s. Ephraim, b. Jan. 29, 1679	OL	35
Thomas, [d.], 1681	ES	16
Thomas, of Milford, m. Rebeccah **BARNES**, of Farmington, Sept. 29, 1713, by Rev. Sam[ue]ll Whitman, of Farmington	1	73
-----, Capt., d. [ ], 1804	BP	8
-----, d. [ ], 1824	BP	50
-----, Capt. his child d. [ ], 1826	BP	54
-----, wid., d. [ ], 1827	BP	56
-----, Capt. his child d. [ ], 1836, ae. 3 y.	BP	76
SATTERLEE, -----, wid., d. [ ], 1827	BP	56
SCOVELL, Mercy, m. Samuel **CAMP**, Jan. 6, 1681	OL	38
SEARS, SEERS, Ann, wid. of J. **BURKE**, d. [ ], 1822, at Jonas Hines	BP	46
Barnabus, d. Jan. 19, 1780, ae. 18	SM	19
Bartholomew, original member of 2nd Church formed in 1742	ES	87
Benjamin, s. John [& Frances], b. Mar. 19, 1746	1	132
Benjamin, d. Apr. [ ], 1777; killed in battle at Danbury	SM	12
Elizabeth, m. Barnabus **WOODCOCK**, May 28, 1736, by Sam[ue]ll Gunn, J.P.	1	106
Elizabeth, d. John [& Frances], b. Aug. 30, 1753	1	132
Elizabeth, m. John **PLUMB**, Jan. 1, 1772. Witnesses Barnabus Woodrock, Daniel Manson	1	172
Eunice, Mrs. her child d. [ ], 1807, ae. 7 y.	BP	15
Francis, d. John [& Frances], b. Oct. 30, 1750	1	132
Hannah, d. John [& Frances], b. May 2, 1744	1	132
John, m. Frances **PLUM**, b. of Milford, Mar. 3, 1740, by Sam[ue]ll Johnson, Missionary	1	132
John, s. John [& Frances], b. Aug. 22, 1742	1	132
John, d. Feb. 10, 1777	SM	11
John, his w. [ ], d. Oct. [ ], 1782 (Was not in Milford at time of death)	SM	24
John, Jr., d. [ ], 1790, at Sea	SM	43
Lucy, wid., d. Apr. 27, 1796	SM	58
Mary, d. John [& Frances], b. Mar. 29, 1748	1	132
Mary, m. Daniel **MUNSON**, May 22, 1766, by Rev. Job. Prudden, Witnesses: Job Fowler, Jr., Susannah Fowler, 2nd	1	168
William, his w. [ ], d. Jan. 26, 1798, ae. 36	SM	63

	Vol.	Page
SEARS, SEERS, (cont.)		
William, his s. [ ], d. Apr. 3, 1798	SM	63
W[illia]m, d. [ ], 1820, at the South	BP	42
W[illia]m Sewell, original member of 2nd Church formed in 1742	ES	87
-----, wid., d. [ ], 1808, ae. 86	BP	17
SELLECK, Sam[ue]ll, a stranger at S. B. Smith's, d. [ ], 1818	BP	38
SEWARD, [see also **STEWARD**, David, d. [ ], 1808, at Sea	BP	17
Daniel, drafted for Continental Army	1	57
Elizabeth, d. Nathaniel, m. Walter **SMITH**, Sept. 26, 1676, by Capt. Tapping	OL	30
John, see John **STEWARD**	SM	17
Mercy, m. Samuel **CAMP**, Jan. 6, 1681	1	18
Obed, m. Bethyah **HAWES**, Oct. 31, 1660	1	4
Obed, m. Bethiah **HAWES**, Oct. 31, 1661, by Robert Treat, Magestrate	OL	13
Obadiah, s. Obed, b. Nov. 1, 1661, "hitherto given into the jurisdiction of New Haven"	1	5
Obadiah, s. Obed, b. Nov. 1, 1661 (2)	OL	14
-----, see **STEWARD** (Mr.)	BP	23
SHAFFER, Henry, d. [ ], 1811	BP	22
SHARP, Andrew, his w. [ ], d. [ ], 1814	BP	27
Hannah, her grandchild d. Sept. 1, 1802	SM	75
Joseph, his d. [ ], d. Oct. 9, 1776, ae. 13	SM	7
Joseph, d. Aug. 16, 1798	SM	64
Joseph, drafted for Continental Army	1	58
SHEPARD, SHEPHARD, SHIPHARD, Abigail, d. John, b. Oct. 22, 1713	1	35
Abigail, d. John, b. Oct. 22, 1713	OL	75
Abigail, m. Peter **PERRITT**, Oct. 31, 1734, by Sam[ue]ll Eells, Asst.	1	101
Abig[ail], m. Peter **PERRET**, [ ], 1734	ES	238
Hannah, d. John, b. Nov. 11, 1715	1	36
Hannah, d. John, b. Nov. 11, 1715	OL	78
John, m. Mrs. Abigail **ALLEN**, Oct. 8, 1707, by Capt. Sam[ue]ll Eells, J.P.	OL	61
John, m. Mrs. Abigail **ALLEN**, Oct. 9, 1707, by Samuel Eells, J.P.	1	28
John, s. John, b. Oct. 26, 1708	1	29
John, s. John, b. Oct. 27, 1708	OL	63
John, of Milford, m. Mary **PARSONS**, of Derby, May [ ], 1732, by John Riggs, J.P.	1	97
Mary, d. John [& Mary], b. June 19, 1733	1	97
Rebecca, d. John, b. Nov. 1, 1710	1	32
Rebecca, d. John, b. Nov. 1, 1710	OL	69
Timothy, s. John, b. Mar. 22, 1718	1	62
SHERMAN, Bazeleel, s. John, bp. [1640], by Rev. Peter Prudden	OL	100
Daniel, s. John, bp. [1642, by Rev. Peter Prudden]	OL	100
Esther, of New Haven, m. Job Prudden, Aug. 22, 1750	ES	238
Esther, of New Haven, m. Rev. Job Prudden, of Milford, Aug. 22, 1750/1, by Rev. Nathan Birdseye, of West Haven	1	128
Esther, of New Haven, m. Rev. Job Prudden, Aug. 22, 1756; d. [ ], in Bethleham	ES	127

MILFORD VITAL RECORDS 165

	Vol.	Page
SHERMAN, (cont.)		
John, Rev., b. [ ], 1613, at Dedham, Essex Co., Eng., graduate of Immanual College; came to America 1634/5; preached his first sermon at Watertown; was twice married; his first w. d. Sept. 8, 1644, at New Haven; had by her six children; his 2nd w. was grand daughter of the Earl of Rivers; had twenty children; d. [ ], 1685, ae. 72 y.	ES	105
John, adm. Church Nov. 8 [1640]; dismissed to Church at Watertown; d. Aug. 8, 1685	OL	97
John, [d.], 1685	ES	16
Josiah, Rev., b. [ ], 1729, at Watertown, Mass.; d. Nov 24, 1789, at Woodbridge, Conn. He left a wid., 2 sons & 4 daughters	ES	128
Josiah, second pastor of 2nd Church, Aug. 23, 1775; dismissed June 21, 1781	ES	93
Mary, w. John, adm. Church Nov. 8, [1640]; d. Sept. 8, 1644, at New Haven	OL	97
Sam[ue]l, d. Sept. 15, 1644, ae. 4 m.	ES	35
Samuel, s. John, bp. [1644, by Rev. Peter Prudden]	OL	101
Samuel, s. Miles, b. Aug. 21, 1656	1	3
SHERWOOD, SHERRWOOD, Mary, m. Josiah **TIBBALS**, July 13, 1670	1	10
Mary, m. John **TIBBALLS**, July 13, 1670	OL	23
SHUTE, SHUTTE, Richard, seaman, m. Sarah **SAMFORD**, d. of Thomas, Aug. 14, 1656, by Mr. Fenn, J.P.	1	3
Richard, seaman, m. Sarah **SAMFORD**, d. Thomas, Aug. 14, 1656, by Mr. Ffenn, Magestrate	OL	10
Richard, came to Milford [ ]	ES	179
Thomas, s. Richard, b. Aug. 5, 1659	1	3
Thomas, s. Richard, b. Aug. 15, 1659	OL	11
SILVERSMITH, N[athanie]l, came to Milford, 1662	ES	179
SIMBONIER, -----, his child d. [ ], 1834	BP	71
SIMSON, Peter, came to Milford, [ ]	ES	179
SLATTERLY, John, d. June 2, 1800, ae. 39	SM	69
SLOUGH, SLOW, [see also **STOW**], Elizabeth, of Milford, m. Roger **PRACHET**, lately, of Springfield, Mass., Dec. 18, 1653, by William Fowler, J.P.	1	1
Elizabeth, of Milford, m. Roger **PRITCHET**, lately of Springfield, Dec. 18, 1653, by Mr. Ffowler,	OL	7
Elizabeth*, w. W[illia]m, came to Milford, 1668 *(Perhaps "Elizabeth **STOW**")	ES	179
Hesediah, d. W[illia]m, b. Nov. 20, 1648	ES	238
Hesadiah, d. William, bp. [1648, by Rev. Peter Prudden]	OL	103
James, s. William, b. Jan. 28, 1649	LL	2
James, s. William, d. Feb. 10, 1649	LL	1
Stephen, Capt., d. Feb. 8, 1777, ae. 57	SM	11
W[illia]m, came to Milford, 1640	ES	179
W[illia]m, "joined 1st Ch. 1646 & excommunicated for humble [ ] for which he was put to death at New Haven"	ES	238
W[illia]m, [d.]	ES	18
SMITH, Abell, s. Nathan, b. Apr. 25, 1752	1	132
Abigail, d. Benjamin, b. Sept. 17, 1666	1	9

	Vol.	Page
SMITH, (cont.)		
Abigail, d. Benjamin, b. Sept. 17, 1668	OL	21
Abigail, d. Caleb [& Abigail], b. Dec. 9, 1730	1	110
Abigaill, d. Nathan & Hannah, b. Jan. 27, 1746/7	1	120
Abigail, wid., d. [ ], 1830, ae. 52	BP	61
Abigail, w. John, d. Jan. 18, 1836	1	50
Abiah, d. Joseph & Mary, b. Sept. 23, 1728	1	89
Abijah, d. [ ], 1809	BP	18
Abraham, his w. [ ], d. Dec. 4, 1781, ae. 68	SM	22
Abraham, d. Jan. 2, 1782	SM	23
Adolphus, d. Oct. 25, 1794	SM	52
Ame, d. Nathan & Hannah, b. Oct. 23, 1760	1	143
Amos, s. Sergt. Joseph, b. Apr. 27, 1732	1	103
Amos, d. [ ], 1824	BP	50
Andrew, s. Nicholas, b. Dec. 3, 1670	1	14
Andrew, s. Nicholas, b. Dec. 3, 1670	OL	28
Andrew, his w. [ ], d. Nov. 16, 1804, ae. 42	SM	81
Andrew, his w. [ ], d. [ ], 1804	BP	10
Andrew, d. [ ], 1836	BP	75
Ann, d. Sergt. Joseph, b. Mar. 12, 1734	1	103
Anna, d. Joseph, b. Mar. 13, 1705/6	1	27
Anna, d. Joseph, b. Mar. 13, 1705/6	OL	57
Anna, [d. Ebenezer], b. Nov. [ ], 1722; d. Dec. 29, 1725	1	78
Anna, wid., d. [ ], 1825, ae. 78	BP	52
Beard, s. John & Mary, b. Nov. 24, 1733; d. Mar. 25, 1736	1	112
Beard Still, [s. John & Mary], b. Nov. 12, 1737	1	112
Benajah, d. [ ], 1818, ae. 70	BP	38
Benj[amin], came to Milford, 1645	ES	179
Benjamin, s. William, of Huntington, m. Mary **BALDWIN**, d. of Timothy, of Milford, Oct. 21, 1660, by Robert Treat, Magistrate	1	4
Benjamin, s. William, of Huntington, m. Mary **BALDWIN**, d. of Timothy, of Milford, Oct. 24, 1660, by Robert Treat, Magestrate	OL	13
Benjamin, s. Benjamin, b. Sept. 17, 1666	1	8
Benjamin, s. Benjamin, b. Sept. 17, 1666	OL	18
Benjamin, m. Sarah **HAUGHTON**, Feb. 9, 1682, by Major Treat	1	18
Benjamin, m. Sarah **HAUGHT[O]N**, Feb. 9, 1682, by Major Treat	OL	38
Benjamin, s. Timothy, b. Apr. 2, 1714	1	35
Benj[ami]n, s. Timothy, b. Apr. 2, 1714	OL	75
Benjamin, Jr., m. Mehetable **BOTSFORD**, June 16, 1747, by Sam[ue]ll Whittlesey, Jr.	1	123
Benjamin, d. Sept. 14, 1748	1	136
Benj[amin], his child d. [ ], 1812	BP	23
Benj[amin], his d. [ ], d. [ ], 1829, ae. 16	BP	60
Caleb, m. Abigail **CLARK**, [ ] 26, 1728, by Sam[ue]ll Gunn, J.P.	1	110
Caleb, his d. [ ], d. Aug. 11, 1795	SM	55
Caleb, d. [ ], 1815, ae. 75	BP	30
Catharine, wid., d. July 19, 1784, ae. 52	SM	27
Charles, his child d. [ ], 1813, N. Milford	BP	26
Charles, his s. [ ], d. [ ], 1838, ae. 8	BP	79

	Vol.	Page
SMITH, (cont.)		
Charles, his child d. [ ], 1836	BP	74
Cornelious, s. Nicholas, b. Dec. 12, 1675	1	15
Cornelius, s. Nicholas, b. Dec. 12, 1675	OL	29
D. C., his infant child d. [ ], 1815	BP	29
Daniel, s. Timothy, b. Oct. 19, 1706	1	28
Daniel, s. Timothy, b. Oct. 19, 1706	OL	61
Daniel, m. Sarah **JOHNSON**, Jan. 17, 1737/8, by Is[aa]c Dickerman, J.P.	1	105
Daniel, d. Feb. 11, 1798, ae. 15	SM	63
Daniel, his w. [ ], d. [ ], 1812	BP	24
David, Jr., his w. [ ], d. [ ], 1822	BP	46
David, Jr., his w. [ ], d. [ ], 1828, ae. 50	BP	58
David, 3rd, his w. [ ], d. [ ], 1840, ae. 56	BP	83
David, [s. Thomas & Mary], b. [ ]	1	51
David C., his child d. [ ], 1822, ae. 10	BP	47
David C., his child d. [ ], 1828	BP	58
Dorothy, d. Walter, b. Mar. 13, 1692	1	24
Dorothy, d. Walter, b. Mar. 13, 1692	OL	50
Ebenezer, s. John, bp. [1650, by Rev. Peter Prudden]	OL	103
Ebenezer, Lieut., m. Sarah **COLLINS**, Jan. 3, 1710, by Samuel Eells, Asst.	1	32
Ebenezer, Lieut., m. Sarah **COLLINS**, Jan. 3, 1710/11, by Sam[ue]ll Eells, Asst.	OL	70
Ebenezer, s. Timothy, b. Sept. 22, 1717	1	67
Ebenezer, m. Hannah **FOWLER**, Jan. 9, 1719, by Major Eells, Asst.	1	78
Eben[eze]r, s. Eben[eze]r, b. Mar. 25, 1720	1	78
Ebenezer, Jr., m. Phebe **CANFIELD**, Aug. 10, 1742, by Rev. Sam[ue]ll Whittlesey	1	118
Ebenezer, s. Eben[eze]r, Jr. & Phebe, b. June 10, 1743	1	118
Ebenezer, s. Nathan, b. Aug. 31, 1748	1	127
Ebenezer, his s. [ ], d. Jan. 24, 1777	SM	11
Ebenezer, his d. [ ], d. Dec. 13, 1783	SM	26
Ebenezer, d. July 6, 1796, ae. 76	SM	59
Eben[eze]r, his child d. [ ], 1809	BP	19
Ebenezer, d. [ ], 1814	BP	26
Elias, his child d. [ ], 1811, at North Milford	BP	21
Elias, his w. [ ], d. [ ], 1813, at N. Milford	BP	25
Elias, his w. [ ], d. [ ], 1824	BP	50
Elias, his child d. [ ], 1825	BP	53
Elias, Jr., his child d. [ ], 1831	BP	65
Elias, Jr., had another child d. [ ], 1831	BP	65
Elijah, Mr., d. [ ], 1816, ae. 22	BP	34
Eliphalet, his wid., d. [ ], 1805	BP	11
Elizabeth, d. Walter, b. Jan. 15, 1702	1	24
Elizabeth, d. Walter, b. Jan. 15, 1702	OL	50
Elizabeth, m. Jonathan **ANDREWS**, Jan. 5, 1726/7, by Rev. Sam[ue]ll Andrews	1	82
Ephraim, pd. £5 for not procuring men for Continental Army	1	55
Ephraim, s. John, bp. [1644, by Rev. Peter Prudden]	OL	101
Ephraim, his child d. [ ], 1838	BP	79
Esther, d. Jonathan, b. Feb. 1, 1705	1	27

	Vol.	Page
SMITH, (cont.)		
Esther, d. Jonathan, b. Feb. 1, 1705	OL	56
Eunice, d. Nathan, b. Sept. 29, 1754	1	134
Eunice, d. Nathan & Hannah, b. Sept. 25, 1758	1	143
Fowler, d. [ ], 1820	BP	42
George, s. Joseph & Mary, b. Oct. 13, 1721	1	89
George, his d. [ ], d. [ ], 1832	BP	66
George, his s. [ ], d. [ ], 1840, ae. 15	BP	83
Gideon, s. Thomas, b. June 13, 1709	1	34
Gideon, s. Thomas, b. June 13, 1709	OL	73
Grace, w. John, adm. Church Sept. 17, [1642]; d. [ ], 1690	OL	98
H., or W. Capt., his child d. [ ], 1825	BP	53
Hannah, d. Benjamin, b. Aug. 14, 1664	1	7
Hannah, d. Benjamin, b. Aug. 14, 1664	OL	18
Hannah, d. Nicholas, b. July 29, 1681	OL	37
Hannah, d. James, Jr. [& Hannah], b. Feb. 16, 1728/9	1	97
Hannah, d. [ ], 1839, ae. 60	BP	81
Hezekiah, his d. [ ], d. Feb. 19, 1783	SM	25
Hezekiah, his w. [ ], d. [ ], 1815, ae. 65 y.	BP	29
Hezekiah, d. [ ], 1823, ae. 74	BP	49
Hiel, d. Apr. [ ], 1782 (Was not in Milford at time of death)	SM	24
Isaac, [Capt.]	ES	41
Isaac, s. Thomas, b. Jan. 31, 1711/12	1	34
Isaac, s. Thomas, b. Jan. 31, 1711/12	OL	73
Isaac, Jr., his d. [ ], d. Aug. 29, 1789, ae. 2 y.	SM	40
Isaac & Phebe, had d. [ ], d. Jan. 17, 1801	SM	71
Isaac, his child d. [ ], 1801	BP	3
Isaac, Capt., d. Apr. 18, 1804, ae. 77	SM	79
Isaac, Capt., d. [ ], 1804	BP	8
Jabez, s. Thomas, b. Nov. 29, 1705	1	34
Jabez, s. Thomas, b. Nov. 29, 1705	OL	73
James, s. Walter, b. Oct. 10, 1689	1	24
James, s. Walter, b. Oct. 10, 1689	OL	50
James, Jr., m. Hannah **NORTHROP**, Mar. 20, 1727/8	1	97
James, s. James, Jr. [& Hannah], b. Aug. 10, 1733	1	97
James, d. Aug. 31, 1796, ae. 20	SM	59
Jehiah, s. Caleb [& Abigail], b. Jan. 6, 1739	1	110
Jeremiah, see John **MCKANE**	1	58
Jeremiah, s. Eben[eze]r, Jr., b. Jan. 31, 1746/7	1	123
Jeremiah, his w. [ ], d. Nov. 11, 1803	SM	78
Jeremey, d. [ ], 1810	BP	21
Jesse, s. Sam[ue]ll, b. Aug. 7, 1708	1	65
Joanna, d. John, of Derby, b. Oct. 20, 1702	1	20
Joanna, d. John, of Derby, b. Oct. 20, 1702	OL	43
Joanna, d. [ ], 1792 (Absentee)	SM	48
Joel, pd. £5 for not procuring men for Continental Army	1	55
Joel, d. [ ], 1812	BP	23
Joel, his s. [ ], d. [ ], 1828, ae. 13	BP	58
Joel, d. [ ], 1834, ae. 56	BP	71
Joel, m. Mary **NORTHROP**, [d. Ephraim & Sarah], [ ]	1	97
John, m. Abigail **LAMBERT**, [d. Jesse & Anne], [ ]	1	50
John, s. John, bp. [1646, by Rev. Peter Prudden]	OL	102
John, blacksmith, m. Sarah **FFOWLER**, d. Lieut. [ ],		

MILFORD VITAL RECORDS

	Vol.	Page
SMITH, (cont.)		
July 19, 1665, by Mr. Ffenn, Magistrate	1	7
John, blacksmith, m. Sarah **FFOWLER**, d. Lieut. William, b. of Milford, July 19, 1665, by Mr. Ffenn, Magestrate	OL	18
John, d. [ ], 1666	ES	238
John, s. John, blacksmith, b. May 11, 1667	OL	19
John, s. John, b. May 11, 1669	1	8
John, in 1671, destroyed the Indian Fort	ES	14
John, s. John, Sr., m. Phebe **CAMPPHIELD**, d. Thomas, Jan. 23, 1672, by John Clark, Com.	OL	25
John, s. John, m. Phebe **CAMPFIELD**, d. Tho[ma]s, Jan. 23, 1672/3, by John Clarke, Commissioner	1	12
John, s. John, Jr., b. June 18, 1674	1	14
John, s. John, Jr., b. June 18, 1674	OL	27
John, s. Nicholas, b. July 20, 1674	1	14
John, s. Nicholas, b. July 20, 1674	OL	27
John, s. Walter, b. Apr. 21, 1696	1	24
John, s. Walter, b. Apr. 21, 1696	OL	50
John, tailor, m. Mary **BRACE**, June 1, 1699, by Robert Treat, Dept. Gov.	1	21
John, tailor, m. Mary **BRACE**, June 1, 1699, by Robert Treat, Dept. Gov.	OL	45
John, blacksmith, d. Apr. 2, 1704	1	42
John, blacksmith, d. Apr. 2, 1704	OL	87
John, Dr., of Bethleham, adm. to Ch. 1738	ES	238
John, adm. to Ch. 1738	ES	238
John, Dr. adm. to Ch. 1739	ES	238
John, s. John & Mary, b. July 8, 1740	1	112
John, original member of 2nd Church formed in 1742	ES	87
John, had negro d. Jan. 21, 1777	SM	11
John, of Chatham, d. Jan. [ ], 1777	SM	10
John, Dea., d. June 8, 1783, ae. 78	SM	26
John, his d. [ ], d. Jan. [ ], 1798	SM	63
John, his child d. [ ], 1806, ae. 7	BP	13
John, d. [ ], 1826, ae. 53	BP	54
Jonah, s. Thomas, b. Apr. 27, 1703	OL	46
Jonah, s. Thomas, b. Apr. 29, 1703	1	22
Jonathan, s. John, b. Sept. 5, 1671	1	11
Jonathan, s. John, b. Sept. 5, 1671	OL	24
Jonathan, adm. to Ch. 1736	ES	238
Jonathan, s. Nathan & Hannah, b. Nov. 3, 1756	1	144
Jonathan, Jr., his w. [ ], d. [ ], 1826	BP	54
Joseph, s. John [black]smith, b. Jan. 15, 1668/9	1	10
Joseph, s. John, [black]smith, b. July 15, 1669	OL	22
Joseph, s. Walter, b. Oct. 16, 1698	1	24
Joseph, s. Walter, b. Oct. 16, 1698	OL	50
Joseph, m. Martha **BRYAN**, July 5, 1711, by Samuel Eells, Asst.	1	33
Joseph, m. Martha **BRYAN**, July 5, 1711, by Sam[ue]ll Eells, Asst.	OL	71
Joseph, m. Mary **CLARK**, July 7, 1720, by Samuel Eells, Asst.	1	67
Joseph, s. Sergt. John, m. Mary **CLARK**, July 7, 1720, by Sam[ue]ll Eells, Asst.	1	89
Joseph, adm. to Ch. 1726	ES	238

SMITH, (cont.)

	Vol.	Page
Joseph, s. Joseph & Mary, b. Mar. 15, 1730	1	89
Joseph, Sr., d. June 30, 1736	1	109
Joseph, s. Nath[anie]ll, b. Nov. 9, 1760	1	146
Joseph, d. [ ], 1812	BP	24
Joseph, adm. to Ch. [ ]	ES	238
Joseph S., d. [ ], 1823, ae. 41	BP	48
Josiah, s. John, b. Sept. 16, 1706	1	27
Josiah, s. John, b. Sept. 16, 1706	OL	59
Julia W., d. [ ], 1828, ae. 17	BP	58
L. N., had child d. [ ], 1832, ae. 5 y.	BP	66
L. N., had another child d. [ ], 1832	BP	66
Launcelot, [s. Thomas & Mary], b. [ ]	1	51
Lewes G., s. Amos & Sally, b. July 13, 1803	1	177
Lydia, d. Timothy, b. Sept. 30, 1710	1	32
Lydia, d. Timothy, b. Sept. last day, 1710	OL	68
Lydia, d. Timothy & Elizabeth, m. Timothy **BOTSFORD**, s. Timothy & Mary, b. of Milford, Nov. 21, 1734, by Sam[ue]ll Gunn, J.P.	1	100
Marg[a]ret, m. Joseph **AMES**, May 30, 1754. Witnesses, John Fowler, David Baldwin	1	138
Martha, d. Nicholas, b. Apr. 7, 1669	1	14
Martha, d. Nicholas, b. Apr. 7, 1669	OL	28
Martha, d. Samuel, b. Nov. 17, 1704	1	25
Martha, d. Samuel [& Rachell], b. Nov. 17, 1704; d. May 2, 1712	OL	52
Martha, d. Samuel, d. May 2, 1712	1	64
Martha, d. Sam[ue]ll, b. May 4, 1713	1	65
Martha, m. John **MILES**, b. of Milford, Nov. 3, 1737, by Sam[ue]ll Eells, Asst.	1	107
Martha, [d. Thomas & Mary], b. [ ]	1	51
Mary, d. John, bp. [1648, by Rev. Peter Prudden]	OL	103
Mary, d. John & Grace S., bp. [1652, by Rev. Peter Prudden]	OL	104
Mary, of New Haven, m. William **CAMP**, of Milford, Jan. 29, 1661, by Mr. Gilbert, Dept. Gov. of New Haven	1	6
Mary, of New Haven, m. William **CAMP**, of Milford, Jan. 29, 1661, by Mr. Gilbert, Dept. Gov. of New Haven	OL	16
Mary, d. Benjamin, b. Mar. 14, 1662	1	5
Mary, d. Benjamin, b. Mar. 14, 1662	OL	14
Mary, d. John, m. Abel **GUN[N]**, s. Joshua, b. of Milford, Oct. 29, 1666, by Mr. Ffenn, Magestrate	OL	19
Mary, d. John, m. Abel **GUNN**, s. Jasper, Oct. 29, 1667, by Mr. Ffenn, Magistrate	1	8
Mary, d. Walter, b. Mar. 27, 1687	1	24
Mary, d. Walter, b. Mar. 27, 1687	OL	49
Mary, d. John, tailor, b. May 6, 1703	1	21
Mary, d. John, tailor, b. May 6, 1703	OL	45
Mary, d. John, b. June 16, 1703	OL	45
Mary, m. Samuel **TERRELL**, Nov. 4, 1707/8 [sic], by Capt. Samuel Eells, J.P.	1	30
Mary, m. Samuel **TERRELL**, Nov. 4, 1707/8, by Sam[ue]ll Eells, J.P.	OL	65
Mary, d. Joseph & Mary, b. July 7, 1727	1	89
Mary, d. John & Mary, b. July 16, 1731	1	112

		Vol.	Page
SMITH, (cont.)			
Mary, Miss, d. Oct. 1, 1795, ae. 81		SM	56
Mary, w. Thomas, d. [ ], 1810		1	51
Mary, Miss, d. [ ], 1816		BP	34
Mary, wid., d. [ ], 1820, ae. 71		BP	41
Mary, wid., d. [ ], 1821, ae. 82		BP	44
Mary, wid., d. [ ], 1835, ae. 92		BP	73
Mary, [d. Thomas & Mary], b. [ ]		1	51
Mary, wid., d. [ ], 1[ ]		ES	238
Mehittabell, d. John, b. Mar. 24, 1654		OL	8
Mehetable, d. John, b. Mar. 24, 1655		1	2
Mehitable, d. John & Grace, bp. [1655, by Rev. Peter Prudden]		OL	105
Mahitable, d. John, Sr., m. Edward **CAMP**, Jan. 15, 1673, by Major Treat		1	13
Mehitabeel, d. John, Sr., m. Edward **CAMPE**, Jan. 15, 1673, by Major Treat		OL	26
Mehitabeel, d. John & Mary, b. Sept. 8, 1735		1	112
Mehitabeel, m. Sam[ue]ll **PECK**, Jr., July 7, 1762, by Rev. Sam[ue]l Whittlesey		1	144
Mehitabeel, m. Sam[ue]ll **PECK**, Jr., July 7, 1762, by Sam[ue]ll Whittlesey		1	149
Mercy, m. Samuel **GUNN**, Nov. 11, 1697		OL	69
Mercy, m. Samuel **GUNN**, Nov. 11, 1698		1	32
Mercy, d. Nathan & Hannah, b. Nov. 1, 1759		1	143
Miles, his other child d. [ ], 1805		BP	11
Miles, his child d. [ ], 1805		BP	11
Nathan, s. Nathan, b. June 21, 1750		1	127
Nathan, his child d. [ ], 1830, ae. 4 y.		BP	62
Nath[anie]ll, m. Catharine **MILLS**, Apr. 23, 1751		1	146
Nathaniel, m. Katharine **MILES**, Apr. 21, 1752, by Rev. Sam[ue]ll Whittlesey		1	133
Nathaniel, s. Nathaniel & Katharine, b. July 18, 1753, N.S.		1	133
Nath[anie]ll, s. Nath[anie]ll, b. July 18, 1753		1	146
Nathaniel, d. June 1, 1776, ae. 52		SM	6
Nathaniel, his d. [ ], d. Feb. [ ], 1777		SM	11
Nathaniel, d. Dec. 18, 1779		SM	18
Nehemiah, d. May 23, 1789, ae. 70		SM	39
Nicholas, m. Mary **TIBBALLS**, July 12, 1664, by Benj[amin] Ffenn		1	6
Nicholas, of Milford, m. Mary **TIBBALLS**, of Milford, July 12, 1664, by Benjamin Fenn		OL	16
Perry, s. John & Abigail (**LAMBERT**), was elected U.S. Senator in May 1836		1	50
Phebe, d. Lieut. Ebenezer, b. Oct. 14, 1711* *(This entry crossed out)		1	39
Phebe, d. Lieut. Ebenezer, b. Oct. 14, 1711		OL	85
Phebe, w. Sergt. John, d. May 3, 1730		1	87
Phebe, m. Isaac **PLATT**, Mar. 12, 1739/40, by Rev. Sam[ue]ll Whittlesey		1	114
Pheebee, d. Eben[eze]r, Jr. & Pheebee, b. July 17, 1744		1	118
Phebe, wid., d. Mar. 6, 1786, ae. 70		SM	31
Phebe, d. Nov. 8, 1790, ae. 18		SM	43

172   BARBOUR COLLECTION

	Vol.	Page
SMITH, (cont.)		
Rebeckah, m. Edward **WILLESON***, July 2, 1672		
*(**WILKINSON**?)	OL	26
Rebecca, d. Walter, b. May 3, 1684	1	24
Rebeckah, d. Walter, b. May 3, 1684	OL	49
Rebecca, w. Walter, d. Dec. 7, 1703	1	42
Rebecah, w. Walter, d. Dec. 7, 1703	OL	88
Richard, d. [ ], 1819	BP	40
Ruth, m. William **WHEELER**, Apr. 10, 1682, by Richard Lawe, of Stamford	1	18
Ruth, m. William **WHEELER**, Apr. 10, 1682, by Richard Law, of Stamford	OL	39
Ruth, m. Samuel **BRISCOE**, Oct. 23, 1707, by Capt. Eells	1	29
Ruth, m. Samuel **BRISCOE**, Oct. 23, 1707, by Capt. Eells	OL	62
S. B., had negro Bills, d. [ ], 1832	BP	67
Sally, d. [ ], 1805	BP	11
Samuel, s. Nicholas, b. Feb. middle, 1664	1	14
Samuel, s. Nicholas, b. Jan. middle, 1674	OL	28
Samuel, s. John, Jr., b. Oct. [Dec.] 8, 1677	1	17
Samuel, s. Walter, b. Feb. 23, 1677/8	1	16
Samuel, s. Walter, b. Feb. 23, 1678	OL	33
Samuel, s. John, Jr., b. Dec. 8, 1679	OL	34
Samuel, m. Rachel **LAMBERT**, d. Jesse & Deborah, Dec. 30, 1703	1	49
Samuel, m. Rachell **LAMBERT**, Dec. 30, 1703, by Thomas Clark, J.P.	OL	52
Samuel, m. Rachel **LAMBERT**, Dec. 31, 1703, by Thomas Clark, J.P.	1	25
Sam[ue]ll, s. Sam[]ue]ll, b. Nov. 12, 1716	1	65
Sam[ue]l, original member of 2nd Church formed in 1742	ES	87
Samuel, d. July 24, 1742	1	112
Samuel, his w. [ ], d. [ ], 1814	BP	26
Samuel B., his infant child d. May 29, 1792	SM	48
Sam[ue]ll Bryan, s. Nath[anie]ll, b. July 18, 1755	1	146
Samuel Bryan, his child d. Oct. 30, 1794	SM	52
Samuel M., his s. [ ], d. July 15, 1801, ae. 3 y.	SM	72
Samuel Miles, his child d. [ ], 1801	BP	4
Samuel Miles, d. [ ], 1822	BP	47
Sarah, d. Benjamin, b. Oct. 28, 1671	OL	24
Sarah, d. Benjamin, b. Oct. 28, 1671/2	1	11
Sarah, d. Nicholas, b. July 19, 1672	1	14
Sarah, d. Nicholas, b. July 19, 1672	OL	28
Sarah, d. Josiah, b. June 16, 1703	1	22
Sarah, m. Joseph **BEARD**, June 27, 1706, by Capt. Samuel Eells, J.P.	1	29
Sarah, m. Joseph **BEARD**, June 27, 1706, by Sam[ue]ll Eells	OL	62
Sarah, m. Nathaniel **BUCKINGHAM**, May 30, 1728, by George Newton, J.P.	1	86
Sarah, d. Caleb [& Abigail], b. Sept. 24, 1734	1	110
Seaman, d. [, 1837	BP	78
Sidney, his child d.], 1825	BP	53
Sidney, d. [, 1831, ae. 30	BP	65

	Vol.	Page
SMITH, (cont.)		
Sidney, [s. Thomas & Mary], b. [ ]	1	51
Simeon, his child d. [ ], 1815, ae. 8 m.	BP	28
Susan, d. [ ], 1825, ae. 22	BP	53
Thaddeus, d. Oct. 16, 1789	SM	40
Theodore, Capt. his child d. Feb. 26, 1799, ae. 3 y.	BP	1
Theodore, his w. [ ], d. [ ], 1819	BP	39
Theophilus, his s. [ ], d. Apr. 27, 1788	SM	36
Theophilus, his twin d. [ ], d. Apr. 22, 1789	SM	39
Theophilus, his twin s. [ ], d. Apr. 29, 1789	SM	39
Theophilus, Capt. his w. [ ], d. May 11, 1789, ae. 29	SM	39
Theophilus, Capt. his s. [ ], d. Feb. 26, 1799, ae. 2 y.	SM	66
Theophilus Mills, [s. Nath[aniell], b. Nov. 8, 1757	1	146
Thomas, s. John, Jr., b. Mar. 17, 1676/7	1	15
Thomas, s. John, Jr., b. Mar. 17, 1676/77	OL	31
Thomas, s. Walter, b. Dec. 23, 1680	OL	37
Thomas, m. Hannah CAMP, Dec. 2, 1699, by Robert Treat, Dept. Gov.	1	22
Thomas, m. Hannah CAMP, Dec. 21, 1699, by Robert Treat, Dept. Gov.	OL	45
Thomas, s. John, Jr., bp. June 16, 1700	1	130
Thomas, m. Mary LAMBERT, [d. David & Martha], [ ]	1	51
Thomas Lambert, [s. Thomas & Mary], b. [ ]	1	51
Timothy, s. Benjamin, b. Nov. 6, 1669	1	9
Timothy, s. Benjamin, b. Nov. 6, 1669	OL	21
Timothy, s. Timothy, b. Feb. 6, 1703/4	1	23
Timothy, s. Timothy, b. Feb. 6, 1703/4	OL	48
Timothy, m. Abigail CAMP, Oct. 29, 1729, by Roger Newton, J.P.	1	84
Timothy, [ ], 1736	ES	238
W., see H. SMITH	BP	53
Walter, m. Elizabeth FARRAND, d. Nathaniel, Sept. 26, 1676, by Capt. Tapping	1	15
Walter, m. Elizabeth SEWARD, d. Nathaniel, Sept. 26, 1676, by Capt. Tapping	OL	30
Walter, m. Rebecca PRIME, Apr. 1, 1677	1	16
Walter, m. Rebecka PRIME, Apr. 1, 1677	OL	33
Walter, d. May 25, 1709	1	64
W[illia]m, came to Milford, 1641	ES	179
W[illia]m, Capt. his child d. Nov. 12, 1781	SM	22
W[illiam, his infant child d. [ ], 1813	BP	31
W[illia]m, his child d. [ ], 1819, ae. 6	BP	40
W[illia]m, Capt., [ ]	ES	41
-----, w. Dea. [ ], d. June 25, 1776	SM	6
-----, Sergt. of Mass., d. Jan. [ ], 1777	SM	9
-----, wid., d. Nov. 10, 1785, ae. 75	SM	30
-----, wid., d. [ ], 1810	BP	20
-----, Mr. of West Haven, d. [ ], 1814, at N. Milford	BP	27
-----, Mr. a stranger at Mr. Burke's, had child d. [ ], 1835	BP	72
-----, Rev. of Oxford, d. [ ], 1836	BP	75
SNOW, John, of Chatham, d. Jan. [ ], 1777	SM	11
SOCKETT, [see under SACKETT]		

	Vol.	Page
SOMERS, [see under **SUMMERS**]		
SOTHERLAND, Mary Fenn, b. Nov. 29, 1758	1	343
SPAULDING, Robert, Lieut., d. Nov. 26, 1776, at the house of Col. Fenn	SM	8
SPENCER, Hannah, m. Benjamin **JONES**, May 2, 1661, by Robert Treat	1	5
Hannah, m. Benjamin **JONES**, May 2, 1661, by Rob[ert] Treat	OL	15
SPENING, Humphrey, d. [ ], 1656	ES	238
SPERRY, SPERREY, Abigail, d. Richard, b. Feb. 11, 1764; d. May 29, 1764	1	149
Caleb, Priv., member of Capt. Samuel Peck's Co., Milford 1776	1	54
Dennis, d. Richard & Rebecca, b. Mar. 31, 1773	1	165
Joel, drafted for Continental Army	1	58
Joel, s. Richard & Abigail, b. Jan. 9, 1757	1	137
Lemuel, s. Richard, b. Jan. 23, 1762	1	146
Lewis, s. Richard & Rebeckah, b. Feb. 4, 1771	1	160
Medad, s. Richard, b. July 6, 1759	1	142
Mehitabel, d. Richard & Rebeckah, b. Mar. 25, 1769	1	160
Rebeckah, d. Richard & Rebeckah, b. May 4, 1767	1	155
Richard, Jr., of New Haven, m. Abigail **NORTHROP**, d. Capt. Joel, of Milford, Dec. 9, 1755, by Rev. Benjamin Woodbridge, of Amity	1	134
Richard, m. Rebeckah **BALDWIN**, Dec. 6, 1764, by Benjamin Woodbridge	1	153
Richard, s. Richard [& Rebeckah], b. Aug. 17, 1765	1	153
STAMFORD, [see under **SANFORD**]		
STARR, Charlotte, colored d. [ ], 1834, in Fairfield	BP	71
Thomas, d. [ ], 1840	BP	83
Timothy, Jr., colored d. [ ], 1834, ae. 26	BP	71
STEELE, Harvey, see under Sally **POTTER**	1	50
STEVENS, Eliphalet, supposed to be dead [ ], 1794	SM	53
W[illia]m, d. [ ], 1807, at Sea	BP	16
STEWARD, [see also **SEWARD**], John, drafted for Continental Army	1	58
John*, his s. [ ], d. June 8, 1779 *(Perhaps "John **SEWARD**")	SM	17
John*, his w. [ ], d. Feb. 26, 1781 *(Perhaps "John **SEWARD**")	SM	21
-----, Mr., d. [ ], 1812 (Perhaps "**SEWARD**")	BP	23
STILES, David, d. [ ], 1805	BP	12
-----, wid., d. Oct. 25, 1801	SM	73
-----, Mrs., d. [ ], 1801	BP	4
STILLMAN, -----, Mr. his child d. Feb. 25, 1799	BP	1
-----, had child d. Feb. 25, 1799	SM	66
W., Mr., d. [ ], 1813	BP	25
STILSON, Abell, s. Joseph, b. Feb. 13, 1754	1	133
Almariellis, d. Joseph & Margaret, b. Sept. 27, 1762	1	146
Ely, s. Joseph, b. Feb. 20, 1764	1	148
Eunice, d. Joseph, b. Sept. 21, 1750	1	129
John, s. Moses, b. Mar. 13, 1708	1	31
John, [s. Moses], b. Mar. 13, 1708	OL	66
Joseph, of Milford, m. Marg[ar]ett **CLINTON**, of West Haven, Nov. 20, 1747, by Rev. Benjamin Woodbridge, of Amity	1	126

MILFORD VITAL RECORDS 175

	Vol.	Page
STILSON, (cont.)		
Josiah, s. Joseph, b. Jan. 14, 1753	1	133
Mary, d. Joseph, b. Sept. 19, 1751	1	129
Mary, of New Town, m. Nathan **PLATT**, of Milford, Jan. 7, 1754, by Rev. Benjamin Woodbridge, of Amity	1	133
Mercy, d. Joseph, b. June 20, 1755	1	135
Moses, m. Charity **LAGLEY**, Mar. 17, 1704/5, by Samuel Eells, J.P.	1	25
Moses, m. Charity **BAYLEY**, Mar. 17, 1704/5, by Sam[ue]ll Eells, J.P.	OL	53
Moses, s. Moses, b. Dec. 25, 1705	1	31
Moses, s. Moses, b. Dec. 25, 1705	OL	66
Rebeckah, d. Joseph & Margaret, b. Mar. 9, 1761	1	143
Sarah, d. Joseph & Marg[a]ret, b. July 28, 1758	1	139
Susanna, d. Vincent, b. Nov. 9, 1680	OL	36
Vinson, came to Milford, 1646	ES	179
STONE, Abel, s. Joseph & Eleanor, b. Mar. 1, 1758	1	139
Demaris, wid., d. [Apr.] [ ], 1795, ae. 81	SM	54
Eliza, d. Aug. 20, 1792	SM	48
Ez[ ], m. Susanna **NEWTON**, d. Rog[er], [ ]	ES	238
Hannah, m. John **DOWN**, Jr., Dec. 14, 1769, by Rev. Job Prudden; Witnesses Samuel Fenn, Jane Treat, Donald Treat, Fitch Welch	1	165
Isaac, d. Nov. 30, 1790, ae. 63	SM	44
Joanna, w. John, d. May 19, 1741	1	123
Jno, came to Milford, [ ]	ES	179
John, m. Johanna **FENN**, Oct. 2, 1740, by Sam[ue]ll Eells, Asst.	1	123
John, of Milford, m. Susannah **MANSFIELD**, of New Haven, Jan. 14, 1741/2, by Jos[eph] Noyes	1	123
John, s. John & Susanna, b. Oct. 13, 1745	1	123
John, d. Apr. 26, 1776	SM	5
Joseph, m. Eleanor **BEECH**, May 11, 1753, by Rev. Sam[ue]ll Whittlesey	1	139
Joseph, s. Joseph & Eleanor, b. Jan. 30, 1756	1	139
Joseph, negro his d. [ ], d. Dec. 18, 1794	SM	53
Joseph, his s. [ ], d. Oct. 16, 1801	SM	73
Joseph, his child d. [ ], 1801	BP	4
Joseph, d. [ ], 1810	BP	21
Joseph, his w. [ ], d. [ ], 1811, North Milford	BP	21
Mary, d. Joseph & Eleanor, b. Mar. 13, 1754	1	139
Samuel, s. John, b. May 27, 1674	1	13
Samuell, s. John, b. May 27, 1674	OL	27
Samuel, d. July 15, 1778	SM	15
Samuel, d. [ ], 1816	BP	35
Samuel M., d. Sept. 20, 1776	SM	7
Sam[ue]ll **MANSFIELD**, s. John & Susannah, b. Nov. 30, 1742	1	123
-----, wid., d. May 4, 1788 (died absent)	SM	38
[**STONEHILL**], **STONHILL**, H., removed to London, 1648	ES	17
Henry, d. [ ], (One of the first planters)	ES	16
Henry, adm. Church June 13, [1641]; dismissed to Church in London	OL	98
STOW, STOWE, STOUGH, [see also **SLOUGH**], A., Capt. had		

	Vol.	Page
STOW, STOWE, STOUGH, [see also **SLOUGH**],		
stranger on board d. [ ], 1818	BP	38
Anthony, Capt. his youngest child d. [ ], 1830, ae. 4	BP	62
Anthony, Capt. his child d. [ ], 1830, ae. 9	BP	63
Cornelius, d. [ ], 1837, ae. 39	BP	78
David, his child d. [ ], 1807	BP	15
David, his child d. [ ], 1820, ae. 1 y.	BP	41
Eleanor, wid., d. Aug. 9, 1798, ae. 77	SM	64
Elisha, his child d. [ ], 1810, ae. 8 y.	BP	20
Elizabeth, Mrs., d. [ ], 1838	BP	79
Fred, Capt. his child d. [ ], 1840, ae. 2	BP	83
Harry, d. Aug. [ ], 1804 (Drowned at Sea aboard Capt. Ferrin Turner's Vessel)	SM	80
Henry, d. [ ], 1804, at Sea	BP	9
Isaac, his d. [ ], d. Feb. 21, 1803	SM	77
Isaac, his child d. [ ], 1803	BP	7
Isaac, his w. [ ], d. [ ], 1834	BP	72
Jedediah, Capt. his d. [ ], d. [ ], 1801	BP	4
Jedediah, Jr., his child d. [ ], 1805	BP	11
Jeremiah, his d. [ ], d. Oct. 18, 1801	SM	73
John, his s. [ ], d. Nov. 27, 1791	SM	47
John, his infant d. [ ], d. Jan. 17, 1798	SM	63
John, his w. [ ], d. [ ], 1838, ae. 69	BP	79
John, d. [ ], 1839, ae. 79	BP	81
Joseph, see Joseph **STONE**	BP	4
Luke, d. [ ], 1824	BP	50
Maria, her child d. [ ], 1831	BP	65
Nelson, d. [ ], 1831, ae. 36, at Georgetown, S.C.	BP	65
Phinehas, d. [ ], 1811	BP	22
Samuel, draafted for Continental Army	1	57
Samuel, Capt., d. [ ], 1831, ae. 73	BP	64
Stephen, Capt., d. [ ], 1819	BP	39
William, adm. Church Mar. 26, [1648]; excummunicated for horrible depravity and put to death at New Haven	OL	99
William, his child d. Aug. 2, 1784	SM	28
William, d. Dec. [ ], 1792, at Sea	SM	48
W[illia]m, s. Capt. J[ ], d. [ ], 1814, ae. 10	BP	26
W[illia]m, m. Elizabeth **PRUDDEN**, d. James, [ ]	OL	98
W[illia]m, m. [ ] **PRUDDEN**, d. James, [ ]	ES	238
-----, wid., d. [ ], 1805, ae. 77	BP	12
-----, Mrs. had stranger d. [ ], 1814, at her home	BP	27
STRATTON, -----, his child d. [ ], 1820, ae. 3 y.	BP	41
STREAM, STREAME, Abigail, d. John, bp. [1654, by Rev. Peter Prudden]	OL	105
Abigail, d. Ens. John, m. Thomas **TIBBALS**, s. Thomas, Dec. 12, 1672, by John Clarke, Commissioner	1	12
Abiga[i]l, d. Ens. John, m. Thomas **TIBBALLS**, s. Thomas, Sr., Dec. 12, 1672, by John Clark, Com.	OL	25
Ephraim, the first settler, m. Mary **BUCKINGHAM**, d. Daniel, [ ]	1	9
John, came to Milford, 1646	ES	179
John, m. Martha **BEARD**, Dec. 20, 1649, by Capt. Asa Woods	LL	1
John, s. John, b. Dec. 27, 1657	1	3

MILFORD VITAL RECORDS 177

	Vol.	Page
STREAM, STREAME, (cont.)		
John, s. John, b. Dec. 27, 1657	OL	11
John, his widow d. June 22, 1706	1	43
Martha, d. John, b. May 6, 1664	1	6
Martha, d. John, b. May 6, 1664	OL	16
Mary, d. John, b. Oct. 12, 1653	1	1
Mary, d. John, b. Oct. 20, 1653	OL	7
Mary, d. John, bp. [1654, by Rev. Peter Prudden]	OL	105
Mary, d. Ens. John, m. David **BALDWIN**, Nov. 11, 1674, by Capt. Thomas Topping	1	14
Mary, d. Ens. John, m. David **BALDWIN**, Nov. 11, 1674, by Thomas Tapping	OL	28
Sarah, d. Sergt. John, b. Feb. 2, 1667	1	9
Sarah, d. Sergt. John, b. Feb. 2, 1667	OL	20
Sarah, m. Ephraim **BURWELL**, May 27, 1698, by Thomas Clark, J.P.	1	22
Sarah, m. Ephraim **BURWELL**, May 27, 1698, by Thomas Clark, J.P.	OL	46
Thomas, s. John, b. Apr. 1, 1661	1	4
Thomas, s. John, b. Apr. 5, 1661	OL	14
-----, wid., d. June 22, 1706	OL	88
STRONG, Ann, d. Ephraim, b. Sept. 25, 1757	1	157
Anthony C., Esq., of Woodbury, m. Julia [**LAMBERT**], [d. Jesse Peck & Amy]	1	51
Catharine Pond, [d. William & Mary H.], b. Nov. 17, 1811	1	177
Charles P., his w. [ ], d. [ ], 1836, ae. 32	BP	74
Charles Pond, [s. William & Mary H.], b. Mar. 24, 1805	1	177
Charles Pond, his child d. [ ], 1830	BP	62
Charlotte, [d. William & Mary H.], b. Aug. 12, 1817	1	177
Elnathan, his w. [ ], d. [ ], 1807	BP	16
Elnathan, d. [ ], 1834	BP	71
Ephraim, m. Mary **BUCKINGHAM**, wid., May 10, 1712, by Capt. Joseph Treat, J.P.	1	76
Ephraim, s. Ephraim [& Mary], b. Mar. 10, 1713/14	1	76
Ep[hraim], b. Mar. 10, 1714	ES	184
Eph[raim], b. July 26, 1716	ES	238
Ephraim, Jr., Elder, original member of 2nd Church formed in 1742	ES	87
Ephraim, member of 2nd Church formed in 1742	ES	87
Ephraim, marks for cattle recorded Aug. 31, 1743	1	114
Ephraim, m. Mary **PRUDDEN**, d. of John, b. of Milford, in the Spring, 1746, by Rev. Mr. Smith; sworn to by his w. Mehitabel Smith, d. Elizabeth Smith, May 24, 1771, before Abram Hatfield, J.P.	1	159
Ephraim, Jr., m. Maj. (?) *Mary **PRUDDEN**, d. John, [ ], 1746, by Rev. John Smith, at White Plains *(Probably Maj. John)	ES	238
Ephraim, s. Ephraim, b. Dec. 11, 1754	1	157
Ephraim, [s. William & Mary H.], b. Sept. 4, 1801	1	177
Ephraim, d. May 12, 1802, ae. 89	SM	74
Eph[rai]m, d. [ ], 1802	BP	5
Eph[rai]m, his w. [ ], d. [ ], 1812, ae. 54 y.	BP	24
Ephraim, d. [ ], 1839, ae. 38, at Petersburg, Va.	BP	81
Eunice, d. Ephraim, b. July 24, 1752	1	157

	Vol.	Page
STRONG, (cont.)		
George, [s. William & Mary H.], b. Feb. 12, 1819	1	177
Hannah, d. [ ], 1826, ae. 17 y.	BP	54
Hannah Platt, [d. William & Mary H.], b. June 15, 1809	1	177
John, s. Ephraim, b. Jan. 26, 1715/16	1	76
John, s. Ephraim, b. July 5, 1760	1	157
John, s. Ephraim, d. Sept. 2, 1763	1	157
John, his w. [ ], d. [ ], 1838	BP	79
John Carrington, [s. William & Mary H.], b. Sept. 5, 1821	1	177
John Prudden, s. Ephraim, b. Aug. 12, 1763	1	157
Martha Miles, [d. William & Mary H.], b. Dec. 29, 1806	1	177
Mary, d. Ephraim [& Mary], b. Aug. 6, 1749	1	156
Mary H., b. June 15, 1779	1	177
Mary Prudden, [d. William & Mary H.], b. Apr. 9, 1803	1	177
Sarah, [d. William & Mary H.], b. July 17, 1813	1	177
Selah, d. [ ], 1823, ae. 27	BP	48
Selah, his child d. [ ], 1830	BP	62
Seth, of Woodbury, m. Harriet [**LAMBERT**, d. Jesse Peck & Amy], [ ], 1831	1	51
Sybil, d. Ephraim [& Mary], b. Jan. 13, 1747	1	156
William, b. Jan. 16, 1781	1	177
William, [s. William & Mary H.], b. July 9, 1815	1	177
-----, wid., d. [ ], 1820	BP	41
STUART, -----, wid., d. [ ], 1825	BP	52
SUMMERS, SOMERS, Abel, d. Jan. 31, 1795	SM	54
Abel, his child d. [ ], 1807	BP	15
Abel, his w. [ ], d. [ ], 1822	BP	47
Abel, d. [ ], 1829	BP	59
Agnes, wid., d. Jan. 15, 1795	SM	54
Benjamin, d. May 10, 1804, ae. 42	SM	80
Benjamin, d. [ ], 1804	BP	9
Curtis, Capt. his w. [ ], d. [ ], 1837	BP	77
Henry, d. May 17, 1799, ae. 64	BP	1
Henry, d. May 18, 1799, ae. 64	SM	66
John, d. [ ], 1813	BP	26
Joseph, of Milford, m. Sarah **JELLET**, Mar. 4, 1729/30, by Roger Newton, J.P.	1	90
Joseph, d. Aug. 27, 1779, ae. 48	SM	18
Levi, d. [ ], 1811	BP	22
Sarah, d. Joseph [& Sarah], b. Jan. 1, 1730/1	1	90
Sarah, Mrs., d. [ ], 1804, ae. 74	BP	9
Stephen, his child d. [ ], 1814, ae. 2 y.	BP	27
Stephen, d. [ ], 1829	BP	60
Stephen, his child d. [ ], 1839	BP	81
William, drafted for Continental Army	1	58
-----, wid., d. Aug. 15, 1804	SM	80
-----, Mrs. d. [ ], 1821, ae. 80	BP	44
[**SUTHERLAND**], [see under **SOTHERLAND**]		
SWEETLAND, Jeptha, Capt., d. [ ], 1822	BP	46
SWESSIH(?), Gabrill, drafted for Continental Army	1	58
SWIFT, Alice W., [d. Homer & Mabel Louisa], b. Nov. 28, 1842	1	52
Elmer L., [s. Homer & Mabel Louisa], b. May 18, 1840	1	52
Homer, of New Lebanon, N.Y., m. Mabel Louisa [**LAMBERT**],		

	Vol.	Page
SWIFT, (cont.)		
d. John & Esther], Apr. 14, 1839; settled at Oyster River, Milford	1	52
Jane W., [d. Homer & Mabel Louisa], b. Jan. 7, 1846	1	52
TALLY, Eunice, wid., d. [ ], 1815, ae. 56	BP	28
TALMAGE, Betty, d. [ ], 1826, ae. 85	BP	55
TAPP, Ann, wid., d. [ ], 1659/60	ES	238
Anne, w. Edmund, adm. Church June 25, [1642]	OL	98
Edmund, original member of First Church gathered at New Haven, Aug. 22, 1639	ES	57
Edmund, d. [ ], 1652	ES	35
Edmund, d. [ ], 1653	ES	16
Edmund, d. [ ], 1653, (One of the first planters)	ES	16
Edmund, d. [ ], 1653, at New Haven	OL	97
Edmund, had d. [ ], who m. Robert TREAT, Gov. of Conn..; they had four sons and four daughters; she d. Apr. 8, 1703	ES	105
Edm[und], agent of the 1ˢᵗ purchase	ES	1
Jane, m. Robert TREAT, [ ], d. Apr. 8, 1703	ES	238
Jane, see Jane TREAT	OL	99
Mary, d. Edmund & Anne, [m.] Capt. William FOWLER, s. William, [ ]; was sister of Jane (TAPP), w. of Geo.* TREAT *(hand corrected to Governor in original manuscript)	1	48
TAPPING, TOPPING, Anna, d. James, b. Sept. 18, 1662	1	5
Anna, d. James, b. Sept. 18, 1662	OL	15
Elnathan, s. Thomas, bp. [1640], by Rev. Peter Prudden	OL	100
Em., w. Thomas, adm. Church July 2, [1640]	OL	97
James, s. Thomas, bp. [1642, by Rev. Peter Prudden]	OL	100
James, d. [ ], 1661	ES	238
Mary, d. Thomas, b. May 26, 1659	1	3
Mary, d. Thomas, b. Mar. 26, 1659	OL	11
Thomas, adm. Church July 2, [1640]; dismissed to Southampton, L.I.; d. [ ], 1684	OL	97
Tho[mas], Capt. dismissed from 1ˢᵗ Ch. Southampton to Ch. in Milford, Nov. 9, 1673	ES	238
Tho[mas], Capt. dismissed from 1ˢᵗ Ch. Southampton, [Nov.] 9, 1673; adm. to 1ˢᵗ Ch. Milford	ES	238
Thomas, d. [ ], 1684 (One of the first planters)	ES	16
-----, wid. [Perhaps d. [ ], 1644]	ES	238
-----, Capt. removed to Southampton but returned in 1673 and went back again; was a Magestrate of Conn.	ES	17
TAUKUS, Betty, Indian, d. June 4, 1794, ae. 63	ES	6
Betty, an Indian, bd. June 4, 1794, ae. 63, in Great Indian Burial Ground at Turkey Hill on the banks of the Housatonic	ES	6
TERRELL, TERREL, TERRELLE, TERRIELL, TERRIL, TERRILL, Aaron, s. Josiah, b. Mar. 23, 1725/6	1	78
Abigail, w. Roger, adm. Church Nov. 3, [1644]	OL	98
Abigail, d. Roger, bp. [1644, by Rev. Peter Prudden]	OL	101
Abigail, d. John, b. June 13, 1681	1	18
Abiga[i]l, d. John, b. June 13, 1681	OL	39
Abraham, s. Sam[ue]ll, b. Sept. 14, 1715	1	65

TERRELL, TERREL, TERRELLE, TERRIELL, TERRIL,
TERRILL, (cont.)

	Vol.	Page
Amos, s. George, b. Apr. 16, 1726	1	78
Amos, s. George, b. Apr. 16, 1726	1	81
Ann, d. George, b. July 16, 1724	1	78
Caleb, s. Daniel, Jr., b. Dec. 18, 1717	1	75
Daniel, s. Roger, b. Mar. 1, 1659/60	1	3
Daniel, m. Abigail **BRISTOL**, Nov. 27, 1712, by Samuel Eells, Asst.	1	33
Dan[ie]l, m. Abigail **BRISTOL**, Nov. 27, 1712, by Sam[ue]ll Eells, Asst.	OL	72
Daniel, m. Zerviah **CANFIELD**, Dec. 12, 1716, by Rev. Sam[ue]ll Andrews	1	75
Daniel, s. Daniel, Jr., b. Dec. 8, 1720	1	76
Daniel, d. June 10, 1727	1	81
Eleazer, s. Roger, b. Sept. 20, 1662	1	5
Eleazer, s. Roger, b. Sept. 20, 1662	OL	14
Eliakim, Priv., member of Capt. Samuel Peck's Co., Milford 1776	1	54
Elizabeth, d. Samuel [& Elizabeth], b. Feb. 28, 1741	1	126
Elizabeth, m. Oliver **BUCKINGHAM**, May 26, 1772, by Job Prudden	1	160
Ephraim, s. Roger, b. Apr. 8, 1655	1	2
Ephraim, s. Roger, b. Apr. 8, 1655	OL	8
Ephraim, s. Roger, bp. [1655, by Rev. Peter Prudden]	OL	105
George, s. Daniel, b. Oct. 31, 1703	1	22
George, s. Daniell, b. Oct. 31, 1703	OL	46
George, m. Abigail **HINE**, Aug. [ ], 1722, by Sam[ue]ll Clarke, J.P.	1	70
Hannah, d. Roger, bp. [1645, by Rev. Peter Prudden]	OL	101
Hannah, m. Richard **BURTON**, Mar. 6, 1723/4	1	73
James, s. Daniel, Jr., b. May 10, 1719	1	76
Jesse, s. Sam[ue]ll, b. Feb. 5, 1710/11	1	65
Jesse, s. Jesse, b. Mar. 20, 1745	1	119
Job, s. Daniel, b. Nov. 6, 1705	1	26
Job, s. Daniell, b. Nov. 6, 1705	OL	54
Job, s. Job & Violet, b. Sept. 9, 1758	1	140
John, s. Roger, bp. [1644, by Rev. Peter Prudden]	OL	101
John, s. John, b. Mar. 10, 1675	1	15
John, s. John, b. Mar. 10, 1675/6	OL	30
Joseph, s. Roger, bp. [1651, by Rev. Peter Prudden]	OL	104
Josiah, m. Mary **GOODWIN**, Jan. 1, 1723/4, by Sam[ue]ll Eells, Asst.	1	73
Mary, d. Roger, b. [ ], 1653	OL	7
Mary, d. Roger, b. Feb. 12, 1653/4	1	1
Mary, d. Roger, bp. [1654, by Rev. Peter Prudden]	OL	104
Mary, d. Roger, d. May 3, 1654, ae. 4 m.	ES	238
Mary, d. Daniel, d. May 2, 1712	1	44
Mary, d. Daniel, d. May 2, 1712	OL	90
Mary, w. Daniel, d. May 8, 1712	1	44
Mary, w. Daniel, d. May 8, 1712	OL	90
Mary, d. Sam[ue]ll, b. Mar. 16, 1713	1	65
Mary, d. Ephraim, b. May 25, 1728	1	87
Mary, d. Samuel, Jr. [& Elizabeth], b. Apr. 2, 1745	1	126

	Vol.	Page
TERRELL, TERREL, TERRELLE, TERRIELL, TERRIL, TERRILL, (cont.)		
Merriam, d. Jesse, b. Dec. 11, 1751	1	127
Merriam, d. Jesse, b. Dec. 11, 1751	1	307
Moses, s. Josiah, b. Oct. 6, 1724	1	78
Noah, s. Jesse, b. May 26, 1749	1	127
Phinehas, of Milford, m. Pheebee **OATMAN**, of Stratford, July 7, 1747, by Sam[ue]ll Adams, J.P.	1	125
Phinehas, s. Phinehas {& Pheebee}, b. May 15, 1748	1	126
Rebeckah, m. Jacob **BALDWIN**, Apr. 11, 1744, by Roger Newton, Asst.	1	122
Robert, s. Robert, b. Aug. 14, 1654	OL	8
Roger, adm. Church July 28, [1644]	OL	98
Rogger, s. Roger, b. Jan. 20, 1649	LL	2
Roger, s. Roger, bp. [1649, by Rev. Peter Prudden]	OL	103
Roger, [d.], 1682	ES	18
Ruth, d. Daniel, d. May 3, 1712	1	44
Ruth, d. Daniel, d. May 3, 1712	OL	90
Samuel, s. Roger, bp. [1647, by Rev. Peter Prudden]	OL	102
Samuel, s. John, b. Apr. 2, 1678	1	16
Samuell, s. John, b. Apr. 2, 1678	OL	32
Samuel, m. Mary **SMITH**, Nov. 4, 1707/8 [sic], by Capt. Samuel Eells, J.P.	1	30
Samuel, m. Mary **SMITH**, Nov. 4, 1707/8, by Sam[ue]ll Eells, J.P.	OL	65
Samuel, s. Samuel, b. Aug. 31, 1708	1	30
Samuel, s. Samuel, b. Aug. 31, 1708	OL	65
Samuel, Jr., m. Abigail **BALDWIN**, Aug. 17, 1710, by Jonathan Law, J.P.	1	33
Samuel, Jr., m. Abigail **BALDWIN**, Aug. 17, 1710, by Jon[a]th[an] Law, J.P.	OL	70
Samuel, s. Samuel, Jr., b. Sept. 10, 1711	1	33
Samuel, s. Samuel, Jr., b. Sept. 10, 1711	OL	71
Samuel, Jr., m. Elizabeth **DOWN**, Oct. 9, 1739	1	126
Sam[ue]l, original member of 2nd Church formed in 1742	ES	87
Sam[ue]ll, s. Samuel [& Elizabeth], b. Dec. 20, 1743	1	126
Samuel, d. June 2, 1782, ae. 74	SM	23
Samuel, his w. [ ], d. [ ], 1815, ae. 71	BP	28
Samuel, d. [ ], 1833, ae. 91	BP	69
Sarah, m. John **HUBBARD**, Nov. 4, 1707/8 [sic], by Capt. Eells, J.P.	1	30
Sarah, m. John **HUBBERT**, Nov. 4, 1707/8, by Capt. Eells, J.P.	OL	65
Sarah, d. Ephraim, b. Dec. 6, 1730	1	87
Sarah, see Sarah **HUBBARD**	1	70
Stephen, s. Daniel, Jr., b. Nov. 11, 1724	1	76
Thomas, s. Roger, b. Oct. 20, 1656	OL	10
Thomas, s. Roger, [b.] Oct. 23, 1656	1	3
-----, wid., d. Feb. 18, 1798	SM	63
THAYER, THARES, Elisha, drafted for Continental Army	1	57
Thomas, Sergt., m. Elizabeth **PECK**, d. Joseph, Oct. [Dec.] 29, 1677, by Major Treat	1	16
THOMAS, Amos, near Dartmouth College, d. Jan. [ ], 1777	SM	11

	Vol.	Page

THOMAS, (cont.)
    Ashael, his w. [   ], d. Aug. 23, 1796, ae. 35   SM   59
    Isaac, Priv., member of Capt. Samuel Peck's Co., Milford 1776   1   54
    Lydia, of New Haven, m. Samuel **NORTHROP**, Jr., of Milford, June 10, 1746, by Isaac Dickerman, J.P.   1   125
    Noah, Priv., member of Capt. Samuel Peck's Co., Milford 1776   1   54
    W[illia]m, not known d. Jan. [   ], 1777   SM   11
THOMLINSON, [see under **TOMLINSON**]
THOMPKINS, [see under **TOMPKINS**]
THOMPSON, -----, his child d. [   ], 1837; burned   BP   77
    -----, at the Point, his child d. [   ], 1837   BP   78
THORNTON, THORNTEN, Thomas, m. Hannah **FFARRAND**, d. Nathaniel, Sr., Aug. 5, 1674, by Major Robert Treat   1   14
    Thomas, m. Hannah **FARRAND**, d. Nathan, Sr., Aug. 5, 1674, by Major Treat   OL   27
TIBBALLS, TIBBALES, TIBBALL, TIBBALS, Abigail, d. Thomas, Jr., b. Mar. 28, 1677   1   15
    Abiga[i]l, d. Thomas, Jr., b. Mar. 28, 1677   OL   31
    Abigail, d. Thomas, b. June 3, 1704   1   23
    Abigall, d. Thomas, b. June 3, 1704   OL   49
    Abigail, d. Samuel & Ruth, b. Feb. 26, 1721/2   1   96
    Abigail, d. Sam[ue]l & Ruth, b. Feb. 26, 1722   1   71
    Abigail, d. Eben[eze]r, m. Nathan **SANFORD**, June 13, 1748, by Nathan Baldwin, J.P.   1   124
    Abner, s. Josiah, Jr. & Mary, b. Mar. 8, 1722/3   1   74
    Abner, s. Josiah, Jr., b. [   ], 1725   1   78
    Ann, d. Thomas, b. Sept. 16, 1707   1   29
    Ann, d. Thomas, b. Sept. 16, 1707   OL   62
    Ann, d. Sam[ue]l & Ruth, b. Apr. 26, 1719   1   71
    Ann, m. Caleb **BALDWIN**, Jr., Jan. 29, 1729, by Sam[ue]ll Eells, Asst.   1   86
    Arnold, Capt., d. June 7, 1795   SM   55
    Arnold, his s. [   ], d. Oct. 8, 1802, ae. 17   SM   76
    Arnold, d. [   ], 1806   BP   13
    Arnold, his w. [   ], d. [   ], 1810   BP   20
    Arnold, d. [   ], 1825, ae. 70   BP   52
    Arnold, Jr., pd. £5 for not procuring men for Continental Army   1   55
    Arnold, Capt., [   ]   ES   41
    Bene[dic]t, pd. £5 for not procuring men for Continental Army   1   55
    Benedict, his infant s. [   ], d. Apr. 23, 1787   SM   33
    Benedict, his d. [   ], d. Sept. 15, 1791, ae. 1 y.   SM   46
    Benedict, d. [   ], 1824, ae. 63   BP   50
    Benedict, his wid. [   ], d. [   ], 1826, ae. 65   BP   55
    Bethiah, w. Josiah, d. Mar. 21, 1714/15   1   44
    Bethiah, w. Josiah, Jr., d. Mar. 21, 1714/15   OL   91
    Deborah, d. John & Deborah, b. Apr. 19, 1750   1   132
    Dorothy, wid., d. [   ], 1812   BP   24
    Eliakim, s. Josiah, Jr., b. [   ], 1735   1   103
    Elias, his child d. [   ], 1834, ae. 4 y.   BP   71
    Elisha, d. [   ], 1836   BP   75
    [Elizabeth], d. Josiah, b. May 18, 1673   1   12
    Elizabeth, m. Samuel **HINE**, Jr., June 9, 1709, by Joseph Treat,

TIBBALLS, TIBBALES, TIBBALL, TIBBALS, (cont.)

	Vol.	Page
J.P.	1	31
Elizabeth, m. Samuel HINE, Jr., June 9, 1709, by Ja[me]s Treat J.P.	OL	66
George, his infant d. [ ], 1839	BP	81
Hannah, d. Thomas, b. Mar. 13, 1656/7	1	3
Hannah, d. Thomas, b. Mar. 13, 1656 or 1657	OL	10
Hannah, d. Josiah, b. Oct. 13, 1676	1	15
Hannah, d. Josiah, b. Oct. 13, 1676	OL	30
Hepzibeth, d. Josiah & Mary, b. Aug. 13, 1728	1	83
James, s. Sergt. Thomas, Jr., b. Aug. 3, 1682	1	18
James, s. Sergt. Thomas, Jr., b. Aug. 3, 1682	OL	38
Jane, d. [ ], 1831	BP	64
John, s. Thomas, bp. [1645, by Rev. Peter Prudden]	OL	102
John, m. Mary SHERRWOOD, July 13, 1670	OL	23
Samuel, s. Samuel & Ruth, b. Mar. 15, 1724/5	1	96
Samuel, s. Samuel & Ruth, d. Jan. 1, 1751/2	1	131
Samuel, his s. [ ], d. Mar. 13, 1780	SM	19
Samuel, Capt. his infant s. [ ], d. May 24, 1786	SM	31
Samuel, his s. [ ], d. June 8, 1791	SM	45
Sam[ue]l, Capt. his 2nd w. [ ], d. Mar. 17, 1796, ae. 38	SM	58
Samuel, Jr., d. Oct. 8, 1801, ae. 22	SM	73
Samuel, d. [ ], 1802, at Sea	SM	74
Samuel, Capt. his w. [ ], d. [ ], 1805	BP	12
Samuel, Capt. his child d. [ ], 1806	BP	13
Samuel, Capt., d. [ ], 1826, ae. 75	BP	54
Samuel, m. Mehetable LAMBERT, [d. Jesse & Anne], [ ]	1	50
Sarah, d. Thomas, b. Nov. 29, 1654	1	2
Sarah, d. Thomas, b. Nov. 29, 1654	OL	8
Sarah, d. Thomas, bp. [1654, by Rev. Peter Prudden]	OL	105
Sarah, d. Thomas, d. June 11, 1712	1	44
Sarah, d. Thomas, d. June 11, 1712	OL	90
Sarah, w. Thomas, d. Jan. 25, 1717/18	1	44
Sarah, w. Thomas, d. Jan. 25, 1717/18	OL	91
Sarah, m. Israel ISBELL, Apr. 18, 1750, by Rev. Samuel Whittlesey	1	126
Thomas, lived to be above 90 y.	ES	17
Thomas, adm. Church Feb. 24, [1645]	OL	98
Thomas, s. Thomas, bp. [1651, by Rev. Peter Prudden]	OL	104
Tho[ma]s, in 1671, destroyed the Indian Fort	ES	14
Thomas, s. Thomas, m. Abigail STREAME, d. Ens. John, Dec. 12, 1672, by John Clarke, Commissioner	1	12
Thomas, s. Thomas, Sr., m. Abiga[i]l STREAME, d. Ens. John, Dec. 12, 1672, by John Clark, Com.	OL	25
Thomas, s. Thomas, Jr., b. Aug. 22, 1679	1	17
Thomas, s. Thomas, Jr., b. Aug. 22, 1679	OL	33
Thomas, Sr., Sergt., d. Apr. 8, 1703	1	40
Thomas, Sr., Sergt., d. Apr. 8, 1703	OL	86
Thomas, [d.], 1703	ES	16
Thomas, member of 2nd Church formed in 1742	ES	87
William, s. William, b. Aug. 24, 1663	OL	15
William, his child d. [ ], 1804	BP	10

	Vol.	Page
TIBBALLS, TIBBALES, TIBBALL, TIBBALS, (cont.)		
William, infant d. Dec. 1, 1804	SM	81
W[illia]m, his infant d. [ ], 1836	BP	74
-----, wid., d. Nov. 28, 1798	SM	65
-----, d. [ ], 1820, at the South	BP	42
-----, his child d. [ ], 1826	BP	55
-----, Mrs., m. Hugh **GRAY**, [ ], by Robert Treat, Justice	1	20
[**TOLLES**], **TOLLS**, Elnathan, drafted for Continental Army	1	58
Jared, Sergt., member of Capt. Samuel Peck's Co., Milford, 1776	1	54
TOMLIN, [see also **TOMLINSON**], Elizabeth, of Milford, m. James **BISHOP**, of New Haven, Dec. 12, 1665, by Benjamin Ffenn, Magestrate	OL	17
TOMLINSON, THOMLINSON, [see also **TOMLIN**], Abraham, s. Abraham, b. Apr. 1, 1765	1	153
Abigail, d. Dr. Abraham & Mary, b. Nov. 23, 1779	1	167
Abigail, d. Dec. 29, 1802, ae. 23	SM	76
Abigail, d. [ ], 1802	BP	6
Abraham, b. Apr. 1, 1765	ES	238
Abraham, Dr. his w. [ ], d. [ ], 1807, ae. 67	BP	15
Abraham, Dr., d. [ ], 1820	BP	41
Abram, Dr., d. [ ], 1816	BP	35
Allice, came to Milford, [1650]	ES	179
Alice, w. Robert, adm. Church Feb. 2, [1653]; dismissed to Stratford	OL	99
Anna, d. David, of Milford, m. as 1ˢᵗ w. Benjamin Lott **LAMBERT**, Mar. 27, 1811; b. Aug. [ ], 1793; d. Jan. 22, 1815	1	53
Caleb, s. Abraham, b. Sept. 29, 1771	1	161
Caleb, d. Aug. 29, 1794; heard of his death at Sea	SM	51
Charles, his child d. [ ], 1837, ae 3 w.	BP	77
David, s. Abraham & Mary, b. Jan. 25, 1767	1	154
David, d. [ ], 1825, ae. 60	BP	53
Henry, came to Milford, [1650]	ES	179
John, s. Abraham, b. June 14, 1769	1	156
John, s. Abraham & Mary, d. Aug. 26, 1773	1	164
John, 2ⁿᵈ, s. Abraham & Mary, b. June 24, 1774	1	164
Rob[ert], came to Milford, 1650	ES	179
William, his w. [ ], d. Sept. 9, 1799	SM	67
W[illia]m, Capt. his w. [ ], d. [ ], 1799, ae. 32	BP	2
W[illia]m, Capt., d. [ ], 1806	BP	14
TOMMANS?, Timothy, d. Nov. 14, 1777	SM	14
TOMPKINS, TOMKINS, THOMPKINS, Abigail, d. Micah, b. Nov. 13, 1655	1	2
Abigail, d. Micah, b. Nov. 13, 1655	OL	9
Abigail, d. Micah, bp. [1655, by Rev. Peter Prudden]	OL	105
David, s. Micah, bp. [1647, by Rev. Peter Prudden]; d. Mar. 5, 1649/50	OL	102
David, d. [ ], 1649, ae. 18 m.	ES	35
Elizabeth, d. Micah, bp. [1644, by Rev. Peter Prudden]	OL	101
Elizabeth, m. James **BISHOP**, of New Haven, Dec. 12, 1665, by Benjamin Ffenn, Magistrate	1	7
Joe, negro his s. [ ], d. Apr. 6, 1799	SM	66

MILFORD VITAL RECORDS 185

	Vol.	Page
TOMPKINS, TOMKINS, THOMPKINS, (cont.)		
Jo, negro had child d. [ ], 1804	BP	9
Jo, colored d. [ ], 1839, ae. 76	BP	81
Jonathan, s. Michael, bp. [1643, by Rev. Peter Prudden]	OL	101
Joseph, his infant s. [ ], d. Sept. 20, 1804	SM	81
Mary, w. Michael or Micah, adm. Church Dec. 12, [1643]	OL	98
Mary, d. [Michael], bp. [1643, by Rev. Peter Prudden]	OL	101
Micah, s. Micah, b. May 9, 1659	1	3
Micah, s. Micah, b. May 9, 1659	OL	11
Micah, [d.]	ES	16
Micah, see Michael **TOMPKINS**	OL	98
Michael*, adm. Church Dec. 12, [1643] *(His name is spelled on Town Records both Michael and Micah)	OL	98
Peg, d. [ ], 1823	BP	48
Rebeckah, d. Michael, b. Nov. 20, 1653	OL	7
Rebecca, d. Michael, b. Nov. 24, 1653	1	1
Rebecca, d. Michael, bp. [1653, by Rev. Peter Prudden]	OL	104
Seth, s. Michael, bp. [1649, by Rev. Peter Prudden]	OL	103
TOPPING, [see under **TAPPING**]		
TRAIN, -----, Rev. his infant d. [ ], 1836	BP	75
TREAT, Abigail, Mrs. adm. To 1st Ch. [ ], 1694	ES	238
Abigail, d. Robert, b. [ ], 1704	ES	238
Abigail, d. Robert, bp. 1704	ES	238
Abigail, d. Sam[ue]l, [ ], 1730	ES	238
Abigail, d. [ ], 1828, ae. 40	BP	57
Abigail, [d. Gov. Robert], b. [ ]	ES	238
Ann, d. Ens. Joseph, bp. [ ], 1700	ES	238
Ann, wid., d. Dec. 15, 1799	SM	68
Ann, wid., d. Dec. 16, 1799, ae. 81	BP	2
Anne, m. Miles **MERWIN**, Sept. 25, 1718, by Rev. Samuel Andrews. Witnesses John Fowler, Susannah Fowler	1	67
Anne, wid., d. [ ], 1806	BP	13
Austin, s. Joseph, of No. Milford, m. Esther Maria [**LAMBERT**], [d. John & Esther], [ ], 1830	1	52
Bethiel, [child of Robert], [ ], 1738	ES	238
B[e]ula, d. Sam[ue]ll, Jr. [& Bula], b. Jan. 15, 1745/6	1	122
B[e]ula, [child of Samuel, Jr. & Beela], b. [ ], 1746	ES	238
Clemence, [child of Joseph & Clement], [ ], 1743	ES	238
Clement, d. Lieut. Joseph, b. July 8, 1743	1	115
Clement, d. Capt. Joseph & Clement, b. July 18, 1743	1	130
Clement, [d. Joseph & Clement], b. [ ], 1743	ES	238
Clement, m. David **INGERSOLL**, Mar. 9, 1768, by Rev. Samuel Whittlesey. Witnesses, Stephen Treat, Rebeckah Powell, Susannah Fowler, Susanna Whittlesey	1	164
Daniel, had s. [ ], d. Feb. 5, 1797, ae. 5 y.	SM	61
Daniel, his w. [ ], & twin d. [ ], d. Jan. 2, 1803	SM	77
Daniel, his child d. [ ], 1803	BP	7
David, had negro man, d. Dec. 23, 1799	SM	68
Donald, his 1st w. [ ], d. Aug. 30, 1785, ae. 45	SM	29
Edmund, s. [Capt. Joseph], b. Nov. 10, 1710	ES	238
Edmund, s. Capt. Joseph, b. Nov. 20, 1710	1	40
Edmund, s. Capt. Joseph, b. Nov. 20, 1710	OL	85
Edmund, [s. Capt. Joseph], [bp.] 1710	ES	238

	Vol.	Page
TREAT, (cont.)		
Edmund, s. Col. Joseph, b. Nov. [ ], 1711	ES	238
Edmond, member of 2nd Church formed in 1742	ES	87
Edmund, his w. [ ], d. June 1, 1785, ae. 69	SM	29
Edmund, d. Sept. 22, 1801, ae. 91	SM	73
Edmund, d. [ ], 1801	BP	4
Elijah, [s. Robert], [ ], 1733	ES	238
Elisha, d. [ ], 1813	BP	26
Elizabeth, [d. Gov. Robert], b. Feb. 8, 1679	ES	238
Elizabeth, w. Robert, adm. to Ch. July 3, 1679	ES	238
Elizabeth, d. Robert, b. Sept. 8, 1679	OL	37
Elizabeth, w. Robert, bp. 1679	ES	238
Elizabeth, Mrs. d. Jan. 10, 1705	1	26
Elizabeth, Mrs., d. Jan. 10, 1705/6	OL	55
Elizabeth, [d. Capt. Joseph], [bp.] 1712	ES	238
Elizabeth, Mrs., m. James **DAVIDSON**, Sept. 2, 1736, by Roger Newton, Asst.	1	104
Elizabeth, d. Sam[ue]ll, Jr. [& Bula], b. Aug. 19, 1747	1	122
Elizabeth, [d. Samuel, Jr. & Beela], b. [ ], 1747	ES	238
Elizabeth, d. Capt. Joseph & Clement, b. Nov. 5, 1752	1	131
Elizabeth, [d. Joseph & Clement], [ ], 1752	ES	238
Elizabeth, w. Robert, d. Jan. [ ]	ES	238
Eunice, [d. Sam[ue]ll], bp. 1729	ES	238
Francis, [d. Joseph & Clement], [ ], 1749	ES	238
Frances, d. Capt. Joseph & Clement, b. Mar. 6, 1750	1	131
Francis, [child of Joseph], b. [ ], 1750	ES	238
Francis, wid., d. [ ], 1806	BP	13
Gideon, s. Joseph & Clement, b. May 1, 1737	1	105
Gideon, s. Capt. Joseph & Clement, b. May 1, 1737; d. [ ]	1	130
Gideon, [s. Joseph & Clement], b. May 1, 1737	ES	238
Gideon, [s. Joseph & Clement], [ ], 1737	ES	238
Gideon, [s. Robert] [ ], 1737	ES	238
Gideon, s. Capt. Joseph, d. Oct. 10, 1746	1	115
Gideon, [s. Joseph & Clement], bp. 1746	ES	238
Gideon, s. Capt. Joseph, b. Oct. 22, 1747	1	115
Gideon, s. Capt. Joseph & Clement, b. Oct. 22, 1747	1	131
Gideon, [s. Joseph], b. [ ], 1747	ES	238
Hannah, d. Robert, b. Jan. 1, 1659	OL	12
Hannah, [d. Gov. Robert], b. Jan. 5, 1659	ES	238
Hannah, d. Robert, b. Jan. 1, 1659/60	1	3
Hannah, d. Joseph & Hannah, b. May 14, 1728	1	83
Hannah, d. Capt. Joseph & Hannah, b. May 14, 1728	1	130
Hannah, [d. Joseph], b. May 14, 1728	ES	238
Hannah, [d. Joseph & Hannah], [ ], 1728	ES	238
Hannah, d. Joseph, bp. 1730	ES	238
Hannah, w. Jos[eph], d. May 25, 1733	1	101
Hannah, w. Capt. Joseph, d. May 25, 1733	1	130
Hannah, w. Joseph, d. [ ], 1733	ES	238
Hannah, w. Joseph, d. May 25, 1739	ES	238
Isaac, [s. Robert], [ ], 1734	ES	238
Isaac, [Capt.], 1775	ES	41
Isaac, Capt. had negro Loudon, d. Sept. 10, 1785	SM	29
Isaac, Capt., d. [ ], 1829, ae. 97	BP	60

MILFORD VITAL RECORDS 187

	Vol.	Page
TREAT, (cont.)		
Jane, d. Edmund Tapp, adm. Church Apr. 19, 1649	OL	99
Jane, d. Robert, b. Jan. 24, 1680	OL	37
Jane, [d. Robert], b. Jan. 24, 1680	ES	238
Jane, d. Robert, bp. [ ], 1680	ES	238
Jane, [d. Ens. Joseph], bp. [ ], 1702	ES	238
Jane, w. Robert, d. Apr. 8, 1703	ES	105
Jane, w. Robert, d. Apr. 8, 1703	ES	238
Jane, w. Col. Tho[ma]s, d. Oct. the last, 1703	1	40
Jane, w. Col. Robert, d. Oct. the last, 1703	OL	86
Jane, [w. Robert], adm. to Ch. 1731	ES	238
Jane, [d. Robert], [ ], 1736	ES	238
Jane, d. Lieut. Jos[eph], b. Aug. 24, 1739	1	113
Jane, [d. Joseph & Clement], b. [ ], 1739	ES	238
Jane, [d. Joseph & Clement], [ ], 1739	ES	238
Jane, d. Aug. 14, 1785, ae. 46	SM	29
Jane, wid., d. Nov. 12, 1793, ae. 93	SM	50
Jean, d. Capt. Joseph, d. Nov. 12, 1723, in the 22nd y. of her age	1	73
Jean, d. Capt. Joseph & Clement, b. Aug. 24, 1739	1	130
John, [s. Gov. Robert], b. Oct. [ ], 1650	ES	238
John, s. Robert, bp. [1650, by Rev. Peter Prudden]; settled in Newark, N.J., and died there very aged	OL	103
John, [s. Gov.] [ ], [bp.] Oct. [16]50	ES	238
John, s. Ens. Joseph, bp. [ ], 1700	ES	238
John, s. Capt. Joseph, d. Nov. 20, 1723, in the 26th y. of his age	1	73
John, s. Joseph, b. Sept. 4, 1724	1	78
John, s. Capt. Joseph & Hannah, b. Sept. 4, 1724	1	130
John, s. Joseph, b. [ ], 1724	ES	238
John, [s. Joseph & Hannah], [ ], 1724	ES	238
John, s. Joseph, bp. 1730	ES	238
John, s. [Sam[ue]l], [ ], 1732	ES	238
John, Jr., his 1st w. [ ], d. Apr. 28, 1792, ae. 25	SM	47
John, d. Oct. 19, 1794, ae. 63	SM	52
John, d. [ ], 1807	BP	16
John, [s. Joseph], b. [ ]	ES	238
John, 2nd s. [Robert], b. [ ], d. young	ES	105
Jonah, his d. [ ], d. Feb. 28, 1801	SM	71
Jonah, his s. [ ], d. Feb. 24, 1801, ae. 1 y. 2 m.	SM	71
Jonathan, s. Robert, b. Mar. 17, 1701	1	22
Jonathan, s. Robert, b. Mar. 17, 1701	OL	46
Jonathan, s. Robert, bp. 1701	ES	238
Jonathan, s. Robert, b. J[ ], 1707	ES	238
Jonathan, s. Jonathan, bp. 1735	ES	238
Jonath[an] & w. Martha, adm. to Ch. 1735	ES	238
Jonathan, had negro Jube, d. Nov. 4, 1777	SM	14
Jonathan, d. June 3, 1779, ae. 78	SM	17
Jonathan, his child d. [ ], 1801	BP	3
Joseph, s. Robert, b. Sept. 17, 1662	1	5
Joseph, s. Robert, b. Sept. 17, 1662	OL	14
Joseph, [s. Gov. Robert], b. Sept. 17, 1662	ES	238
Joseph, [s. Gov. [ ], [bp.] Sept. 24, [16]62	ES	238
Joseph, adm. to 1st ch. [ ], 1700	ES	238
Joseph, s. Ens. Joseph, bp. [ ], 1700	ES	238

BARBOUR COLLECTION

TREAT, (cont.)

	Vol.	Page
Joseph, his w. adm. to 1st Ch. [ ], 1700; d. Feb. 21, 1703	ES	238
Joseph, Lieut., widower, m. Mrs. Elizabeth **MARVIN**, Nov. 8, 1705, by Robert Treat, Dept. Gov.	1	26
Joseph, Lieut. m. 2nd w. Mrs. Elizabeth **MARWIN**, [b.] of Milford, Nov. 8, 1705, by Robert Treat, Dept. Gov.	OL	54
Joseph, Jr., Capt. 1708	ES	40
Joseph, Capt., 1712; d. [ ], 1721	ES	40
Joseph, m. Hannah **BUCKINGHAM**, June 9, 1720, by Sam[ue]ll Eells, Asst.	1	68
Joseph, m. Hannah **BUCKINGHAM**, d. of John, June 9, 1720	1	130
Joseph, m. Hannah **BUCKINGHAM**, July 9, 1720	ES	238
Joseph, s. Capt. Joseph & Hannah, b. July 9, 1721; d. Aug. 12, 1721	1	130
Joseph, s. Joseph [& Hannah], b. July 9, 1721; d. Aug. 12, 1721	1	68
Joseph, Capt., d. Aug. 9, 1721	ES	238
Joseph, Capt., d. Aug. 9, 1721	1	69
Joseph, Capt., d. Aug. 9, 1721	ES	238
Joseph, s. Joseph & Hannah, b. Nov. 28, 1722	1	73
Joseph, s. Capt. Joseph & Hannah, b. Nov. 28, 1722	1	130
Joseph, [s. Joseph], b. Nov. 28, 1722	ES	238
Joseph, [s. Joseph & Hannah], [ ], 1722	ES	238
Joseph, [s. Joseph], bp. 1730	ES	238
Joseph, m. Clement **BUCKINGHAM**, (2nd w.), Feb. *26, 1734 *(Probably "Sept.")	ES	238
Joseph, m. Clement **BUCKINGHAM**, Sept. 26, 1734, by Roger Newton, J.P.	1	101
Joseph, Capt., m. Clement **BUCKINGHAM**, Sept. 26, 1734	1	130
Joseph, m. Clement **BUCKINGHAM**, [ ], 1734	ES	238
Joseph, Capt., d. [ ], 1772, ae. 86	ES	180
Joseph, his negro man, d. July 28, 1785	SM	29
Joseph, Dea., d. July 28, 1791, ae. 69	SM	46
Joseph, Jr., his child d. [ ], 1805	BP	12
Joseph, Jr., of N. Milford, d. [ ], 1812	BP	24
Joseph, 4th s. [Robert], b. [ ]	ES	105
Joseph, m. [ ] **BRYAN**, d. of Richard, [ ]	ES	238
Julia, d. [Dec.] [ ], 1795	SM	56
Mary, [d. Gov. [ ], [bp.] May 28, [16]52	ES	238
Mary, [d. Gov. Robert], b. May 28, 1652	ES	238
Mary, d. Robert, bp. [1652, by Rev. Peter Prudden]	OL	104
Mary, d. Sam[ue]ll, Jr. [& Bula], b. Oct. 29, 1744	1	122
Mary, wid., d. July 22, 1803	SM	78
Mary, Mrs., d. [ ], 1803	BP	7
Mary T., [d. Sam[ue]ll, Jr. & Beela], b. [ ], 1744	ES	238
Pamelia, wid., d. [ ], 1836	BP	74
Philo, his negro man, d. Mar. 18, 1784	SM	27
Philo S., d. May 3, 1798	SM	63
Richard, s. Capt. Joseph, b. Sept. 28, 1708	1	40
Rich[ar]d, s. Capt. Joseph, b. Sept. 28, 1708	OL	85
Richard, s. Capt. Joseph, b. Sept. 28, 1708	ES	238
Richard, s. Col. Joseph, b. Oct. [ ], 1708	ES	238
Richard, s. Capt. Joseph, bp. 1708	ES	238

MILFORD VITAL RECORDS 189

	Vol.	Page
TREAT, (cont.)		
Richard, s. Joseph & Clement, [ ], 1735	ES	238
Richard, s. Capt. Joseph & Clement, b. Feb. 2, 1735	1	130
Richard, s. Joseph & Clement, b. Feb. 2, 1735/6	1	104
Richard, s. Sergt. Joseph, [ ], 1736	ES	238
Richard, [s. Joseph & Clement], b. Feb. 2, 1736	ES	238
Richard, Priv., member of Capt. Samuel Peck's Co., Milford, 1776	1	54
Richard, his d. [ ], d. Sept. 22, 1790	SM	42
Richard, had child d. May 7, 1798	SM	63
Richard, his w. [ ], d. Aug. 30, 1799, ae. 66	SM	67
Richard, his w. [ ], d. [ ], 1819	BP	40
Richard, his w. [ ], d. [ ], 1830, ae. 55	BP	61
Richard, d. [ ], 1832	BP	66
Robert, Gov. of Conn., b. [ ], 1621, in England; d. July 12, 1710, in his 89th y. His 1st w. was d. Edmund TAPP; she d. Apr. 8, 1703; had by her 4 sons & 4 daughters, m. 2nd w. Elizabeth BRYAN, wid., Oct. 22, 1705	ES	105
Robert, b. [ ], 1621, in England; m. Jane TAPP, [ ]; m. 2nd w. Elizabeth BRYAN, Oct. 22, 1705; d. July 12, 1710, in his 89th y.	ES	238
Robert, Gov. member of Ch. in Wethersfield and his w. [ ], 1648	ES	238
Robert, adm. Church Apr. 19, 1649	OL	99
Robert, [s. Gov.[ ], [bp.] Feb. [16]54	ES	238
Robert, [s. Gov. Robert], b. July [ ], 1654	ES	238
Robert, s. Robert, b. Aug. 14, 1654	1	1
Robert, s. Robert, bp. [1654, by Rev. Peter Prudden]	OL	105
Robert, agent of the 2nd purchase, Oct. [ ], 1660	ES	1
Robert, Capt., 1662; Major 1670; Col. 1675; d. [ ], 1690	ES	40
Robert, adm. to 1st Ch. 1689; d. Mar. [ ], 1721	ES	238
Robert, s. Robert, bp. 1694	ES	238
Robert, Sr., m. Mrs. Elizabeth BRYAN, Oct. 24, 1705, by Rev. Samuel Andrew	1	26
Robert, Sr., m. Mrs. ElizabethBRYAN, Oct. 24, 1705, by Rev. Samuel Andrews	OL	54
Robert, Rev., s. Hon. Joseph & grandson of Gov. Robert, b. [ ], 1708	ES	121
Robert, [d.], 1710	ES	18
Robert, Jr., adm. to Ch. 1719	ES	238
Robert, s. Robert, [ ], 1730	ES	238
Robert, adm. to Ch. 1731	ES	238
Robert, infant, d. July 28, 1777	SM	13
Robert*, his d. [ ], d. July 21, 1794 *(Jr.)	SM	51
Robert, his w. [ ], d. Aug. 30, 1799, ae. 66	BP	2
Robert, had negro woman, d. [ ], 1806	BP	13
Robert, d. [ ], 1807, ae. 76	BP	16
Robert, 3rd s. [Robert], b. [ ]	ES	105
S. A., Major d. [ ], 1819, New York	BP	39
Samuel, [s. Gov. Robert], b. Aug. [ ], 1648	ES	238
Samuel, Rev. eldest s. Gov. [Robert], b. Sept. 1, 1648; m. Elizabeth MAYO, [ ]; had 11 children; m. 2nd w. Abigail WILLARD, d. Rev. Samuel; had 2 children; d. Mar. 18, 1717, at East Haven	ES	105

	Vol.	Page
TREAT, (cont.)		
Samuel, [s. Gov. [ ], [bp] Sept. [16]48	ES	238
Samuel, s. Robert, bp. [1648, by Rev. Peter Prudden]; "Member of the Church at Wethersfield, Conn.; was a minister of the Gospel; settled at Eastham, Mass.; his descendents are now there and in Maine"	OL	103
Sam[ue]ll, s. Robert, b. [ ], 1696	ES	238
Samuel, s. Robert, bp. 1697	ES	238
Sam[ue]ll & w. Anna, adm. to Ch. 1729	ES	238
Sam[ue]ll, [s. Sam[ue]ll], bp. 1729	ES	238
Sam[ue]ll, Jr., m. Beela JENNING, of Fairfield, Oct. 26, 1742	ES	238
Samuel, Jr., of Milford, m. Bula JENNINGS, of Fairfield, Oct. 26, 1743, by Sam[ue]ll Whittlesey, Jr.	1	122
Samuel, s. Samuel, m. Frances BRYAN, d. Richard & Sarah, June 27, 1751, by Rev. Samuel Whittlesey	1	127
Samuel, s. Samuel, m. Frances BRYAN, d. Richard & Sarah, June 27, 1751	ES	238
Sam[ue]ll, Jr. & w. Frances [adm. to Ch.] 1752	ES	238
Sam[ue]ll, chosen Dea. Aug. 31, 1786	ES	238
Samuel, d. July 17, 1787, ae. 59	SM	34
Samuel, his 1st w. [ ], d. June 25, 1793, ae. 32	SM	49
Sarah, [d. Gov. Robert], b. Oct. [ ], 1655	ES	238
Sarah, d. Robert, b. Oct. 9, 1656	1	3
Sarah, d. Robert, b. Oct. 10, 1656	OL	9
Sarah, 2nd, [d. Gov. Robert], b. 1656; d. Mar. [ ], 1721	ES	238
Sarah, Mrs., m. Richard BRYAN, Mar. 15, 1721/2, by Rev. Sam[ue]ll Andrews	1	100
Sarah, d. Lieut. Joseph, b. July 20, 1745	1	115
Sarah, d. Capt. Joseph & Clement, b. July 20, 1745	1	130
Sarah, [d. Joseph], b. July 20, 1745	ES	238
Sarah, [d. Joseph & Clement], [ ], 1745	ES	238
Stephen, s. Lieut. Jos[eph], b. June 22, 1741	1	113
Stephen, s. Capt. Joseph & Clement, b. June 22, 1741	1	130
Stephen, [s. Joseph & Clement], b. [ ], 1741	ES	238
Stephen, his 1st w. [ ], d. June 18, 1782, ae. 30	SM	23
Stephen, of Milford, m. Sarah LAMBERT, [d. Jesse & Anne], Dec. 25, 1785	1	50
Stephen, d. [ ], 1807	BP	16
Stephen, his wid. [ ], d. [ ], 1825	BP	53
Stephen A., d. [ ], 1838, ae. 25	BP	80
Susan, d. of Jonah, of Orange, m. as 2d w. Benjamin Lott LAMBERT, June 23, 1848	1	53
Susannah, d. Nov. 19, 1777, ae. 7	SM	14
Sibel*, d. May 26, 1782, ae. 8 *(Sybil)	SM	23
Thomas, s. Ens. Joseph, bp. [ ], 1700	ES	238
-----, Dea. his negro Rachel, d. July 27, 1788	SM	37
-----, wid., d. [ ], 1822, ae. 77	BP	47
TROWBRIDGE, Joseph, of Norwalk, d. Jan. [ ], 1777	SM	10
*TULLER entered under FULLER *(Hand printed in original manuscript)		
TUCK, W[illia]m, came to Milford, [ ]	ES	179
TURNER, Constant, of Middletown, d. Jan. [ ], 1777	SM	9

	Vol.	Page
TURNER, (cont.)		
Edward, came to Milford, [ ]	ES	179
Good, came to Milford, 1658	ES	179
H., Capt. his twin child d. [ ], 1802	BP	5
H., Capt. his infant child d. [ ], 1802	BP	5
H., Capt. his child d. [ ], 1815	BP	28
Henry, his twin daughters [ ], d. July 22, 1802	SM	75
Henry, Capt. his child d. [ ], 1807	BP	16
Henry, Capt. his child d. [ ], 1815	BP	29
Mary, d. Edward, b. Mar. 13, 1662	1	5
Mercy, d. Edward, b. Mar. 13, 1662	OL	14
Thomas, Priv., member of Capt. Samuel Peck's Co., Milford, 1776; killed or taken	1	54
TUTTLE, TUTTLES, TUTHILL, Andrew, m. Ann **WOODRUFF**, Aug. 7, 1729, by Sam[ue]ll Eells, Asst.	1	99
Andrew, d. Mar. 9, 1783, ae. 90	SM	25
Andrew, d. Oct. 23, 1794	SM	52
Ann, d. Andrew & Ann, b. July 2, 1730	1	99
Bethuel, d. [ ], 1778	SM	16
Daniel, d. June 12, 1787, ae. 22	SM	33
Eunice, wid., d. Apr. 6, 1795	SM	54
Gardner, Jr., his 1st w. [ ], d. Sept. 7, 1776, ae. 41	SM	7
Hannah, d. Andrew & Ann, b. Nov. 18, 1733	1	99
John, d. May 14, 1796	SM	58
Samuel, of Norwich, d. Jan. [ ], 1777	SM	10
-----, wid., d. Feb. 27, 1787	SM	33
-----, d. [ ], 1811	BP	22
TYLER, [see also **TYLEY**], Jon[a]th[an], his infant child d. [ ], 1807	BP	15
W[illia]m, came to Milford, 1646	ES	179
TYLEY, [see also **TYLER**], Katharince, d. Samuel, b. Apr. 15, 1710	1	32
Katharine, d. Samuel & Eliphall(?), b. Apr. 15, 1710	OL	69
UFFOOT, UFFET, UFFIT, UFFITT, UFFOT, UFFORT, UFFUT, UFIT, Elizabeth, d. John, b. Feb. 19, 1672	OL	25
Elizabeth, d. John, b. Feb. 19, 1672/3	1	12
Ephraim, d. Sept. 4, 1774	1	165
Isabel, w. Thomas, adm. Church Jan.[ ], 1645	OL	98
John, s. John, b. Feb. 3, 1665	1	7
John, s. John, b. Feb. 3, 1665	OL	18
John, s. John, b. Jan. 21, 1666	1	7
John, s. John, b. Jan. 21, 1666	OL	18
John, s. John, decd., b. Aug. 6, 1713	1	34
John, s. John, decd., b. Aug. 6, 1713	OL	74
John, s. Thomas, of Milford, m. Hannah **NETTLETON**, d. Samuel, of Branford, [ ], by Mr. Ffenne, Magestrate	OL	10
Liddiah, m. Thomas **CAMP**, Jr., Feb. 1, 1704/5, by Thomas Clark, J.P.	1	25
Liddiah, m. Samuel **CAMP**, Jr., Feb. 1, 1704/5, by Thomas Clark, J.P.	OL	52
Martha, d. John, b. Aug. 12, 1659	1	7
Martha, d. John, b. Aug. 12, 1659	OL	18
Mary, d. John, b. June 20, 1661	1	7

	Vol.	Page
UFFOOT, UFFET, UFFIT, UFFITT, UFFOT, UFFORT, UFFUT, UFIT, (cont.)		
Mary, d. John, b. June 20, 1661	OL	18
Samuel, s. John, b. June 21, 1670	1	10
Samuell, s. John, b. June 21, 1670	OL	22
Thomas, adm. Church Feb. 11, [1645]	OL	98
Thomas, s. John, b. Aug. 20, 1657	1	3
Thomas, s. John, b. Aug. 20, 1657	OL	10
Thom[as], s. Thomas, m. Hannah **NETTLETON**, d. Samuel, of Branford, [ ], by Mr. Fenn, J.P.	1	3
ULMSTEAD, UMSTEAD, [see under **OLMSTEAD**]		
UNDERWOOD, John, (Welch), drafted for Continental Army	1	58
UPHAM, Ebenezer, of killingly, d. Jan. [ ], 1777	SM	10
VALLOW, Mary, Mrs., m. William **RULLAN**, Sept. 23, 1714, by Rev. Samuel Andrews	1	64
VAN AUTEN, Esther, d. [ ], 1811, ae. 52	BP	21
VAN DUSER, VANDUZER, John, d. Feb. [ ], 1795, at Carolina (non resident)	SM	57
-----, Mr. d. [ ], 1811, at Loudon	BP	22
VIGISON, John, drafted for Continental Army	1	57
WADSWORTH, -----, Gen. see under Capt. Samuel **PECK**	1	179
WAGGENER, Freelove, Mrs. her d. [ ], d. Aug. 1, 1781	SM	22
WALES, John, Rev., s. Rev. John, b. [ ], at Roynham, Mass., d. Feb. 18, 1794; he left a wid., 3 sons, daughter	ES	121
Samuel, succeeded to ministry of First Church Dec. 19, 1770; dismissed May 15, 1782 to become Prof. of Divinity at Yale; d. Feb. 18, 1794	ES	57
Samuel, Rev. of New Haven, d. [ ], 1794	SM	53
WALKER, Joseph, m. Abigail **PRUDEN**, d. Peter, decd., Nov. 14, 1667, by Mr. Ffenn, Magistrate	1	9
Robert, s. Joseph, b. Aug. 5, 1668	1	9
WALLACE, WALLIS, Charles, not drafted for Continental Army	1	57
Nathan Little, d. Oct. 10, 1785, ae. 34	SM	30
Nathaniel, of Litchfield, d. Oct. 18, 1785	SM	30
WALTERS, WALTER, [see also **WATERS**], Joseph, m. Abigail **PRUDEN**, d. Peter, decd., Nov. 14, 1667, by Mr. Ffenn, Magestrate	OL	21
Joseph, m. Abigail **PRUDDEN**, d. Rev. Peter & Johannah, [ ], 1667	ES	104
Joseph, m. Abigail **PRUDDEN**, d. Peter, [ ], 1667	ES	182
	OL	21
Robert, s. Joseph [& Abigail], b. Aug. 5*, 1668 *(Aug 1 (?)	BP	15
WARD, Archibald, negro, d. [ ], 1807	BP	10
Betty, wid., d. [ ], 1805 (negro)	1	17
Hannah, m. Jonathan **BALDWIN**, Nov. 2, 1677, by John Ward	OL	34
Hannah, m. Jonathan **BALDWIN**, Nov. 2, 1677, by Jno Ward	SM	69
Hannah, d. May 14, 1800	SM	74
John, d. Apr. 17, 1802, ae. 23	BP	5
John, negro, d. [ ], 1802	SM	26
Peter, d. [ ], 1783; drowned at Sea	SM	41
Peter, his d. [ ], d. Apr. 8, 1790	SM	48
Peter, d. July 20, 1792	OL	28
Susanna, Mrs., m. Benjamin **FFENN**, Sr., Mar. 12, 1663		

	Vol.	Page
WARD, (cont.)		
Susanna, m. Benj[ami]n **FENN**, Mar. 12, 1663	ES	180
Tho[mas], came to Milford, 1657	ES	179
Titus, his child d. [ ], 1824	BP	50
-----, Capt. of West Haven, d. [ ], 1839	BP	82
-----, colored girl d. [ ], 1889, ae. 22	BP	81
WARNER, A., came to Milford, [ ]	ES	179
Abigaill, d. Andrew, b. Nov. 20, 1660	OL	13
Abigail, d. Andrew, b. Dec. 7, 1660	1	4
Andrew, of Hartford, m. Rebecca **FFLETCHER**, d. of John, of Milford, Oct. 10, 1653, by William Fowler, J.P.	1	1
Andrew, of Stratford*, m. Rebeckah **FFLETCHER**, d. John, of Milford, Dec. 10, 1653, by Mr. Ffowler, Magestrate *(Overwritten to read "Hartford?")	OL	7
Frances, Mrs., d. Sept. 3, 1792 (Absentee)	SM	48
Rebecka, w. Andrew & d. Mr. **FLETCHER**, adm. Church Sept. 17, [1653], by Mr. Prudden	OL	99
-----, Mrs. her infant child d. [ ], 1812	BP	24
WATERMAN, -----, Mr., d. [, 1813]	BP	33
WATERS, [see also **WALTERS**], Joseph, adm. Church June 27, [1653]	OL	99
Joseph(?), came to Milford, 1658	ES	179
Mehitabeel, of Stratford, m. John **HINE**, Jr., of Milford, Dec.31, 1725, by Sam[ue]ll Clark, J.P.	1	101
WATKINS, Joanna, wid. of Joseph, of Stratford & d. of Samuel **BUCKINGHAM**, [m.] Jesse **LAMBERT**, [ ]	1	49
WAY, Elisha, negro d. [ ], 1803, at Sea with Capt. Turner	BP	8
Elisha, d. Dec. [ ], 1803 (drowned at Sea, Capt. Turner)	SM	78
WEBSTER, Amillar, w. Thomas, d. [ ], 1831	BP	64
WELCH, **WELSH**, Elizabeth, wid., m. Eleazer **BEECHER**, Nov. 30, 1704, by Robert Treat, Dept. Gov.	1	26
Elizabeth, wid., m. Eleazer **BEECHER**, Nov. 30, 1704, by Robert Treat, Dept. Gov.	OL	55
Elizabeth, m. William **GILLETT**, Nov. 14, 1722, by Sam[ue]ll Clark, J.P.	1	74
Elizabeth, d. Thomas & Sarah, b. Apr. 31 [sic], 1733	1	110
Fitch, s. Thomas & Sarah, b. Sept. 1, 1735	1	110
Fitch, d. Oct. 12, 1787	SM	34
Hannah, d. Thomas, bp. [1652, by Rev. Peter Prudden]	OL	104
Hannah, d. Thomas, b. Oct. 21, 1729	1	110
John, his s. [ ], d. May 12, 1801	SM	72
John, his child d. [ ], 1801	BP	3
Lidiah, d. Thomas, b. Nov. 10, 1669	1	9
Liddiah, d. Thomas, b. Nov. 10, 1669	OL	22
Lidiah, d. Thomas, b. Nov. 27, 1669	OL	21
Mary, d. Thomas, b. Aug. 14, 1655	1	2
Mary, d. Thomas, b. Aug. 14, 1655	OL	9
Mary, d. Thomas, bp. [1655, by Rev. Peter Prudden]	OL	105
Mary, m. Israel **HOLBROOK**, Nov. 20, 1677, by Major Treat	1	18
Mary, m. Israel **HOLBROOK**, Dec. 20, 1677, by Major Treat	OL	35
Mary, d. Thomas & Sarah, b. Oct. 19, 1740	1	110
Mary, wid., d. June 23, 1790, ae. 62	SM	42

	Vol.	Page
WELCH, WELSH, (cont.)		
Sarah, d. Thomas, b. Dec. 7, 1660	1	4
Sarah, d. Thomas, b. Dec. 7, 1660	OL	13
Sarah, d. Thomas & [Sarah], b. Apr. 21, 1724	1	76
Sarah, w. Thomas, d. Oct. 26, 1740	1	110
Thomas, original member of First Church gathered at New Haven Aug. 22, 1639	ES	57
Thomas, s. Thomas, b. Jan. 28, 1657	1	3
Thomas, s. Thom[as], b. Jan. 28, 1657	OL	11
Thomas, d. Aug. 12, 1681	ES	16
Thomas, d. Aug. 12, 1681 (One of the first planters)	ES	16
Thomas, d. Aug. 12, 1681	OL	97
Thomas, m. Sarah **WHITMAN**, May 9, 1723, by Sam[ue]ll Clark, J.P.	1	76
Thomas, s. Thomas & Sarah, b. May 30, 1727	1	81
Thomas, member of 2nd Church formed in 1742	ES	87
Thomas, d. Oct. 9, 1782	SM	24
Thomas, his 1st w. [ ], d. May 21, 1790, ae. 42	SM	42
Thomas, his child d. May [ ], 1790	SM	42
Whitman, s. Thomas & Sarah, b. Jan. 5, 1738	1	110
Whitman, s. Tho[mas] & Sarah, [ ], 1738	ES	238
Whitman, Rev., (Heard of his death June 9, 1776; he was formerly of this place)	SM	6
-----, Mr. lived to above 90 y.	ES	17
WEST, Sal, Town Poor, d. [ ], 1823	BP	48
WETTERMORE, [see also **WHITMORE**], Dorothy, m. Samuel **CAMP**, s. Edward, July 17, 1712, by Samuel Eells, Asst.	1	33
Dorothy, m. Samuel **CAMP**, s. Edward, July 17, 1712, by Sam[ue]ll Eells, Asst.	OL	71
WHEELER, Abigail, d. Ephraim, b. Feb. 8, 1683	1	19
Abigail, d. Ephraim, b. Feb. 8, 1683	OL	41
Abigaill, of Durham, m. Joseph **MERCHANT**, of Milford, Oct. 27, 1714, by Joseph Treat, J.P.	1	109
Anna, d. Joseph, b. Feb. 20, 1680	OL	37
Ebenezer, m. Mary **HOLBROOK**, d. Richard, Sept. 8, 1675, by Alexander Bryan, Asst.	1	14
Eleazer, s. Thomas, bp. [1648, by Rev. Peter Prudden]; d. [ ]	OL	103
Eleazer, bd. Aug. 10, 1649	ES	238
Eleazer, d. [ ], 1649, ae. 15 m.	ES	35
Elizabeth, d. William, b. Jan. 12, 1696	1	22
Elizabeth, d. William, b. Jan. 12, 1696	OL	45
Elizabeth, d. Thomas, Jr., b. June 9, 1705	1	26
Elizabeth, d. Thomas, Jr., b. June 9, 1705	OL	53
Ephraim, s. Thomas, bp. [1646, by Rev. Peter Prudden]	OL	102
Ephraim, m. Mary **HOLBROOK**, d. Richard, Sept. 8, 1675, by Alexander Bryan, Asst.	OL	29
Ephraim, had s. [ ], b. June 25, 1680	OL	36
Ephraim, s. Ephraim, b. Jan. 5, 1681	OL	37
George, his s. [ ], d. June [ ], 1779	SM	17
Jane, w. Thomas, adm. Church Sept. 27, [1640]; bd. June 11, 1673	OL	97
John, s. Thomas, bp. [1640], by Rev. Peter Prudden	OL	100
John, of Woodbury, m. Mrs. Ruth **PLUM**, of Milford, July 3,		

MILFORD VITAL RECORDS 195

	Vol.	Page
WHEELER, (cont.)		
1706, by Samuel Eells, J.P.	1	27
John, of Woodbury, m. Mrs. Ruth PLUM, of Milford, July 3, 1706, by Sam[ue]ll Eells, J.P.	OL	57
Joseph, s. Thomas, b. Nov. 23, 1655	1	2
Joseph, s. Thomas, b. Nov. 20, 1655; d. [ ]	OL	9
Joseph, s. Thomas, bp. [1655, by Rev. Peter Prudden]	OL	105
Joseph, s. Thomas, b. Mar. 13, 1656/7	1	3
Joseph, s. Thomas, b. Mar. 13, 1656/7	OL	10
Joseph, m. Patience HOLBROOK, June [ ], 1678, by Major Treat	1	17
Joseph, m. Patience HOLBROOK, June [ ], 1678, by Major Treat	OL	35
Joseph, s. Joseph, b. Dec. 1, 1683	1	19
Joseph, s. Joseph, b. Dec. 1, 1683	OL	40
Joseph, Jr., m. Sarah CRANE, Mar. 27, 1707, by Samuel Andrews	1	28
Joseph, Jr., m. Sarah CRANE, Mar. 27, 1707, by Sam[ue]ll Andrews	OL	60
Josiah, s. Thomas, bp. [1653, by Rev. Peter Prudden]	OL	104
Mary, d. Ephraim, b. Feb. [ ], 1677	1	15
Mary, d. Ephraim, b. Feb. [ ], 1677	OL	30
Mehitable, d. Mrs. [ ], of Boston, [ ], 1701	ES	238
Nathaniel, s. Thomas, bp. [1641, by Rev. Peter Prudden]	OL	100
Nathaniel, m. Hestter BETHSFORD*, d. Henry, June 27, 1665, by Benjamin Ffenn, Magistrate *(Probably "BOCHFORD")	1	6
Nathaniell, m. Easther BOTCHFORD, d. Henry, b. of Milford, June 27, 1665, by Benjamin Ffenn, Magestrate	OL	17
Nathaniell, m. Easther BOTCHFORD, d. Henry, b. of Milford, [ ] 27, [ ], by Benjamin Ffenn, Magestrate	OL	17
Obadiah, s. Thomas, bp. [1644, by Rev. Peter Prudden]	OL	101
Obadiah, s. Ephraim, b. June 15, 1676	1	15
Obadiah, s. Ephraim, b. June 15, 1676	OL	30
Patience, d. Joseph, b. June 7, 1679	1	17
Patience, d. Joseph, b. June 7, 1679	OL	35
Rhoda, d. William, b. Dec. 9, 1701	1	22
Rhoda, d. William, b. Dec. 9, 1701	OL	45
Ruth, w. William, d. Sept. 28, 1705	1	42
Ruth, w. William, d. Sept. 28, 1705	OL	88
Ruth, d. William, b. Jan. 14, 1682	1	18
Ruth, d. William, b. Jan. 14, 1682	OL	39
Samuel, s. [Thomas, bp. [1640], by Rev. Peter Prudden	OL	100
Samuel, s. William, d. Oct. 22, 1705	1	42
Samuel, s. William, d. Oct. 22, 1705	OL	88
Sarah, m. James BRISCOE, Nov. 6, 1676, by Capt. Tapping	1	15
Sarah, m. James BRISCOE, Dec. 6, 1676, by Capt. Tapping	OL	30
Thomas, adm. Church Aug. 9, [1640]; d. Nov. 25, 1672	OL	97
Thomas, s. Thomas, bp. [1650, by Rev. Peter Prudden]	OL	103
Thomas, d. Nov. 26, 1672 (One of the first planters)	ES	16
Thomas, d. Nov. 26, 1672	ES	16
Thomas, of Milford, m. Anna FRENCH, d. Francis, of Derby, June 1, 1685	1	21

	Vol.	Page
WHEELER, (cont.)		
Thomas, of Milford, m. Anna **FRENCH**, d. Francis, of Derby, June 1, 1685, at the house	OL	42
William, m. Ruth **SMITH**, Apr. 10, 1682, by Richard Lawe, of Stamford	1	18
William, m. Ruth **SMITH**, Apr. 10, 1682, by Richard Law, of Stamford	OL	39
William, d. Nov. 12, 1705	1	42
William, d. Nov. 12, 1705	OL	88
WHITE, George, Esq., m. Louis **LAMBERT**, [d. David & Louis], [ ]	1	52
John, Corp., member of Capt. Samuel Peck's Co., Milford, 1776	1	54
John, of New London, d. Jan. [ ], 1777	SM	11
Timothy, ens., member of Capt. Samuel Peck's Co., Milford, 1776	1	54
WHITING, Elisha, d. [ ], 1778	SM	16
Elisha Gregory, d. May 21, 1797, ae. 18	SM	61
Esther, d. Oct. 20, 1795	SM	56
John, chosen Dea. Sept. 26, 1802	ES	238
Joseph, Capt. his d. [ ], d. Oct. 23, 1795	SM	56
Jos[eph], Capt., d. [ ], 1820	BP	43
Martha, Mrs., d. John **WHITING**, of Hartford, m. Samuel **BRYAN**, Dec. 25, 1683, by Maj. John Talcott, Asst.	1	19
Martha, Mrs., d. John **WHITING**, of Stratford*, m. Samuel **BRYAN**, of Milford, Dec. 25, 1683, by Major John Talcott, Asst. *(Overwritten to read "Hartford")	OL	40
Nancy, d. [ ], 1832, ae. 68	BP	66
Samuel, original member of 2nd Church formed in 1742	ES	87
Samuel, of Stratford, d. Jan. [ ], 1777	SM	9
WHITMAN, WHITTMAN, Damaris, w. Zachariah, adm. to Ch. 1711	ES	238
Elizabeth, [d. Zachariah & Damaris], [ ], 1710	ES	238
Frances, [d. Zachariah & Damaris], [ ], 1720	ES	238
Sam[ue]ll, Minister at Farmington, 1713	ES	238
Sarah, w. Zachariah, adm. Church Dec. 27, [1640]; bd. Jan. 2, 1670	OL	98
Sarah, d. Zachariah, b. Nov. 16, 1705	1	26
Sarah, d. Zachariah [& Sarah], b. Nov. 16, 1705	OL	55
Sarah, w. Zachariah, d. Nov. 27, 1705	1	42
Sarah, w. Zachariah, d. Nov. 27, 1705	OL	88
Sarah, [d. Zachariah & Damaris], [ ], 1709	ES	238
Sarah, m. Thomas **WELCH**, May 9, 1723, by Sam[ue]ll Clark, J.P.	1	76
Zach[aria]h, agent of the 1st purchase	ES	1
Zachariah, original member of First Church gathered at New Haven Aug. 22, 1639	ES	57
Zach[ariah], ordained Elder, June [ ], 1648	ES	180
Zachariah, d. Apr. 25, 1666 (One of the first planters)	ES	16
Zachariah, d. Apr. 25, 1666	OL	97
Zachariah, m. Mrs. Sarah **FITCH**, Jan. 6, 1702/3, by Robert Treat, Dept. Gov.	1	26
Zachariah, m. Mrs. Sarah **FITCH**, Jan. 6, 1702/3, by Robert Treat, Dept. Gov.	OL	55
Zachariah, s. Zachariah [& Sarah], b. Oct. 23, 1704; d. Nov. 1,		

	Vol.	Page
WHITMAN, WHITTMAN, (cont.)		
1704	OL	55
Zachariah, s. Zachariah, b. Oct. 23, 1704/5; d. Nov. 1, 1704	1	26
Zachariah, m. Demaris CARR, Mar. 18, 1705, by Major Johnson	1	27
Zachariah, m. Damaris CARR, Mar. 18, 1705/6, by Major Johnson	OL	56
Zachariah, adm. to Ch. 1711	ES	238
Zach[ariah], Rev. of Hull, d. Sept. 5, 1726, ae. 82	ES	238
-----, Mr. his other child d. [ ], 1813	BP	32
-----, Mr. his child d. [ ], 1813	BP	32
-----, Mr., d. [ ], 1820, ae. 90	BP	41
WHITMORE, WHITEMORE, WHITTEMORE, [see also WETTEMORE], Amey, d. Josiah, b. Feb. 17, 1703/4	1	23
Amey, d. Joseph, b. Feb. 17, 1703/4	OL	48
Eunice, d. Solomon & Eunice, b. July 17, 1751	1	131
Mary, m. Silvanus NETTLETON, Apr. 24, 1729, by Sam[ue]ll Eells, Asst.	1	93
Solomon, m. Eunice FOWLER, June 14, 1749, by Jno Fowler, J.P.	1	131
WHITTLESEY, WHETTLESEY, Roger N., [s. Samuel & Susannah], b. Feb. 24, 1754	ES	238
Roger Newton, [s. Samuel & Susannah], b. Feb. 6, 1754	ES	238
Roger Newton, s. Sam[ue]ll & Susannah, b. Feb. 24, 1754	1	151
Roger Newton, s. Rev. Sam[ue]ll, b. Feb. 24, 1754	1	153
Roger Newton, [s. Rev. Samuel & Susannah], b. Feb. 24, 1754	ES	238
Roger Newton, [s. Rev. Samuel & Susannah,]	ES	121
Samuel, Rev. s. Rev. Samuel, b. 1714; m. Susannah NEWTON, d. (eldest) of Col. Roger, Sept. 21, 1743; d. Oct. [ ], 1768; had children, Samuel, Susannah, Roger Newton, Sarah	ES	121
Sam[ue]ll, m. Mrs. Susannah NEWTON, Sept. 21, 1743, by Roger Newton, Asst.	1	151
Sam[ue]ll, Rev., m. Mrs. Susanna NEWTON, Sept. 21, 1743, by Roger Newton	1	153
Samuel, m. Susannah NEWTON, Sept. 21, 1743	ES	238
Samuel, Rev. s. Rev. Samuel, of Wallingford, b. [ ]; m. Susannah NEWTON, d. Col. Roger, Sept. 21, 1743; d. Oct. 22, 1768, ae. 56 y.	ES	238
Sam[ue]ll, s. Sam[ue]ll & Susannah, b. Aug. 3, 1745	1	151
Sam[ue]ll, s. Rev. Sam[ue]ll [& Susanna], b. Aug. 3, 1745	1	153
Sam[ue]l, Jr. [s. Samuel & Susannah], b. Aug. 3, 1745	ES	238
Sam[ue]l, Jr., Rev., s. Rev. Samuel, b. Aug. 3, 1745; m. [ ] HUBBARD, d. Rev. Mr. [ ], [ ]; d. Feb. 9, 1776, ae. 31	ES	121
Samuel, Jr., [s. Rev. Samuel & Susannah], b. Oct. 3, 1745	ES	238
Samuel, succeeded to ministry of First Church Nov. 9, 1737*; d. Oct. 22, 1768 *(Arnold Copy has "1637")	ES	57
Samuel, Jr., physician and Town Clerk, b. Aug. 3, 1745; m. [ ] HUBBARD, d. Dr. [ ], of New Haven; d. Feb. 9, 1776, ae. 31 y.	ES	238
Samuel, Dr., d. Feb. 9, 1776	1	165
Sam[ue]l, Town Clerk, d. Feb. 9, 1776	ES	238
Samuel, Dr., d. Feb. 9, 1776, ae. 30	SM	5

	Vol.	Page
WHITTLESEY, WHETTLESEY, (cont.)		
Samuel, [s. Rev. Samuel & Susannah], [ ]	ES	121
Sarah, d. Rev. Sam[ue]ll [& Susanna], b. Oct. 31, 1749	1	153
Sarah, [d. Rev. Samuel & Susannah], b. Oct. 31, 1749	ES	238
Sarah, [d. Samuel & Susannah], b. Oct. 31, 1749	ES	238
Sarah, [d. Rev. Samuel & Susannah,]	ES	121
Susanna, d. Rev. Sam[ue]ll [& Susanna], b. Jan. 26, 1747	1	153
Susannah, [d. Samuel & Susannah], b. Jan. 26, 1747	ES	238
Susannah, [d. Rev. Samuel & Susannah], b. July* 26, 1747; m. Dr. Edward **CARRINGTON**, [ ] *(Probably "Jan.")	ES	238
Susannah, d. Sam[ue]ll [& Susannah], b. Oct. 31, 1747* *(Pencil note says "Jan. 26, 1747")	1	151
Susannah, [d. Samuel & Susannah], b. Oct. 31, 1747	ES	238
Susannah, [d. Rev. Samuel & Susannah,]	ES	121
-----, wid. of Rev. Sam[ue]l, Jr., m. Rev. Mr. **LEWIS**, [ ]	ES	121
-----, wid. of Samuel, Jr., physician and town clerk, m. 2nd h. Rev. Mr. **LEWIS**, of Rocky Hill, [ ]	ES	238
WICKES, Peter, d. [ ], 1778	SM	16
WILCOX, Mark, his infant child d. [ ], 1829	BP	59
Mark, his w. [ ], d. [ ], 1840	BP	84
Mark, m. as 1st h. Mary Emeline **LAMBERT**, [d. John & Esther], Apr. 15, 1849	1	52
WILDMAN, -----, Mr., d. [, 1813]	BP	33
WILKINSON, Abigail, m. David **BALDWIN**, Feb. 20, 1707/8, by Capt. Samuel Eells, J.P.	1	29
Abigail, m. David **BALDWIN**, Feb. 12, 1707/8, by Capt. Eells, J.P.	OL	63
Edw[ard], came to Milford, 1645	ES	179
Edward, in 1671, destroyed the Indian Fort	ES	14
Edward, m. Rebecca **SMITH**, July 2, 1672	1	13
Edward, m. Rebeckah **SMITH**, July 2, 1672 *(Written "Edward **WILLESON**")	OL	26
Edward, s. Edward, b. Mar. 5, 1678/9	1	16
Edward, s. Edward, b. Mar. 5, 1678/9	OL	33
Elizabeth, d. Edward, b. May 30, 1674	1	13
Elizabeth, d. Edward, b. May 30, 1674	OL	27
Hannah, d. Edward, b. Nov. 1, 1684	1	19
Hannah, d. Edward, b. Nov. 1, 1684	OL	41
John, m. Hannah **LONGSTAFFE**, Jan. [ ], 1717/18, by Samuel Eells, Asst.	1	64
John, s. Lewis, b. Dec. 19, 1723	1	99
Lewis, s. Lewis & Sarah, b. Sept. 20, 1722	1	70
Lewis, m. wid. Sarah **HUBBARD**, d. of John Terrell, Dec. 4, 1722*, by Jon[a]th[an] Law, Asst. *(1721/2 ?)	1	70
Rebecca, d. Edward, b. Aug. 8, 1676	1	15
Rebecca, d. Edward, b. Aug. 8, 1676	OL	30
Ruth, d. Edward, b. Oct. 23, 1681	1	18
Ruth, d. Edward, b. Oct. 23, 1681	OL	38
Ruth, m. Daniel **COLLINS**, Dec. 7, 1699, by Robert Treat, Dept. Gov.	1	22
Ruth, m. Daniel **COL[L]INS**, Dec. 7, 1699, by Rob[er]t Treat,		

MILFORD VITAL RECORDS

	Vol.	Page
WILKINSON, (cont.)		
Dept. Gov.	OL	46
Sarah, d. Lewis, b. Nov. 13, 1726	1	99
-----, his w. [ ], d. [ ], 1839, ae. 27	BP	82
WILLARD, Abigail, d. Rev. Samuel, m. Rev. Samuel **TREAT**, s. Gov. Robert, [ ]; had 2 children	ES	105
WILLESON, [see under **WILKINSON**]		
WILLET, WILLETT, Joanna, returned to Milford from 1ˢᵗ Ch. in Rehobath, 1674	ES	238
-----, Capt. of Plymouth, m. Mrs. Johannah **PRUDDEN**, wid. of Peter, Sept. 19, 1671, by Benjamin Ffenne, Asst.	1	11
-----, Capt. of Plimouth, m. Mrs. Johannah **PRUDEN**, of Milford, Sept. 19, 1671, by Benjamin Ffenn, Asst.	OL	24
-----, Capt. of Plimouth, m. Johanna **PRUDDEN**, d. Rev. Peter & Johannah, Sept. 19, 1671	ES	104
-----, Capt. of Plymouth, m. Joanna **PRUDDEN**, Sept. [ ], 1671; (see Joanna **PRUDDEN**)	ES	182
-----, Capt. of Plimouth, m. Joanna **PRUDDEN**, w. Peter, Sept. 19, 1672	OL	97
WILMOT, WILMOTT, David, Priv., member of Capt. Samuel Peck's Co., Milford 1776	1	54
Mary, m. Richard **BRYAN**, July 15, 1679	1	18
Mary, m. Rich[ard] **BRYAN**, July 15, 1679	OL	35
Timothy, Priv., member of Capt. Samuel Peck's Co., Milford 1776	1	54
WILSON, Benjamin, s. Thomas, b. July 8, 1673	1	13
Benjamin, s. Thomas, b. July 8, 1673	OL	26
John, m. Mrs. Sarah **NEWTON**, July 4, 1683	1	19
John, m. Mrs. Sarah **NEWTON**, July 4, 1683	OL	39
John, m. Mrs. Sarah **NEWTON**, [ ], 1683	ES	185
-----, Capt. his child d. [ ], 1831, ae. 18 m.	BP	65
WILTON, Nathan, of Conn., d. Jan. [ ], 1777	SM	10
WISE, Duncan, b. [ ], in Scotland, d. Apr. 21, 1775	1	343
Mehitable, [d. Duncan & Mehitable], b. June 12, 1767	1	343
Mehitable, w. Duncan, d. July 2, 1774	1	343
Samuel, [s. Duncan & Mehitable], b. July 30, 1764	1	343
Samuel, d. [ ], 1827	BP	56
WOLCOTT, WOLCOT, WOOLCOT, WOOLCOTT, Elijah, a child d. Nov. 15, 1804	SM	81
John, his infant s. [ ], d. Feb. 15, 1790	SM	41
John, his s. [ ], d. Nov. 13, 1794, ae. 6 m.	SM	53
John, his d. [ ], d. Apr. 3, 1798; a twin (?)	SM	63
Samuel, his child d. [ ], 1814, ae. 5 y.	BP	26
-----, Mr. his child d. [ ], 1804, at W. Haven	BP	9
-----, Mr., d. [ ], 1826, ae. [ ]	BP	55
-----, Mr., d. [ ], 1827	BP	56
WOOD, WOODS, An[n]e, her d. [ ], d. Oct. 1, 1794 (now of Long Island, a resident of Milford nine months	SM	52
Eunice, d. Justus, d. Mar. 17, 1797, ae. [ ]	SM	61
George, his infant twins d. July 1, 1790	SM	42
Justus, his d. [ ], d. Oct. [ ], 1795, ae. 1 ½ y.	SM	56
Justus, his w. [ ], d. [ ], 1831	BP	65
Justus, d. [ ], 1840, ae. 87	BP	83

WOOD, WOODS, (cont.)

	Vol.	Page
Justus, drafted for Continental Army	1	57
Lewis, his child d. [ ], 1832	BP	66
Rebecca, her child d. Sept. 2, 1799	BP	2
Rebecka, her s. [ ], d. Sept. 2, 1799, ae. 2 w.	SM	67
Rebecka, Mrs., d. [ ], 1818	BP	38
Richard, d. [ ], 1790, at Sea	SM	43
Sidney, d. [ ], 1822, ae. 12	BP	46
Susannah, Mrs., m. Benjamin FFENNE, Sr., Mar. 12, 1663	1	14
-----, Mrs., d. [ ], 1836, at Poor House	BP	75

WOODBURY, Elizabeth, m. Joseph **PLATT**, Jan. 19, 1701/2, by Rob[er]t Treat, Dept. Gov. — OL 49

Elizabeth, m. Joseph **PLATT**, Jan. 19, 1711/12, by Robert Treat, Dept. Gov. — 1 23

WOODCOCK, Barnabus, m. Elizabeth **SEARS**, May 28, 1736, by Sam[ue]ll Gunn, J.P. — 1 106

	Vol.	Page
Barnabus, d. Nov. 15, 1804, in Peekskill	SM	81
Nehemiah, s. Barnabus, b. Aug. 25, 1737	1	106
-----, Capt., d. [ ], 1804	BP	10
-----, Mrs., d. [ ], 1808	BP	17

WOODHULL, Sam[ue]ll, tailor, of Bridgeport, m. Mary Ann **BULL**, d. Henry & Harriet, [ ]; settled in Utica, N.Y. — 1 174

WOODRUFF, WOODROOFFE, WOODRUFFE, WOODSRAFFE, WOODRUFE, WOODEROUFFE, Abel, his wid., d. [ ], 1818 — BP 38

	Vol.	Page
Ann, d. [John], bp. 1707	ES	238
Ann, [d. John], bp. 1709	ES	238
Ann, d. Lieut. John, b. Mar. 2, 1711; recorded Oct. 12, 1721	1	68
Ann, m. Andrew **TUTTLE**, Aug. 7, 1729, by Sam[ue]ll Eells, Asst.	1	99
Anna, d. John, b. Feb. 25, 1708/9	1	30
Anna, d. Jno, b. Feb. 25, 1708/9	OL	65
Benjamin, d. Nov. 18, 1781, ae. 21	SM	22
David, d. [ ], 1787 (non resident)	SM	35
Edward, s. John & Hannah, b. Feb. 28, 1761	1	167
Edwin, m. Anna T. **LAMBERT**, [d. Benjamin Lott & Anna], May 14, 1837; moved to Tallmadge, Ohio	1	53
Eli, his s. [ ], d. Nov. 8, 1800, ae. 6 m.	SM	70
Eli, his child d. [ ], 1807	BP	15
Eli, d. [ ], 1818	BP	38
Eli, his wid. [ ], d. [ ], 1835; bd. at N. Milford	BP	72
Enoch, Capt. his d. [ ], d. Jan. 1, 1779	SM	17
Enoch, Capt. his s. [ ], d. Dec. 6, 1781	SM	22
Enoch, Capt. his negro woman, d. Jan. 12, 1783	SM	25
Enoch, Capt., d. Mar. 6, 1786, ae. 44	SM	31
Enoch, Capt., 1785; d. May 6, 1786	ES	41
Esther, d. Matthew & Esther (**BULL**), of No. Milford, m. John **LAMBERT**, 5th s. David & Martha, Jan. 3, 1799	1	52
Esther, d. Matthew & Esther (**BULL**), m. John **LAMBERT**, s. David, [ ]	1	152
Hannah, [w. John], adm. to Ch. 1734	ES	238
Hannah, d. John & Hannah, b. Jan. 21, 1771	1	167

MILFORD VITAL RECORDS 201

	Vol.	Page
WOODRUFF, WOODROOFFE, WOODRUFFE, WOODSRAFFE, WOODRUFE, WOODEROUFFE, (cont.)		
Hannah, w. John, d. Feb. 22, 1813	1	49
Ichabod, d. [July], 1799	BP	2
Ichabod, his s. [ ], d. Aug. 28, 1799, ae. 8 m.	SM	67
Ichabod, his s. [ ], d. [ ], 1820, North Milford	BP	43
Isaac, formerly of Milford, d. Apr. [ ], 1782	SM	24
Jane, d. John & Hannah, b. Feb. 10, 1766	1	167
Job, drafted for Continental Army	1	57
Joel, his child d. [ ], 1801	BP	3
Joel, d. Feb. 16, 1801	SM	71
Joel, d. [ ], 1808, in New Milford, ae. 30	BP	17
John, m. Hannah **LAMBERT**, d. Jesse [& Mary], [ ]; moved to Watertown, Conn.	1	106
John, s. Matthew, b. Feb. 1, 1672/3	1	12
John, s. Matthew, b. Feb. 5, 1672	OL	25
John, m. Mary **PLATT**, Dec. 22, 1698, by Robert Treat, Gov.	1	20
John, m. Mary **PLATT**, Dec. 22, 1698, by Robert Treat, Gov.	OL	43
John, Capt., 1699 & 1726	ES	41
John, Capt. adm. To Ch. 1699; d. [ ], 1726	ES	238
John, s. John, b. May 26, 1703	1	20
John, s. John [& Mary], b. May 26, 1703	OL	43
John, s. John, bp. 1703	ES	238
John, adm. to Ch. 1734	ES	238
John, Capt., 1750	ES	41
John, m. Hannah **LAMBERT**, [d. Jesse & Mary], Mar. 13, 1757; settled in Watertown, Conn.	1	49
John, s. John & Hannah (**LAMBERT**), b. Sept. 29, 1757	1	167
Joseph, s. John, bp. 1704	ES	238
Joseph, s. John, b. Feb. 18, 1704/5	1	26
Joseph, s. John, b. Feb. 18, 1704/5	OL	54
Joseph, m. [ ] **NEWTON**, sister of Col. [ ], [ ], 1720	ES	238
Joseph, m. Phebe **NEWTON**, Jan. 22, 1728/9, by Roger Newton, J.P.	1	92
Joseph, s. Joseph, b. Apr. 18, 1733	1	100
Joseph, [ ], 1736	ES	238
Joseph, d. Aug. 13, 1777, ae. 44	SM	13
Jos[eph], his infant child d. [ ], 1813	BP	31
Joseph, d. [ ], 1822	BP	47
Joseph, his w. [ ], d. [ ], 1838	BP	79
Lambert, s. John & Hannah, b. June 28, 1763	1	167
Mary, d. Matthew, b. Dec. 27, 1670	1	10
Mary, d. Matthew, b. Dec. 27, 1670	OL	23
Mary, d. John [& Mary], b. Mar. 3, 1699	OL	43
Mary, d. John, b. Mar. 3, 1699/1700	1	20
Mary, m. Tho[mas] **BUCKINGHAM**, July 9, 1724	ES	238
Mary, d. Joseph, b. Mar. 14, 1740/1	1	113
Mary, d. [ ], 1835, ae. 65	BP	72
Mary B., m. Thomas **BUCKINGHAM**, Jan. 9, 1723/4, by Sam[ue]ll Eells, Asst.	1	73
Matthew, s. Matthew, b. Feb. 1, 1668	1	9

	Vol.	Page
WOODRUFF, WOODROOFFE, WOODRUFFE, WOODSRAFFE, WOODRUFE, WOODEROUFFE, (cont.)		
Matthew, s. Matthew, b. Feb. 8, 1668	OL	21
Matthew, m. Mary **PLUMB**, June 16, 1668, by Mr. Ffeenn	1	9
Matthew, m. Mary **PLUMB**, [ ], 1668, by Mr. Ffenn, Magestrate	OL	21
Matthew, his s. [ ], d. Nov. 14, 1793, ae. 4 y.	SM	50
Matthew, his s. [ ], d. Nov. 15, 1793, ae. 1 y.	SM	50
Matthew, his w. [ ], d. [ ], 1806	BP	13
Matthew, m. Esther **BULL**, d. Benjamin & Easther, [ ]	1	152
Nancy, d. John & Hannah, b. Feb. 18, 1769	1	167
Nehemiah, [s. Joseph & [ ] (**NEWTON**), b. J[ ] 15, 1735	ES	238
Nehemiah, s. Joseph, b. Jan. 15, 1735/6	1	113
Nehemiah, of N. Milford, his child d. [ ], 1809	BP	19
Phebe, d. Joseph & Phebe, b. Oct. 28, 1729	1	92
Phebe, wid., d. Dec. 21, 1790, ae. 84	SM	44
Samuel, s. John & Hannah, b. Apr. 10, 1759	1	167
Samuel, d. [ ], 1836, ae. 69	BP	74
Sarah, d. John, b. Dec. 20, 1711	1	20
Sarah, d. John [& Mary], b. Dec. 20, 1701	OL	43
Susanah, d. John, b. May 3, 1707	1	28
Susannah, d. John, b. May 3, 1707	OL	61
Susannah, m. Thomas **CLARK**, s. Capt. Sam[ue]l, Dec. 15, 1725, by Sam[ue]ll Eells, Asst.	1	81
Susanna, m. Tho[mas] **CLARK**, s. Capt. Sam[ue]l, [ ], 1725	ES	238
-----, wid. had negro Tony d. Jan. 12, 1776	SM	5
-----, wid., d. Feb. 21, 1779	SM	17
WOOSTER, WORSTER, WOSSTER, Edw[ard], came to Milford, 1651	ES	179
Henry, s. Edward, b. Aug. 18, 1666	1	11
Hennary, s. Edward, b. Aug. 18, 1666	OL	23
Mary, d. Edward, b. Nov. 2, 1654	1	2
Mary, d. Edward, b. Nov. 2, 1654	OL	8
Ruth, d. Edward, b. Apr. 8, 1668	1	11
Ruth, d. Edward, b. Apr. 8, 1668	OL	23
Timothy, s. Edward, b. Nov. 12, 1670	1	11
Timothy, s. Edward, of Pagaset, b. Nov. 12, 1670	OL	24
WRIGHT, Thomas, of Simsbury, d. Jan. [ ], 1777	SM	9
-----, Sergt., of Bolton, d. Jan. [ ], 1777	SM	9
YALE, Samuel, of Wrentham, d. Jan. [ ], 1777	SM	10
YORK, Pigg, colored, d. [ ], 1834, ae. 77	BP	72
ZADO, Congo, drafted for Continental Army	1	57
NO SURNAME, Abel, negro his child d. [ ], 1816	BP	34
Abel, negro had child d. [ ], 1822	BP	46
Abigail, m. Joseph **FENN**, Dec. 26, 1716, by Jonathan Law, J.P.	1	38
Abigail, m. Joseph **FFENN**, Dec. 26, 1716, by Jon[a]th[an] Law, J.P.	OL	83
Abram, d. [ ], 1823, ae. 89	BP	48
Alber, a German, ordained Elder, May 3, 1673; d. Jan. [ ] 1674	ES	238

	Vol.	Page
NO SURNAME, (cont.)		
Arnold, negro d. [ ], 1822	BP	46
Benjamin, negro his s. [ ], d. Aug. 11, 1797	SM	62
Betsey, m. Daniel **BULL**, s. Benjamin, [ ]; moved to Plymouth, Conn.	1	152
Cambridge, negro d. Nov. 6, 1777	SM	14
Cate, negro d. Aug. 29, 1791	SM	46
Cato, his child d. Jan. 20, 1795	SM	54
Cato, negro d. [ ], 1820	BP	41
Cato, colored man, d. [ ], 1829	BP	60
Cloe, negro, d. [ ], 1803	BP	7
Clary, negro her child d. [ ], 1815	BP	28
Congo, d. Dec. 10, 1798	SM	65
Cubitt, m. Em [ ], of West India, b. Indians, Nov. 11, 1709	OL	66
Cyrus, negro (Waiter), Priv., member of Capt. Samuel Peck's Co., Milford, 1776	1	54
Dan, [s.] of Congo, d. Apr. 17, 1787	SM	33
Edward, s. James, d. [ ], 1834, at New Haven (colored)	BP	71
Elijah, negro d. [ ], 1811, at Sea	BP	22
Elisha, colored his child d. [ ], 1830	BP	62
Em, of West India, m. Cubitt [ ], b. Indians, Nov. 11, 1709	OL	66
Francis, colored d. [ ], 1832	BP	66
Francisco, negro had child d. [ ], 1828	BP	57
Frederick, d. [ ], 1802	ES	165
Harden, d. [ ], 1823	BP	48
Harry, negro d. Feb. 22, 1799, ae. 60	BP	1
James, negro, d. [ ], 1806, ae. 22	BP	13
James, negro d. [ ], 1811	BP	22
Jeffries, negro his w. [ ], d. [ ], 1811	BP	22
Jeffs, had negro woman d. [ ], 1806	BP	14
Jennette, colored her child d. [ ], 1833	BP	68
Jinney, negro d. [ ], 1812	BP	23
Jenny, negro d. [ ], 1819, ae. 80	BP	40
Jenny, colored had s. [ ], d. [ ], 1828, ae. 15	BP	57
Jim, colored, d. [ ], 1829	BP	59
Joel, [ ]	1	83
John, negro, d. [ ], 1805, drowned at Sea	BP	12
John, d. [ ], 1810, at Sea	BP	21
John, [ ]	1	109
Joseph, Jr., his 2nd w. [ ], d. July 26, 1787, ae. 64	SM	34
Josiah, Rev. s. W[illia]m, of Stoughton, Mass., s. John, s. of Capt. John, who came from Dedham, Eng., to Watertown, 1634/5	ES	128
Jube, negro, drafted for Continental Army	1	57
Kittery, sailor d. [ ], 1819, abroad	BP	40
Louisa, Mrs., d. [ ], 1808, ae. 90	BP	17
Luck, negro, d. June 10, 1800	SM	69
Margaret, colored d. [ ], 1837, ae. 14 y.	BP	77
Margaret, colored, her child "sometime since" d. [ ], 1837	BP	77
Maria, colored d. Elisha, d. [ ], 1839, ae. 24	BP	81
Martha, m. Thomas **CLARK**, Nov. 22, 1703, by Thomas Hart, J.P.	1	23

NO SURNAME, (cont.)

	Vol.	Page
Martha, m. Thomas **CLARK**, Jr., Nov. 22, 1703, by Thomas Hart, J.P.	OL	48
Martha, negro girl, d. Mar. 14, 1784	SM	27
Martha, wid. of Simon, d. Apr. 1, 1797	SM	61
Martin, d. [ ], 1804	BP	9
Martin, see [ ] N.R.	SM	80
Mary, wid., d. Aug. 16, 1796	SM	59
Meriam, colored d. [ ], 1830, ae. 110 (supposed to be very aged)	BP	61
N.R., called Martin, d. May 10, 1804, ae. 44	SM	80
Nando, negro man, d. Feb. 16, 1795	SM	54
Nandros, negro had child d. [ ], 1808	BP	18
Nathan, [ ]	1	117
Nimrod, negro d. [ ], 1808	BP	17
Nodina, negro had child d. [ ], 1808	BP	17
Olive, negro d. [ ], 1822, ae. 50	BP	46
Peg, negro female, d. [ ], 1807, ae. 78	BP	16
Peter, negro, drafted for Continental Army	1	57
Peter, & Billy, negros had s. Peter, b. Oct. 3, 1761 & Billy, negro, had d. Billy, b. Oct. 21, 1764	1	154
Phillis, negro had child d. [ ], 1806	BP	14
Phillis, negro d. [ ], 1813	BP	32
Pitty, m. Charles **DEALE**, July 3, 1672, by John Clarke, Commissioner	1	12
Pomps, had negro girl d. Dec. 26, 1794	SM	53
Pomp, negro his child d. [ ], 1804	BP	10
Pomp, negro had child d. [ ], 1809	BP	19
Pomp, negro d. [ ], 1826	BP	55
Pomp, colored d. [ ], 1837	BP	78
Primus, negro d. [ ], 1804	BP	8
Primus, negro d. [ ], 1816, ae. 78	BP	34
Richard, negro had child d. [ ], 1828	BP	58
Richard, colored had child d. [ ], 1830, ae. 5 d.	BP	62
Roda, negro d. [ ], 1809, ae. 68	BP	19
Roe, found dead on shore, July 8, 1799	SM	67
Rose, child d. Apr. 23, 1783	SM	25
Sarah, [ ], 1730	ES	238
Sarah, d. J[ ] & Eunice, [bp.] 1737	ES	238
Sarah, negro, d. Nov. 21, 1799	SM	68
Seylla, negro woman, d. Oct. 5, 1781	SM	22
Simon, d. July 20, 1791	SM	46
Susan, colored, d. [ ], 1832, ae. 64	BP	67
Susan, colored, d. [ ], 1836	BP	75
Tambo, or Tamer had infant child d. [ ], 1819	BP	39
Tamer, see. [ ] Tambo	BP	39
Tine, negro at B[urwell] Farms, d. [ ], 1802	BP	5
Tobey, negro d. [ ], 1809	BP	18
Tony, negro, heard of death Aug. [ ], 1777	SM	13
Tryal, d. [ ], 1824 (black)	BP	51
Wando, negro had child d. [ ], 1815	BP	29
Wando, his child d. [ ], 1816	BP	35
Wanda, negro had child d. [ ], 1821	BP	44

		Vol.	Page

NO SURNAME, (cont.)

	Vol.	Page
Wando, negro d. [ ], 1824, ae. 70	BP	50
York, negro d. [ ], 1811, ae. 71	BP	21
-----, negro d. [ ], at New Haven	ES	165
-----, a Dutchman from Penn., d. Jan. [ ], 1777	SM	9
-----, a Dutchman, d. Jan. [ ], 1777	SM	9
-----, a Spainard, d. Jan. [ ], 1777	SM	10
-----, man found dead May 28, 1794, on shore	SM	53
-----, man found dead on shore of Burwell Farm, May 20, 1800	SM	69
-----, negro d. [ ], 1801	BP	3
-----, child d. [ ], 1801, at the Gulph	BP	4
-----, 2 negroes d. [1801]	BP	4
-----, Mrs., d. [ ], 1802	BP	5
-----, child of negro, d. [ ], 1806	BP	14
-----, Indian woman, of Bridgeport, d. [ ], 1807	BP	16
-----, negro child d. [ ], 1810, at N. Milford	BP	20
-----, negro child d. [ ], 1810, at N. Milford	BP	21
-----, negro d. [ ], 1811; lost at Sea, sailing from West Indies	BP	22
-----, negro d. [ ], 1813, at N. Milford	BP	25
-----, negro child d. [ ], 1813	BP	25
-----, Indian d. [ ], 1814, at N. Milford	BP	27
-----, Indian d. [ ], 1814, at N. Milford	BP	27
-----, negro child d. [ ], 1815, at N. Milford	BP	29
-----, negro at North Milford, d. [ ], 1815	BP	30
-----, stranger drowned in Harbor, [ ], 1816	BP	34
-----, Indian called the Indian Dr., d. [ ], 1817	BP	37
-----, child d. [ ], 1818, at North Milford	BP	38
-----, negro had child d. [ ], 1821	BP	44
-----, negro woman had infant child d. [ ], 1821	BP	44
-----, stranger drowned in storm, [ ], 1821	BP	44
-----, stranger d. [ ], 1822 "Washed up on shore"	BP	46
-----, negro woman, d. [ ], 1824	BP	50
-----, infant child d. [ ], 1824	BP	51
-----, infant d. [ ], 1824	BP	51
-----, colored child at Oyster River, d. [ ], 1829	BP	60
-----, young man from E. Florida, d. [ ], 1833	BP	69
-----, a squaw d. [ ], 1835	BP	73
-----, child d. [ ], 1836, at Poor House	BP	75
-----, person d. [ ], 1839, at West Haven, bd. in Milford	BP	82

NEW CANAAN VITAL RECORDS
1801 - 1854

Page

ABBOTT, Hannah E., m. Samuel M. **NEWEL**, of Mass., Nov. 30, 1843, by
David Ogden — 62
Hazar, m. Mary Ann **AYRES**, b. of New Canaan, Dec. 6, 1825, by Origen
P. Holcomb — 11
Henrietta, of New Canaan, m. James N. **COOLEY**, of Dutchess Co., N.Y.
July 4, 1847, by Rev. D. H. Short — 65
Mary Elizabeth, m. Edward **DEFOREST**, b. of New Canaan, [   ],
by Rev. J. Lyman Clark. Recorded Apr. 7, 1836 — 28
AICCOX, Pennina, of Canaan, m. Ezra **HOIT**, of Wilton, Apr. 21, 1798 — 3
AKIN, William E., m. Angeline E. **ROOT**, b. of New Canaan, Oct. 28, 1840, by
Theophilus Smith — 55
ANDRAS, ANDREAS, Sarah, of Darien, m. Enos **WEED**, Apr. 1, 1821, [Cong.
Ch. Rec.] — 192
William, m. Meriam **CRAFTE**, Sept. 10, 1797 — 3
ARNOLD, Cynthia, of New Canaan, m. William **GRIFFETH**, of Norwalk, June
17, 1821, by William Bonney — 6
AVERY, Marcus S., of New York, m. Hannah **BENEDICT**, of New Canaan,
May 29, 1836, by Rev. Edwin Hall, of Norwalk — 29
AYRES, Amos, m. Hannah **LOCKWOOD**, Nov. 26, 1797 — 3
Ann Malvina, of New Canaan, m. Lewis E. P. **SMITH**, of New York City,
Dec. 23, 1851, by Rev. Theophilus Smith — 75
Calsine, of Wilton, m. Eliphalet **HANFORD**, of New Canaan, Nov. 25,
1823, by Rev. William Bonney — 9
Caroline C., m. Rev. Benoni Y. **MESSENJER**, of Ohio, May 31, 1830, by
William Bonney — 19
Darius S., m. Anna E. **COMSTOCK**, b. of New Canaan, Dec. 24, 1849, by
Rev. Theophilus Smith — 69
Delia M., of New Canaan, m. Dr. Thomas **RITTER**, of Wethersfield,
June 16, 1830, by S. Haight — 19
Ebenezer, m. Rhoda **BOUTON**, Nov. [   ], 1817 [Cong. Ch. Rec.] — 192
Edward, of Norwalk, m. Matilda **HAYES**, of New Canaan, Apr. 21, 1839,
by Rev. Lyman H. Atwater — 31
Eliza Jane, of New Canaan, m. Vincent **ST. JOHN**, of Binghamton, N.Y.
Oct. 17, 1839, by Theophilus Smith — 33
Ezra, of Poundridge, m. Abbey **KELLOGG**, of Canaan, Nov. 16, 1796,
(Cong. Ch. Rec.) — 2
Hannah Eliza, m. Edwin S. **SEYMOUR**, b. of New Canaan, May 3, 1829,
by William Bonney — 17
Harriet, m. Zalmon **CARTER**, Aug. 21, 1820, by William Bonney — 4
Harriet, m. Zalmon **CARTER**, Aug. 21, 1820 [Cong. Ch. Rec.] — 192
Hezron L., m. Sally **BROWN**, Apr. 22, 1821, by William Bonney — 6
Hezron L., see also Nozron L. **AYRES**
James S., of New York, m. Clarinda **FITCH**, of New Canaan, Feb. 21,
1836, by Theophilus Smith

	Page
AYRES, (cont.)	
Jared, m. Polly **LOCKWOOD**, Feb. 20, 1800	0
Jared, m. Dinah **BENEDICT**, Oct. 9, 1803	1
Jonathan E., m. Jane **CHAPMAN**, Nov. 7, 1827, by William Bonney	15
Julia Ann, of New Canaan, m. Josiah Mason **CARTER**, of New York, June 23, 1841, by Rev. Theophilus Smith	57
Lavina, of New Canaan, m. John **PURVIS** (Rev.), of Danbury, Apr. 10, [1844], in St. Marks Church, by David Ogden	63
Lewis B., m. Clarina B. **HOYT**, b. of New Canaan, Sept. 6, 1840, by Theophilus Smith	34
Mary Ann, m. Hazar **ABBOTT**, b. of New Canaan, Dec. 6, 1825, by Origen P. Holcomb	11
Mary E., of New Canaan, m. Warring S. **WEED**, of Binghamton, N.Y., June 6, 1842, by Theophilus Smith [crossed out]	59
Mary E., of New Canaan, m. Waring S. **WEED**, of Binghamton, N.Y., June 6, 1842, by Rev. Theophilus Smith	59
Mary E., of New Canaan, m. S. M. **LOCKWOOD**, of Stamford, Dec. 12, 1850, by Rev. Theophilus Smith	72
Minott, of New Canaan, m. Hannah **KELLOGG**, of Norwalk, Apr. 10, 1821, by William Bonney	5
Minott, m. Hannah **KELLOGG**, of Norwalk, Apr. 10, 1821 [Cong. Ch.Rec.]	192
Minot, m. Sarah J. **WEED**, b. of New Canaan, June 27, 1843, by Rev. Theophilus Smith	61
Nozron L., m. Sally **BROWN**, Apr. 22, 1821 [Cong. Ch. Rec.]	192
Nozron L., see also Hezron L. **AYRES**	
Sally Ann, of New Canaan, m. Daniel **BUTTON**, of North Haven, July 12, 1820, by William Bonney	4
Sally Ann, m. Daniel **BUTTON**, July 12, 1820 [Cong. Ch. Rec.]	192
William Henry, s. Frederick, m. Eliza Jane **BENEDICT**, d. Caleb, b. of New Canaan, Jan. 7, 1834, by Theophilus Smith	25
BADEAU, [see also **BARTOW**], Mary A., m. Henry W. **WOOD**, Oct. 9, 1842, by Peter Smith, J.P.	59
BAILEY, Harvey, of North Salem, West Chester Co., N.Y., m. Delia Davis, of New Canaan, Mar. 16, 1846, by Rev. George Waterbury	64
BARACLOUGH, BARRACLOUGH, Mary, m. William J. **FINDLEY**, b. of New Canaan, Oct. 20, 1834, by Theophilus Smith	27
William, m. Polly **CURTIS**, Apr. 1, 1810, [Cong. Ch. Rec.]	191
BARTOW, BARTO, [see also **BADEAU**], Chauncey, of Wilton, m. Merinda **NASH**, of New Canaan, Oct. 15, 1820, by William Bonney	4
Chauncey, of Wilton, m. Merinda **NASH**, of New Canaan, Oct. 15, 1820, [Cong. Ch. Rec.]	192
George A., of New Canaan, m. Harriet A. **WEBB**, of Walton, N.Y., May 13, 1850, by Rev. Theophilus Smith	69
Lucy A., m. Leander S. **PARKETON**, b. of New Canaan, Dec. 7, 1849, by Rev. Theophilus Smith	68
Sophronia E., of New Canaan, m. Henry* M. **WEBB**, of Walton, N.Y., Nov 30, 1852, by Rev. Theophilus Smith *(Written "Harry M. **WEBB**" in Index)	80
Stephen, of Sidney, N.Y., m. Sally **CLINTON**, Apr. 20, 1820, [Cong. Ch. Rec.]	192
BATES, Benjamin, of Middlesex, m. Ester **ST. JOHN**, Aug. 30, 1798	3

NEW CANAAN VITAL RECORDS

	Page
BATES, (cont.)	
Martha Ann, of Darien, m. Henry **DOSSAERD**(?)*, of Westport, Nov. 24, 1852, in St. Marks Church, by W[illia]m Long *(Copied as nearly as made out. Written "**DOWNING** or **DUNNING**" in Index)	78
BEARDSLEY, Maryette, m. Levi **CLARK**, b. of New Canaan, Aug. 26, 1839, by David Ogden	32
Sarah Jane, m. Joseph H. **MEAD**, b. of New Canaan, June 6, 1847, by Rev. D. H. Short	65
BEERS, Daniel, of Poundridge, N.Y., m. Anna **WATERBURY**, of New Canaan, July 6, 1831, by William Bonney	21
BELDEN, Amos, m. Levina **SEYMOUR**, of Canaan, June 23, 1803	0
Benjamin, of Wilton, m. Grace **RICHARDS**, of New Canaan, (colored), Mar. 24, 1831, by William Bonney	22
Dennis, of Troy, m. Anna **LOCKWOOD**, of New Canaan, Apr. 15, 1813, [Cong. Ch. Rec.]	191
BELL, Phebe, of Darien, m. Darius M. **HOYT**, of New Canaan, Sept. 22, 1844, by Rev. Theophilus Smith	63
BELLWOOD, Rebecca, m. Samuel Augustus **WEED**, b. of New Canaan, May 1, 1849, by Rev. Theophilus Smith	68
BENEDICT, Abigail, of Canaan, m. W[illia]m **DAVENPORT**, Sept. 12, 1802	0
Amelia C., m. Charles **BENEDICT**, b. of New Canaan, June 13, 1843, by Rev. Theophilus Smith	61
Andrew, s. Jonathan B., m. Emily **HOYT**, d. Samuel, b. of New Canaan, Oct. 15, 1833, by Theophilus Smith	25
Anson, m. Mary **BOUTON**, May 9, 1819, [Cong. Ch. Rec.]	192
Anson R.*, m. Esther **HOYT**, b. of New Canaan, Sept. 1, 1844, by Peter Smith, J.P. *(Written "Anson B." in Index)	63
Antoinette, m. Rufus **FANCHER**, Mar. 3, 1822, by William Bonney	8
Bille, m. Anne **EELS**, Jan. 30, 1800	0
Caleb, Jr., m. Elis **ST. JOHN**, Aug. 23, 1801	0
Caleb S., m. Hannah E. **CRESSEY**, b. of New Canaan, Nov. 9, 1826, by William Bonney	12
Charles, m. Amelia C. **BENEDICT**, b. of New Canaan, June 13, 1843, by Rev. Theophilus Smith	61
Scinthia, m. Rufus **FANCHER**, of Franklin, S.N., Mar. 30, 1800 *(Cynthia)	0
David, m. Hannah **FITCH**, Dec. 22, 1796	3
Deborah, m. Bradley **NASH**, July 2, 1817, [Cong. Ch. Rec.]	192
Deborah A., m. John F. **RAYMOND**, b. of New Canaan, Sept. 11, 1825, by William Bonney	11
Dinah, m. Jared **AYRES**, Oct. 9, 1803	1
Dina, m. Eliakim **SMITH**, Jan. 7, 1805	1
Eliza Jane, d. Caleb, m. William Henry **AYRES**, s. Frederick, b. of New Canaan, Jan. 7, 1834, by Theophilus Smith	25 191
Elizabeth, m. Seth **HICKOK**, Mar. 26, 1810, [Cong. Ch. Rec.]	192
Eunice, m. Adoniram **SKEELS**, Oct. 17, 1816, [Cong. Ch. Rec.]	0
Ezra, m. Hannah **COMSTOCK**, Dec. 1, 1799	
Ezra, m. Sarah **COMSTOCK**, b. of New Canaan, Jan. 22, 1846, by Rev. Theophilus Smith	64
Hannah, d. Ezra, of New Canaan, m. Smith B. **KEELER**, of Ridgefield, Aug. 4, 1834, by Theophilus Smith	26
Hannah, of New Canaan, m. Marcus S. **AVERY**, of New York, May 29,	

	Page
BENEDICT, (cont.)	
1836, by Rev. Edwin Hall, of Norwalk	29
Irena, m. Moses **LION**, of Wilton, Aug. 18, 1799	3
James M., m. Mary E. **WATERBURY**, b. of New Canaan, Oct. 12, 1831, by Theophilus Smith	21
John, s. Caleb, m. Mary **MILLS**, d. Eldne, b. of New Canaan, Apr. 26, 1835, by Theophilus Smith	27
Lockard, m. Betsey **WEED**, May 12, 1800	0
Lockwood, m. Betsey **WEED**, May 12, 1800	2
Loraina, of New Canaan, m. Emery **WHITLOCK**, of Wilton, Nov. 28, 1843, by Rev. Theophilus Smith	62
Mary, m. Rufus **RICHARDS**, b. of New Canaan, May 25, 1826, by William Bonney	11
Mary E., m. Robert **LAMBERT**, b. of New Canaan, May 27, 1840, by Theophilus Smith	34
Mary Jane, m. William Edmund **HUSTED**, Sept. 1, 1851, by Rev. D. H. Short	74
Matthias, m. Polly **HUSTED**, Sept. 18, 1803	1
Molly, m. Hennery **SEYMOUR**, Nov. 28, 1799	0
Orestes H., of Lewisboro, N.Y., m. Martha A. **SLAUSON**, of New Canaan, Apr. 28, 1851, by Rev. Theophilus Smith	73
Rachel Emilia, d. Lockwood & Betsey, b. Feb. 16, 1801	189
Roswel, m. Minerva **CARTER**, b. of New Canaan, Sept. 1, 1840, by Theophilus Smith	34
Royal F., m. Delia **BOUTON**, b. of New Canaan, Nov. 12, 1826, by William Bonney	12
Royal F., m. Delia **BOUTON**, b. of New Canaan, Nov. 12, 1826, by William Bonney	13
Rufus, m. Mariah **LINES**, b. of New Canaan, Feb. 9, 1851, by Rev. Theophilus Smith	72
Ruth, of Canaan, m. Jacob **REED**, May 5, 1803	0
Ruth, m. James B. **EELLS**, Aug. 3, 1820, by William Bonney	4
Ruth, m. James B. **EELLS**, Aug. 3, 1820 [Cong. Ch. Rec.]	192
Sally, m. Zalmon **HOYT**, Oct. 25, 1820, by William Bonney	4
Sally, m. Zalmon **HOYT**, Oct. 25, 1820, [Cong. Ch. Rec.]	192
Sally, m. Ira **WEED**, b. of New Canaan, Apr. 11, 1827, by William Bonney	14
Scinthia, see under Cynthia	
Siley, m. Stephen **HOYT**, Jr., b. of New Canaan, Oct. 29, 1823, by William Bonney	9
Thankful, m. Bouton **HOIT**, Feb. 8, 1800	0
BETTS, [see also **BOTT** & **BUTTS**], Ellis A., m. Abraham **CRISSY**, July 29, 1817, [Cong. Ch. Rec.]	192
Harriet, m. Elisha L. **SILLIMAN**, Dec. 25, 1815, [Cong. Ch. Rec.]	192
Harriet, of Wilton, m. Samuel P. **TUTTLE**, of New Canaan, Apr. 11, 1848, by Rev. D. H. Short	67
Sally, m. Justus **HOYT**, Jr., b. of New Canaan, Oct. 28, 1821, by William Bonney	7
Samuel, see under Samuel **BOTT**	
BIGSBY, William, of Norwalk, m. Betsey **PETTIT**, of New Canaan, Aug. 26, 1819, [Cong. Ch. Rec.]	192
	81
BIRCHARD, Eli, m. Jemima **JONES**, Nov. 21, 1853, by Rev. L. D. Nickerson	
BIRDSEL, Charles, of South Salem, N.Y., m. Emeline **TUTTLE**, of New	

	Page
BIRDSEL, (cont.)	
Canaan, Nov. 28, 1830, by Samuel Raymond, J.P.	18
BISHOP, Anne, of Canaan, m. Benjamin **WEBB**, of New York, Dec. 25, 1803	1
David, m. Mary **FINCH**, Nov. 22, 1795 (Cong. Ch. Rec.)	2
BLOOMER, Edgar, of Stamford, m. Eliza **PALMER**, of New Canaan, Aug. 3, 1851, by Rev. Jacob Shaw	73
BOSSEE, Nerbert, of Quebec, Can., m. Rebecca Ann **WATERBURY**, of New Canaan, Dec. 13, 1852, in St. Marks Church, by William Long	78
BOSTWICK, Alanson, m. Abigail E. **CRISSY**, b. of New Canaan, Sept. 5, 1841, by Rev. Theophilus Smith	58
Daniel, of Stanwich, m. Sarah **PENNOYER**, of New Canaan, Mar. 12, 1809	1
George L., m. Harriet **CRISSY**, b. of New Canaan, Feb. 8, 1841, by Theophilus Smith	56
Sarah J., m. Moses **RAYMOND**, b. of New Canaan, Sept. 4, 1839, by Theophilus Smith	32
BOTT, [see also **BETTS**], Samuel, m. Mary **WEBB**, Jan. 3, 1798	3
BOUTON, Aaron, of New Canaan, m. Anna **KEELER**, of Ridgbury, Oct. 6, 1807, by Rev. Samuel Goodrich. Witnesses Daniel Bouton & Abagail Keeler	2
Ann E., m. Orrin A. **DOTY**, b. of New Canaan, Feb. 25, 1846, by Rev. Theophilus Smith	64
Augustus, of Darien, m. Eliza **ST. JOHN**, of New Canaan, Apr. 14, 1829, by William Bonney	17
Daniel, of New Canaan, m. Hannah **HOYT**, of Stamford, Oct. 17, 1803, by Rev. Daniel Smith. Witness Aaron Bouton	2
Daniel W., of Darien, m. Almina **ST. JOHN**, of New Canaan, Aug. 28, 1827, by William Bonney	15
Daniel Webb, s. Jared & Polly, b. Feb. 26, 1805	189
Delia, m. Royal F. **BENEDICT**, b. of New Canaan, Nov. 12, 1826, by William Bonney	12
Delia, m. Royal F. **BENEDICT**, b. of New Canaan, Nov. 12, 1826, by William Bonney	13
Elizabeth, of New Canaan, m. William B. **HOYT**, of Lewisboro, Westchester Co., N.Y., Dec. 11, 1842, by Peter Smith, J.P.	60
Emma Matilda, of New Canaan, m. Ralph E. **WASHBURH**, of Charlestown, Mass., Jan. 20, 1851, by Rev. Theophilus Smith	72
Harriett, of New Canaan, m. John **BROWN**, of Norwalk, [ ], by Rev. Edwin Hall, of Norwalk	24
Harvey, m. Emily **HANFORD**, b. of New Canaan, Oct. 18, 1826, by William Bonney	14
James S., m. Emeline **LEWIS**, b. of New Canaan, May 5, 1851, by Rev. D. H. Short	73
Jared, of New Canaan, m. Polly **WEBB**, of Stamford, Oct. 7, 1802	2
Josiah, s. Stephen & Hannah, b. Mar. 17, 1802	189
Mary, m. Anson **BENEDICT**, May 9, 1819, [Cong. Ch. Rec.]	192
Nathaniel, of N.S., m. Rachel **STEVENS**, Mar. 22, 1801	0
Nathaniel Augustus, s. Jared & Polly, b. Aug. 4, 1803	189
Polly, d. Aaron & Anna, b. Mar. 31, 1810	190
Polly, m. Minor **LOUNSBURY**, b. of New Canaan, Dec. 24, 1828, by William Bonney	16
Rhoda, m. Ebenezer **AYRES**, Nov. [ ], 1817, [Cong. Ch. Rec.]	192

	Page
BOUTON, (cont.)	
Robert P., m. Betsey S. **WARRING**, Aug. 9, 1821, by William Bonney	6
Ruth, m. Elliott **RAYMOND**, Feb. 20, 1821, by William Bonney	5
Ruth, m. Elliott **RAYMOND**, Feb. [ ], 1821, [Cong. Ch. Rec.]	192
Sally, d. Aaron & Anna, b. Dec. 14, 1811; d. Dec. 24, 1811	190
Samuel, s. Aaron & Anna, b. Sept. 3, 1817	190
BOYER, David H., m. Esther **SCOFIELD**, Feb. 26, 1837, by Edwin Hall	30
BRINKERHOOF, Edward H., of Poundridge, N.Y., m. Julia E. **CHICHESTER**, of New Canaan, July 25, 1852, by Rev. Theophilus Smith	77
BRITTS, Sophia, m. Silvester **BRITTS**, b. of Wilton, July [ ], 1840, by Joseph Silliman, J.P.	34
Silvester, m. Sophia **BRITTS**, b. of Wilton, July [ ], 1840, by Joseph Silliman, J.P.	34
BROWN, Ann, of New Canaan, m. William **RUSCO**, of Greenwich, Sept. 2, 1830, by Rev. Samuel Cochrane	19
Barbary, m. Nathan **NASH**, of Middlesex, Jan. 1, 1797	3
Bradley, see Burdby **BROWN**	
Burdby*, of Norwalk, m. Sarah Ann **WEBB**, of New Canaan, Nov. 11, 1830, by Rev. Samuel Cochrane *(Written "Bradley" in Index)	18
David C., of Stamford, m. Mary Adeline **LOCKWOOD**, of New Canaan, [ ], by Rev. David H. Short. Recorded Jan. 1, 1851	71
Eber, m. Anna **STEVENS**, b. of New Canaan, June 18, 1837, by Theophilus Smith	30
John, m. Ellis J. **VERVALAN**(?), b. of New Canaan, Dec. 10, 1843, by Daniel W. Bouton, J.P.	62
John, of Norwalk, m. Harriett **BOUTON**, of New Canaan, [ ], by Rev. Edwin Hall, of Norwalk. Recorded Apr. 8, 1833	24
Levi, of Norwalk, m. Emily **PLATT**, of New Canaan, Nov. 19, 1840, by Edwin Hall	55
Lyman, m. Polly **HOYT**, Oct. 10, 1826, by William Bonney	12
Mary A., m. George**ELLS**, Mar. 7, 1843, by Rev. Charles F. **PELTON**	60
Mary Ann, of New Canaan, m. Theodore **TAYLOR**, of Westport, Feb. 23, 1852, by Rev. Theophilus Smith	76
Mary E., of Norwalk, m. George **FANCHER**, Sept. 5, 1841, by Peter Smith, J.P.	58
Sally, m. Hezron L. **AYRES**, Apr. 22, 1821, by William Bonney	6
Sally, m. Nozron L. **AYRES**, Apr. 22, 1821, [Cong. Ch. Rec.]	192
Susanna, m. William **ST. JOHN**, Apr. 7, 1799	3
BRUNSON, Nancy, of New Canaan, m. Nelson **THATCHER**, of Danbury, Mar. 2, 1853, by Rev. L. D. Nickerson	80
BURTON, Oliver, m. Ruth Ann **SMITH**, b. of New Canaan, Dec. 10, 1851, by Rev. Theophilus Smith	74
BUTLER, Daniel, of Norwalk, m. H. **EELLS**, of New Canaan, Sept. 5, 1813, [Cong. Ch. Rec.]	191
-----, m. Jemima **TAYLOR**, of Greens Farms, Oc. 29, 1802	0
BUTTERY, William, Jr., m. Sally Ann **PARSELA**, of New York, Aug. 13, 1832, by William Bonney	23
Zachariah, m. Sally **BUTTS**, of Wilton, Jan. 6, 1805	1
Zachariah, of Wilton, m. Sarah **SHUTE**, of New Canaan, Dec. 26, 1830, by J. B. Benedict, J.P.	18
BUTTON, Daniel, of North Haven, m. Sally Ann **AYRES**, of New Canaan, July	

	Page
BUTTON, (cont.)	
12, 1820, by William Bonney	4
Daniel, m. Sally Ann **AYRES**, July 12, 1820, [Cong. Ch. Rec.]	192
BUTTS, [see also **BETTS**], Sally, of Wilton, m. Zachariah **BUTTERY**, Jan. 6, 1805	1
BUXTON, Julia Ann, of New Canaan, m. Charles **JONES**, of Dantown, Feb. 10, 1839, by Samuel W. King	31
BYINGTON, Henry, m. Betsy **WEEKS**, May 14, 1837, by Nath[an] Comstock, J.P.,	30
CAMP, Harvey, of Norwalk, m. Currence* **HAYES**, of New Canaan, Oct. 6, 1818, [Cong. Ch. Rec.]	192
CAMPBELL, Joseph, m. Sarah C. **CHAMBERS**, July 7, 1850, at Albany, N.Y., by Rev. J. H. Reade. Witnesses Eliza Shaw & Thomas Hoyt	74
CANFIELD, Mary E., m. Andrew J. **SLAWSON**, b. of New Canaan, Feb. 17, 1846, by Rev. Theophilus Smith	64
Polly, of New Canaan, m. Charles **WEBB**, of Wilton, Oct. 8, 1809	1
CARTER, Caroline E., of New Canaan, m. George M. **HANFORD**, of Wilton, Apr. 6, 1852, by Rev. Jacob Shaw	77
Eben, Jr., m. Eliza **WEED**, Jan. 14, 1819, [Cong. Ch. Rec.]	192
Eliza, of New Canaan, m. Samuel **HUNT**, of Teroksbury, Mass., Sept. 26, 1814, [Cong. Ch. Rec.]	191
Emma M., m. Andrew K. **COMSTOCK**, b. of New Canaan, Mar. 22, 1848, by Rev. Theophilus Smith	66
Emma M., m. Andrew K. **COMSTOCK**, b. of New Canaan, Mar. 22, 1848, by Rev. Theophilus Smith	67
Emma M., m. Andrew K. **COMSTOCK**, b. of New Canaan, Mar. 22, 1848, by Rev. Theophilus Smith	81
George, m. Sarah E. **VALENTINE**, b. of New Canaan, May 9, 1836, by Theophilus Smith	28
Hanford, m. Mabel **FITCH**, Oct. 12, 1817, [Cong. Ch. Rec.]	192
Hannah, of New Canaan, m. Benjamin **NORTH**, of Walton, N.Y., Sept. 26, 1814, [Cong. Ch. Rec.]	191
Hannah J., m. William **ST. JOHN**, b. of New Canaan, Mar. 13, 1843, by Rev. Theophilus Smith	61
Josiah Mason, of New York, m. Julia Ann **AYRES**, of New Canaan, June 23, 1841, by Rev. Theophilus Smith	57
Mary Ann, m. William **DRUMMOND**, b. of New Canaan, May 24, 1833, by Theophilus Smith	24
Minerva, m. Roswel **BENEDICT**, b. of New Canaan, Sept. 1, 1840, by Theophilus Smith	34
Thomas, m. Esther **GREENBY***, b. of New Canaan, July 21, 1824, by William Bonney *(Perhaps "**GRUNBY**". See Index)	10
	4
Zalmon, m. Harriet **AYRES**, Aug. 21, 1820, by William Bonney	192
Zalmon, m. Harriet **AYRES**, Aug. 21, 1820, [Cong. Ch. Rec.]	192
CHAMBERS, Henry, m. Hannah **ST. JOHN**, Apr. [ ], 1817, [Cong. Ch. Rec.]	
Sarah C., m. Joseph **CAMPBELL**, July 7, 1850, at Albany, N.Y., by Rev. J. H. Read. Witnesses Eliza Shaw & Thomas Hoyt	74
	15
CHAPMAN, Jane, m. Jonathan E. **AYRES**, Nov. 7, 1827, by William Bonney	
CHASE, Daniel, of Norwalk, m. Esther **CROFOOT**, of New Canaan, Jan. 5, 1823, by Sylvester Eaton	9
CHICHESTER, Aaron, m. Betsey **EDWARDS**, b. of Wilton, Mar. 24, 1833, by William Bonney	24

	Page
CHICHESTER, (cont.)	
Alanson, m. Sally **WEED**, Nov. 30, 1815, [Cong. Ch. Rec.]	192
Clarissa, d. Nathan & Theodocia, b. Oct. 23, 1801	189
Cynthia, of New Canaan, m. Samuel **DEAN**, of Stamford, Aug. 29, 1819, [Cong. Ch. Rec.]	192
David, m. Phebe **LOCKWOOD**, Aug. 26, 1813, [Cong. Ch. Rec.]	191
Edward Lewis, s. Lewis & Sophronia, b. Oct. 27, 1820	190
James Hervey, m. Julia Eliza **LOCKWOOD**, b. of New Canaan, Jan. 24, 1827, by Rev. Orin P. Holcomb	14
Julia E., of New Canaan, m. Edward H. **BRINKERHOOF**, of Poundridge, N.Y., July 25, 1852, by Rev. Theophilus Smith	77
Lewis, m. Sophronia **WOOD**, Oct. [ ], 1819, [Cong. Ch. Rec.]	192
Mary Ann, m. Carlile **LOCKWOOD**, b. of New Canaan, Oct. 8, 1823, by William Bonney	9
Nancy, of New Canaan, m. Abijah **HANFORD**, of Norwalk, Sept. 24, 1816, [Cong. Ch. Rec.]	192
CLARK, Levi, m. Maryette **BEARDSLEY**, b. of New Canaan, Aug. 26, 1839, by David Ogden	32
Mary Elizabeth, of Norwalk, m. Isaac G. **TRAPHAGEN**, of Stamford, Jan. 19, 1852, by D. H. Short	76
Oliver, of Danbury, m. Abigail A. **TALLMADGE**, of New Canaan, Mar. 22, 1853, by Rev. Lorenzo D. Nickerson	80
CLINTON, Esther, m. David **OLMSTEAD**, of Wilton, Dec. 29, 1808	
Sally, m. Stephen **BARTO**, of Sidney, N.Y., Apr. 20, 1820, [Cong. Ch. Rec.]	192
CLOCK, Henry, of Darien, m. Hannah **RAYMOND**, of New Canaan, Jan. 9, 1821, by G. S. Webb	5
COMSTOCK, Andrew K., m. Emma M. **CARTER**, b. of New Canaan, Mar. 22, 1848, by Rev. Theophilus Smith	66
Andrew K., m. Emma M. **CARTER**, b. of New Canaan, Mar. 22, 1848, by Rev. Theophilus Smith	67
Andrew K., m. Emma M. **CARTER**, b. of New Canaan, Mar. 22, 1848, by Rev. Theophilus Smith	81
Anna E., m. Darius S. **AYRES**, b. of New Canaan, Dec. 24, 1849, by Rev. Theophilus Smith	69
Betsey, m. Zenas **WEED**, Nov. 17, 1816 [Cong. Ch. Rec.]	192
Betty, m. John **PIONOYER**, Feb. 25, 1800	0
Deborah, m. Andras **POWERS**, Nov. 2, 1797	3
Deborah, of New Canaan, m. Arnet A. **NASH**, of Norwalk, Dec. 28, 1828, by William Bonney	15
Diana, of New Canaan, m. Rev. Chester **ISHAM**, of Taunton, Mass., Apr. 21, 1824, by William Bonney	10
Elisha, of Norwalk, m. Harriet **DAVENPORT**, of New Canaan, Oct. 3, 1842, by Rev. Theophilus Smith	59
Elizabeth, m. William **WEED**, of North Stamford, Feb. 5, 1804	1 0
Hannah, m. Ezra **BENEDICT**, Dec. 1, 1799	0
Lucretia, m. Gould **ST. JOHN**, Nov. 1, 1801	
Margarett, m. Darius W. **TODD**, b. of New Canaan, Feb. 4, 1829, by Rev. Daniel DePinng	18
Mary A., m. Arastus **SEELEY**, Nov. 11, 1818, [Cong. Ch. Rec.]	192
Matilda, of New Canaan, m. Roswel A. **RAYMOND**, of Norwalk, Feb. 22, 1837, by Rev. Edwin Hall, of Norwalk	30

NEW CANAAN VITAL RECORDS 215

	Page
COMSTOCK, (cont.)	
Mijah, Jr., m. Polly **COMSTOCK**, of Canaan, Oct. 21, 1802	0
Moses, m. Lois **HOIT**, Sept. 23, 1805	1
Nancy, m. James I. **EETS***, b. of New Canaan, Feb. 22, 1802 *(**EELLS**?)	0
Polly, of Canaan, m. Mijah **COMSTOCK**, Jr., Oct. 21, 1802	0
Rose, m. Robbert **MANNING**, negro, Nov. [ ], 1803	1
Sarah, m. Ezra **BENEDICT**, b. of New Canaan, Jan. 22, 1846, by Rev. Theophilus Smith	64
Sip, m. Sarah **FLETCHER**, [colored], Jan. 12, 1818, [Cong. Ch. Rec.]	192
Thomas, m. Catharine A. **PERKINS**, b. of New Canaan, Sept. 3, 1850, by Rev. Jacob Shaw	70
Thomas A., m. Polly **LOCKWOOD**, b. of New Canaan, Oct. 10, 1836, by Theophilus Smith	30
Xenophen, s. Caleb & Lucy, b. Sept. 28, 1801	189
CONLEY, Alanson, m. Polly **DEFOREST**, Mar. 9, 1817, [Cong. Ch. Rec.]	192
Daniel, m. Deborah **HANFORD**, b. of New Canaan, Nov. 8, 1821, by William Bonney	7
COOLEY, James N., of Dutchess Co., N.Y., m. Henrietta **ABBOTT**, of New Canaan, July 4, 1847, by Rev. D. H. Short	65
CRAFTE, Meriam, m. William **ANDRAS**, Sept. 10, 1797	3
Polly, m. Isaac **LEWIS**, of Hungtington, Sept. 24, 1797	3
CRANE, Sally, of Wilton, m. John **LOUNSBURY**, Oct. 21, 1813, [Cong. Ch. Rec.]	191
CRISSY, CRESSEY, CRISSEY, Abigail E., m. Alanson **BOSTWICK**, b. of New Canaan, Sept. 5, 1841, by Rev. Theophilus Smith	58
Abraham, m. Jane **TALLMADGE**, Nov. 26, 1815, [Cong. Ch. Rec.]	192
Abraham, m. Ellis A. **BETTS**, July 29, 1817, [Cong. Ch. Rec.]	192
Charlotte, of New Canaan, m. Wyx **SEELY**, of Darien, Sept. 17, 1832, by Rev. John Lovejoy	23
Ebenezer, m. Julia **SELLECK**, b. of New Canaan, Sept. 25, [1854], by Rev. F. W. Williams	81
Hannah E., m. Caleb S. **BENEDICT**, b. of New Canaan, Nov. 9, 1826, by William Bonney	12
Harriet, m. James **MITCHELL**, b. of New Canaan, Mar. 6, 1832, by Rev. Henry Fuller	23
Harriet, m. George L. **BOSTWICK**, b. of New Canaan, Feb. 8, 1841, by Theophilus Smith	56
Hiram, m. Polly **PENNOYER**, b. of New Canaan, Jan. 15, 1823, by William Bonney	8
Jared, m. Polly **CRISSY**, Nov. 24, 1813, [Cong. Ch. Rec.]	191
Maria, of New Canaan, m. Selleck **JONES**, of Stamford, Jan. 18, 1829, by Rev. Harvey Fuller, of North Stamford	17
Nancy, m. Isaac **WATERBURY**, b. of New Canaan, Feb. 3, 1834, by William Bonney	26
	191
Polly, m. Jared **CRISSY**, Nov. 24, 1813, [Cong. Ch. Rec.]	
Polly, of New Canaan, m. Hickford **MARSHALL**, of New York, Sept. 12, 1833, by Rev. Henry **FULLER**, of North Stamford	25
	191
Prudence, m. Thomas S. **HUSTED**, Jan. 24, 1813, [Cong. Ch. Rec.]	
Sally, m. Sylvanus **SEELY**, b. of New Canaan, Aug. 29, 1831, by William Bonney	21
	3
Samuel, m. [ ] **HOYT**, of North Stamford, Sept. 28, 1797	1
-----, m. [ ] **MILLS**, of North Stamford, Dec. 2, 1804	

	Page
CROFOOT, Betsey Ann, m. Darius **ST. JOHN**, b. of New Canaan, Oct. 16, 1829, by Rev. M. Eli Daviston	17
Charles, s. Minot & Nancy, b. Apr. 20, 1841	191
Cyrus, m. Clarissa **SLAUSON**, Mar. 1, 1843, by Rev. Charles F. Pelton	60
Electa, m. Matthew **KELLOGG**, b. of New Canaan, Nov. 21, 1830, by Rev. Daniel I. Wright	18
Esther, of New Canaan, m. Daniel **CHASE**, of Norwalk, Jan. 5, 1823, by Sylvester Eaton	9
Matilda, m. Rev. Eli **DENNISTON**, Oct. 16, 1823, by Rev. Aaron Hunt	9
Minott, m. Nancy **HOYT**, b. of New Canaan, Apr. 1, 1840, by Rev. Cyrus Fon	34
Minott, of New Canaan, m. Rhuamy **LOUNSBURY**, of Prattsville, N.Y., Dec. 23, 1852, by Rev. S. VanDusen. Witnesses A. M. Hought & Elizabeth Vandusen	80
CROSBY, Frederick, m. Julia Ann **PENDER**, b. of New Canaan, Nov. 2, 1842, by Charles F. Pelton	60
CROSSMAN, Lewis, of Norwalk, m. Matilda **DOTY**, Apr. 29, 1827, by William Bonney	14
CURTIS, Polly, m. William **BARRACLOUGH**, Apr. 1, 1810, [Cong. Ch. Rec.]	191
CURZON, James, m. Catharine **TRISTRAM**, June 14, 1843, by Rev. J. Hunt	61
DAMBY, William, of Ridgefield, m. Harriet Elizabeth **RAYMOND**, of New Canaan, Sept. 2, 1839, by [ ]	32
DAN, Maria, Mrs. of New Canaan, m. Nathan **JONES**, of Norwalk, Ohio, Oct. 26, 1851, by Rev. Jacob Shaw	75
Sally M., m. Russell G. **RAYMOND**, b. of New Canaan, Dec. 14, 1835, by Rev. Davis Stocking	28
DAVENPORT, Abby, of North Stamford, m. Lebens **REED**, of Canaan, Oct. [ ], 1795, (Cong. Ch. Rec.)	2
Anna, m. Thomas **WARRING**, b. of New Canaan, May 3, 1807	2
Betsey, of Wilton, m. Charles **NAP**, Dec. 29, 1800	0
Emily, m. Harvey **SANDERSON**, b. of New Canaan, Feb. 4, 1836, by Theophilus Smith	28
Hanford, m. Hannah **ST. JOHN**, Sept. 10, 1817, [Cong. Ch. Rec.]	192
Harriet, of New Canaan, m. Elisha **COMSTOCK**, of Norwalk, Oct. 3, 1842, by Rev. Theophilus Smith	59
Joseph, m. Julia M. **YOUNG**, b. of New Canaan, Sept. 15, 1824, by Rev. Henry Fuller, of North Stamford	10
Polly, of New Canaan, m. Amzi **SCOFIELD**, of Stamford, Nov. 24, 1819, [Cong. Ch. Rec.]	192
W[illia]m, m. Abigail **BENEDICT**, of Canaan, Sept. 12, 1802	0
DAVIS, A[a]ron, of Stamford, m. Sarah **LOCKWOOD**, of New Canaan, May 2, 1816, [Cong. Ch. Rec.]	192
Delia, of New Canaan, m. Harvey **BAILEY**, of North Salem, West Chester Co., N.Y., Mar. 16, 1846, by Rev. George Waterbury	64
DEAN, Samuel, of Stamford, m. Cynthia **CHICHESTER**, of New Canaan, Aug. 29, 1819, [Cong. Ch. Rec.]	192
DEFOREST, DEFREES, Edward, m. Mary Elizabeth **ABBOTT**, b. of New Canaan, [ ], by Rev. J. Lyman Clark. Recorded Apr. 7, 1836	28
George W., of New Canaan, m. Sally Ann **PALMER**, of Ridgefield, June 8, 1834, by Theophilus Smith	26
Harriett, m. Frederick **NOBLE**, Jan. 30, 1833, by Theophilus Smith	24

	Page
DEFOREST, DEFREES, (cont.)	
Harvey, of Wilton, m. Mary **RICHARDS**, of New Canaan, Sept. 18, [1854], by Rev. I. P. Lestrade, of New York	81
Polly, m. Alanson **CONLEY**, Mar. 9, 1817, [Cong. Ch. Rec.]	192
Polly, m. Albinus **JOHNSON**, Oct. 10, 1822, by William Bonney	8
Polly, of New Canaan, m. Alanson **HAWLEY**, of Monroe, Apr. 28, 1839, by Watts Comstock, J.P.	32
Sabia, m. Ira **WADDY**, Sept. 6, 1810, [Cong. Ch. Rec.]	191
Seth, m. Rachel **WEED**, Feb. 25, 1798	3
DENNISTON, Eli, Rev., m. Matilda **CROFOOT**, Oct. 16, 1823, by Rev. Aaron Hunt	9
DICKENS, Amos, of Ridgefield, m. Polly **STAPLES**, of Wilton, Nov. 28, 1826, by William Bonney	13
Amos B., m. Delia A. **MONROE**, b. of New Canaan, Jan. 1, 1828, by William Bonney	17
David, m. Clarinda **LOCKWOOD**, b. of New Canaan, Oct. 17, 1832, by Rev. John Lovejoy	23
DONOVAN, Robert, of Bridgeport, m. Abigail **TUTTLE**, of New Canaan, Jan. 20, 1819, [Cong. Ch. Rec.]	192
DOSSAERD*, Henry, of Westport, m. Martha Ann **BATES**, of Darien, Nov. 24, 1852, in St. Marks Church, by W[illia]m Long *(Copied as nearly as made out. Written "DOWNING" in Index)	78
DOTY, Matilda, m. Lewis **CROSSMAN**, of Norwalk, Apr. 29, 1827, by William Bonney	14
Orrin A., m. Ann E. **BOUTON**, b. of New Canaan, Feb. 25, 1846, by Rev. Theophilus Smith	64
Orvin* **AMBROSE**, m. Lydia M. **HICKOK**, b. of New Canaan, Oct. 6, 1834, by Theophilus Smith *(Probably "Orrin")	27
DOWNES, Benjamin S., of Greenwich, m. Abigail **TYRRELL**, of New Canaan, Feb. 28, 1854, by Rev. L. D. Nickerson	81
DOWNING, Henry, see Henry **DOSSAERD**	
DRUMMOND, DRUMMON, William, m. Sally **JOHNSON**, May 17, 1820, [Cong. Ch. Rec.]	192
William, m. Mary Ann **CARTER**, b. of New Canaan, May 24, 1833, by Theophilus Smith	24
DUNNING, Henry, see under Henry **DOSSAERD**	
EDWARDS, Betsey, m. Aaron **CHICHESTER**, b. of Wilton, Mar. 24, 1833, by William Bonney	24
EELLS, EELS, ELLS, [see also **EETS**], Anne, m. Bille **BENEDICT**, Jan. 30, 1800	0
Betsey, m. Joseph **NORTHROP**, June 17, 1810, [Cong. Ch. Rec.]	191
George, m. Mary A. **BROWN**, Mar. 7, 1843, by Rev. Charles F. Pelton	60
H., of New Canaan, m. Daniel **BUTLER**, of Norwalk, Sept. 5, 1813, [Cong. Ch. Rec.]	191
James B., m. Ruth **BENEDICT**, Aug. 3, 1820, by William Bonney	4
James B., m. Ruth **BENEDICT**, Aug. 3, 1820, [Cong. Ch. Rec.]	192
Sally, m. James* **PERSEVIL**, b. of New Canaan, May 29, 1836, by Rev. Davis Stocking *(Written "John" in Index)	29
	191
-----, m. [ ] **FAIRBANKS**, [ ], [Cong. Ch. Rec.]	0
EETS, [see also **EELLS**], Betsey, m. Josiah **SMITH**, of Norwalk, Jan. 9, 1800	0
James I., m. Nancy **COMSTOCK**, b. of New Canaan, Feb. 22, 1802	
EVERETT, EVERET, EVERIT, EVORIT, Hannah, d. Joseph & Hannah, b.	

	Page
EVERETT, EVERET, EVERIT, EVORIT, (cont.)	
Sept. 7, 1801	189
Hannah, of New Canaan, m. Nathaniel **LOCKWOOD**, of Stamford, June 5, 1839, by Theophilus Smith	32
Juliett, of New Canaan, m. David B. **MATHER**, of Darien, Nov. 10, 1841, by Rev. Theophilus Smith	58
Samuel, of Salif, m. Anna **ST. JOHN**, Dec. 9, 1801	0
FAIRBANKS, -----, m. [ ] **EELLS**, [ ], [Cong. Ch. Rec.]	191
FAIRTEE, James, of New Canaan, m. Eliza **MONROE**, of New Canaan, Jan. 19, 1830, by Rev. Daniel DeVinne	20
FANCHER, Eliza, m. Henry **HUSTED**, Oct. 15, 1816, [Cong. Ch. Rec.]	192
George, m. Mary E. **BROWN**, of Norwalk, Sept. 5, 1841, by Peter Smith, J.P.	58
Jane, m. Riley A. **HOYT**, Oct. 13, 1825, by Rev. Origen P. Holcomb	11
Polly, m. Lewis **ST. JOHN**, b. of New Canaan, Apr. 10, 1833, by Theophilus Smith	24
Rufus, m. Antoinette **BENEDICT**, of New Canaan, Mar. 3, 1822, by William Bonney	8
Rufus, of Franklin, S.N., m. Scinthia **BENEDICT**, Mar. 30, 1800	0
Stephen, of South Salem, m. Catharine Jane **LOCKWOOD**, Oct. 27, 1831, by Theophilus Smith	21
FAYERWEATHER, FAIRWEATHER, Elizabeth Maria. of New Canaan, m. Julian M. Sturdevant (Rev.), of New Haven, Aug. 31, 1829, by William Bonney	17
Richard, of N.W., m. Hannah **RICHARDS**, Dec. 11, 1803	1
FELAND*, John, m. Prudence Lemira **HUSTED**, Mar. 20, 1832, by Theophilus Smith *(Written "PHELAND" in Index)	23
FERRIS, Mary, of New Canaan, m. Alfred B. **NASH**, of Troy, N.Y., June 3, 1847, by Rev. Theophilus Smith	65
FINCH, Abigail Ann, m. John B. **MILLER**, b. of New Canaan, Nov. 25, 1830, by Rev. Henry Fuller, of North Stamford	18
Betsey, d. Caleb & Abigail, b. Aug. 3, 1797	189
Caleb, s. Titus & Hannah, b. July 5, 1772	189
Caleb, m. Abigail **SCOFIELD**, Dec. 31, 1796	2
David, s. Titus & Hannah, b. Mar. 31, 1782	189
Edwin, m. Sally Ann **MUNROE**, b. of New Canaan, Sept. 17, 1837, by Theophilus Smith	31
Mary, m. David **BISHOP**, Nov. 22, 1795, [Cong. Ch. Rec.]	2
Polly, d. Caleb & Abigail, b. Feb. 24, 1799	189
Sherman, s. Caleb & Abigail, b. July 5, 1802	189
Thankful, b. July 24, 1766; m. Asahel **WEED**, [ ]	189
Thankful, m. Asahel **WEED**, May 16, 1793	2
FINDLEY, William J., m. Mary **BARACLOUGH**, b. of New Canaan, Oct. 20, 1834, by Theophilus Smith	27
FINNEY, FENNY, Alanson F., of Norwalk, m. Sally K. **ST. JOHN**, Apr. 22, 1819, [Cong. Ch. Rec.]	192
John A., of Stamford, m. Mary Ann **MERRITT**, of Stamford, Sept. 1, 1830, by Rev. Samuel Cochrane	19
FITCH, Clarinda, of New Canaan, m. James S. **AYRES**, of New York, Feb. 21, 1836, by Theophilus Smith	28
Hannah, m. David **BENEDICT**, Dec. 22, 1796	3
Hannah, of Canaan, m. Sherman **MITCHELL**, of Spence I., Jan. 5, 1806	1

NEW CANAAN VITAL RECORDS 219

	Page
FITCH, (cont.)	
Harry, m. Sally **INGERSOLL**, (colored), Nov. 27, 1799	0
Joseph, Jr., m. Sally **REED**, of New Canaan, Feb. 26, 1809	1
Leman, m. Caroline M. **KELLOGG**, b. of New Canaan, Dec. 13, 1820, by William Bonney	5
Leman, m. Caroline M. **KELLOGG**, Dec. 13, 1820, [Cong. Ch. Rec.]	192
Mabel, m. Hanford **CARTER**, Oct. 12, 1817, [Cong. Ch. Rec.]	192
Mary A., m. James I. **LOUNSBURY**, b. of New Canaan, Nov. 16, 1835, by Theophilus Smith	27
FLETCHER, Sarah, m. Sip **COMSTOCK** (colored), Jan. 12, 1818, [Cong. Ch. Rec.]	192
FOOT, Maria, m. David B. **HOYT**, b. of New Canaan, Feb. 12, 1840, by Theophilus Smith	33
FORBS, Cleopatra, of Brooklyn, N.Y., m. Nehemiah **STEVENS**, of New Canaan, Jan. 6, 1851, by Jacob Shaw	81
Cleopatra C., of Brooklyn, N.Y., m. Nehemiah **STEVENS**, of New Canaan, Jan. 6, 1851, by Jacob Shaw	73
GARNER, Mabel, m. John **TUTTLE**, Nov. 26, 1795, [Cong. Ch. Rec.]	2
GEDDIS, John A., m. Olive **GREGORY**, b. of New Canaan, Sept. 28, 1845, by Rev. Theophilus Smith	63
GILBERT, A[a]ron B., m. Zilpah **HOYT**, Feb. 3, 1822, by William Bonney	8
Caroline, of New Canaan, m. Nehemiah **GREGORY**, of Norwalk, Dec. 24, 1833, by Theophilus Smith	25
Daniel, of Wilton, m. Betsey **HARLBUTT**, of New Canaan, Sept. 20, 1826, by William Bonney	13
Delia, m. Daniel G. **WEED**, b. of New Canaan, Jan. 12, 1831, by Rev. Samuel Cochrane	22
GODFREY, [Ann]*, of New Canaan, m. Theophilas **PARTRICK**, of Ridgefield, May 5, 1830, by William Bonney *(Supplied from Index)	20
GREENBY, [see under **GREENLY**]	
GREENLY, GREENBY, Eliza, d. Thomas, of New Canaan, m. Isaac H. **LEWIS**, of New York, Sept. 29, 1834, by Theophilus Smith	27
Emma L., of New Canaan, m. Asahil S. **HOYT**, of Poundridge, N.Y. Oct. 13, 1852, by Rev. Theophilus Smith	80
Esther, m. Thomas **CARTER**, b. of New Canaan, July 21, 1824, by William Bonney	10
Julia E., of New Canaan, m. William **MCDUFFIE**, of Bedford, N.Y., Nov. 11, 1851, by Rev. Theophilus Smith	74
Matilda A., of New Canaan, m. Jacob **HOYT**, of Lewisboro, N.Y., Oct. 17, 1843, by Rev. Theophilus Smith	61
GREGORY, Fitch, m. Nancy **SEYMOUR**, Oct. 23, 1800	0
Nehemiah, of Norwalk, m. Caroline **GILBERT**, of New Canaan, Dec. 24, 1833, by Theophilus Smith	25
Olive, m. John A. **GEDDIS**, b. of New Canaan, Sept. 28, 1845, by Rev. Theophilus Smith	63
GRIFFETH, Henery B., of Norwalk, m. Louisa **REED**, of New Canaan, Sept. 18, 1825, by William Bonney	11
William, of Norwalk, m. Cynthia **ARNOLD**, of New Canaan, June 17, 1821, by William Bonney	6
GRIFFING, GRIFFIN, Abigail, m. Joseph **SCOFIELD**, b. New Canaan, May 4, 1831, by William Bonney	22
Seeley, m. Deborah S. **WEED**, Mar. 19, 1820, [Cong. Ch. Rec.]	192

	Page
GRUNBY, Esther, see Esther GREENBY	
GUERNSEY, GURNSEY, Jesse H., m. Clarry* PATRICK, July 21, 1830, by Aaron W. Whiting *(Written "Charry" in Index)	20
Walter, m. Polly NORTHROP, b. of New Canaan, Nov. 1, 1821, by Aaron Comstock, J.P.	7
HALL, William E., of Norwalk, m. Calsine PENNOYER, of New Canaan, Feb. 19, 1850, by Rev. D. H. Short	69
HAMILTON, Mary Ann, of New Canaan, m. William P. HAYES, of New Canaan, Apr. 11, 1847, by Rev. A. H. Furgerson	64
HANDS, Lucy, of New Canaan, m. Stephen B. MUNROE, of Stamford, Nov. 17, 1842, by Rev. Theophilus Smith	60
HANFORD, Abijah, of Norwalk, m. Nancy CHICHESTER, of New Canaan, Sept. 24, 1816, [Cong. Ch. Rec.]	192
Ann Frances, m. Bartholomew TRISTRAM, b. of New Canaan, Nov. 2, 1852, by Rev. Lorenzo D. Nickerson	78
Benjamin F.*, m. Mary L. REED, b. of New Canaan, Oct. 6, 1846, by Rev. A. H. Ferguson *(Written "Benjamin F. HANFRED" in Index)	64
Deborah, m. Daniel CONLEY, b. of New Canaan, Nov. 8, 1821, by William Bonney	7
Eliphalet, of New Canaan, m. Calsine AYRES, of Wilton, Nov. 25, 1823, by Rev. William Bonney	9
Elizabeth, m. Charles LOUNSBURY, b. of New Canaan, Apr. 29, 1851, by Rev. Jacob Shaw	73
Elizabeth, m. Charles LOUNSBURY, b. of New Canaan, Apr. 29, 1851, by Rev. Jacob Shaw	81
Emily, m. Harvey BOUTON, b. of New Canaan, Oct. 18, 1826, by William Bonney	14
Eveline, Mrs., m. Stephen SEELY, of Norwalk, Apr. 7, 1841, in St. Marks Church, by David Ogden	56
George M., of Wilton, m. Caroline E. CARTER, of New Canaan, Apr. 6, 1852, by Rev. Jacob Shaw	77
Hannah, m. Martin HANFORD, Aug. 25, 1799	3
Jaber, of Norwalk, m. Abigal RICHARDS, Aug. [ ], 1803	1
Juliet, m. James H. HOYT, Nov. 28, 1823, by Rev. Eli Denniston	9
Lucretia, m. Holly SEYMOUR, Dec. 19, 1810, [Cong. Ch. Rec.]	191
Lydia, of New Canaan, m. Alanson HOYT, of Litchfield, Oct. 19, 1834, by William Bonney	26
Martin, m. Hannah HANFORD, Aug. 25, 1799	3
Nathan, m. Mary ST. JOHN, Oct. 8, 1795, [Cong. Ch. Rec.]	2
Sally, of New Canaan, m. Harvey SAUNDERS, of Norwalk, Nov. 24, 1819, [Cong. Ch. Rec.]	192 191
Sarah, m. Ezra SEYMOUR, Sr., June 24, 1810, [Cong. Ch. Rec.]	2
Thaddeus, m. Sally ST. JOHN, Mar. [ ], 1796, [Cong. Ch. Rec.]	
HARROWAY, Elias, of New York, m. Dinah THOMPSON, Dec. 2, 1819, [Cong. Ch. Rec.]	192
HAUGHTON*, George Washington, of New York City, m. Ann Comstock ST. JOHN, of New Canaan, Nov. 16, 1826, by William Bonney *(Written "HOUGHTON" in Index)	13
HAWLEY, Alanson, of Monroe, m. Polly DEFOREST, of New Canaan, Apr. 28, 1839, by Watts Comstock, J.P.	32
Eliza J., of Darien, m. Daniel SMITH, of Stamford, Jan. 26, 1853, by Rev. Lorenzo D. Nickerson	78

NEW CANAAN VITAL RECORDS   221

	Page
HAYES, Cunnence*, of New Canaan, m. Harvey **CAMP**, of Norwalk, Oct. 6, 1818, [Cong. Ch. Rec.] *(Currence?)	192
Hannah, m. Ebenezer **HOIT**, Feb. 24, 1796, [Cong. Ch. Rec.]	2
Mary, wid., m. Mathew **HOYT**, Apr. [ ], 1817, [Cong. Ch. Rec.]	192
Matilda, of New Canaan, m. Edward **AYRES**, of Norwalk, Apr. 21, 1839, by Rev. Lyman H. Atwater	31
William P., of New Canaan, m. Mary Ann **HAMILTON**, of New Canaan, Apr. 11, 1847, by Rev. A. H. Furgerson	64
HEATH, Benjamin N., m. Sarah **ST. JOHN**, b. of New Canaan, Jan. 1, 1840, by Theophilus Smith	33
Benjamin N., m. Julia **HOYT**, b. of New Canaan, Oct. 9, 1850, by Rev. Theophilus Smith	71
HENDRIX, HENDRICK, Abigail, of New Canaan, m. William **POWERS**, Mar. 11, 1804	1
David, m. Sally **HOIT**, Jan. 4, 1800	0
Salome, m. Isaac **PERRY**, of Weston, Mar. 10, 1800	0
HICKOK, Amanda, m. Lambert **HOYT**, b. of New Canaan, Nov. 28, 1822, by William Bonney	8
Huldah, m. Chauncy **HOYT**, b. of New Canaan, Nov. 23, 1825, by William Bonney	11
Keziah, d. Dea. Seth, m. Elias **LOCKWOOD**, s. Northrop, Nov. 6, 1833, by Theophilus Smith	25
Lydia M., m. Orrin* Ambrose **DOTY**, b. of New Canaan, Oct. 6, 1834, by Theophilus Smith *(Orvin)	27
Margaret*, m. John **UNCLES**, b. of New Canaan, Jan. 5, 1846, by Rev. Theophilus Smith *(Written "Margaret G." in Index)	63
Martha E., of New Canaan, m. Franklin B. **TAYLOR**, of Warren, Apr. 14, 1840, by Theophilus Smith	34
Peninnah, m. Silas **OLMSTEAD**, Mar. 31, 1812, [Cong. Ch. Rec.]	191
Preson, s. Seth & Kezia, b. Feb. 22, 1802	189
Seth, m. Elizabeth **BENEDICT**, Mar. 26, 1810, [Cong. Ch. Rec.]	191
HOLMES, James, m. Anna **WEED**, Dec. 27, 1797	3
HOUGHTON, George Washington, see under George Washington **HAUGHTON**	
HOWEL, William M., of Hector, Tompkins Co., N.Y., m. Esther **ST. JOHN**, of New Canaan, Apr. 21, 1839, by Rev. Lyman H. Atwater	31
HOWLET, Herman, of Philadelphia, m. Hannah **STEVENS**, of New Canaan, Mar. 13, 1820, [Cong. Ch. Rec.]	192
HOYT, HOIT, Alanson, of Litchfield, m. Lydia **HANFORD**, of New Canaan, Oct. 19, 1834, by William Bonney	26
Asahil S., of Poundridge, N.Y., m. Emma L. **GREENLY**, of New Canaan, Oct. 13, 1852, by Rev. Theophilus Smith	80
Benjamin, m. Sally C. **HOYT**, b. of New Canaan, Oct. 13, 1828, by William Bonney	16
Betsey, m. Rufus **WEED**, b. of New Canaan, Oct. 29, 1820, by G. S. Webb	5
Bouton, m. Thankful **BENEDICT**, Feb. 8, 1800	0
Charles, of Pound Ridge, m. Lydia H. [ ], Nov. 25, 1804	1
Charlotte, m. Daniel **ST. JOHN**, b. of New Canaan, Oct. 15, 1826, by William Bonney	14
Chauncy, m. Huldah **HICKOK**, b. of New Canaan, Nov. 23, 1825, by William Bonney	11
Clarina B., m. Lewis B. **AYRES**, b. of New Canaan, Sept. 6, 1840, by	

HOYT, HOIT, (cont.)

	Page
Theophilus Smith	34
Clarissa, m. Samuel B.* **HOYT**, b. of New Canaan, Sept. 26, 1847, by Rev. Theophilus Smith *(Written "R." in Index)	65
Darius M., of New Canaan, m. Phebe **BELL**, of Darien, Sept. 22, 1844, by Rev. Theophilus Smith	63
David, m. Hannah **JENNINGS**, b. of New Canaan, Nov. 18, 1832, by Theophilus Smith	23
David B., m. Maria **FOOT**, b. of New Canaan, Feb. 12, 1840, by Theophilus Smith	33
Deborah, of Canaan, m. [ ] **WASHBORN**, Mar. 30, 1802	0
Deborah, m. Gilbert **MARSHALL**, b. of New Canaan, Oct. 21, 1834, by Rev. Abraham S. Francis	26
Ebenezer, m. Hannah **HAYES**, Feb. 24, 1796, [Cong. Ch. Rec.]	2
Eliza J., of New Canaan, m. Chauncey **RUSCO**, of South Salem, N.Y., Oct. 17, 1839, by Theophilus Smith	33
Elizabeth, m. Lewis **HOIT**, Sept. 17, 1797	3
Emily, d. Samuel, m. Andrew **BENEDICT**, s. Jonathan B., b. of New Canaan, Oct. 15, 1833, by Theophilus Smith	25
Ester, m. Jonathan **WARING**, Sept. [ ], 1797	3
Esther, m. Anson R.* **BENEDICT**, b. of New Canaan, Sept. 1, 1844, by Peter Smith, J.P. *(Written "Anson B." in Index)	63
Ezra, of Wilton, m. Pennina **AICCOX**, of Canaan, Apr. 21, 1798	3
Hannah, of Stamford, m. Daniel **BOUTON**, of New Canaan, Oct. 17, 1803, by Rev. Daniel Smith. Witness Aaron Bouton	2
Hannah, m. Alfred **SEELY**, b. of New Canaan, Oct. 25, 1820, by G. S. Webb	5
Hannah E., of New Canaan, m. Lewis S. **OLMSTED**, of Wilton, Oct. 30, 1850, by Rev. Jacob Shaw	71
Hetty, m. Elias **LOCKWOOD**, b. of New Canaan, June 21, 1821, by William Bonney	6
Jacob, of Lewisboro, N.Y., m. Matilda A. **GREENLY**, of New Canaan, Oct. 17, 1843, by Rev. Theophilus Smith	61
James H., m. Juliet **HANFORD**, Nov. 28, 1823, by Rev. Eli Denniston	9
Jane A., of New Canaan, m. Edward A. **KNAPP**, of Greenwich, Nov. 16, 1842, by Rev. Theophilus Smith	60
Jesse, of New Canaan, m. Charlotte **WEBB**, of Ridgefield, Feb. 10, 1833, by William Bonney	24
Joel, m. Esther **RICHARDS**, Jan. 17, 1799	3
Joel, m. Mercy **SCOFIELD**, b. of New Canaan, Sept. 10, 1828, by William Bonney	16
Julia A., m. Benjamin N. **HEATH**, b. of New Canaan, Oct. 9, 1850, by Rev. Theophilus Smith	71
Justus, Jr., m. Sally **BETTS**, b. of New Canaan, Oct. 28, 1821, by William Bonney	7
Lambert, m. Amanda **HICKOK**, b. of New Canaan, Nov. 28, 1822, by William Bonney	8
Lambert, of New Canaan, m. Sally A. **MILLER**, of Patterson, N.J., Jan. 6, 1850, by Rev. Theophilus Smith	69
Lewis, m. Elizabeth **HOIT**, Sept. 17, 1797	3
Lewis K., m. Sarah G. **SLAWSON**, b. of New Canaan, Sept. 25, 1842, by Rev. Charles F. Pelton	59

	Page
HOYT, HOIT, (cont.)	
Lois, m. Moses **COMSTOCK**, Sept. 23, 1805	1
Mary, m. Andrew **MESSNARD**, Jan. 1, 1797	3
Mathew, m. wid. Mary **HAYES**, Apr. [ ], 1817, [Cong. Ch. Rec.]	192
Mehetabil, m. George **SELLECK**, Dec. 1, 1819, [Cong. Ch. Rec.]	192
Nancy, m. Minott **CROFOOT**, b. of New Canaan, Apr. 1, 1840, by Rev. Cyrus Fon	34
Phebe, m. Joseph **PIATT**, of Stuben, Feb. 20, 1800	0
Polly, m. Nathaniel **STERLING**, of Wilton, May 7, 1801	0
Polly, m. Lyman **BROWN**, Oct. 10, 1826, by William Bonney	12
Polly*, m. Rodney S. **LOCKWOOD**, June 2, 1828, by William Bonney. *(Written "Polly A. **HOYT**" in Index)	16
Riley A., m. Jane **FANCHER**, Oct. 13, 1825, by Rev. Origen P. Holcomb	11
Sally, m. David **HENDRIX**, Jan. 4, 1800	0
Sally C., m. Benjamin **HOYT**, b. of New Canaan, Oct. 13, 1828, by William Bonney	16
Samuel B.*, m. Clarissa **HOYT**, b. of New Canaan, Sept. 26, 1847, by Rev. Theophilus Smith *(Written "R." in Index)	65
Sarah, of New Canaan, m. Lockwood **PALMER**, of Stamford, Oct. 28, 1821, by Rev. Henry Fuller, of North Stamford	7
Selleck, of Stamford, m. wid. Mary **STEVENS**, of New Canaan, Oct. 18, 1830, by Rev. Henry Fuller, of North Stamford	19
Stephen, Jr., m. Siley **BENEDICT**, b. of New Canaan, Oct. 29, 1823, by William Bonney	9
Susan, m. William L. **WARING**, b. of New Canaan, Aug. 28, 1836, by Theophilus Smith	29
Thankful Mariah, of New Canaan, m. Timothy **MARVIN**, of Churlton, N.Y., Apr. 16, 1844, by Rev. Theophilus Smith	62
William, m. Sarah **WEED**, Nov. 19, 1822, by William Bonney	8
William B., of Lewisboro, Westchester Co., N.Y., m. Elizabeth **BOUTON**, of New Canaan, Dec. 11, 1842, by Peter Smith, J.P.	60
Zalmon, m. Sally **BENEDICT**, Oct. 25, 1820, by William Bonney	4
Zalmon, m. Sally **BENEDICT**, Oct. 25, 1820, [Cong. Ch. Rec.]	192
Zilpah, m. A[a]ron B. **GILBERT**, Feb. 3, 1822, by William Bonney	8
-----, of North Stamford, m. Samuel **CRISSEY**, Sept. 28, 1797	3
HUBBARD, John, of Darien, m. Louisania* **SELLECK**, of New Canaan, (colored), Jan. 23 (?), 1830, by William Bonney *(Written "Lousannia" in Index)	20
	0
HUNT, Daniel, of Salem, m. Hannah **SILLIC**, Dec. 25, 1799	
Samuel, of Teroksbury, Mass., m. Eliza **CARTER**, of New Canaan, Sept. 26, 1814, [Cong. Ch. Rec.]	191
	0
HUNTINGTON, Jonathan, m. Dinah **SILLIMAN**, Nov. 25, 1800	
HURLBUTT, HARLBUTT, Betsey, of New Canaan, m. Daniel **GILBERT**, of Wilton, Sept. 20, 1826, by William Bonney	13
Hannah, m. Andrew **STEVENS**, b. of New Canaan, Feb. 25, 1827, by William Bonney	15
Sarah M., m. Album J. **SIMS**, b. of New Canaan, July 1, 1850, by Rev. Theophilus Smith	192
HUSTED, Abigail, of Stamford, m. Charles G. **SMITH**, of New Canaan, May 14, 1821, by William Bonney	6
Abigail, of Stamford, m. Charles G. **SMITH**, May 14, 1821, [Cong. Ch. Rec.]	192

	Page
HUSTED, (cont.)	
Caroline A., of New Canaan, m. Augustus **PAGE**, of New Haven, Apr. 26, 1853, in St. Marks Church, by Rev. William Long	80
Henry, m. Eliza **FANCHER**, Oct. 15, 1816, [Cong. Ch. Rec.]	192
Mary Elizabeth, m. William Henry **WHEELER**, b. of New Canaan, Sept. 28, 1840, by Theophilus Smith	55
Polly, m. Matthias **BENEDICT**, Sept. 18, 1803	1
Prudence Lemira, m. John **FELAND***, Mar. 20, 1832, by Theophilus Smith *(Written "**PHELAND**" in Index)	23
Thomas S., m. Prudence **CRISSEY**, Jan. 24, 1813, [Cong. Ch. Rec.]	191
William Edmund, m. Mary Jane **BENEDICT**, Sept. 1, 1851, by Rev. D. H. Short	74
INGERSOLL, Sally, m. Harry **FITCH** (colored), Nov. 27, 1799	0
ISHAM, Chester, Rev. of Taunton, Mass., m. Diana **COMSTOCK**, of New Canaan, Apr. 21, 1824, by William Bonney	10
JARVIS, Charlotte, m. John **SEYMOUR**, Dec. 12, 1810, [Cong. Ch. Rec.]	191
JENNINGS, Aaron, of New York, m. Sally **SEELY**, of New Canaan, Oct. 6, 1813, [Con. Ch. Rec.]	191
Caroline E., m. Aaron C. **SEELY**, b. of New Canaan, July 15, 1850, by Rev. Theophilus Smith	70
Cynthia E., m. Eber **STEVENS**, Sept. 16, 1821, by William Bonney	7
Hannah, m. David **HOYT**, b. of New Canaan, Nov. 18, 1832, by Theophilus Smith	23
Jesup Taylor, of Fairfield, m. Isabella **SEELY**, of New Canaan, Mar. 27, 1821, by William Bonney	5
Jessup Taylor, m. Isabella **SEELEY**, Mar. 27, 1821, [Cong. Ch. Rec.]	192
Sally, m. Harvey **MUNROW**, b. of New Canaan, Nov. 11, 1821, by William Bonney	7
JESUP, Zadoc R., of Charleston, S.C., m. Gertrude **RICHARDS**, of New Canaan, May 4, 1848, by Rev. Theophilus Smith	67
JOHNSON, Albinus, m. Polly **DEFOREST**, Oct. 10, 1822, by William Bonney	8
Charles, of Norwalk, m. Joanna S. **RICHARDS**, of New Canaan, June 8, 1836, by Rev. I. Lyman Clark	29
Hannah K., Mrs. of New Canaan, m. Henry S. **OSBORNE**, of Haverstraw, N.Y., Mar. 27, 1853, in St. Marks Church, by Rev. William Long	80
James, of Darien, m. Hannah R.* **WEED**, of New Canaan, Dec. 13, 1840, by David Ogden *(Perhaps "K"?)	56
Polly A., of New Canaan, m. Abijah F. **TAYLOR**, of New York, June 14, 1830, by William Bonney	19
Sally, m. William **DRUMMON**, May 17, 1820, [Cong. Ch. Rec.]	192
JONES, Charles, of Dantown, m. Julia Ann **BUXTON**, of New Canaan, Feb. 10, 1839, by Samuel W. King	31
Charlotte, m. James A. **SMALLHORN**, Nov. 21, 1853, by Rev. L. D. Nickerson	81
Jemima, m. Eli **BIRCHARD**, Nov. 21, 1853, by Rev. L. D. Nickerson	81
Nathan, of Norwalk, Ohio, m. Mrs. Maria **DAN**, of New Canaan, Oct. 26, 1851, by Rev. Jacob Shaw	75
Patty, m. Ishmael **TUCKER**, Oct. 8, 1809, [Cong. Ch. Rec.]	191
Selleck, of Stamford, m. Maria **CRISSY**, of New Canaan, Jan. 18, 1829, by Rev. Harvey Fuller, of North Stamford	17
JUDSON, Charles, m. Betsey **STEVENS**, b. of New Canaan, Nov. 14, 1827, by	

	Page
JUDSON, (cont.)	
William Bonney	15
Samuel, m. Sarah **TUTTLE**, Dec. 28, 1825, by William Bonney	11
KEELER, Anna, of Ridgbury, m. Aaron **BOUTON**, of New Canaan, Oct. 6, 1807, by Rev. Samuel Goodrich. Witnesses Daniel Bouton & Abigail Keeler	2
Daniel, m. Mary **PONOIER**, Oct. 2, 1798	3
Ester, m. Uriah **RICHARDS**, Sept. 17, 1800	0
Phebe, m. William G. **WEBB**, b. of New Canaan, Sept. 11, 1838, by Theophilus Smith	31
Phebe Baxter, m. Hezekiah **ST. JOHN**, Jr., Aug. 20, 1798	3
Sally, m. John **SLAUSON**, Sept. 23, 1817, [Cong. Ch. Rec.]	192
Sally, of New Canaan, m. Rufus **SEYMOUR**, of Wilton, Mar. 26, 1834, by Theophilus Smith	26
Smith B., of Ridgefield, m. Hannah **BENEDICT**, d. Ezra, of New Canaan, Aug. 4, 1834, by Theophilus Smith	26
-----, Capt., m. Mary **ST. JOHN**, Jan. [ ], 1812, [Cong. Ch. Rec.]	191
KELLOGG, Abbey, of Canaan, m. Ezra **AYRES**, of Poundridge, Nov. 16, 1796, [Cong. Ch. Rec.]	2
Caroline M., m. Leman **FITCH**, b. of New Canaan, Dec. 13, 1820, by William Bonney	5
Caroline M., m. Leman **FITCH**, Dec. 13, 1820, [Cong. Ch. Rec.]	192
Hannah, of Norwalk, m. Minott **AYRES**, of New Canaan, Apr. 10, 1821, by William Bonney	5
Hannah, of Norwalk, m. Minott **AYRES**, Apr. 10, 1821, [Cong. Ch. Rec.]	192
Mary, m. David **LOCKWOOD**, Feb. 21, 1810, [Cong. Ch. Rec.]	191
Matthew, of Norwalk, m. Sally **SEELY**, of New Canaan, June 13, 1821, by William Bonney	6
Matthew, of Norwalk, m. Sally **SEELY**, of New Canaan, June 13, 1821, [Cong. Ch. Rec.]	192
Matthew, m. Electa **CROFOOT**, b. of New Canaan, Nov. 21, 1830, by Rev. Daniel I. Wright	18
Seth, m. Matilda **LOCKWOOD**, Jan. 4, 1799	3
KNAPP, NAP, Charles, m. Betsey **DAVENPORT**, of Wilton, Dec. 29, 1800	0
Edward A., of Greenwich, m. Jane A. **HOYT**, of New Canaan, Nov. 16, 1842, by Rev. Theophilus Smith	60
KNIGHT, NIGHT, Darius, m. Hannah **ST. JOHN**, June 22, 1797	3
LAMBERT, Jane, of New Canaan, m. Edward B. **OSBORNE**, of Danbury, Oct. 7, 1840, by E. P. Vrmby, Elder, of New York	55
Robert, m. Mary E. **BENEDICT**, b. of New Canaan, May 27, 1840, by Theophilus Smith	34
LEWIS, Emeline, m. James S. **BOUTON**, b. of New Canaan, May 5, 1851, by Rev. D. H. Short	73
Isaac, of Huntington, m. Polly **CRAFTE**, Sept. 24, 1797	3
Isaac H., of New York, m. Eliza **GREENLY**, d. Thomas, of New Canaan, Sept. 29, 1834, by Theophilus Smith	27
LINES, Mariah, m. Rufus **BENEDICT**, b. of New Canaan, Feb. 9, 1851, by Rev. Theophilus Smith	72
Susan, of Redding, m. Samuel W. **STEVINS**, of New Canaan, Oct. 3, 1847, by Rev. D. H. Short	66
LINN, Martha Y.*, of New Canaan, m. Benjamin **SMITH**, of Bridgeport, May 16, 1852, by Rev. Jacob Shaw *(Written "Martha J." in Index)	77

LION, [see under LYON]
LOCKWOOD, Aaron, of Redding, m. Polly STEVENS, of New Canaan, Oct. 9, 1839, by Rev. S. W. King — 32
Anna, of New Canaan, m. Dennis BELDEN, of Troy, Apr. 15, 1813, [Cong. Ch. Rec.] — 191
Carlile, m. Mary Ann CHICHESTER, b. of New Canaan, Oct. 8, 1823, by William Bonney — 9
Catharine Jane, m. Stephen FANCHER, of South Salem, Oct. 27, 1831, by Theophilus Smith — 21
Chauncey R.*, s. Samuel, of New Canaan, m. Polly Ann TERREL, of Wilton, May 4, 1834, by Theophilus Smith   *(Written "Chauncey K." in Index) — 26
Clarinda, m. David DICKENS, b. of New Canaan, Oct. 17, 1832, by Rev. John Lovejoy — 23
David, m. Elizabeth RICHARDS, Dec. 27, 1804 — 1
David, m. Mary KELLOGG, Feb. 21, 1810, [Cong. Ch. Rec.] — 191
Edwin, m. Sarah PENNOYER, b. of New Canaan, Jan. 19, 1826, by Rev. A. S. Todd, of Stamford — 12
Elias, m. Hetty HOYT, b. of New Canaan, June 21, 1821, by William Bonney — 6
Elias, s. Northrop, m. Keziah HICKOK, d. Dea. Seth, Nov. 6, 1833, by Theophilus Smith — 25
Elizabeth R., m. Lewis G. STEELE, Oct. 23, 1831, by Chauncey Wilcox — 21
George, m. Amelia RAYMOND, b. of New Canaan, Nov. 14, 1847, by Rev. D. H. Short — 66
Hannah, m. Amos AYRES, Nov. 26, 1797 — 3
Harvey, m. Susan NASH, Feb. 27, 1820, [Cong. Ch. Rec.] — 192
James Nelson, m. Nancy LOCKWOOD, b. of New Canaan, June 23, 1853, by Rev. L. D. Nickerson — 80
John, m. [   ] WEED, of North Stamford, Dec. 24, 1809, [Cong. Ch. Rec.] — 191
Julia Eliza, m. James Hervey CHICHESTER, b. of New Canaan, Jan. 24, 1827, by Rev. Orin P. Holcomb — 14
Mary Adeline, of New Canaan, m. David C. BROWN, of Stamford, [   ], by Rev. David H. Short. Recorded Jan. 1, 1851 — 71
Matilda, m. Seth KELLOGG, Jan. 4, 1799 — 3
Michael, m. Selina NASH, b. of New Canaan, Feb. 1, 1824, by William Bonney — 10
Nancy, m. James Nelson LOCKWOOD, b. of New Canaan, June 23, 1853, by Rev. L. D. Nickerson — 80
Nathaniel, of Stamford, m. Hannah EVERET, of New Canaan, June 5, 1839, by Theophilus Smith — 32, 191
Phebe, m. David CHICHESTER, Aug. 26, 1813, [Cong. Ch. Rec.] — 0
Polly, m. Jared AYRES, Feb. 20, 1800
Polly, m. Thomas A. COMSTOCK, b. of New Canaan, Oct. 10, 1836, by Theophilus Smith — 30
Rodney S., m. Polly* HOYT, June 2, 1828, by William Bonney   *(Written "Polly A. HOYT" in Index) — 16
S. M., of Stamford, m. Mary E. AYRES, of New Canaan, Dec. 12, 1850, by Rev. Theophilus Smith — 72
Sarah, of New Canaan, m. A[a]ron DAVIS, of Stamford, May 2, 1816, [Cong. Ch. Rec.] — 192

	Page
LOCKWOOD, (cont.)	
Sarah, m. Benjamin **SMITH**, b. of New Canaan, [Feb.] 26, [1824], by Rev. Origen P. Holcomb	10
Sarah, of New Canaan, m. Lewis **STEBBINS**, of Ithica, N.Y., Sept. 4, 1836, by Theophilus Smith	29
Sarah L., of New Canaan, m. Samuel B. **MIDDLEBROOK**, of Wilton, Oct. 10, 1854, in St. Marks Church, by Rev. William Long	81
LOUNSBURY, Charles, of Stamford, m. Sally Ann **WEED**, of New Canaan, Mar. 23, 1841, by David Ogden	56
Charles, m. Elizabeth **HANFORD**, b. of New Canaan, Apr. 29, 1851, by Rev. Jacob Shaw	73
Charles, m. Elizabeth **HANFORD**, b. of New Canaan, Apr. 29, 1851, by Rev. Jacob Shaw	81
James I., m. Mary A. **FITCH**, b. of New Canaan, Nov. 16, 1835, by Theophilus Smith	27
John, m. Sally **CRANE**, of Wilton, Oct. 21, 1813, [Cong. Ch. Rec.]	191
Minor, m. Polly **BOUTON**, b. of New Canaan, Dec. 24, 1828, by William Bonney	16
Rhuamy, of Prattsville, N.Y., m. Minott **CROFOOT**, of New Canaan, Dec. 23, 1852, by Rev. S. VanDusen. Witnesses A. M. Hought & Elizabeth Vandusen	80
Sidney R., of Stamford, m. Hannah C. **ROOT**, of New Canaan, Mar. 21, 1852, by Rev. Theophilus Smith	76
William Henry, of New York City, m. Ann Eliza **TAYLOR**, of New Canaan, Nov. 13, 1851, by Rev. Jacob Shaw	75
LYON, LION, Moses, of Wilton, m. Irena **BENEDICT**, Aug. 18, 1799	3
MCCAULEY, Grace, m. Ned **NOYES**, negro, Dec. 9, 1804	1
MCDUFFIE, William, of Bedford, N.Y., m. Julia E. **GREENLY**, of New Canaan, Nov. 11, 1851, by Rev. Theophilus Smith	74
MANNING, Robbert, negro, m. Rose **COMSTOCK**, Nov. [ ], 1803	1
MARSHALL, Gilbert, m. Deborah **HOYT**, b. of New Canaan, Oct. 21, 1834, by Rev. Abraham S. Francis	26
Hickford, of New York, m. Polly **CRISSEY**, of New Canaan, Sept. 12, 1833, by Rev. Henry Fuller, of North Stamford	25
MARVIN, James H., of Troy, N.Y., m. Mahettable H. **SELLECK**, of New Canaan, Mar. 28, 1842, by Rev. Theophilus Smith	58
Timothy, of Churlton, N.Y., m. Thankful Mariah **HOYT**, of New Canaan, Apr. 16, 1844, by Rev. Theophilus Smith	62
MATHER, David B., of Darien, m. Juliett **EVERETT**, of New Canaan, Nov. 10, 1841, by Rev. Theophilus Smith	58
MEAD, MEED, Joseph H., m. Sarah Jane **BEARDSLEY**, b. of New Canaan, June 6, 1847, by Rev. D. H. Short	65
Nehemiah, of Horse Neck, m. Ruth **RICHARDS**, Nov. 5, 1795, [Cong. Ch. Rec.]	2
MERRIL, John H., m. Adeline A. **SEYMOURE**, b. of New Canaan, Nov. 6, 1848, by Rev. Theophilus Smith	67
MERRITT, Mary Ann, of Stamford, m. John A. **FINNEY**, of Stamford, Sept. 1, 1830, by Rev. Samuel Cochrane	19
MESSENJER, Benoni Y., Rev. of Ohio, m. Caroline C. **AYRES**, May 31, 1830, by William Bonney	19
MESSNARD, Andrew, m. Mary **HOIT**, Jan. 1, 1797	3
MIDDLEBROOK, Samuel B., of Wilton, m. Sarah L. **LOCKWOOD**, of New	

	Page
MIDDLEBROOK, (cont.)	
Canaan, Oct. 10, 1854, in St. Marks Church, by Rev. William Long	81
MILLER, John B., m. Abigail Ann **FINCH**, b. of New Canaan, Nov. 25, 1830, by Rev. Henry Fuller, of North Stamford	18
Sally A., of Patterson, N.J., m. Lambert **HOYT**, of New Canaan, Jan. 6, 1850, by Rev. Theophilus Smith	69
Stephen I., m. Nancey **WEED**, b. of New Canaan, July 5, 1826, by Rev. Henery Fuller, of North Stamford	12
MILLS, Charlotte, of New Canaan, m. Morris **SANFORD**, of Reading, Nov. 12, 1826, by William Bonney	12
Charlotte, of New Canaan, m. Morris **SANFORD**, of Reading, Nov. 12, 1826, by William Bonney	13
Mary, d. Eldne, m. John **BENEDICT**, s. Caleb, b. of New Canaan, Apr. 26, 1835, by Theophilus Smith	27
-----, of North Stamford, m. [ ] **CRISSEY**, Dec. 2, 1804	1
MITCHELL, Betsey, of Canaan, m. Charles **THOMPSON**, of Spencer Town, Nov. 1, 1801	0
James, m. Harriet **CRISSY**, b. of New Canaan, Mar. 6, 1832, by Rev. Henry Fuller	23
Martha Ann, m. Joseph **SILLIMAN**, b. of New Canaan, Mar. 13, 1839, by Theophilus Smith	31
Sherman, of Spence, I., m. Hannah **FITCH**, of Canaan, Jan. 5, 1806	1
MONROE, MUNROW, Delia A., m. Amos B. **DICKENS**, b. of New Canaan, Jan. 1, 1828, by William Bonney	17
Eliza, of New Canaan, m. James **FAIRTEE**, of New Canaan, Jan. 19, 1830, by Rev. Daniel DeVinne	20
Harvey, m. Sally **JENNINGS**, b. of New Canaan, Nov. 11, 1821, by William Bonney	7
Lucius M., m. Sarah **WATERS**, b. of New Canaan, Jan. 13, 1851, by Rev. D. H. Short	76
Sally Ann, m. Edwin **FINCH**, b. of New Canaan, Sept. 17, 1837, by Theophilus Smith	31
Stephen B., of Stamford, m. Lucy **HANDS**, of New Canaan, Nov. 17, 1842, by Rev. Theophilus Smith	60
NASH, Abigail, of New Canaan, m. Aaron **STEVENS**, of Poundridge, Oct. 9, 1831, by Theophilus Smith	21
Alfred B., of Troy, N.Y., m. Mary **FERRIS**, of New Canaan, June 3, 1847, by Rev. Theophilus Smith	65
Arnet A., of Norwalk, m. Deborah **COMSTOCK**, of New Canaan, Dec. 28, 1828, by William Bonney	15, 192
Bradley, m. Deborah **BENEDICT**, July 2, 1817, [Cong. Ch. Rec.]	
Hannah C., m. Edward S. Ogden, of Fairfield, Nov. 12, 1842, by David Ogden	60
Merinda, of New Canaan, m. Chauncey **BARTO**, of Wilton, Oct. 15, 1820, by William Bonney	4
Merinda, of New Canaan, m. Chauncey **BARTO**, of Wilton, Oct. 15, 1820, [Cong. Ch. Rec.]	192
Nathan, of Middlesex, m. Barbary **BROWN**, Jan. 1, 1797	3
Selina, m. Michael **LOCKWOOD**, b. of New Canaan, Feb. 1, 1824, by William Bonney	10
Susan, m. Harvey **LOCKWOOD**, Feb. 27, 1820, [Cong. Ch. Rec.]	192
Susan, of New Canaan, m. P. Ashly **SIMONSON**, of New York, Jan. 6,	

NEW CANAAN VITAL RECORDS

	Page
NASH, (cont.)	
1851, by Rev. D. H. Short	72
William H.*, m. Charlotte **RAYMOND**, b. of New Canaan, Nov. 5, 1828, by William Bonney *(Written "K." in Index)	16
NEWELL, NEWEL, Allen R., of Pittsfield, Mass., m. Hannah **PENNOYER**, of New Canaan, Jan. 27, 1831, by William Bonney	22
Samuel M., of Mass., m. Hannah E. **ABBOTT**, Nov. 30, 1843, by David Ogden	62
NEWMAN, John, of Lewisboro, N.Y., m. Mary Elizabeth **SLAWSON**, of New Canaan, Nov. 25, 1846, by Rev. George Waterbury	64
NIGHT, [see under **KNIGHT**]	
NOBLE, Frederick, m. Sally M. **ST. JOHN**, Oct. [ ], 1819, [Cong. Ch. Rec.]	192
Frederick, m. Harriett **DEFOREST**, Jan. 30, 1833, by Theophilus Smith	24
NORMAN, Edward, of Norwalk, m. Nancy **WHALEY**, Mar. 19, 1804	1
NORTH, Benjamin, of Walton, N.Y., m. Hannah **CARTER**, of New Canaan, Sept. 26, 1814, [Cong. Ch. Rec.]	191
NORTHROP, Joseph, m. Betsey **EELLS**, June 17, 1810, [Cong. Ch. Rec.]	191
Polly, m. Walter **GURNSEY**, b. of New Canaan, Nov. 1, 1821, by Aaron Comstock, J.P.	7
NOYES, Ned, negro, m. Grace **MCCAULEY**, Dec. 9, 1804	1
OGDEN, Edward S., of Fairfield, m.Hannah C. **NASH**, Nov. 12, 1842, by David Ogden	60
George W., m. Maria **OLMSTED**, Feb. 25, 1844, by Daniel W. Bouton, J.P.	62
OLMSTED, OLMSTEAD, David, of Wilton, m. Esther **CLINTON**, Dec. 29, 1808	1
Hannah, of New Canaan, m. Isaac **SMITH**, of Greenville, Green Co., N.Y. Sept. 1, 1826, by William Bonney	12
Hezekiah, m. Rhoda **STEPHENS**, Sept. 29, 1805	1
Jalmes, of New Haven, m. Sophia **RICHARDS**, of New Canaan, Oct. 19, 1847, by Rev. Theophilus **SMITH**	66
Lewis S., of Wilton, m. Hannah E. **HOYT**, of New Canaan, Oct. 30, 1850, by Rev. Jacob Shaw	71
Maria, m. George W. **OGDEN**, Feb. 25, 1844, by Daniel W. Bouton, J.P.	62
Sally Ann, of New Canaan, m. Charles **PARKETON**, of Darien, Apr. 28, 1839, by Rev. William Biddle	32
Silas, m. Peninnah **HICKOK**, Mar. 31, 1812, [Cong. Ch. Rec.]	191
Smith W., of Wilton, m. Caroline **REED**, of New Canaan, Oct. 8, 1828, by Sylvanus Haight	16
OSBORN, OSBORNE, Edward B., of Danbury, m. Jane **LAMBERT**, of New Canaan, Oct. 7, 1840, by E. P. Vrmby, Elder, of New York	55
Henry S., of Haverstraw, N.Y., m. Mrs. Hannah K. **JOHNSON**, of New Canaan, Mar. 27, 1853, in St. Marks Church, by Rev. William Long	80
-----, of Weston, m. Sarah **SMITH**, of Canaan, Apr. 25, 1804	1
OSTRANDER, Jacob W., m. Sarah E. **SEELY**, b. of New Canaan, Sept. 30, 1850, by Rev. Theophilus Smith	71
PAGE, Augustus, of New Haven, m. Caroline A. **HUSTED**, of New Canaan, Apr. 26, 1853, in St. Marks Church, by Rev. William Long	80
PALMER, Eliza, of New Canaan, m. Edgar **BLOOMER**, of Stamford, Aug. 3, 1851, by Rev. Jacob Shaw	73
Lockwood, of Stamford, m. Sarah **HOYT**, of New Canaan, Oct. 28, 1821, by Rev. Henry Fuller, of North Stamford	7

	Page
PALMER, (cont.)	
Sally Ann, of Ridgefield, m. George W. **DEFOREST**, of New Canaan, June 8, 1834, by Theophilus Smith	26
PARKETON, Charles, of Darien, m. Sally Ann **OLMSTED**, of New Canaan, Apr. 28, 1839, by Rev. William Biddle	32
Leander S., m. Lucy A. **BARTOW**, b. of New Canaan, Dec. 7, 1849, by Rev. Theophilus Smith	68
PARSELS, Sally Ann, of New York, m. William **BUTTERY**, Jr., Aug. 13, 1832, by William Bonney	23
PARTRICK, Clarry*, m. Jesse H. **GUERNSEY**, July 21, 1830, by Aaron W. Whiting *("Charry" in Index)	20
Theophilas, of Ridgefield, m. [Ann*] **GODFREY**, of New Canaan, May 5, 1830, by William Bonney *(Supplied from Index)	20
PENDER, Julia Ann, m. Frederick **CROSBY**, b. of New Canaan, Nov. 2, 1842, by Charles F. Pelton	60
PENNOYER, PIONOYER, PONOIER, Calsine, of New Canaan, m. William E. Hall, of Norwalk, Feb. 19, 1850, by Rev. D. H. Short	69
Garrit, m. Eliza Jane **WATERBURY**, b. of New Canaan, Nov. 13, 1839, by Rev. Samuel W. King	34
Hannah, of New Canaan, m. Allen R. **NEWELL**, of Pittsfield, Mass. Jan. 27, 1831, by William Bonney	22
John, m. Betty **COMSTOCK**, Feb. 25, 1800	0
Mary, m. Daniel **KEELER**, Oct. 2, 1798	3
Polly, m. Hiram **CRISSEY**, b. of New Canaan, Jan. 15, 1823, by William Bonney	8
Sarah, of New Canaan, m. Daniel **BOSTWICK**, of Stanwich, Mar. 12, 1809	1
Sarah, m. Edwin **LOCKWOOD**, b. of New Canaan, Jan. 19, 1826, by Rev. A. S. Todd, of Stamford	12
PERKINS, Catharine A., m. Thomas **COMSTOCK**, b. of New Canaan, Sept. 3, 1850, by Rev. Jacob Shaw	70
PERRY, Isaac, of Weston, m. Salome **HENDRIX**, Mar. 10, 1800	0
PERSEVIL, PERCEVIL, James*, m. Sally **ELLS**, b. of New Canaan, May 29, 1836, by Rev. Davis Stocking *(Written "John" in Index)	29
John, see under James	
PETTIT, Betsey, of New Canaan, m. William **BIGSBY**, of Norwalk, Aug. 26, 1819, [Cong. Ch. Rec.]	192
PHELAND, John, see under John **FELAND**	0
PIATT, Joseph, of Stuben, m. Phebe **HOIT**, Feb. 20, 1800	
PLATT, Emily, of New Canaan, m. Levi **BROWN**, of Norwalk, Nov. 19, 1840, by Edwin Hall	55
POWERS, Andras, m. Deborah **COMSTOCK**, Nov. 2, 1797	3
Sally, m. Edmund **RAYMOND**, Aug. 14, 1803	0
William, m. Abigail **HENDRICK**, of New Canaan, Mar. 11, 1804	1
PRIME, Violet Ann, m. Pomp **SELLECK**, b. of New Canaan, May 18, 1835, by Theophilus Smith	27
PROVOST, William, Jr., m. Mariah **SCOFIELD**, b. of New Canaan, July 7, 1824, by Nobles W. Thomas, Elder	10
PURDY*, Berling D., of Stamford, m. Caroline **WILMOT**, of New Canaan, Oct. 30, 1836, by Rev. Davis Stocking *(Written "PERDY" in Index)	30
PURVIS, John, Rev., of Danbury, m. Lavina **AYRES**, of New Canaan, Apr. 10, [1844], in St. Marks Church, by David Ogden	63

NEW CANAAN VITAL RECORDS

	Page
RAYMOND, Amelia, m. George LOCKWOOD, b. of New Canaan, Nov. 14, 1847, by Rev. D. H. Short	66
Charles, m. Eliza WATSON, Sept. 30, 1833, by Rev. W. Patton, of New York. Witnesses Joseph William Hyne, Julia Hyne	57
Charles, Jr., s. Charles & Eliza, b. June 3, 1841	190
Charles S., m. Louisa WAKEMAN, b. of New Canaan, Sept. 15, 1850, by Rev. D. H. Short	70
Charlotte, m. William H.* NASH, b. of New Canaan, Nov. 5, 1828, by William Bonney *(Written "K." in Index)	16
Charlotte, d. Charles & Eliza, b. Oct. 9, 1837	190
Edmund, m. Sally POWERS, Aug. 14, 1803	0
Elliott, m. Ruth BOUTON, Feb. 20, 1821, by William Bonney	5
Elliott, m. Ruth BOUTON, Feb. [ ], 1821, [Cong. Ch. Rec.]	192
Francis C., m. Hannah M. WOOD, b. of New Canaan, Feb. 22, 1846, by Rev. Theophilus Smith	64
Hannah, of New Canaan, m. Henry CLOCK, of Darien, Jan. 9, 1821, by G. S. Webb	5
Harriet Elizabeth, of New Canaan, m. William DAMBY, of Ridgefield, Sept. 2, 1839, by [ ]	32
James W., s. Charles & Eliza, b. Apr. 12, 1835	190
John F., m. Deborah A. BENEDICT, b. of New Canaan, Sept. 11, 1825, by William Bonney	11
Julian, d. John, Jr. & Ruth, b. Jan. 29, 1802	189
Moses, m. Sarah J. BOSTWICK, b. of New Canaan, Sept. 4, 1839, by Theophilus Smith	32
Polly Asenath, d. Russel G., of New Canaan, m. Samuel SCRIBNER, of Wilton, Jan. 1, 1834, by Theophilus Smith	25
Roswel A., of Norwalk, m. Matilda COMSTOCK, of New Canaan, Feb. 22, 1837, by Rev. Edwin Hall, of Norwalk	30
Russell G., m. Sally M. DAN, b. of New Canaan, Dec. 14, 1835, by Rev. Davis Stocking	28
REED, Caroline, of New Canaan, m. Smith W. OLMSTED, of Wilton, Oct. 8, 1828, by Sylvanus Haight	16
Jacob, m. Ruth BENEDICT, of Canaan, May 5, 1803	0
Jesse, of Clinton, S.N., m. Hannah SEELEY, of N.E., Dec. 29, 1802	0
Lebens, of Canaan, m. Abby DAVENPORT, of North Stamford, Oct. [ ], 1795, [Cong. Ch. Rec.]	2
Louisa, of New Canaan, m. Henery B. GRIFFETH, of Norwalk, Sept. 18, 1825, by William Bonney	11
Mary L., m. Benjamin F. HANFORD*, b. of New Canaan, Oct. 6, 1846, by Rev. A. H. Ferguson *(Written "HANFRED" in Index)	64
Sally, m. Joseph FITCH, Jr., Feb. 26, 1809	1
	1
RICHARDS, Abigal, m. Jaber HANFORD, of Norwalk, Aug. [ ],1803	
Alfred, m. Ardima STEVENS, b. of New Canaan, Feb. 23, 1840, by Rev. Samuel W. King	33
Elizabeth, m. David LOCKWOOD, Dec. 27, 1804	1
Esther, m. Joel HOIT, Jan. 17, 1799	3
Gertrude, of New Canaan, m. Zadoc R. JESUP, of Charleston, S.C., May 4, 1848, by Rev. Theophilus Smith	67
Grace, of New Canaan, m. Benjamin BELDEN, of Wilton, (colored), Mar. 24, 1831, by William Bonney	22
	3
Hannah, of Canaan, m. Samuel ST. JOHN, Mar. 1, 1798	

	Page
RICHARDS, (cont.)	
Hannah, m. Richard **FAIRWEATHER**, of N.W., Dec. 11, 1803	1
Joanna S., of New Canaan, m. Charles **JOHNSON**, of Norwalk, June 8, 1836, by Rev. I. Lyman Clark	29
Lewis, m. Mary **SELLECK**, b. of New Canaan, Jan. 17, 1827, by William Bonney	14
Mary, of New Canaan, m. Harvey **DEFOREST**, of Wilton, Sept. 18, [1854], by Rev. I. P. Lestrade, of New York	81
Rufus, m. Mary **BENEDICT**, b. of New Canaan, May 25, 1826, by William Bonney	11
Ruth, m. Nehemiah **MEED**, of Horse Neck, Nov. 5, 1795, [Cong. Ch. Rec.]	2
Sophia, of New Canaan, m. William G. **WOOD**, of Skanesteles, N.Y., Jan. 31, 1815, [Cong. Ch. Rec.]	191
Sophia, of New Canaan, m. Jalmes **OLMSTED**, of New Haven, Oct. 19, 1847, by Rev. Theophilus Smith	66
Uriah, m. Ester **KEELER**, Sept. 17, 1800	0
RITTER, Thomas, Dr. of Wethersfield, m. Delia M. **AYRES**, of New Canaan, June 16, 1830, by S. Haight	19
ROCKWELL, Isaac, of Salem, m. Polly **HOWES**, of Canaan, Sept. 15, 1796	3
ROOT, Angeline E., m. William E. **AKIN**, b. of New Canaan, Oct. 28, 1840, by Theophilus Smith	55
Hannah C., of New Canaan, m. Sidney R. **LOUNSBURY**, of Stamford, Mar. 21, 1852, by Rev. Theophilus Smith	76
RUNDSEY, Daniel, of Balls Town, m. Isabel **HOWS**, of Canaan, Apr. 21, 1796, [Cong. Ch. Rec.]	2
RUSCO, Chauncey, of South Salem, N.Y., m. Eliza J. **HOYT**, of New Canaan, Oct. 17, 1839, by Theophilus Smith	33
Floyd, of South Salem, m. Clarinda **ST. JOHN**, of New Canaan, Nov. 20, 1831, by Rev. Daniel I. Wright	20
William, of Greenwich, m. Ann **BROWN**, of New Canaan, Sept. 2, 1830, by Rev. Samuel Cochrane	19
ST. JOHN, Abigail D., m. William **SILLIMAN**, Apr. 20, 1817, [Cong. Ch. Rec.]	192
Abraham W., m. Deborah **WATERBURY**, Oct. 24, 1820, by William Bonney	4
Abraham W., m. Deborah **WATERBURY**, Oct. 24, 1820, [Cong. Ch. Rec.]	192
Alice, see under Elis	
Almina, of New Canaan, m. Daniel W. **BOUTON**, of Darien, Aug. 28, 1827, by William Bonney	15
Ann Comstock, of New Canaan, m. George Washington **HAUGHTON***, of New York City, Nov. 16, 1826, by William Bonney *(Written "**HOUGHTON**" in Index)	13
Anna, m. Samuel **EVORIT**, of Salif, Dec. 9, 1801	0
Betsey, m. Jesse **SEELY**, Oct. 15, 1801	0
Birchard, m. Mary **WHALEY**, Sept. 21, 1804	1
Clarinda, of New Canaan, m. Floyd **RUSCO**, of South Salem, Nov. 20, 1831, by Rev. Daniel I. Wright	20
Cook, m. Polly **SEYMOUR**, Dec. 21, 1796	3
	1
Sinthia, of North Stamford, m. Elijah **SCOFIELD**, Dec. 8, 1803	
Daniel, m. Charlotte **HOYT**, b. of New Canaan, Oct. 15, 1826, by William Bonney	14
Darius, m. Betsey Ann **CROFOOT**, b. of New Canaan, Oct. 16, 1829, by Rev. M. Eli Daviston	17

	Page
ST. JOHN, (cont.)	
Elis, m. Caleb **BENEDICT**, Jr., Aug. 23, 1801	0
Eliza, of New Canaan, m. Augustus **BOUTON**, of Darien, Apr. 14, 1829, by William Bonney	17
Ephraim, s. Peter & Rachel, b. June 29, 1801	189
Ester, m. Benjamin **BATES**, of Middlesex, Aug. 30, 1798	3
Esther, of New Canaan, m. William M. **HOWEL**, of Hector, Tompkins Co., N.Y., Apr. 21, 1839, by Rev. Lyman H. Atwater	31
Gould, m. Lucretia **COMSTOCK**, Nov. 1, 1801	0
Hannah, m. Darius **NIGHT**, June 22, 1797	3
Hannah, m. Henry **CHAMBERS**, Apr. [ ], 1817, [Cong. Ch. Rec.]	192
Hannah, m. Hanford **DAVENPORT**, Sept. 10, 1817, [Cong. Ch. Rec.]	192
Hannah, 2nd, of New Canaan, m. Theophilus **SMITH**, of Halifax, Vt., June 27, 1831, by William Bonney	22
Hezekiah, Jr., m. Phebe Baxter **KEELER**, Aug. 20, 1798	3
Hiram, of New Canaan, m. Julia Ann **SWAN**, of Greenwich, Feb. 11, 1630, by William Bonney	20
Jesse, m. Sally **WEED**, Apr. 20, 1819, [Cong. Ch. Rec.]	192
Lewis, m. Polly **FANCHER**, b. of New Canaan, Apr. 10, 1833, by Theophilus Smith	24
Mary, m. Nathan **HANFORD**, Oct. 8, 1795, [Cong. Ch. Rec.]	2
Mary, m. Capt. [ ] **KEELER**, Jan. [ ], 1812, [Cong. Ch. Rec.]	191
Polly, m. Elijah **WEED**, Jan. 24, 1801	0
Sally, m. Thaddeus **HANFORD**, Mar. [ ], 1796, [Cong. Ch. Rec.]	2
Sally K., m. Alanson F. **FENNY**, of Norwalk, Apr. 22, 1819, [Cong. Ch. Rec.]	192
Sally M., m. Frederick **NOBLE**, Oct. [ ], 1819, [Cong. Ch. Rec.]	192
Samuel, m. Hannah **RICHARDS**, of Canaan, Mar. 1, 1798	3
Sarah, m. Benjamin N. **HEATH**, b. of New Canaan, Jan. 1, 1840, by Theophilus Smith	33
Selleck Y., m. Mary L. **SEYMOUR**, b. of New Canaan, Dec. 1, 1840, by Rev. John A. Sillick	55
Theophilus Worthington, see Theophilus Worthington **SMITH**	
Vincent, of Binghamton, N.Y., m. Eliza Jane **AYRES**, of New Canaan, Oct. 17, 1839, by Theophilus Smith	33
William, m. Susanna **BROWN**, Apr. 7, 1799	3
William, m. Hannah J. **CARTER**, b. of New Canaan, Mar. 13, 1843, by Rev. Theophilus Smith	61
SANDERSON, Harvey, m. Emily **DAVENPORT**, b. of New Canaan, Feb. 4, 1836, by Theophilus Smith	28
SANFORD, Morris, of Reading, m. Charlotte **MILLS**, of New Canaan, Nov. 12, 1826, by William Bonney	12
Morris, of Reading, m. Charlotte **MILLS**, of New Canaan, Nov. 12, 1826, by William Bonney	13
SAUNDERS, Harvey, of Norwalk, m. Sally **HANFORD**, of New Canaan, Nov. 24, 1819, [Cong. Ch. Rec.]	192
	2
SCOFIELD, Abigail, m. Caleb **FINCH**, Dec. 31, 1796	
Abigail, m. Joseph **SCOFIELD***, b. of New Canaan, May 4, 1831, by William Bonney *(Written "**GRIFFING**" in Index)	22
	2
Abijah, m. Hannah **WILMOT**, Apr. 1, 1806	
Amzi, of Stamford, m. Polly **DAVENPORT**, of New Canaan, Nov. 24, 1819, [Cong. Ch. Rec.]	192

SCOFIELD, (cont.)

	Page
Anna, m. Elijah **WEED**, of Stamford, Dec. 21, 1796	2
Charles W., of Stamford, m. Harriet E. **YOUNG**, of New Canaan, Jan. 9, 1833, by Rev. Henry Fuller, of North Stamford	24
Elijah, m. Sinthia ST. **JOHN**, of North Stamford, Dec. 8, 1803	1
Esther, m. David H. **BOYER**, Feb. 26, 1837, by Edwin Hall	30
Joseph, m. Abigail **SCOFIELD***, b. of New Canaan, May 4, 1831, by William Bonney *(Written "**GRIFFING**" in Index"	22
Lewis, m. Eliza Augusta **SEELY**, b. of New Canaan, Feb. 11, 1849, by Rev. David H. Short	68
Maria, d. Abijah & Hannah, b. Apr. 1, 1807	189
Mariah, m. William **PROVOST**, Jr., b. of New Canaan, July 7, 1824, by Nobles W. Thomas, Elder	10
Mercy, m. Joel **HOYT**, b. of New Canaan, Sept. 10, 1828, by William Bonney	16

SCRIBNER, Samuel, of Wilton, m. Polly Asenath **RAYMOND**, d. Russel G., of New Canaan, Jan. 1, 1834, by Theophilus Smith — 25

SEELEY, SEELY, Aaron C., m. Caroline E. **JENNINGS**, b. of New Canaan, July 15, 1850, by Rev. Theophilus Smith — 70

Abijah Whitlock, s. Abijah & Johannah, b. Oct. 4, 1805	189
Alfred, m. Hannah **HOYT**, b. of New Canaan, Oct. 25, 1820, by G. S. Webb	5
Carleton White, s. Abijah & Johannah, b. Sept. 30, 1802	189
Eliza Augusta, m. Lewis **SCOFIELD**, b. of New Canaan, Feb. 11, 1849, by Rev. David H. Short	68
Arastus*, m. Mary A. **COMSTOCK**, Nov. 11, 1818, [Cong. Ch. Rec.] *(Erastus)	192
Hannah, of N.E., m. Jesse **REED**, of Clinton, S.N., Dec. 29, 1802	0
Henry Bates, s. Abijah & Johannah, b. Mar. 25, 1800	189
Isabella, of New Canaan, m. Jesup Taylor **JENNINGS**, of Fairfield, Mar. 27, 1821, by William Bonney	5
Isabella, m. Jessup Taylor **JENNINGS**, Mar. 27, 1821, [Cong. Ch. Rec.]	192
Jesse, m. Betsey ST. **JOHN**, Oct. 15, 1801	0
Joseph, Jr., m. Sally **WARING**, Apr. 25, 1799	3
Julia A.*, m. William P. **TRISTRAM**, b. of New Canaan, Oct. 16, 1850, by Rev. Jacob Shaw *(Written "Julia H." in Index)	71
Mary, m. Henry R. **WEED**, b. of New Canaan, Dec. 26, 1832, by Rev. Ambrose J. Todd, of Stamford	22
Sally, of New Canaan, m. Aaron **JENNINGS**, of New York, Oct. 6, 1813, [Cong. Ch. Rec.]	191
Sally, of New Canaan, m. Matthew **KELLOGG**, of Norwalk, June 13, 1821, by William Bonney	6
Sally, of New Canaan, m. Matthew **KELLOGG**, of Norwalk, June 13, 1821, [Cong. Ch. Rec.]	192
Sarah E., m. Jacob W. **OSTRANDER**, b. of New Canaan, Sept. 30, 1850, by Rev. Theophilus Smith	71
Stephen, of Norwalk, m. Mrs. Evelina **HANFORD**, Apr. 7, 1841, in St. Marks Church, by David Ogden	56
Sylvanus, m. Sally **CRISSY**, b. of New Canaan, Aug. 29, 1831, by William Bonney	21
Thomas, s. Abijah & Johannah, b. Nov. 20, 1797	189
Walter, s. Abijah & Johannah, b. Mar. 6, 1810	189

	Page
SEELEY, SEELY, (cont.)	
Wyx, of Darien, m. Charlotte **CRISSY**, of New Canaan, Sept. 17, 1832, by Rev. John Lovejoy	23
SELLECK, SILLIC, George, m. Mehetabil **HOYT**, Dec. 1, 1819, [Cong. Ch. Rec.]	192
Hannah, m. Daniel **HUNT**, of Salem, Dec. 25, 1799	0
Judah Ann, m. Leander **SMITH**, Sept. 4, 1827, by William Bonney	15
Julia, m. Ebenezer **CRISSY**, b. of New Canaan, Sept. 25, [1854], by Rev. F. W. Williams	81
Louisania*, of New Canaan, m. John **HUBBARD**, of Darien (colored), Jan. 23,(?), 1830, by William Bonney *(Written "Lousannia" in Index)	20
Mary, m. Lewis **RICHARDS**, b. of New Canaan, Jan. 17, 1827, by William Bonney	14
Mary J., m. John **SLAWSON**, Feb. 7, 1854, by Rev. L. D. Nickerson	81
Mahettable H., of New Canaan, m. James H. **MARVIN**, of Troy, N.Y., Mar. 28, 1842, by Rev. Theophilus Smith	58
Pomp, m. Violet Ann **PRIME**, b. of New Canaan, May 18, 1835, by Theophilus Smith	27
SEYMOUR, SEYMOURE, Adeline A., m. John H. **MERRIL**, b. of New Canaan, Nov. 6, 1848, by Rev. Theophilus Smith	67
Edwin S., m. Hannah Eliza **AYRES**, b. of New Canaan, May 3, 1839, by William Bonney	17
Ezra, Sr., m. Sarah **HANFORD**, June 24, 1810, [Cong. Ch. Rec.]	191
Hennery, m. Molly **BENEDICT**, Nov. 28, 1799	0
Holly, m. Lucretia **HANFORD**, Dec. 19, 1810, [Cong. Ch. Rec.]	191
John, m. Charlotte **JARVIS**, Dec. 12, 1810, [Cong. Ch. Rec.]	191
Levina, of Canaan, m. Amos **BELDEN**, June 23, 1803	0
Mary L., m. Selleck Y. **ST. JOHN**, b. of New Canaan, Dec. 1, 1840, by Rev. John A. Sillick	55
Nancy, m. Fitch **GREGORY**, Oct. 23, 1800	0
Polly, m. Cook **ST. JOHN**, Dec. 21, 1796	3
Rufus, of Wilton, m. Sally **KEELER**, of New Canaan, Mar. 26, 1834, by Theophilus Smith	26
-----, of Ridgefield, m. [ ] **STUART**, Sept. [ ], 1811, [Cong. Ch. Rec.]	191
SHERWOOD, Sylvester, m. Catharine A. **WOOD**, b. of New Canaan, Aug. 25, 1852, by Theophilus Smith	77
SHUTE, Sarah, of New Canaan, m. Zachariah **BUTTERY**, of Wilton, Dec. 26, 1830, by J. B. Benedict, J.P.	18
SILLIMAN, Dinah, m. Jonathan **HUNTINGTON**, Nov. 25, 1800	0
Elisha L., m. Harriet **BETTS**, Dec. 25, 1815, [Cong. Ch. Rec.]	192
Joseph, m. Martha Ann **MITCHELL**, b. of New Canaan, Mar. 13, 1839, by Theophilus Smith	31
Joseph Fitch, s. Joseph & Martha A., b. Feb. 7, 1840	190
Samuel C., Jr., m. Sarah G. **SMITH**, b. of New Canaan, May 21, 1841, by Rev. Eli Denniston. Witnesses Robert Morrison & W. B. Smith	57
William, m. Abigail D. **ST. JOHN**, Apr. 20, 1817, [Cong. Ch. Rec.]	192
SIMONSON, P. Ashly, of New York, m. Susan **NASH**, of New Canaan, Jan. 6, 1851, by Rev. D. H. Short	72
SIMS, Album J., m. Sarah M. **HURLBUTT**, b. of New Canaan, July 1, 1850, by Rev. Theophilus Smith	70
SKEELS, Adoniram, m. Eunice **BENEDICT**, Oct. 17, 1816, [Cong. Ch. Rec.]	192

236 BARBOUR COLLECTION

	Page
SLAWSON, SLAUSON, Andrew J., m. Mary E. CANFIELD, b. of New Canaan, Feb. 17, 1846, by Rev. Theophilus Smith	64
Clarissa, m. Cyrus CROFOOT, Mar. 1, 1843, by Rev. Charles F. Pelton	60
John, m. Sally KEELER, Sept. 23, 1817, [Cong. Ch. Rec.]	192
John, m. Mary J. SELLECK, of New Canaan, Feb. 7, 1854, by Rev. L. D. Nickerson	81
Martha A., of New Canaan, m. Orestes H. BENEDICT, of Lewisboro, N.Y., Apr. 28, 1851, by Rev. Theophilus Smith	73
Mary Elizabeth, of New Canaan, m. John NEWMAN, of Lewisboro, N.Y., Nov. 25, 1846, by Rev. George Waterbury	64
Sarah G., m. Lewis K. HOYT, b. of New Canaan, Sept. 25, 1842, by Rev. Charles F. Pelton	59
SMALLHORN, James A., m. Charlotte JONES, Nov. 21, 1853, by Rev. L. D. Nickerson	81
SMITH, Benjamin, m. Sarah LOCKWOOD, b. of New Canaan, [Feb.] 26, [1824], by Rev. Origen P. Holcomb	10
Benjamin, of Bridgeport, m. Martha Y.* LINN, of New Canaan, May 16, 1852, by Rev. Jacob Shaw *(Written "Martha J. LINN" in Index)	77
Charles G., of New Canaan, m. Abigail HUSTED, of Stamford, May 14, 1821, by William Bonney	6
Charles G., m. Abigail HUSTED, of Stamford, May 14, 1821, [Cong. Ch. Rec.]	192
Daniel, of Stamford, m. Eliza J. HAWLEY, of Darien, Jan. 26, 1853, by Rev. Lorenzo D. Nickerson	78
Eliakim, m. Dina BENEDICT, Jan. 7, 1805	1
Hannah B., [d. Theophilus & Caroline St. John], b. Mar. 7, 1834	190
Hannah Benedict, d. Theophilus & Caroline St. John, b. Mar. 27, 1832	190
Harriet Mariah, of New Canaan, m. John TAYLOR, of New York City, Jan. 1, 1852, by Rev. Theophilus Smith	75
Isaac, of Greenville, Green Co., N.Y., m. Hannah OLMSTEAD, of New Canaan, Sept. 1, 1826, by William Bonney	12
Isaac M., of Stamford, m. Ethelinda WEBB, of Onondaga, N.Y., Sept. 1, 1830, by Rev. Samuel Cochrane	19
Josiah, of Norwalk, m. Betsey EETS, Jan. 9, 1800	0
Leander, m. Judah Ann SELLECK, Sept. 4, 1827, by William Bonney	15
Lewis E. P., of New York City, m. Ann Melvina AYRES, of New Canaan, Dec. 23, 1851, by Rev. Theophilus Smith	75
Ruth Ann, m. Oliver BURTON, b. of New Canaan, Dec. 10, 1851, by Rev. Theophilus Smith	74
Samuel St. John, [s. Theophilus & Caroline St. John], b. Mar. 1, 1837	190
Sarah, of Canaan, m. [ ] OSBORN, of Weston, Apr. 25, 1804	1
Sarah G., m. Samuel C. SILLIMAN, Jr., b. of New Canaan, May 21, 1841, by Rev. Eli Denniston. Witnesses Robert Morrison & W. B. Smith	57
Theophilus, of Halifax, Vt., m. Hannah B. ST. JOHN, 2nd, of New Canaan, June 27, 1831, by William Bonney	22
Theophilus Worthington*, s. Theophilus & Hannah B., b. Mar. 5, 1840 *(Indexed as "Theophilus Worthington ST. JOHN")	190
STAPLES, Polly, of Wilton, m. Amos DICKENS, of Ridgefield, Nov. 28, 1826, by William Bonney	13
STEBBINS, Lewis, of Ithica, N.Y., m. Sarah LOCKWOOD, of New Canaan, Sept. 4, 1836, by Theophilus Smith	29
STEELE, Lewis G., m. Elizabeth R. LOCKWOOD, Oct. 23, 1831, by	

	Page
STEELE, (cont.)	
Chauncey Wilcox	21
STERLING, Nathaniel, of Wilton, m. Polly HOIT, May 7, 1801	0
STEVENS, STEVINS, Aaron, of Poundridge, m. Abigail NASH, of New Canaan, Oct. 9, 1831, by Theophilus Smith	21
Andrew, m. Hannah HURLBUTT, b. of New Canaan, Feb. 25, 1827, by William Bonney	15
Anna, m. Eber BROWN, b. of New Canaan, June 18, 1837, by Theophilus Smith	30
Ardima, m. Alfred RICHARDS, b. of New Canaan, Feb. 23, 1840, by Rev. Samuel W. King	33
Betsey, m. Charles JUDSON, b. of New Canaan, Nov. 14, 1827, by William Bonney	15
Betsey Ann, m. Robert H. TRISTRAM, b. of New Canaan, Jan. 16, 1832, by Rev. Daniel I. Wright	23
Eber, m. Cynthia E. JENNINGS, Sept. 16, 1821, by William Bonney	7
Edwin H., s. David & Saloma, b. Apr. 22, 1816	190
Elisha Edward, [s. David & Saloma], b. Sept. 11, 1818	190
Hannah, of New Canaan, m. Herman HOWLET, of Philadelphia, Mar. 13, 1820, [Cong. Ch. Rec.]	192
Isaac Norton, [s. David & Saloma], b. July 12, 1822	190
John Westly, s. [David & Saloma], b. June 9, 1817	190
Mary, of New Canaan, wid., m. Selleck HOYT, of Stamford, Oct. 18, 1830, by Rev. Henry Fuller, of North Stamford	19
Nehemiah, of New Canaan, m. Cleopatra C. FORBS, of Brooklyn, N.Y., Jan. 6, 1851, by Jacob Shaw	73
Nehemiah, of New Canaan, m. Cleopatra FORBS, of Brooklyn, N.Y., Jan. 6, 1851, by Jacob Shaw	81
Polly, of New Canaan, m. Aaron LOCKWOOD, of Redding, Oct. 9, 1839, by Rev. S. W. King	32
Rachel, m. Nathaniel BOUTON, of N.S., Mar. 22, 1801	0
Rhoda, m. Hezekiah OLMSTED, Sept. 29, 1805	1
Samuel W., of New Canaan, m. Susan LINES, of Redding, Oct. 3, 1847, by Rev. D. H. Short	66
Theodore Nelson, [s. David & Saloma], b. May 14, 1820	190
STUART, -----, m. [ ] SEYMOUR, of Ridgefield, Sept. [ ], 1811, [Cong. Ch. Rec.]	191
STURDEVANT, Julian M., Rev. of New Haven, m. Elizabeth Maria FAYERWEATHER, of New Canaan, Aug. 31, 1829, by William Bonney	17
SWAN, Julia Ann, of Greenwich, m. Hiram ST. JOHN, of New Canaan, Feb. 11, 1830, by William Bonney	20
TALMADGE, TALLMADGE, Abigail A., of New Canaan, m. Oliver CLARK, of Danbury, Mar. 22, 1853, by Rev. Lorenzo D. Nickerson	80
Henry, m. Rachel WATERBURY, Apr. 12, 1812 [Cong. Ch. Rec.]	191
Jane, m. Abraham CRISSY, Nov. 26, 1815, [Cong. Ch. Rec.]	192
-----, m. Hezekiah WEED, Oct. 5, 1817, [Cong. Ch. Rec.]	192
TAYLOR, Abijah F., of New York, m. Polly A. JOHNSON, of New Canaan, June 14, 1830, by William Bonney	19
Ann Eliza, of New Canaan, m. William Henry LOUNSBURY, of New York, Nov. 13, 1851, by Rev. Jacob Shaw	75
Franklin B., of Warren, m. Martha E. HICKOK, of New Canaan, Apr. 14,	

	Page
TAYLOR, (cont.)	
1840, by Theophilus Smith	34
Jemima, of Greens Farms, m. [ ] **BUTLER**, Oct. 29, 1802	0
John, of New York City, m. Harriot Mariah **SMITH**, of New Canaan, Jan. 1, 1852, by Rev. Theophilus Smith	75
Theodore, of Westport, m. Mary Ann **BROWN**, of New Canaan, Feb. 23, 1852, by Rev. Theophilus Smith	76
TERREL[L], TYRRELL, Abigail, of New Canaan, m. Benjamin S. **DOWNES**, of Greenwich, Feb. 28, 1854, by Rev. L. D. Nickerson	81
Polly Ann, of Wilton, m. Chauncey R.* **LOCKWOOD**, s. Samuel, of New Canaan, May 4, 1834, by Theophilus Smith *(Written "Chauncey K." in Index)	26
THATCHER, Nelson, of Danbury, m. Nancy **BRUNSON**, of New Canaan, Mar. 2, 1853, by Rev. L. D. Nickerson	80
THOMPSON, Charles, of Spencer Town, m. Betsey **MITCHELL**, of Canaan, Nov. 1, 1801	0
Dinah, m. Elias **HARROWAY**, of New York, Dec. 2, 1819, [Cong. Ch. Rec.]	192
TODD, Darius W., m. Margarett**COMSTOCK**, b. of New Canaan, Feb. 4, 1829, by Rev. Daniel DePinng	18
TRAPHAGEN, Isaac G., of Stamford, m. Mary Elizabeth **CLARK**, of Norwalk, Jan. 19, 1852, by D. H. Short	76
TREADWELL, Mary, d. Stephen W. & Lucinda, b. Apr. 6, 1842	191
TRISTRAM, Bartholomew, m. Ann Frances **HANFORD**, b. of New Canaan, Nov. 2, 1852, by Rev. Lorenzo D. Nickerson	78
Catharine, m. James **CURZON**, June 14, 1843, by Rev. J. Hunt	61
Robert H., m. Betsey Ann **STEVENS**, b. of New Canaan, Jan. 16, 1832, by Rev. Daniel I. Wright	23
William P., m. Julia A. **SEELY**, b. of New Canaan, Oct. 16, 1850, by Rev. Jacob Shaw *(Written "Julia H." in Index)	71
TUCKER, Ishmael, m. Patty **JONES**, Oct. 8, 1809, [Cong. Ch. Rec.]	191
TUTTLE, Abigail, of New Canaan, m. Robert **DONOVAN**, of Bridgeport, Jan. 20, 1819, [Cong. Ch. Rec.]	192
Eliza A., of New Canaan, m. Hiram **WOOD**, of Hartford, Apr. 10, 1843, by Rev. Theophilus Smith	61
Emeline, of New Canaan, m. Charles **BIRDSEL**, of South Salem, N.Y., Nov. 28, 1830, by Samuel Raymond, J.P.	18
Harmony, m. Smith **TUTTLE**, b. of New Canaan, Apr. 7, 1836, by Rev. J. Lyman Clark	28
John, m. Mabel **GARNER**, Nov. 26, 1795, [Cong. Ch. Rec.]	2
Samuel P., of New Canaan, m. Harriet **BETTS**, of Wilton, Apr. 11, 1848, by Rev. D. H. Short	67
Sarah, m. Samuel **JUDSON**, Dec. 28, 1825, by William Bonney	11
Sarah A., m. James **WHITNEY**, b. of New Canaan, Nov. 15, 1848, by Rev. J. D. Marshall	68
Smith, m. Harmony **TUTTLE**, b. of New Canaan, Apr. 7, 1836, by Rev. J. Lyman Clark	28
TYRRELL, [see under **TERRELL**]	
UNCLES, John, m. Margaret* **HICKOK**, b. of New Canaan, Jan. 5, 1846, by Rev. Theophilus Smith *(Written "Margaret G. **HICKOK**" in Index)	63
VALENTINE, Sarah E., m. George **CARTER**, b. of New Canaan, May 9, 1836,	

NEW CANAAN VITAL RECORDS

	Page
VALENTINE, (cont.)	
by Theophilus Smith	28
VERVALAN(?), Ellis J., m. John **BROWN**, b. of New Canaan, Dec. 10, 1843,	
by Daniel W. Bouton, J.P.	62
WADDY, Ira, m. Sabia **DEFOREST**, Sept. 6, 1810, [Cong. Ch. Rec.]	191
WAKEMAN, Louisa, m. Charles S. **RAYMOND**, b. of New Canaan, Sept. 15,	
1850, by Rev. D. H. Short	70
WARING, WARRING, WARIN, Betsey S., m. Robert P. **BOUTON**, Aug. 9,	
1821, by William Bonney	6
Ephraim, s. Thomas & Anna, b. Mar. 13, 1808	190
Jerusha, m. David **WEED**, of North Stamford, Aug. 10, 1797	3
Jonathan, m. Ester **HOIT**, Sept. [ ], 1797	3
Sally, m. Joseph **SEELY**, Jr., Apr. 25, 1799	3
Thomas, m. Anna **DAVENPORT**, b. of New Canaan, May 3, 1807	2
William L., m. Susan **HOYT**, b. of New Canaan, Aug. 28, 1836, by	
Theophilus Smsith	29
WASHBURN, WASHBORN, Ralph E., of Charlestown, Mass., m. Emma	
Matilda **BOUTON**, of New Canaan, Jan. 20, 1851, by Rev.	
Theophilus Smith	72
-----, m. Deborah **HOIT**, of Canaan, Mar. 30, 1802	0
WATERBURY, Anna, of New Canaan, m. Daniel **BEERS**, of Poundridge, N.Y.,	
July 6, 1831, by William Bonney	21
Betsey, of New Canaan, m. Abram **WEED**, of Sharron, Feb. 15, 1847, by	
Rev. Theophilus Smith	64
Deborah, m. Abraham W. **ST. JOHN**, Oct. 24, 1820, by William Bonney	4
Deborah, m. Abraham W. **ST. JOHN**, Oct. 24, 1820, [Cong. Ch. Rec.]	192
Eliza Jane, m. Garrit **PENNOYER**, b. of New Canaan, Nov. 13, 1839, by	
Rev. Samuel W. King	34
Isaac, m. Nancy **CRISSEY**, b. of New Canaan, Feb. 3, 1834, by William	
Bonney	26
Mary E., m. James M. **BENEDICT**, b. of New Canaan, Oct. 12, 1831, by	21
Theophilus Smith	191
Rachel, m. Henry **TALLMADGE**, Apr. 12, 1812, [Cong. Ch. Rec.]	
Rebecca Ann, of New Canaan, m. Nerbert **BOSSEE**, of Quebec, Can., Dec.	
13, 1852, in St. Marks Church, by William Long	78
WATERS, Sarah, m. Lucius M. **MONROE**, b. of New Canaan, Jan. 13, 1851,	76
by Rev. D. H. Short	
WATSON, Ann, of New Canaan, m. Joel **WITHERBY**, of New York City, May	21
25, 1831, by William Bonney	
Eliza, m. Charles **RAYMOND**, Sept. 30, 1833, by Rev. W. Patton, of New	57
York. Witnesses Joseph William Hyne & Julia Hyne	1
WEBB, Benjamin, of New York, m. Anne **BISHOP**, of Canaan, Dec. 25, 1803	1
Charles, of Wilton, m. Polly **CANFIELD**, of New Canaan, Oct. 8, 1809	
Charlotte, of Ridgefield, m. Jesse **HOYT**, of New Canaan, Feb. 10, 1833,	24
by William Bonney	
Ethelinda, of Onondaga, N.Y., m. Isaac M. **SMITH**, of Stamford, Sept. 1,	19
1830, by Rev. Samuel Cochrane	
Harriet A., of Walton, N.Y., m. George A. **BARTOW**, of New Canaan,	69
May 13, 1850, by Rev. Theophilus Smith	
Harry M., see Henry M. **WEBB**	
Henry* M., of Walton, N.Y., m. Sophronia E. **BARTOW**, of New Canaan,	
Nov. 30, 1852, in Rev. Theophilus Smith *(Written "Harry M." in	

	Page
WEBB, (cont.)	
Index)	80
Mary, m. Samuel **BOTT**, Jan. 3, 1798	3
Polly, of Stamford, m. Jared **BOUTON**, of New Canaan, Oct. 7, 1802	2
Sarah Ann, of New Canaan, m. Buedby* **BROWN**, of Norwalk, Nov. 11, 1830, by Rev. Samuel Cochrane *(Written "Bradley" in Index)	18
William G., m. Phebe **KEELER**, b. of New Canaan, Sept. 11, 1838, by Theophilus Smith	31
WEED, Abram, of Sharron, m. Betsey **WATERBURY**, of New Canaan, Feb. 15, 1847, by Rev. Theophilus Smith	64
Angeline, d. Elijah & Anna, b. May 27, 1804	190
Anna, m. James **HOLMES**, Dec. 27, 1797	3
Asahel, s. Joel, b. Jan. 16, 1766; m. Thankful **FINCH**, [ ]	189
Asahel, m. Thankful **FINCH**, May 16, 1793	2
Betsey, m. Lockard **BENEDICT**, May 12, 1800	0
Betsey, m. Lockwood **BENEDICT**, May 12, 1800	2
Daniel G., m. Delia **GILBERT**, b. of New Canaan, Jan. 12, 1831, by Rev. Samuel Cochrane	22
David, of North Stamford, m. Jerusha **WARIN**, Aug. 10, 1797	3
Deborah S., m. Seeley **GRIFFIN**, Mar. 19, 1820, [Cong. Ch. Rec.]	192
Edmund, s. Elijah & Anna, b. Mar. 16, 1802	190
Elijah, of Stamford, m. Anna **SCOFIELD**, Dec. 21, 1796	2
Elijah, m. Polly **ST. JOHN**, Jan. 24, 1801	0
Eliza, m. Eben **CARTER**, Jan. 14, 1819, [Cong. Ch. Rec.]	192
Enos, m. Sarah **ANDREAS**, of Darien, Apr. 1, 1821, [Cong. Ch. Rec.]	192
Hannah R.*, of New Canaan, m. James **JOHNSON**, of Darien, Dec. 13, 1840, by David Ogden *(Perhaps "K."?)	56
Henry R., m. Mary **SEELY**, b. of New Canaan, Dec. 26, 1832, by Rev. Ambrose J. Todd, of Stamford	22
Hezekiah, s. Elijah & Anna, b. June 6, 1799	190
Hezekiah, m. [ ] **TALMADGE**, Oct. 5, 1817, [Cong. Ch. Rec.]	192
Ira, m. Sally **BENEDICT**, b. of New Canaan, Apr. 11, 1827, by William Bonney	14
Isaac, s. Elijah & Anna, b. Apr. 27, 1814	190
Nancey, m. Stephen I. **MILLER**, b. of New Canaan, July 5, 1826, by Rev. Henery Fuller, of North Stamford	12
Rachel, m. Seth **DEFREES**, Feb. 25, 1798	3
Reuben Scofield, s. Elijah & Anna, b. Dec. 26, 1806	190
Rufus, m. Betsey **HOYT**, b. of New Canaan, Oct. 29, 1820, by G. S. Webb	5
Sally, m. Alanson **CHICHESTER**, Nov. 30, 1815, [Cong. Ch. Rec.]	192
Sally, m. Jesse **ST. JOHN**, Apr. 20, 1819, [Cong. Ch. Rec.]	192
Sally Ann, of New Canaan, m. Charles **LOUNSBURY**, of Stamford, Mar. 23, 1841, by David Ogden	56
Samuel Augustus, m. Rebecca **BELLWOOD**, b. of New Canaan, May 1, 1849, by Rev. Theophilus Smith	68
Sarah, m. William **HOYT**, Nov. 19, 1822, by William Bonney	8
Sarah J., m. Minot **AYRES**, b. of New Canaan, June 27, 1843, by Rev. Theophilus Smith	61
Stephen, s. Elijah & Anna, b. Jan. 15, 1810	190
Waring S., of Binghamton, N.Y., m. Mary E. **AYRES**, of New Canaan, June 6, 1842, by Rev. Theophilus Smith	59
Warring S., of Binghamton, N.Y., m. Mary E. **AYRES**, of New Canaan,	

NEW CANAAN VITAL RECORS 241

	Page
WEED, (cont.)	
June 6, 1842, by Theophilus Smith *(Crossed out)	59
William, of North Stamford, m. Elizabeth **COMSTOCK**, Feb. 5, 1804	1
William, s. Elijah & Anna, b. Dec. 13, 1811	190
Zenas, m. Betsey **COMSTOCK**, Nov. 17, 1816, [Cong. Ch. Rec.]	192
-----, of North Stamford, m. John **LOCKWOOD**, Dec. 24, 1809, [Cong. Ch. Rec.]	191
WEEKS, Betsy, m. Henry **BYINGTON**, May 14, 1837, by Nath[an] Comstock, J.P.	30
WHALEY, Mary, m. Birchard **ST. JOHN**, Sept. 21, 1804	1
Nancy, m. Edward **NORMAN**, of Norwalk, Mar. 19, 1804	1
WHEELER, William Henry, m. Mary Elizabeth **HUSTED**, b. of New Canaan, Sept. 28, 1840, by Theophilus Smith	55
WHITLOCK, Emery, of Wilton, m. Loraina **BENEDICT**, of New Canaan, Nov. 28, 1843, by Rev. Theophilus Smith	62
WHITNEY, James, m. Sarah A. **TUTTLE**, b. of New Canaan, Nov. 15, 1848, by Rev. J. D. Marshall	68
WILMOT, Caroline, of New Canaan, m. Berling D. **PURDY***, of Stamford, Oct. 30, 1836, by Rev. Davis Stocking *(Written "**PERDY**" in Index)	30
Hannah, m. Abijah **SCOFIELD**, Apr. 1, 1806	2
WITHERBY, Joel, of New York City, m. Ann **WATSON**, of New Canaan, May 25, 1831, by William Bonney	21
WOOD, Catharine A., m. Sylvester **SHERWOOD**, b. of New Canaan, Aug. 25, 1852, by Rev. Theophilus Smith	77
Hannah M., m. Francis C. **RAYMOND**, b. of New Canaan, Feb. 22, 1846, by Rev. Theophilus Smith	64
Henry W., m. Mary A. **BADEAU**, Oct. 9, 1842, by Peter Smith, J.P.	59
Hiram, of Hartford, m. Eliza A. **TUTTLE**, of New Canaan, Apr. 10, 1843, by Rev. Theophilus Smith	61
Sophronia, m. Lewis **CHICHESTER**, Oct. [ ], 1819, [Cong. Ch. Rec.]	192
William G., of Skanesteles, N.Y., m. Sophia **RICHARDS**, of New Canaan, Jan. 31, 1815, [Cong. Ch. Rec.]	191
YOUNG, Harriet E., of New Canaan, m. Charles W. **SCOFIELD**, of Stamford, Jan. 9, 1833, by Rev. Henry Fuller, of North Stamford	24
Julia M., m. Joseph **DAVENPORT**, b. of New Canaan, Sept. 15, 1824, by Rev. Henry Fuller, of North Stamford	10
NO SURNAME, Lydia H., m. Charles **HOIT**, of Pound Ridge, Nov. 25, 1804	1

NEW HARTFORD VITAL RECODS
1740 - 1854

	Vol.	Page
ADAMS, Ann, of New Hartford, m. Thaddeus **DAILEY**, of Burlington, Feb. 1, 1821, by Cyrus Yale	3	4
ALEXANDER, William, m. Amarelia **CURTIS**, b. of New Hartford, Nov. 10, 1833, by Rev. John Nickerson	3	20
ALLEN, [see also **ALLYN**], Alfred, m. Emeline A. **GRISWOLD**, b. of New Hartford, Sept. 26, 1850, by Rev. John H. Betts	3	37
ALLYN, [see also **ALLEN**], Anna, d. Peletiah & Sarah, b. Oct. 27, 1753	1	46
Joannah, d. Peletiah & Sarah, b. June 5, 1751; d. Jan. 2, 1753, O.S.	1	46
Peletiah, m. Sarah **MOODEY**, May 23, 1750	1	28
Peletiah, s. Peletiah & Sarah, b. Feb. 5, 1756	1	46
AMES, Hannah, m. Dr. Eldad **MERRELL**, b. of New Hartford, Dec. 17, 1778	2	1
Joshua, m. Harriet **STEDMAN**, b. of New Hartford, Sept. 15, 1822, by Cyrus Yale	3	7
Phebe, of New Hartford, m. Harmon **DAILEY**, of Waterbury, Oct. 6, 1820, by Cyrus Yale	3	3
ANDERSON, John, of Kinderhook, N.Y., m. Sarah M. **ATKINS**, of New Hartford, Oct. 8, 1837, by Rev. Orsamus Allen, of Bristol	3	23
ANDREWS, [see also **ANDRUS**], Elizabeth, d. Eber & Elizabeth, b. July 19, 1743	1	25
Laura, of New Hartford, m. Edward E. **HEWITT**, of Winsted, Sept. 4, 1851, by Rev. John H. Betts	3	39
ANDRUS, ANDRAS, ANDROS, ANDRUSS, ANDROUS, Abigail, d.	1	35
John, b. Sept. 21, 1740	1	35
Asa, s. John & Sarah, b. Sept. 30, 1749; d. Mar. 8, 1749/50	1	55
Asa, s. John, Jr. & Sarah, b. May 2, 1762	2	53
Asa, m. Temperance Colt **PELTON**, Dec. 16, 1813	1	35
Benjamin, s. John, b. Nov. 26, 1746		
Cornelier, m. James Spencer **DOUGLASS**, b. of New Hartford, Nov. 24, 1853, by Rev. John H. Betts	3	55
Cornelia, m. James Spencer **DOUGLASS**, Nov. 24, 1853, by Rev. J. H. Betts	3	56
Elisha, s. John, b. Aug. 3, 1750	1	35
Elizabeth, d. John, Jr. & Sarah, b. Oct. 10, 1769	2	53
Emory Augustus, s. Asa & Temperance, b. Feb. 9, 1821	1	26
Ephraim, s. Ephraim, b. Jan. 9, 1738/9	1	35
Esther, d. John, b. Aug. 13, 1743	2	53
Franklin Horton, s. Asa & Temperance, b. Jan. 12, 1819		
Hannah, d. Ephraim & Hannah, b. Oct. 30, 1757* *(Written over "1751")	1	38
Hannah, d. Ithamer & Hannah, b. Aug. 18, 1759	1	55
Hannah, d. Ephraim & Hannah, b. Aug. 9, 1760	1	52

	Vol.	Page
ANDRUS, ANDRAS, ANDROS, ANDRUSS, ANDROUS, (cont.)		
Israel, of New Hartford, m. Martha **PELTON**, Mar. 7, 1827, by Andrew Abernethy, J.P.	3	13
John, Jr., m. Sarah **IVES**, Oct. 17, 1749	1	29
Julia Ann, d. Asa & Temperance, b. Feb. 1, 1817	2	53
Justus, s. Ithamer & Hannah, b. Feb. 18, 1758	1	55
Lyda, d. John, b. Nov. 13, 1741	1	35
Mary, d. Ephraim & Hannah, b. June 16, 1754	1	47
Mary, d. John & Sarah, b. Jan. 5, 1757	1	47
Nehemiah, of Crawford, N.Y., m. Asantha **GITTELL***, of New Hartford, Jan. 8, 1846, by Rev. Cyrus Yale *("**GILLETT**"?)	3	32
Phebe, m. Israel **LOOMIS**, b. of New Hartford, Dec. 7, 1820, by Cyrus Yale	3	4
Sarah, d. John & Sarah, b. Mar. 1, 1741/2* *(Written over "1751/2")	1	35
Sarah Elizabeth, d. Asa & Temperance, b. Sept. 21, 1814	2	53
Sibel, d. John, b. Dec. 16, 1744	1	35
ARMSTRONG, Jabez D., m. Mary M. **HITCHCOCK**, b. of New Hartford, Apr. 26, 1821, by Rev. C. Yale	3	5
ATKINS, Chester R., of Cheshire, m. Huldah **DOWD**, of New Hartford, Aug. 10, 1841, by Samuel S. Bates, J.P.	3	36
Sarah M., of New Hartford, m. John **ANDERSON**, of Kinderhook, N.Y., Oct. 8, 1837, by Rev. Orsamus Allen, of Bristol	3	23
ATWOOD, Emily L., m. Fayette **MERRELL**, b. of New Hartford, Dec. 18, 1838, by Rev. Cyrus Yale	3	26
Herbert A., of Watertown, m. Sarah A. **RYDER**, of New Hartford, Mar. 2, 1846, by Rev. Cyrus Yale	3	32
James M., of Watertown, m. Helen E. **MERRELL**, of New Hartford, Sept. 4, 1850, by Rev. Cyrus Yale	3	36
AUSTIN, Archibald, [s. Joseph & Hannah], b. Dec. 29, 1783	2	28
Elizabeth, m. Daniel **ROYCE**, May 17, 1840, by Rev. Cyrus Yale	3	27
Harvey, s. Robert & Mary, b. Feb. 15, 1785	2	24
Helen, m. Henry **BECKWITH**, b. of New Hartford, Sept. 17, 1827, by Cyrus Yale	3	13
Joseph, m. Hannah **KELLOGG**, Dec. 18, 1782	2	28
Lewis, of Torringford, m. Elizabeth P. **SADD**, of New Hartford, Oct. 4, 1826, by Cyrus Yale	3	12
Louisa, m. George **BECKWITH**, May 16, 1827, by Cyrus Yale	3	13
Lucina, m. David **LYMAN**, b. of New Hartford, July 13, 1826, by Cyrus Yale	3	12
Mindwell, w. Samuell, Jr., d. Feb. 1, 1764	1	57
Norman, [s. Joseph & Hannah], b. Apr. 12, 1785	2	28
Phebe, d. Robert & Mary, b. Jan. 29, 1782	2	24
Reuben, s. Robert & Mary, b. Feb. 8, 1787	2	24
Robert, m. Mary **HAWLEY**, Oct. 26, 1780	2	24
Robert Hawley, s. Robert & Mary, b. Aug. 11, 1781	2	24
Russell, s. Joseph & Hannah, b. May 17, 1787	2	28
BACON, Joseph, m. Mary **DOUGLASS**, Dec. 2, 1752	1	28
Roswell, Jr., of Burlington, m. Betsey **SMITH**, of New Marlborough, Jan. 4, 1831, by Rev. Alden Handy	3	17
BAILEY, Abiram, of New Hartford, m. Mrs. Hannah **COOK**, of Harwington, Apr. 9, 1853, by Rev. James C. Haughton	3	49

	Vol.	Page
BAILEY, (cont.)		
Ellen, of New Hartford, m. William **DAILEY**, of Goshen, Nov. 30, 1845, by Rev. Cyrus Yale	3	32
Frederic, m. Clarissa **WITNEY**, Nov. 2, 1853, by Rev. David Miller	3	50
Martha A., m. Jesse D. **WARREN**, Jan. 2, 1853, by Rev. John H. Betts	3	48
BAKER, Anthony, m. Eliza **GOODWIN**, b. of New Hartford, Jan. 22, 1824, by Cyrus Yale	3	9
Caroline, of New Hartford, m. Thomas **GILKS**, of Leamington, Eng., Oct. 24, 1852, by Rev. J. A. Saxton	3	47
Elvira, m. Crosby **SIKES**, b. of New Hartford, Aug. 11, 1842, by Roger H. Mills, J.P.	3	28
Hannah, of New Hartford, m. Joseph **CHURCH**, of Barkhamsted, Dec. 20, 1820, by Datus Ensign	3	4
Scott, 2nd, m. Abby E. **BURWELL**, Sept. 20, 1846, by Rev. Jno Morrison Reid	3	33
William S., m. Fanny M. **RODGERS**, b. of New Hartford, Nov. 15, 1840, by Rev. Aaron Gates	3	26
BALCOM, Phebe, m. Ezekiel **MARKHAM**, Mar. 10, 1774	2	13
BALDWIN, Esther A., m. John C. **GUY**, b. of New Hartford, Oct. 11, 1847, by Rev. Alexander Leadbetter	3	35
Noys, m. Deborah **SPENCER**, b. of New Hartford, May 1, 1823, by Cyrus Yale	3	8
Sophia, of New Hartford, m. Jonathan **DEMMING**, Jr., of Sandisfield, Mass., Feb. 4, 1829, by Cyrus Yale	3	16
W[illia]m W., of West Granvill, Mass., m. Jane M. **LYMAN**, of New Hartford, June 13, 1849, by Rev. Judson G. Lyman, of Huntington	2	52
BARBOUR, BARBER, Clarissa, Mrs. of New Hartford, m. Judson **WADSWORTH**, of Wellington, O., May 4, 1852, by Rev. J. A. Saxton	3	42
Elam, m. Mary Jane **SMITH**, b. of New Hartford, Sept. 19, 1852, by Rev. James C. Haughton	3	46
Ellen M., m. Herbert A. **STEELE**, Apr. 19, 1852, by Rev. J. A. Saxton	3	41
Hiram, m. Clarissa **CASE**, May 3, 1830, by Rev. George Phippen, of Canton	3	16
Lovina, m. Elijah **STRONG**, b. of New Hartford, July 18, 1821, by Cyrus Yale	3	5
Luke, of New Hartford, m. Lavinia **HOSMER**, of East Hartford, Apr. 24, 1845, by Alexander Leadbetter	3	32
BARKER, Hart, of Harwinton, m. Susan M. **CADWELL**, of Winsted, Oct. 13, 1842, by Rev. Cyrus Yale	3	29
	2	12
BARNES, BARNS, Albert, [s. Michael & Charlotte], b. Mar. 14, 1814	2	5
Bartholomew, s. Joseph [& Huldah], b. May 2, 1798	2	12
Charlotte, [d. Michael & Charlotte], b. Apr. 13, 1802		
Charlotte, m. Joel **FOSKET**, Jr., Nov. 25, 1823, by Tubal Wakefield	3	10
Edward, [s. Michael & Charlotte], b. Mar. 10, 1809	2	12
Eliza P., m. Alfred E. **MERRELL**, b. of New Hartford, May 3, 1853, by Rev. James C. Haughton	3	48

	Vol.	Page
BARNES, BARNS, (cont.)		
Emeline, of New Hartford, m. John E. **BENJAMIN**, of New Haven, June 30, 1847, by Rev. James Burt, of Canton	3	34
Eunice Ann, d. Joseph [& Huldah], b. Oct. 29, 1805	2	5
Fan[n]y, [d. Michael & Charlotte], b. July 18, 1798	2	12
Franklin, [s. Michael & Charlotte], b. Aug. 21, 1806	2	12
Huldah, d. Joseph & Huldah, b. May 9, 1796	2	5
Huldah, m. Isaac **DOWD**, b. of New Hartford, May 30, 1830, by Rev. Cyrus Yale	3	16
Isaac M., of Burlington, m. Phebe **SPENCER**, of New Hartford, Mar. 5, 1854, by Rev. Frederick Marsh	3	53
Jairus, s. Joseph [& Huldah], b. Nov. 18, 1808	2	5
Joseph, m. Huldah **BARTHOLOMEW**, Sept. 14, 1794	2	5
Joseph, of New Hartford, m. Maria **MATTHEWS**, of Bristol, Aug. 21, 1820, by Cyrus Yale	3	2
Kesiah, d. Joseph [& Huldah], b. July 24, 1800	2	5
Levi, m. Anstra **GROSS**, b. of New Hartford, Feb. 16, 1822, by William G. Williams, J.P.	3	7
Margaret, d. Stephen & Azubah, b. Feb. 25, 1775	1	67
Marilla, m. Absalom **WELLS**, Jr., Jan. 1, 1811	2	52
Michael, [s. Michael & Charlotte], b. June 17, 1804	2	12
Richard Wheaton, s. Joseph & Huldah, b. Mar. 14, 1803	2	5
Ruth, d. Stephen & Azubah, b. [ ] 3, 1773	1	67
Sextus, [s. Michael & Charlotte], b. Feb. 21, 1811	2	12
Stephen, [s. Michael & Charlotte], b. Apr. 25, 1816	2	12
Stephen, of New Hartford, m. Sally **OLMSTED**, of Canton, Oct. 8, 1832, by Rev. David Miller	3	19
Zenas, [s. Michael & Charlotte], b. Dec. 28, 1799	2	12
Zenas, m. Flora **GOODWIN**, b. of New Hartford, Dec. 22, 1825, by Cyrus Yale	3	12
BARRIET, Belinda M., of Barkhamsted, m. Richard **HOPKINS**, of New Hartford, Nov. 23, 183, by Rev. Cyrus Yale	3	30
BARTHOLOMEW, Huldah, m. Joseph **BARNES**, Sept. 14, 1794	2	5
BATTELL*, Henry, m. Mary Ann **CASE**, b. of New Hartford, Nov. 9, 1837, by Rev. Willis Lord *(Overwritten to read "**BARTLETT**")	3	24
BEACH, Electa M., m. Gilbert A. **CANE**, b. of New Hartford, July 3, 1842, by Rev. Erastus Doty, of Colebrook	3	29
Moses, of Harwinton, m. Harriet **CATLIN**, of New Hartford, Sept. 12, 1826, by Erastus Clapp, V.D.M.	3	12
Susan, m. Garret B. **WARNER**, Oct. 4, 1835, by Rev. Seth Higby	3	22
BEADLE, Elias R., of New Orleans, La., m. Martha R. **YALE**, of New Hartford, Aug. 31, 1852, by Rev. Cyrus Yale	3	46
BEARDSLEY, -----, of Sandisfield, Mass., m. Laura **WILCOX**, of Canton, Nov. 30, 1825, by Isaac Kellogg, J.P.	3	12
BECKWITH, George, m. Louisa **AUSTIN**, May 16, 1827, by Cyrus Yale	3	13
Henry, m. Helen **AUSTIN**, b. of New Hartford, Sept. 17, 1827, by Cyrus Yale	3	13
BELDEN, Rhoda, m. David **LYMAN**, Jr., Apr. 9, 1801	2	44
BELLAMY, Hiram D., of Collinsville, m. Mary Ann **CLEMENCE**, of New Hartford, Nov. 15, 1843, by Rev. Cyrus Yale	3	30

	Vol.	Page
BELLAMY, (cont.)		
Ralsamon O., m. Minerva **DUTTON**, b. of New Hartford, Nov. 20, 1828, by Cyrus Yale	3	15
BENEDICK, Harriet, m. George **FARNSWORTH**, b. of Burlington, Oct. 8, 1832, by Rev. David Miller	3	19
BENHAM, Allen, m. Jerusha **KELLOGG**, b. of New Hartford, Feb. 7, 1822, by Cyrus Yale	3	6
Alpheas W., m. Betsey **GOODWIN**, b. of New Hartford, Oct. 22, 1832, by Rev. Cyrus Yale	3	19
Asahael, s. Samuell & Phebe, b. Dec. 15, 1754	1	42
Elias, s. Samuel & Phebe, b. Jan. 8, 1749/50	1	35
James, s. Samuel, b. Feb. 10, 1739/40	1	26
John, s. Sam[ue]l & Phebe, b. Nov. 15, 1745* *("1740"?)	1	27
John, s. Samuell & Phebe, b. Mar. 8, 1758	1	48
John, s. Samuell & Phebe, d. Dec. 29, 1757	1	48
Pane A., of New Hartford, m. Edward P. **ROBERTS**, of Winsted, Sept. 22, 1850, by Rev. Cyrus Yale	3	37
Phebe, d. Samuell & Phebe, b. July 2, 1747	1	21
Samuel, s. Samuel & Phebe, b. Jan. 12, 1742/3	1	25
Trumbull, m. Sefroma **STONE**, Nov. 10, 1822, by Asa Goodwin, J.P.	3	8
BENJAMIN, John E., of New Haven, m. Emeline **BARNES**, of New Hartford, June 30, 1847, by Rev. James Burt, of Canton	3	34
BIDWELL, Achsah, d. Riverius & Phebe, b. Mar. 14, 1783	2	48
Esther, d. Riverius & Phebe, b. Oct. 6, 1786	2	48
Jasper, s. Thomas & Esther, b. Aug. 30, 1775	1	69
Jehial, s. Thomas & Esther, b. Jan. 10, 1761	1	54
Jehiel, s. Riverius & Phebe, b. Apr. 7, 1785	2	48
Lois, d. Thomas & Esther, b. May 22, 1772	1	65
Norman, s. Thomas & Esther, b. Feb. 8, 1769	1	62
Phebe, d. Riverius & Phebe, b. May 31, 1788	2	48
Riverivus, s. Thomas & Esther, b. Aug. 20, 1763	1	56
Riverius, m. Phebe [ ], Sept. 8, 1782	2	48
Riverius, s. Riverius & Phebe, b. Sept. 5, 1790	2	48
Sophia, d. Riverius & Phebe, b. Feb. 3, 1797	2	48
Susan, m. Charles D. **KELLOGG**, b. of New Hartford, Jan. 19, 1845, by Rev. Cyrus Yale	3	31
Thomas, Jr., s. Thomas & Esther, b. May 4, 1766	1	60
Wayne, s. Riverius & Phebe, b. Dec. 17, 1793	2	48
BIRD, Daniel S., m. Julia **DRIGGS**, b. of New Hartford, Oct. 17, 1821, by Cyrus Yale	3	6
Daniel S., m. Julia **DRIGGS**, Oct. 17, 1821	2	36
Eliza M., of New Hartford, m. George W. **GRANGER**, of Tolland, Mass., Sept. 26, 1843, by Rev. J. Burt	3	29
Richard Hiram, s. Daniel & Julia, b. July 17, 1822	2	36
BIRGE, John, of Torringford, m. Lucy **GOODWIN**, of New Hartford, Feb. 5, 1824, by Cyrus Yale	3	9
Luther, of Torrington, m. Harriet **CURTIS**, of New Hartford, May 13, 1822, by Epaphras Goodman	3	6
Roswell, of Torrington, m. Amanda **WHITING**, of New Hartford, June 27, 1826, by Rev. Epaphras Goodman	3	12
BISSELL, Cyrus, of Torringford, m. Amanda **CASE**, of New Hartford,		

	Vol.	Page
BISSELL, (cont.)		
Sept. 14, 1825, by Cyrus Yale	3	11
BLISS, Charles, of Collinsville, m. Delia **GARRETT**, of New Hartford, Feb. 12, 1834, by Rev. Cyrus Yale	3	20
Edward, s. Edward & Susannah, b. May 3, 1768	1	61
BLOICE, Richard, s. Richard & Ruth (now w. of W[illia]m **NOLLING**), d. Sept. 25, 1746	1	21
BOLLES, Henry D., m. Miriam W. **GOODWIN**, Nov. 26, 1829, by Rev. Cyrus Yale	3	16
BOUGHTON, Catharine M., of Torrington, m. Oscar M. **WALDEN**, of New Hartford, Dec. 31, 1851, by Rev. James C. Houghton	3	41
BRADLEY, Briant, of Harwinton, m. Anna **ROSSITER**, of New Hartford, Nov. 17, 1824, by Cyrus Yale	3	11
Esther, m. Michael **GILLET**, June 13, 1782	2	4
Joanna, m. Martin **DRIGGS**, Sept. 25, 1785	2	36
John, m. Minerva L. **SMITH**, b. of New Hartford, Mar. 28, 1841, by Rev. Cyrus Yale	3	27
BREWSTER, Worthy, of Granby, m. Lydia **DELOON**, of New Hartford, Nov. 25, 1830, by Asa Goodwin, J.P.	3	17
BRONSON, Emeline M., of New Hartford, m. Wesley **CHURCHILL**, of Litchfield, Apr. 25, 1852, by Rev. Edward N. Crossman, of Bakerville	3	43
BROOKS, Edward A., m. Lucy A. **JONES**, Sept. 19, 1844, by Alexander Leadbetter. Int. Pub.	3	31
Sally, m. John **WHITING**, Oct. 8, 1826, by Rev. Etbert Osborn	3	13
BROUGHTON, Mehetable, m. Ithuriel **FLOWER**, Dec. 10, 1782	2	17
BROWN, Abigail, of Sandisfield, Mass., m. Harry **COWLES**, of New Hartford, Dec. 13, 1810	2	46
Eliza, m. Darius B. **SMITH**, b.of New Hartford, Nov. 28, 1844, by Alexander Leadbetter. Int. Pub.	3	31
Elizur O., of Canton, m. Mary A. **LOOMIS**, of New Hartford, Nov. 7, 1853, by Rev. F. A. Spencer	3	50
John, Dea., m. wid. Abi **CASE**, June 11, 1844, by Alexander Leadbetter. Int. Pub.	3	31
BUELL, Anna, m. Phinehas **MERRELL**, Mar. 10, 1781	2	39
Truman, of Simsbury, m. Lois **SPENCER**, of New Hartford, Aug. 19, 1835, by Rev. Epaphras Goodman	3	22
BULL, Aaron, s. Asher & Hannah, b. May 19, 1780	2	12
Asher, m. Hannah **HOPKINS**, May 23, 1776	2	12
Calvin, s. Asher & Hannah, b. Oct. 23, 1777	2	12
Haris Hopkins, s. Asher & Hannah, b. Jan. 24, 1779	2	12
BUNN, Almeron, of Winsted, m. Mary E. **HENDERSON**, of New Hartford, Sept. 1, 1852, by Rev. James C. Haughton	3	45
BUNNEL, Elbert, of Burlington, m. Mary E. **POTTER**, of Milton, Aug. 31, 1845, by Rev. Cyrus Yale	3	31
BURDICK, Clark, m. Almira **WINSLOW**, b. of New Hartford, Nov. 18, 1821, by Cyrus Yale	3	6
BURNELL, Marian E., of New Hartford, m. James H. **SPENCER**, of Humphreyville, Dec. 23, 1849, by Rev. Joel R. Arnold	2	52
BURNS, Frederick D., of Winsted, m. Francis E. **TAYLOR**, of New Hartford, Jan. 21, 1854, by James C. Haughton	3	52
BURR, Alonzo, of Torringford, m. Dorcas L. **CASE**, of New Hartford,		

	Vol.	Page
BURR, (cont.)		
Oct. 25, 1852, by Rev. John H. Betts	3	47
BURWELL, Abby E., m. Scott **BAKER**, 2nd, Sept. 20, 1846, by Rev. Jno Morrison Reid	3	33
Angeline L., of Barkhamsted, m. Charles E. **SEYMOUR**, of Waterbury, Jan. 2, 1854, by Rev. F. A. Spencer	3	51
Robert M., m. Elizabeth **WOODRUFF**, June 1, 1847, by Cyrus Yale	3	34
BUSHNELL, Orpah, of New Hartford, m. Edward **RANNEY**, of Augusta, N.Y., Mar. 7, 1847, by George Kerr	3	33
BUTLER, Aurelia, [d. William & Jemima], b. Aug. 20, 1805	2	53
Celestia, [d. William & Jemima], b. Dec. 20, 1807	2	53
Celestia, of New Hartford, m. Samuel **TYLER**, of Branford, Nov. 17, 1830, by Rev. Cyrus Yale	3	18
Harriet, [d. William & Jemima], b. July 20, 1815	2	53
Harriet M., m. Ichabod R. **MERRELL**, b. of New Hartford, Mar. 31, 1845, by Rev. Cyrus Yale	3	31
Jane, [d. William & Jemima], b. Apr. 4, 1821	2	53
Jane L., m. Marshall **MERRELL**, b. of New Hartford, Feb. 21, 1842, by Rev. Cyrus Yale	3	28
Jemima, [d. William & Jemima], b. Oct. 6, 1812	2	53
Jenette J., of New Hartford, m. Milton B. **JARVIS**, M.D., of Dover, N.Y., Feb. 25, 1836, by William Case	3	23
Julia, [d. William & Jemima], b. Sept. 9, 1823; d. Oct. 14, 1825	2	53
Lorain, [s. William & Jemima], b. Oct. 27, 1818	2	53
Loraine K., m. Henry A. **KELLOGG**, b. of New Hartford, Sept. 29, 1841, by Rev. Cyrus Yale	3	28
Roman, [s. William & Jemima], b. Sept. 26, 1803	2	53
Roman M., m. Chloe M. **MASON**, Nov. 29, 1827, by Rev. Cyrus Yale	3	17
William, m. Jemima **PITKIN**, [ ]	2	53
William M., [s. William & Jemima], b. Feb. 14, 1810	2	53
William S., of Edinburgh, N.Y., m. Delight G. **MILLS**, of New Hartford, Sept. 6, 1827, by Jairus Burton	3	14
CADWELL, Deliverance, m. Seth **SMITH**, Feb. 17, 1757	1	28
Susan M., of Winsted, m. Hart **BARKER**, of Harwinton, Oct. 13, 1842, by Rev. Cyrus Yale	3	29
CAHILL, Margaret, m. John **PHELAN**, June 15, 1851, by Rev. John H. Betts	3	39
CAMP, Meriaette A., of New Hartford, m. Duncan **THOMPSON**, of North East, N.Y., Oct. 13, 1847, by Rev. C. H. Topliff, of Collinsville	3	34
CANE, Gilbert A., m. Electa M. **BEACH**, b. of New Hartford, July 3, 1842, by Rev. Erastus Doty, of Colebrook	3	29
CANFIELD, Albert A., m. Jane A. **SMITH**, Nov. 17, 1844, by Alexander Leadbetter. Int. Pub.	3	31
William G., m. Elmina **SMITH**, Nov. 17, 1844, by Alexander Leadbetter. Int. Pub.	3	31
CARDER, Henry, of Killingworth, m. Fanny **KELLOGG**, of New Hartford, Oct. 4, 1832, by Rev. Cyrus Yale	3	18
CARPENTER, Emily, m. Henry **HOLCOMB**, b. of New Hartford, June 5, 1854, by Rev. J. H. Betts	3	56

	Vol.	Page
CARPENTER, (cont.)		
Mary, m. James J. **WHEELER**, b. of New Hartford, Nov. 2, 1845, by Alexander Leadbetter	3	32
CARR, Helen M., of New Hartford, m. Charles H. **GUILFORD**, of Waterbury, June 14, 1839, by Rev. John Higbey	3	26
CARTER, Caroline, m. Samuel D. **HURLBURT**, b. of New Hartford, Oct. 30, 1843, by Rev. Cyrus Yale	3	30
CASE, Abi, wid., m. Dea. John **BROWN**, June 11, 1844, by Alexander Leadbetter. Int. Pub.	3	31
Amanda, of New Hartford, m. Cyrus **BISSELL**, of Torringford, Sept. 14, 1825, by Cyrus Yale	3	11
Clarissa, m. Hiram **BARBER**, May 3, 1830, by Rev. George Phippen, of Canton	3	16
Daniel, m. Mrs. Almira **WALTER**, b. of New Hartford, Mar. 1, 1847, by Roger H. Mills, J.P.	3	33
Dorcas L., of New Hartford, m. Alonzo **BURR**, of Torringford, Oct. 25, 1852, by Rev. John H. Betts	3	47
Lucinda, of New Hartford, m. James **WISWALL**, of Franklin, N.Y., Nov. 13, 1851, by Rev. J. H. Betts	3	43
Mary Ann, m. Henry **BATTELL***, b. of New Hartford, Nov. 9, 1837, by Rev. Willis Lord *(Written over "**BARTLETT**")	3	24
Melissa, m. Ithuel **GRIDLEY**, b. of Canton, Apr. 24, 1844, by Charles B. McLean	3	30
Wells, m. Ruth **TROWBRIDGE**, Nov. 3, 1845, by Isaac Kellogg, J.P.	3	31
Wilson, of Granby, m. Mary **LEWIS**, of New Hartford, Sept. 8, 1846, by Rev. Alexander Leadbetter. Int. Pub.	3	33
CATLIN, Cloe, of New Hartford, m. Henry **COTT***, of Torrinford, Oct. 19, 1829, by Rev. George E. Pierce *(Perhaps "**COLT**"?)	3	17
Harriet, of New Hartford, m. Moses **BEACH**, of Harwinton, Sept. 12, 1826, by Erastus Clapp, V.D.M.	3	12
Lucretia, of New Hartford, m. W[illia]m **LEWIS**, of Bristol, Nov. 10, 1835, by Richard M. Chipman, V.D.M.	3	22
Luman, Jr., of Harwinton, m. Calestia **WETMORE**, of New Hartford, Jan. 19, 1831, by Rev. Epaphras Goodman	3	17
Stanley, of Harwinton, m. Candace **WILLIAMS**, of New Hartford, Apr. 28, 1831, by Cyrus Yale	3	18
CHAPIN, Abigail, d. David & Martha, b. Jan. 19, 1749/50	1	35
David, s. David & Martha, b. Aug. 1, 1762	1	55
David, d. Sept. 15, 1762, at Havana	1	57
David, d. Sept. 15, 1762, at Havanah	1	58
Hannah, d. David & Martha, b. Nov. 4, 1751	1	36
Herman, m. Catharine **MERRELL**, b. of New Hartford, May 18, 1828, by Cyrus Yale	3	14
Loruhamah, d. David & Martha, b. June 11, 1758	1	46
Martha, d. David & Martha, b. Aug. 19, 1753	1	42
Martha, m. Joseph **MERRELL**, Feb. 16, 1769	1	65
Phinehas, s. David & Martha, b. Mar. 15, 1759	1	49
Rachel, d. David & Martha, b. Feb. 16, 1761	1	53
Sabery, d. David & Martha, b. July 7, 1755	1	42
CHAPMAN, Luman Joseph, s. Joseph & Ursula, b. Sept. 1, 1817	2	45

	Vol.	Page
CHIDSEY, Abraham, of Avon, m. Lavinia **MERRELL**, of New Hartford, Sept. 17, 1851, by Rev. John H. Betts	3	39
CHUBB, CHUB, Allaxonder, s. Stephen & Rebecca, b. June 1, 1761	1	53
Deidamia, d. Stephen & Rebeca, b. Feb. 2, 1759	1	47
Rebecca, d. Stephen & Rebecca, b. Apr. 16, 1752	1	43
Rebecca, w. Stephen, d. Feb. 16, 1769	1	56
Ruth, d. Stephen & Rebeckah, b. July 26, 1756	1	43
Stephen, Jr., s. Stephen & Rebecca, b. Feb. 15, 1754	1	43
CHURCH, Abigail, d. Daniel & Eunice, b. Oct. 2, 1751	1	36
Abigail, d. Daniel & Eunice, b. Oct. 2, 1757* *(Written over "1751")	1	36
Daniel*, m. Eunice **KELLEY***, Dec. 1, 1743 *(First written "Joseph") *("KELSEY"?)	1	28
Daniel, s. Daniel & Eunice, b. Nov. last day, 1747	1	21
Daniel, s. Daniel & Eunice, b. Sept. 15, 1753	1	42
Eunice, d. Daniel & Eunice, b. Apr. 2, 1749	1	36
Eunice, d. Daniel & Eunice, b. Apr. 2, 1759* *(Changed to "1749)	1	36
Henry, of Barkhamsted, m. Mary **WENTWORTH**, of New Hartford, Aug. 18, 1846, by Rev. Alexander Leadbetter. Int. Pub.	3	33
Joseph*, m. Eunice **KELLEY***, Dec. 1, 1743 *("Daniel" overwritten) *("KELSEY"?)	1	28
Joseph, s. Dan[ie]l & Eunice, b. Mar. 29, 1745	1	22
Joseph, of Barkhamsted, m. Hannah **BAKER**, of New Hartford, Dec. 20, 1820, by Datus Ensign	3	4
CHURCHILL, Laura, of New Hartford, m. Lora(?) **WATERS**, of Berlin, Oct. 28, 1834, by Rev. Cyrus Yale	3	21
Wesley, of Litchfield, m. Emeline M. **BRONSON**, of New Hartford, Apr. 25, 1852, by Rev. Edward N. Crossman, of Bakerville	3	43
CLARK, Abby B., m. Judson G. **LYMAN**, b. of New Hartford, June 21, 1848, by Rev. C. H. Topliff, of Collinsville. Int. Pub.	3	35
Abijah, [s. Joseph decd. & [ ] after w. Daniel **SHEPARD**], b. Apr. 29, 1729	1	26
Andrew, Jr., m. Mary F. **GERRETT**, b. of New Hartford, Sept. 10, 1845, by Rev. Aaron Gates	3	31
Betsey, m. William **PIERPOINT**, May 24, 1821, by Daniel Coe	3	5
Betsey, m. William **PIERPOINT**, May 24, 1821	2	24
Charles, of Burlington, m. Mary **HURLBURT**, of Winchester, Sept. 26, 1820, by Cyrus Yale	3	2
Jemimah, [d. Joseph, decd. & [ ] after w. of Daniel **SHEPARD**], b. Aug. 17, 1724	1	26
Joseph, [s. Joseph, decd. & [ ] after w. of Daniel **SHEPARD**], b. Dec. 3, 1726	1	26
Nathaniel, of Seymouth, m. Mary **YALE**, of Mereden, Sept. 23, 1827, by Cyrus Yale	3	14
Victoria, m. Calvin **MARANDUS** (colored), b. of Southington, Mar. 15, 1854, by J. C. Haughton	3	52
CLEMENCE, Elmina M., of New Hartford, m. Gilbert S. **RICHMOND**, of Madison, May 9, 1852, by Rev. James C. Houghton	3	42

	Vol.	Page
CLEMENCE, (cont.)		
Mary Ann, of New Hartford, m. Hiram D. **BELLAMY**, of Collinsville, Nov. 15, 1843, by Rev. Cyrus Yale	3	30
CLEVELAND, Louisa S., m. Austin **KELLOGG**, b. of New Hartford, Dec. 18, 1837, by Rev. Willis Lord	3	24
Maria Jerusha, m. Reuel A. **WATSON**, Oct. 11, 1836	2	52
CLINTON, -----, b. [ ]	1	21
COE, Elizabeth, of Torrington, m. Dr. Eldad **MERRELL**, of New Hartford, Aug. 21, 1773	2	1
COLE, [see also **COWLES**], Annah, m. John **MARSH**, Jr., Aug. 18, 1791	2	41
COLLER, Hannah, d. Stephen & Sarah, b. Nov. 15, 1759	1	57
John, s. Stephen & Sarah, b. Feb. 15, 1763	1	57
COLLINS, Amanda H., of Simsbury, m. William H. **SHELBY**, of New Hartford, Apr. 24, 1853, by Rev. Cyrus Yale	3	49
COLT(?), Henry, of Torringford, m. C[h]loe **CATLIN**, of New Hartford, Oct. 19, 1829, by Rev. George E. Pierce *(Perhaps "**COTT**" or **CATT**"?)	3	17
COLTON, Edward, of New Hartford, m. Mary **WINCHESTER**, of Torringford, Mar. 17, 1824, by Cyrus Yale	3	9
CONDON, John, of New Haven, m. Mary C. **RYAN**, of New Hartford, Mar. 4, 1870, by Rev. J. H. Betts, of St. John's Ch.	3	57
CONE, John, m. Catharine **CROWLEY**, b. of New Hartford, July 4, 1854, by Rev. Thomas Hendricken	3	54
COOK, Chloe G., of New Hartford, m. Anson **HOTCHKISS**, of Wayne, O., Oct. 25, 1821, by Cyrus Yale	3	6
Delia, d. William & Theodosia, b. Mar. 29, 1794	2	33
Hannah, Mrs. of Harwington, m. Abiram **BAILEY**, of New Hartford, Apr. 9, 1853, by Rev. James C. Haughton	3	49
Laura, d. William & Theodosia, b. July 23, 1789	2	33
Phedelia, m. Harvey S. Sage, Oct. 2, 1844, by Alexander Leadbetter. Int. Pub.	3	31
Roswell, of Harwinton, m. Sarah **KELLOGG**, of New Hartford, Jan. 14, 1830, by Rev. Cyrus Yale	3	16
Theodosia, d. William & Theodosia, b. Nov. 14, 1791	2	33
Theodosia, of New Hartford, m. Harlow **SPENCER**, St. Louis, Mo., Oct. 16, 1820, by Cyrus Yale	3	3
William, m. Theodosia **GILBERT**, Feb. 14, 1788	2	33
W[illia]m, Jr., m. Eliza **WEBSTER**, b. of New Hartford, Oct. 12, 1820, by Cyrus Yale	3	3
COOPER, John C., m. Elen **RICE**, b. of New Hartford, Oct. 12, 1845, by Alexander Leadbetter	3	32
Julia Ann, m. Henry J. **HALLOCK**, Jan. 3, 1847, by Benjamin G. Loomis, J.P.	3	33
COPELAND, Alfred, of Hartford, m. Emma Augusta **HOWD**, of New Hartford, Sept. 1, 1829, by Cyrus Yale	3	14
COTT*, Henry, of Torringford, m. Cloe **CATLIN**, of New Hartford, Oct. 19, 1829, by Rev. George E. Pierce *(Perhaps "**COLT**"?)	3	17
COTTON, Lucy, m. Ashbel **KELLOGG**, Sept. 20, 1780	2	34
COUCH, Chester S., of Sandisfield, Mass., m. Mary B. **PARSONS**, of Windsor, Jan. 4, 1831, by Rev. Epaphras Goodman	3	17

	Vol.	Page
COWLES, COWLS, [see also **COLE**], Abigail, d. Joseph & Sarah, b. Sept. 4, 1757	1	49
Abigail, m. Francis **LYMAN**, May 4, 1780	2	2
Abigail Ann, d. Harry & Abigail, b. Sept. 14, 1824	2	46
Anna, d. Theodore & Mary, b. Aug. 17, 1791; d. Apr. 10, 1792	2	46
Asa, s. Joseph & Sarah, b. Dec. 17, 1766	1	60
Carrel, s. Theodore & Margaret, b. Oct. 2, 1796	2	46
Carol, m. Betsey **NORTH**, b. of New Hartford, Oct. 3, 1822, by Cyrus Yale	3	7
George, s. Theodore & Margaret, b. Mar. 11, 1798	2	46
Hannah, m. Daniel **GOODWIN**, [ ]	2	30
Harry, s. Theodore & Mary, b. Feb. 12, 1786	2	46
Harry, of New Hartford, m. Abigail **BROWN**, of Sandisfield, Mass., Dec. 13, 1810	2	46
Henry Brown, s. Harry & Abigail, b. Sept. 23, 1811	2	46
John, s. Joseph & Sarah, b. Apr. 30, 1750; d. Sept. 26, 1750	1	49
John, 2nd, s. Joseph & Sarah, b. July 13, 1751	1	49
Joseph, s. Joseph & Sarah, b. July 12, 1755; d. July 29, 1755	1	49
Joseph, 2nd, s. Joseph & Sarah, b. Aug. 19, 1759	1	49
Mary, w. Theodore, d. July 11, 1792, in the 28th y. of her age	2	46
Mary Anne, d. Theodore & Margaret, b. June 8, 1803	2	46
Ovid, s. Theodore & Margaret, b. Jan. 26, 1795	2	46
Polly, d. Theodore & Mary, b. Oct. 17, 1787	2	46
Richard, s. Theodore & Mary, b. Apr. 1, 1789; d. July 27, 1799	2	46
Richard B., s. Theodore & Margaret, b. Nov. 10, 1800	2	46
Sarah, d. Joseph & Sarah, b. Sept. 6, 1753	1	49
Sarah, Jr., m. Dr. Eldad **MERRELL**, Apr. 4, 1782	2	1
Sibel, d. Joseph & Sarah, b. July 22, 1764	1	58
Theodore, s. Joseph & Sarah, b. Jan. 26, 1762	1	54
Theodore, s. Joseph & Sarah, b. June* 26, 1762 *(Marked over "Jan.")	1	56
Theodore, m. Mary **GILBERT**, Aug. [ ], 1785	2	46
Theodore, m. Margaret **DEMING**, Feb. 26, 1794	2	46
Theodore Gilbert, s. Harry & Abigail, b. Mar. 31, 1815	2	46
CRISSE, Mary, m. Joseph **LOOMIS**, Jan. 10, 1796* *(Written over "1786")	2	31
CROMEE, Lucretia A., of Burlington, m. Harley M. **SPENCER**, of New Hartford, May 27, 1841, by Rev. Cyrus Yale	3	28
CROSBY, Ephraim G., m. Huldah E. **HENSHAW**, b. of New Hartford, Sept. 21, 1820, by Cyrus Yale	3	2
CROSS, Anstra, m. Levi **BARNES**, b. of New Hartford, Feb. 16, 1822, by William G. Williams, J.P.	3	7
Mary A., m. Abram **SPENCER**, Mar. 31, 1807	2	50
CROWE, CROW, Jane, m. Norman J. **HARRIS**, b. of New Hartford, Dec. 31, 1854, by Rev. F. A. Spencer	3	55
Shubael, s. Roger & Anna, b. Nov. 7, 1764	2	6
CROWLEY, Catharine, m. John **CONNELL**, b. of New Hartford, July 4, 1854, by Rev. Thomas Hendricken	3	54
CURTIS, Amarelia, m. William **ALEXANDER**, b. of New Hartford, Nov. 10, 1833, by Rev. John Nickerson	3	20
Cyrus, s. Zebulon & Hannah, b. Nov. 3, 1794	2	29
Elizur, s. Job, b. Dec. 26, 1778; d. Sept. 7, 1781	2	29

	Vol.	Page
CURTIS, (cont.)		
Elizur, [s. Job], b. Sept. 11, 1782	2	29
Elizur, m. Naomi **KELLOGG**, Nov. 25, 1802	2	47
Elizur, m. Amanda **STEEL**, Nov. 25, 1804	2	47
Emeline, d. Elizur & Amanda, b. Aug. 3, 1807	2	47
Eunice, d. Job, b. June 23, 1775	2	29
Hannah, d. John & Hannah, b. Nov. 13, 1771	1	66
Hannah, w. John, d. Aug. 18, 1773	1	66
Hannah, d. Zebulon & Hannah, b. May 4, 1798	2	29
Harmon, s. Elizur & Amanda, b. Jan. 5, 1810	2	47
Harriet, of New Hartford, m. Luther **BIRGE**, of Torrington, May 13, 1822, by Epaphras Goodman	3	6
Jabez G., m. Louisa **WETMORE**, b. of New Hartford, Oct. 21, 1830, by Rev. Epaphras Goodman	3	17
John, m. wid. Hannah **MILLER**, Feb. 1, 1770	1	66
Julia, d. Elizur & Amanda, b. Jan. 7, 1818	2	47
Julia A., of New Hartford, m. Richard W. **GRISWOLD**, of Torringford, Apr. 16, 1838, at the house of Dea. Elizur Curtis, by Rev. Herman L. Vaill, of Torringford	3	25
Julius, s. Elizur & Amanda, b. Sept. 3, 1805	2	47
Kezia, [d. Job], b. Dec. 2, 1784	2	29
Lucius, s. Elizur & Amanda, b. Nov. 16, 1812	2	47
Martin, s. John & Hannah, b. July 21, 1773	1	66
Mary Eliza, d. Elizur & Amanda, b. Jan. 18, 1816	2	47
Naomi, d. Elizur & Naomi, b. Jan. 22, 1804	2	47
Naomi, w. Elizur, d. Feb. 3, 1804	2	47
Truman, s. Zebulon & Hannah, b. June 6, 1793	2	29
William P., of Stratford, m. Adaline L. **WRIGHT**, of New Hartford, Oct. 29, 1851, by Rev. Alexander Leadbetter. Int. Pub.	3	40
Zebulon, m. Hannah **PARSONS**, Jan. 5, 1792	2	29
DAILEY, Harmon, of Waterbury, m. Phebe **AMES**, of New Hartford, Oct. 6, 1820, by Cyrus Yale	3	3
Lyman, m. Susan **NICHOLS**, Apr. 22, 1852, by Rev. Edward N. Crossman, of Bakerville	3	43
Thaddeus, of Burlington, m. Ann **ADAMS**, of New Hartford, Feb. 1, 1821, by Cyrus Yale	3	4
William, of Goshen, m. Ellen **BAILEY**, of New Hartford, Nov. 30, 1845, by Rev. Cyrus Yale	3	32
DANVILL, Mary Ann, of New Hartford, m. Samuel B. **WELLES**, of Sandisfield, Mass., Feb. 19, 1846, by Rev. Alexander Leadbetter. Int. Pub.	3	33
DAWSON, Eliza, of New Hartford, m. Solomon **JOHNSON**, of New Haven, Sept. 30, 1822, by Cyrus Yale	3	7
Jennette, m. Barzillai **MOSS**, Aug. 28, 1823, by Tubal Wakefield	3	9
John, s. Titus & Sibel, b. July 27, 1779	2	25
Martha, d. Titus & Sibel, b. Dec. 16, 1781	2	25
Timothy, m. Lucina **MARSH**, b. of New Hartford, Sept. 26, 1822, by Asa Goodwin, J.P.	3	7
Titus, m. Sibel **DENISON**, Aug. 26, 1778	2	25
DAYTON, Marcus, of Wolcottville, m. Diadama J. **STOCKWELL**, of New Hartford, Sept. 26, 1852, by Rev. E. N. Crossman, of Bakerville	3	46

	Vol.	Page
DELOON, [see also **DELOOR**], Lucinda, of New Hartford, m. Henry Seumac, of Norwich, July 7, 1829, by Asa Goodwin, J.P.	3	15
Lydia, of New Hartford, m. Worthy **BREWSTER**, of Granby, Nov. 25, 1830, by Asa Goodwin, J.P.	3	17
DELOOR, [see also **DELOON**], Polly, of New Hartford, m. Jacob **WAY**, of Farmington, Oct. 13, 1822, by William G. Williams, J.P.	3	7
DEMING, DEMMING, Asher, of Collinsville, m. Martha **OAKLEY**, of New Hartford, July 2, 1854, by Rev. F. A. Spencer	3	54
Chester M., of Canaan, m. Ellen **WOODRUFF**, of New Hartford, Apr. 22, 1846, by Rev. Cyrus Yale	3	32
Jonathan, Jr., of Sandisfield, Mass., m. Sophia **BALDWIN**, of New Hartford, Feb. 4, 1829, by Cyrus Yale	3	16
Margaret, m. Theodore **COWLES**, Feb. 26, 1794	2	46
DENISON, Sibel, m. Titus **DAWSON**, Aug. 26, 1778	2	25
DEWEY, Franklin S., of Westfield, Mass., m. Maria E. **GOODWIN**, of New Hartford, Sept. 6, 1852, by Rev. J. A. Saxton	3	45
Wilson, of Granby, m. Mary M. **SPENCER**, of New Hartford, Sept. 28, 1841, by Rev. Cyrus Yale	3	28
DICKINSON, Esther, m. Eliphalet **ENSIGN**, Jr., Nov. 20, 1777	2	38
DOOLITTLE, Jerusha, d. David & Saphath, b. Dec. 22, 1781	2	14
Jesse, s. Jesse & Mary, b. Nov. 16, 1764	1	61
Mary, d. Jesse & Mary, b. Aug. 9, 1767	1	61
Ruth, d. Jesse & Mary, b. Dec. 13, 1763	1	61
Zebina, d. Jesse & Mary, b. Jan. 7, 1772	1	65
Zerah, s. Jesse & Mary, b. Feb. 15, 1770	1	62
DOUGLASS, DOWGLASS, DOUGLAS, Abigail, d. Sam[ue]ll & Abigail, b. Dec. last day, 1771	1	66
Chester, [s. Moses & Anne], b. Dec. 25, 1785	2	5
Earl R., m. Elizabeth **MCNARY**, b. of New Hartford, Apr. 22, 1846, by Rev. Alexander Leadbetter. Int. Pub.	3	33
Hannah, d. Samuell & Mary, b. Feb. 16, 1741/2	1	37
Hannah, d. [ ]	1	25
James Spencer, m. Cornelier **ANDRUS**, b. of New Hartford, Nov. 24, 1853, by Rev. John H. Betts	3	55
James Spencer, m. Cornelia **ANDRUS**, Nov. 24, 1853, by Rev. J. H. Betts	3	56
John, [s. Moses & Anne], b. Oct. 8, 1782	2	5
Loes, d. Samuel & Mary, b. Oct. 26, 1749	1	36
Lois, m. Matthew **GILLETT**, Jr., Oc. 6, 1768	1	28
Mary, d. Samuel & Mary, b. June the last, 1736	1	25
Mary, m. Joseph **BACON**, Dec. 2, 1752	1	28
Merriam, twin with Moses, d. Samuell & Mary, b. Sept. 23, 1745	1	22
Moses, twin with Merriam, s. Samuell & Mary, b. Sept. 23, 1745	1	22
Moses, m. Anne **SPENCER**, June 28, 1781	2	5
Moses M., of Winsted, m. Juliaette M. **GARRET**, of New Hartford, July 14, 1852, by Rev. J. C. Haughton	3	44
Samuel, s. Samuel & Mary, d. Dec. 2, 1738	1	25
Samuel, s. Samuel & Mary, b. Apr. 27, 1740	1	25
Samuell, d. Oct. 14, 1766, in the 59th y. of his age	1	60
Sarah, d. Samuel & Mary, b. June 12, 1732	1	25
Sarah, [d. Moses & Anne], b. June 24, 1784	2	5

	Vol.	Page
DOUGLASS, DOWGLASS, DOUGLAS, (cont.)		
Sibel, d. Samuel & Mary, b. Aug. 18, 1738	1	25
Silas, s. Samuell & Abigail, b. July 24, 1765	1	58
DOWD, DOUD, Chester C., m. Orvilla N. **SPENCER,** of New Hartford, Oct. 1, 1839, by Rev. Cyrus Yale	3	27
Deborah, m. John **SPENCER,** Jr., Nov. 19, 1765	1	69
Huldah, of New Hartford, m. Chester R. **ATKINS,** of Cheshire, Aug. 10, 1841, by Samuel S. Bates, J.P.	3	36
Isaac, m. Huldah **BARNES,** b. of New Hartford, May 30, 1830, by Rev. Cyrus Yale	3	16
DRAKE, Mary Esther, of New Hartford, m. Horace **WESTCOTT,** of Cheshire, June 2, 1851, by Rev. John Herbert Betts	3	38
DRIGGS, Andrew, s. Martin & Joanna, b. Oct. 30, 1786	2	36
Anson, s. Martin & Joanna, b. June 18, 1789	2	36
Eliza, d. Martin & Joannar, b. Mar. 6, 1804	2	36
Eliza, m. Orrin **GOODWIN,** b. of New Hartford, Nov. 16, 1826, by Cyrus Yale	3	13
Hiram, s. Martin & Joanna, b. July 18, 1794	2	36
Julia, d. Martin & Joanna, b. Nov. 14, 1797	2	36
Julia, m. Daniel S. **BIRD,** b. of New Hartford, Oct. 17, 1821, by Cyrus Yale	3	6
Julia, m. Daniel S. **BIRD,** Oct. 17, 1821	2	36
Laura, d. Martin & Joanna, b. Nov. 17, 1791	2	36
Martin, m. Joanna **BRADLEY,** Sept. 25, 1785	2	36
Sterling G., s. Martin & Joannar, b. June 20, 1801; d. Dec. 22, 1803	2	36
DUNBAR, Esther, of Torrington, m. James **PALMER,** of Litchfield, Aug. 10, 1834, by Rev. David Miller	3	20
Niel, of Southington, m. Parnal **TYLER,** of New Hartford, Apr. 20, 1824, by Cyrus Yale	3	10
DUTTON, Henry S., s. Jesse & Roxy, b. Nov. 14, 1806	2	45
Jesse, m. Roxy **LANE,** Nov. 26, 1803	2	45
Mariah, d. Jesse & Roxy, b. Feb. 13, 1811	2	45
Minerva, d. Jesse & Roxy, b. Dec. 23, 1808	2	45
Minerva, m. Ralsamon O. **BELLAMY,** b. of New Hartford, Nov. 20, 1828, by Cyrus Yale	3	15
Sally, d. Jesse & Roxy, b. June 26, 1804	2	45
Sally, m. Horace **ROWLEY,** b. of New Hartford, June 21, 1827, by Rev. Cyrus Yale	3	14
EDDY, George W., of Berlin, m. Maria **MERRELL,** of New Hartford, Apr. 25, 1838, by Rev. Cyrus Yale	3	25
'EDGECOMB], EDGCOM, EDGCOME, EDGCOMB, Ammi, d. John & Phebe, b. Feb. 20, 1745/6	1	35
Elizabeth, had d. Betsey **JERRELLS,** b. July 4, 1780; father Fitch **JERRELLS**	2	2
Elizabeth, w. John & d. of Roger **OLMSTEAD,** decd. & Eunice, d. Nov. 17, 1801, in the 26th y. of her age	2	3
Ezra, s. John & Phebe, b. May 3, 1748	1	35
Huldah, d. John & Phebe, b. June 28, 1749	1	35
John, s. John & Phebe, b. Mar. 16, 1738	1	27
Jonathan, s. Ezra & Elizabeth, b. Jan. 5, 1774	1	66
Uriah, s. John & Phebe, b. Mar. 24, 1740	1	27

NEW HARTFORD VITAL RECORDS 257

	Vol.	Page
ELWELL, Gaius, s. Jonas, b. Dec. 21, 1792	2	30
Jonas, Jr., s. Jonas, b. June 18, 1787	2	30
ENSIGN, Anna, d. Eliphalet & Esther, b. Mar. 12, 1786	2	38
Bela, s. Samuell & Mary, b. Feb. 13, 1770	1	66
Chauncey, s. David & Elizabeth, b. Aug. 4, 1755	1	42
David, s. David & Elizabeth, b. June 1, 1754	1	42
Dorcas, d. Eliphalet & Esther, b. Apr. 9, 1791	2	38
Elias, s. Eliphalet & Dorkis, b. Dec. 26, 1750	1	38
Elias, s. Eliphalet & Esther, b. Apr. 17, 1780; d. June 22, 1783	2	38
Elias, 2nd, s. Eliphalet & Esther, b. Jan. 7, 1784	2	38
Eliphalet, m. Dorkise WEBSTER, Feb. 12, 1739/40	1	28
Eliphalet, s. Eliphalet & Dorkis, b. Aug. 16, 1748	1	38
Eliphalet, Jr., m. Esther DICKINSON, Nov. 20, 1777	2	38
Eliphalet, s. Eliphalet & Esther, b. Nov. 25, 1788	2	38
Eliphalet, Sr., d. July 21, 1792, in the 75th y. of his age	2	38
Elizabeth, d. David & Elizabeth, b. Oct. 17, 1760, at Windsor	1	54
Esther, d. Eliphalet, Jr. & Esther, b. July 31, 1778	2	38
Harvey, s. David & Elizabeth, b. Mar. 4, 1760	1	48
Ichabod, m. Elizabeth STEVISON, July 4, 1753	1	28
Jerushah, d. Eliphalet & Dorkish, b. Nov. 18, 1742	1	22
Jerusha, d. Eliphalet & Dorkis, b. Nov. 18, 1742	1	38
Jerusha, m. Daniel SHEPARD, Jr., b. of New Hartford, Jan. 25, 1770	1	28
Jerusha, had illeg. s. Isaac PAYNE, b. Jan. 23, 1787; f. Isaac PAYNE	2	30
John, s. Eliphalet & Dorkis, b. Dec. 20, 1754; d. Dec. 23, [1754]	1	46
Linus, s. Samuell & Mary, b. Apr. 10, 1772	1	67
Lucy, d. Eliphalet & Esther, b. July 10, 1793	2	38
Catis, s. Eliphalet & Dorkis, b. Dec. 23, 1739	1	22
Oatis, s. Eliphalet & Dorkis, b. Dec. 23, 1740	1	38
Polly, d. Eliphalet & Esther, b. Jan. 29, 1782	2	38
Sally, d. Eliphalet & Esther, b. Nov. 2, 1795	2	38
Samuel, s. Eliphalet & Dorkis, b. Sept. 6, 1745	1	22
Samuel, s. Eliphalet & Dorkis, b. Sept. 6, 1745	1	38
Samuell, m. Mary IVES, Sept. 3, 1767	1	66
Samuell, s. Samuel & Mary, b. Aug. 2, 1768	1	66
Seba, child of Samuell & Mary, b. Mar. 20, 1774; d. May 2, 1774	1	67
Seth, s. Eliphalet & Dorcis, b. Apr. 10, 1755; d. Mar. 9, 1757	1	46
Silas, s. David & Elizabeth, b. Dec. 1, 1756	1	47
Susanna, d. Eliphalet & Esther, b. Jan. 15, 1798, in Chemung, Cty. of Tioga, N.Y.	2	38
Titus, s. Eliphalet & Esther, b. Feb. 13, 1801, in State of Penn., Luzerne Cty. Town of Ulster	2	38
FARNSWORTH, George, m. Harriet BENEDICK, b. of Burlington, Oct. 8, 1832, by Rev. David Miller	3	19
Mary, of New Hartford, m. Isaac OLCOTT, of Wolcott, Oct. 27, 1841, by Rev. David Miller	3	28
FARRELL, Thomas, of Collinsville, m. Margret HOGAN, of New Hartford, June 11, 1854, by Rev. T. Hendricken	3	54
FENN, W[illia]m Henry, of Plymouth, m. Adah N. WEBSTER, of New Hartford, Nov. 29, 1827, by Rev. Cyrus Yale	3	17
FERRY, Mary P., of West Granby, m. Horatio N. SMITH, of New		

	Vol.	Page
FERRY, (cont.)		
Hartford, Sept. 9, 1849, by William Goodwin	2	53
FILLEY, Abram, m. Lucretia **MERRELLS,** July 28, 1790	2	37
Medad, s. Abraham & Lucretia, b. Sept. 25, 1793	2	37
Roxy, d. Abram & Lucretia, b. May 30, 1791	2	37
FISH, Ark W., of Hartford, m. Betsey **WHITE,** of New Hartford, Jan. 10, 1827, by Cyrus Yale	3	13
FLETCHER, Charlotte, m. Zachariah **SPENCER,** b. of New Hartford, Jan. 16, 1822, by Datus Ensign, Elder	3	6
FLOWER, FLOWERS, Abigail, d. Elijah & Abigail, b. July 4, 1745	1	22
Benjamin, s. John & Elizabeth, b. Apr. 30, 1732; d. Nov. 13, 1736, in the 5th y. of his age	1	26
Cornelius, s. John & Elizabeth, b. Dec. 2, 1726	1	26
Elijah, s. Elijah & Abigail, b. June 22, 1743; d. same day	1	22
Elisha, s. John & Elizabeth, b. May 16, 1729	1	26
Elisha, s. John & Elizabeth, d. Feb. 8, 1733/4 in the 5th y. of his age	1	26
Ely, s. Ely* & Abigail, b. June 19, 1750 *(Written over "Elijah")	1	53
George, s. Ely & Abigail, b. Apr. 26, 1760	1	53
Isaac, s. Ely* & Abigail, b. Aug. 16, 1755 *("Elijah")	1	53
Ithuriel, m. Mehetable **BROUGHTON,** Dec. 10, 1782	2	17
Ithuriel, Jr., s. Ithuriel & Mehetabel, b. Aug. 11, 1783	2	17
John, s. John & Elizabeth, b. Aug. 1, 1718	1	26
Lydia, d. Ely* & Abigail, b. Apr. 25, 1748 *(Written over "Elijah")	1	52
Nancy, d. Ely* & Abigail, b. Jan. 17, 1753; d. July 3, 1757 *(Written over "Elijah")	1	53
Nancy, d. Ely* & Abigail, b. Dec. 18, 1757 *("Elijah")	1	53
Nathaniel, s. John & Elizabeth, b. July 29, 1720	1	26
Reuben, s. John & Elizabeth, b. May 27, 1722	1	26
Violet, d. Jno & Elizabeth, b. Aug. 14, 1724	1	26
FORD, Sabra E., m. Hiram M. **TALLMADGE,** b. of New Hartford, Dec. 24, 1853, by Rev. J. H. Betts	3	56
Stephen, Jr., of Harwinton, m. Harriet **LOOMIS,** of New Hartford, Mar. 14, 1832, by Asa Goodwin, J.P.	3	19
FOSKET, Joel, Jr., m. Charlotte **BARNES,** Nov. 25, 1823, by Tubal Wakefield	3	10
FOSTER, Hiram, of Mereden, m. Maretta **HAMLIN,** of New Hartford, Feb. 14, 1836, by William Case	3	23
FOX, Delilah, of New Hartford, m. Benjamin **WILCOX,** of Voluntown, Sept. 22, 1824, by Cyrus Yale	3	10
Mariah H., of New Hartford, m. Edward **SMITH,** of Glastonbury, May 1, 1847, by Rev. George B. Atwell, of Pleasant Valley	3	34
RRISBIE, Enos, Jr., of Harwinton, m. Candace **WHITING,** of New Hartford, Apr. 18, 1827, by Rev. George E. Pierce	3	14
FURLONG, Elizabeth, m. Truman A. **HART,** b. of New Hartford, Feb. 11, 1854, by Rev. J. H. Betts	3	56
GAINS, Nelson, m. Margaretta **GLAPON*,** b. of New Hartford, Oct. 26, 1851, by Rev. J. H. Betts *("GLASSON"?)	3	43
GARNER, Franklin, s. Lorenzo, b. Oct. 1, 1840	2	47
Jane, d. Lorenzo **GARNER,** b. Dec. 1, 1837	2	47

	Vol.	Page
GARRETT, GARRET, GERRETT, Anna A., m. Aaron GATES, Jr., Sept. 5, 1838, by Rev. Aaron Gates, of Hartland]	3	25
Bigelow C., m. Sabrina C. MARSH, Oct. 8, [1833?], by Thomas Watson, Jr., J.P.	3	20
Delia, of New Hartford, m. Charles BLISS, of Collinsville, Feb. 12, 1834, by Rev. Cyrus Yale	3	30
Juliaette M., of New Hartford, m. Moses M. DOUGLASS, of Winsted, July 14, 1852, by Rev. J. C. Haughton	3	44
Mary F., m. Andrew CLARK, Jr., b. of New Hartford, Sept. 10, 1845, by Rev. Aaron Gates	3	31
Theda, m. Allen MOORE, b. of New Hartford, Oct. 8, 1822, by C. Yale	3	7
Watson, m. Huldah SPENCER, b. of New Hartford, Mar. 25, 1833, by Rev. Cyrus Yale	3	20
GATES, Aaron, Jr., m. Anna A. GARRETT, Sept. 5, 1838, by Rev. Aaron Gates, of Hartland	3	25
GAYLORD, Parintha, of Torringford, m. Henry W. WEDGE, May 5, 1840, by Rev. Cyrus Yale	3	27
GEAR, Mary W., m. Edwin E. HOWD, b. of New Hartford, May 6, 1824, by Cyrus Yale	3	10
GILBERT, Alma, d. Joseph & Miriam, b. June 28, 1794	2	42
Asa, s. Theodore & Mary, b. Nov. 14, 1708* *(Written over "1755")	1	43
Asa, m. Mary GOODWIN, July 22, 1784	2	19
Chloe, d. John & Theodosia, b. Sept. 14, 1779	2	18
Chloe, d. Joseph & Miriam, b. Apr. 21, 1796	2	42
Clarise, d. Joseph & Miriam, b. June 30, 1783	2	42
Edwin, s. Joseph & Miriam, b. Feb. 12, 1798	2	42
Elias, s. Joseph & Miriam, b. Nov. 29, 1776	2	42
Elizabeth, d. John & Theodosia, b. Mar. 6, 1777	2	18
Erastus, s. Asa & Mary, b. Apr. 11, 1790	2	19
Esther, d. John & Theodosia, b. July 15, 1770	1	69
Freeman, s. Joseph & Miriam, b. May 13, 1790	2	42
Giles, s. John & Theodosia, b. Mar. 15, 1775	1	69
Harriet, d. Asa & Mary, b. Aug. 31, 1788	2	19
Henry, m. Harriet MILLS, Sept. 20, 1829, by Cyrus Yale	3	16
Hiram, s. John & Theodosia, b. Oct. 24, 1785	2	18
John, Jr., s. John & Theodosia, b. Sept. 14, 1772	1	69
John, 2nd, s. John & Theodosia, b. Aug. 26, 1782	2	18
Joseph Marshfield, s. Joseph & Miriam, b. Nov. 2, 1778	2	42
Lucy, d. Joseph & Miriam, b. Aug. 28, 1774	2	42
Luman, s. Joseph & Miriam, b. Apr. 24, 1785	2	42
Mary, m. Theodore COWLES,, Aug. [ ], 1785	2	46
Miriam Webster, d. Joseph & Miriam, b. June 3, 1780	2	42
Nancy, d. Asa & Mary, b. Jan. 7, 1787	2	19
Orrin, s. Joseph & Miriam, b. Dec. 30, 1792	2	42
Polly Brace, d. Asa & Mary, b. Dec. 12, 1791	2	19
Theodore, m. Mary WATERS, June 11, 1750	1	28
Theodore, s. Theodore & Mary, b. Oct. 5, 1751 O.S.	1	38
Theodosia, d. John & Theodosia, b. Jan. 25, 1768	1	69
Theodosia, d. Joseph & Miriam, b. Apr. 28, 1787	2	42
Theodosia, m. William COOK, Feb. 14, 1788	2	33

	Vol.	Page
GILKS, Thomas, of Leamington, Eng., m. Caroline BAKER, of New Hartford, Oct. 24, 1852, by Rev. J. A. Saxton	3	47
GILLETT, GILLET, GILLETTE, GELLET, Adna, Jr., s. Adna & Jane, b. Aug. 23, 1788	2	33
Asantha, see Asantha GITTELL	3	32
Amanda, d. Michael & Esther, b. Feb. 25, 1791	2	4
Ann, d. Matthew & Ann, b. Nov. 19, 1750	1	36
Ann, w. Matthew, d. Dec. 22, 1783	2	4
Sinthy*, d. Matthew, Jr. & Lois, b. Sept. 19, 1769 *("Cynthia"?)	1	62
Esther, d. Michael & Esther, b. Mar. 26, 1785; d. Mar. 28, 1785	2	4
Esther, 2nd, d. Michael & Esther, b. May 15, 1786	2	4
George N., of Granville, m. Sylvia C. GILLETT, of New Hartford, Sept. 17, 1846, by Rev. Alexander Leadbetter. Int. Pub.	3	33
Heman, s. Adna & Jane, b. Jan. 12, 1781	2	33
Joseph, m. Sabrina MERRELL, b. of New Hartford, Mar. 22, 1821, by Cyrus Yale	3	5
Joseph, m. Abigail LOOMIS, Mar. 11, 1850, by Rev. Cyrus Yale	3	36
Lindey, d. Michael & Esther, b. Apr. 7, 1783	2	4
Linus, s. Michael & Esther, b. Oct. 7, 1800	2	4
Mabel, d. Michael & Esther, b. July 3, 1798	2	4
Mary, d. Matthew & Ann, b. Aug. 24, 1758	1	51
Mary, d. Adna & Jane, b. Mar. 8, 1783	2	33
Matthew, s. Matthew & Ann, b. Apr. 10, 1747	1	21
Matthew, Jr., m. Lois DOUGLASS, Oct. 6, 1768	1	28
Matthew, d. Dec. 24, 1789	2	4
Michael, s. Matthew & Ann, b. May 27, 174[ ]	1	25
Michael, s. Matthew & Ann, d. Sept. 9, 1757	1	51
Michael, s. Matthew & Ann, b. Jan. 22, 1761	1	52
Michael, m. Esther BRADLEY, June 13, 1782	2	4
Michael, s. Michael & Esther, b. Oct. 6, 1788	2	4
Miles, s. Michael & Esther, b. Dec. 1, 1795	2	4
Moses, s. Matthew, Jr. & Lois, b. Apr. 19, 1776	1	70
Nathan, m. Anne LOOMIS, Jan. 13, 1741/2	1	28
Phinehas, s. Matthew & Ann, b. July 6, 1754; d. Sept. 16, 1757	1	51
Phinehas, s. Matthew, Jr. & Lois, b. Mar. 16, 1771	1	62
Phinehas, s. Michael & Esther, b. July 4, 1793	2	4
Phinehas, m. Clarissa PITKIN, b. of New Hartford, Oct. 5, 1820, by Cyrus Yale	3	2
Sarah, d. Matthew, Jr. & Lois, b. Aug. 2, 1773	1	70
Sylvia C., of New Hartford, m. George N. GILLETT, of Granville, Sept. 17, 1846, by Rev. Alexander Leadbetter. Int. Pub.	3	33
GILMAN, Chester W., of Hartford, m. Antoinette SMITH, of East Haddam, Sept. 29, 1846, by Rev. Alexander Leadbetter. Int. Pub.	3	33
GITTELL*, Asantha, of New Hartford, m. Nehemiah ANDRUS, of Crawford, N.Y., Jan. 8, 1846, by Rev. Cyrus Yale *("GILLETT"?)	3	32
GLAPON, [see also GLASSON], Margaretta*, m. Nelson GAINS, b. of New Hartford, Oct. 26, 1851, by Rev. J. H. Betts *("Margaretta GLASSON"?)	3	43

	Vol.	Page
GLASSON, [see also **GLAPON**], Sophia, of New Hartford, m. Langston **WATT**, of New York City, Oct. 11, 1847, by Roger H. Mills, J.P.	3	34
GOODSEL[L], Dennis, of Burlington, m. Asenath **TYLER**, of New Hartford, Nov. 29, 1820, by Cyrus Yale	3	3
GOODWIN, Adaline, of New Hartford, m. Thaddeus L. **ROOT**, of Winchester, Dec. 27, 1854, by Rev. David Miller	3	56
Allen, m. Eunice M. **MARAH**, b. of New Hartford, Oct. 18, 1840, by Rev. Cyrus Yale	3	27
Amanda, of New Hartford, m. Carlow **SMITH**, of Sheffield, Mass., Sept. 12, 1820, by Cyrus Yale	3	2
Asa, s. Jonathan & Esther, b. Dec. 22, 1766	1	60
Asa, m. Polly **PEASE**, Nov. 14, 1793	2	40
Asa, Jr., s. Asa & Polly, b. Oct. 17, 1802	2	40
Betsey, d. Asa & Polly, b. Oct. 5, 1807	2	40
Betsey, m. Alpheas W. **BENHAM**, b. of New Hartford, Oct. 22, 1832, by Rev. Cyrus Yale	3	19
Daniel, m. Hannah **COWLES**, [ ]	2	30
Daniel, d. [ ]	2	30
Eleazer & Hannah, had d. [ ], s.b. May 4, 1738	1	51
Eleazer, Jr., s. Eleazer & Hannah, b. June 27, 1741	1	51
[Eleazer] & Hannah, had s. [ ], s.b. Dec. 14, 1748	1	51
Eleazer, s. Daniel & Hannah, b. Jan. 29, 1800	2	30
Elijah, s. Jonathan & Esther, b. Oct. 5, 1773	1	64
Elijah, m. Matilda **PEASE**, Jan. 5, 1797	2	45
Elijah, [s. George M.], b. Oct. 28, 1838	2	53
Elijah, Dea., d. Nov. 18, 1844	2	45
Elijah H., m. Harriet K. **WILLIAMS**, b. of New Hartford, Aug. 4, 1824, by Cyrus Yale	2	32
Elijah K.*, m. Harriet K. **WILLIAMS**, b. of New Hartford, Aug. 4, 1824, by Cyrus Yale *("H." overwritten)	3	10
Elijah Norton*, s. Elijah & Matilda, b. Sept. 26, 1802 *(Changed to "**HORTON**")	2	45
Eliza, m. Anthony **BAKER**, b. of New Hartford, Jan. 22, 1824, by Cyrus Yale	3	9
Elizabeth, d. Eleazer & Hannah, b. July 30, 1739	1	51
Emory, s. Asa & Polly, b. Nov. 23, 1796	2	40
Emory, m. Mary **KING**, b. of New Hartford, Oct. 20, 1825, by Cyrus Yale	3	11
Esther, d. Jonathan & Esther, b. Jan. 29, 1761	1	54
Esther, wid. Jonathan, d. June 20, 1811, ae. 74 y.	2	40
Flora, d. Asa & Polly, b. Apr. 9, 1805	2	40
Flora, m. Zenas **BARNES**, b. of New Hartford, Dec. 22, 1825, by Cyrus Yale	3	12
Frederick, [s. George M.], b. July 23, 1851	2	53
George Williams, [s. Elijah H. & Harriet K.], b. Mar. 25, 1828	2	32
Hannah, Jr., d. Eleazer & Hannah, b. Aug. 9, 1743	1	51
Hannah, m. Solom **WOODRUFF**, Nov. 20, 1766	1	29
Hannah, d. Jonathan & Esther, b. June 24, 1771	1	62
Hannah, d. Jonathan & Esther, b. July 25, 1776	1	64
Hannah, d. Daniel & Hannah, b. Apr. 6, 1804	2	30
Hannah, d. Elijah & Matilda, b. May 6, 1805	2	45

	Vol.	Page
GOODWIN, (cont.)		
Hannah, w. Daniel, d. [ ]	2	30
Hiram Gould, s. Jeduthan & Proserpine, b. May 18, 1808	2	51
Horace, m. Monemia J. **THORP**, b. of New Hartford, Jan. 25, 1838, by Rev. Cyrus Yale	3	24
Ira, s. Charles & Thankfull, b. Apr. 19, 1770	1	62
James Walter, [s. Elijah H. & Harriet K.], b. Nov. 30, 1835	2	32
Jeduthan, m. Pina **KING**, Oct. 2, 1803, by Amasa Jerome	2	51
Jeduthan & Pina, had 1st child s.b. Oct. 12, 1805	2	51
Juduthan, d. Feb. 13, 1809	2	51
Jonathan, s. Eleazer & Hannah, b. Oct. 13, 1731	1	51
Jonathan, s. Asa & Polly, b. Nov. 15, 1794; d. Feb. 22, 1801	2	40
Jonathan, Sr., d. May 15, 1797, ae. 65	2	40
Joseph G., m. Sarah A. **SMITH**, b. of New Hartford, Dec. 24, 1838, by Rev. Cyrus Yale	3	26
Levinia, b. Jan. 8, 1765; m. Isaac **STEEL**, Oct. [ ], 1792	2	27
Lewis, [s. George M.], b. Mar. 18, 1833	2	53
Lucy, of New Hartford, m. John **BIRGE**, of Torringford, Feb. 5, 1824, by Cyrus Yale	3	9
Lydia, d. Jesse & Rachel, b. Oct. 2, 1769	1	62
Margaret Tryphena, [d. Elijah H. & Harriet K.], b. Apr. 26, 1841	2	32
Maria E., of New Hartford, m. Franklin S. **DEWEY**, of Westfield, Mass., Sept. 6, 1852, by Rev. J. A. Saxton	3	45
Mary, d. Jesse & Rachel, b. Apr. 14, 1766	1	58
Mary, m. Asa **GILBERT**, July 22, 1784	2	19
Matilda, d. Elijah & Matilda, b. Oct. 3, 1797	2	45
Matilda, d. Elijah & Matilda, d. Jan. 29, 1816, ae. 18 y. 3 m. 26 d.	2	45
Mehetable, d. Eleazer & Hannah, b. Nov. 8, 1733	1	51
Michael, s. Eleazer & Hannah, b. Jan. 25, 1736	1	51
Miriam W., m. Henry D. **BOLLES**, Nov. 26, 1829, by Rev. Cyrus Yale	3	16
Moses, s. Eleazer & Hannah, b. Apr. 10, 1750	1	51
Norman, s. Asa & Polly, b. Dec. 19, 1809	2	40
Norman, m. Harriet P. **MERRELL**, b. of New Hartford, Nov. 3, 1844, by Rev. Cyrus Yale	3	30
Orrin, m. Eliza **DRIGGS**, b. of New Hartford, Nov. 16, 1826, by Cyrus Yale	3	13
Polly, d. Asa & Polly, b. Feb. 25, 1799; d. Jan. 9, 1800	2	40
Polly, d. Asa & Polly, b. Jan. 15, 1801	2	40
Polly, d. Daniel & Hannah, b. Nov. 8, 1811	2	30
Polly, m. Nelson **MERRELL**, b. of New Hartford, June 6, 1822, by Cyrus Yale	3	7
Polly, w. Asa, d. Dec. 7, 1836	2	40
Rebecca, d. Charles & Thankfull, b. Apr. 19, 1768	1	61
Reuby, d. Daniel & Hannah, b. Mar. 11, 1806	2	30
Rhoda, m. Wyllys **MARSH**, Dec. 23, 1807	2	47
Robert Pease, [s. Elijah H. & Harriet K.], b. Jan. 18, 1831	2	32
Roswell King, [s. Elijah H. & Harriet K.], b. Mar. 2, 1826	2	32
Russell, s. Elijah & Matilda, b. Aug. 23, 1799; d. Mar. 14, 1801	2	45
Ruth, d. Jonathan & Esther, b. June 8, 1763	1	56
Ruth, d. Jonathan & Esther, b. May 14, 1769	1	62
Sarah, d. Jonathan & Hester, b. Oct. 8, 1758	1	48

	Vol.	Page
GOODWIN, (cont.)		
Sarah M., [d. George M.], b. Nov. 8, 1852	2	53
Seth, s. Charles & Thankfull, b. Aug. 4, 1763	1	57
Siras*, s. Charles & Thankfull, b. Aug. 26, 1765 *(Changed to "Tyrus")	1	58
Susannah, d. Eleazar & Hannah, b. Feb. 26, 1746	1	51
Thankfull, d. Charles & Thankfull, b. May 22, 1762* *(Changed to "1761")	1	54
Warren, s. Daniel & Hannah, b. Mar. 26, 1808	2	30
William, [s. George M.], b. Nov. 10, 1842	2	53
William Horton, [s. Elijah H. & Harriet K.], b. Jan. 4, 1834	2	32
GRANGER, George W., of Tolland, Mass., m. Eliza M. BIRD, of New Hartford, Sept. 26, 1843, by Rev. J. Burt	3	29
GRIDLEY, Ithuel, m. Melissa CASE, b. of Canton, Apr. 24, 1844, by Charles P. McLean	3	30
GRIFFIN, Erastus, of Kinman, O., m. Emily LEET, of Canton, June 11, 1822, by Cyrus Yale	3	8
GRISWOLD, Ann, w. Seth, d. Sept. 16, 1774	1	67
Anna, d. Seth & Ann, b. May 5, 1763	1	55
Chauncey, of Barkhamsted, m. Frances W. RALSTON, of New Hartford, Dec. 3, 1854, by Rev. F. A. Spencer	3	55
Emeline A., m. Alfred ALLEN, b. of New Hartford, Sept. 26, 1850, by Rev. John H. Betts	3	37
Lewis W., m. Mary L. RIGLEY, b. of New Hartford, May 5, 1851, by Rev. John Herbert Betts	3	38
Richard W., of Torringford, m. Julia A. CURTIS, of New Hartford, Apr. 16, 1838, at the house of Dea. Elizur Curtis, by Rev. Herman L. Vaill, of Torringford	3	25
Seth, s. Seth & Ann, b. July 11, 1774	1	67
Susanna, d. Seth & Ann, b. June 4, 1761	1	53
Susanna, m. Jesse KELLOGG, May 10, 1781	2	31
GROSS, George W., of Torringford, m. Charlotte HEATON, of New Hartford, Oct. 11, 1842, by Rev. Cyrus Yale	3	29
GUILFORD, Charles H., of Waterbury, m. Helen M. CARR, of New Hartford, June 14, 1839, by Rev. John Higbey	3	26
GUY, John C., m. Esther A. BALDWIN, b. of New Hartford, Oct. 11, 1847, by Rev. Alexander Leadbetter	3	35
William Baldwin, s. John C. & Esther A., b. July 31, 1848	3	35
HALE, Clarisa, d. Reuben & Esther, b. Mar. 22, 1799	2	37
Eugene, d. Reuben & Esther, b. Nov. 12, 1788	2	37
Levi, s. Reuben & Esther, b. Sept. 6, 1791	2	37
Orpah, d. Reuben & Esther, b. Nov. 25, 1793	2	37
Tamar, d. Reuben & Esther, b. Apr. 6, 1801	2	37
William, of Collinsville, m. Lydia A. ROGERS, of New Hartford, Sept. 24, 1837, by Rev. Orsamus Allen, of Bristol	3	23
HALLOCK, Henry J., m. Julia Ann COOPER, Jan. 3, 1847, by Benjamin G. Loomis, J.P.	3	33
HAMLIN, Maretta, of New Hartford, m. Hiram FOSTER, of Mereden, Feb. 14, 1836, by William Case	3	23
HARRIS, John, s. Philip & Rhoda, b. Oct. 12, 1753	1	42
Norman J., m. Jane CROWE, b. of New Hartford, Dec. 31, 1854, by Rev. F. A. Spencer	3	55

	Vol.	Page
HARRIS, (cont.)		
Oliver, m. Diadama **SMITH**, b. of Glastonbury, June 29, 1835, by Asa Goodwin, J.P.	3	21
Rufus, of Glastonbury, m. Betsey **MIX**, of New Hartford, Feb. 28, 1828, by C. Yale	3	14
HART, Simeon, of Burlington, m. Mrs. Pamelia **PETTIBONE**, of New Hartford, Jan. 30, 1822, by Cyrus Yale	3	6
Truman A., m. Elizabeth **FURLONG**, b. of New Hartford, Feb. 11, 1854, by Rev. J. H. Betts	3	56
HAWLEY, Mary, m. Robert **AUSTIN**, Oct. 26, 1780	2	24
Sarah A., of New Hartford, m. Jacob **WITHNER**, of Troy, N.Y., July 19, 1854, by Rev. F. A. Spencer	3	55
[**HAYDEN**], **HEYDON**, Mary, m. Gideon Ackley **KNOWLTON**, Nov. 22, 1781	2	30
HAYS, Henry Elizur, of Oregon, m. Sarah Lavinia **WOODRUFF**, of New Hartford, Feb. 6, 1853, by Rev. Jame C. Haughton	3	49
HEATON, Charlotte, of New Hartford, m. George W. **GROSS**, of Torringford, Oct. 11, 1842, by Rev. Cyrus Yale	3	29
Jane, of New Hartford, m. Eli J. **TRUMBULL**, of Barkhamsted, June 2, 1840, by Rev. Cyrus Yale	3	27
HEMENWAY, Nathan, of Shoreham, Vt., m. Rachel **SPENCER**, of New Hartford, May 16, 1841, by Rev. Charles Bentley, of Harwinton	3	27
HENDERSON, HANDERSON, Edwin, m. Ann M. **LOOMIS**, b. of New Hartford, Nov. 27, 1828, by Cyrus Yale	3	16
Gordon W., m. Candace **MERRELL**, b. of New Hartford, Nov. 12, 1835, by Rev. William Case	3	22
Grove W., of New Hartford, m. Elizabeth A. **WILMOT**, of Plymouth, May 19, 1841, by Rev. Cyrus Yale	3	28
Jerusha, m. John **SPENCER**, Jr., June 1, 1775	1	70
John, m. Amelia **WOODFORD**, b. of New Hartford, May 4, 1831, by Cyrus Yale	3	18
Mary E., of New Hartford, m. Almeron **BUNN**, of Winsted, Sept. 1, 1852, by Rev. James C. Haughton	3	45
Sally, m. Heman **WATSON**, Jan. 4, 1803	2	50
Shubael H., m. Anna **MERRELL**, b. of New Hartford, Nov. 10, 1842, by Rev. Cyrus Yale	3	29
Susanna, m. Nathaniel **IVES**, Apr. 11, 1775	2	40
HENSHAW, Andrew Wheeler, s. [Benjamin, Jr. & Elsa], b. Mar. 13, 1794	2	39
Asher Miller, s. Benjamin & Elsa, b. Sept. 5, 1796	2	39
Benjamin, Jr., m. Elsa **WHEELER**, Aug. 18, 1791, at the house of Benjamin **HENSHAW**, f. of Benjamin, Jr., by Rev. Jonathan Marsh	2	39
Benjamin Hayward, [s. Benjamin, Jr. & Elsa], b. Apr. 10, 1795	2	39
Elizabeth Lord, d. Benjamin, Jr. & Elsa, b. Dec. 21, 1792	2	39
Huldah E., m. Ephraim G. **CROSBY**, b. of New Hartford, Sept. 21, 1820, by Cyrus Yale	3	2
HEWITT, Edward E., of Winsted, m. Laura **ANDREWS**, of New Hartford, Sept. 4, 1851, by Rev. John H. Betts	3	39
HIBBARD, William, m. Lucina **LOWREY**, Sept. 3, 1833, by Rev. Isaac Dwinel	3	19

	Vol.	Page
HIGLEY, Martha, of Canton, m. Edward WILCOX, of New Hartford, July 4, 1852, by Rev. John H. Betts	3	44
HILLIS, Cynthia, m. Charles D. KELLOGG, b. of New Hartford, Oct. 12, 1820, by Cyrus Yale	3	3
HITCHCOCK, Mary M., m. Jabez D. ARMSTRONG, b. of New Hartford, Apr. 26, 1821, by Rev. C. Yale	3	5
HODSDILL, Luther, of New Marlboro, m. Clarissa WEBSTER, of New Hartford, Sept. 15, 1828, by Cyrus Yale	3	15
HOGAN, Margret, of New Hartford, m. Thomas FARRELL, of Collinsville, June 11, 1854, by Rev. T. Hendricken	3	54
HOLCOMB, Elizabeth A., m. Frederick MERRELL, Apr. 18, 1838, by Rev. Cyrus Yale	3	24
Friend, m. Lydia ROBERTS, Mar. 22, 1821, by Cyrus Yale	3	5
Henry, m. Emily CARPENTER, b. of New Hartford, June 5, 1854, by Rev. J. H. Betts	3	56
Nancy S., m. Roger MILLS, b. of New Hartford, Sept. 7, 1828, by Cyrus Yale	3	15
Phinehas, m. Jerusha KELLOGG, b. of New Hartford, Dec. 12, 1826, by Cyrus Yale	3	13
Sophronia G., m. Douglass WILLIAM, b. of New Hartford, Sept. 2, 1828, by Rev. Cyrus Yale	3	14
HOLLEY, Francis N., of Wolcottville, m. Eliza A. HOTCHKISS, of New Hartford, May 27, 1846, by Rev. Alexander Leadbetter. Int. Pub.	3	33
HOPKINS, Abigail, m. Michael OLMSTED, Jan. 29, 1795	2	44
Consider, s. Consider & Lydia, b. July 21, 1752	1	38
Elias, s. Elias & Mirriam, b. Oct. 12, 1751	1	38
Elias, m. Meriam WEBSTER, May 10, 1752	1	28
Hannah, m. Asher BULL, May 23, 1776	2	12
Richard, of New Hartford, m. Belinda M. BARRIET, of Barkhamsted, Nov. 23, 1843, by Rev. Cyrus Yale	3	30
HOSMER, Lavinia, of East Hartford, m. Luke BARBER, of New Hartford, Apr. 24, 1845, by Alexander Leadbetter	3	32
HOTCHKISS, Abigail M., of New Hartford, m. Selden MILLARD, of Manchester Ioway (Territory), Mar. 15, 1842, by Rev. Cyrus Yale	3	28
Anson, of Wayne, O., m. Chloe G. COOK, of New Hartford, Oct. 25, 1821, by Cyrus Yale	3	6
Eliza A., of New Hartford, m. Francis N. HOLLEY, of Wolcottville, May 27, 1846, by Rev. Alexander Leadbetter. Int. Pub.	3	33
Julius C., of Burlington, m. Laura NEWELL, of New Hartford, Dec. 1, 1820, by Cyrus Yale	3	4
HOWD, Edwin E., m. Mary W. GEAR, b. of New Hartford, May 6, 1824, by Cyrus Yale	3	10
Emma Augusta, of New Hartford, m. Alfred COPELAND, of Hartford, Sept. 1, 1829, by Cyrus Yale	3	14
HUBBARD, Hannah, m. Ebenezer KELLEY*, May 11, 1739, by William Russel *("KELSEY"?)	1	28
	1	29
Mary, m. John SPENCER, Apr. 14, 1764		
HUBBELL, Ira, of Southington, m. Irena STRONG, of New Hartford, Sept. 2, 1820, by Cyrus Yale	3	2

	Vol.	Page
HUMPHREY, HUMPHREYS, Adna, of Simsbury, m. Caroline STOW, of New Hartford, May 3, 1827, by Cyrus Yale	3	13
Almirah, d. Alvin & Almirah, b. Dec. 3, 1795	2	46
Alvin, Jr., s. Alvin & Almirah, b. Aug. 13, 1790	2	46
Aness, m. Aaron **MERRELL**, Apr. 18, 1775	2	17
Ansel, s. Alvin & Almirah, b. June 1, 1792	2	46
Belinda, of Canton, m. Nelson **SMITH**, of Burlington, Dec. 11, 1828, by C. Yale	3	16
Cesta, child of Alvin & Almirah, b. Sept. 7, 1797	2	46
Dwight, s. Alvin & Almirah, b. Sept. 5, 1799	2	46
Milton, s. Alvin & Almirah, b. Feb. 23, 1794	2	46
Orrin, s. Alvin & Almirah, b. Aug. 27, 1801	2	46
HURLBURT, Lewis G., of West Hartford, m. Elizabeth D. **KELLOGG**, of New Hartford, Sept. 18, 1844, by Rev. Cyrus Yale	3	30
Mary, of Winchester, m. Charles **CLARK**, of Burlington, Sept. 26, 1820, by Cyrus Yale	3	2
Samuel D., m. Caroline **CARTER**, b. of New Hartford, Oct. 30, 1843, by Rev. Cyrus Yale	3	30
IVES, Abel, Jr., s. Abel & Lois, b. Oct. 6, 1762; d. Apr. 28, 1765	2	14
Abel, 2nd, s. Abel & Lois, b. June 13, 1766; d. Mar. 23, 1773	2	14
Amos, s. Abel & Lois, b. Aug. 28, 1768	2	14
Candace, d. Joseph & Rhoda, b. Dec. 31, 1773	1	69
Chauncey, s. Nathaniel & Susanna, b. Oct. 18, 1791	2	40
Lois, d. Abel & Lois, b. Aug. 23, 1764	2	14
Mary, m. Samuell **ENSIGN**, Sept. 3, 1767	1	66
Molly, d. Abel & Lois, b. July 19, 1771	2	14
Nathaniel, m. Susanna **HENDERSON**, Apr. 11, 1775	2	40
Nathaniel, Jr., s. Nathaniel & Susanna, b. May 23, 1783	2	40
Ruth, d. Abel & Lois, b. Apr. 2, 1761	2	14
Samuel, s. Nathaniel & Susanna, b. Oct. 15, 1777	2	40
Sarah, m. John **ANDRUS**, Jr., Oct. 17, 1749	1	29
Sebe, s. Abel & Lois, b. May 17, 1776	2	14
Seth, s. Abel & Lois, b. Jan. 27, 1774	2	14
Susanna, d. Nathaniel & Susanna, b. Feb. 11, 1780	2	40
JAQUA, James H., of Winsted, m. Amelia S. **KELLOGG**, of New Hartford, June 14, 1843, by Rev. Cyrus Yale	3	29
JARVIS, Milton B., M.D., of Dover, N.Y., m. Jenette J. **BUTLER**, of New Hartford, Feb. 25, 1836, by William Case	3	23
JERRELLS, Betsey, d. Fitch & Elizabeth **EDGCOMB**, b. July 4, 1780	2	2
JEWELL, George R., m. Sarah E. **ROCKWELL**, b. of New Hartford, Feb. 22, 1838, by Rev. Willis Lord	3	25
JOHNSON, Elizur, m. Maria **JONES**, Sept. 2, 1829, by Rev. David Miller	3	15
Ellen, of Winsted, m. John A. **WOODWARD**, of Watertown, Jan. 2, 1853, by Rev. John H. Betts	3	48
Henry, of Norfolk, m. Julia **JOHNSON**, of Orcutt, Pa., June 11, 1827, by Cyrus Yale	3	14
Julia, of Orcutt, Pa., m. Henry **JOHNSON**, of Norfolk, June 11, 1827, by Cyrus Yale	3	14
Solomon, of New Haven, m. Eliza **DAWSON**, of New Hartford, Sept. 30, 1822, by Cyrus Yale	3	7

	Vol.	Page
JONES, Eunice, w. Asahel, d. May 4, 1790, in the 42nd y. of her age	2	30
Henry, m. Catharine **MILLS**, b. of New Hartford, Jan. 25, 1826, by Cyrus Yale	3	12
L. Lysander, of New York City, m. Eliza Ann **MILLS***, of New Hartford, Oct. 31, 1842, by Rev. Cyrus Yale *(Should be "Ann Maria")	3	29
Lucy A., m. Edward A. **BROOKS**, Sept. 19, 1844, by Alexander Leadbetter. Int. Pub.	3	31
Maria, m. Elizur **JOHNSON**, Sept. 2, 1829, by Rev. David Miller	3	15
JOP, Elizabeth, m. Roger **OLMSTED**, Jr., Dec. 10, 1788	2	37
JUDD, Samuel E., of Farmington, m. Mary L. **STRONG**, of New Hartford, Apr. 6, 1836, by William Case	3	23
JUDSON, Damaris, m. Jonathan **MERRELL**, May 16, 1825, by Andrew Abernethy, J.P.	3	11
KAPLE, Charles, of Woster, N.Y., m. Delilah **SPENCER**, of New Hartford, Oct. 21, 1824, by Datus Engsign, Elder	3	11
KEETH(?), Maryan, Mrs., m. Rev. Jonathan **MARSH**, May 27, 1751	1	37
KELLEY*, Abel, s. Ebenezer & Hannah, b. Aug. 12, 1753 *("KELSEY"?)	1	42
Abigail*, d. Ebenezer & Hannah, b. June 6, 1746 *("Abigail **KELSEY**"?)	1	22
Daniel*, s. Samuell & Mary, b. Nov. 25, 174[3] *("Daniel **KELSEY**")	1	25
Davilly*, d. Ebenezer & Hannah, d. Jan. 22, 1768 *(Written over "Davilly **KELSEY**")	1	61
Ebenezer*, m. Hannah **HUBBARD**, May 11, 1739, by William Russel *("Ebenezer **KELSEY**"?)	1	28
Ebenezer*, twin with Loes, s. Ebenezer & Hannah, b. Aug. 18, 1744 *("Ebenezer **KELSEY**"?)	1	25
Ebenezer*, twin with Lois, s. Ebenezer & Hannah, b. Aug. 18, 1744 *("Ebenezer **KELSEY**"?)	1	28
Ebenezer*, s. Ebenezer & Hannah, b. Oct. 14, 1750 *("Ebenezer **KELSEY**"?)	1	36
Elisha*, s. Ebenezer & Hannah, b. Apr. 8, 1756 *("Elisha **KELSEY**"?)	1	46
Eunice*, m. Joseph* **CHURCH**, Dec. 1, 1743 *("Eunice **KELSEY**"?) *("Daniel" overwritten)	1	28
Hannah*, d. Ebenezer & Hannah, b. Mar. 27, 1740 *("Hannah **KELSEY**"?)	1	28
Jonathan*, m. Mary **STANDCLEF**, Jan. 26, 1742/3 *("Jonathan **KELSEY**"?)	1	28
Loes*, twin with Ebenezer, d. Ebenezer & Hannah, b. Aug. 18, 1744 *("Loes **KELSEY**"?)	1	25
Lois*, twin with Ebenezer, d. Ebenezer & Hannah, b. Aug. 18, 1744 *("Lois **KELSEY**"?)	1	28
Loes*, d. Eben[eze]r & Hannah, b. Oct. 1, 1763 *(Written over "Loes **KELSEY**")	1	58
Luce*, d. Samuell & Mary, b. Nov. 1, 1749 *("Luce **KELSEY**"?)	1	35
Rhoda*, d. Ebenezer & Hannah, b. May 8, 1742 *("Rhoda **KELSEY**"?)	1	25
Samuell*, s. Samuell & Mary, b. Mar. 30, 1756 *(Written		

	Vol.	Page
KELLEY*, (cont.)		
"Samuell **KELSEY**")	1	43
Sarah*, d. Samuell & Mary, b. May 29, 1753 *("Sarah **KELSEY**"?)	1	42
Sarah*, d. Stephen, d. Oct. 17, 1756 *("Sarah **KELSEY**"?)	1	46
KELLOGG, Abigail, d. Ashbel & Sarah, b. Mar. 16, 1760	1	57
Abigail, d. Ashbel & Sarah, b. Mar. 16, 1760	2	34
Abraham, m. Sarah **MARSH**, June 17, 1747	2	18
Abram, m. Sarah **MARSH**, June 17, 1747	1	28
Abram, s. Abram & Sarah, b. Jan. 27, 1749/50	1	38
Abram, [s. Abraham & Sarah], b. Jan. 27, 1750	2	18
Abram, Jr., b. Jan. 27, 1750; m. Sarah **SEYMOUR**, Feb. 6, 1772	2	25
Abram, [s. Abram, Jr. & Sarah], b. Sept. 28, 1774	2	25
Abram, m. Sarah **MERRELL**, Jan. 6, 1803	2	25
Amelia S., of New Hartford, m. James H. **JAQUA**, of Winsted, June 14, 1843, by Rev. Cyrus Yale	3	29
Ansel, [s. Jesse & Susanna], b. Oct. 21, 1786	2	31
Aranda, s. Ashbel & Lucy, b. Sept. 8, 1790	2	34
Asahel, m. Amanda **SPENCER**, Jan. 9, 1809	2	34
Ashbel, m. Sarah **LOOMIS**, Apr. 5, 1759	2	34
Ashbel, [s. Ashbel & Sarah], b. Oct. 18, 1763	2	34
Ashbel, m. Lydia **STEEL**, July 17, 1766	2	34
Ashbel, m. Lucy **COTTON**, Sept. 20, 1780	2	34
Ashbel, [s. Ashbel & Lucy], b. Sept. 13, 1783	2	34
Ashbel, Jr., m. Martha Bacon **WARD**, June 3, 1790	2	18
Ashbel, s. Ashbel, Jr. & Martha, b. Oct. 27, 1791	2	18
Ashbel, Sr., d. Feb. 7, 1806, ae. 73 y. 3 m. 8 d.	2	34
Austin, m. Louisa S. **CLEVELAND**, b. of New Hartford, Dec. 18, 1837, by Rev. Willis Lord	3	24
A zubah, d. Joseph & Esther, b. Aug. 18, 1754	1	43
Charles D., m. Cynthia **HILLIS**, b. of New Hartford, Oct. 12, 1820 by Cyrus Yale	3	3
Charles D., m. Susan **BIDWELL**, b. of New Hartford, Jan. 19, 1845, by Rev. Cyrus Yale	3	31
Chloe, [d. Ashbel & Lydia], b. Mar. 16, 1774	2	34
Chloe, [d. Ashbel & Lydia], d. Sept. 5, 1776	2	34
Clarre, [d. Noah & Clemence], b. May 19, 1777	2	14
Clemenc[e], d. Noah & Clemene, b. Feb. 18, 1758	1	47
Clemence, [s. Noah & Clemence], b. Feb. 18, 1758	2	14
Cotton, [s. Ashbel & Lucy], b. Aug. 18, 1785	2	34
Daniel, s. Isaac, Jr. & Martha, b. Apr. 5, 1758	1	46
Eleazer, s. Jude*, Jr. & Martha, b. Apr. 10, 1749 *(Overwritten to read "Isaac")	1	35
Eleazer, s. Isaac, Jr. & Martha, b. Apr. 10, 1749	1	46
Elias, twin with Moses, s. Abram & Sarah, b. Feb. 3, 1754	1	42
Elias, twin withMoses, d. [Abraham & Sarah], b. Feb. 3, 1754	2	18
Elijah, [s. Ashbel & Lydia], b. July 12, 1770	2	34
Eliza, of New Hartford, m. George M. **WELCH**, of Hartford, Oct. 5, 1853, by Rev. F. A. Spencer	3	50
Elizabeth, [d. Abraham & Sarah], b. June 17, 1768	2	18
Elizabeth D., of New Hartford, m. Lewis G. **HURLBURT**, of West Hartford, Sept. 18, 1844, by Rev. Cyrus Yale	3	30

	Vol.	Page
KELLOGG, (cont.)		
Esther, d. Abram & Sarah, b. Mar. 24, 1748	1	21
Esther, [d. Abraham & Sarah], b. Mar. 24, 1748	2	18
Fanna, [d. Jesse & Susanna], b. June 13, 1784	2	31
Fanny, of New Hartford, m. Henry **GARDER**, of Killingworth, Oct. 4, 1832, by Rev. Cyrus Yale	3	18
Frederick H., of Terryville, m. Polly **STEELE**, of New Hartford, Jan. 1, 1845, by Rev. Cyrus Yale	3	30
Frederick Webster, [s. Abraham & Sarah], b. Jan. 31, 1761	2	18
Green, [s. Solomon & Ruthe], b. Sept. 14, 1782	2	32
Hannah, [d. Abram, Jr. & Sarah], b. Oct. 29, 1772; d. May 3, 1774	2	25
Hannah, [d. Abram, Jr. & Sarah], b. Mar. 18, 1776	2	25
Hannah, m. Joseph **AUSTIN**, Dec. 18, 1782	2	28
Harvey, [s. Solomon & Ruthe], b. Sept. 29, 1784	2	32
Helmont, s. Samuell & Mary, b. Mar. 17, 1762	1	54
Henry A., m. Loraine E. **BUTLER**, b. of New Hartford, Sept. 29, 1841, by Rev. Cyrus Yale	3	28
Henry C., m. Mariette **SPRAGUE**, b. of New Hartford, May 1, 1854, by Rev. F. A. Spencer	3	53
Horace, [s. Abram, Jr. & Sarah], b. Oct. 1, 1780	2	25
Horace, m. Orpah **PRATT**, Oct. 21, 1807, by Isaac Porter	2	49
Hulda Lovisa, d. Noah & Clement, b. Sept. 13, 1763	1	58
Huldah Lavina, [d. Noah & Clemence], b. Sept. 13, 1763	2	14
Isaac, Jr., m. Martha **MERRILL**, Jan. 26, 1748	1	11
Isaac, d. July 3, 1787, in the 91st y. of his age	2	34
Jimme, [s. Solomon & Ruthe], b. Feb. 14, 1787	2	32
James, m. Harriet M. **MERRILL**, May 1, 1850, by Rev. Cyrus Yale	3	36
Jerusha, m. Allen **BENHAM**, b. of New Hartford, Feb. 7, 1822, by Cyrus Yale	3	6
Jerusha, m. Phinehas **HOLCOMB**, b. of New Hartford, Dec. 12, 1826, by Cyrus Yale	3	13
Jesse, s. Noah & Clemence, b. Sept. 25, 1759	1	49
Jesse, [s. Noah & Clemence], b. Sept. 25, 1759	2	14
Jesse, m. Susanna **GRISWOLD**, May 10, 1781	2	31
Joana, d. Noah & Clemene, b. Jan. 15, 1768	1	61
Joanna, [d. Noah & Clemence], b. Jan. 15, 1768	2	14
John P., m. Achsa A. **MERRELL**, b. of New Hartford, Sept. 21, 1843, by Rev. Cyrus Yale	3	29
Julia Caroline, d. Asahel & Amanda, b. Nov. 17, 1810	2	34
Laura, m. Ashbel **MARSH**, b. of New Hartford, Sept. 2, 1826, by Cyrus Yale	3	12
Leonard F., m. Francis F. **MERRELL**, May 27, 1847, by Rev. Cyrus Yale	3	34
Lucy, [d. Ashbel & Lydia], b. Feb. 26, 1773	2	34
Lurannah, d. Isaac, Jr. & Martha, b. Dec. 25, 1765	1	67
Lydia, [d. Ashbel & Lydia], b. Dec. 19, 1768	2	34
Lydia, w. Ashbel, d. Nov. 14, 1779	2	34
Margaret, m. Chandler **ROSSETER**, Mar. 15, 1829, by Cyrus Yale	3	16
Martha, d. Isaac, Jr. & Martha, b. Sept. 19, 1751	1	46
Martin, s. Abram & Sharah, b. July 16, 1756* *(Written		

	Vol.	Page
KELLOGG, (cont.)		
over "1758")	1	49
Martin, [s. Abraham & Sarah], b. July 16, 1758	2	18
Mary, 1st d. Isaac, Jr. & Martha, b. Jan. 17, 1754; d. Jan. 23, 1754	1	46
Mary, 2nd, d. Isaac, Jr. & Martha, b. May 9, 1756	1	46
Mary Ann, d. Ashbel & Sarah, b. Oct. 9, 1761	1	57
Mary Ann, [d. Ashbel & Sarah], b. Oct. 9, 1761	2	34
Mela, d. Isaac, Jr. & Martha, b. Feb. 12, 1763	1	56
Meriam, d. Noah & Clement, b. Sept. 6, 1765	1	58
Meriam, [d. Noah & Clemence], b. Sept. 6, 1765	2	14
Miriam, m. Noah **SEYMOUR**, Dec. 17, 1784	2	42
Michael,]s. Noah & Clemence], b. Mar. , 1770	2	14
Moses, twin with Elias, s. Abram & Sarah, b. Feb. 3, 1754	1	42
Moses, twin with Elias, s. [Abraham & Sarh], b. Feb. 3, 1754	2	18
Nancy, [d. Ashbel & Lydia], b. Apr. 2, 1776	2	34
Naomi, m. Elizur **CURTIS**, Nov. 25, 1802	2	47
Noah, m. Clemmence **MERRELL**, Nov. 18, 1754	1	28
Noah, m. Clemence **MERRELL**, Nov. 18, 1754	2	14
Noah, s. Noah & Clemene, b. Aug. 8, 1756	1	47
Noah, Jr., [s. Noah & Clemence], b. Aug. 8, 1756	2	14
Norman, m. Fanny **STEEL**, b. of New Hartford, Jan. 3, 1821, by Cyrus Yale	3	4
Orpah Ann, of New Hartford, m. Elijah **WOODWARD**, of Torringford, Nov. 6, 1850, by Rev. Cyrus Yale	3	37
Philo, of Manlius, N.Y., m. Nancy **RILEY**, of New Hartford, Oct. 14, 1821, by Cyrus Yale	3	6
Phinehas, s. Abram & Sarah, b. June 7, 1756	1	43
Phinehas, [s. Abraham & Sarah], b. June 7, 1756	2	18
Rachel, d. Isaac, Jr. & Martha, b. May 1, 1760	1	54
Rhoderick, [s. Ashbel & Lydia], b. Dec. 24, 1777	2	34
Ruthe, m. Solomon **KELLOGG**, Nov. 16, 1773	2	32
Ruth, [d. Solomon & Ruthe], b. Aug. 12, 1774	2	32
Sarah, [d. Noah & Clemence], b. Sept. 28, 1761	2	14
Sarah, [d. Abraham & Sarah], b. June 3, 1763	2	18
Sarah, w. Ashbel, d. June 22, 1765	2	34
Sarah, d. Ashbel & Lydia, b. May 19, 1767	2	34
Sarah, [d. Ashbel & Lydia], d. Oct. 5, 1776	2	34
Sarah, m. Daniel **SANDEFORTH**, May 10, 1781	2	16
Sara, [d. Abram, Jr. & Sarah], b. July 4, 1783	2	25
Sarah, [s. Ashbel & Lucy], b. Feb. 21, 1788	2	34
Sarah, w. Abram, d. Mar. 4, 1802	2	25
Sarah, of New Hartford, m. Roswell **COOK**, of Harwinton, Jan. 14, 1830, by Rev. Cyrus Yale	3	16
Silas, [s. Solomon & Ruthe], b. Mar. 30, 1776	2	32
Silva, [d. Jesse & Susanna], b. Feb. 15, 1782	2	31
Solomon, s. Abram & Sarah, b. Dec. 10, 1751	1	38
Solomon, [s. Abraham & Sarah], b. Dec. 10, 1751	2	18
Solomon, m. Ruthe **KELLOGG**, Nov. 16, 1773	2	32
Solomon, Jr., [s. Solomon & Ruthe], b. Apr. 4, 1778	2	32
Sophia, of New Hartford, m. William **LOVEJOY**, of Wolcott, N.Y., Feb. 17, 1824, by Cyrus Yale	3	9
Timothy, s. Samuell & Mary, b. Sept. 3, 1745	1	22

	Vol.	Page
KELLOGG, (cont.)		
Truman, [s. Abraham & Sarah], b. Jan. 3, 1766	2	18
Truman, m. Fanny **MARSH**, b. of New Hartford, Aug. 25, 1825, by Cyrus Yale	3	11
Virgil, [s. Abram, Jr. & Sarah], b. June 29, 1785	2	25
Warren, [s. Abram, Jr. & Sarah], b. Jan. 5, 1779	2	25
Washington, [s. Solomon & Ruthe], b. July 2, 1780	2	32
KELSEY*, Abel, s. Ebenezer & Hannah, b. Aug. 12, 1753 *(Arnold Copy has "**KELLEY**")	1	42
Abigail, d. Ebenezer & Hannah, b. June 5, 1746	1	22
Daniel, s. Samuell & Mary, b. Nov. 25, 174[3]	1	25
Davilly, d. Ebenezer & Hannah, d. Jan. 22, 1768	1	61
Ebenezer*, m. Hannah **HUBBARD**, May 11, 1739, by William Russel[l] *(Arnold Copy has "Ebenezer **KELLEY**")	1	28
Ebenezer*, twin with Loes, s. Ebenezer & Hannah, b. Aug. 18, 1744 *(Arnold Copy has "Ebenezer **KELLEY**")	1	25
Ebenezer, twin with Lois, s. Ebenezer & Hannah, b. Aug. 18, 1744	1	28
Ebenezer, s. Ebenezer & Hannah, b. Oct. 14, 1750	1	36
Elisha, s. Ebenezer & Hannah, b. Apr. 8, 1756	1	46
Eunice, m. Joseph* **CHURCH**, Dec. 1, 1743 *("Daniel" overwritten)	1	28
Hannah, d. Ebenezer & Hannah, b. Mar. 27, 1740	1	28
Jonathan, m. Mary **STANDCLEF**, Jan. 26, 1742/3	1	28
Loes, twin with Ebenezer, d. Ebenezer & Hannah, b. Aug. 18, 1744	1	25
Lois, twin with Ebenezer, d. Ebenezer & Hannah, b. Aug. 18, 1744	1	28
Loes, d. Eben[eze]r & Hannah, b. Oct. 1, 1763	1	58
Luce, d. Samuell & Mary, b. Nov. 1, 1749	1	35
Rhoda, d. Ebenezer & Hannah, b. May 8, 1742	1	25
Samuell, s. Samuell & Mary, b. Mar. 30, 1756	1	43
Sarah, d. Samuell & Mary, b. May 29, 1753	1	42
Sarah, d. Stephen, d. Oct. 17, 1756	1	46
KEMBLE, Harriet, m. Eliphalet **SMITH**, b. of Goshen, Nov. 9, 1824, by Eli Barrett, Elder	3	11
KILBOURNE, KILLBOURNE, John, m. Deborah **SMITH**, Aug. 20, 1785	2	34
Laura Ann, m. Otis T. **PECK**, July 18, 1830, by Andrw Abernethy,, J.P.	3	18
KING, Arnold, m. Melinda **STONE**, Oct. 3, 1824, by Asa Goodwin, J.P.	3	10
Charity, w. Gideon, d. July 27, 1810	2	48
Charles H., m. Ellen **STANCLIFFE**, Sept. 26, 1852, by Rev. John H. Betts	3	47
Gideon, d. Dec. 11, 1802	2	48
Gideon Smith, s. Plato & Betsey, b. Feb. 25, 1812	2	48
Mary, m. Emory **GOODWIN**, b. of New Hartford, Oct. 20, 1825, by Cyrus Yale	3	11
Mary French, d. Plato & Betsey, b. Oct. 5, 1804	2	48
Pina, m. Jeduthan **GOODWIN**, Oct. 2, 1803, by Amasa Jerome	2	51
Plato, of New Hartford, m. Betsey **MARAH**, of East Hartford, Dec. 7, 1800	2	48

	Vol.	Page
KING, (cont.)		
Plato & Betsey, had s. [ ], b. Sept. 23, 1801; d. Oct. 1, 1801	2	48
Sherman, s. Plato & Betsey, b. Dec. 14, 1806	2	48
KNOWLTON, Ackley, [s. Gideon Ackley & Mary], b. June 25, 1786	2	30
Gideon Ackley, m. Mary **HEYDON**, Nov. 22, 1781	2	30
Harry, [d. Gideon Ackley & Mary], b. Sept. 22, 1784	2	30
Lydia Smith, [d. Gideon Ackley & Mary], b. Jan. 31, 1783	2	30
Polly, d. Gideon A. & Mary, b. May 9, 1788	2	30
LANDSON, Jairus, m. Aeta M. **SEGAR**, b. of New Hartford, Mar. 24, 1830, by Rev. Cyrus Yale	3	17
LANE, Mindwell, m. John **ROBERTS**, Sept. 16, 1780	2	15
Roxy, m. Jesse **DUTTON**, Nov. 26, 1803	2	45
LANGDON, Nathaniel G., of Canton*, m. Ursula **SEGAR**, of New Hartford, Nov. 29, 1827, by Rev. Cyrus Yale *(Note says "New Hartford")	3	17
Orrin M., of Bristol, m. Harriet **SEGAR**, of New Hartford, Nov. 25, 1830, by Rev. Cyrus Yale	3	18
LEE, Anna Harris, d. Samuel W. & Mehetabel, b. Nov. 21, 1795	2	36
Hetty, d. Samuel W. & Mehetabel, b. Mar. 9, 1786	2	36
Polly W., d. Samuel W. & Mehetabel, b. Nov. 15, 1790	2	36
Robert, s. Samuel W. & Mehetabel, b. Feb. 1, 1784	2	36
Samuel W., m. Mehetabel **ROBBINS**, May 22, 1783	2	36
Samuel Waters, s. Samuel W. & Mehetabel, b. Nov. 21, 1795	2	36
Thomas, of New Britain, m. Esther L. **LUSH**, of New Hartford, Jan. 3, 1838, by Rev. Willis Lord	3	24
LEET, Emily, of Canton, m. Erastus **GRIFFIN**, of Kinman, O., June 11, 1822, by Cyrus Yale	3	8
LEWIS, Chloe, d. Charles & Rhoda, of Barkhamstead, b. Nov. 9, 1762, in Barkhamstead	1	57
Elizabeth, d. Charles & Rhoda, of Barkhamstead, b. Dec. 23, 1760, in Barkhamstead	1	57
Mary, of New Hartford, m. Wilson **CASE**, of Granby, Sept. 8, 1846, by Rev. Alexander Leadbetter. Int. Pub.	3	33
Nath[anie]ll, s. Charles & Rhoda, of Barkhamstead, b. Apr. 24, 1759, in Barkhamstead	1	57
W[illia]m, of Bristol, m. Lucretia **CATLIN**, of New Hartford, Nov. 10, 1835, by Richard M. Chipman, V.D.M.	3	22
LOOMIS, Abigail, d. Lieut.Israel & Sarah, b. May* 6, 1753 *(Overwritten to read "Aug.")	1	42
Abigail, d. Israel & Sarah, d. Oct. 12, 1757	1	52
Abigail, d. Joseph & Mary, b. Jan. 4, 1795	2	31
Abigail, m. Joseph **GILLETTE**, Mar. 11, 1850, by Rev. Cyrus Yale	3	36
Andrew H., m. Laura C. **MERRELL**, b. of New Hartford, Aug. 21, 1831, by Rev. Cyrus Yale	3	18
Ann M., m. Edwin **HENDERSON**, b. of New Hartford, Nov. 27, 1828, by Cyrus Yale	3	16
Anne, m. Nathan **GILLET**, Jan. 13, 171/2	1	28
Ashbel, s. Israel & Sarah, d. Oct. 16, 1757	1	52
Ashbel, s. Althea **TERRELL**, b. Apr. 9, 1792	2	17
Caroline Marsh, d. Luther & Esther, b. Oct. 16, 1821	2	31

	Vol.	Page
LOOMIS, (cont.)		
Desiah, d. Lieut. Israel & Sarah, d. Dec. 15, 1762	1	56
Eliza Maria, d. Luther & Esther, b. June 16, 1820	2	31
Emeline, of New Hartford, m. Harry **PECK**, of Bristol, Apr. 23, 1838, by Rev. Cyrus Yale	3	25
Esther C., [d. Luther & Esther], b. Sept. 21, 1823	2	31
Hannah, d. Israel & Sarah, b. May 4, 1744	1	25
Harriet, of New Hartford, m. Stephen **FORD**, Jr., of Harwinton, Mar. 14, 1832, by Asa Goodwin, J.P.	3	19
Isaac, s. Israel & Sarah, b. July 3, 1750	1	38
Israel, m. Sarah **SIMONS**, Nov. [ ], 1737	1	52
Israel, s. Israel, b. Aug. 17, 1738	1	26
Israel, Dea., d. Sept. 10, 1781, in the 78th y. of his age	1	39
Israel, s. Joseph & Mary, b. Nov. 29, 1789	2	31
Israel, m. Phebe **ANDRUS**, b. of New Hartford, Dec. 7, 1820, by Cyrus Yale	3	4
Jeremiah, of Springfield, Mass., m. Hannah **WILMOT**, of New Hartford, Dec. 2, 1835, by Rev. Seth Higbey	3	22
Joseph, s. Israel & Sarah, b. June 17, 1747	1	39
Joseph, s. Joseph & Mary, b. June 18, 1788	2	31
Joseph, m. Mary **CRISSE**, Jan. 10, 1796* *(Overwritten to read "1786")	2	31
Kezia, d. Israel & Sarah, b. Feb. 10, 1741/2	1	27
Laura A., m. Albert P. **PHELPS**, b. of New Hartford, May 5, 1852, by Rev. Cyrus Yale	3	43
Luther, s. Joseph & Mary, b. Dec. 21, 1791	2	31
Luther, m. Esther **MARSH**, July 8, 1819	2	31
Mary, d. Joseph & Mary, b. Jan. 21, 1787	2	31
Mary A., of New Hartford, m. Elizur O. **BROWN**, of Canton, Nov. 7, 1853, by Rev. F. A. Spencer	3	50
Mary Ann, [d. Luther & Esther], b. June 5, 1826	2	31
Philo A., m. Polly Ann **WATSON**, Oct. 22, 1835, by R. M. Chipman, V.D.M.	3	22
Sarah, d. Jereall & Sarah, b. Jan. 5, 1739/40	1	27
Sarah, m. Ashbel **KELLOGG**, Apr. 5, 1759	2	34
Sarah, w. Israel, d. Nov. 17, 1791, in the 80th y. of her age	1	39
Sarah Jane, [d. Luther & Esther], b. Aug. 5, 1833	2	31
Simeon, of Torrington, m. Flora **WOODRUFF**, of New Hartford, Apr. 20, 1834, by Rev. Cyrus Yale	3	21
LOVEJOY, William, of Wolcott, N.Y., m. Sophia **KELLOGG**, of New Hartford, Feb. 17, 1824, by Cyrus Yale	3	9
LOWREY, Lucina, m. William **HIBBARD**, Sept. 3, 1833, by Rev. Isaac Dwinel	3	19
William, of Burlington, m. Lucinda **VOSE**, of New Hartford, Apr. 4, 1830, by Rev. David Bennett	3	16
LUSH, Elizabeth C., of New Hartford, m. Curtis **WHAPLE**, of New Britain, May 9, 1838, by Rev. Willis Lord	3	25
Esther L., of New Hartford, m. Thomas **LEE**, of New Britain, Jan. 3, 1838, by Rev. Willis Lord	3	24
LYMAN, Anna, [d. Francis & Abigail], b. Dec. 7, 1780	2	2
Benjamin, s. David & Rhoda, b. July 8, 1819	2	44
Clarinda Mary, d. John & Salome, b. Sept. 29, 1805	2	49

	Vol.	Page
LYMAN, (cont.)		
Daniel, s. David & Mary, b. Apr. 18, 1784	2	3
David, Jr., m. Rhoda **BELDEN**, Apr. 9, 1801	2	44
David, m. Lucina **AUSTIN**, b. of New Hartford, July 13, 1826, by Cyrus Yale	3	12
David Belden, s. David & Rhoda, b. July 29, 1803	2	44
Edward, s. David & Rhoda, b. Aug. 5, 1810	2	44
Electa J., of New Hartford, m. Leavit D. **MILLS**, of Burlington, Mar. 14, 1848, by Rev. William N. Morse	3	34
Elijah, s. David & Rhoda, b. Feb. 6, 1808	2	44
Emily, d. John & Salome, b. Aug. 22, 1809	2	49
Emily, of New Hartford, m. George W. **STONE**, of Warren, Apr. 17, 1838, at the house of John Lyman, by Rev. Herman L Vaill, of Torringford	3	25
Epaphras, [s. Francis & Abigail], b. Feb. 2, 1784	2	2
Francis, m. Abigail **COWLS**, May 4, 1780	2	2
Gaylord Porter, s. David & Rhoda, b. Sept. 6, 1821	2	44
George, s. David & Rhoda, b. Apr. 17, 1806	2	44
Harvey, s. Josiah & Deborah, b. Dec. 13, 1794	2	35
James, s. David & Rhoda, b. Feb. 14, 1813; d. May 17, 1813	2	44
James D., m. Rhoda E. **MARSH**, b. of New Hartford, Nov. 24, 1853, by Rev. F. A. Spencer	3	51
Jane M., of New Hartford, m. W[illia]m W. **BALDWIN**, of West Granvill, Mass., June 13, 1849, by Rev. Judson G. Lyman, of Huntington	2	52
Jerusha, d. Josiah & Deborah, b. June 1, 1801	2	35
John, s. David & Mary, b. Oct. 5, 1778, at Litchfield	2	3
John, m. Salome **MALTBY**, Mar. 19, 1801	2	49
John Bennet, s. John & Salome, b. Feb. 5, 1802	2	49
Josiah, m. Deborah **WESTLAND**, Mar. 1, 1790	2	35
Judson G., m. Abby B. **CLARK**, b. of New Hartford, June 21, 1848, by Rev. C. H. Topliff, of Collinsville. Int. Pub.	3	35
Julia Ann, d. David & Rhoda, b. May 24, 1824	2	44
Julius, s. John & Salome, b. Aug. 21, 1808; d. Aug. 28, 1808	2	49
Laura, m. Zadoc **STEEL**, Feb. 11, 1805	2	35
Laura, d. John & Salome, b. Sept. 24, 1811	2	49
Luther Franklin, s. David & Rhoda, b. Oct. 1, 1814	2	44
Norman, s. David & Mary, b. Sept. 6, 1787	2	3
Oringe, s. David & Mary, b. July 26, 1780	2	3
Polly, d. David & Mary, b. Aug. 18, 1789	2	3
Rhoda, w. David, d. July 28, 1825	2	44
Rhoda P., m. Luther **MILLER**, Nov. 16, 1836	2	52
Rhoda Phelps, d. David & Rhoda, b. Nov. 22, 1816	2	44
Robzamon, s. Josiah & Deborah, b. May 7, 1797	2	35
Sally, [d. Francis & Abigail], b. Apr. 28, 1782	2	2
Salome Marilla, d. John & Salome, b. Jan. 14, 1807	2	49
Samuel, s. David & Mary, b. Feb. 8, 1793	2	3
William Maltby, s. John & Salome, b. Jan. 27, 1804	2	49
MACKINTIER, Benjamin, s. Joseph & Lydia, b. Aug. 27, 1744	1	36
Elijah, s. Joseph & Lydia, b. Dec. 29, 1746	1	37
Joseph, s. Joseph & Lydia, b. May [ ], 1739	1	36
Lydia, d. Joseph & Lydia, b. June 7, 1742	1	25

	Vol.	Page
MACKINTIER, (cont.)		
Lydia, d. Joseph & Lydia, b. June 7, 1742	1	36
Mary, d. Joseph & Lydia, b. Sept. 8, 1751	1	37
Richard, s. Joseph & Lydia, b. July 13, 1749	1	37
MCNARY, Elizabeth, m. Earl R. **DOUGLASS**, b. of New Hartford, Apr. 22, 1846, by Rev. Alexander Leadbetter. Int. Pub.	3	33
Frederick, s. George & Jerusha, b. June 1, 1811; d. Sept. 23, 1813	2	52
George, m. Jerusha **SPENCER**, Apr. 20, 1807	2	52
Jerusha, d. George & Jerusha, b. Oct. 19, 1813	2	52
Juliann, d. George & Jerusha, b. Feb. 11, 1808	2	52
Lucia, m. George **SOSER***, b. of New Hartford, Nov. 26, 1834, by Rev. Junius Burt *(Perhaps "**TOZER**")	3	20
MALISON, Emeline M., m. Frederick S. **PRITCHARD**, b. of New Hartford, May 5, 1841, by Rev. Cyrus Yale	3	27
MALTBY, Salome, m. John **LYMAN**, Mar. 19, 1801	2	49
MARANDUS, Calvin, of Winsted, m. Victoria **CLARK**, b. of Southington, (colored), Mar. 15, 1854, by J. C. Haughton	3	52
MARKHAM, Aralsamon, s. Ezekiel & Phebe, b. May 3, 1791	2	13
Bele, s. Ezekiel & Phebe, b. Mar. 15, 1777	2	13
Bele, [s. Ezekiel & Phebe], d. Oct. 12, 1793	2	13
Brainard, s. Ezekiel & Phebe, b. Apr. 20, 1785	2	13
Brainard, [s. Ezekiel & Phebe], d. Oct. 12, 1793	2	13
Chester, s. Ezekiel & Phebe, b. Apr. 13, 1793	2	13
Ezekiel, m. Phebe **BALCOM**, Mar. 10, 1774	2	13
Hosea, s. Ezekiel & Phebe, b. Mar. 23, 1789	2	13
Nabby, d. Ezekiel & Phebe, b. Aug. 2, 1782	2	13
Sarah, d. Ezekiel & Phebe, b. July 1, 1775	2	13
Sebe, s. Ezekiel & Phebe, b. June 2, 1780	2	13
Seba, [s. Ezekiel & Phebe], d. Oct. 12, 1793	2	13
MARSH, Adeline, m. Frederick **WOODRUFF**, b. of New Hartford, Apr. 22, 1840, by Rev. James Beach, of Winsted	3	26
Amos, s. Job & Jemimah, b. Feb. 6, 1757	1	43
Ann, d. Rev. Jonathan & Elizabeth, b. Feb. 22, 1740/1	1	37
Archibald, s. Wyllys & Rhoda, b. Sept. 24, 1808	2	47
Ashbel, s. Jonathan, Jr. & Theodosia, b. July 13, 1762	1	55
Ashbel, m. Abigail **WARD**, Nov. 27, 1788	2	50
Ashbel, Jr., [s. Ashbel & Abigail], b. Oct. 28, 1795	2	50
Ashbel, m. Lanra **KELLOGG**, b. of New Hartford, Sept. 2, 1826, by Cyrus Yale	3	12
Betsey, of East Hartford, m. Plato **KING**, of New Hartford, Dec. 7, 1800	2	48
Chloe, d. Jonathan, Jr. & Theodosia, b. Nov. 12, 1751	1	55
Chloe, [d. Ashbel & Abigail], b. Sept. 21, 1793	2	50
Cynthia, d. Jonathan, Jr. & Damaris, b. Oct. 16, 1791	2	43
Daniel, s. Rev. Jonathan & Elizabeth, b. Feb. 4, 1746	1	37
Electa, d. Jonathan, Jr. & Damaris, b. Feb. 18, 1787; d. July 7, 1787	2	43
Electa, 2nd, d. Jonathan, Jr. & Damaris, b. Mar. 1, 1789	2	43
Elizabeth, d. Rev. Jonathan & Elizabeth, b. May 10, 1749	1	37
Elizabeth, w. Rev. Jonathan, d. May 20, 1749	1	37
Elizabeth, d. Jonathan, Jr. & Theodosia, b. Oct. 13, 1759	1	55
Elizabeth, m. Roswell G. **STEEL**, b. of New Hartford, Apr. 19,		

	Vol.	Page
MARSH, (cont.)		
1854, by Rev. Frederick Marsh	3	54
Esther, [d. Ashbel & Abigail], b. Mar. 17, 1792	2	50
Esther, m. Luther **LOOMIS**, July 8, 1819	2	31
Eunice M., m. Allen **GOODWIN**, b. of New Hartford, Oct. 18, 1840, by Rev. Cyrus Yale	3	27
Fanny, m. Truman **KELLOGG**, b. of New Hartford, Aug. 25, 1825, by Cyrus Yale	3	11
Frederick, s. Jonathan, Jr. & Damaris, b. Sept. 18, 1780	2	43
Frederick, Rev., m. Parnal **MERRELL**, May 22, 1809	2	43
George, [s. Ashbel & Abigail], b. Apr. 27, 1799	2	50
Grove Sheldon, [s. Ashbel & Abigail], b. Aug. 7, 1803	2	50
Hannah, m. Caleb **WATSON**, Nov. 13, 1779	2	15
Harriet, d. John, Jr. & Annah, b. Aug. 4, 1792	2	41
Henry, [s. Wyllys & Rhoda], b. Mar. 4, 1817	2	47
Isaac, s. Rev. Jonathan & Elizabeth, b. Oct. 18, 1747	1	37
James, s. John & Sarah, b. June 1, 1767	1	60
James, [s. Ashbel & Abigail], b. Sept. 27, 1806	2	50
Jerusha, d. Rev. Jonathan & Elizabeth, b. Aug. 20, 1744	1	37
Job, s. Job & Jemimah, b. May 12, 1757* *(Marked "1755")	1	43
John, m. Asena **SEYMOUR**, Feb. 2, 1756	1	28
John, s. John & Susina, b. Nov. 25, 1758	1	47
John, Jr., m. Annah **COLE**, Aug. 18, 1791	2	41
John Cole, s. John, Jr. & Annah, b. Mar. 14, 1796	2	41
John L., m. Mrs. Lucy **MARSH**, Oct. 10, 1796, by Israel Jones, Jr., J.P.	2	38
Jonathan, Rev., m. Mrs. Maryan **KEETH**(?), May 27, 1751	1	37
Jonathan, 3rd, s. Jonathan, Jr. & Theodosia, b. Mar. 1, 1757	1	55
Jonathan, Jr., m. Damaris **PITKIN**, June 29, 1780	2	43
Jonathan, Rev., d. July 5, 1794, in the 81st y. of his age and 55th y. of his ministry	2	38
Jonathan, s. Jonathan, Jr. & Damaris, b. Oct. 18, 1795; d. Feb. 18, 1796	2	43
Jonathan Pitkin, s. Jonathan, Jr. & Damaris, b. Feb. 13, 1798	2	43
Joseph Whiting, s. Rev. Jonathan & Elizabeth, b. Feb. 6, 1742/3	1	37
Lusiana, d. John & Sarah, b. June 15, 1764	1	58
Lucina, m. Timothy **DAWSON**, b. of New Hartford, Sept. 26, 1822, by Asa Goodwin, J.P.	3	7
Lucy, d. Jonathan, Jr. & Damaris, b. Nov. 20, 1784	2	43
Lucy, Mrs., m. John L. **MARSH**, Oct. 10, 1796, by Israel Jones, Jr., J.P.	2	38
Mary, d. Jonathan, Jr. & Theodosia, b. July 23, 1754	1	55
Matilda, [d. Wyllys & Rhoda], b. May 10, 1820	2	47
Miles, m. Esther **WATSON**, b. of New Hartford, Apr. 3, 1827, by Rev. Epaphras Goodman	3	14
Minerva, [d. Ashbel & Abigail], b. Mar. 19, 1794	2	50
Nabby, d. Ashbel & Abigail, b. Aug. 23, 1790	2	50
Naby, eldest child Ashbel & Abigail, d. Mar. 31, 1795, ae. 4 y. 7 m. 8 d.	2	50
Nathaniell, s. John & Lusina, b. July 22, 1761	1	53
Nathaniel, s. John, Jr. & Annah, b. Sept. 4, 1794	2	41
Nelson Gilbert, s. Wyllys & Harriet, b. Oct. 23, 1828	2	47

	Vol.	Page
MARSH, (cont.)		
Rhoda, w. Wyllys, d. June 26, 1823	2	47
Rhoda E., m. James D. **LYMAN**, b. of New Hartford, Nov. 24, 1853, by Rev. F. A. Spencer	3	51
Rhoda Electa, d. Wyllys & Harriet, b. Oct. 28, 1824	2	47
Ruth, d. Jonathan, Jr. & Theodosia, b. July 14, 1749	1	55
Sabrina C., m. Bigelow C. **GARRETT**, Oct. 8, [1833?], by Thomas Watson, Jr., J.P.	3	20
Sarah, m. Abram **KELLOGG**, June 17, 1747	1	28
Sarah, m. Abraham **KELLOGG**, June 17, 1747	2	18
Sarah, d. John & Sarah, b. Dec. 16, 1769	1	61
Sarah, d. John & Sarah, b. June 16, 1772	1	67
Theodosia, d. John, Jr. & Theodosia, b. July 13, 1751* *(Written over "1747")	1	55
Wolcott, s. Wyllys & Rhoda, b. June 5, 1810	2	47
Wyllys, s. Jonathan, Jr. & Damaris, b. Sept. 23, 1782	2	43
Wyllys, m. Rhoda **GOODWIN**, Dec. 23, 1807	2	47
Wyllys, of New Hartford, m. Harriet **MUNSON**, of Barkhamsted, Nov. 12, 1823, by Cyrus Yale	3	9
Wyllys, m. Marriet **MUNSON**, Nov. 13, 1823	2	47
Wyllys Goodwin, [s. Wyllys & Rhoda], b. Jan. 19, 1814	2	47
MARTIN, Carmine, of Sharon, m. Caroline **MERRELL**, of New Hartford, Sept. 19, 1833, by Rev. Cyrus Yale	3	20
MASON, Ann, m. Jeffery **WILCOX**, Nov. 25, 1822, by Samuel Griswold	3	8
Chloe M., m. Roman M. **BUTLER**, Nov. 29, 1827, by Rev. Cyrus Yale	3	17
MATTHEWS, Charles, m. Lydia **MERRELL**, b. of New Hartford, Aug. 14, 1828, by Rev. Epaphras Goodman	3	15
Levinia, of New Hartford, m. Andrew J. **MERRELL**, of Waterbury, Dec. 25, 1837, by Rev. Willis Lord	3	24
Maria, of Bristol, m. Joseph **BARNES**, of New Hartford, Aug. 21, 1820, by Cyrus Yale	3	2
MEIGS, Sarah M., of New Hartford, m. Erastus **WILLIAMS**, of Knox, N.Y., Mar. 8, 1827, by Cyrus Yale	3	13
MERRIAM, Polly, w. Stephen Rice, d. May 22, 1817	2	44
Stephen R., m. Belinda Neal, Sept. 18, 1817	2	44
MERRILL, MERRELL, MERRELLS, Aaron, m. Aness **HUMPHREY**, Apr. 18, 1775	2	17
Abi, d. Jonathan, Jr. & Hannah, b. Jan. 2, 1767	1	69
Abigail, d. Joseph & Abigail, b. Sept. 16, 1747	1	21
Abigail, w. Joseph, d. May 3, 1768	1	60
Achsa A., m. John P. **KELLOGG**, b. of New Hartford, Sept. 21, 1843, by Rev. Cyrus Yale	3	29
Alfred E., m. Eliza P. **BARNES**, b. of New Hartford, May 3, 1853, by Rev. James C. Haughton	3	48
Amanda, d. Ichabod & Mary, b. Nov. [ ], 1776	1	72
Andrew J., of Waterbury, m. Levinia **MATTHEWS**, of New Hartford, Dec. 25, 1837, by Rev. Willis Lord	3	24
Anna, m. Shubael H. **HENDERSON**, b. of New Hartford, Nov. 10, 1842, by Rev. Cyrus Yale	3	29
Asher, s. Ely* & Rachel, b. June 28, 1756 *("Elijah")	1	43

	Vol.	Page
MERRILL, MERRELL, MERRELLS, (cont.)		
Asher, Jr., m. Eliza **OLMSTED**, [ ] 2, 1823, by Cyrus Yale	3	8
Bennajah, s. Jonathan, Jr. & Hannah, b. June 8, 17[ ]	1	69
Bildad, s. Eliakim & Sarah, b. Jan. 28, 1749	1	52
Bildad, m. Damaris **MIX**, Jan. 16, 1774	2	35
Bildad, Jr., s. Bildad & Damaris, b. Sept. 9, 1777	2	35
Candace, d. Phinehas & Anna, b. July 11, 1781	2	39
Candace, m. Gordon W. **HENDERSON**, b. of New Hartford, Nov. 12, 1835, by Rev. William Case	3	22
Carolina, d. George & Sarah, b. Apr. 15, 1770	1	62
Caroline, m. Harry **SEYMOUR**, June 20, 1821, by Rev. Rodney Rosseter, of Plymouth	3	5
Caroline, of New Hartford, m. Carmine **MARTIN**, of Sharon, Sept. 19, 1833, by Rev. Cyrus Yale	3	20
Catharine, m. Herman **CHAPIN**, b. of New Hartford, May 18, 1828, by Cyrus Yale	3	14
Charles, s. Eliakim & Sarah, b. Mar. 26, 1746	1	52
Chloe, d. Zebulon & Susannah, b. Aug. 12, 1746, at Hartford	1	51
Chloe, d. George & Sarah, b. Jan. 18, 1772	1	65
Clement*, d. Joseph & Mary, b. Sept. 12, 1734 *("Clemence")	1	52
Clemmence, m. Noah **KELLOGG**, Nov. 18, 1754	1	28
Clemence, m. Noah **KELLOGG**, Nov. 18, 1754	2	14
Cyrenius **BISSELL**, [s. Aaron & Aness], b. Oct. 4, 1775	2	17
Daniel, s. Jonathan & Mary, b. Feb. 10, 1730	1	27
Daniel, b. Mar. 24, 1759	2	24
Diadema, d. Ichabod & Mary, b. Sept. 6, 1778	1	72
Eldad, Dr., of New Hartford, m. Elizabeth **COE**, of Torrington, Aug. 21, 1773	2	1
Eldad, Dr., m. Hannah **AMES**, b. of New Hartford, Dec. 17, 1778	2	1
Eldad, Jr., s. Dr. Eldad & Hannah, b. Oct. 4, 1779; d. Jan. 10, 1780	2	1
Eldad, Dr., m. Sarah **COWLS**, Jr., Apr. 4, 1782	2	1
Eldad William, s. Sela & Lydia, b. May 12, 1807	2	47
Ely*, s. Ely* & Rachel, b. June 13, 1754 *("Elijah")	1	43
Eli, s. Ichabod & Mary, b. Oct. 1, 1772	1	72
Eliakim, s. Eliakim & Sarah, b. Feb. 10, 1741/2	1	25
Eliakim, s. Eliakim & Sarah, b. Feb. 9, 1742	1	52
Elias, s. Eliakim & Sarah, b. June 23, 1744	1	52
Elizabeth, w. Dr. Eldad, d. Mar. 12, 1775	2	1
Elizabeth, [ ]	2	24
Emeline, m. Ira **MERRELL**, b. of New Hartford, Sept. 30, 1841, by Rev. Cyrus Yale	3	28
Esther, d. Noah & Esther, b. Mar. 2, 1730	1	22
Ester, d. Eliakim & Sarah, b. Feb. 5, 1758	1	52
Esther, 3rd, d. Joseph, 2nd & Mary, b. Nov. 20, 1762; d. Apr. 5, 1763	1	57
Esther, d. Ichabod & Mary, b. Oct. 6, 1770	1	72
Fayette, m. Emily L. **ATWOOD**, b. of New Hartford, Dec. 18, 1838, by Rev. Cyrus Yale	3	26
Francis F., m. Leonard F. **KELLOGG**, May 27, 1847, by Rev. Cyrus Yale	3	34

NEW HARTFORD VITAL RECORDS 279

	Vol.	Page
MERRILL, MERRELL, MERRELLS, (cont.)		
Frederick, m. Elizabeth A. **HOLCOMB**, Apr. 18, 1838, by Rev. Cyrus Yale	3	24
George, s. Jonathan & Mary, b. Sept. 18, 1746	1	21
Hannah, d. Jonathan & Mary, b. Jan. 13, 1739/40	1	27
Hannah, d. Elijah & Rachel, b. Jan. 15, 1765	1	65
Hannah, d. George & Sarah, b. Apr. 18, 1767	1	61
Hannah, d. Jonathan, Jr. & Hannah, b. Mar. 11, 1770	1	69
Hannah, w. Dr. Eldad, d. Apr. 16, 1780	2	1
Harriet, d. Phinehas & Anna, b. Mar. 31, 1784; d. Sept. 4, 1828	2	39
Harriet, of New Hartford, m. Norman **MILLS**, of Farmington, Mar. 10, 1833, by Roger Mills, J.P.	3	19
Harriet H., of New Hartford, m. Walter L. **TYLER**, of Plymouth, Apr. 12, 1846, by Rev. Cyrus Yale	3	32
Harriet M., m. James **KELLOGG**, May 1, 1850, by Rev. Cyrus Yale	3	36
Harriet P., m. Norman **GOODWIN**, b. of New Hartford, Nov. 3, 1844, by Rev. Cyrus Yale	3	30
Helen E., of New Hartford, m. James M. **ATWOOD**, of Watertown, Sept. 4, 1850, by Rev. Cyrus Yale	3	36
Hepsibah, d. Jonathan & Mary, b. May 6, 1744	1	21
Icabod, s. Noah & Esther, b. Sept. 2, 1728	1	22
Ichabod, m. Mary **MERRELL**, Mar. 15, 1761	1	29
Ichabod R., m. Harriet M. **BUTLER**, b. of New Hartford, Mar. 31, 1845, by Rev. Cyrus Yale	3	31
Ira, s. Bildad & Damaris, b. Oct. 29, 1779	2	35
Ira, m. Emeline **MERRELL**, b. of New Hartford, Sept. 30, 1841, by Rev. Cyrus Yale	3	28
Irena, d. Bildad & Damaris, b. Dec. 29, 1774; d. Sept. 29, 1776	2	35
Irena, d. Bildad & Damaris, b. Jan. 8, 1784	2	35
Isaac, s. Eliakim & Sarah, b. Feb. 6, 1760	1	52
Isaac, s. Bildad & Damaris, b. Dec. 8, 1781	2	35
Isaiah, s. Nehemiah & Lydia, b. May 30, 1756; d. Sept. 6, 1756	1	60
Isaiah, 2nd, s. Nehemiah & Lydia, b. Oct. 30, 1757	1	60
James, s. Joseph & Abigail, b. Jan. 11, 1758	1	52
James, s. Phinehas & Anna, b. Dec. 20, 1792	2	39
Jared, s. Nehemiah & Lydia, b. Aug. 28, 1760	1	60
Jemima, d. Ichabod & Mary, b. Jan. 29, 1763; d. Feb. 5, 1764	1	71
Jemima, 2nd, d. Ichabod & Mary, b. Oct. 15, 1765; d. July 2, 1771	1	71
Jerijah, s. Zebulon & Susannah, b. July 25, 1749, at Hartford	1	51
Joanah, d. Joseph & Abigail, b. Mar. 20, 1761	1	56
John, s. Samuell & Mary, b. Jan. 28, 1762	1	56
Jonathan, s. Jonathan & Mary, b. Sept. 6, 1737	1	27
Jonathan, s. Jonathan, Jr. & Hannah, b. May 28, 1764	1	67
Jonathan, m. Damaris **JUDSON**, May 16, 1825, by Andrew Abernethy, J.P.	3	11
Joseph, s. Noah & Esther, b. Jan. 25, 1732	1	22
Joseph, m. Abigail **STONE**, Mar. last day, 1742	1	28
Joseph, s. Joseph & Abigail, b. Mar. 4, 1744	1	25
Joseph, 2nd, m. Mery **MERRELL**, Mar. 7, 1762	1	55
Joseph, m. Martha **CHAPINS**, Feb. 16, 1769	1	65
Joseph, 2nd, of New Hartford, m. Kezia **SEYMOUR**, of Hartford,		

	Vol.	Page
MERRILL, MERRELL, MERRELLS, (cont.)		
Feb. 11, 1778	2	1
Kezia, d. Nehemiah & Lydia, b. July 26, 1767	1	60
Laura C., m. Andrew H. **LOOMIS**, b. of New Hartford, Aug. 21, 1831, by Rev. Cyrus Yale	3	18
Lavinia, of New Hartford, m. Abraham **CHIDSEY**, of Avon, Sept. 17, 1851, by Rev. John H. Betts	3	39
Lloyd, m. Fanny M. **WATSON**, b. of New Hartford, July 6, 1824, by Rev. Epaphras Goodman	3	10
Lorinda S., m. Herman **STEDMAN**, b. of New Hartford, Mar. 27, 1834, by Rev. Cyrus Yale	3	20
Lucretia, m. Abram **FILLEY**, July 28, 1790	2	37
Lucy, d. Ichabod & Mary, b. Feb. 8, 1762	1	54
Luman, [s. Aaron & Aness], b. Oct. 16, 1784	2	17
Lydia, d. Nehemiah & Lydia, b. Dec. 28, 1753	1	60
Lydia, d. Joseph, Jr. & Lydia, b. Sept. 17, 1770; d. Sept. 17, 1770	1	66
Lydia, 2nd, d. Joseph, Jr. & Lydia, b. July 15, 1772	1	66
Lydia, m. Charles **MATTHEWS**, b. of New Hartford, Aug. 14, 1828, by Rev. Epaphras Goodman	3	15
Mabel, d. Elijah & Rachel, b. Mar. 6, 1763	1	65
Marcy, d. Joseph & Abigail, b. Dec. 7, 1749	1	35
Maria, of New Hartford, m. George W. **EDDY**, of Berlin, Apr. 25, 1838, by Rev. Cyrus Yale	3	25
Marshall, m. Jane L. **BUTLER**, b. of New Hartford, Feb. 21, 1842, by Rev. Cyrus Yale	3	28
Martha, d. Jonathan & Mary, b. Jan. 24, 1727/8	1	27
Martha, m. Isaac **KELLOGG**, Jr., Jan. 26, 1748	1	11
Martin, s. Eliakim & Sarah, b. Apr. 17, 1754	1	52
Martin, of Barkhamsted, m. Clarisse **NEWTON**, of New Hartford, May 28, 1823, by Cyrus Yale	3	8
Mary, d. Jonathan & Mary, b. July 27, 1734	1	27
Mary, d. Joseph & Abigail, b. Mar. 28, 1743	1	25
Mary, m. Ichabod **MERRELL**, Mar. 15, 1761	1	29
Mary, m. Joseph **MERRELL**, 2nd, Mar. 7, 1762	1	55
Mary, w. Joseph, 2nd, d. May 25, 1763	1	57
Mary, d. Elijah & Rachel, b. Apr. [ ], 1767	1	65
Mary, d. Ichabod & Mary, b. Apr. 24, 1775	1	72
Mary Penny, d. George & Sarah, b. Aug. 23, 1773	1	66
Medad Warner, [s. Aaron & Aness], b. Oct. 5, 1777	2	17
Mehitabel, d. Noah & Esther, b. May 25, 1734	1	22
Mehetable, m. William **SEYMOUR**, Dec. 27, 1753	2	13
Mehetable, d. Ely* & Rachel, b. Mar. 6, 1763 *(Written over "Elijah")	1	56
Melissa, of New Hartford, m. Hector T. **RUICK**, of West Granby, Sept. 17, 1851, by Rev. John H. Betts	3	39
Michael, s. Joseph & Abigail, b. Aug. 20, 1745	1	22
Michael, s. Joseph & Abigail, d. Sept. 5, 1762	1	56
Michael, s. Joseph & Martha, b. May 26, 1770	1	65
Nehemiah, s. Nehemiah & Lydia, b. Sept. 22, 1751	1	60
Nelson, m. Polly **GOODWIN**, b. of New Hartford, June 6, 1822, by Cyrus Yale	3	7
Noah, s. Noah & Esther, b. Dec. 24, 1735	1	22

	Vol.	Page
MERRILL, MERRELL, MERRELLS, (cont.)		
Noah, s. Ichabod & Mary, b. Dec. 7, 1765	1	72
Norman, s. Phinehas & Anna, b. July 2, 1787; d. May 4, 1861	2	39
Parnal, m. Rev. Frederick **MARAH**, May 22, 1809	2	43
Phinehas, s. Joseph & Abigail, b. Feb. 19, 1755	1	52
Phinehas, m. Anna **BUELL**, Mar. 10, 1781	2	39
Prosper, [s. Aaron & Aness], b. July 18, 1781	2	17
Prudence, d. Joseph & Abigail, b. Mar. 27, 1752	1	52
Prudence, b. Jan. 5, 1791; m. Noah B. **NORTON**, May 10, 1812	2	15
Rachel, d. Ely* & Rachel, b. July 21, 1752 *(Written "Elijah")	1	43
Rachel, d. Jonathan, Jr. & Hannah, b. Apr. 21, 1763	1	67
Rhoda, [ ]	2	24
Roswell M., m. Frances C. M. **TURNER**, b. of New Hartford, Oct. 1, 1837, by Rev. Willis Lord	3	24
Roxa, [d. Aaron & Aness], b. Mar. 18, 1783	2	17
Sabrina, m. Joseph **GILLET**, b. of New Hartford, Mar. 22, 1821, by Cyrus Yale	3	5
Samuel, s. Samuel & Mary, b. Dec. 13, 1767	2	25
Sarah, d. Eliakim & Sarah, b. Feb. 26, 1752	1	52
Sarah, d. Elijah & Rachel, b. May 28, 1758	1	48
Sarah, d. George & Sarah, b. Feb. 18, 1769	1	62
Sarah, m. Abram **KELLOGG**, Jan. 6, 1803	2	25
Sarah, [ ]	2	24
Selah, s. Dr. Eldad & Sarah, b. Nov. 2, 1783	2	1
Sela, m. Lydia **STEEL**, Apr. 26, 1803	2	47
Seth, m. Zebulon & Susannah, b. Mar. 30, 1760	1	51
Shubel, s. George & Sarah, b. Mar. 12, 1766	1	61
Shubael, s. George & Sarah, b. Apr. 21, 1775	1	69
Silvanius, s. Nehemiah & Lydia, b. May 3, 1770	1	65
Susanna, d. Jonathan & Mary, b. Nov. 9, 1741	1	21
Susannah, d. Zebulon & Susannah, b. Apr. 13, 1754	1	51
Susannah, d. Jonathan, Jr. & Hannah, b. Nov. 10, 1773	1	69
Thankfull, d. Nehemiah & Lydia, b. Oct. 30, 1763	1	60
Theodore, s. Ely* & Rachel, b. Jan. 16, 1761 *(Written over "Elijah")	1	56
Theodosia, d. Zebulon & Susannah, b. Dec. 9, 1747, at Hartford	1	51
Theodosia, m. Solomon **WOODRUFF**, Oct. 3, 1771	1	65
William, s. Jonathan & Mary, b. Mar. 10, 1732	1	27
Zebulon, Jr., s. Zebulon & Susannah, b. Mar. 17, 1756	1	51
Zelinda, d. Bildad & Damaris, b. June 16, 1786	2	35
MESSENGER, Eliza, m. Mark **MOSES**, b. of Barkhamsted, Jan. 31, 1844, by Salmon Merrell, J.P.	3	30
Phebe, of New Hartford, m. Zerah **PRESTON**, of Weathersfield, Mar. 27, 1822, by Cyrus Yale	3	7
MILLARD, Selden, of Manchester, Loway (Territory), m. Abigail M. **HOTCHKISS**, of New Hartford, Mar. 15, 1842, by Rev. Cyrus Yale	3	28
MILLER, MILLAR, Ashbel, s. John & Hannah, b. Oct. 30, 1762	1	56
Hannah, d. John & Hannah, b. May 15, 1757; d. Dec. 16, 1758	1	54
Hannah, wid., m. John **CURTIS**, Feb. 1, 1770	1	66
John, s. John & Hannah, b. Dec. 30, 1760, at Weathersfield	1	54
John, d. Oct. 4, 1763, at Havanah	1	56

	Vol.	Page
MILLER, MILLAR, (cont.)		
Lewis B., of Torringford, m. Jane **TRUMBULL**, of New Hartford, Oct. 11, 1842, by Rev. Cyrus Yale	3	29
Luther, m. Rhoda P. **LYMAN**, Nov. 16, 1836	2	52
Ruth, d. John & Hannah, b. Dec. 10, 1758	1	54
Sarah A., of Farmington, m. David B. **UNDERWOOD**, of Montwell, O., May 20, 1833, by Rev. David Miller	3	19
MILLS, Alfred, [s. Moses & Zeruiah], b. July 26, 1783	2	29
Anna, [d. Moses & Zeruiah], b. Mar. 4, 1773	2	29
Asher, [s. Moses & Zeruiah], b. Feb. 17, 1781	2	29
Catharine, m. Henry **JONES**, b. of New Hartford, Jan. 25, 1826, by Cyrus Yale	3	12
Delight G., of New Hartford, m. William S. **BUTLER**, of Edinburgh, N.Y., Sept. 6, 1827, by Jairus Burton	3	14
Ebenezer, [s. Moses & Zeruiah], b. Oct. 5, 1777	2	29
Eliza Ann*, of New Hartford, m. L. Lysander **JONES**, of New York City, Oct. 31, 1842, by Rev. Cyrus Yale *(Should be "Ann Maria")	3	29
Harriet, m. Henry **GILBERT**, Sept. 20, 1829, by Cyrus Yale	3	16
Leavit D., of Burlington, m. Electa J. **LYMAN**, of New Hartford, Mar. 14, 1848, by Rev. William N. Morse	3	34
Moses, m. Zeruiah **WALLER**, Mar. 12, 1767	2	29
Moses, s. Moses & Zeruiah, b. Sept. 12, 1768	1	62
Moses, [s. Moses & Zeruiah], b. Sept. 12, 1768	2	29
Norman, of Farmington, m. Harriet **MERRELL**, of New Hartford, Mar. 10, 1833, by Roger Mills, J.P.	3	19
Roger, m. Nancy S. **HOLCOMB**, b. of New Hartford, Sept. 7, 1828, by Cyrus Yale	3	15
Sarah, of Simsbury, m. Nathan **NEWEL**, of New Hartford, Dec. 3, 1739, by Jno Humphries, J.P.	1	29
Thomas, [s. Moses & Zeruiah], b. Mar. 26, 1771	2	29
Zeruiah, [d. Moses & Zeruiah], b. Sept. 11, 1775	2	29
Zeruiah, w. Moses, d. Dec. 15, 1785, in the 41st y. of her age	2	29
MINTHORN, John, s. W[illia]m, Jr. & Hannah, b. Oct. 4, 1769	2	4
Lucy, d. W[illia]m, Jr. & Hannah, b. Oct. 3, 1772	2	4
Mary, d. W[illia]m, Jr. & Hannah, b. July 17, 1766	2	4
Michael, s. William, Jr. & Hannah, b. Oct. 20, 1764	2	4
Nancy, d. W[illia]m, Jr. & Hannah, b. Mar. 23, 1776	2	4
Norman, s. W[illia]m, Jr. & Hannah, b. Feb. 25, 1778	2	4
William, 3rd, s. W[illia]m, Jr. & Hannah, b. Oct. 28, 1767	2	4
MIX, Amanda, m. Norris **SEGAR**, b. of New Hartford, Dec. 9, 1824, by Cyrus Yale	3	11
Betsey, of New Hartford, m. Rufus **HARRIS**, of Glastonbury, Feb. 28, 1828, by C. Yale	3	14
Damaris, m. Bildad **MERRELL**, Jan. 16, 1774	2	35
MOODEY, Adonijah, m. Sarah **SMITH**, Nov. 9, 1742	1	28
	1	21
Adonijah, d. Jan. 4, 1746/7	1	62
Adonijah, s. Ebenezer & Zeruiah, b. May 16, 1771	2	28
Adonijah, [s. Ebenezer & Zeruiah], b. May 16, 1771	2	28
Anna, [d. Ebenezer & Zeruiah], b. Dec. 21, 1783	2	28
Anson, [s. Ebenezer & Zeruiah], b. Feb. 13, 1778	2	28
Ebenezer, s. Adonijah & Sarah, b. Jan. 9, 1743/4	1	22

	Vol.	Page
MOODEY, (cont.)		
Ebenezer, m. Zeruiah **SEYMOUR**, Nov. 17, 1768	2	28
Ebenezer, [twin with Epaphras, s. Ebenezer & Zeruiah], b. Nov. 11, 1775	2	28
Epaphras, [twin with Ebenezer, s. Ebenezer & Zeruiah], b. Nov. 11, 1775	2	28
Ludy, [twin with Lusina, d. Ebenezer & Zeruiah], b. Feb. 28, 1773	2	28
Lusina, [twin with Lucy, d. Ebenezer & Zeruiah], b. Feb. 28, 1773	2	28
Roxselana, [d. Ebenezer & Zeruiah], b. Feb. 9, 1780	2	28
Sarah, d. Adonijah & Sarah, b. June 8, 1747	1	21
Sarah, m. Peletiah **ALLYN**, May 23, 1750	1	28
Susanna, d. Adonijah & Sarah, b. Sept. 13, 1745	1	22
Susannah, m. Zachariah **WATSON**, Nov. 12, 1767	2	15
Zeniah, [child of Ebenezer & Zeruiah], b. Feb. 12, 1782	2	28
MOORE, MOOR, Allen, m. Theda **GARRET**, b. of New Hartford, Oct. 8, 1822, by C. Yale	3	7
Anna, m. David **WATSON**, May 11, 1795	2	41
Caroline, m. Sylvester **VINTON**, b. of New Hartford, Oct. 31, 1852, by Rev. John H. Betts	3	48
Margaret, d. Joseph & Margaret, b. July 11, 1760	1	54
Salvanus, m. Lucina **SPENCER**, b. of New Hartford, Oct. 19, 1824, by Eli Barrett, Elder	3	11
MOSES, Maria E., m. James E. **SMITH**, b. of New Hartford, Aug. 17, 1851, by Rev. Alexander Leadbetter. Int. Pub.	3	39
Mark, m. Eliza **MESSENGER**, b. of Barkhamsted, Jan. 31, 1844, by Salmon Merrell, J.P.	3	30
MOSS, Barzillai, m. Jennette **DAWSON**, Aug. 28, 1823, by Tubal Wakefield	3	9
MOURREY, George A., of Smithfield, R.I., m. Mary **SPENCER**, of New Hartford, May 13, 1832, by Cyrus Yale	3	18
MUNSON, Harriet, of Barkhamsted, m. Wyllys **MARSH**, of New Hartford, Nov. 12, 1823, by Cyrus Yale	3	9
Harriet, m. Wyllys **MARSH**, Nov. 13, 1823	2	47
MURPHY, Mary Jane, m. Timothy **RAUDEN**, b. of Bakerville, May 2, 1854, by Rev. Thomas Hendrickson	3	53
MYNOTT, Betsey, of Oxford, m. Ira **STOVEL**, of New Hartford, Oct. 23, 1820, by Cyrus Yale	3	3
NEAL, Belinda, m. Stephen R. **MERRIAM**, Sept. 18, 1817	2	44
NEWELL, NEWEL, Laura, of New Hartford, m. Julius C. **HOTCHKISS**, of Burlington, Dec. 1, 1820, by Cyrus Yale	3	4
Medad, s. Nathan & Sarah, b. Aug. 18, 1741	1	27
Nathan, of New Hartford, m. Sarah **MILLS**, of Simsbury, Dec. 3, 1739, by Jno Humphries, J.P.	1	29
NEWTON, Clarisse, of New Hartford, m. Martin **MERRELL**, of Barkhamsted, May 28, 1823, by Cyrus Yale	3	8
NICHOLS, Susan, m. Lyman **DAILEY**, Apr. 22, 1852, by Rev. Edward N. Crossman, of Bakerville	3	43
NICHOLSON, Clarissa, d. John & Sarah, b. Jan. 23, 1785	2	5
James, s. John & Sarah, b. July 28, 1771	2	5
Jemimah, d. John & Sarah, b. May 9, 1773	2	5
Mary, d. John & Sarah, b. July 20, 1775	2	5
Persa, d. John & Sarah, b. Jan. 6, 1787		

	Vol.	Page
NICHOLSON, (cont.)		
Sarah, d. John & Sarah, b. Sept. 24, 1777	2	5
NOLLING, Ruth, see Richard **BLOICE**	1	21
NORTH, Betsey, m. Carol **COWLES**, b. of New Hartford, Oct. 3, 1822, by Cyrus Yale	3	7
NORTON, Nathaniel White, s. Noah B. & Prudence, b. Apr. 18, 1822	2	15
Noah B., b. Jan. 1, 1790; m. Prudence **MERRELL**, May 10, 1812	2	15
Noah B., m. Polly **OLMSTED**, b. of New Hartford, Mar. 4, 1824, by Cyrus Yale	3	9
Prudence, w. Noah B., d. Aug. 12, 1822	2	15
Riley Merrell, s. Noah B. & Prudence, b. May 3, 1816; d. Jan. 7, 1820	2	15
Roman Loomis, s. Noah B. & Prudence, b. July 14, 1813	2	15
OAKLEY, Isaac T., of Jewett City, m. Jane Louisa **RING**, of New Hartford, Feb. 19, 1854, by Rev. J. H. Betts	3	56
Martha, of New Hartford, m. Asher **DEMING**, of Collinsville, July 2, 1854, by Rev. F. A. Spencer	3	54
OLCOTT, Abel, s. Thomas, Jr. & Lydia, b. Oct. 26, 1768	1	61
Isaac, s. Thomas & Lydia, b. May 28, 1764	1	61
Isaac, of Wolcott, m. Mary **FARNSWORTH**, of New Hartford, Oct. 27, 1841, by Rev. David Miller	3	28
Lydia, d. Thomas, Jr. & Lydia, b. Mar. 7, 1761	1	61
Thomas, 3rd, s. Thomas, Jr. & Lydia, b. Oct. 27, 1766* *(Written over "1765")	1	61
OLMSTED, OLMSTEAD, Abigail, d. Michael & Abigail, b. Sept. 18, 1812	2	44
Andrew, s. Michael & Abigail, b. Dec. 30, 1800	2	44
Elijah, s. Roger & Eunice, b. Oct. 21, 1782	2	3
Eliza, m. Asher **MERRELL**, Jr., [ ] 2, 1823, by Cyrus Yale	3	8
Elizabeth, d. Roger, Jr. & Elizabeth, b. Feb. 11, 1800	2	37
Elizabeth, d. Roger, decd. & Eunice & w. of John **EDGCOM**, d. Nov. 17, 1801, in the 26th y. of her age	2	3
Elizabeth, d. Michael & Abigail, b. Sept. 24, 1803	2	44
Eunice, d. Roger & Eunice, b. July 9, 1767	1	10
Eunice, wid., d. May 24, 1807, in the 71st y. of her age	2	37
Gamaliel, s. Roger & Eunice, b. June 14, 1759	1	48
George, s. Roger, Jr. & Elizabeth, b. Sept. 7, 1792	2	37
Hannah, d. Roger & Elizabeth, b. Mar. 1, 1806; d. Aug. 2, 1808	2	37
Hannah Jopp, d. Roger & Elizabeth, b. May 18, 1808	2	37
Jesse, s. Roger, Jr. & Elizabeth, b. July 13, 1794; d. Mar. 16, 1795; ae. 8 m. 3 d.	2	37
Jesse, s. Roger, Jr. & Elizabeth, b. Mar. 28, 1796	2	37
Joseph Alden, s. Roger, Jr. & Elizabeth, b. Feb. 14, 1798	2	37
Laura, d. Michael & Abigail, b. Jan. 10, 1799	2	44
Michael, s. Roger & Eunice, b. July 14, 1770	1	10
Michael, m. Abigail **HOPKINS**, Jan. 29, 1795	2	44
Michael, s. Michael & Abigail, b. Apr. 25, 1808	2	44
Philo, s. Roger & Elizabeth, b. Mar. 8, 1804	2	37
Polly, d. Michael & Abigail, b. Sept. 19, 1796	2	44
Polly, m. Noah B. **NORTON**, b. of New Hartford, Mar. 4, 1824,		

	Vol.	Page
OLMSTED, OLMSTEAD, (cont.)		
by Cyrus Yale	3	9
Roger, s. Roger & Eunice, b. Aug. 25, 1764	1	10
Roger, Jr., m. Elizabeth **JOP**, Dec. 10, 1788	2	37
Roger, Sr., d. June 6, 1800, in the 72nd y. of his age	2	37
Roger, Jr., s. Roger & Elizabeth, b. Apr. 21, 1802	2	37
Sally, of Canton, m. Stephen **BARNES**, of New Hartford, Oct. 8, 1832, by Rev. David Miller	3	19
Sarah, d. Roger & Eunice, b. Oct. 14, 1773	1	66
Warren W., s. Michael & Abigail, b. Nov. 26, 1805	2	44
William, s. Roger, Jr. & Elizabeth, b. Sept. 6, 1789; d. Dec. 29, 1789	2	37
William, s. Roger, Jr. & Elizabeth, b. Nov. 6, 1790	2	37
PALMER, James, of Litchfield, m. Esther **DUNBAR**, of Torrington, Aug. 10, 1834, by Rev. David Miller	3	20
PARK, PARKS, Chloe, d. John & Sarah, b. June 10, 1784	2	2
Lois, d. John & Sarah, b. June 12, 1782	2	2
Sally, d. John & Sarah, b. Jan. 16, 1779	2	2
PARSONS, PERSONS, Benjamin, s. Benjamin, b. Jan. 20, 1757	1	46
Hannah, m. Zebulon **CURTIS**, Jan. 5, 1792	2	29
Lois, d. Benjamin, b. Mar. 24, 1758	1	46
Mary, d. Benjamin, b. Aug. 26, 1755	1	46
Mary B., of Windsor, m. Chester S. **COUCH**, of Sandisfield, Mass., Jan. 4, 1831, by Rev. Epaphras Goodman	3	17
PAYNE, Isaac, s. Isaac **PAYNE** & Jerusha **ENSIGN**, b. Jan. 23, 1787	2	30
PEASE, Mailda, m. Elijah **GOODWIN**, Jan. 5, 1797	2	45
Polly, m. Asa **GOODWIN**, Nov. 14, 1793	2	40
PECK, Harry, of Bristol, m. Emeline **LOOMIS**, of New Hartford, Apr. 23, 1838, by Rev. Cyrus Yale	3	25
Otis T., m. Laura Ann **KILBOURNE**, July 18, 1830, by Andrew Abernethy, J.P.	3	18
PELTON, Martha, m. Israel **ANDRUS**, Mar. 7, 1827, by Andrew Abernethy, J.P.	3	13
Temperance Colt, m. Asa **ANDRUSS**, Dec. 16, 1813	2	53
PERKINS, Elisha, s. John & Mary, b. June 23, 1754	1	42
John, s. John & Mary, b. July 28, 1751	1	37
Mary, d. John & Mary, b. Dec. 11, 1752	1	38
PERRY, David L., of Sharon, m. Margaret **WILLIAMS**, of New Hartford, May 9, 1838, by Rev. Willis Lord	3	25
Mary J.*, of West Granby, m. Horatio N. **SMITH**, of New Hartford, Sept. 9, 1849, by Rev. William Goodwin *(Perhaps "Mary J. **FERRY** or **TERRY**"?)	3	40
PETTIBONE, Charlotte, d. Capt. Abram, b. Apr. 25, 1772	1	67
Jerusha, alias Jerusha **SPENCER**, m. Seth **SPENCER**, May 20, 1779	2	43
Norman, s. Capt. Abram, b. Oct. 30, 1774	1	67
Pamelia, Mrs. of New Hartford, m. Simeon **HART**, of Burlington, Jan. 30, 1822, by Cyrus Yale	3	6
PHELAN, John, m. Margaret **CAHILL**, June 15, 1851, by Rev. John H. Betts	3	39
PHELPS, Albert P., m. Laura A. **LOOMIS**, b. of New Hartford, May 5, 1852, by Rev. Cyrus Yale	3	43

	Vol.	Page
PIERPOINT, Harriet E., 3rd d. William & Betsey, b. May 14, 1827	2	24
Hestor Ann, 2nd d. William & Betsey, b. Nov. 20, 1824	2	24
Sabra Ann, d. William & Betsey, b. June 27, 1822	2	24
William, m. Betsey CLARK, May 24, 1821	2	24
William, m. Betsey CLARK, May 24, 1821, by Daniel Coe	3	5
PIKE, Julia A., of Canton, m. William T. WILCOX, of New Hartford, Nov. 18, 1845, by Alexander Leadbetter	3	32
PINNEY, Charles H., M.D. of Derby, m. Maria WATSON, of New Hartford, Apr. 4, 1854, by J. C. Haughton	3	52
PITKIN, Caleb, m. Damerous PORTER, Nov. 7, 1751	1	28
Caleb, 3rd, s. Caleb & Camaris, b. Aug. 9, 1752	1	38
Caleb, d. Oct. 2, 1768	1	61
Clarissa, m. Phinehas GILLET, b. of New Hartford, Oct. 5, 1820, by Cyrus Yale	3	2
Damares, d. Caleb & Damares, b. Oct. 20, 1756	1	60
Damaris, m. Jonathan MARSH, Jr., June 29, 1780	2	43
Dorothy, d. Caleb & Damares, b. Sept. 28, 1758	1	60
Dorothy, m. Isaac STEEL, Sept. 10, 1777	2	27
Hannah, d. Caleb & Damares, b. Apr. 16, 1763	1	61
Jemima, m. William BUTLER, [ ]	2	53
John, s. Caleb & Damares, b. Jan. 5, 1761	1	61
Stephen, s. Caleb & Damares, b. Sept. 19, 1754	1	42
Timothy, s. Caleb & Damares, b. Aug. 6, 1765	1	61
PITMAN, Thomas G., of New Haven, m. Harriet A. VANDEUSEN, of New Hartford, Jan. 17, 1853, by Rev. John H. Betts	3	48
POND, Julius R., of Ansonia, m. Martha A. WATSON, of Torringford, July 1, 1850, by Rev. William H. Moore	3	36
PORTER, Damerous, m. Caleb PITKIN, Nov. 7, 1751	1	28
POTTER, Mary E., of Milton, m. Elbert BUNNEL, of Burlington, Aug. 31, 1845, by Rev. Cyrus Yale	3	31
PRATT, Orpah, m. Horace KELLOGG, Oct. 21, 1807, by Isaac Pratt	2	49
PRESTON, Zerah, of Weathersfield, m. Phebe MESSENGER, of New Hartford, Mar. 27, 1822, by Cyrus Yale	3	7
PRITCHARD, Frederick S., m. Emeline M. MALISON, b. of New Hartford, May 5, 1841, by Rev. Cyrus Yale	3	27
QUOMANY, Humphrey, of New Hartford, m. Perintha TAYLOR, of Canton, Aug. 16, 1823, by Isaac Kellogg, J.P.	3	10
RALSTON, Frances W., of New Hartford, m. Chauncey GRISWOLD, of Barkhamsted, Dec. 3, 1854, by Rev. F. A. Spencer	3	55
RANNEY, Edward, of Augusta, N.Y., m. Orpah BUSHNELL, of New Hartford, Mar. 7, 1847, by George Kerr	3	33
RAUDEN, Timothy, m. Mary Jane MURPHY, b. of Bakerville, May 2, 1854, by Rev. Thomas Hendrickson	3	53
RAYMOND, Antonette, [d. Riley & Lucy], b. May 19, 1831	2	33
Edwin W., [s. Riley & Lucy], b. June 11, 1815	2	33
Emory E., [s. Riley & Lucy], b. Apr. 14, 1822	2	33
Frederick A., [s. Riley & Lucy], b. Apr. 6, 1820	2	33
George R., [s. Riley & Lucy], b. July 18, 1813	2	33
Hershehl P., [s. Riley & Lucy], b. July 6, 1826	2	33
John R., [s. Riley & Lucy], b. June 18, 1829; d. July 13, 1833	2	33
Juliette, [d. Riley & Lucy], b. Apr. 13, 1824	2	33
Lucy A., m. Bradley TERRELL, Apr. 14, 1841, by Rev. Cyrus		

	Vol.	Page
RAYMOND, (cont.)		
Yale	3	27
Lucy Ann, [d. Riley & Lucy], b. Sept. 21, 1817	2	33
Mary Curtis, [d. Riley & Lucy], b. Aug. 4, 1811	2	33
William Riley, [s. Riley & Lucy], b. July 5, 1810; d. July 21, 1810	2	33
READ, Abijah, s. Jacob & Rebeckah, b. Mar. 10, 1783	2	32
Chauncey, s. Jacob & Rebeckah, b. May 25, 1786	2	32
Elizabeth, d. Jacob & Rebeckah, b. May 19, 1777	2	32
REYNOLDS, Rufus, of Barkhamsted, m. Susan **THORP**, of New Hartford, July 13, 1821, by Cyrus Yale	3	4
RICE, [see also **ROYCE**], Elen, m. John C. **COOPER**, b. of New Hartford, Oct. 12, 1845, by Alexander Leadbetter	3	32
Isaac, s. Asa & Anna, b. Oct. 14, 1765	1	60
RICHARDS, Anne, d. James & Anne, b. Apr. 3, 1743	1	25
Charles Buck, s. Aaron, b. Feb. 6, 1779	2	12
George, of Farmington, m. Lucy **WILLIAMS**, of New Hartford, May 6, 1824, by Cyrus Yale	3	10
Hannah, d. Jona[than], b. Apr. 12, 1739	1	26
Sam[ue]ll, s. Hezekiah & Sarah, b. Apr. 22, 1763	1	66
Timothy, s. Jonah & Mary, b. Sept. 13, 1741	1	27
Timothy, s. Hezekiah & Sarah, b. Mar. 3, 1760	1	66
RICHMOND, Gilbert S., of Madison, m. Elmina M. **CLEMENCE**, of New Hartford, May 9, 1852, by Rev. James C. Houghton	3	42
RIGHT, [see under **WRIGHT**]		
RIGLEY, Mary L., m. Lewis W. **GRISWOLD**, b. of New Hartford, May 5, 1851, by Rev. John Herbert Betts	3	38
RILEY, Nancy, of New Hartford, m. Philo **KELLOGG**, of Manlius, N.Y., Oct. 14, 1821, by Cyrus Yale	3	6
RING, Jane Louisa, of New Hartford, m. Isaac T. **OAKLEY**, of Jewett City, Feb. 19, 1854, by Rev. J. H. Betts	3	56
ROBBINS, Mehetabel, m. Samuel W. **LEE**, May 22, 1783	2	36
ROBERTS, Benjamin, s. John & Mindwell, b. Sept. 17, 1781	2	15
Edward P., of Winsted, m. Pane A. **BENHAM**, of New Hartford, Sept. 22, 1850, by Rev. Cyrus Yale	3	37
Hannah, d. John & Mindwell, b. July 17, 1782	2	15
John, m. Mindwell **LANE**, Sept. 16, 1780	2	15
Lucinda, m. Eliphas **SPENCER**, b. of New Hartford, Nov. 8, 1820, by Cyrus Yale	3	3
Lydia, m. Friend **HOLCOMB**, Mar. 22, 1821, by Cyrus Yale	3	5
Rube, d. John & Mindwell, b. Nov. 14, 1784	2	15
ROCKWELL, Sarah E., m. George R. **JEWELL**, b. of New Hartford, Feb. 22, 1838, by Rev. Willis Lord	3	25
ROGERS, RODGERS, Fanny M., m. William S. **BAKER**, b. of New Hartford, Nov. 15, 1840, by Rev. Aaron Gates	3	26
Lydia A., of New Hartford, m. William **HALE**, of Collinsville, Sept. 24, 1837, by Rev. Orsamus Allen, of Bristol	3	23
ROOT, Thaddeus L., of Winchester, m. Adaline **GOODWIN**, of New Hartford, Dec. 27, 1854, by Rev. David Miller	3	56
ROSSITER, ROSSETER, Anna, of New Hartford, m. Briant **BRADLEY**, of Harwinton, Nov. 17, 1824, by Cyrus Yale	3	11
Chandler, m. Margaret **KELLOGG**, Mar. 15, 1829, by Cyrus Yale	3	16

288　　　BARBOUR COLLECTION

	Vol.	Page
ROWE, Cynthia, d. Ari & Wealthy, b. Feb. 2, 1797	2	45
Martin, s. Ari & Wealthy, b. Apr. 21, 1799	2	45
Norman, s. Ari & Wealthy, b. Jan. 2, 1795	2	45
Samuel, s. Ari & Wealthy, b. Apr. 22, 1801	2	45
ROWLEY, Horace, m. Sally DUTTON, b. of New Hartford, June 21, 1827, by Rev. Cyrus Yale	3	14
ROYCE, ROYS, Barnabus, s. Assa & Anna, b. June 26, 1760	1	53
Daniel, m. Elizabeth AUSTIN, May 17, 1840, by Rev. Cyrus Yale	3	27
Lovisa Anne, d. Lieut. Asa & Anna, b. Nov. 16, 1762	1	56
Seth, s. Asa & Anna, b. July 13, 1769	1	61
RUICK, Hector T., of West Granby, m. Melissa MERRELL, of New Hartford, Sept. 17, 1851, by Rev. John H. Betts	3	39
RUSSELL, RUSSEL, Anna, d. Elisha, b. Nov. 13, 1781	2	7
Anna, d. Elisha & Anna, b. Nov. 15, 1781	2	16
Elisha, Jr., s. Elisha, b. Jan. 20, 1777	2	7
Hannah Harrington, d. Elisha & Anna, b. Aug. 3, 1784	2	7
John, s. Elisha, b. Oct. 17, 1779	2	7
John, s. Elisha & Anna, b. Oct. 17, 1779	2	16
Josiah, s. Elisha, b. Apr. 26, 1775	2	7
Sally Winship, d. Elisha & Anna, b. June 2, 1787	2	7
Stephen, Jr., s. Stephen, b. Mar. 22, 1796	2	33
RUST, Elisha, Jr., of Barkhamsted, m. Emeline TUCKER, of New Hartford, Sept. 11, 1828, by Cyrus Yale	3	15
RYAN, Mary C., of New Hartford, m. John CONDON, of New Haven, Mar. 4, 1870, by Rev. J. H. Betts, of St. John's Ch.	3	57
RYDER, Mary Jane, of New Hartford, m. Beardsley W. SMITH, of Waterbury, Sept. 25, 1853, by Rev. Cyrus Yale	3	49
Sarah A., of New Hartford, m. Herbert A. ATWOOD, of Watertown, Mar. 2, 1846, by Rev. Cyrus Yale	3	32
SADD, Elizabeth P., of New Hartford, m. Lewis AUSTIN, of Torringford, Oct. 4, 1826, by Cyrus Yale	3	12
SAGE, Harvey S., m. Phedelia COOK, Oct. 2, 1844, by Alexander Leadbetter. Int. Pub.	3	31
SANDEFORTH, Daniel, m. Sarah KELLOGG, May 10, 1781	2	16
Sale, d. Daniel & Sarah, b. Feb. 27, 1782	2	16
SCOVILLE, Irene, m. Merritt E. SMITH, Oct. 10, 1851, by Rev. Harley Goodwin, of South Canaan	3	40
SEGAR, SEGER, Aeta M., m. Jairus LANDSON, b. of New Hartford, Mar. 24, 1830, by Rev. Cyrus Yale	3	17
Harriet, of New Hartford, m. Orrin M. LANGDON, of Bristol, Nov. 25, 1830, by Rev. Cyrus Yale	3	18
John L., m. Jane TROWBRIDGE, b. of New Hartford, July 3, 1851, by Rev. Alexander Leadbetter. Int. Pub.	3	38
Mehetabel, m. Jesse STEEL, Dec. 18, 1777	2	26
Norris, m. Amanda MIX, b. of New Hartford, Dec. 9, 1824, by Cyrus Yale	3	11
Ursula, of New Hartford, m. Nathaniel G. LANGDON, of Canton*, Nov. 29, 1827, by Rev. Cyrus Yale *(Note says "New Hartford")	3	17
SESSIONS, Eunice, of Lee, m. Harvey SHEPARD, of York, N.C., Sept. 2, 1820, by Cyrus Yale	3	2

	Vol.	Page
SEUMAC, Henry, of Nowich, m. Lucinda DELOON, of New Hartford, July 7, 1829, by Asa Goodwin, J.P.	3	15
SEYMOUR, Ann M., m. Edmund WATSON, b. of New Hartford, Jan. 27, 1836, by William Case	3	23
Asena, m. John MARSH, Feb. 2, 1756	1	28
Asenath, m. Constantine SEYMOUR, Feb. 17, 1791	2	26
Asenath Hurlbut, d. Elias & Tryphena, b. Apr. 5, 1768	2	6
Charles E., of Waterbury, m. Angeline L. BURWELL, of Barkhamsted, Jan. 2, 1854, by Rev. F. A. Spencer	3	51
Constantine, m. Asenath SEYMOUR, Feb. 17, 1791	2	26
David, s. John & Hannah, b. Aug. 7, 1748	1	48
Elias, s. John & Hannah, b. Aug. 23, 1738	1	48
Elias, Jr., s. Elias & Tryphena, b. Nov. 6, 1771	2	6
Elij[ah], s. John & Hannah, b. Aug. 6, 1744	1	48
Eliza, m. Royal J. WATSON, b. of New Hartford, June 2, 1823, by Cyrus Yale	3	8
Elizabeth, d. John & Hannah, b. Nov. 14, 1736	1	48
Ester, [d. William & Mehetable], b. Apr. 4, 1762; d. Feb. 18, 1774	2	13
Ester, [d. William & Mehetable], b. Sept. 4, 1774	2	13
Esther, d. Noah & Miriam, b. Mar. 14, 1796	2	42
Hannah, d. John & Hannah, b. Aug. 3, 1735; d. Sept. 21, 1737	1	48
Hannah, twin with Hezekiah, d. John & Hannah, b. July 7, 1740	1	48
Harry, m. Caroline MERRELL, June 20, 1821, by Rev. Rodney Rosseter, of Plymouth	3	5
Hezekiah, twin with Hannah, s. John & Hannah, b. July 7, 1740	1	48
Horace, s. Noah & Miriam, b. Jan. 26, 1801	2	42
Huldah, d. Noah & Miriam, b. Mar. 15, 1794	2	42
Jesse, [s. William & Mehetable], b. Dec. 4, 1763	2	13
Joel, [s. William & Mehetable], b. June 28, 1772	2	13
John, d. July 25, 1758	1	48
Josiah, s. Elias & Tryphena, b. Oct. 11, 1769	2	6
Kezia, of Hartford, m. Joseph MERRELL, 2nd, of New Hartford, Feb. 11, 1778	2	1
Lauren, s. Noah & Miriam, b. June 15, 1790	2	42
Lot Norton, s. Noah & Miriam, b. Mar. 3, 1788	2	42
Lucinda, [d. William & Mehetable], b. Nov. 12, 1767	2	13
Lydia, [d. William & Mehetable], b. Mar. 1, 1770	2	13
Mary S., m. Hezekiah H. STONE, b. of New Hartford, Jan. 1, 1854, by Rev. F. A. Spencer	3	51
Mehetabel, m. William SEYMOUR, Dec. 27, 1753	1	28
Mehetabel, d. William & Mehetable, b. Oct. 18, 1756; d. Oct. 25, 1756	1	47
Mehetable, Jr., [d. William & Mehetable], b. Nov. 3, 1757	2	13
Mehetable, 2nd, d. William & Mehetable, b. Nov. 3, 1757	1	47
Nath[anie]ll, s. John & Hannah, b. Oct. 11, 1742	1	48
Nath[anie]ll, s. John & Hannah, supposed he d, Oct. 20, 1760, at Crown Point	1	56
Noah, [s. William & Mehetable], b. Nov. 10, 1759	2	13
Noah, m. Miriam KELLOGG, Dec. 17, 1784	2	42
Norman, s. Noah & Miriam, b. Dec. 11, 1785	2	42
Philomela, d. Elias & Tryphena, b. July 27, 1774	2	6
Sarah, d. John & Hannah, b. July 12, 1750	1	48

	Vol.	Page
SEYMOUR, (cont.)		
Sarah, b. July 12, 1750; m. Abram **KELLOGG**, Jr., Feb. 6, 1772	2	25
Silas, [s. William & Mehetable], b. May 7, 1777	2	13
Solomon J., m. Martha **SPENCER**, b. of New Hartford, Apr. 13, 1846, by Rev. Cyrus Yale	3	32
Tryphena, Jr., d. Elias & Tryphena, b. Apr. 13, 1777	2	6
Uriah, s. John & Hannah, b. Sept. 7, 1733	1	48
William, m. Mehetable **MERRELL**, Dec. 27, 1753	2	13
William, m. Mehetabel **SEYMOUR**, Dec. 27, 1753	1	28
William, s. William & Mehetabel, b. Nov. 15, 1754	1	42
William, Jr., [s. William & Mehetable], b. Nov. 15, 1754	2	13
Zerviah, d. John & Hannah, b. Oct. 18, 1746	1	48
Zeruiah, m. Ebenezer **MOODEY**, Nov. 17, 1768	2	28
SHELBY, William H., of New Hartford, m. Amanda H. **COLLINS**, of Simsbury, Apr. 24, 1853, by Rev. Cyrus Yale	3	49
SHEPARD, Aaron, s. Daniel, Jr. & Jerusha, b. Sept. 10, 1775	1	67
Alvan, s. Daniel, Jr. & Jerusha, b. Nov. 30, 1778	1	43
Daniel, Jr., [s. Daniel], b. Oct. 18, 1739	1	26
Daniel, Jr., m. Jerusha **ENSIGN**, b. of New Hartford, Jan. 25, 1770	1	28
Daniel, s. Daniel, Jr. & Jerusha, b. June 10, 1771	1	65
Daniel, s. Daniel, Jr. & Jerusha, d. Mar. 24, 1776	1	69
Daniel, s. Daniel, Jr. & Jerusha, b. Mar. 11, 1779	2	7
Daniel, Sr., d. Aug. 18, 1784	2	7
Ebenezer, s. Zebulon & Elizabeth, b. Dec. 30, 1745	1	36
Elizabeth, d. Zebulon & Elizabeth, b. Apr. 7, 1749	1	36
Elizabeth, d. Zebulon & Elizabeth, b. Nov. 7, 1761	1	56
Esther, d. Daniel, Jr. & Jerusha, b. May 21, 1777	2	7
Harvey, of York, N.C., m. Eunice **SESSIONS**, of Lee, Sept. 2, 1820, by Cyrus Yale	3	2
Harvey, of York, Upper Canada, m. Lucy Tracy **YALE**, of Lee, Mass., Nov. 20, 1825, by Cyrus Yale	3	12
Heman, s. Daniel & Jerusha, b. Aug. 9, 1782	2	7
Peletiah, s. Zebulon & Elizabeth, b. Aug. 30, 1747	1	36
Phinehas, s. Zebulon & Elizabeth, b. June 19, 1757	1	47
Seth, s. Daniel, Jr. & Jerusha, b. June 15, 1772	1	65
Seth, s. Daniel, Jr. & Jerusha, d. Mar. 13, 1776	1	69
Seth, s. Daniel, Jr. & Jerusha, b. Jan. 31, 1781	2	7
Susanna, [d. Daniel], b. July 4, 1734	1	26
William, s. Zebulon & Elizabeth, b. Jan. 16, 1755	1	42
Zebulon, s. Zebulon & Elizabeth, b. Apr. 21, 1751	1	36
SIKES, Crosby, m. Elvira **BAKER**, b. of New Hartford, Aug. 11, 1842, by Roger H. Mills, J.P.	3	28
Nelson, m. Marilla **TYLER**, b. of New Hartford, July 6, 1836, by William Case	3	23
SIMONS, Luther, of Winchester, m. Minerva **WEBSTER**, of Barkhamsted, July 25, 1852, by Rev. J. A. Saxton	3	44
Sarah, m. Israel **LOOMIS**, Nov. [ ], 1737	1	52
SMITH, Amelia, d. Seth & Deliverance, b. Jan. 26, 1758	1	58
Antoinette, of East Haddam, m. Chester W. **GILMAN**, of Hartford, Sept. 29, 1846, by Rev. Alexander Leadbetter. Int. Pub.	3	33

NEW HARTFORD VITAL RECORS 291

	Vol.	Page
SMITH, (cont.)		
Beardsley W., of Waterbury, m. Mary Jane **RYDER**, of New Hartford, Sept. 25, 1853, by Rev. Cyrus Yale	3	49
Betsey, of New Marlborough, m. Roswell **BACON**, Jr., of Burlington, Jan. 4, 1831, by Rev. Alden Handy	3	17
Candace, d. Seth & Deliverance, b. Aug. 1, 1762	1	58
Carlow, of Sheffield, Mass., m. Amanda **GOODWIN**, of New Hartford, Sept. 12, 1820, by Cyrus Yale	3	2
Caroline Matilda, d. Seth & Deliverance, b. May 12, 1764	1	58
Darius B., m. Eliza **BROWN**, b. of New Hartford, Nov. 28, 1844, by Alexander Leadbetter. Int. Pub.	3	31
Deborah, m. John **KILLBOURNE**, Aug. 20, 1785	2	34
Deliverance, d. Seth & Deliverance, b. Feb. 23, 1766	1	58
Diadama, m. Oliver **HARRIS**, b. of Glastonbury, June 29, 1835, by Asa Goodwin, J.P.	3	21
Edward, of Glastonbury, m. Mariah H. **FOX**, of New Hartford, May 1, 1847, by Rev. George B. Atwell, of Pleasant Valley	3	34
Eleazer, s. Martin & Sarah, b. Apr. 21, 1722; d. Mar. 28, 1749	1	21
Eliazer, s. Seth & Deliverance, b. Nov. 18, 1757; d. Dec. 2, 1757	1	58
Eliphalet, m. Harriet **KEMBLE**, b. of Goshen, Nov. 9, 1824, by Eli Barrett, Elder	3	11
Elmina, m. William G. **CANFIELD**, Nov. 17, 1844, by Alexander Leadbetter. Int. Pub.	3	31
Ferdinand, s. Seth & Deliverance, b. Nov. 14, 1760	1	58
Horatio N., of New Hartford, m. Mary P. **FERRY**, of West Granby, Sept. 9, 1849, by William Goodwin	2	53
Horatio N., of New Hartford, m. Mary J. **PERRY**, of West Granby, Sept. 9, 1849, by Rev. William Goodwin	3	40
James K., m. Maria E. **MOSES**, b. of New Hartford, Aug. 17, 1851, by Rev. Alexander Leadbetter. Int. Pub.	3	39
Jane A., m. Albert A. **CANFIELD**, Nov. 17, 1844, by Alexander Leadbetter. Int. Pub.	3	31
Joseph, of Burlington, m. Florilla A. **SPENCER**, of New Hartford, Nov. 27, 1828, by Cyrus Yale	3	15
Lois, d. Martin & Sarah, b. Aug. 13, 1725	1	35
Martin, s. Martin & Sarah, b. Mar. 15, 1728	1	35
Mary Jane, m. Elam **BARBER**, b. of New Hartford, Sept. 19, 1852, by Rev. James C. Haughton	3	46
Merritt E., m. Irene **SCOVILLE**, of New Hartford, Oct. 10, 1851, by Rev. Harley Goodwin, of South Canaan	3	40
Minerva L., m. John **BRADLEY**, b. of New Hartford, Mar. 28, 1841, by Rev. Cyrus Yale	3	27
Nelson, of Burlington, m. Belinda **HUMPHREY**, of Canton, Dec. 11, 1828, by C. Yale	3	16
Rebeckah, d. Martin & Ruth, b. Feb. 3, 1715/6	1	21
Sarah, d. Martin & Sarah, b. Oct. 30, 1717	1	21
Sarah, m. Adonijah **MOODEY**, Nov. 9, 1742	1	28
Sarah A., m. Joseph G. **GOODWIN**, b. of New Hartford, Dec. 24, 1838, by Rev. Cyrus Yale	3	26
Seth, s. Martin & Sarah, b. Mar. 22, 1732	1	35
Seth, m. Deliverance **CADWELL**, Feb. 17, 1757	1	28
Seth, s. Seth & Deliverance, b. Sept. 10, 1767	1	58

	Vol.	Page
SOSER(?)*, George, m. Lucia **MCNARY**, b. of New Hartford, Nov. 26, 1834, by Rev. Junius Burt *(Perhaps "**TOZER**")	3	20
SPENCER, Abraham, s. Seth & Jerusha, b. June 23, 1786	2	43
Abram, m. Mary A. **CROSS**, Mar. 31, 1807	2	50
Alanson, s. Seth & Jerusha, b. Aug. 7, 1792	2	43
Amanda, m. Asahel **KELLOGG**, Jan. 9, 1809	2	34
Amelia, d. Nathan & Lois, b. Oct. 21, 1770	1	65
Anna, wid. Isaac, d. Jan. 19, 1778	2	2
Anne, m. Moses **DOUGLASS**, June 28, 1781	2	5
Deborah, w. John, Jr., d. Nov. 2, 1773	1	70
Deborah, m. Noys **BALDWIN**, b. of New Hartford, May 1, 1823, by Cyrus Yale	3	8
Delilah, of New Hartford, m. Charles **KAPLE**, of Woster, N.Y., Oct. 21, 1824, by Datus Ensign, Elder	3	11
Dorcas, d. John & Mary, b. May 9, 1754	1	42
Eliphas, m. Lucinda **ROBERTS**, b. of New Hartford, Nov. 8, 1820, by Cyrus Yale	3	3
Ezra, s. John & Mary, b. May 20, 1752	1	42
Florilla, d. Seth & Jerusha, b. Dec. 17, 1797	2	43
Florilla A., of New Hartford, m. Joseph **SMITH**, of Burlington, Nov. 27, 1828, by Cyrus Yale	3	15
Halsey, s. Seth & Jerusha, b. Apr. 24, 1788; d. Oct. 30, 1789	2	43
Halsey, s. Seth & Jerusha, b. May 2, 1790	2	43
Harley M., of New Hartford, m. Lucretia A. **CROMBEE**, of Burlington, May 27, 1841, by Rev. Cyrus Yale	3	28
Harlow, of St. Louis, Mo., m. Theodosia **COOK**, of New Hartford, Oct. 16, 1820, by Cyrus Yale	3	3
Harvey, s. Abram & Mary, b. Jan. 7, 1808	2	50
Huldah, m. Watson **GARRETT**, b. of New Hartford, Mar. 25, 1833, by Rev. Cyrus Yale	3	20
Isaac, s. John, Jr. & Deborah, b. Feb. 12, 1773	1	70
Isaac, s. John, Jr. & Deborah, d. Sept. 20, 1776	1	70
Isaac, Jr., s. Isaac & Anna, b. Oct. 23, 1777	2	2
Isaac, d. Jan. 1, 1778	2	2
James H., of Humphreyville, m. Marian E. **BURNELL**, of New Hartford, Dec. 23, 1849, by Rev. Joel R. Arnold	2	52
Jerusha, alias Jerusha **PETTIBONE**, m. Seth SPENCER, May 20, 1779	2	43
Jerusha, m. George **MCNARY**, Apr. 20, 1807	2	52
John, s. John & Mary, b. Jan. 26, 1742	1	25
John, m. Mary **HUBBARD**, Apr. 14, 1764	1	29
John, Jr., m. Deborah **DOUD**, Nov. 19, 1765	1	69
John, Jr., m. Jerusha **HANDERSON**, June 1, 1775	1	70
Lois, d. Nathan & Lois, b. Aug. 29, 1772	1	65
Lois, of New Hartford, m. Truman **BUELL**, of Simsbury, Aug. 19, 1835, by Rev. Epaphras Goodman	3	22
Lucina, m. Salvenus **MOORE**, b. of New Hartford, Oct. 19, 1824, by Eli Barrett, Elder	3	11
Lydia, d. Nathaniell & Lois, b. Sept. 15, 1776	2	3
Marilla, of New Hartford, m. Edward **WOODRUFF**, of Farmington, July 23, 1828, by Rev. Epaphras Goodman	3	15
Martha, m. Solomon J. **SEYMOUR**, b. of New Hartford, Apr. 13,		

	Vol.	Page
SPENCER, (cont.)		
1846, by Rev. Cyrus Yale	3	32
Mary, d. John & Mary, b. Feb. 4, 1749	1	42
Mary, of New Hartford, m. George A. **MOURREY**, of Smithfield, R.I., May 13, 1832, by Cyrus Yale	3	18
Mary Anne, d. Abram & Mary, b. Dec. 2, 1809	2	50
Mary M., of New Hartford, m. Wilson **DEWEY**, of Granby, Sept. 28, 1841, by Rev. Cyrus Yale]	3	28
Michael, s. John & Mary, b. Mar. 9, 1746	1	21
Michael, s. John & Mary, d. Jan. 12, 1756	1	46
Michael, s. John, Jr. & Deborah, b. Sept. 8, 1766	1	69
Nathaniell, Jr., s. Nathaniell & Lois, b. Aug. 1, 1774	2	3
Norman, s. Seth & Jerusha, b. May 5, 1795	2	43
Olive, d. John, Jr. & Deborah, b. Nov. 19, 1768	1	70
Orvilla N., m. Chester C. **DOWD**, Oct. 1, 1839, by Rev. Cyrus Yale	3	27
Phebe, of New Hartford, m. Isaac M. **BARNES**, of Burlington, Mar. 5, 1854, by Rev. Frederick Marsh	3	53
Phinehas, s. John, Jr. & Deborah, b. Nov. 23, 1770	1	70
Phinehas, s. John, Jr. & Deborarh, d. Sept. 25, 1776	1	70
Rachel, of New Hartford, m. Nathan **HEMENWAY**, of Shoreham, Vt., May 16, 1841, by Rev. Charles Bentley, of Harwinton	3	27
Rusha, d. Seth & Jerusha, b. Apr. 22, 1784	2	43
Samuel, s. Seth & Jerusha, b. Nov. 7, 1779	2	43
Seth, m. Jerusha **PETTIBONE** alias Jerusha **SPENCER**, May 20, 1779	2	43
Submit, d. John & Mary, b. Aug. 15, 1756; d. Nov. 2, 1756	1	46
Susanna, d. John & Mary, b. Sept. 20, 1747	1	21
Zachariah, m. Charlotte **FLETCHER**, b. of New Hartford, Jan. 16, 1822, by Datus Ensign, Elder	3	6
SPRAGUE, James C., of Pomfret, m. Mariette **STEELE**, of New Hartford, Apr. 26, 1831, by Cyrus Yale	3	18
Mariette, m. Henry C. **KELLOGG**, b. of New Hartford, May 1, 1854, by Rev. F. A. Spencer	3	53
STANCLIFFE, STANDCLEF, Ellen, m. Charles H. **KING**, Sept. 26, 1852, by Rev. John H. Betts	3	47
Mary, m. Jonathan **KELLEY***, Jan. 26, 172/3 *("**KELSEY**"?)	1	28
STEDMAN, Harriet, m. Joshua **AMES**, b. of New Hartford, Sept. 15, 1822, by Cyrus Yale	3	7
Herman, m. Lorinda S. **MERRELL**, b. of New Hartford, Mar. 27, 1834, by Rev. Cyrus Yale	3	20
STEELE, STEEL, Abigail, d. Timothy & Abigail, b. Nov. 9, 1773	2	19
Amanda, d. Isaac & Dorothy, b. Apr. 7, 1783	2	27
Amanda, m. Elizur **CURTIS**, Nov. 25, 1804	2	47
Andrew, s. Lovina **STEEL**, b. Mar. 22, 1809	2	27
Ann, d. James & Lois, b. Nov. 5, 1764	1	57
Anna, [d. Isaac & Dorothy], b. Oct. [ ], 1788	2	27
Anthy, d. Isaac & Dorothy, b. Dec. 22, 1785	2	27
Carrel, s. William, Jr. & Polly, b. Oct. 3, 1804	2	51
Catharine M., of New Hartford, m. James G. **WOODWARD**, of Torringford, Sept. 22, 1847, by Rev. Cyrus Yale	3	34
Chloe, d. James & Huldah, b. Feb. 4, 1781	2	26

294 BARBOUR COLLECTION

	Vol.	Page
STEELE, STEEL, (cont.)		
Chloe, d. James & Huldah, d. June 18, 1782, ae. 16 m. 14 d.	2	26
Chloe, d. William & Hannah, b. May 13, 1791; d. Aug. 17, 1794	2	27
Dolly, [d. Isaac & Levinia], b. Aug. 22, 1794	2	27
Dorothy, w. Isaac, d. Mar. [ ], 1792	2	27
Eli, s. James & Huldah, b. Oct. 24, 1772	2	26
Elizabeth, d. James & Lois, b. Mar. 28, 1765* *(Written "1763")	1	57
Elizabeth, d. Jesse & Mehetabel, b. Aug. 2, 1778	2	26
Enos, s. James & Huldah, b. May 4, 1778	2	26
Eunice, d. Timothy & Abigail, b. May 16, 1772	2	19
Ezekiel, s. William, Jr. & Hannah, b. Aug. 20, 1774	1	67
Ezekiel, s. William & Hannah, b. Aug. 20, 1774	2	27
Fanna, [d. Isaac & Levinia], b. Dec. 29, 1797	2	27
Fanny, m. Norman **KELLOGG**, b. of New Hartford, Jan. 3, 1821, by Cyrus Yale	3	4
Frederick, s. William & Polly, b. Oct. 7, 1807	2	51
Gaylord, s. William, Jr. & Polly, b. Sept. 21, 1802	2	51
Hannah, d. W[illia]m & Hannah, b. Aug. 18, 1779	2	27
Herbert A., m. Ellen M. **BARBER**, Apr. 19, 1852, by Rev. J. A. Saxton	3	41
Huldah, d. William & Lydia, b. Aug. 12, 1759* *(Overwritten to read "1749")	2	19
Huldah, m. James **STEEL**, Nov. 10, 1768	2	26
Huldah, d. James & Huldah, b. Nov. 15, 1774	2	26
Ira, s. James & Huldah, b. Dec. 3, 1789	2	26
Isaac, s. William & Lydia, b. Oct. 14, 1752	2	19
Isaac, m. Dorothy **PITKIN**, Sept. 10, 1777	2	27
Isaac, m. Levinia **GOODWIN**, Oct. [ ], 1792	2	27
Isaac, Jr., [s. Isaac & Levinia], b. Aug. 16, 1793	2	27
Isaac P., twin with Sally B., s. [Isaac & Levinia], b. Oct. 28, 1799	2	27
James, s. James & Lois, b. July 7, 1746	1	43
James, m. Huldah **STEEL**, Nov. 10, 1768	2	26
James, s. James & Huldah, b. Jan. 13, 1770	2	26
Jesse, s. James & Lois, b. Aug. 18, 1755	1	43
Jesse, m. Mehetabel **SEGER**, Dec. 18,1777	2	26
Joannah, d. Jesse & Mehetabel, b. Jan. 10, 1780	2	26
John, s. James & Lois, b. Oct. 24, 1753	1	43
John, s. Jesse & Mehetabel, b. Feb. 25, 1782	2	26
Levinia, [d. Isaac & Levinia], b. Mar. 27, 1796	2	27
Lois, d. James & Lois, b. May 15, 1748	1	43
Lovina, d. William & Hannah, b. Nov. 10, 1785	2	27
Lovina, had s. Andrew, b. Mar. 22, 1809	2	27
Lovisa, d. William & Hannah, b. Sept. 8, 1789	2	27
Lydia, d. William & Lydia, b. Mar. 26, 1747/8	1	21
Lydia, m. Ashbel **KELLOGG**, July 17, 1766	2	34
Lydia, d. Timothy & Abigail, b. July 9, 1776; d. Feb. 3, 1777	2	19
Lydia, d. W[illia]m & Hannah, b. Mar. 29, 1782	2	27
Lydia, m. Sela **MERRELL**, Apr. 26, 1803	2	47
Mabel, d. Jesse & Mehetabel, b. Nov. 7, 1784	2	26
Mariette, of New Hartford, m. James C. **SPRAGUE**, of Pomfret, Apr. 26, 1831, by Cyrus Yale	3	18
Noah, s. William & Hannah, b. Dec. 21, 1783	2	27

	Vol.	Page
STEELE, STEEL, (cont.)		
Norman, s. James & Huldah, b. Aug. 9, 1783	2	26
Polly, d. Isaac & Dorothy, b. Oct. 22, 1780	2	27
Polly, d. William & Polly, b. Mar. 21, 1813	2	51
Polly, of New Hartford, m. Frederick H. **KELLOGG**, of Terryville, Jan. 1, 1845, by Rev. Cyrus Yale	3	30
Rodrick, s. William & Lydia, b. Aug. 4, 1755	2	19
Rodrick, s. Isaac & Dorothy, b. July 27, 1778	2	27
Roswell G., m. Elizabeth **MARSH**, b. of New Hartford, Apr. 19, 1854, by Rev. Frederick Marsh	3	54
Sally B., twin with Isaac P., d. [Isaac & Levinia], b. Oct. 28, 1799	2	27
Sarah, d. James & Lois, b. Nov. 18, 1750	1	43
Seth, s. William & Lydia, b. Apr. 12, [ ]	2	19
Susanna, d. James & Lowis, b. May 30, 1760	1	55
Timothy, s. William & Lydia, b. Nov. 3, 1745	1	21
Truman, s. James & Huldah, b. July 22, 1786	2	26
William, s. William & Lydia, b. May 27, 1742	1	21
William, m. Hannah **WEBSTER**, Jan. 31, 1770	2	27
William, s. William, Jr. & Hannah, b. Feb. 16, 1773	1	67
William, s. William & Hannah, b. Feb. 16, 1773	2	27
William, Jr., m. Polly **CONE**, Oct. 12, 1801	2	51
William, Sr., d. May 9, 1806, ae. 64 y.	2	27
William, Jr., s. William & Polly, b. Aug. 16, 1816	2	51
Wolcott, s. Zadoc & Laura, b. Oct. 29, 1805	2	35
Zadock, s. W[illia]m & Hannah, b. Oct. 21, 1776; d. Feb. 10, 1777	2	27
Zadock, 2nd, s. William & Hannah, b. Dec. 4, 1780	2	27
Zadock, m. Laura **LYMAN**, Feb. 11, 1805	2	35
STEVISON, Elizabeth, m. Ichabod **ENSIGN**, July 4, 1753	1	28
STEWARD, George W., m. Mrs. Susan **SWEET**, b. of Barkhamsted, Aug. 27, 1843, by Rev. Erastus Doty, of Colebrook	3	29
STOCKWELL, Diadama J., of New Hartford, m. Marcus **DAYTON**, of Wolcottville, Sept. 26, 1852, by Rev. E. N. Crossman, of Bakerville	3	46
STONE, Abigail, m. Joseph **MERRILL**, Mar. last day, 1742	1	28
George W., of Warren, m. Emily **LYMAN**, of New Hartford, Apr. 17, 1838, at the house of John Lyman, by Rev. Herman L. Vaill, of Torringford	3	25
Hezekiah H., m, Mary S. **SEYMOUR**, b. of New Hartford, Jan. 1, 1854, by Rev. F. A. Spencer	3	51
Melinda, m. Arnold **KING**, Oct. 3, 1824, by Asa Goodwin, J.P.	3	10
Sefroma, m. Trumbull **BENHAM**, Nov. 10, 1822, by Asa Goodwin, J.P.	3	8
STOVEL(?), Ira, of New Hartford, m. Betsey **MYNOTT**, of Oxford, Oct. 23, 1820, by Cyrus Yale	3	3
STOW, Caroline, of New Hartford, m. Adna **HUMPHREYS**, of Simsbury, May 3, 1827, by Cyrus Yale	3	13
Eliza, of New Hartford, m. Charles **RIGHT**, of New Marlborough, Mass., Nov. 23, 1820, by James Beach	3	4
Louisana, of New Hartford, m. Horace **WILCOX**, of Stockbridge, Mass., Nov. 4, 1824, by Cyrus Yale	3	11
STRONG, Elijah, m. Lovina **BARBER**, b. of New Hartford, July 18, 1821, by Cyrus Yale	3	5

	Vol.	Page
STRONG, (cont.)		
Irena, of New Hartford, m. Ira **HUBBELL**, of Southington, Sept. 2, 1820, by Cyrus Yale	3	2
Mary L., of New Hartford, m. Samuel E. Judd, of Farmington, Apr. 6, 1836, by William Case	3	23
SWEET, Susan, Mrs., m. George W. **STEWARD**, b. of Barkhamsted, Aug. 27, 1843, by Rev. Erastus Doty, of Colebrook	3	29
TALLMADGE, Hiram M., m. Sabra E. **FORD**, b. of New Hartford, Dec. 24, 1853, by Rev. J. H. Betts	3	56
TAYLOR, David, Jr., s. David & Lusyna, b. Sept. 23, 1785, at New Hartford	2	31
Francis E., of Hew Hartford, m. Frederick D. **BURNS**, of Winsted, Jan. 21, 1854, by James C. Haughton	3	52
Ozias, s. William & Ruth, b. Mar. 19, 1760	1	48
Perintha, of Canton, m. Humphrey **QUOMANY**, of New Hartford, Aug. 16, 1823, by Isaac Kellogg, J.P.	3	10
William, s. William & Ruth, b. July 13, 1757	1	48
TERRELL, Althea, had s. Ashbel **LOOMIS**, b. Apr. 9, 1792	2	17
Bradley, m. Lucy A. **RAYMOND**, Apr. 14, 1841, by Rev. Cyrus Yale	3	27
THOMPSON, Duncan, of North East, N.Y., m. Meriaette A. **CAMP**, of New Hartford, Oct. 13, 1847, by Rev. C. H. Topliff, of Collinsville	3	34
THORP, Monemia J., m. Horace **GOODWIN**, b. of New Hartford, Jan. 25, 1838, by Rev. Cyrus Yale	3	24
Susan, of New Hartford, m. Rufus **REYNOLDS**, of Barkhamsted, July 13, 1821, by Cyrus Yale	3	4
TOZER*, George, m. Lucia **MCNARY**, b. of New Hartford, Nov. 26, 1834, by Rev. Junius Burt *("**SOSER**"?)	3	20
TROWBRIDGE, Jane, m. John L. **SEGAR**, b. of New Hartford, July 3, 1851, by Rev. Alexander Leadbetter. Int. Pub.	3	38
Ruth, m. Wells **CASE**, Nov. 3, 1845, by Isaac Kellogg, J.P.	3	31
TRUMBULL, Eli J., of Barkhamsted, m. Jane **HEATON**, of New Hartford, June 2, 1840, by Rev. Cyrus Yale	3	27
Jane, of New Hartford, m. Lewis B. **MILLER**, of Torringford, Oct. 11, 1842, by Rev. Cyrus Yale	3	29
TUCKER, **TOCKER**, Emeline, of New Hartford, m. Elisha **RUST**, Jr., of Barkhamsted, Sept. 11, 1828, by Cyrus Yale	3	15
Ephraim, s. Ephraim & Susanna, b. July 12, 1732	1	25
TURNER, Frances C. M., m. Roswell M. **MERRELL**, b. of New Hartford, Oct. 1, 1837, by Rev. Willis Lord	3	24
TYLER, Amos, Jr., s. Amos & Esther, b. Mar. 25, 1785	2	18
Asenath, of New Hartford, m. Dennis **GOODSEL**, of Burlington, Nov. 29, 1820, by Cyrus Yale	3	3
Marilla, m. Nelson **SIKES**, b. of New Hartford, July 6, 1836, by William Case	3	23
Parnal, of New Hartford, m. Niel **DUNBAR**, of Southington, Apr. 20, 1824, by Cyrus Yale	3	10
Samuel, of Branford, m. Celestia **BUTLER**, of New Hartford, Nov. 17, 1830, by Rev. Cyrus Yale	3	18
Walter L., of Plymouth, m. Harriet H. **MERRELL**, of New Hartford, Apr. 12, 1846, by Rev. Cyrus Yale	3	32

	Vol.	Page
UNDERWOOD, David B., of Montwell, O., m. Sarah A. **MILLER**, of Farmington, May 20, 1833, by Rev. David Miller	3	19
VANDEUSEN, Harriet A., of New Hartford, m. Thomas G. **PITMAN**, of New Haven, Jan. 17, 1853, by Rev. John H. Betts	3	48
VINTON, Sylvester, m. Caroline **MOORE**, b. of New Hartford, Oct. 31, 1852, by Rev. John H. Betts	3	48
VOSE, Lucinda, of New Hartford, m. William **LOWREY**, of Burlington, Apr. 4, 1830, by Rev. David Bennett	3	16
WADSWORTH, Judson, of Wellington, O., m. Mrs. Clarissa **BARBOUR**, of New Hartford, May 4, 1852, by Rev. J. A. Saxton	3	42
WALDEN, Oscar M., of New Hartford, m. Catharine M. **BOUGHTON**, of Torrington, Dec. 31, 1851, by Rev. James C. Houghton	3	41
WALLER, Zeruiah, m. Moses **MILLS**, Mar. 12, 1767	2	29
WALLING, Daniel, s. Daniel & Elener, b. Mar. 5, 1757	1	47
Elisha, s. Peter & Martha, b. Mar. 14, 1756	1	43
Hannah, d. Daniel & Elener, b. Feb. 2, 1754	1	47
Heber, s. Thomas & Mary, b. Oct. 26, 1791	2	40
Lois, d. Daniel & Elener, b. May 6, 1752	1	47
Lydia, d. Ezekiel & Lydia, b. Sept. 10, 1761	1	58
Thomas, Jr., s. Thomas & Mary, b. Jan. 6, 1793	2	40
WALTER, Almira, Mrs., m. Daniel **CASE**, b. of New Hartford, Mar. 1, 1847, by Roger H. Mills, J.P.	3	33
Ruth, d. Jaob & Hepsibah, b. Dec. 16, 1751	1	37
WARD, Abigail, m. Ashbel **MARSH**, Nov. 27, 1788	2	50
Martha Bacon, m. Ashbel **KELLOGG**, Jr., June 3, 1790	2	18
WARNER, Garret B., m. Susan **BEACH**, Oct. 4, 1835, by Rev. Seth Higby	3	22
WARREN, Jesse D., m. Martha A. **BAILEY**, Jan. 2, 1853, by Rev. John H. Betts	3	48
WATERS, Lora(?), of Berlin, m. Laura **CHURCHILL**, of New Hartford, Oct. 28, 1834, by Rev. Cyrus Yale	3	21
Mary, m. Theodore **GILBERT**, June 11, 1750	1	28
WATSON, Abigail, w. Cyprian, d. Dec. 16, 1757	1	47
Allin, s. Zachariah & Susanna, b. Sept. 16, 1783	2	15
Ammari, s. Cyprian & Abigail, d. Feb. 24, 1746	1	47
Ammariah, s. Zachariah & Hannah, b. May 8, 1748; d. Sept. 23, 1750	1	53
Ammariah, 2nd, s. Zachariah & Hannah, b. Feb. 7, 1751	1	53
Caleb, s. Zachariah & Hannah, b. Dec. 5, 1753	1	54
Caleb, m. Hannah **MARSH**, Nov. 13, 1779	2	15
Calvin, s. Caleb & Hannah, b. Oct. 4, 1780	2	15
Cyprian, s. John & Sarah, d. Dec. 30, 1753	1	47
David, m. Anna **MOORE**, May 11, 1795	2	41
David & Anna, had s. [ ], b. Mar. 19, 1803; d. Apr. 10, 1803	2	41
David, Jr., s. David & Anna, b. Sept. 29, 1810	2	41
Eathon*, s. Zachariah & Susannah, b. Jan. 11, 1780 *(Overwritten to read "Heman")	2	15
Edmund, m. Ann M. **SEYMOUR**, b. of New Hartford, Jan. 27, 1836, by William Case	3	23
Elizabeth, d. Zachariah & Hannah, b. Mar. 21, 1750	1	53

	Vol.	Page
WATSON, (cont.)		
Esther, d. David & Anna, b. Mar. 29, 1796	2	41
Esther, m. Miles **MARSH**, b. of New Hartford, Apr. 3, 1827, by Rev. Epaphras Goodman	3	14
Fanny, d. David & Anna, b. Aug. 23, 1804	2	41
Fanny M., m. Lloyd **MERRELL**, b. of New Hartford, July 6, 1824, by Rev. Epaphras Goodman	3	10
Florilla, d. David & Anna, b. Apr. 28, 1800	2	41
Florilla A., of New Hartford, m. Elias **WILCOX**, of Harwinton, Nov. 27, 1828, by Rev. Epaphras Goodman	3	15
Hannah, d. Zachariah & Susannah, b. Apr. 21, 1768	2	15
Harvey, [twin with [ ], s. Heman & Sally], b. June 22, 1808	2	50
Heman, s. Zachariah & Susannh, b. Dec. 8, 1776	2	15
Heman, s. Zachariah & Susannah, b. Jan. 11, 1780	2	15
Heman, m. Sally **HANDERSON**, Jan. 4, 1803	2	50
Heman Handerson, s. Heman & Sally, b. Feb. 8, 1804	2	50
Joel, s. David & Anna, b. Sept. 11, 1808	2	41
Levi, Sr., d. May 27, 1798, in the 72nd y. of his age	2	41
Maria, of New Hartford, m. Charles H. **PINNEY**, M.D., of Derby, Apr. 4, 1854, by J. C. Haughton	3	52
Martha A., of Torringford, m. Julius R. **POND**, of Ansonia, July 1, 1850, by Rev. William H. Moore	3	36
Norrace, s. David & Anna, b. Jan. 15, 1798	2	41
Polly, d. David & Anna, b. Apr. 18, 1807	2	41
Polly Ann, m. Philo A. **LOOMIS**, Oct. 22, 1835, by R. M. Chipman, V.D.M.	3	22
Reuel A., m. Maria Jerusha **CLEVELAND**, Oct. 11, 1836	2	52
Royal J., m. Eliza **SEYMOUR**, b. of New Hartford, June 2, 1823, by Cyrus Yale	3	8
Sarah, d. Zachariah & Susannah, b. July 7, 1774	2	15
Sarah Lucretia, d. Heman [& Sally], b. Dec. 19, 1806	2	50
Susa, d. Zachariah & Susannah, b. Sept. 14, 1770; d. Apr. 18, 1771	2	15
Susa, d. Zachariah & Susannah, b. Apr. 19, 1772	2	15
Thomas, s. Cyprian & Abigail, d. Oct. 20, 1757	1	47
Zachariah, s. Zachariah & Hannah, b. Aug. 5, 1745	1	53
Zachariah, s. Cyprian, d. June 21, 1757	1	53
-----, [twin with Harvey, s. Heman & Sally], b. June 25, 1808; d. at birth	2	50
WATT, Langston, of New York City, m. Sophia **GLASSON**, of New Hartford, Oct. 11, 1847, by Roger H. Mills, J.P.	3	34
WAX, Jacob, of Farmington, m. Polly **DELOOR**, of New Hartford, Oct. 13, 1822, by William G. Williams, J.P.	3	7
WEBSTER, Adah N., of New Hartford, m. W[illia]m Henry **FENN**, of Plymouth, Nov. 29, 1827, by Rev. Cyrus Yale	3	17
Clarissa, of New Hartford, m. Luther **HODSDILL**, of New Marlboro, Sept. 15, 1828, by Cyrus Yale	3	15
Dorkise, m. Eliphalet **ENSIGN**, Feb. 12, 1739/40	1	28
Eliza, m. W[illia]m **COOK**, Jr., b. of New Hartford, Oct. 12, 1820, by Cyrus Yale	3	3
Hannah, m. William **STEEL**, Jan. 31, 1770	2	27
Meriam, m. Elias **HOPKINS**, May 10, 1752	1	28

	Vol.	Page
WEBSTER, (cont.)		
Minerva, of Barkhamsted, m. Luther **SIMONS**, of Winchester, July 25, 1852, by Rev. J. A. Saxton	3	44
WEDGE, Henry W., m. Parintha **GAYLORD**, of Torringford, May 5, 1840, by Rev. Cyrus Yale	3	27
WELCH, George M., of Hartford, m. Eliza **KELLOGG**, of New Hartford, Oct. 5, 1853, by Rev. F. A. Spencer	3	50
WELLES, WELLS, Absalom, Jr., m. Marilla **BARNES**, Jan. 1, 1811	2	52
Absalom Barnes, s. Absalom & Marilla, b. Sept. 26, 1826	2	52
Anna, d. Absalom, Jr. & Marilla, b. Oct. 6, 1814	2	52
Catharine, of New Hartford, m. Seneca **CONE**, of Augusta, Ga., May 20, 1824, by Cyrus Yale	3	10
Harriet, d. Absalom, Jr. & Marilla, b. Jan. 17, 1819	2	52
Henry, s. Absalom, Jr. & Marilla, b. Feb. 3, 1812	2	52
Marilla, d. Absalom, Jr. & Marilla, b. Oct. 9, 1823	2	52
Ralph, s. Absalom, Jr. & Marilla, b. May 15, 1821	2	52
Samuel B., of Sandisfield, Mass., m. Mary Ann **DANVILL**, of New Hartford, Feb. 19, 1846, by Rev. Alexander Leadbetter. Int. Pub.	3	33
Timothy, s. Samuell & Susannah, b. May 20, 1745	1	22
WENTWORTH, Mary, of New Hartford, m. Henry **CHURCH**, of Barkhamsted, Aug. 18, 1846, by Rev. Alexander Leadbetter. Int. Pub.	3	33
WESTCOTT, Horace, of Cheshire, m. Mary Esther **DRAKE**, of New Hartford, June 2, 1851, by Rev. John Herbert Betts	3	38
WESTLAND, Deborah, m. Josiah **LYMAN**, Mar. 1, 1790	2	35
WETMORE, Celestia, of New Hartford, m. Luman **CATLIN**, Jr., of Harwinton, Jan. 19, 1831, by Rev. Epaphras Goodman	3	17
Louisa, m. Jabez G. **CURTIS**, b. of New Hartford, Oct. 21, 1830, by Rev. Epaphras Goodman	3	17
WHAPLE, Curtis, of New Britain, m. Elizabeth C. **LUSH**, of New Hartford, May 9, 1838, by Rev. Willis Lord	3	25
WHEELER, Elsa, m. Benjamin **HENSHAW**, Jr., Aug. 18, 1791, at the house of Benjamin **HENSHAW**, f. of Benjamin, Jr., by Rev. Jonathan Marsh	2	39
James J., m. Mary **CARPENTER**, b. of New Hartford, Nov. 2, 1845, by Alexander Leadbetter	3	32
WHITE, Betsey, of New Hartford, m. Ark W. **FISH**, of Hartford, Jan. 10, 1827, by Cyrus Yale	3	13
WHITING, Amanda, d. Harvey & Olive, b. Nov. 2, 1798	2	36
Amanda, of New Hartford, m. Roswell **BIRGE**, of Torrington, June 27, 1826, by Rev. Epaphras Goodman	3	12
Candace, of New Hartford, m. Enos **FRISBIE**, Jr., of Harwinton, Apr. 18, 1827, by Rev. George E. Pierce	3	14
Henry Franklin, s. Harvey & Olive, b. Oct. 26, 1804	2	36
John, m. Sally **BROOKS**, Oct. 8, 1826, by Rev. Etbert Osborn	3	13
WILCOX, Benjamin, of Voluntown, m. Delilah **FOX**, of New Hartford, Sept. 22, 1824, by Cyrus Yale	3	10
Edward, of New Hartford, m. Martha **HIGLEY**, of Canton, July 4, 1852, by Rev. John H. Betts	3	44
Elias, of Harwinton, m. Florilla A. **WATSON**, of New Hartford, Nov. 27, 1828, by Rev. Epaphras Goodman	3	15

	Vol.	Page
WILCOX, (cont.)		
Horace, of Stockbridge, Mass., m. Louisana **STOW**, of New Hartford, Nov. 4, 1824, by Cyrus Yale	3	11
Jeffrey, m. Ann **MASON**, Nov. 25, 1822, by Samuel Griswold	3	8
Laura, of Canton, m. [ ] **BEARDSLEY**, of Sandisfield, Mass., Nov. 30, 1825, by Isaac Kellogg, J.P.	3	12
William T., of New Hartford, m. Julia A. **PIKE**, of Canton, Nov. 18, 1845, by Alexander Leadbetter	3	32
WILLIAMS, Candace, of New Hartford, m. Stanley **CATLIN**, of Harwinton, Apr. 28, 1831, by Cyrus Yale	3	18
Douglass, m. Sophronia G. **HOLCOMB**, b. of New Hartford, Sept. 2, 1828, by Rev. Cyrus Yale	3	14
Erastus, of Knox, N.Y., m. Sarah M. **MEIGS**, of New Hartford, Mar. 8, 1827, by Cyrus Yale	3	13
Harriet K., m. Elijah K.* **GOODWIN**, b. of New Hartford, Aug. 4, 1824, by Cyrus Yale *("H" overwritten)	3	10
Harriet K., m. Elijah H. **GOODWIN**, b. of New Hartford, Aug. 4, 1824, by Cyrus Yale	2	32
Lucy, of New Hartford, m. George **RICHARDS**, of Farmington, May 6, 1824, by Cyrus Yale	3	10
Margaret, of New Hartford, m. David L. **PERRY**, of Sharon, May 9, 1838, by Rev. Willis Lord	3	25
WILMOT, Elizabeth A., of Plymouth, m. Grove W. **HENDERSON**, of New Hartford, May 19, 1841, by Rev. Cyrus Yale	3	28
Hannah, of New Hartford, m. Jeremiah **LOOMIS**, of Springfield, Mass., Dec. 2, 1835, by Rev. Seth Higbey	3	22
WINCHESTER, Mary, of Torringford, m. Edward **COLTON**, of New Hartford, Mar. 17, 1824, by Cyrus Yale	3	9
WINSLOW, Almira, m. Clark **BURDICK**, b. of New Hartford, Nov. 18, 1821, by Cyrus Yale	3	6
WISWALL, James, of Franklin, N.Y., m. Lucinda **CASE**, of New Hartford, Nov. 13, 1851, by Rev. J. H. Betts	3	43
WIT, Harriet, d. Oliver & Eunice, b. Aug. 18, 1792	2	17
WITHNER, Jacob, of Troy, N.Y., m. Sarah A. **HAWLEY**, of New Hartford, July 19, 1854, by Rev. F. A. Spencer	3	55
WITNEY, Clarissa, m. Frederic **BAILEY**, Nov. 2, 1853, by Rev. David Miller	3	50
WOODFORD, Amelia, m. John **HENDERSON**, b. of New Hartford, May 4, 1831, by Cyrus Yale	3	18
WOODRUFF, Edward, of Farmington, m. Marilla **SPENCER**, of New Hartford, July 23, 1828, by Rev. Epaphras Goodman	3	15
Elizabeth, m. Robert M. **BURWELL**, June 1, 1847, by Cyrus Yale	3	34
Ellen, of New Hartford, m. Chester M. **DEMING**, of Canaan, Apr. 22, 1846, by Rev. Cyrus Yale	3	32
Flora, of New Hartford, m. Simeon **LOOMIS**, of Torrington, Apr. 20, 1834, by Rev. Cyrus Yale	3	21
Frederick, m. Adeline **MARSH**, b. of New Hartford, Apr. 22, 1840, by Rev. James Beach, of Winsted	3	26
Hannah, d. Solomon & Hannah, b. Mar. 26, 1769	1	62
Sarah Lavinia, of New Hartford, m. Henry Elizur **HAYS**, of Oregon, Feb. 6, 1853, by Rev. James C. Haughton	3	49

NEW HARTFORD VITAL RECORDS

	Vol.	Page
WOODRUFF, (cont.)		
Silas, s. Solomon & Hannah, b. July 28, 1772	1	62
Solom[on], m. Hannah **GOODWIN**, Nov. 20, 1766	1	29
Solomon, Solomon & Hannah, b. July 3, 1767	1	60
Solomon, m. Theodosia [**MERRELL**] **WOODRUFF**, Oct. 3, 1771	1	65
Theodosia [**MERRELL**], m. Solomon **WOODRUFF**, Oct. 3, 1771	1	65
WOODWARD, Elijah, of Torringford, m. Orpah Ann **KELLOGG**, of New Hartford, Nov. 6, 1850, by Rev. Cyrus Yale	3	37
James G., of Torringford, m. Catharine M. **STEELE**, of New Hartford, Sept. 22, 1847, by Rev. Cyrus Yale	3	34
John A., of Watertown, m. Ellen **JOHNSON**, of Winsted, Jan. 2, 1853, by Rev. John H. Betts	3	48
WRIGHT, RIGHT, Adaline L., of New Hartford, m. William P. **CURTIS**, of Stratford, Oct. 29, 1851, by Rev. Alexander Leadbetter. Int. Pub.	3	40
Charles, of New Marlborough, Mass., m. Eliza **STOW**, of New Hartford, Nov. 23, 1820, by James Beach	3	4
Esther, d. Earl & Esther, b. May 17, 1754	1	42
YALE, Lucy Tracy, of Lee, Mass., m. Harvey **SHEPARD**, of York, Upper Canada, Nov. 20, 1825, by Cyrus Yale	3	12
Martha R., of New Hartford, m. Elias R. **BEADLE**, of New Orleans, La., Aug. 31, 1852, by Rev. Cyrus Yale	3	46
Mary, of Mereden, m. Nathaniel **CLARK**, of Seymouth, Sept. 23, 1827, by Cyrus Yale	3	14
NO SURNAME, Phebe, m. Riverius **BIDWELL**, Sept. 8, 1782	2	48

www.ingramcontent.com/pod-product-compliance
Lightning Source LLC
Chambersburg PA
CBHW050624300426
44112CB00012B/1652